Employment Regulation in the Workplace

D1470564

Employment Regulation in the Workplace

Basic Compliance for Managers

Second Edition

**Robert K. Robinson and
Geralyn McClure Franklin**

Routledge
Taylor & Francis Group

LONDON AND NEW YORK

First published 2014 by M.E. Sharpe

Published 2015 by Routledge
2 Park Square, Milton Park, Abingdon, Oxon OX14 4RN
711 Third Avenue, New York, NY 10017, USA

Routledge is an imprint of the Taylor & Francis Group, an informa business

Copyright © 2014 Taylor & Francis. All rights reserved.

No part of this book may be reprinted or reproduced or utilised in any form or by
any electronic, mechanical, or other means, now known or hereafter invented,
including photocopying and recording, or in any information storage or retrieval
system, without permission in writing from the publishers.

Notices
No responsibility is assumed by the publisher for any injury and/or damage to
persons or property as a matter of products liability, negligence or otherwise,
or from any use of operation of any methods, products, instructions or ideas
contained in the material herein.

Practitioners and researchers must always rely on their own experience and
knowledge in evaluating and using any information, methods, compounds, or
experiments described herein. In using such information or methods they should
be mindful of their own safety and the safety of others, including parties for
whom they have a professional responsibility.

Product or corporate names may be trademarks or registered trademarks, and
are used only for identification and explanation without intent to infringe.

Library of Congress Cataloging-in-Publication Data

Robinson, Robert K.
  Employment regulation in the workplace : basic compliance for managers / by Robert K. Robinson and
Geralyn McClure Franklin. — Second Edition.
     pages cm
  Includes index.
  ISBN 978-0-7656-4080-2 (pbk. : alk. paper)
1. Labor laws and legislation—United States. 2. Personnel management—United States. I. Franklin, Geralyn
McClure. II. Title.

KF3319.R6349 2014
658.3—dc23   2013025357

ISBN 13: 978076540802 (pbk)

Dedicated to

The memory of my father, Lt. Col. Robert Gene Robinson, USAF (1924–2008)
and the important women in my life: Rosemary Patricia Robinson, Betty Jean Robinson,
Rachael Ann Robinson Davis, Mackenzie Nicole Robinson, and
Mary Patricia Robinson Viguerie, Ph.D.
Soli Deo Gloria
RKR

My husband, Kenny, and son, Tanner, who accept and support me always; and
my parents, Gerald C. and Marie McClure, who made me who I am in so many ways
GMF

CONTENTS

PREFACE AND ACKNOWLEDGMENTS

The American workplace is becoming an increasingly difficult place to navigate for practicing managers and human resource (HR) professionals. The United States of America has become a culture obsessed with rights, both real and imagined. One consequence is that Congress and government agencies have felt pressure to promulgate more regulations and statutes as time progresses. These in turn have increased the compliance requirements on businesses and heightened the potential for employment litigation.

As the cost of litigation reduces an organization's financial resources, fewer resources are left for product development, market research, or capital investment. All of these activities have a positive effect on productivity improvements and job creation; hence, reducing them has the opposite effect.

There is little doubt that the United States has become an exceedingly litigious society. According to a report by the Towers Watson, over 1.8 percent of the gross domestic product of the United States is spent on civil lawsuits.[1] It has been estimated by the U.S. Chamber of Commerce that litigation cost small businesses approximately $105.4 billion in 2008, imposing significantly higher legal costs for U.S. companies than those in other industrialized nations.[2] This trend may even have a chilling effect on foreign investment, as a 2008 survey by the Department of Commerce identified the U.S. legal system as one of the concerns that foreign companies have when investing in facilities in the United States.[3] Unquestionably, this trend toward settling disputes through litigation has had an impact on the American workplace, regardless of whether the entity is American or foreign owned.

One major factor contributing to the rise in workplace litigation is the commonly held belief that employees possess a vast array of inalienable rights on which their employers cannot infringe. Because of this rights-entitlement belief, employees are far more likely to resort to litigation in order to protect these rights—whether real or perceived.

It is unfortunate that in some instances, perhaps even many, organizational managers have no better understanding of these rights than do their employees. This often results in confusion regarding when an employee's concerns are legitimate or not, and this confusion can lead to resolution by an outside entity—either a regulatory agency or a court. Misconceptions arise from employer obligations under employment laws, and regulations may result in employers' maintaining policies and practices that violate the law and unnecessarily expose the organization to litigation. Another consequence of management misconceptions may be the implementation of unnecessary workplace policies that actually impede the efficient operation of the organization. In either case, the organization is adversely affected.

To further compound matters, the legal environment is in a constant state of flux due to political dynamics. This only adds to the difficulty of remaining current on the law. As practitioners already know, and students will soon learn, a practice that was lawful yesterday may be unlawful tomorrow. As a practical example, yesterday's permissive affirmative action program could be tomorrow's reverse-discrimination lawsuit, due to a change in the composition of the Supreme Court.

In short, regulatory compliance has become an even more vital component of all management activities. Failure to execute compliance obligations properly can have material and intangible consequences for employers. Without question, federal regulation affects every activity involving human endeavor in the organization. Recruiting, selection, placement, promotions, transfers, and compensation all must be carried out in accordance with the equal employment opportunity (EEO) provisions mandated by Title VII of the Civil Rights Act of 1964, the Age Discrimination in Employment Act (ADEA), and the Americans with Disabilities Act (ADA). Compensation and benefits administrators are responsible for ensuring that pay and benefits programs are in compliance with the Equal Pay Act, the Employee Income and Security Act (ERISA), the Consolidated Omnibus Budget and Reconciliation Act (COBRA), the Health Insurance Portability and Accountability Act (HIPAA), and the Patient Protection and Affordable Care Act (PPACA), to name a few.

When delving into the world of regulations, one quickly begins to notice the proliferation of acronyms. Since the subject matter of this text deals with government bureaucracies and the legal profession, the reader will be introduced to the technical language (which includes a plethora of acronyms). By the end of the book, the authors hope to reduce the mystery surrounding these terms and concepts for the reader.

Because all managers, by definition, must get their assigned goals and objectives accomplished through the efforts of their employees, any employment practices in which they engage (i.e., hiring, discipline, terminations, work assignments, and performance management) have the potential to expose employers to employment litigation. It is, therefore, essential that all managers have a basic knowledge of their compliance obligations in order to avoid unnecessary legal complications for their employers. One indication of the increasing importance of regulatory compliance lies in the fact that approximately one-third of the examination for certification as a professional in human resources (PHR) evaluates some aspect of test-taker knowledge of employment or labor law. It is hardly surprising that the Society for Human Resource Management would place employment law and employee and labor relations as required content areas in its 2010 undergraduate curriculum guidelines.[4]

The authors do not wish to imply that it is only HR professionals who have to be knowledgeable on regulatory responsibilities. *Any manager* who actively engages in decisions regarding employees will be affected by government regulation. Any personnel decision made by a manager who impermissibly considers the employee's or applicant's race, color, religion, sex, national origin, age, or disability not only taints the entire process but also exposes the organization to litigation. Lawsuits and charges that contain the language "the employer did . . ." or "the employer failed to . . ." invariably mean that the employer's representative did something wrong or failed to do something right. The owners of businesses usually are not the individuals violating laws or regulations, it is their managers.

Every year, workplace practices and behaviors come under more government scrutiny and regulation, often resulting in changes in existing regulations and sometimes leading to new regulations. These regulatory changes invariably affect an organization's daily operation, as well as adding to the cost of doing business. In 2012 the Competitive Enterprise Institute estimated that regulatory compliance cost American business $1.75 trillion per annum.[5] This book examines the impact of federal regulation on employment activities and introduces readers to the more common practices that may trigger scrutiny under the law.

PURPOSE

The purpose of this book is to acquaint readers with the major federal statutes and regulations that control management and employment practices in the American workplace. The authors have, therefore, focused discussion on the effect of employment practices and the subsequent impact that these practices have on employees in relation to existing federal statutes, regulations, and court decisions.

This book endeavors to present a comprehensive, but practical, view of the regulatory environment under which practicing managers must operate. Most businesspeople are not motivated in their decision making by racial, gender, or ethnic biases. Frankly, such decisions are bad for business. Many merely blunder into noncompliance through ignorance of the law rather than through discriminatory intent. The sin is often one of omission rather than one of commission. Therefore, we have worked diligently to make this text legally correct rather than politically correct. Again, our concern is compliance with existing employment law, which we view as an externality with which all affected organizations must deal.

Other texts attempt to approach the regulation of employment practices in a manner that evaluates all organizational activities on a broad range of economic, social, legal, and institutional contexts. The scope of this book is limited to only the legal context. Following the old axiom that "there is right, there is wrong, and there is the law," the authors concentrate on the legal obligations imposed on organizations. If the reader is looking for a text that either justifies or challenges the current state of federal regulations, this is not it.

The material in this textbook is presented from the viewpoint that HR professionals and managers are the employer's representatives and are, therefore, responsible for protecting the employer's interests by reducing the employer's exposure to litigation through monitoring activities and viable employee policies. The text is designed as a tool for today's business and management professionals. If we have a bias, it is likely to be pro-business or pro-management.

Through our discussions of compliance obligations, readers will develop a basic understanding and appreciation for the challenges confronting practicing managers in formulating and implementing strategies and policies that enable organizations to attain a sustained competitive advantage. Additionally, the text will enhance the reader's ability to interpret and understand the legal requirements that all managers must meet in order to comply with equal employment opportunity, wage and hour, safety and health, and other statutes and regulations governing workplace behavior. We have endeavored to develop a framework of analysis to enable readers to identify central issues and problems in personnel activities and then evaluate their potential for noncompliance.

ORGANIZATION

This book is organized in four parts that include fifteen chapters. Chapter 1, "Impact of Regulation on Human Resource Practices," sets the stage by introducing readers to the federal regulatory environment and discussing its evolution, the principal sources of regulatory obligations, and the judicial system and how it works.

Chapter 2, "Equal Employment Opportunity: Regulatory Issues," provides the reader with a historical background of the federal regulation of private sector employers. It introduces Title VII of the Civil Rights Act of 1964 and explains how complaints are filed, how the Equal Employment Opportunity Commission (EEOC) investigates such complaints, and what outcomes can be expected from the investigations.

The next six chapters examine specific aspects of equal employment opportunity (EEO) prohibitions. Chapter 3, "Intentional Discrimination: Disparate Treatment," focuses on complaining parties establishing a *prima facie* case of intentional discrimination and on employer defenses. Chapter 4, "Unintentional Discrimination: Disparate Impact," examines Title VII prohibitions on employment discrimination with a detailed discussion of unintentional discrimination. Issues specifically related to sex discrimination, including sexual harassment, are addressed in Chapter 5, "Discrimination Based on Sex." Discrimination against other protected classes (i.e., religion, national origin, age, and disability) is the focus of Chapter 6, "Discrimination Based on Religion, Age, and Disability." Chapter 7, "National Origin Discrimination and Immigration Issues," centers on national origin issues such as unlawful discrimination based on ethnicity, English-only work rules, and immigration issues. The EEO chapters conclude with Chapter 8, "Affirmative Action," which investigates the complex issue of affirmative action programs in light of their permissibility under both Title VII and the Equal Protection Clause of the Fourteenth Amendment.

This volume also includes two chapters devoted to compensation. Chapter 9, "Compensation: Wage, Hour, and Related Statutes," examines statutes that relate to wages and hours in the workplace. A good deal of attention is given to the provisions of the Fair Labor Standards Act (FLSA) and determining who is an exempt employee under that act. Chapter 10, "Compensation: Benefits," focuses primarily on benefits regulation. Particular attention is given to the Family and Medical Leave Act (FMLA), the Consolidated Omnibus Reconciliation Act (COBRA), Health Insurance Portability and Accountability

Act (HIPAA), Patient Protection and Affordable Care Act (PPACA), and the Uniformed Services Employment and Reemployment Rights Act (USERRA).

Chapter 11, "Laws Affecting Workplace Health and Safety," deals with compliance issues arising from workers' compensation laws and the Occupational Safety and Health Act (OSHA). Also addressed are emerging health and safety issues such as work-related stress, work-related musculoskeletal disorders, and sick building syndrome.

Chapter 12, "Employment-at-Will, Employee Discipline, and Negligent Hiring Issues," diverges from federal law and looks into the state-based employment-at-will (EAW) doctrine. Special consideration is dedicated to both the statutory and common law exceptions. Because of their growing importance, both negligent hiring and negligent retention are also examined.

Chapter 13, "Privacy and Recent Developments in Employment Regulation," addresses privacy related to disclosure of employee information, video monitoring, and electronic monitoring of employees in a work setting. Employee personal expression as it conflicts with employer dress codes/appearance policies is addressed. Among the developing issues in employee privacy is DNA testing, which was substantially limited in 2008 with the passage of the Genetic Information Nondiscrimination Act (GINA).

The final two chapters, Chapter 14, "Job Analysis: The Foundation of Employment Decision Making," and Chapter 15, "Establishing Job-Relatedness Validation," were purposely placed at the end of the book. These chapters are specifically provided for those instructors who desire to go into more depth on job-relatedness/business necessity defenses for disparate impact allegations. For those instructors desiring not to do so, these chapters can be easily omitted. Chapter 14 looks at how to conduct job analysis, while Chapter 15 explains how validation is conducted, including specific examples of how criterion-related validation is performed.

Each of the fifteen chapters begins with a scenario based on an actual court case or workplace event that is related to the chapter's subject. These opening scenarios are intended not only to provide an example of a real workplace problem confronting an employer, but to also provide a practice or policy to which the chapter subject matter may be applied. It is one thing to discuss what the compliance requirements are; it is yet another to understand how they are applied.

It is our intention that this textbook should provide a practical benefit to readers. We have attempted to translate the "legalese" into English as much as possible without sacrificing accuracy. However, the reader will also become familiar with the language of the regulatory agencies, allowing him or her not only to communicate on their level, but to better understand what the enforcement agencies desire. Should you find any errors or other points within our book upon which you would like to comment, we would appreciate hearing from you. By incorporating your ideas, we hope to continue writing a book that best serves you and future readers.

We are HR professionals and have approached the subject matter in this book from that perspective. Our objective is strictly informative in nature—to make readers aware of their general compliance obligations. Because of the dynamic nature of regulatory issues, readers must be forewarned that though this book's contents were current at the time this book went to press, subsequent legislation or, even more likely, federal court decisions may have rendered some of the contents out-of-date.

Finally, the authors warn the reader that we are not attorneys and are not offering legal advice. This book *is not* intended to offer legal recommendations for specific legal problems. Readers who are involved in legal disputes are advised to seek competent legal counsel.

ACKNOWLEDGMENTS

We would like to recognize and thank the following individuals for their assistance; without their support, this textbook would not have been completed. First, we wish to express our sincerest appreciation to the M.E. Sharpe support staff, including Harry M. Briggs, executive editor, and Elizabeth Parker, associate editor. Also, special thanks to Ana Erlic, production editor and Sandy Koppen, proofreader, for their efforts in making the second edition happen. Additional thanks go to Bob Robinson's Employee Relations (MGMT 582) classes at the University of Mississippi for being the "guinea pigs" for early drafts of this book.

Bob Robinson would especially like to recognize the hard work of his wife, Betty, for the many long hours she spent proofreading drafts and making critical contributions to this textbook. He would also like to recognize colleagues who, in one way or another, aided in the creation of this book. These include Samuel Causley, University of Mississippi; Steve Crow, University of New Orleans; Randy Evans, University of Tennessee at Chattanooga; Clay Dibrell, University of Mississippi; Ross L. Fink, Bradley University; Joseph Goodman, Illinois State University; William Jackson, University of South Florida St. Petersburg; Neal Mero, Kennesaw State University; Dave L. Nichols, University of Mississippi; Gregory Rose, University of Washington; William Rose, Texas Christian University; Larry Tunnell, New Mexico State University; Scott Vitell, University of Mississippi; Robert Van Ness, University of Mississippi; and David Wyld, Southeastern Louisiana University.

Bob would further like to thank the Michael S. Starnes Foundation for funding his research activities for nearly a decade, as well as making it possible for him to attend certification programs in employment law offered by the Society for Human Resource Management and the Institute of Applied Management and Law. These programs contributed greatly to the currency of the subject matter contained in this textbook. He also wishes to recognize support he has received from Dr. Ken Cyree, Dean of the School of Business Administration of the University of Mississippi, for his unwavering support of research across all business disciplines.

Geralyn Franklin would like to thank her husband, Kenny, and son, Tanner, for their sacrifices over the years for her publications like this book. She would also like to express her appreciation to many of the same colleagus that Bob Robinson acknowledged earlier. In addition, Geralyn wishes to recognize her mentors from Stephen F. Austin State University (where she received the BBA degree in 1982, MBA degree in 1985, served as an administrator and faculty member from 1987–1998, and returned as an administrator and faculty member in 2011) including Janelle C. Ashley, Nancy C. Speck, Dillard Tinsley, and the late Bobby G. Bizzell and Marlin C. Young. She also wishes to acknowledge her mentors from the University of North Texas, where she received a Ph.D. degree in 1989, including J.D. Dunn, Elvis C. Stephens, William L. McKee, and the late Walton H. Sharp. Finally, Geralyn owes special gratitude to the administration, faculty, staff, and students at Stephen F. Austin State University, where in July of 2012 she began serving as interim dean of the Nelson Rusche College of Business.

NOTES

1. Towers Watson, *2011 Update on U.S. Tort Cost Trends* (New York: Towers Watson & Co., 2012).

2. U.S. Chamber Institute for Legal Reform, *Tort Liability Costs for Small Business* (Washington, DC: U.S. Chamber of Commerce, July 2010).

3. U.S. Department of Commerce, *The U.S. Litigation Environment and Foreign Direct Investment* (Washington, DC: GPO, 2008), p. 6.

4. N.A. Woolever, D. Cohen, A. Benedict, S. Williams, B. Schaefer, and S. Bergman, *SHRM Human Resource Curriculum: An Integrated Approach to HR Education* (Alexandria, VA: Society for Human Resource Management, 2010).

5. C.W. Crews, *Ten Thousand Commandments: An Annual Snapshot of the Federal Regulatory State, 2012 Edition* (Washington, DC: Competitive Enterprise Institute, 2012).

Employment Regulation in the Workplace

PART I

REGULATORY IMPACT

IMPACT OF REGULATION ON HUMAN RESOURCE PRACTICES

LEARNING OBJECTIVES

- Understand the different regulatory environments for all union and nonunion employees.
- Discuss the evolution of government regulation in the workplace.
- Understand the costs associated with government regulation in the workplace.
- Discuss the sources of laws and government regulations in the workplace.
- Identify the responsibilities and enforcement powers of the principal regulatory agencies overseeing the workplace.
- Describe the federal judicial system and how its decisions affect workplace practices.

OPENING SCENARIO

Milorad's Lawn Service in Oxford, MS, employed seventeen full-time workers of whom five were illegal aliens: Evita, a 53-year-old female from Nicaragua; Tony, a 40-year-old male from Canada; Pedro, a 36-year-old male from Honduras; Ramona, a 52-year-old female from Mexico; and her 15-year-old son, Hector. All of the undocumented workers in question, except Tony, were paid $5.00 per hour to perform manual labor in the company's landscaping unit for four fifteen-hour shifts per week. Tony was paid $7.25 per hour for the same work.

On August 22, Evita presented a petition to Bob, her supervisor, demanding that she and her undocumented coworkers receive the same health benefits as her coworkers who were U.S. citizens. Bob told Evita, "All you Mexicans are breaking the law by coming into the U.S. and ought to be happy I'm giving you a job. You got to understand that you as illegal aliens don't have the same rights as 'real employees.'" Evita was then promptly fired. Bob also fired Ramona, stating that she was getting too old for this kind of work and he wanted to hire a younger person for her position.

The following day, Bob was confronted by one of the other undocumented employees, Pedro, who also claimed to be the spiritual leader of the Roman Catholic workers. Pedro stated that he was upset by Bob's treatment of the undocumented workers and then threatened to file a complaint at the Memphis District Office of the EEOC over Evita's termination. After berating Pedro for being both an ingrate and a snitch, Bob promptly fired him as well.

ARE EMPLOYMENT LAWS BEING BROKEN?

Based upon this scenario, there are indications that a number of federal employment laws were potentially violated by Bob's actions. In this and the following chapters, the reader will be introduced to the variety of federal regulations and laws that govern employee-management relations. Through this reading, students will develop an appreciation for observing workplace behaviors and ascertaining whether certain laws are being violated *and* on what grounds. For example, if an employer is unaware of the first-level supervisor's actions, is the organization "off the hook" for any liability? The answer is no. Employers are, in most instances, liable for the actions of their management representatives, often whether or not they knew of these actions. Employers can take certain actions to limit this liability, which will be discussed later in this book.

Returning to the opening scenario, we can estimate the extent of unlawful activity by using the Steps in Conducting Case Analysis recommended in Chapter 2 (see pages 58–59). The answers to these questions would be as follows: First, by knowingly hiring undocumented workers, the employer has violated the Immigration Reform and Control Act.[1] Second, we find that the Fair Labor Standards Act of 1938 (FLSA) was likely violated on three counts (see Chapter 9). First, the undocumented employees are being paid below the minimum wage.[2] Next, no one is being paid overtime for those hours worked over 40 in a 168 consecutive-hour workweek.[3] Finally, the FLSA's child labor provisions are violated when a fifteen-year-old is being worked in excess of 40 hours (if he was working during a school week, he could not work in excess of 18 hours).[4]

Because Bob paid the illegal Latino workers less than the illegal non-Latinos (Tony, the Canadian), Milorad's Lawn Service is also violating Title VII of the Civil Rights Act of 1964—different compensation and terms of employment based on national origin, an issue discussed in Chapter 7.[5] Note that even though the company is a small business, it employs seventeen individuals, which is above the threshold of the fifteen necessary to be covered by Title VII.[6] Title VII is that part of the Civil Rights Act of 1964 that makes it unlawful to discriminate in employment because of an individual's race, color, religion, or *national origin*. Additionally, Title VII was violated again when Pedro was fired for making the EEO complaint about Evita's treatment.[7] This is called "retaliation," which is discussed in Chapter 3.

What about religious discrimination? Didn't Bob fire Pedro, who was the spiritual leader of the Roman Catholic employees? Yes, Bob did indeed fire Pedro, but not because of his Roman Catholicism. Pedro was fired because he threatened to go to the EEOC and report Bob's firing of Evita. Retaliation, not religion, was the motive behind Pedro's discharge.

What about the Age Discrimination in Employment Act (ADEA)? Didn't Bob fire

Ramona, stating that "she was getting too old for this kind of work"? Yes he did, but the company might be able to avoid an actionable age discrimination charge if they are timely in notifying the court that they are not an employer covered under the ADEA. The ADEA covers employers with twenty or more employees.[8] Milorad's Lawn Service is below this threshold (see Chapter 6). Though Bob's action is reprehensible, it is not necessarily actionable.

This exercise demonstrates several issues that will recur throughout this book. First, a practical exhibition of the workplace protections afforded to employees by various employment laws is given. Second, the employers who are required to comply with specific requirements vary from law to law. The size of the employer is often a determinant of whether a statute applies. Finally, just because an employee is a member of a protected group does not automatically prove that the employer's action was motivated by the employee's protected class status. The employee must produce evidence that his or her class was a motivating factor in the employer's decision.

UNION VERSUS NONUNION WORK ENVIRONMENTS

This book examines the impact of federal regulation in one of two distinct types of work environments—union and nonunion. It is important to make this distinction because of the differences in their respective legal environments.

In 2011, employees who were union members represented less than 11.9 percent of all employees, public and private, in the United States.[9] Public sector workers (government employees) continue to have a substantially higher unionization rate (37.0 percent) than workers in the private sector (6.9 percent).[10]

In organized work environments, the terms, conditions, and privileges of employment are specified under a contractual arrangement called a **collective bargaining agreement (CBA)**. Representatives of the employees meet with the employer to negotiate the provisions of this CBA. Thus, many employment practices and employee rights are formalized and guaranteed in this "contract."

For example, most CBAs stipulate benefit packages for all employees in the bargaining unit. The agreement is also likely to govern employee discipline and terminations. From the latter half of the nineteenth century through the first half of the twentieth century, workers were drawn to unions because of the protection the CBA provided. Under such contractual arrangements, workers received protection from arbitrary and capricious treatment by employers. Through the collective bargaining process, employees in organized workplaces have the opportunity to negotiate for more favorable working conditions, employment practices, and treatment. In essence, the negotiation process allows employees to establish contractual rights that their employer is legally required to honor.

Labor relations is that part of human resource management (HRM) that addresses employment issues arising from the organized workplace. In such a work environment, human resource (HR) professionals and managers are not only responsible for ensuring compliance with the federal and state employment laws that govern *all* workplaces, but they also must be familiar with federal and state labor laws.

Does this mean that employees who do not work in organized workplaces have little or no protection? Not at all. A growing body of employment law provides an increasing number of safeguards for employees working in nonunion environments, and this body of law is the primary focus of this book.

Before proceeding further, the authors wish to make a semantic distinction between *employment law,* which applies to *all* workplaces, and *labor law,* which applies only to *unionized* workplaces. When we refer to regulatory compliance, it is in respect to *employment law.*

As an indicator of why the study of compliance responsibilities is germane to a manager's career development, consider the results of two studies conducted by the Society for Human Resource Management (SHRM). In a 2005 survey of 422 early, mid, and senior level HR professionals, respondents were asked to identify the knowledge, skills, and abilities (KSA) critical for professional success. Knowledge of employment law was ranked among the top five critical KSAs.[11] In another study on undergraduate education, knowledge of employment law was ranked second only to communications skills as a requisite skill for a successful career.[12]

The HR activity that deals with the legal relationship between managers and employees in a regulated, but nonunionized, work environment is called **HR compliance**. HR compliance emphasizes employee rights and employer responsibilities in areas such as health, safety, security, and equal employment opportunity (EEO). In practice, this involves developing, communicating, and monitoring HR policies that ensure obedience to government regulations and laws. It also emphasizes the necessity for all managers to be knowledgeable of the laws, agency regulations, and court decisions that affect employment practices. Though states and, in some cases, municipalities have created laws and ordinances that regulate employment practices, the greatest source of workplace regulation is the federal government.

This textbook focuses primarily on the effects of federal regulation. The first thirteen chapters examine employers' responsibilities in these areas and the laws affecting them. The remaining two chapters focus on techniques related to ensuring compliance, such as job analysis and validation.

A BRIEF HISTORY OF GOVERNMENT REGULATION OF THE WORKPLACE

Before the twentieth century, there were very few federal laws that governed employee–employer relations. The Civil Rights Act of 1866 removed annual labor contracts (discussed in greater detail in Chapter 2), and the Civil Service Reform Act of 1883 provided protection for civil servants from the spoils system. However, it was not until the 1920s and 1930s that the first major wave of federal regulation began (see Table 1.1).

The First Period of Federal Regulation

The first large-scale attempt by the federal government to restrict management's actions in the workplace was the Railway Labor Act of 1926. This legislation gave employees in the railway industry the right to organize labor unions and bargain collectively for wages and working conditions. This law was motivated by the frequent strikes that plagued the railroad industry during the post–World War I era. It is important to remember that railroads were *the* means of transportation during this period. When railroad management refused to allow workers to form unions or ignored their demands, the workers would strike. The strike would shut down the specific railroad, and all commerce dependent upon that rail line would grind to a halt. Congress eventually intervened under pressure from the businesses affected by railroad strikes. The Railway Labor Act was very narrow in scope: it applied only to workers in the railway and steamship industries. A 1936 amendment added airline employees.[13]

As the Great Depression loomed, labor agitation heightened and civil unrest became an increasing concern. In an attempt to appease the growing labor movement, Congress enacted the Labor Disputes Act of 1932, commonly known as the Norris-LaGuardia Act. Although it made "yellow-dog contracts"—contracts under which workers promised not to join unions—unenforceable in federal courts and made it more difficult to obtain federal injunctions against strikers, it had little effect on state courts. The Norris-LaGuardia Act was quickly seen as a "paper tiger." It sounded good, but it did little to change the plight of industrial workers. As a result, greater pressure was placed on the Roosevelt administration and Congress to provide genuine labor reform.

The needed reforms came with the National Labor Relations Act of 1935 (NLRA; also known as the Wagner-Connerly Act or sometimes just the Wagner Act). This legislation guaranteed the right of private sector employees to organize and bargain collectively in much the same manner that the Railway Labor Act had done for railroad employees. To ensure that employees' rights to organize and bargain were not interfered with by management, the Act also established definitions of unfair labor practices by management. Additionally, the NLRA created an agency responsible for enforcing the Act, the National Labor Relations Board (NLRB). This federal agency was responsible for overseeing certification elections and investigating complaints of unfair labor practices. Some historians consider this to be the beginning of the movement toward "big government."[14] As laws were enacted, new bureaucracies were created to enforce them. As the federal government enacted more laws, the federal workforce increased accordingly.

When the NLRA was enacted, its intrusions into the workplace and restrictions on employers' property rights were considered outrageous.[15] The new law was immediately challenged in court. However, in *NLRB v. Jones & Laughlin Steel Corp.,*[16] the Supreme Court upheld the Act's constitutionality. A new era of "big government" was beginning.

The NLRA proved to be a less-than-perfect remedy for America's growing labor problems and serves as an example of the law of unintended consequences. Instead of reducing labor unrest, it may have made it worse. Following the enactment of the NLRA, work stoppages (strikes) actually increased from 2,014 in 1935, to 4,956 in 1944, a time when the United States was at war.[17]

One of the problems that arises from legislation designed to remedy a specific problem is that it can create a different problem. This is a phenomenon that Robert Merton referred to as the "law of unintended consequences." Essentially, the actions of government

Table 1.1

Sources of Regulation

Date	Statute	Enforcement Agency	Provisions
First-Wave Regulations			
1926	Railway Labor Act	National Railroad Adjustment Board (NRAB) National Mediation Board (NMB)	Permits employees in the railroad, airline, and steamship industries to organize and bargain collectively
1932	Labor Disputes Act (Norris-LaGuardia Act)	None	Made "yellow dog" contracts unenforceable in federal court. Made it more difficult to secure a federal court injunction for labor disputes
1935	National Labor Relations Act (Wagner Act)	National Labor Relations Board (NLRB)	Permits most private sector employees to organize and bargain collectively and created unfair labor practices (ULPs) for management
1935	Social Security Act	Social Security Administration	Provides for unemployment compensation
1938	Fair Labor Standards Act	Wage and Hour Division, Department of Labor	Regulates child labor and provides for minimum wage and overtime
1947	Labor-Management Relations Act (Taft-Hartley Act)	National Labor Relations Board (NLRB)	Balances power in labor-management relations by creating unfair labor practices (ULPs) for the union
1959	Labor Management Reporting and Disclosure Act (Landrum-Griffin Act)	Employee Standards Administration, Department of Labor	Provides protection for union members against abuses by the union
Second-Wave Regulations			
1963	Equal Pay Act	Equal Employment Opportunity Commission (EEOC)	Prohibits differentials in wages and benefits based on an employee's sex
1964	Civil Rights Act (as amended) (CRA 64)	Equal Employment Opportunity Commission (EEOC)	Prohibits discrimination in the conditions and privileges of employment based on an individual's race, color, religion, sex, or national origin
1967	Age Discrimination in Employment Act (as amended) (ADEA)	Equal Employment Opportunity Commission (EEOC)	Prohibits discrimination in the conditions of employment based on an individual's age (persons 40 years or older)
1970	Occupational Safety and Health Act	Occupational Safety and Health Administration (OSHA)	Regulates worker safety and health in the workplace
1972	Equal Employment Opportunity Commission (EEOC)	Equal Opportunity Commission (EEOC)	Amended CRA 64 to include private sector employers with fifteen or more employees and added state and local governments to Title VII coverage
1973	Vocational Rehabilitation Act	EEOC (§§ 501 & 505) and Office of Federal Contract Compliance Programs (OFCCP) (§ 503)	Holders of federal contracts or subcontracts in excess of $2,500 cannot discriminate against qualified individuals with physical or mental handicaps and must take affirmative action to hire such individuals
1974	Employee Retirement Income Security Act (ERISA)	Pension and Welfare Benefits Administration (PWBA) and Internal Revenue Service (IRS)	Regulates employees' pension programs

Date	Statute	Enforcement Agency	Provisions
1974	Vietnam Era Veteran's Readjustment Assistance Act	Office of Federal Contract Compliance Programs (OFCCP)	Holders of federal contracts or subcontracts in excess of $10,000 cannot discriminate against Vietnam era veterans and must take affirmative action to hire such individuals
1978	Pregnancy Discrimination Act	Equal Employment Opportunity Commission (EEOC)	Prohibits discrimination in the conditions of employment based on pregnancy and related medical conditions
1978	Civil Service Reform Act (CRSA 78)	Federal Labor Relations Authority (FLRA)	Prohibits discrimination in the conditions of federal employment based on an individual's race, color, religion, sex, or national origin
1986	Immigration Reform and Control Act (IRCA)	Office of Special Counsel for Immigration-Related Unfair Employment Practices (OSC)	Prohibits hiring of undocumented workers while prohibiting discrimination based on national origin and citizenship
1986	Consolidated Omnibus Budget Reconciliation Act (COBRA)	Internal Revenue Service (IRS)	Mandates extended health care coverage for retirees and some classes of terminated employees and dependents
1988	Worker Adjustment and Retraining Notification Act (WARN)		Requires certain employers to provide a 60-day advanced notification of "mass" layoffs and plant closings
1988	Drug-Free Workplace Act		Holders of federal contracts or subcontracts in excess of $100,000 must implement programs reasonably expected to reduce and eliminate employee drug use
1988	Polygraph Protection Act	Wage and Hour Division, Department of Labor	Restricts the use of polygraph testing in hiring and other employment decisions
1990	Americans with Disabilities Act (ADA)	Equal Employment Opportunity Commission (EEOC)	Title I prohibits discrimination in the conditions of employment based on an individual's physical or mental disability provided the individual is qualified for the position, or could be qualified through reasonable accommodation
1991	Civil Rights Act (CRA 91)	Equal Employment Opportunity Commission (EEOC)	Provides for punitive and compensatory damages in some instances of disparate treatment, provides for jury trials, and extends Title VII extraterritorially
1993	Family and Medical Leave Act (FMLA)	Wage and Hour Division, Department of Labor	Mandates up to 12 weeks unpaid leave for covered employees to care for family or medical emergencies as defined in the act
1994	Uniformed Services Employment and Reemployment Rights Act (USERRA)	Office of the Assistant Secretary for Veteran' Employment and Training DOL; Office of Special Counsel (OSC), DOJ	Guarantees civilian employment and reemployment rights of military veterans, members of the armed reserve, and National Guard
1996	Health Insurance Portability and Accountability Act (HIPAA)		Title I protects health coverage of employees who change jobs

invariably have unanticipated effects.[18] Such was the case of the NLRA, which made it unlawful for management to interfere with an employee's right to organize, but failed to place labor unions under comparable limitations. As a result, many unions operated without restraint, harming employers and union members alike. During the period immediately following the enactment of the NLRA, some labor unions had engaged in questionable activities such as extorting exorbitant dues and fees from members, coercing workers to join unions, striking neutral companies, and employing take-it-or-leave-it bargaining tactics. To rectify these abuses, Congress amended the NLRA in 1947 by enacting the Labor-Management Relations Act (LMRA; also known as the Taft-Hartley Act). The LMRA curbed the power of unions by instituting unfair labor practices by unions,[19] which created more regulation.

During this first wave of federal regulation, most government efforts concentrated on establishing procedures by which employees could organize. If these efforts were successful, then the union, as the employees' representative, could create a contractual relationship with the employer to ensure higher wages, better working conditions, and greater job security. Two other statutes enacted during this period were also designed to encourage union organizing. The Davis-Bacon Act of 1931 was designed to remove the incentive for hiring nonunion labor in federal government construction contracts exceeding $2,000. Any employer with such a contract was required to pay the "prevailing wage" for the geographic area in which the construction was taking place. The **prevailing wage** was based on the average union scale in the area. Hence, the employer was required to pay nonunion employees just as much as union workers. The incentive for cheaper nonunion labor was removed. Five years later, Congress enacted the Walsh-Healey Act to accomplish the same ends in federal supply contracts exceeding $10,000.

The Second Period of Federal Regulation

The second wave of federal regulation of the workplace began in the early 1960s under John Kennedy's New Frontier and more notably under Lyndon Johnson's Great Society. This wave continues today and is characterized by increasing government regulation of daily operations in the workplace.

Without a doubt, the most far-reaching legislation affecting employee relations in the United States is the Civil Rights Act of 1964.[20] Many of the subsequent employment laws are actually amendments to this Act. The relevant part of this statute for managers is Title VII. This is the portion of the Civil Rights Act of 1964 that mandates equal employment opportunity and is the central focus of Chapters 2 through 8 of this textbook. In short, Title VII makes it unlawful for any employer covered by the Act to discriminate against any individual in the conditions and privileges of employment because of that individual's race, color, religion, sex, or national origin.[21] The five categories of people against whom discrimination is prohibited are referred to as the **protected classes**. In the original legislation, the protected classes were based on race, color, religion, sex, and national origin. The simplest example of the type of discrimination that Title VII makes unlawful would be refusing to hire a qualified engineer because he is an African

American. The decision not to hire the engineer is not based on his qualifications but on his protected class status (in this instance, his race). Similarly, refusing to hire an applicant for a job based solely on the fact that she is a woman would be an example of discrimination on the basis of sex.

Since enactment of the Civil Rights Act in 1964, the protected classes of workers now include workers over the age of forty and those with physical or mental disabilities who can still perform their work with reasonable accommodation. This last class, qualified individuals with a disability, was added to the growing list of protected classes by the enactment of the Americans with Disabilities Act of 1990. According to the Bureau of Labor Statistics (BLS), approximately 62 percent of Americans in the labor force are members of at least one protected class (female, minority, over 40, etc.).[22] When one considers that men are protected against sex discrimination, and whites are protected against race discrimination, then 100 percent of the labor force is protected by at least one equal employment opportunity statute.

The second most influential statute affecting employment discrimination after the Civil Rights Act of 1964, is the Civil Rights Act of 1991. Chapter 3 will point out some of the provisions of this statute that have had a dramatic effect on increasing Title VII complaints. This Act not only provided for punitive and compensatory damages in specific cases of intentional employment discrimination,[23] but also permitted employment discrimination cases to be heard by a jury. Prior to the Civil Rights Act of 1991, all Title VII suits were heard before a federal judge only. The Act also expanded the jurisdiction of Title VII to the overseas plants, offices, and facilities of American-owned companies. Previously, Title VII was enforced only within the United States and its territories.

Besides focusing its attention on employment law, the federal government also involved itself in other workplace issues. In 1970, the Occupational Safety and Health Act was passed with the expressed purpose of making American factories and businesses safer places to work (see Chapter 11). Not only does this statute attempt to curb workplace accidents and injuries, it is also concerned with workplace illnesses. The Occupational Safety and Health Administration (OSHA), the agency responsible for enforcing the Act, also publishes the *Occupational Safety and Health Standards* (all 563 pages) to provide further explanation.[24]

The federal government has not only regulated the workplace by banning certain practices, as it did with the Polygraph Protection Act of 1988, but it also requires employers to engage in certain practices. The most recent example of the increasing administrative burdens on employers (thus making managing human resources more complicated) came in the form of the Family and Medical Leave Act (FMLA). This 1993 law requires employers with fifty or more full-time employees to grant up to twelve weeks of unpaid leave to qualified employees to attend to serious family or medical problems. Some of the situations that would justify this leave are: (1) the birth or adoption of a child; (2) serious injury or illness of a spouse, child, or parent; or (3) serious injury or illness of the employee.

Unfortunately, due to vague language in the FMLA, many employees are using this act to take unfair advantage of their employers. For example, by merely getting a certificate

Figure 1.1 Current Employment Practices Governed by Federal and State Laws

- Disciplinary action
- Harassment
- Layoffs
- Performance appraisal
- Promotions
- Recruiting
- Selection/hiring

- Training and development
- Terminations
- Wage and salary administration
- Work assignments
- Worker safety
- Worker security

---

of a medical condition from a local physician, an employee may use the FMLA to gain an unscheduled week of unpaid leave in order to extend a vacation. The FMLA, as noted in Chapter 9, has very little popular support among employers.

Additionally, the Patient Protection and Affordable Care Act of 2010, and its subsequent amendments in the Health Care and Education Affordability Reconciliation Act of 2010, mandated group health insurance coverage of employees for those firms with 50 or more employees. It also imposes "taxes" on employees as well as employers. A cumbersome and extremely ambiguous piece of legislation, its new employer obligations will have an impact on regulatory compliance for years. Its more basic provisions are also presented in Chapter 9.

The second wave of federal regulation laws appears to have expanded since its inception. Over time, more and more employee "rights" are turned into legal requirements with which management must comply. In a constantly evolving legal environment, it becomes absolutely essential that managers and HR professionals remain abreast of these latest developments (see Figure 1.1).

During the second wave, the courts were busy as well. The judicial activism of the Supreme Court was developing employment discrimination law through numerous landmark decisions. **Judicial activism** is the concept that judges must go beyond their power of merely interpreting the law to actually making law. There are liberal and conservative judicial activists. Judicial restraint is the antithesis of judicial activism.[25] The most noteworthy decision illustrating judicial activism was *Griggs v. Duke Power Co.,*[26] which created a new form of unlawful discrimination, *disparate impact* (discussed in Chapter 4). Two years later, in 1973, the Supreme Court standardized the process for determining whether *disparate treatment*, the other form of unlawful discrimination, had occurred in its ruling in *McDonnell-Douglas Corp. v. Green*[27] (as discussed in Chapter 3).

The concept of *sexual harassment* is a judicial invention as well.[28] This "new" Title VII violation is now the fastest-growing EEO complaint. Sexual harassment has evolved from a prohibition of coercing sexual favors in exchange for tangible job benefits to the expectation that employers will create work environments that are free of sexual innuendo and reference (see Chapter 5).

Federal courts have had a greater impact on the evolution and transformation of EEO laws than the other two branches of government. In the 1979 case *Steelworkers v. Weber,* the Supreme Court held that formal, voluntary affirmative action programs (AAPs) did not necessarily violate Title VII, and then it outlined the conditions under which such programs were permissible.[29] These decisions have had a profound effect on how AAPs are structured. Through the 1980s and 1990s, the Supreme Court would devote much energy to further defining disparate impact and disparate treatment, sexual harassment, and permissible affirmative action.

Despite some instances of abuse, all federal employment laws were enacted for the best of reasons. Some of these objectives include protecting workers' rights to organize, ending discriminatory practices, creating job opportunities for certain groups in society, and promoting safe work environments. However, along with these actual or intended benefits are the costs that such programs impose on both public and private sector employers. Whether in the form of a constraint on management actions or a monetary expenditure, compliance imposes definite costs on the organizations it affects. Under ideal conditions, these costs are offset by the law's intended benefits. As with any costs, the employer who is able to minimize them, relative to competitors, will usually achieve an advantage. Therefore, an important duty of both managers and HR professionals is to help reduce compliance costs.

If the costs of compliance are an issue, the costs of noncompliance are of even greater concern. The penalties for noncompliance not only result in fines, legal expenses, and damage awards but also in bad publicity that could damage a firm's image. What follows is an overview of the compliance costs confronting organizations.

COSTS OF COMPLIANCE

Most federal employment laws impose some compliance reporting requirements on employers. Employers are usually required to document their activities and maintain reports for periodic review or inspection by the specific regulatory agency. Failure to maintain such records or submit the required reports could result in the employer's being fined, losing their government contracts, to being subjected to other measures that the regulatory agency deems appropriate. To avoid these negative consequences, HR staffs must collect, compile, and synthesize relevant employment information. They are then required to document these data on the appropriate government form in the approved format.

One example of this reporting requirement is the Employer Employment Report (EEO-1), which is required of all employers with 100 or more employees who are subject to Title VII of the Civil Rights Act of 1964. The employers must submit an EEO-1 annually to the Equal Employment Opportunity Commission (EEOC).[30] The EEO-1 report requires employers to provide employment data for five racial/ethnic classifications, by gender, in ten job categories (see Figure 1.2). It is the HR staff's responsibility to compile and store this information. The HR staff is also responsible for compiling the report, assuring its accuracy, and ensuring that it is submitted in a timely manner. If the employer holds a federal contract or subcontract, an additional EEO-1 report must be sent to the Office of Federal Contract Compliance Programs (OFCCP). Failure to properly provide this information can result in fines or loss of government contracts.

An example of the importance of this reporting and documentation obligation is demonstrated in the Immigration Reform and Control Act (IRCA) of 1986. All employers are required to verify the eligibility of all employees who work in the United States with

14

Figure 1.2 **EEO-1 Report**

Source: The U.S. Equal Employment Opportunity Commission, 2008 EEO-1 Survey. http://www.eeoc.gov/eeo1survey/.

the U.S. Citizenship and Immigration Services (USCIS), and an Employee Eligibility Verification Form (Form I-9) must be maintained on file. All new employees are required to complete the Form I-9 within three business days of hiring.

The HR staff must collect and process the relevant personnel information required by this statute. Once collected, the information must then be protected and made readily accessible to the appropriate federal regulatory agency (in this case, Immigration and Customs Enforcement, or ICE) upon demand.

Sometimes the requirement involves more than completing and maintaining government forms. If the employer holds a federal contract or subcontract, receives federal grant or aid money, or is a depository of federal funds, there is an obligation under several statutes and regulations to develop and maintain formal affirmative action programs.[31] Meeting the government's requirements for a permissible AAP requires complicated utilization analysis (discussed in Chapter 9) and the development of realistic goals and timetables. All of this takes time and expertise if it is to be done properly. If it is not done correctly, the employer could be exposed to unnecessary litigation. These are only a few examples of the documentation requirements placed upon employers.

Naturally, HR professionals are responsible for knowing the current regulatory requirements and ensuring that they are properly followed. In larger companies, this is often a full-time job. In very large companies, it could require the services of several staffers. In any case, data gathering, analysis, and record keeping translate into money in the form of the HR staff's salaries. Compliance requires a good deal of data retrieval and record keeping. Naturally, the greater the need for documentation, the larger the HR staff, not to mention the time required by line mangers to furnish necessary information to HR. Even by the federal government's own estimate, in a report for the Small Business Administration, compliance costs for American businesses were estimated to be $970 billion.[32]

Fines or Loss of Contract

An unpleasant cost associated with regulatory compliance rules is the penalty for noncompliance. Fines frequently result from an employer's failure to maintain proper documentation. Remember IRCA's requirement to maintain a Form I-9 and supporting documentation? This means that all employees hired after November 6, 1986, must have the required immigration form in their personnel files. IRCA also requires that each employee's identity and status be appropriately verified (two forms of identification), and there must be some tangible proof of this verification. Keep in mind that the purpose of this law was to make it unlawful to hire undocumented workers (illegal aliens) and to protect jobs for citizens and resident aliens. Prior to its enactment, it was unlawful for an illegal alien to work in the United States, but it was not unlawful to hire them. IRCA documentation requirements immediately resulted in the modification of recruiting and selection procedures for virtually all business and public sector organizations nationwide. Additionally, employers had to absorb the time and cost of preparing and communicating new policies.

But these were only the initial compliance costs; noncompliance with these requirements can expose the organization to even greater costs. Under IRCA, any employer who fails to maintain the appropriate documentation faces a fine ranging from $110 to $1,100 for *each employee* without a Form I-9 and supporting records.[33] Furthermore, the fine for failure to maintain required documents can be imposed regardless of whether or not the organization actually hired any illegal aliens. The fine, straightforwardly, is for failing to comply with IRCA's record-keeping requirements, not for having undocumented workers on the payroll.

The employer may also be subject to further fines for hiring undocumented workers. In the case of government contractors or subcontractors, the worst penalty is often the loss of the current contract and ineligibility for future contracts. The same is true for financial institutions that hold federal funds—those deposits would be removed. Further, institutions that currently receive federal grant or aid money, such as universities, risk having the aid withdrawn as a consequence of any noncompliance.

Many of the federal statutes discussed in this textbook provide for direct noncompliance costs (fines or loss of contracts) as well as indirect noncompliance costs. The indirect noncompliance costs often result from conciliation agreements with the regulatory agency involving reinstating affected employees or applicants, paying back pay, paying front pay, or any legal expenses incurred by the employee or candidate. However, even greater costs can be incurred if the matter must be resolved through litigation.

Litigation Costs

Perhaps no cost currently heightens employers' compliance concerns more than the fear of litigation. The United States is one of the most litigious societies in the world, and American businesses are painfully aware of this phenomenon. The Judicial Conference Committee on Long-Range Planning estimated that nearly thirty million lawsuits are filed each year in the American judicial system,[34] and this trend is showing no signs of slowing. A 2011 Tower and Perrin report estimated that costs generated by the U.S. tort system rose to approximately $264.6 billion in 2010.

From a business perspective, employment litigation can translate into real business costs and many of these costs affect HRM. According to a survey conducted by the law firm of Jackson, Lewis, Schnitzler and Krupman for the Society for Human Resource Management,[35] 57 percent of the responding firms had experienced at least one employment litigation during the previous five years.

With average awards in employment cases exceeding $242,000,[36] it is easy to understand how such litigation can affect the organization's bottom line. Unfortunately, even when employers win a case, they still lose, since in the vast majority of cases, even when a company wins, it still must pay court costs and attorney fees. This creates a very strong incentive for managers to quickly identify compliance problems and take steps to resolve them internally. In this manner, HR professionals and line managers provide a tangible return to their organizations by reducing compliance costs.

To further complicate the litigation problem, many employees believe they have certain rights in the workplace upon which their employers may not infringe. Consequently,

Table 1.2

EEO Charge Receipts 1988–2012

Year	Receipts	Year	Receipts
1988	58,853	2001	80,840
1989	55,952	2002	84,442
1990	59,426	2003	81,293
1991	62,806	2004	79,432
1992	70,399	2005	75,428
1993	87,942	2006	75,768
1994	91,189	2007	82,792
1995	87,529	2008	95,402
1996	77,990	2009	93,277
1997	80,680	2010	99,922
1998	79,591	2011	99,947
1999	77,444	2012	99,412
2000	79,896		

Source: U.S. Equal Employment Opportunity Commission, All Statutes FY 1997–FY 2012, http://www.eeoc.gov/eeoc/statistics/enforcement/all.cfm (accessed March 31, 2013).

employees are far more prone to use litigation to protect these real or perceived rights. Many employees assume that they have the right to freedom of speech in the workplace. In most private employment situations this "right" may not exist, and in most instances, a private employer, as a private entity, is allowed to abridge an employee's free speech rights without violating public policy.[37] Our right to freedom of expression guaranteed under the Constitution protects us against any government restricting our speech, but imposes no such obligation on private entities (with a few rare exceptions).

In a similar vein, many employees believe they enjoy the right to freely date whomever they please. Moreover, these employees believe that any employer's nonfraternization policy, which prohibits coworkers from dating, violates their right to free association. Though the enforceability of these policies varies from state jurisdiction to state jurisdiction, "no dating" policies have been upheld in a number of courts.[38]

Besides legally protected rights (i.e., right to workplace health and safety, right to join a labor union, etc.), some workers and worker advocates believe workers are entitled to an even broader range of rights, many of which are currently without legal recognition. For example, some workplace rights advocates believe workers have the right to meaningful work, the right to self-management, the right to freedom of expression (such as wearing particular clothing), and many other "rights" not recognized by federal statutes or regulations.[39] This concern among employees for "rights," and the resulting belief that they are entitled to them, makes some employees more prone to litigate. Not surprisingly, after over thirty-six years of EEO laws, litigation is increasing rather than decreasing (see Table 1.2).

Since the laws that regulate employment practices are in a constant state of flux, managers and HR professionals are constantly reviewing their existing policies to ensure that they remain in compliance with the ever-changing legal environment.

As new laws or regulations are created and existing ones are modified or amended, HR professionals must update and adapt their policies and practices to these changes, or develop new ones. The impact of litigation cannot be overstated. Consequently, both managers and HR professionals are constantly under pressure to stay familiar with an increasing number of potential legal liabilities.[40]

Opportunity Costs

A direct result of the escalation in litigation has been what some authors call the "culture of fear."[41] In this instance, the fear is of being sued. In order to avoid litigation, some argue that intimidated companies may consciously eliminate product lines that are susceptible to lawsuits along with the jobs that go with them. In some situations, employers' concerns regarding potential product liability may be so severe that they choose not to offer a new product.[42] However, since employers do not report such decisions, it is extremely difficult to project the actual extent of this activity and its related costs.

Regretfully, fear of litigation can also affect an organization's management of its human resources. Some employers may retain less productive and more disruptive employees over fear that terminations would result in legal action. After all, EEO complaints arising from terminations are four times greater than all other sources combined.[43] Failing to take corrective action against "problem" employees might actually increase, rather than diminish, the potential for litigation.

These practices not only expose employers to potential reverse discrimination litigation (discussed in Chapter 8) but also create a dangerous precedent in allowing substandard performance or disruptive behavior to gain a degree of acceptance in the workplace. This not only has undesirable organizational consequences for the employer but also may expose the organization to litigation if it attempts to take corrective action later.

To illustrate this point, assume that a plant superintendent has allowed certain employees, who happen to be Hispanic, to leave early for lunch and return late. The reason she has permitted this to occur is a result of these employees' negative reactions when she first attempted to correct them. When confronted, some of the tardy Hispanic employees accused her of discriminating against them because they were Hispanic. Wishing to minimize conflict in the workplace, the plant superintendent gave up on taking action against these employees and hoped the situation would correct itself. Unfortunately, other employees are now taking longer-than-authorized lunch breaks. What is the likely response from a non-Hispanic employee when he or she is disciplined for not obeying the work rules on lunch break? The response in today's diverse workplace would most likely be, why are you punishing me for not coming back to work on time when you allow the Hispanic employees to do it all the time? By not equitably enforcing a work rule against a group of disruptive employees, the plant superintendent has created several new problems.

First, other employees see offenders being given slack and might conclude that the work rule in question is no longer being enforced. Second, when "other" employees are disciplined, they think it is unfair, and rightly so. Finally, because the "other" employees are being disciplined for breaking the work rule because they are *not* Hispanic (obviously the Hispanic employees were not disciplined because they *were* Hispanic), the "other" employees have grounds for filing a Title VII complaint. And all of this resulted because the plant superintendent was afraid the Hispanic employees would file a Title VII complaint—on an allegation that, by the way, was without merit.

Corporate Legitimacy

Another concern for organizations is the adverse effect noncompliance may have on their corporate legitimacy. **Corporate legitimacy** is the extent to which an organization's objectives, actions, and activities are viewed as being consistent with society's expectations. When an organization conforms to these societal expectations, it may enjoy a positive public image. When, however, an organization's actions are contrary to societal expectations, that organization loses its legitimacy—this translates into loss of public support and may place it at a competitive disadvantage.[44]

It is only natural that organizations are concerned about their public image. A poor image can have undesirable consequences for a firm's financial future. If the public as a whole feels that a given firm has acted in an irresponsible manner, a boycott of its products or services could easily result. This in turn could have a direct effect on the company's ability to compete in its industry. If the company's conduct is particularly outrageous, the public could call on their representatives in government to enact more restrictive laws and regulations. The old adage rings true that organizations that behave irresponsibly eventually cause laws to be enacted that affect *all* organizations, even the responsible ones.[45]

In the public arena, no organization wants to appear to be unfair, arbitrary, insensitive, or discriminatory. Negative media coverage resulting from an alleged violation of federal employment laws may be sufficient to damage a firm's reputation. Even when allegations are untrue, the firm's public image can be damaged. Such was the case when the *New York Times* reported that Texaco executives were using racial epithets when referring to African American employees.[46] Although the paper eventually admitted to gross inaccuracies in its story,[47] the damage to the company's reputation had been done.

GOVERNMENT LAWS AND REGULATIONS

Since laws and government regulations have such a substantial impact on HRM, a brief description of their sources is in order. It is not surprising that each of the three traditional branches of government (legislative, executive, and judicial) is a producer of laws or regulations that affect the workplace. Each branch of government imposes some requirements to which employers are expected to comply.

Statutory Law

Legislative bodies create statutes. In the strictest sense, when someone uses the term "law" they are referring to a "statute." In the federal government, enacting **statutory law** is strictly the right of the Congress of the United States. Congress receives this authority from Article I of the Constitution of the United States, which empowers it, among other things, to "regulate commerce with foreign nations and among the several States."[48] This is the Commerce Clause, which is the legal foundation for most of the labor and employment laws passed by Congress.

In terms of employment law, most statutes tend to be restrictive in nature. They identify specific employment practices in which employers are prohibited from engaging. In general, these prohibitions are broadly worded and, therefore, broad in scope. Too often, the details tend to be vague. To resolve this inherent ambiguity and the problems that arise from the day-to-day enforcement, many statutes either create or designate an enforcement agency. As more laws are enacted, more regulatory agencies are created or existing ones are expanded.

Classes of Employees Protected by the Act

It is important for managers to determine which employees are protected by a specific law and which are not. In some instances, like the Civil Rights Act of 1964, an extremely broad range of employees is covered, with very few exceptions (for example, independent contractors, parents, children, elected officials, and their personal staffs). In other statutes, several substantial classes of employees may be specifically excluded or exempted from the law's provisions. In others, like the National Labor Relations Act, supervisory personnel are excluded.[49]

To illustrate the importance of knowing who is entitled to a statute's protection, let's look at a possible complaint made by an employee that her employer is violating the Fair Labor Standards Act, the federal statute that requires employers to pay covered employees 1½ times their hourly rate of pay for each hour worked in excess of forty in a 168 consecutive hour workweek.[50] This act also makes a distinction between classes of employees who are entitled to overtime (nonexempt employees) and those who are not (exempt employees). The employee is concerned that she has not been paid overtime. The employee has proof that she has worked at least fifty hours in each of the three preceding workweeks.

However, before we can conclude that the employer has violated the FLSA, we must first determine whether the employee is entitled to the overtime mandated in the Act, that is, whether she is a nonexempt or an exempt employee. To do this, the manager must examine the employee's job classification, particularly the tasks, duties, and responsibilities of the job in question. In this illustration, let's assume the employee making the complaint was employed as an "outside salesperson" and that our review of her job description confirms this.

Her job duties reveal that she is primarily engaged in making sales away from the employer's place of business. Because she is a *bona fide* outside salesperson, she is among those job categories specifically exempted from the FLSA's minimum-wage and overtime provisions.[51] In other words, the FLSA does not require the employer to pay overtime to this employee. On the other hand, if the employee was not an exempted employee, she would have been entitled to overtime payments. The distinctions between exempt and nonexempt employees are discussed in greater detail in Chapter 8.

In most statutes, the section or part titled "definitions" defines both the "employees" who are entitled to the statute's protection as well as the "employers" who must comply. Because federal laws are designed to cover a broad range of employers and employees, it is often more effective for many of the laws discussed in this text to simply identify employers and employees they do not cover.

To illustrate this point, let's briefly return to this chapter's opening scenario. Remember that the supervisor informed the undocumented workers that because they were not U.S. citizens or resident aliens, they were not entitled to protection under U.S. employment laws. This assumption was false. Even though these workers were working illegally in the United States (both they and the employer were violating IRCA),[52] undocumented workers are nevertheless protected by most U.S. employment laws. They are entitled to the minimum wage and overtime under the FLSA[53] even though they have no legal right to be in the country. Furthermore, they are protected under the NLRA in regard to their right to organize a union free of interference from management.[54]

The rationale for this apparently paradoxical state of affairs lies squarely in the definition of "employee" in each of the affected statutes. Since the definitions do not specifically exclude undocumented workers (in fact, they are not mentioned at all), federal courts have concluded that illegal aliens are entitled to the same protection as any other employee.[55] Again, the lesson learned from this is simple: unless it is explicitly stated in a given statute that a specific class of employees is not covered, assume that class is covered.

Administrative Regulations

The executive branch of the government is charged with the responsibility of enforcing the laws enacted by the legislative branch. In the federal government, the executive branch draws its power from Article II of the Constitution.[56] As previously mentioned, more laws enacted by Congress create regulatory agencies to enforce the law in question or assign them to an existing agency. These regulatory agencies operate under the executive branch of government. A few of these agencies operate directly under the control of the president and report only to him. These so-called **independent agencies** like the EEOC and the NLRB operate with a greater degree of autonomy since their respective heads are appointed by the president, confirmed by the Senate, and are subject to removal only in the event of misconduct.

Most agencies are under the authority of a cabinet officer. For example, the Office of Federal Contract Compliance Programs, ICE, and the Wage and Hour Division of the Department of Labor.

As previously mentioned, most regulatory agencies arise from statutes, a legislative action. Typically, the Civil Rights Act of 1964 created the EEOC to enforce its provisions.[57] Similarly, the NLRB was created by the National Labor Relations Act to enforce that statute.[58] Some regulatory agencies, however, were not created by Congress, but instead were created by executive order. That is to say, the president created the agency to enforce either a statute or executive order. Such was the case for the OFCCP, which was created to monitor and enforce AAPs mandated by Executive Order 11246.[59]

In carrying out the day-to-day administration of a particular statute, regulatory agencies create definitive regulations. Since the statutes are broadly worded, the regulations fill in the details. For example, Title VII of the Civil Rights Act of 1964 makes it an unlawful employment practice to fail or refuse to hire, or to discharge, any individual or otherwise to discriminate against any individual with respect to his compensation, terms, conditions, or privileges of employment, because of said individual's race, color, religion, sex, or national origin.[60]

However, the statute does not go into the "specifics" of just exactly what a term, condition, or privilege of employment is. Neither does it tell us how to determine whether or not unlawful discrimination has actually occurred. These details usually fall within the jurisdiction of the regulatory agency.

For example, to define what is lawful and unlawful in the hiring or promotion of an employee, the EEOC developed the twenty-six-page *Uniform Guidelines on Employee Selection Procedures* (commonly referred to as the *Uniform Guidelines*).[61] These administrative regulations tell the employer how the EEOC determines whether or not a given employment practice is in violation of Title VII. It further provides the standards for determining whether or not a given selection criterion is job related (a process called *validation*) and tells the employer what records it is expected to maintain.

In addition to the *Uniform Guidelines*, the EEOC has also developed regulations for investigating allegations of sex discrimination,[62] religious discrimination,[63] national origin discrimination,[64] age discrimination,[65] and reverse discrimination.[66] Still, this only scratches the surface. The Title 29 of the *Code of Federal Regulations,* those federal regulations that apply to civil rights, exceeds 6,200 total pages, and these are expanded every year. The Title 42, which deals with public health welfare and civil rights, exceeds 1,200 pages.

THE REGULATORY AGENCIES

A regulatory agency exercises a great deal of power through its specific statute. It is up to the agency to interpret its statute and create regulations. Once the regulations are in place, the agency is in a position to conduct investigations to ensure that employers are in compliance with the statute and the subsequent regulations. Many agencies exercise the power to impose fines, penalties, and remedies. For example, the NLRB may enforce the NLRA through the use of administrative law judges. These agencies can enjoin (a legal term meaning that a court orders a person to either perform or refrain from performing some action) employers from carrying out certain decisions like employee terminations, promotions, and assignments; they may impose fines; or they may require employers to reinstate specific employees or eliminate certain employment practices.

Equal Employment Opportunity Commission

The Equal Employment Opportunity Commission is the primary federal agency responsible for overseeing federal EEO laws. Though initially created by Congress to enforce Title VII of the Civil Rights Act of 1964, the EEOC has since become responsible for enforcing the following statutes:

- Equal Pay Act of 1963
- Age Discrimination in Employment Act of 1967
- Sections 501 and 505 of the Rehabilitation Act of 1973
- Title I of the Americans with Disabilities Act of 1990
- Genetic Information Nondiscrimination Act of 2008

The EEOC is comprised of five commissioners. Each commissioner is appointed by the president and confirmed by the Senate to serve a five-year term. The terms are staggered to ensure that no two commissioners rotate off the commission in a given year. The president designates a chairman and vice chairman of the EEOC.

National Labor Relations Board

Like the EEOC, the National Labor Relations Board is an independent federal agency.[67] Similarly, its board is comprised of five members, each of whom serves a staggered five-year term. A member is appointed by the president of the United States and approved by the Senate. The duties of the NLRB in enforcing the national labor codes are twofold:

- Oversee employee free choice as to whether or not they will be represented by a labor union through democratic secret-ballot elections
- Investigate violations of the national labor code by either the employer or the union (such violations are known as *unfair labor practices*)

Occupational Safety and Health Administration

OSHA is the division of the Department of Labor responsible for enforcing the provisions of the Occupational Safety and Health Act of 1970. OSHA accomplishes its duties by:

- Establishing standards for workplace safety
- Investigating complaints of unsafe conditions or serious workplace accidents

Workplace safety and health issues, as well as OSHA's role, will be examined in Chapter 11.

Office of Federal Contract Compliance Programs

The Office of Federal Contract Compliance Programs is also a division within the Department of Labor. As its name implies, the OFCCP's efforts are concentrated on enforcing the antidiscrimination provisions of various federal laws pertaining to government contracts and subcontracts.[68] Such laws require contractors and subcontractors *not* to discriminate against protected groups and to establish AAPs for any groups that are *underrepresented* in the contractor's workforce. To serve this end, the OFCCP:

- Conducts compliance reviews of federal contractors' HR policies and practices
- Monitors federal contractors' progress toward achieving affirmative action goals
- Investigates complaints of discrimination

The OFCCP is the agency that establishes the federal standards for AAPs. These guidelines are commonly referred to as *Revised Order No. 4.*[69] The provisions of *Revised Order No. 4* and permissible AAPs are discussed in detail in Chapter 8.

Office of Labor Management Standards

The Office of Labor Management Standards is another division of the Department of Labor. Its major functions entail ensuring that labor unions are in compliance with their obligations to provide internal union democracy and are meeting the financial integrity requirements imposed under the Labor Management Reporting and Disclosure Act of 1959.

Wage and Hour Division

The Wage and Hour Division is an agency of the Department of Labor and has a broad range of federal statutes to enforce.[70] The Wage and Hour Division is responsible for administering:

- Minimum-wage provisions under the Fair Labor Standards Act, Davis-Bacon Act, Walsh-Healey, and Service Contract Act
- Child labor restrictions under the Fair Labor Standards Act
- Overtime provisions under the Fair Labor Standards Act, Davis-Bacon Act, Walsh-Healey, and Service Contract Act
- Restrictions in the use of polygraphs in employment decisions under the Polygraph Protection Act
- Grants of emergency employee leave with job security under the Family and Medical Leave Act
- Additional requirements on construction contracts arising out of the American Recovery and Reinvestment Act of 2009

The Wage and Hour Division's role in enforcement is discussed in Chapters 9 and 10.

THE FEDERAL JUDICIAL SYSTEM

The third source of employment law is the judiciary, which produces case law. Since 1964, the federal judiciary has been responsible for the majority of the significant changes in EEO laws and their application. Through their power of judicial review, activist courts have created many more conscientious theories of discrimination than the other two branches of government. Both disparate impact[71] and sexual harassment[72] were court

Figure 1.3   **Structure of the Federal Court System**

- Supreme Court
- Circuit Courts of Appeal
  (11 Geographic Circuits + the District of Columbia and Federal Circuits)
- Federal District Courts
  (94 districts)

creations. Additionally, the standards for permissible affirmative action programs evolved through the judicial, rather than the legislative, branch of government.[73] Because of its impact on EEO and other workplace laws, a brief discussion of the federal court system is provided.

Federal District Courts

The federal courts are arranged in a hierarchy of courts beginning with the federal district courts and culminating with the U.S. Supreme Court (see Figure 1.3). There are ninety-four district courts located in the fifty states as well as the District of Columbia and Puerto Rico. Three of these district courts cover the territories of the Virgin Islands, Guam, and the Northern Mariana Islands.

There are more than 600 district court judges authorized to preside over cases in the ninety-four federal districts.[74] The number of district court judges in each district is largely determined by the caseload arising from the specific district.

Federal district courts exercise original jurisdiction over most of the federal criminal and civil suits arising within the geographical boundaries of their districts (First through Eleventh Circuits, the District of Columbia Circuit, and the Federal Circuit). Original jurisdiction means that this court has the right to try a case and pass judgment based on the law and the facts of the case. This is also the court that can impose a remedy (injunction or fine). Violations of federal employment laws are civil matters, and most violations of the laws discussed in this textbook would originate in the federal district courts. In the event that either party to a District Court ruling feels that the Court made an error of law in their case, the party may appeal it to the appropriate Court of Appeals.

U.S. Courts of Appeals

The federal courts of appeals are organized in thirteen circuits. Eleven of these circuits, sometimes called the geographic circuits, are identified by ordinal numbers, the First through Eleventh Circuits, and consist of three or more states (see Figure 1.4). As their name implies, the geographic courts hear cases on appeal from the federal district courts within their geographical jurisdiction. Each court of appeals consists of at least six judges, depending on the given circuit's caseload. The smallest court, in terms of judges, is the First Circuit in Boston, Massachusetts, with five circuit judges.[75] The largest court is the Ninth Circuit in San Francisco, California, with twenty-eight judges.[76]

Figure 1.4   **The Thirteen Federal Circuits**

Circuit	States/Territories/Courts of Jurisdiction
First	Massachusetts, Maine, New Hampshire, Rhode Island, and Puerto Rico
Second	Connecticut, New York, and Vermont
Third	Delaware, New Jersey, Pennsylvania, and the Virgin Islands
Fourth	Maryland, North Carolina, South Carolina, Virginia, and West Virginia
Fifth	Louisiana, Mississippi, and Texas
Sixth	Kentucky, Michigan, Ohio, and Tennessee
Seventh	Illinois, Indiana, and Wisconsin
Eighth	Arkansas, Iowa, Minnesota, Missouri, Nebraska, North Dakota, and South Dakota
Ninth	Alaska, Arizona, California, Hawaii, Idaho, Montana, Nevada, Oregon, Washington, Guam, and the Northern Mariana Islands
Tenth	Colorado, Kansas, New Mexico, Oklahoma, Utah, and Wyoming
Eleventh	Alabama, Florida, and Georgia
Federal	Various courts
District of Columbia	District of Columbia

Source: Emory Law Library, U.S. Circuit Court Directories. U.S. Federal Courts Finder. Available at www.law.emory.edu/FEDCTS/.

One court of appeals, the U.S. Court of Appeals for the Federal Circuit, was created primarily to hear cases appealed from the U.S. Court of Federal Claims, Court of International Trade, Court of Veterans Appeals, Merit Service Protection Board, and the Patent and Trademark Office. Under certain circumstances, the Court of Appeals for the Federal Circuit will hear appeals from district courts involving patents and minor claims against the federal government including issues arising from federal employment.

The Thirteenth Circuit is the U.S. Court of Appeals for the District of Columbia. This circuit addresses appeals originating in the District of Columbia and hears cases arising from legislation affecting the departments and agencies of the federal government. As previously mentioned, some statutes create regulatory agencies that often operate like quasi-judicial bodies. For example, the NLRB is authorized by the National Labor Relations Act to resolve labor disputes. Any appeal against a NLRB decision is filed in the U.S. Court of Appeals for the District of Columbia rather than the nearest federal district court.

Regardless of the circuit, the federal courts of appeals all have the same basic functions:

- Review district court cases for errors of law—misinterpretation of federal law
- In extremely rare instances, overturn district court decisions on factual grounds;[77] this occurs only when the appellate court has strong evidence that the lower court was wholly unreasonable in considering the facts of the case.

Most often, the court of appeals rules on the district court's interpretation of the law it used in making its decision. If the court of appeals concludes that the district court's interpretation and application of the law was appropriate, then the court of appeals will *affirm* the lower court's decision. This essentially means the district court's decision will stand, as will the remedies it imposed.

If it is concluded that the lower court made an error in applying the law, the court of appeals may **vacate** or *reverse* the district court's decision. This means that the district court's decision has been overturned or voided. Sometimes the court of appeals may vacate part of the decision, instruct the lower court where it erred (improperly interpreted the law), and then return the case (a process called **remand**) to the district court for re-examination under the courts of appeals' previous instructions on the point of the law. If either party feels that the court of appeals made an error in its interpretation of the law, that party can attempt to appeal the case to the Supreme Court.

The Supreme Court

At the very top of the federal judicial hierarchy is the Supreme Court of the United States. This court hears cases on appeal from the U.S. Courts of Appeals and state supreme courts. Appeals to the Supreme Court are not automatic. A party requesting an appeal applies for a **writ of certiorari**. If approved, the writ would compel the court of appeals to provide records of a case for review by the Supreme Court. Simply stated, the writ of certiorari indicates that the Supreme Court will hear the appeal. In order for a writ of certiorari to be granted, at least four of the nine justices of the Supreme Court must agree to hear the case in question; otherwise the appeal is automatically denied. This means that the decision of the court of appeals stands.

To demonstrate how this works, let us assume that a party in Muncie, Indiana, sued his employer for reverse discrimination. The suit was first heard in the U.S. District Court for the Northern District of Indiana, the federal court exercising original jurisdiction. The district court concluded that the employer's AAP was permissible and its actions did not violate the Civil Rights Act of 1964.

Feeling that the district court erred in its interpretation of the law, the complaining party appealed this decision to the appropriate court of appeals, in this case the U.S. Court of Appeals for the Seventh Circuit. On appeal, the Seventh Circuit concluded that the lower court had erred (perhaps it failed to consider whether the employer's actions created an absolute bar) and, therefore, reversed the district court's decision. The employer now feels that the court of appeals' decision is in error, and petitions the Supreme Court to hear the case in the hope that the Seventh Circuit's decision will be reversed. As an appellate court, the Supreme Court can affirm, reverse, or remand a case just like the circuit courts. In this example, let us assume that four justices did not agree to hear the case and certiorari is denied. This would mean that the decision rendered by the Seventh Circuit would stand, as would its standard for judging similar claims of reverse discrimination. However, the standards would apply only to federal district courts within the jurisdiction of the Seventh Circuit (Indiana, Illinois, and Wisconsin). The Seventh Circuit's decision would not affect federal district courts in the Eleventh Circuit (Alabama, Georgia, and Florida) or any other circuit.

If, on the other hand, a writ of certiorari were granted and the case were heard by the Supreme Court, the Court's decision would apply to all federal courts in all thirteen circuits. Assume that the employer has argued that its affirmative action goal is to mirror the relevant external labor market and that the AAP would cease to operate when this end is accomplished. The complaining party argues that the employer must establish an identifiable numerical goal (not a vague "when it mirrors the relevant labor market") in order to determine when the AAP has achieved its goal and is no longer needed. The legal issue is which of these two approaches should be determinant of the AAP's termination?

Assume the Seventh Circuit agreed with the complaining party, but the employer still feels its standard would satisfy the requirement that its plan is temporary and, therefore, permissible under Title VII. If the Supreme Court hears the case and concludes that the employer's action is correct, this standard will now be applied to future cases addressing the issue of AAPs being temporary.

This means that in all ninety-four federal districts and thirteen circuits, affirmative action goals could be stated as achieving proportional representation with their relevant labor markets and *not* violate the temporary-in-nature requirement. On the other hand, had the certiorari been denied, then only stated numerical goals would be permissible, but this would apply only within the jurisdiction of the Seventh Circuit. Another circuit could permit the "mirroring the relevant labor market" standard.

Case Law

The judicial branch, through court decisions, sometimes produces what is referred to as common law. These are "laws" that result from a process known as judicial review. This process is based upon a court's interpretation of the Constitution, statutes, or administrative regulation. Particularly in instances where a statute is especially vague, or fails to adequately address the issue in question, the court may actually create law by resolving the ambiguity. "Disparate impact" was one such instance in which a court, in this case the Supreme Court, effectively created law. Prior to the *Griggs v. Duke Power Company* decision, unlawful discrimination was limited to intentional discrimination against an individual because of that individual's race, color, religion, sex, or national origin (a form of discrimination known as disparate treatment). The Supreme Court's decision in *Griggs* created a second form of actionable discrimination by making it unlawful when a selection procedure results in a statistical imbalance of one of the protected classes and the procedure *cannot* be shown to be job related.[78] Interestingly, the EEOC defined what that statistical imbalance was in its *Uniform Guidelines*, an example of case law resulting in administrative law. The term **actionable discrimination** merely means that a person is seeking legal redress for the discrimination under a specific statute.

When creating case law, the courts are expected to follow two guiding principles—congressional intent and precedent. **Congressional intent** means that the court must view the issue in terms of what Congress was trying to accomplish *at the time the statute was enacted*. To illustrate congressional intent, let us look at the Supreme Court's decision in *EEOC v. Arabian American Oil Co.* In this case, the employee sued his employer because he was being harassed at a Middle Eastern processing plant. The employee was a naturalized U.S. citizen born in Lebanon and was being harassed by foreign employees at the site because of his national origin (Lebanese) and his religion (Christianity). The employee claimed that the employer has a responsibility under Title VII to provide a harassment-free work environment. The employer contended that Title VII applied only within the boundaries of the United States and its territories. Since the plant is located on foreign soil, only the host country's laws and not United States' laws (to include Title VII) apply. Under the concept of congressional intent, the Court had to determine, based on the wording of Title VII, whether or not Congress (in 1964) intended the Civil Rights Act to be enforced beyond the territorial boundaries of the United States. When this issue appeared before the Supreme Court, it concluded that the 91st Congress (the Congress that had enacted the Civil Rights Act of 1964) had not intended for Title VII to be applied extraterritorially (beyond the boundaries of the United States or its territories).[79] As a result of this interpretation of congressional intent, United States EEO laws did not receive extraterritorial applications until the Civil Rights Act of 1991.[80]

Congressional intent is drawn from the legislative branch of government, but precedent is drawn from the judicial. **Precedent** is based on the legal principle of *stare decisis*, which means adherence to decided cases.[81] When judges are required to make a decision on a case in which statutory guidance is vague or absent, they rely on legal interpretations from previous cases on the same subject. For example, a case involving a voluntary AAP would refer to the Supreme Court decision in *Steelworkers v. Weber*[82] to determine if the program was in compliance with Title VII. Consequently, all such cases refer back to this landmark ruling to determine whether or not a given AAP is permissible. The *Steelworkers v. Weber* decision provides the precedent for all subsequent rulings.

One school of judicial thought, **judicial activism**, views the judicial branch of government as a means to achieve social justice. The federal courts are used as a means to extend civil rights protections in the workplace. Proponents of judicial activism, therefore, call on the courts to make social policy, particularly in the area of protecting minority rights and the public interest from the hands of majorities motivated by folly or injustice.[83] In practice, this means that a court makes significant changes in public policy, particularly in policies made by other governmental institutions.[84]

The avoidance of judicial activism is **judicial restraint**.[85] Essentially the court refrains from law making and restricts its activities to the settlement of legal conflicts. Proponents of judicial restraint tend to see judicial activism as the courts' exceeding their authority and advocate that courts should restrict their activities to enforcing existing laws, not creating new ones.

There can be little doubt that the federal court system has exercised an increasingly activist role in government policy making. Though this has resulted in national policies regarding such issues as abortion, birth control, capital punishment, and school prayer (to name a few), the decisions involving the ethnic and gender composition of the workplace are the major concern for an organization's managers. Therefore, HR professionals and managers must remain alert to the changes imposed by the courts.

Understanding Legal Citations

Since so much of compliance is concerned with legal documents (statutes, agency regulations, and court cases), it is necessary that managers understand the mysteries of legal citations. Many government and legal documents are referenced under what is called *A Uniform System of Citation*. What follows is a very cursory explanation of how this system works. Take, for example, the legal citation for the landmark Supreme Court decision on the permissibility of affirmative action plans under Title VII, *Steelworkers v. Weber*, 443 U.S. 193, 208 (1979). If you wanted to locate a copy of this decision and read it yourself, the citation provides all the information you need. First, it provides the title of the decision, *Steelworkers v. Weber*. Next, the citation tells you the volume of the particular legal reporter that contains the case. In this instance, the decision is found in the 443rd volume of *United States Reports* (that is what the "U.S." stands for in the citation). *United States Reports* is provided by the Supreme Court and printed by the Government Printing Office; it contains only decisions rendered by the U.S. Supreme Court. Next, the citation tells the reader on which page in volume 443 the *Steelworkers v. Weber* decision begins. In this instance, the citation indicates page 193. Finally, the citation informs the researcher that this ruling occurred in 1979; the year in parentheses is the year of the decision.

Sometimes other numbers are added to the citation. This usually is done to identify a specific page in the text of a decision containing an important legal point or explanation. For example, a researcher wants to reference the four standards that an employer's affirmative action plan must satisfy in order to avoid a Title VII. This information is found on page 208 of the legal reporter.

To reiterate, this location would be conveyed in the following citation form: *Steelworkers v. Weber*, 443 U.S. 193, 208 (1979). The number 208 following the number 193 (the page on which the decision begins) tells the researcher that the specific information sought is found on page 208 of the 443rd volume of *United States Reports*.

Statutes are handled in the same manner as cases, though their form changes once they are codified. The Civil Rights Act of 1964 provisions prohibiting discrimination in employment on the basis of race, color, religion, sex, or national origin were initially found, after enactment, in a legal reporter called *Statutes at Large* in the following format: 78 Stat. 255 (1964). Like the case format, the first number, 78, tells the researcher that the information is found in the 78th volume of *Statutes at Large* (Stat.) and is found on page 255. This same section of the 1964 act is also found in its codified form as: 42 U.S.C. § 2000e–2. This indicates that it can be found in the Title 42 of the *United States Code*. However, this time, instead of referring the reader to a page, the reader is referred to a section (§), specifically § 2000e-2. Figure 1.5 provides the abbreviations for the most common legal sources containing information used in this textbook.

MANAGING RISK IN A LEGAL ENVIRONMENT

Due to the litigious nature of American society, it is becoming increasingly important for managers to fully understand the impact of federal regulation of HR practices in their

Figure 1.5   **Common Abbreviations Used in Legal Citations**

Abbreviations	Law Reporter	Material Reported
U.S.	*United States Reports*	U.S. Supreme Court decisions
S.Ct.	*Supreme Court Reporter*	U.S. Supreme Court decisions
F.3d	*Federal Reporter, 3rd Series*	Federal appeals court decisions
F.2d	*Federal Reporter, 2nd Series*	Federal appeals court decisions
F.Supp.2d	*Federal Supplement, 2nd Series*	Federal district court decisions
F.Supp.	*Federal Supplement*	Federal district court decisions
U.S.C.	*United States Code*	Federal statutes
Stat.	*Statutes at Large*	Federal statutes
C.F.R.	*Code of Federal Regulations*	Federal agency regulations

workplaces. This includes being aware of the sources of such regulation (legislative, executive, and judicial). It further means that managers must understand their obligations in conducting investigations and how these will affect, or be affected by, the investigations of the regulatory agencies and the courts. It is equally crucial that these professionals understand the importance of their roles in reducing their organizations' exposure to employment litigation and the related costs of compliance.

How do managers and HR professionals assist their organizations in reducing compliance costs? They do so by:

- Monitoring the legal environment for changes in compliance requirements
- Updating existing personnel policies when necessitated by changes in the legal environment
- Continually monitoring employment practice to ensure compliance
- Providing training and information to management and supervisory employees
- Providing training and information to nonsupervisory employees

In order to reduce exposure to litigation from noncompliance, managers should consider including a risk analysis of the legal implication of major human resource decisions. This has become such a concern in human resource practices that the SHRM Employment Practices Committee encourages the use of risk management techniques. The five basic steps of classic risk management theory are:

1. Identify and evaluate loss exposure
2. Develop policies and procedures for minimizing and preventing loss
3. Disseminate the policies and procedures
4. Provide training
5. Implement organization policies and procedures[86]

SUMMARY

This chapter provides an overview of the federal system and its effect on HR practices. You have been introduced to the differences between union and nonunion workplaces, the different sources of "law" for these workplaces, and the impact of regulation on HR practices.

Labor relations is the part of HRM that addresses employment issues arising from the organized workplace, a workplace in which a union represents the interests of the employees. The area of HRM that deals with the relationship between managers and employees in a regulated, but nonunionized, environment is called HR compliance.

Before the twentieth century, there were very few federal laws that governed employee–employer relations. Since that time, there have been two waves of federal regulation. The first wave began with the passage of the Railway Labor Act of 1926 and included the major legislation related to unions. The second wave began in the early 1960s with the passage of the Civil Rights Act of 1964 and is still in process. This wave includes all of the EEO/AA laws. Such government regulation has had an impact on employers through administrative costs of compliance, fines or contract losses, litigation costs, and opportunity costs.

This chapter also introduced the federal judicial system and regulatory agencies, both of which have a direct effect on risk management for any organization and the resulting costs associated with compliance. The knowledge of the origins of federal regulations, statutes, and decisions is essential if organizations are to operate effectively in the current legal environment.

The laws that regulate the workplace come from many sources. With three branches of government (legislative, executive, and judicial), it is not surprising that each produces laws or regulations that affect the workplace.

The remaining chapters in this textbook provide the basic knowledge and understanding of federal laws and regulations necessary to meet the organization's legal obligations and still achieve organizational objectives. The legal environment of HR practices will continue to increase in complexity, and it is incumbent upon all managers and HR professionals to remain abreast of these developments.

KEY TERMS AND CONCEPTS

Actionable discrimination
Collective bargaining agreement (CBA)
Congressional intent
Corporate legitimacy
HR compliance
Independent agencies
Judicial activism
Judicial restraint

Labor relations
Precedent
Protected classes
Remand
Statutory law
Vacate
Writ of certiorari

DISCUSSION QUESTIONS

1. How does labor law differ from employment law?
2. Discuss the significance of the first and second waves of federal legislation.

3. What are the protected classes covered under Title VII of the Civil Rights Act of 1964? From what are they protected?
4. What is the impact of government regulation on the workplace?
5. What are the three sources of employment law?
6. Identify and briefly describe the functions of the regulatory agencies.
7. Where would one look for the following legal information: 443 U.S.193, 91 F.3d 1547, 933 F.Supp. 1157, 42 U.S.C. § 2000e, and 29 C.F.R. §1604.11?

NOTES

1. 8 U.S.C. § 1324a(1).
2. 29 U.S.C. § 206.
3. 29 U.S.C. § 207.
4. 29 U.S.C. § 212; 29 C.F.R. § 570.35.
5. 42 U.S.C. § 2000e-2(a)(1).
6. 42 U.S.C. § 2000e (b).
7. 42 U.S.C. § 2000e-3(a).
8. 29 U.S.C. § 630(b).
9. U.S. Bureau of Labor Statistics, "Union Members in 2011," *Union Members Summary* (January 25, 2012), www.bls.gov/news.release/union2.nr0.htm (accessed October 20, 2012).
10. Ibid.
11. J. Dooney, N. Smith, and S. Williams, *Graduate Curriculum Study* (Alexandria, VA: SHRM Research, 2005), pp. 38–41.
12. L. Kluttz, and D. Cohen, *SHRM Undergraduate HR Curriculum Study* (Alexandria, VA: SHRM Research, 2003), pp. 18–22.
13. 25 U.S.C. § 181 (2007).
14. J.F. Walker and H.G. Vatter, *The Rise of Big Government in the United States* (Armonk, NY: M.E. Sharpe, 1997); L. Bennett and S. Bennett, *Living with Leviathan: Americans Coming to Terms with Big Government* (Lawrence: University of Kansas Press, 1990).
15. W. Manchester, *The Glory and the Dream: A Narrative History of America, 1932–1972* (Boston, MA: Little, Brown, 1974), pp. 133–134.
16. 301 U.S. 1 (1937).
17. U.S. Bureau of the Census, *Statistical Abstract of the United States: 1951*, 71st ed. (Washington, DC: Government Printing Office, 1951).
18. R.K. Merton, "The Unanticipated Consequences of Purposive Social Action," *Sociological Review* 1 (6) (December, 1936): 894–904.
19. 29 U.S.C. § 158(b) (2007).
20. 42 U.S.C. § 2000e *et. seq.* (2007).
21. 42 U.S.C. § 2000e-2(a)(1).
22. U.S. Bureau of Labor Statistics, Employment Status of the Civilian Noninstitutional Population by Age, Sex, and Race, 2007, ftp://ftp.bls.gov/pub/special.requests/lf/aat3.txt (accessed August 20, 2008).
23. 42 U.S.C. § 1981, 9(a).
24. 29 C.F.R. Part 1910.
25. K.L. Hall, ed., *The Oxford Companion to the Supreme Court of the United States* (New York: Oxford University Press, 1992), p. 454.
26. 401 U.S. 424 (1971).
27. 411 U.S. 792, 802 (1973).
28. *Williams v. Saxbe,* 413 F. Supp. 654 (D. D.C. 1976).

29. 411 U.S. 972 (1973).

30. 29 C.F.R. § 1602.7.

31. E.O. 11246; 42 U.S.C. § 2000e.

32. N.C. Crain and W.M. Crain, *The Impact of Regulatory Costs on Small Firms,* Washington, DC: SBA Office of Advocacy (September 2010).

33. 8 U.S.C. § 1324 (5).

34. Judicial Conference Committee on Long-Range Planning, *Conserving Core Values. Report on the Judiciary* (Washington, DC: Government Printing Office, 1995), p. 11.

35. J.C. Sharf and D.P. Jones, "Employment Risk Management," in *Managing Selection in Changing Organizations,* ed. J.F. Kehoe (New York: John Wiley & Sons, 2000), pp. 271–318.

36. Ibid.

37. *Teleflex Information Systems, Inc. v. Arnold,* 513 S.E.2d 85, 88 (N.C. App. 1999).

38. *Smith v. Wal-Mart Stores,* 891 F.2d 1177, 1180 (5th Cir. 1990); *Wilson v. Scruggs,* 1999 U.S. Dist. LEXIS 2607 (N.D. Miss. 1999).

39. G. Ezorsky, ed., *Moral Rights in the Workplace* (Albany: State University of New York Press, 1977).

40. R.B. Edwards, "Legal Skills Important Part of HR Professional's Tool Kit," *HR News* 17 (5): 26.

41. P.M. Garry, *A Nation of Adversaries: How the Litigation Explosion Is Reshaping America* (New York: Plenum Press, 1997); P.K. Howard, *The Death of Common Sense* (New York: Random House, 1994).

42. Ibid.

43. U.S. Equal Employment Opportunity Commission, *Annual Report 1985 Combined Annual Report 1986, 1987, 1988; Annual Report 1989; Annual Report 1990; Combined Annual Report 1991 and 1992; Annual Report 1993;* and *Annual Report 1994* (Washington, DC: Government Printing Office).

44. T. Parsons and C. Perrow, *Complex Organizations,* 2d ed. (Glenview, IL: Scott, Foresman, 1979).

45. K. Davis, "The Meaning and Scope of Social Responsibility," in *Contemporary Management: Issues and Viewpoints,* ed. J.W. McGuire (Englewood Cliffs, NJ: Prentice-Hall, 1974), p. 631.

46. K. Eichenwald, "Texaco Executives, on Tape, Discussed Impeding a Bias Suit," *New York Times,* November 4, 1996, p. A1.

47. K. Eichenwald, "Investigation Finds no Evidence of Slur on Texaco Tapes," *New York Times,* November 11, 1996, p. A1.

48. U.S. Constitution, Article 1, § 8, clause 3.

49. 29 U.S.C. § 152(3) (2012).

50. 29 U.S.C. § 207.

51. 29 U.S.C. § 541.500.

52. 8 U.S.C. § 1324a(a).

53. *NLRB v. Apollo Tire Co., Inc.,* 604 F.2d 1180 (9th Cir. 1979).

54. *Sure-Tan, Inc. v. NLRB,* 467 U.S. 883 (1984).

55. Ibid., at 892; *Apollo Tire Co.,* 604 F.2d at 1184; *Fuentes v. INS,* 765 F.2d 886, 888 (9th Cir. 1985); *DeCanas v. Bica,* 424 U.S. 351, 356–357 (1976).

56. U.S. Constitution, Article 2, § 3.

57. 42 U.S.C. § 2000e-4.

58. 29 U.S.C. § 153.

59. 28 Fed. Reg. 11717 (1965).

60. 42 U.S.C. § 2000e-2.

61. 29 C.F.R. Part 1607.

62. 29 C.F.R. Part 1604.

63. 29 C.F.R. Part 1605.

64. 29 C.F.R. Part 1606.

65. 29 C.F.R. Part 1625.

66. 29 C.F.R. Part 1606.

67. 29 U.S.C. § 153.

68. 29 C.F.R. §§ 7 & 8.

69. 41 C.F.R. Part 60–2.

70. 29 U.S.C. § 204.

71. *Griggs v. Duke Power Company,* 401 U.S. 424 (1971).

72. *Meritor Savings Bank v. Vinson,* 477 U.S. 57 (1986).

73. H. Belz, *Equality Transformed: A Quarter-Century of Affirmative Action* (New Brunswick, NJ: Transaction Publishers, 1992).

74. U.S. District Courts, *U.S. Courts* (2008), www.uscourts.gov/districtcourts.html (accessed August 20, 2008).

75. The First Circuit consists of Massachusetts, Maine, New Hampshire, Rhode Island, and Puerto Rico.

76. The Ninth Circuit consists of Alaska, Arizona, California, Hawaii, Idaho, Montana, Nevada, Oregon, Washington, Guam, and the Northern Mariana Islands.

77. *DeJarnette v. Corning, Inc.,* 133 F.3d 293, 297 (4th Cir. 1998).

78. 401 U.S. 424 (1971).

79. *EEOC v. Arabian American Oil Co.,* 499 U.S. 244 (1991).

80. 42 U.S.C. § 2000e(f).

81. H.C. Black, *Black's Law Dictionary* (St. Paul, MN: West Publishing, 1990), p. 1406.

82. 443 U.S. 193 (1979).

83. K.M. Holland, *Judicial Activism in Comparative Perspective* (New York: St. Martin's Press, 1991).

84. B.C. Canon, "A Framework for the Analysis of Judicial Activism," in *Supreme Court Activism and Restraint,* ed. S.C. Halpern and C.M. Lamb (Lexington, MA: Lexington Books, 1982), pp. 385–419.

85. L. Baum, *The Supreme Court,* 6th ed. (Washington, DC: CQ Press, 1998).

86. Edwards, "Legal Skills Important Part of HR Professional's Tool Kit"; P.J. Petesch, "The ADA, HIV, and Risk Management Strategies," *Legal Report* (May 1998), pp. 1–6.

PART II

REGULATION OF EQUAL EMPLOYMENT OPPORTUNITY

2

EQUAL EMPLOYMENT OPPORTUNITY

Regulatory Issues

LEARNING OBJECTIVES

- Understand the evolution of equal employment opportunity laws in the context of American history.
- Explain what employment practices are unlawful under Title VII.
- Identify the classes of employers and types of people required to comply with Title VII.
- Describe how an equal employment opportunity (EEO) complaint is filed with the Equal Employment Opportunity Commission (EEOC) or a fair employment practice agency.
- Explain how "reasonable cause" is determined by an investigative agency.

OPENING SCENARIO

Malcolm, an Asian American, applies for a management position with the employer, Eternal Therapies (ET), a small pharmaceutical marketing research company employing ten full-time and four part-time employees. Malcolm is well qualified; he has a B.S. in biology from Cornell University and a Pharm.D. from Auburn University. He also has seven years' experience in pharmacy sales and marketing research. Additionally, he recently obtained an Executive M.B.A. from the Wharton School of Business. ET interviewed Malcolm and eight other candidates. Malcolm was one of two finalists brought back for a final round of interviews.

On January 3, 2012, ET's selection committee ultimately chose Robert, a white male who had no marketing research experience and whose highest degree was an online MBA. When Malcolm asked why a substantially less qualified individual was hired instead of him, Malcolm was told Robert received the job offer because he had work experience with a competitor. The employer told Malcolm that given Robert's experience, it believed the company would gain the most competitive benefit by hiring Robert.

Malcolm later found a less desirable job with another company. However, he continued to feel that ET had treated him unfairly, a thought that bothered him more and more as time progressed. After much discussion with his friends and family, Malcolm finally decided to file a complaint with the EEOC on February 14, 2013, claiming that ET had unlawfully discriminated against him on the basis of his race.

Can Malcolm make a Title VII claim that he was unlawfully discriminated against because of his race? By the end of this chapter, you should be able to make that determination.

THE HISTORICAL BACKGROUND OF EQUAL OPPORTUNITY

The history of federal civil rights law begins with the end of the Civil War and the abolition of slavery. Following the abolition of slavery by the Thirteenth Amendment to the Constitution, many states had passed **Black Codes** to prevent freedmen, newly emancipated slaves, from enjoying the full benefits of citizenship.[1] Among the rights denied freedmen by these black codes were the rights to bear arms, to assemble after sunset, to serve on juries, and to vote. In some states it was unlawful for freedmen to marry whites. There were laws and ordinances that even limited the professions in which African Americans could engage (usually to domestic servants or agricultural laborers), and some required African Americans to sign annual employment contracts.[2] In a few states, laws even restricted the right of newly emancipated slaves to purchase, hold, or convey property.

Contrary to popular belief, these limitations on the rights of African American citizens were not confined to the southern states. At the end of the Civil War, only five northern states allowed African American citizens to vote on the same terms as whites.[3] Even prior to the war free Blacks were denied basic civil liberties. As an example, the 1848 state constitution of Illinois[4] and the 1851 state constitution of Indiana[5] denied voting rights to Blacks. In the then territory of Oregon, Blacks could not own real property, vote, initiate lawsuits, or even migrate into the territory.[6] Because of this environment of unequal treatment by state governments, the first federal civil rights act was passed, the Civil Rights Act of 1866. Among its provisions was the first federal prohibition on discrimination in employment. Because newly emancipated blacks were required to sign annual employment contracts (which contained severe penalties for noncompliance), and nonblacks were not, this first civil rights law made such race-based contracts unlawful and permitted the aggrieved party to sue for punitive and compensatory damages.[7] One residual effect of the Civil Rights Act of 1866 is that this statute became the basis for imposing punitive and compensatory damages under the Civil Rights Act of 1991.

For the next ninety-eight years, the terms "civil rights," "equal rights," and "equal opportunity" would be primarily focused on eliminating government-sanctioned racial discrimination. The Civil Rights Act of 1866, as a first attempt to remove the effects of *de jure* discrimination (discrimination that is required by law), had minimal impact in practice. The primary objectives of this statute were to guarantee that African Americans were granted the same rights enjoyed by white citizens to own or rent property, to have access to the courts, and to make and enforce contracts.[8] Other than eliminating the oppressive annual labor contracts that some states forced on African American citizens, it accomplished little. Today, this statute has been held to protect any citizen against intentional discrimination on the basis of race, sex, or national origin.[9]

Because state governments were circumventing the Civil Rights Act of 1866, Congress sent the Fourteenth Amendment to the Constitution (the second of the so-called Reconstruction Amendments) to the states for ratification.[10] Ratification occurred on July 9, 1868.[11] The Fourteenth Amendment compelled all state governments to treat all of their citizens equally under state laws. Specifically, a state government or agency is prohibited from denying "any person within its jurisdiction the equal protection of the laws."[12] This so-called equal protection clause was passed to remedy the problem of second-class citizenship. In theory, a state could not pass a law that applied to members of only one race. In practice, however, discrimination on the basis of race continued.

The Civil Rights Act of 1866 was followed by the Civil Rights Act of 1875, which provided for equal access to all public accommodations for African Americans with one noted exception, schools. Public accommodation means that any individual has the right to enter and use facilities that are open to the public in general (libraries, government buildings, stores, parks, eating establishments, etc.).

By the end of the nineteenth century, "Jim Crow" laws proliferated throughout the nation. **Jim Crow laws**, named for a character in minstrel shows, were a means for state governments to get around the Civil Rights Acts of 1866, 1870, 1871, and 1875. States circumvented the federal civil rights laws by establishing a race relations system based on the concept of separate but equal accommodations. Under the concept of separate but equal, states passed legislation that provided for separate schools, separate railcars on trains, separate restrooms, and separate counters in eating establishments to accommodate their African American constituents. In most instances they were hardly equal. Nevertheless, the Supreme Court ruled that this separate but equal arrangement was lawful in the 1896 *Plessy v. Ferguson* decision.[13]

Only one justice on the 1896 Supreme Court, John Marshall Harlan, took exception to the *Plessy v. Ferguson* ruling. In his dissent, Justice Harlan wrote that the high court was in error. He based this on his conclusion that the Constitution was a color-blind document and that no government could rightfully treat a citizen differently because of his race.[14] But Justice Harlan's opinion was not with the majority, and the concept of separate but equal would continue until 1954, when it was at last overturned by another Supreme Court decision, *Brown v. Topeka Board of Education*.[15] Still, it would be years—not until 1964—before equal treatment in the workplace would emerge as a national policy.

Executive Orders

In addition to the federal civil rights laws passed by Congress, the executive branch made several attempts to guarantee equal employment opportunity, at least where federal contracts were concerned. Among the first of these executive actions was President Franklin Roosevelt's Executive Order 8802, which prohibited discrimination based on race in federal employment and by private companies holding federal defense contracts. It affected only private enterprises which received defense contracts or subcontracts. It did not impose any requirements on the vast majority of businesses in the country. This order also created the Fair Employment Practice Commission (the precursor to the Office of Federal Contract Compliance Programs) to enforce its provisions.

Similarly, the Truman, Eisenhower, and Kennedy administrations would all initiate executive orders that continued to expand the prohibition on racial discrimination by federal contractors.[16] However, these orders affected only a small percentage of private employers, those who held federal contracts, and the only penalty they imposed for noncompliance was the loss of the contract. Their impact was negligible as none of these executive actions had any effect on employee–management relations among the vast majority of private sector employers who did not hold federal contracts or subcontracts.

The Civil Rights Act of 1964

The struggle for equal treatment in the workplace reached its zenith with the Civil Rights Act of 1964. This federal statute is the most comprehensive ever to regulate employee–employer relations. This legislation was enacted to ensure that employers and managers did not take any individual's race, color, religion, sex, or national origin into account when making an employment decision. In 1890, Justice Harlan, in his dissenting opinion in *Plessy v. Ferguson*, had stated his conviction that the Constitution was color-blind. Nearly seventy-four years later, in 1964, Congress would mandate a color-blind workplace when it passed **Title VII**, which is that portion of the Civil Rights Act of 1964 that governs discrimination in the workplace. Because the primary social concerns in 1964 focused on race relations, the remainder of this chapter will focus on racial discrimination prohibited by the Civil Rights Act of 1964's Title VII.

Individual Versus Group Rights Perspectives

As Congress debated the new civil rights law, three distinct factions took shape: those who opposed the legislation, those who wanted it to protect individual rights, and those who desired it to protect group rights. The first group is of little consequence: those who opposed the Civil Rights Act were defeated and have largely faded from history and the body politic. However, the other two factions, which represent two distinct views of what equal employment opportunity should be, are very much with us today.

It is important to understand the historical context under which Title VII was debated if one is to understand the many apparent contradictions in EEO law and regulations (i.e., the Title VII prohibition against race-conscious decisions and affirmative action's encouragement of race-conscious decisions) that later emerged (see Figure 2.1). Because government regulation is the result of a political process, understanding political motivations can help explain how and why some employment requirements have evolved.

Individual Rights Approach to EEO. What we will call the individual rights faction held a different view of what EEO should be than the group rights faction. As the name implies, the new civil rights act was intended to protect the rights of individuals against the denial

Figure 2.1   **Two Views of Equal Employment Opportunity**

Individual Prospective	Group Prospective
Prospective	Retrospective
Individual rights focus	Group rights focus
Protected class-blind	Protected class-conscious
Antidiscrimination	Compensatory/remedial
Equal treatment	Equal results

of employment opportunities based on membership in a particular group. The underlying proposition of the individual rights party was that it had been morally wrong to deny an individual the opportunity to compete for employment opportunities merely because he or she was the member of a particular group for which the decision maker harbored a bias. The damage suffered was by the individual, and it was the individual who needed protection. Consequently, the new law should be prospective in nature,[17] that is to say, looking toward the future. Title VII would serve the purpose of outlawing discrimination based on race, color, religion, sex, and national origin from a particular point in time forward. The past could not be undone, but discrimination could be prohibited in the present and future.

Under this view of EEO, employers would make all employment decisions in a color-blind manner, or more accurately, in a protected class-blind manner. The ultimate end was to create a workplace that guarantees equal treatment.

Group Rights Approach to EEO. As the individual rights party was prospective, the group rights party was retrospective. The underlying proposition of the group rights party was that certain groups had been historically wronged and that it was the government's responsibility to make them whole, to make up for past discrimination. This view was, therefore, remedial in nature. It attempted to compensate groups for past injuries. Instead of being *protected class-blind*, the group rights party advocated[18] that employment practices needed to be *protected class-conscious,* giving protection and a helping hand to historically oppressed classes. Under this philosophy of EEO, the ultimate end is to create a workplace that guarantees equal results among the different gender and ethnic groups.

Initially, the individual rights party would prevail in Congress by getting its view codified in Title VII. Note throughout the wording of § 703 the repeated reference to the individual:

> It shall be an unlawful employment practice for an employer—(1) to fail or refuse to hire or to discharge *any individual* or otherwise to discriminate against *any individual* with respect to his compensation, terms, conditions, or privileges of employment, because of such *individual's* race, color, religion, sex, or national origin. . . .[19]
> (emphasis added by the authors)

That the individual rights faction prevailed in getting its vision of equal employment opportunity incorporated in the Civil Rights Act of 1964 is clearly demonstrated by the statute's repeated references to "any individual" and "such individual's." However, the group rights perspective would emerge within one year of Title VII's enactment in such later innovations of the executive and judicial branch as affirmative action[20] and disparate impact.[21]

THE PURPOSE OF TITLE VII

Title VII is the foundation of most of the laws and regulations affecting equal employment opportunity in the workplace. To understand how comprehensive Title VII's concept of equal employment opportunity is, one must first understand Section 703, the section that specifically prohibits certain forms of discrimination in employment. According to Section 703,

> It shall be an unlawful employment practice for an employer—(1) to fail or refuse to hire or to discharge *any individual* or otherwise to discriminate against *any individual* with respect to his compensation, terms, conditions, or privileges of employment, because of *such individual's* race, color, religion, sex, or national origin; or (2) to limit, segregate, or classify his employees or applicants for employment in any way which would deprive or tend to deprive *any individual* of employment opportunities or otherwise adversely affect his status as an employee, because of *such individual's* race, color, religion, sex, or national origin.[22] (emphasis added by the authors)

Specifically, Section 703 forbids any employer to use an applicant's race, color, religion, sex, or ethnicity in making any employment-related decision. Thus, a Title VII violation potentially occurs if, at any time, the employer considers an applicant's race (i.e., African American) when making an employment-related decision. If an employer wants to promote a candidate because she is female, Title VII is violated. If an employer has a preference for hiring Catholics over Protestants, Title VII is violated. If a Pakistani applicant is not given consideration because an employer dislikes all persons from Pakistan, Title VII is violated on the basis of national origin. The bottom line is that Title VII mandates employers to make employment decisions based on an individual's qualifications and not on race, color, religion, sex, or national origin. Figure 2.2 lists typical employment decisions that could trigger a Title VII violation.

Congress intended Title VII to create a work environment in which an individual's qualifications and performance were the only appropriate considerations for hiring, firing, or any other employment outcome. This ban is on different treatment (which by definition is unequal) of employees. As will be examined later in this book, people making a claim under Title VII are *not* required to demonstrate that they were treated badly, but that they were treated differently than someone who was not in their class.[23] In its application, Title VII is interpreted broadly and does not consider whether the individual in question is being treated in an unfavorable or favorable manner, again, only that he is being treated differently. Treating persons well because of their ethnicity is no different, in the eyes

Figure 2.2   **Workplace Decisions That Affect Compensation, Terms, Conditions, or Privileges of Employment**

- Apprenticeships
- Benefits
- Layoffs
- Performance appraisal
- Promotion
- Recruiting
- Selection
- Terminations
- Training
- Transfers
- Wages
- Work assignments
- Working conditions

Figure 2.3   **Protected Classes**

Under Title VII:
- Race
- Color
- Religion
- Sex
- National origin (Ethnicity)

Under the Age Discrimination in Employment Act:
- Persons 40 years of age or older

Under the Americans with Disabilities Act:
- Qualified persons with a disability

Under the Pregnancy Discrimination Act:
- Pregnant women
- Women with medical conditions related to pregnancy

of the law, than treating them poorly because of their ethnicity. The bottom line is that employer decisions cannot be made based on an employee's protected class status. The term **protected class** will be used throughout this book to identify the classification of employees who are expressly protected by Title VII's antidiscrimination provisions. The classes of employees who are protected by Title VII are identified in Figure 2.3. The one notable exception to this principle is preferential treatment authorized under a formal *permissible* affirmative action, which will be discussed at length in Chapter 8.

Essentially, the equal employment opportunity guaranteed under Title VII is a guarantee that all employees or applicants will be treated according to their qualifications, education, experience, and/or performance. This position is demonstrated in the case of *McDonald v. Santa Fe Transportation Company,* in which three employees of a shipping company were caught stealing merchandise from a shipping container.[24] The company's long-standing policy had been that any employee caught pilfering company or customer property would be terminated. After an investigation, all three employees were found guilty of the theft, but only two (both white) were fired. The third employee (an African American) was reprimanded but returned to his job on the grounds that the company had very few African American employees and desired to increase representation of African Americans in its workforce.

Recalling Section 703, do you believe Title VII was violated? Was the employer's decision to terminate or retain certain employees based on whether an individual employee was a member of a protected class or on the employee's violation of the work rule? In this instance, the Supreme Court concluded Title VII was violated. All three employees were similarly situated, that is, they were all equally guilty of breaking the company's nonpilferage rule. Yet two were fired while the other was allowed to return to work. The Supreme Court found that the similarly situated employees were treated differently for the same misconduct. After further examination, it was concluded that the only factor accounting for the different treatment (who was fired and who was retained) was the race of the individual employee. Even though race earned the African American employee more favorable treatment than his peers, that favorable treatment violated Title VII.[25]

As a consequence of the *McDonald* ruling, the Supreme Court concluded that Title VII protected white employees from racial discrimination just as it protected African Americans from racial discrimination. The company had unlawfully violated Title VII when it discriminated against the two whites by firing them but not firing the African American for the same misconduct.

Race in the context of Title VII means all races. According to the U.S. Census Bureau, Americans are classified *racially* into the following categories: Black/African American, White, Asian, Native Hawaiian/Pacific Islander, American Indian/Alaska Native or Two or more races.[26] In 2007, the EEOC changed its racial and ethnic reporting to conform with these categories. The text of Title VII does not exclude any specific race from protection, hence all are protected. As a technical note, the EEOC does not treat Hispanics or Latinos as a race but as an ethnic group. As a result, there are only two ethnic classifications recognized by the EEOC, Hispanic or Latino, and Non Hispanic or Latino.[27]

Employers Covered by Title VII

Like many federal statutes, Title VII is not universally applied to all employers. Only those entities specifically included in the Act's definition of "employer" are required to follow its provisions.[28] Covered employers include all state and local governments and their subdivisions. Hence, police departments, fire departments, and public utilities are all covered. Additionally, all educational institutions, both public and private, are employers under the Act. Labor unions with fifteen or more members in twenty or more calendar weeks in the current or preceding calendar year are required to comply with Title VII's antidiscrimination provisions, as are all joint (labor–management) committees for apprenticeship and training. Finally, all employment agencies, regardless of size, in both the public and private sectors are covered for compliance purposes.

All private sector employers who employ fifteen or more employees for each working day in each of twenty or more calendar weeks in the current or preceding calendar year are defined as an "employer" under the Act.[29] There are seven Title VII employees enumerated in Figure 2.4.

It should be further noted that since the statute does not explicitly specify full-time employees, part-time employees are to be counted in meeting this minimum. Hence,

Figure 2.4 **Employers Covered Under Title VII**

- Private sector employers with fifteen or more employees for twenty or more calendar weeks
- All educational institutions (public or private)
- All labor unions with fifteen or more members
- All employment agencies (public and private)
- All state and local governments
- All joint (labor–management) committees for apprenticeship and training
- Employees of the U.S. Congress (Civil Rights Act of 1991)

an employer with fifteen full-time employees is obviously covered under the Act, but so is an employer with eight full-time and seven part-time employees. However, if an employer does not have the requisite numerical threshold (fifteen or more employees), the employer is not covered.

Arbaugh v. Y & H Corporation and the Numerosity Requirement

There is one important caveat. According to the Supreme Court in *Arbaugh v. Y & H Corporation*,[30] the objection that the employer is not covered under Title VII may not be raised once a verdict has been rendered. If a respondent raises the issue after the conclusion of a trial, the respondent will be treated as though he or she was a covered entity. It is very important for employers to know whether they are a covered entity, as their attorneys or the EEOC might overlook the fifteen-employee numerosity requirement, which could subsequently be discovered too late.[31]

This ruling has its greatest impact on small businesses, and there are examples where enterprises have avoided liability or expensive conciliation by a timely challenge that they do not meet the minimum employee threshold for coverage under the statute in question. In these instances in which the employer had fewer than fifteen employees, he or she won a quick dismissal of a complaint.[32] Small business owners are cautioned that even a pre-trial dismissal entails an expensive legal defense.

Thinking about our opening scenario, the reader will recall that ET had ten full-time employees and four part-time employees, totaling fourteen. This is below the threshold of fifteen employees necessary for employer coverage under Title VII. Provided that ET informs the court prior to a verdict, Title VII would not apply.

A notable exclusion from the list of "employers" is the nation's single largest employer, the government of the United States. It is not an uncommon practice for the federal government to exclude itself from the legislation and regulations it imposes on state and local governments and the private sector. An exception to this practice is the inclusion of the U.S. Congress on the list of "employers" in the Civil Rights Act of 1991 (including employees of the Architect of the Capitol, the Congressional Budget Office, the General Accounting Office, the Government Printing Office, the Office of Technology Assessment, and the United States Botanic Garden).[33] But this applies only to the legislative branch and not the rest of the federal government.

Employees Not Protected by Title VII

There are some employees who do not receive Title VII protection even if the employment action is based on their race, color, religion, sex, or national origin. First, any person who works for an organization that does not meet the Act's definition of "employer" would not be covered. As noted previously, the term "employer" does not include the U.S. government or any corporation wholly owned by the federal government, nor any employer having fewer than fifteen employees.[34] Also omitted are Indian tribes because they are covered by treaties. Some job classifications are also expressly excluded from the statute. Primarily, these encompass elected officials and their personal staffs.

You probably realize that the federal government is the largest employer not covered by Title VII. Before continuing, there are two points that need to be made about the federal government exclusion. First, those individuals who are employed directly by the U.S. Congress are now covered by Title VII as a result of the Civil Rights Act of 1991.[35] However, this inclusion is very limited and applies only to the approximately 30,600 employees of the legislative branch.[36] It does not include the roughly 2.8 million federal civilian employees who do not work for Congress.[37] This does not mean, however, that other federal employees are not protected from employment discrimination. Under the Civil Service Reform Act of 1978, all other federal employees receive employment protection against personnel practices that discriminate on the basis of race, color, national origin, religion, sex, age or disability.[38] This act provides most federal employees with essentially the same antidiscrimination protection as their counterparts in the private sector, state, and local governments.

Elected officials and individuals appointed to such officials' personal staff are also excluded from Title VII protection.[39] As a member of an elected official's personal staff, an individual would exercise some degree of discretion or autonomy in carrying out assigned duties, serve in some advisory capacity, or have access to confidential information. For example, a governor's public relations director would not be eligible for Title VII protection as he/she is a personal staff member. On the other hand, the receptionist for the public relations director would be entitled to full Title VII protection because his or her job does not exercise discretion or regularly give advice to the elected official on policy matters.

Though the Act does protect U.S. citizens working for American firms at facilities outside the United States and its territories under certain circumstances[40] (discussed in Chapter 7 under extraterritorial applicant), Title VII does not apply to citizens of other countries working for a U.S. firm outside the United States and its territories.[41]

However, Title VII protects all foreign nationals who are working *within* the United States and its territories. Furthermore, it does not matter if the foreign national is in the country legally or illegally. Title VII even protects *illegal aliens* from discrimination on the basis of race, color, religion, sex, or national origin in the terms and conditions of their employment.[42]

The only other employee classification that is not protected under Title VII is actually a holdover from the Cold War. Members of the Communist Party or any other organization required to register as a Communist-front organization under the Subversive Activities Control Act of 1950 do not come under the Act's prohibition of employment discrimination.[43]

As a final point, there are some religious exemptions permitted under Title VII. Under section 702 of the Civil Rights Act of 1964, religious corporations, associations, educational institutions, and societies may give preference to members of their religion in hiring. This is not a carte blanche preference. The religious preference must be for work and activities that are connected to the religious purpose of the corporation, association, educational institution, or society. This issue will be examined in greater detail in Chapter 6.

FILING COMPLAINTS AND CHARGES

Filing a Charge with the EEOC

If an employee believes he or she has been discriminated against in employment or workplace decisions, the employee can file a complaint with the EEOC. Figure 2.5 provides an overview of the complaint process.

The party making the complaint (under the Civil Rights Act of 1991 this person is technically known as the **complaining party**)[44] can contact the EEOC by phone, letter, or making a visit to a regional office. The complaining party then fills out a charge sheet, or, if necessary, an EEOC staff member can assist in the preparation of the complaint. It is important to note that even though a complaint may appear frivolous, the EEOC is under an obligation to investigate all charges.[45]

The Civil Rights Act of 1991 identifies the party against whom the complaint is made, typically the employer, as the **respondent**.[46] This standardization of terminology may cause less confusion among laymen, but some in the legal and regulatory community may become confused because the term "respondent" also means the party against whom an appeal is taken.[47]

Deferral to a State Agency

If a state has its own antidiscrimination laws with a state enforcement agency to investigate unlawful discrimination, the charge may be filed under state antidiscrimination law with the state agency first. Since the names of these agencies vary from state to state (i.e., Minnesota Department of Human Rights, Ohio Civil Rights Commission, Wyoming Fair Employment Practices Commission, etc.), they are collectively referred to as **Fair Employment Practices Agencies** or **FEPAs**). Table 2.1 contains a list of charges deferred to FEPAs.

Deferral means that the federal EEOC can choose to forward a charge for investigation by the state or local FEPA. In short, a case that is filed with the EEOC can be deferred to a state FEPA having jurisdiction over the alleged discrimination.[48] In the case of a deferral, the complaining party can later file a complaint with the EEOC within 300 days of

Figure 2.5   **EEO Complaint Process**

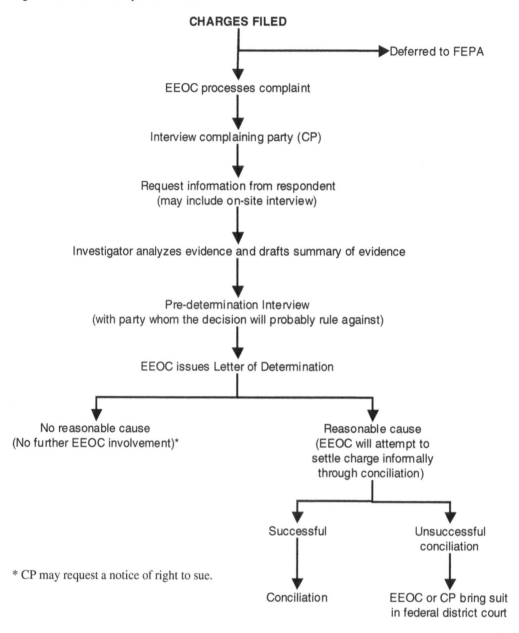

the alleged discriminatory act, or within 30 days of the state FEPA closing the charge.[49] Because deferral to FEPAs was first authorized under section 706 of Title VII,[50] FEPAs are sometimes referred to as *section 706 agencies.*

However, nine states have FEPAs that are not certified for deferrals under EEOC regulations. They are: Alabama, Arkansas, Georgia, Kentucky, Louisiana, Mississippi, North Carolina, North Dakota, and Virginia.[51] In these states, the timeliness period for filing is

Table 2.1

Charges Deferred to Fair Employment Practice Agencies, 1987–2012

Year	EEOC Charge Receipts	FEPA Charge Receipts	Total Charge Receipts
1987	65,844	49,692	115,536
1988	63,778	54,154	117,936
1989	59,411	48,995	108,406
1990	62,135	50,493	112,628
1991	62,806	53,961	116,767
1992	70,399	54,080	124,479
1993	87,942	61,389	149,231
1994	91,189	64,423	155,612
1995	87,529	67,453	154,982
1996	77,990	66,242	144,232
1997	80,680	69,854	150,534
1998	79,591	65,678	145,269
1999	77,444	61,708	139,152
2000	79,896	*	
2001	80,840	58,303	139,143
2002	84,442	62,774	147,216
2003	81,293	61,998	143,291
2004	79,432	57,318	136,750
2005	75,428	55,928	131,356
2006	75,768	48,926	124,694
2007	82,792	52,854	135,646
2008	95,402	56,897	152,299
2009	93,277	53,028	146,305
2010	99,922	50,014	149,936
2011	99,947	46,120	146,067
2012	99,412	Data not available	Data not available

Source: U.S. Equal Employment Opportunity Commission (January 12, 2000), *Enforcement Statistics & Litigation,* www.eeoc.gov/stats/all.html; Annual Reports for fiscal years 1985 to 1994; and U.S. Equal Employment Opportunity Commission (April 10, 2000), FEPA Receipts Nationwide. *National Database* (Washington, DC: EEOC Automatic Reporting Facility); U.S. Equal Employment Opportunity Commission (March 11, 2009), *All Statutes.*, www.eeoc.gov/stats/all.html (accessed July 1, 2009); U.S. Equal Employment Opportunity Commission (February 2011), Table 6: State and Local Workload Projections, Fiscal Year 2011 Congressional Budget Justification, http://www.eeoc.gov/eeoc/plan/2011budget.cfm#IA (accessed October 25, 2012); U.S. Equal Employment Opportunity Commission (February 2012), Chart 7: State and Local Workload Projections Fiscal Year 2009 to Fiscal Year 2015, Fiscal Year 2013 Congressional Budget Justification, http://www.eeoc.gov/eeoc/plan/2013budget.cfm#IA (accessed October 25, 2012).

*FEPA data unavailable.

limited to 180 days. This is important as it will determine whether the complaining party made his or her complaint in a timely manner. Failure to do so can result in dismissal of the case (discussed below).

Note that in the opening scenario, Malcolm had waited over thirteen months to make his claim (from January 3, 2012, when the discrimination occurred, until February 14, 2013, when he filed his complaint—a passage of 407 days). As a consequence, Malcolm's claim is too old to pursue under Title VII and will likely be administratively closed.

Timeliness for Compensation Matters:
The Lilly Ledbetter Fair Pay Act of 2009

The Lilly Ledbetter Fair Pay Act was signed into law on January 29, 2009. Title I, the Lilly Ledbetter Fair Pay Act, was specifically enacted to overturn the 2007 Supreme Court decision, *Ledbetter v. Goodyear Tire & Rubber Co.,* by amending Title VII of the Civil Rights Act of 1964, the Age Discrimination in Employment Act of 1967, the Americans with Disabilities Act of 1990, and the Rehabilitation Act of 1973. Title II, the Paycheck Fairness Act, amends the Fair Labor Standards Act of 1938.[52]

In *Ledbetter v. Goodyear Tire & Rubber Co.,*[53] the complaining party, Lilly Ledbetter, had worked for Goodyear for approximately twenty-one years. After taking early retirement, she filed an Equal Employment Opportunity complaint under Title VII of the Equal Pay Act of 1963, claiming that several supervisors had given her poor evaluations early in her employment because she was a woman. She further claimed that this unlawful discrimination resulted in her receiving less pay than similarly situated male coworkers *over the course of her employment.* Title VII requires a complaining party to file an EEOC charge within 300 days (180 days in nondeferral states) "after the alleged unlawful employment practice occurred."[54] Since Ms. Ledbetter worked at a facility in the state of Alabama (a nondeferral state), she would have had to make her Title VII complaint within 180 days from the unlawful discrimination's occurrence. As a consequence, the Supreme Court held that the complaint about pay discrimination that occurred more than 180 days prior to her retirement was not filed in a timely manner, and to allow it to stand would create a "paycheck accrual rule."[55] That is, the Supreme Court did not allow Ms. Ledbetter, the complaining party, to claim that decades-old alleged discriminatory actions will later impact wages or pension benefits.

The Ledbetter Fair Pay Act has now created such a "paycheck accrual rule." For all intents and purposes, each paycheck, even if it is not tainted with discriminatory intent, triggers a new EEOC charging period during which the complainant may properly challenge any previous discriminatory conduct that might have affected that paycheck's amount, regardless of how long ago that discrimination may have occurred. To alleviate confusion, assume that an employee of your company had been denied a pay raise because she was a woman (based on her sex) twenty years ago. At that time she chose not to file an EEO complaint. Since that time no other unlawful discrimination has occurred. Now the female employee files a complaint alleging that because she was discriminated against two decades ago that she is entitled to restitution for the cumulative effect on all of her subsequent compensation. This complaint is now possible because the 180- or 300-day EEOC charging period for making a claim of unlawful discrimination in compensation (and compensation claims only) begins anew with each paycheck.[56]

INVESTIGATION OUTCOMES

Whether the complaint is investigated by the EEOC or the FEPA, an investigator is assigned to the case and the employer is notified. Investigators may then question relevant witnesses and might even require employers to provide pertinent personnel records and documents or other evidence as needed. Once the initial investigation is completed, the complaint is assigned one of three outcomes:

- Reasonable cause
- No reasonable cause
- Dismissal

Reasonable Cause

Under **reasonable cause**, the EEOC's investigation has found enough evidence to believe that an unlawful employment practice has occurred.[57] In making such a determination, the EEOC uses either direct evidence of unlawful discrimination or acquires sufficient circumstantial evidence to establish a *prima facie* case for the particular discrimination alleged. What constitutes a *prima facie* case will be discussed in greater detail in later chapters in this book. In the event that the EEOC or FEPA investigator has determined that there is reasonable cause, the employer is formally notified. Even when cause was indeed found, the matter is not automatically concluded. The employer might request that the EEOC reconsider the matter. A request for reconsideration might be based on new evidence that has surfaced since the initial investigation. Failing that, the employer is left with only the options of **conciliation** (a negotiated settlement with the complaining party) or litigation.

No Cause

Under a **no cause** determination, the investigation failed to produce sufficient evidence to establish that an unlawful employment practice has likely occurred.[58] In the ten-year period from 1996 to 2006, 612,526 of the 1,012,769 charges resolved by the EEOC (approximately 60.5 percent) ended in a finding of no cause (see Table 2.2). Managers and HR professionals should take note that even though the EEOC's investigation may have concluded with a finding of no cause, the complaining party can still bring suit against the employer in federal court. Provided that the complaining party requests a **notice of right to sue** (sometimes referred to as a "right to sue letter")[59] within ninety days of being formally notified of the EEOC's no cause determination, the agency must issue the notice.[60] So even if the EEOC or FEPA investigation finds no cause, the complaining party can still be issued a notice of right to sue upon demand.

Dismissal

The EEOC may dismiss a complaint for a number of reasons (see Figure 2.6). When such a decision is made it is referred to as an administrative withdrawal or **dismissal**. Essentially, the EEOC stops the investigation without any determination being made. One of the common reasons for a dismissal is that the complaint was not made in a timely manner.

Table 2.2

Percentage of EEOC Resolutions Resulting in No Cause Determinations, 1987–2012

Fiscal Year	Total EEOC Resolutions	No Cause Determinations	Percentage of No Cause
1987	53,482	29,578	55.3
1988	70,749	35,148	49.7
1989	66,209	35,896	54.2
1990	67,415	38,537	57.2
1991	64,342	38,369	59.6
1992	68,366	41,736	61.0
1993	71,716	40,183	56.0
1994	71,563	34,451	48.1
1995	91,774	46,700	50.9
1996	103,467	63,216	61.1
1997	106,312	64,567	60.7
1998	101,470	61,794	60.9
1999	97,846	58,174	59.5
2000	93,672	54,578	58.3
2001	90,106	51,562	57.2
2002	95,222	56,514	59.3
2003	87,755	55,359	63.1
2004	85,259	53,183	62.4
2005	77,352	48,079	62.2
2006	74,308	45,500	61.2
2007	72,442	42,979	59.3
2008	81,081	47,152	58.2
2009	85,980	52,363	60.9
2010	104,999	67,520	64.3
2011	112,499	74,198	66.0
2012	111,139	75,511	67.9

Source: U.S. Equal Employment Opportunity Commission, Litigation Statistics, http://www.eeoc.gov/eeoc/statistics/enforcement/all.cfm (accessed March 25, 2013).

Typically, the complaining party has waited too long and filed the complaint more than 180 days after the alleged unlawful discrimination occurred (300 days after in the case of a state-covered practice).[61]

In some instances, the party filing the complaint cannot be located after the initial charge was filed. Without a complaining party, the investigation can hardly proceed. Occasionally, the complaining party fails to provide the EEOC with requested information. In other cases, the complaining party may have refused or failed to appear at scheduled interviews or conferences. In general, a dismissal results under most circumstances in which a complaining party refuses to otherwise cooperate with the investigation.[62]

Conciliation

If conciliation is chosen, the EEOC will attempt to work out a mutually agreeable settlement between the complaining party and the employer. This option is actually preferred by the EEOC; in fact, it is encouraged even before the determination of reasonable cause is reached.[63]

Figure 2.6   **Reasons EEOC Closes a File on a Charge**

1. The facts alleged in the charge fail to state a claim under any statutes enforced by the EEOC.
2. The allegations did not involve a disability as defined under the Americans with Disabilities Act.
3. The respondent employs less than the required number of employees and is not otherwise covered by the statutes.
4. The charge was not timely filed with EEOC; in other words, the complaining party waited too long after the date of the alleged discrimination to file a charge.
5. The EEOC issues the following determination: Based upon its investigation, the EEOC is unable to conclude that the information obtained establishes violations of the statutes. This does not certify that the respondent is in compliance with the statutes. No finding is made as to any other issues that might be construed as having been raised by this charge.
6. The EEOC has adopted the findings of the state or local fair employment practices agency that investigated this charge.
7. Other

Source: EEOC Form 161 (November 2009).

To illustrate this point, let us assume that an employee has filed a charge with the EEOC alleging that she was terminated from her position because of her race and the investigation is well under way. In the complaint, it is alleged that the employer keeps African American employees on the payroll only for as long as it takes to find a non–African American to replace them. The EEOC investigates and discovers, according to payroll records, that no African American employee has been employed by the company for a period longer than two months. The EEOC further notes that the only requirements for the job are that an applicant possesses a high school diploma and a valid driver's license, both of which are possessed by the complaining party. No other evidence is presented by either the complaining party or by her employer. Based on this evidence, the EEOC would most likely conclude that there was reasonable cause or sufficient circumstantial evidence to indicate that a Title VII violation had occurred. In other words, there is sufficient evidence to establish a *prima facie* case of unlawful discrimination. At this juncture, the authors wish to make it clear that establishing a *prima facie* case is not, of and by itself, proof of unlawful discrimination. It merely indicates that Title VII (or any other EEO statute for that matter) may have been violated. The employer is still afforded the opportunity to defend his or her employment practice.

Bringing this to the employer's attention, the EEOC would attempt to encourage the employer to initiate a remedy that is mutually acceptable to the complaining party. The intent is that the employer should meet with the complaining party and attempt to produce an agreeable solution. In this case, an attempted settlement might begin with an offer by the employer to reinstate the complaining party (essentially rehire her) and pay her estimated wages from the time she was fired to the time she was reinstated (back pay). The complaining party might offer the counterproposal that she also be allowed to accrue seniority for the time period between her termination and reinstatement. If this counterproposal is accepted by the employer, the EEOC is notified and the matter is closed.

Litigation

If the parties cannot agree to conciliation, or the employer refuses to even consider conciliation, the EEOC has the option of filing suit on behalf of the complaining party. When the EEOC decides to litigate a complaint, it uses the resources of its own Solicitor General's Office, essentially its own legal staff. Typically the EEOC commits its legal resources only to cases that promise large monetary settlements or would create judicial precedent favorable to the agency.

Because of its aforementioned limited legal resources, it is very rare that the EEOC litigates a complaint itself. If the agency chooses not to file suit, as it does in the vast majority of complaints, complaining parties are issued a notice of right to sue. Table 2.3 lists the number of cases handled by the EEOC.

Managers are cautioned not to forget a disturbing fact about a notice of right to sue: it is available upon request.[64] Even if the EEOC or FEPA investigations resulted in findings of no cause, the complaining party is still entitled to request the notice of right to sue, and the agency must fulfill that request.

Who Litigates?

Whether the litigation is initiated by the complaining party using a notice of right to sue, or whether it is filed by the EEOC's Solicitor General's Office, the case will be tried in a federal district court. This is the court of original jurisdiction, meaning that this court has the authority to hear and decide the specific case. The federal district court is characteristically the court that exercises the authority to impose a legal remedy for the injured party, whether it is monetary relief (i.e., back pay, punitive damages, etc.) or enforcement of a right (i.e., stop harassment, reinstatement, etc.).[65]

Prior to 1991, all EEO cases were heard before a judge only, in what is known as "bench trial."[66] Since the enactment of the Civil Rights Act of 1991, complaining parties have the right to request jury trials under specific circumstances in litigation arising from disparate treatment. In fact, either party may request a trial by jury if a complaining party is seeking compensatory or punitive damages.[67] Complaining parties are far more likely to request trial by jury than employers. First, by selecting jurors with certain demographic and socioeconomic backgrounds, attorneys can create a jury with a predisposition toward a particular outcome.[68] Second, jurors may be swayed by emotional appeals rather than the facts, resulting in a case that may be won on appeal, but lost in the initial trial.[69] Consequently, employers are reluctant to request jury trials for Title VII complaints. After all, how many employers sit on a jury?

In the event that either party believes the ruling in the district court (either as a result of a trial by jury or a bench trial by a judge) is in error, and many do, the case can then be appealed to a federal appellate court (see Chapter 1).

Though appellate courts were not created to impose remedies, they can overturn the remedies imposed by a district court. If an appellate court wants to modify a remedy, it **vacates** the remedy of the lower court (this means that the original damage award is

Table 2.3

Two Decades of Cases Litigated by the Solicitor General's Office

Fiscal Year	Suits Filed By EEOC	Total Charge Receipts
1987	527	68,822
1988	555	70,749
1989	598	66,209
1990	643	67,415
1991	593	68,366
1992	447	70,399
1993	481	87,942
1994	425	91,189
1995	373	87,529
1996	193	77,990
1997	338	80,680
1998	405	79,591
1999	465	77,444
2000	329	79,896
2001	428	80,840
2002	370	84,442
2003	400	81,293
2004	421	79,432
2005	416	75,428
2006	403	75,768
2007	362	82,792
2008	325	95,402
2009	314	93,277
2010	271	99,922
2011	300	99,947
2012	155	99,412

Source: The U.S. Equal Employment Opportunity Commission, *EEOC Litigation Statistics*, http://www.eeoc.gov/eeoc/statistics/enforcement/litigation.cfm (accessed March 25, 2013).

now annulled or canceled),[70] and then sends the case back to the district court (the court exercising original jurisdiction) with instructions on how a new remedy should be fashioned. The legal term used for this process of returning an appealed case to the court of original jurisdiction is **remand**.

Frivolous Appeals

An appeal to an appellate court can occur only if one of the parties shows that the lower court made an error in its interpretation or application of the law. If it can be clearly shown that a party has made an appeal that is blatantly without merit, the appeal is said to be frivolous.[71] At least seven U.S. Circuit Courts of Appeal have held parties, and sometimes those parties' attorneys, liable for legal costs if the appeal was obviously frivolous, assessing double legal costs to that party and that party's attorney.[72] In an instance in which the complaining party initiates a frivolous appeal, that individual would also incur his or her employer's legal expenses. If the employer initiated the meritless or vexatious appeal, then he or she would be responsible for the complaining party's expenses.[73] Such penalties are to curb those appeals that are filed for the purposes of delaying outcomes, harassing the other party, or for any other improper purposes.[74]

TWO THEORIES OF DISCRIMINATION

Can any applicant or employee make an allegation of unlawful discrimination and take legal action against their employer? It is not as simple as that. In order for a discrimination claim to get into court it must first be "actionable," that is to say, it must give sufficient grounds for a lawsuit.[75] Under Title VII, there are two basic theories of actionable unlawful discrimination: disparate treatment and disparate impact. **Disparate treatment** results from treating individuals in the workplace differently because of their membership in a protected class. It is intentional and is characterized by imposing different standards on different people. **Disparate impact** is a child of the courts, born of the *Griggs v. Duke Power Company* decision. Disparate impact focuses managers' and HR professionals' attention on statistical imbalances in their workforces. It is often unintentional and is characterized by imposing the same facially neutral standards on all employees with different outcomes for different groups. A detailed examination of disparate impact is covered in Chapter 4.

Disparate Treatment Theory of Discrimination

When the Civil Rights Act of 1964 was first enacted, there was essentially only one form of unlawful discrimination—disparate treatment. To engage in disparate treatment, an employer, or its agent, treats applicants or employees differently because of their protected class status. Thus, there are different standards for applicants, or employees, based on an individual's race, color, religion, sex, or national origin.

The most blatant example of imposing different standards would be a company in which no women were ever promoted to management positions because the owner felt that women do not make good leaders. As a consequence of this personal bias, no female applying for a management position is ever seriously considered. Another way of viewing this is that all female candidates for promotion are automatically "deselected" because of their sex before any relevant job qualifications are considered. The candidate's sex simply and exclusively disqualifies her for the job. The same would hold true if an employer believed that people of Italian ancestry were lacking in leadership ability. Every candidate with an Italian surname would be disqualified strictly because of, and for no other reason than, national origin. The discrimination in either case is intentional and based on personal prejudices rather than on the individual candidate's ability to do the job in question.

STEPS IN CONDUCTING CASE ANALYSIS

When confronted with a workplace practice that is potentially a violation of Title VII, it is important to investigate it in a systematic manner (see Figure 2.7). The employer

Figure 2.7   **Steps in Conducting Case Analysis**

1. What law applies to the situation?
2. Is the employer covered? Is the organization an "employer" under that statute?
3. Was the complaint filed in a timely manner?
4. Is the employee covered (some employees may be exempted)?
5. Can the employee make a *prima facie* case?
6. Does the employer have a nondiscriminatory rebuttal?
7. Can the employee refute the employer's rebuttal?

or his/her representative will need to make an assessment of the situation in order to formulate a proper response. For example, if the investigation indicates that a violation of the law has occurred, then perhaps the appropriate course of action would be to make some sort of conciliation with the affected employee(s). If, on the other hand, an employee is found to be making an unfounded complaint, or the employer is becoming the victim of a "shakedown," the employer may want to fight the matter. A shakedown is a slang expression referring to extortion, in this case by lawyers filing nuisance suits.[76] In essence, the employer is being forced to choose between high litigation costs or settle a nonmeritorious claim out of court.

A good point at which to begin this systematic analysis is to ascertain which law applies to the situation at hand. Once you have determined which law governs the issue, then determine whether or not the employer is covered. Many laws have a threshold requirement based on the number of employees. For example, Title VII requires 15 employees, the Age Discrimination in Employment Act requires 20, and the Family Medical Leave Act requires 50.

Did the complaining party initiate the complaint in a timely manner? In some states a Title VII complaint must be filed in 180 days, in others, 300 days. As already discussed, failing to file within the time constraints may result in the complaint being dismissed.

Is the employee covered? Remember that some employees may be exempted. If they are, then the Act affords them no protection. If a particular law does apply, the employer is covered under that law, the employee is also covered, and the complaint was filed in a timely manner, then it is time to look at the evidence to see if the complaining party can establish a *prima facie* case. If the *prima facie* case is established, then can the employer muster a rebuttal to show that the decision was not based on illegal discrimination? Once the employer's rebuttal is accepted, can the employee now provide evidence that the employer's rebuttal is flawed? These last three steps are the central issues in our next chapter.

SUMMARY

This chapter provided a historical overview of equal employment opportunity. Particular attention was given to Title VII of the Civil Rights Act of 1964. The Civil Rights Act was enacted to ensure that employers and managers did not take any individual's race, color, religion, sex, or national origin into consideration when making employment decisions.

Title VII is the foundation of most of the laws and regulations related to equal employment opportunity.

Employees who feel they have been discriminated against in employment or workplace decisions can file a complaint with the EEOC or FEPA. There is an established process for handling such complaints, as was discussed in this chapter.

KEY TERMS AND CONCEPTS

Black Codes	No cause
Complaining party	Notice of right to sue
Conciliation	Protected class
Dismissal	Reasonable cause
Disparate treatment	Remand
Disparate impact	Respondent
Fair Employment Practice Agencies (FEPAs)	Title VII
Jim Crow laws	Vacate

DISCUSSION QUESTIONS

1. Once you have been notified that the EEOC has received a complaint from one of your employees, what are the three possible outcomes after the investigation begins?
2. What are the five protected classes under Title VII?
3. What are the seven classifications of employers who are covered under Title VII?
4. What are the statutes of limitation (time limits) for filing a Title VII complaint? What determines the length of the time limit?
5. Describe the process by which a Title VII complaint is filed. What are the three possible outcomes once the complaint has been filed?
6. Under what circumstances is the EEOC or a FEPA likely to dismiss a complaint?

CASE

As an activity therapist coordinator, Raymond Rayburn organizes and supervises recreational activities for patients at the Rosey Fink Mental Health Center, a facility operated by the Illinois Department of Human Services (IDHS). He has worked at the health center since 2005 and has been employed by the IDHS since 2001. For many years, Rayburn has organized a luncheon at the health center to recognize Black History Month.

Rayburn's long career at the health center hit a bump in the road in early 2012. On February 5, 2012, Rayburn complained in writing to William Thomas, EEO officer for the IDHS, that he was being discriminated against and harassed. His letter detailed various perceived injustices and reported a lack of coordination between health center employees, including Rayburn's direct supervisor, Umberto Duenos. The letter uses the word "discrimination" twice, but gives no hint that Rayburn is complaining about racial, gender-based, or any other form of legally prohibited discrimination. Rather, Rayburn seems to be complaining simply that he felt that he was being singled out for unfair treatment as compared with coworkers.

On February 26, Rayburn apparently abandoned his assigned work area in order to attend a staff training session for which he had not signed up in advance. And on March 3, a coworker complained that Rayburn had been playing basketball with staff from the Engineering Department while a nude patient he was supposed to be supervising wandered off down a hallway unattended.

Rayburn responded to these alleged infractions by claiming that either (1) he did nothing wrong, or (2) he was disciplined more harshly than his white coworkers. Rayburn alleges that Activity Therapist Kathy Bennett had abandoned her assigned work area on the very same day, February 26, on which he was accused of abandoning his. However, her supervisor was unaware of her absence and, therefore, imposed no disciplinary action.

Furthermore, Rayburn argues that because he attended a staff training session during his lunch break, he should not be required to notify his supervisor that he was out of the area. Finally, Rayburn charges that lots of other activity therapists let down their guards while supervising nude patients and nothing has ever happened to them, though he can give no names nor give specifics.

It is true that all of the coworkers in Rayburn's allegations are white, and that none of them have personnel records indicating that they had been disciplined. In response, the health center notes that with regard to Kathy Bennett, Rayburn provided no evidence to show that she had abandoned her work area.

Unquestionably, Rayburn attended classes without notifying his supervisor and without arranging for a replacement to cover his assigned work area. Even though it was during his lunch period, health center policy required him to inform his supervisor of his whereabouts in case of an emergency.

As for the "nude patient" claim, the supervisor responded that the policy is to keep the patient in view at all times. Rayburn failed to follow that policy and that is what precipitated the disciplinary action. As for the allegations that other employees did the same thing, Umberto Duenos responded that they were not under his charge, but had they been, and had he caught them, they too would have been disciplined.

Rayburn was suspended for violating the policy beginning on March 7 and ending on March 14, 2012. He eventually filed a formal complaint with the Equal Employment Opportunity Commission on January 17, 2013. Rayburn alleges that his suspension constituted intentional racial discrimination.

   a. Will the EEOC investigate Rayburn's complaint? Why or why not?
   b. Which of the three investigation outcomes discussed in the chapter is most likely to occur?

NOTES

1. J.R. Hummed, *Emancipating Slaves, Enslaving Free Men* (Chicago: Open Court, 1996), p. 298.

2. L. Cox and J.H. Cox, *Reconstruction, the Negro, and the New South* (Columbia: University of South Carolina Press, 1973), pp. 211–248.

3. E. Foner, *Reconstruction: America's Unfinished Revolution, 1863–1877* (New York: Harper & Row, 1988), p. 222.

4. Illinois Constitution, article VI § 1 and article VIII § 7 (1848).

5. Indiana Constitution, article XIII (1851).

6. Oregon Constitution, article II § 6 and article XVIII § 2 (1857).

7. 42 U.S.C. § 1981a.

8. 42 U.S.C. § 1982.

9. 42 U.S.C. § 1981a(a) & (b).

10. J. Forman, "Juries and Race in the Nineteenth Century," *Yale Law Journal* 113 (2004): 895–938.

11. D.H. Bryant, "Unorthodox and Paradox: Revisiting the Ratification of the Fourteenth Amendment," *Alabama Law Review* 53 (2002): 555–581.

12. U.S. Const., Amend. XIV, § 1.

13. *Plessy v. Ferguson,* 163 U.S. 537 (1896).

14. Id. (Harlan dissenting) at 552–562.

15. 347 U.S. 483 (1954).

16. Executive Order 10309 (1951); Executive Order 10590 (1955); Executive Order 10925 (1961).

17. Herman Belz, *Equality Transformed: A Quarter-Century of Affirmative Action* (New Brunswick, NJ: Transaction Publishers, 1992), p. 29.

18. 42 U.S.C. § 2000e-2(a).

19. Ibid.

20. Executive Order 11246, 30 Fed. Reg. 12,319 (Sept. 24, 1965).

21. *Griggs v. Duke Power Co.,* 401 US 424 (1971).

22. 42 U.S.C. § 2000e-2(a).

23. *McDonnell Douglas Corp. v. Green,* 411 US 792 (1973).

24. 427 U.S. 273 (1976).

25. *McDonald v. Santa Fe Transportation Co.,* 427 U.S. 273, 283–284 (1976).

26. U.S. Census Bureau, *Racial and Ethnic Classifications Used in Census 2000 and Beyond* (Washington, DC: U.S. Census Bureau, 2009).

27. Equal Employment Opportunity Commission, *Employer Information Report EEO-1 Instruction Booklet* (Washington, DC: Equal Employment Opportunity Commission, 2007).

28. 42 U.S.C. § 2000e(b).

29. Ibid.

30. 546 U.S. 500 (2006).

31. *Rodriguez v. Diego's Restaurant, Inc.,* 619 F. Supp. 2d 1345 (S.D. Fla. 2009).

32. *Mason v. Invision, LLC,* 347 Fed. Appx. 257, 2009 U.S. App. LEXIS 21843 (8th Cir. 2009).

33. 2 U.S.C. § 601 (2007).

34. 42 U.S.C. § 2000e(b).

35. Public Law 102–166 §117(b).

36. U.S. Census Bureau (2012). "Federal Civilian Employment by Branch and Agency: Table 499. Federal Civilian Employment by Branch and Agency: 1990 to 2010." *Statistical Abstract of the United States: 2012* (Washington, DC: GPO).

37. U.S. Office of Personnel Management, "Total Government Employment Since 1962." *Historical Federal Workforce Tables.* http://www.opm.gov/feddata/HistoricalTables/TotalGovernment Since1962. asp (accessed November 23, 2012).

38. 5 U.S.C. § 7201.

39. 42 U.S.C. § 2000e(f).

40. 42 U.S.C. § 2000e(f).

41. 42 U.S.C. § 2000e-1(a).

42. *Rivera v. NIBCO, Inc.* 364 F.3d 1057, 1064 n.4 (9th Cir. 2004).

43. 42 U.S.C. § 2000e-2(f).

44. 42 U.S.C. § 2000e(1).

45. 29 C.F.R. § 1601 (2011).

46. 42 U.S.C. § 2000e(n).

47. H.C. Black, *Black's Law Dictionary* (St. Paul, MN: West Publishing, 1990), p. 1312.

48. 29 C.F.R. § 1601.13.

49. 29 C.F.R. § 1601.13 (b).

50. 42 U.S.C. § 2000e-5.

51. 29 C.F.R. § 1601.80.

52. S. 181, 111th Congress (1st Sess. 2009) §§ 3–5.

53. 550 U.S. 618 (2007).

54. 42 U.S.C. §2000e–2(a) (1).

55. 550 U.S. 618, 633 (2007).

56. S. 181, 111th Congress (1st Sess. 2009), § 3(A).

57. 29 C.F.R. § 1601.21.

58. 29 C.F.R. § 1601.19.

59. 29 C.F.R. § 1601.28.

60. 29 C.F.R. § 1601.19(a).

61. 29 C.F.R. § 1603.107.

62. Ibid.

63. 29 C.F.R. § 1601.20.

64. 29 C.F.R. § 1601.27.

65. Black, *Black's Law Dictionary*, p. 1099.

66. Ibid., p. 156.

67. 42 U.S.C. § 1981a(c).

68. P. Mogin, "Why Judges, Not Juries, Should Set Punitive Damages," *University of Chicago Law Review* 65 (1998): 179–223; M. Forbes, "Juries and Jurors: Juries on Trial; Constitutional Right Versus Judicial Burden: An Analysis of Jury Effectiveness and Alternative Methods for Deciding Cases," *Oklahoma Law Review* 48 (1995): 563–592; F. Strier and D. Shetowsky, "Profiling the Profilers: A Study of the Trial Consulting Profession, Its Impact on Trial Justice and What, If Anything to Do About It," *Wisconsin Law Review* (1999): 441–498; M.E. Lee, "Twelve Carefully Selected Not So Angry Men: Are Jury Consultants Destroying the American Legal System?" *Suffolk University Law Review* 32 (1999): 463–480.

69. N.J. Kressel and D.F. Kressel, *Stack and Sway: The New Science of Jury Consulting* (Boulder, CO: Westview Press, 2004).

70. Black, *Black's Law Dictionary,* p. 1548.

71. *Carmon v. Lubrizol Corp.,* 17 F.3d 791, 795 (5th Cir. 1994).

72. *Thomas v. Digital Equipment Corp.,* 880 F.2d 1486, 1491 (1st Cir. 1989); *Quiroga v. Hasbro, Inc.,* 943 F.3d 346, 347 (3rd Cir. 1991); *Williams v. Phillips Petroleum Co.,* 23 F.3d 930, 941 (5th Cir. 1994); *Damron v. Yellow Freight Systems,* 1999 U.S. App. LEXIS 20330, *5 (6th Cir. 1999); *Smeigh*

v. Johns Manville, Inc., 643 F.3d 554, 565 (7th Cir. 2011); *Marino v. Fred Meyer, Inc.* 1995 U.S. App. LEXIS 17280, *7 (9th CIR. 1995); and *Casillan v. Regional Transportation District,* 1993 U.S. App. LEXIS 32668 (10th Cir. 1993).

73. Federal Rule of Appellate Procedure 38.

74. *NLRB v. Cincinnati Bronze, Inc.* 829 F.2d 585, 591 (6th Cir. 1987).

75. Black, *Black's Law Dictionary,* p. 29.

76. S.R. Bagenstos, "The Perversity of Limited Civil Rights Remedies: The Case of 'Abusive' ADA Litigation." *The Regents of the University of California UCLA Law Review* 54 (2006): 1.

3

INTENTIONAL DISCRIMINATION

Disparate Treatment

LEARNING OBJECTIVES

- Explain what employment practices are unlawful under Title VII.
- Describe the burdens of proof for both the complaining party and the respondent under the disparate treatment theory of discrimination.
- Describe the conditions under which religion, sex, or national origin could be a *bona fide* occupational qualification.
- Identify the traditional remedies available to the complaining party under Title VII.
- Explain the circumstances under which an employer is liable for punitive and compensatory damages under Title VII.
- Explain practices that employers can pursue that would reduce the likelihood of disparate treatment claims.
- Differentiate direct and indirect retaliation.
- Describe under what circumstances an employer is liable for retaliation under Title VII.

OPENING SCENARIO

In May 2013, the board of education accepted a recommendation from the superintendent of schools to reduce the teaching staff in the Business Department at Central High School by one. Such decisions were normally based on seniority, with the most junior faculty member being eliminated. The problem confronting the superintendent was that the two junior teachers in the department were of equal seniority, both having begun their employment with the school on the same day nine years earlier.

Of particular concern to the superintendent was that one of those teachers was white and the other was an African American. The African American teacher was the only minority teacher among the faculty in the Business Department, though not in the school.

State law greatly restricted local school board decisions regarding layoffs and reductions in force. Nontenured faculty must be terminated first and subsequent reductions among tenured teachers in the affected subject area or grade level must proceed in reverse order of seniority. Seniority for this purpose is calculated according to specific guidelines set by state law. Thus, local boards lack discretion to choose between employees for layoff, except in the rare instance of a tie in seniority between the two or more employees eligible to fill the last remaining position.

The board determined that it was facing such a rare circumstance in deciding whom to retain between the white and African American teachers. In prior decisions involving the layoff of employees with equal seniority, the board had broken the tie through "a random process which included drawing numbers out of a container, drawing lots, or having a lottery." In none of those instances, however, had the teachers involved been of different races.

According to the school board's vice president, after the board recognized that the two teachers were of equal seniority, it further assessed their classroom performance, evaluations, volunteerism, and certifications and determined that they were "two teachers of equal ability" and "equal qualifications."

It was then that the superintendent made the recommendation that the African American teacher be retained and the white teacher be laid off "because he believed both teachers had equal seniority, were equally qualified, and because one of the teachers was the only African American teacher in the Business Department." The board made a discretionary decision to support the recommendation to break the tie between the white and African American teachers. The white teacher was informed that she was being laid off in order to preserve the diversity of the department, because there was already a sufficient number of white teachers in the department.[1]

Upon learning of this rationale, the white teacher immediately filed a charge with the Equal Employment Opportunity Commission claiming that she had been intentionally discriminated against because of her race—in direct violation of Title VII.

Was the white teacher unlawfully discriminated against because of her race? By the end of this chapter, you should be able to make that determination.

INTENTIONAL DISCRIMINATION

Title VII, as we remember, makes it an unlawful employment practice for a covered employer to "discriminate against any individual with respect to his compensation, terms, conditions, or privileges of employment, because of such individual's race, color, religion, sex, or national origin."[2] But how does one prove that an employer has unlawfully discriminated? The Act is mute on this subject. However, the courts and the EEOC (the regulatory agency for Title VII) have solved this problem by developing two methods to prove that Title VII may have been violated.

A complaining party can prove discrimination in one of two ways: The individual can meet the burden of proof by offering *direct evidence* of discriminatory intent, or the individual can rely on the burden-shifting method of proof set forth in the *McDonnell Douglas Corp. v. Green* decision to establish *circumstantial evidence* of violation.[3] In

Figure 3.1 **Disparate Treatment Proofs**

Prima Facie Case:
- Complaining party member is a member of a protected class,
- Complaining party was qualified for the job in question,
- Complaining party suffered from an adverse employment action, and
- A similarly situated individual (one with equal or fewer qualifications than the complaining party) from another class was treated differently.

Respondent's Rebuttal:
- The respondent's actions are based on legitimate nondiscriminatory reasons, and/or
- The respondent's actions are based on a bona fide occupational qualification.

Complaining Party's Rebuttal:
- The respondent's legitimate nondiscriminatory reasons are a pretext (a reason given to hide the respondent's real reason for the employment action).

EEO matters, the term "complaining party" is used to identify the individual initiating the EEO charge, the term "respondent" refers to the party against whom the complaint is filed, usually the employer. One way to establish direct proof of unlawful discrimination occurs when an employer makes a statement before credible witnesses. For example, a manager states, "as long as I am plant superintendent, XYZ Company will never hire an Asian supervisor" in the presence of several first-level supervisors and clerical staff. This would be direct evidence that the reason that a qualified Asian applicant was not hired was race. In the half century since Title VII was enacted, it is very rare for an employer to publicly announce his or her intention to openly violate the Act.

The *McDonnell Douglas* burden-shifting, or indirect, method is based upon producing sufficient circumstantial evidence to indicate that Title VII may have been violated. This is by far the more common method of initiating an unlawful employment practice suit. This method requires investigation of the allegation in a systematic manner following a set of prescribed legal criteria, or proofs. Under this formula, the burden of proving disputed facts shifts from party to party. Typically the initial burden of providing evidence indicating that Title VII may have been violated falls on the complaining party. This is known as establishing the *prima facie* case. Once the *prima facie* case has been established, the burden then shifts to the respondent. Should the respondent fail to rebut the complaining party's *prima facie* case, the complaining party prevails. If, however, the respondent can disprove the complaining party's *prima facie* allegation, the burden then shifts back to the complaining party to prove that the respondent's rebuttal is flawed. Figure 3.1 summarizes these shifting burdens of proof.

THE *PRIMA FACIE* CASE

The complaining party has the initial burden of proving that a Title VII violation may have occurred. In legal terminology, this is called establishing a *prima facie* case. The term *prima facie* literally means "first face" or "first appearance." In its legal sense, it means there is enough evidence to establish that Title VII has been violated unless the respondent can refute, or disprove, this evidence. The operative word in this process is *evidence*. A mere allegation is not sufficient to establish a *prima facie* case. There is no violation of Title VII unless the respondent's rebuttal fails.

To establish the *prima facie* case of disparate treatment using the *McDonnell Douglas* burden-shifting method, the complaining party must first demonstrate that he or she is a member of a protected class. This may appear nonsensical to some, but it is important to remember that Title VII only prohibits discrimination based on race, color, religion, sex, or national origin—nothing else. If the individual cannot demonstrate that he or she is a member of a protected class, Title VII is not applicable. This means that if the complaining party is seeking Title VII protection on any grounds other than race, color, religion, sex or national origin, the Act's protection cannot be invoked. If a Texas business owner refuses to hire any applicant from the state of Oklahoma, those applicants cannot make a claim under Title VII. Though this hiring practice may not be fair to qualified Oklahomans, it is not prohibited under Title VII. Being born in a particular state is not a class of employees protected under Title VII.

Furthermore, there is nothing in Title VII that guarantees that employees be treated well.

Member of a Protected Class

Most often the "member of a protected class" proof is invoked when complaining parties attempt to file unlawful discrimination complaints on the basis of sexual preference/orientation. Is discrimination on the basis of "sexual preference/orientation" the same as discrimination on the basis of "sex"? Federal courts have held that "sex" is a biological condition that does not encompass sexual orientation or preference.[4] In essence, sexual orientation discrimination is not actionable under Title VII[5] (though in some states, it is prohibited under state law, which is discussed in greater detail in Chapter 5).

Was Qualified and Applied

The second stage of *McDonnell Douglas*'s burden-shifting analysis involves demonstrating that the candidate who applied for the position in question met the qualifications for the position. In the first part, a person who did not apply for a position could hardly claim discrimination, since the individual cannot prove that he or she suffered any injury from the employer. You cannot be denied a job if you did not first apply, nor can you lose a job that you did not first hold.

If the individual did not meet the minimum requirements for the position vacancy, the individual can hardly make the argument that his or her protected class membership was the reason for rejection. If the individual were not qualified, the individual would not have been hired. This is why it is so important for employers to conduct good job analysis and to clearly communicate the minimum qualifications for any employment decision outcome.

If the person is truly unqualified for the job, the *prima facie* case is not made and the complaint will be dismissed. Title VII does not guarantee a job to every person regardless of qualifications. Even under a permissible affirmative action program, the applicant receiving preferential treatment must at least meet minimum job qualifications.[6] Simply stated, there is nothing in Title VII that requires an employer to hire or retain an unqualified employee.

Suffering an Adverse Employment Action

Unless the complaining party experiences some type of adverse employment consequence, she or he has no standing. Invariably, disparate treatment cases arise from rejection from employment, layoffs, denial of promotions, disciplinary actions, and so forth. If the applicant or employee has not experienced a tangible consequence, how can he or she claim that discrimination in compensation, terms, or conditions of employment has occurred? There can be no unlawful employment discrimination without evidence of its effects.

Different Treatment for Different Classes

The basic premise in **disparate treatment** is that the employee or applicant is intentionally being treated differently because of his or her membership in a particular racial, ethnic, gender, or religious group. As such, the fourth proof focuses on whether an individual of another class who was similarly situated was treated in a different manner.[7] The issue is not that a member of another class was treated differently, but that the individual was *similarly situated* and was treated differently. Similarly situated means that in a comparison, the individual from the other class either had equal or fewer qualifications,[8] or that the individual was guilty of similar misconduct.

The fourth proof under the *McDonnell Douglas* burden-shifting analysis leads to an argument over the applicant's qualifications. The employer's argument will be that the complaining party is qualified, but less qualified than the other candidates for the position. The complaining party must cast doubt on this assertion by providing evidence that he or she is more qualified than the other candidate. If the complaining party is successful in doing so, it will shift the burden to the employer to prove that the selected candidate was the more qualified.

As an illustration of a failure to establish the fourth proof, a female officer was recently transferred from a drug enforcement unit to a patrol unit for insubordination and exhibiting a poor attitude toward her duties. The complaining party alleges that this employment action (reassignment to a patrol unit) was predicated on her sex. She is able to establish the first three proofs: she is a member of a protected class (sex), she was qualified and held the position of undercover detective, and she suffered an adverse employment action (transferred to the patrol unit). However, she offers no evidence that a male detective with comparable performance to hers was *not* similarly transferred.[9] To make her case, she needed to show that a specific male detective who was evaluated as confrontational with a poor attitude and as having insubordinate/disrespectful behavior was not transferred. When the employment action involves layoffs or terminations, a Title VII claim arises when someone from another class with fewer qualifications was retained.

There is no unlawful discrimination in those instances where an individual was not qualified for the job, or the individual who was laid off was less qualified than those who were retained. The major exception to these circumstances is when the employment decision is affected by a *bona fide* seniority system, which will be discussed later under legitimated nondiscriminatory reasons.

To illustrate how the fourth proof could be established; let us assume that an employer has just interviewed a job applicant for a position as a sales representative to market health and fitness products. Roberto, a thirty-five-year-old Hispanic, applies for the job. He is 5'9" tall, weighs 230 pounds, and has a physique that could best be described as flabby. The interviewer informs Roberto that he does not fit the product image the company wants to portray. More to the point, Roberto is told that he is overweight and too flabby for this job. The job instead is given to Ralph, a white male who is 6'1" tall, weighs 190 pounds, and has a physique that could be described as athletic. The other applicant is outraged and claims that this action violates Title VII, but does it? Is the applicant entitled to protection under Title VII? Is the physically less-fit a class protected under Title VII? No.

To make his case, Roberto must show that his race, color, religion, sex, or national origin affected the employer's decision. Title VII does not protect applicants from being denied opportunities based on grooming and appearance,[10] but it does protect against different treatment based on ethnicity, race, or sex. Now also suppose that the job Roberto applied for was eventually given to Mark, a white male who is 6'1" tall, weighs 290 pounds, and has a physique that can also be described as overweight and flabby. If being flabby disqualified Roberto, a Hispanic, then why did it not disqualify Mark, a flabby white male, as well? With this evidence in hand, Roberto will be able to establish his *prima facie* case.

Less Qualified Members of the Same Class

Title VII is not violated when the complaining party was denied the employment benefit (i.e., hiring, promotion, assignment, etc.) and it was given instead to an applicant of equal or fewer qualifications of the same protected class. A *prima facie* case can be established only when an applicant of equal or fewer qualifications from another protected class receives the offer. As an example, assume that Allison O'Reilly, a female engineering graduate, applied for the following position: Industrial Engineer Needed. Candidates should have a minimum of four years' experience in light manufacturing. A B.S. degree in industrial or mechanical engineering is essential.

O'Reilly received her degree in industrial engineering from Massachusetts Institute of Technology (MIT) in 1995 and has spent the previous six years working for an electronic parts manufacturer in Sioux City, Iowa. She is very disappointed when she discovers that the job was given to Dee Dee Burt, a female sales representative with a degree in marketing and no manufacturing experience. O'Reilly decides to file a sex discrimination complaint.

If we were to apply the proofs for disparate treatment to the situation with O'Reilly, our analysis would reveal the following: (1) O'Reilly is a member of a protected class based on her sex, (2) O'Reilly was qualified for the position and applied for it, (3) O'Reilly was rejected, and (4) the position remained open and was filled by someone with fewer qualifications; in fact, it was filled by someone who was unqualified. However, O'Reilly has no Title VII claim. Why?

Because the "someone" who was less qualified (Burt) is also a member of O'Reilly's protected class. O'Reilly can hardly claim that the employer discriminated against her because of her sex, if the employer hired another woman. Obviously, the decision was not based on the applicant's qualifications, but neither was it based on sex. Title VII does not protect applicants against bad decisions, only decisions based on the applicant's protected class.

RESPONDENT'S REBUTTAL

Once a complaining party has successfully established the *prima facie* case, the burden of proof shifts to the respondent. At this juncture the respondent can pursue one of two avenues. The organization can justify its employment decision as being based on a legitimate nondiscriminatory reason, or it can contend that the decision is based on a *bona fide* occupational qualification (BFOQ). Since it is far more difficult to establish a BFOQ than a legitimate nondiscriminatory reason, this defense will be discussed first.

BFOQs

BFOQs are extremely rare and very limited in their application. They are further limited only to the protected classes of sex, religion, and national origin. The federal courts have long declared that there is no BFOQ for race. Note that in this chapter's opening scenario, the Board of Education would not be permitted to defend its layoff decision as a BFOQ, because race can never be used as a BFOQ. In other categories, a BFOQ essentially allows an employer to use the applicant's sex, religion, and national origin as a prerequisite for the job in question. The use of BFOQs in employment decisions is specifically authorized by Section 703(e) of the Civil Rights Act of 1964. Section 703(e) says, "[I]t shall not be an unlawful employment practice for an employer to hire and employ employees . . . on the basis of [their] religion, sex, or national origin in those certain instances where religion, sex, or national origin is a **bona fide occupational qualification** reasonably necessary to the normal operation of that particular business or enterprise."

This means that there may be specific instances when an employer can, for example, hire only females for a particular job. Or, there may be circumstances in which members of a particular religion would be considered for a job and members of other religions could legally be excluded. This is not nearly as large a loophole as one might imagine.

In the case of *Diaz v. Pan American Airways* (1971), a federal appeals court interpreted the BFOQ as being "reasonably necessary to the normal operation of a particular employer" to actually mean that the BFOQ must be at the very essence of the business.[11] In other words, the very essence of the business is threatened by not hiring members of one specific class. In *Diaz*, a man filed an EEOC complaint alleging sex discrimination on the grounds that Pan American Airlines would hire only female applicants for the position of flight attendant (at that time they were still called stewardesses). The complaining party noted that the principal function of the airline was to safely transport passengers from one airport to another. Any function not directly tied to passenger safety while in flight is not part of the essence of the business. Even if passengers preferred female attendants, so long as men can perform safely and efficiently the duties of a flight attendant, the men should not be excluded. In *Diaz*, the Court concluded that sex was not a BFOQ for being a flight attendant.

In determining whether or not a BFOQ based on sex, religion, or national origin can be used, two criteria should be considered. First, the essence of the business operation would be undermined by not hiring members of one protected class. Second, there is a factual basis for believing that all, or substantially all, members of the protected class in question cannot perform the principal duties of the job. In *Dothard v. Rawlinson*, the Supreme Court stated that sex discrimination is valid only when the essence of the business operation would be undermined if the practice were eliminated.[12]

In one case, a psychiatric hospital specializing in treating sexually abused adolescents was permitted to discriminate on the basis of sex in making shift assignments because some of the patients responded better to female staff than to male staff.[13] Similarly, a county jail was able to use a BFOQ defense in assigning a female jailer to the 12:00 A.M. to 8:00 A.M. shift because of a regulation requiring a female jailer be present at all times when female prisoners are incarcerated.[14]

For another example of a situation under which a BFOQ would be upheld, consider a meat-packing plant that excludes all non-Jews from its kosher foods processing unit. Under a religious BFOQ, it is permissible because foods that are marketed as kosher must meet strict preparation standards, and the preparation is further tied to a religious ritual that must be performed by a member of the Jewish faith. Therefore, no non-Jew can even assist in the preparation of meat marketed "kosher." Other common instances in which BFOQs are permitted are situations requiring female or male models and actors.

BFOQs have also been permitted by the courts on the grounds of safety to others. Such was the case in *Dothard v. Rawlinson*, in which a female applicant sued the state of Alabama because she was denied a position as a guard at a male maximum-security facility. The Supreme Court ruled that discriminating on the basis of sex was a BFOQ because "the likelihood that inmates would assault a woman because she was a woman would pose a real threat not only to the victim of the assault but also to the basic control of the penitentiary and protection of its inmates and other security personnel."[15]

However, the courts have been consistent in excluding customer preferences from the determination of "essence of the business." If, for example, customers prefer female flight attendants to male ones, this preference would not establish a BFOQ based on sex. In a similar vein, coworkers' preferences have also been excluded as a legitimate criterion for determining BFOQs. Because BFOQs are so narrowly applied, they are rarely used to justify employer decisions that are challenged under disparate treatment theory. By far the most commonly used disparate treatment defense is legitimate nondiscriminatory reasons. BFOQs on the basis of age are also permitted under the Age Discrimination in Employment Act.[16]

Figure 3.2   **Legitimate Nondiscriminatory Defenses Used to Justify Promotions, Raises, Layoffs, and Terminations**

Bona fide seniority systems	To be defensible, the seniority system must be consistently applied to all affected employees and not adopted for discriminatory purposes.
Merit	To be defensible, it must be based on objective performance, not subjective criteria.
Quality of production	To be defensible, it must be based on clearly defined, measurable, and disseminated standards.
Quantity of production	To be defensible, it must be based on clearly defined, measurable, and disseminated standards.
Job-related experience	To be defensible, the experience should enhance job performance.
Job-related training	To be defensible, the training should be applicable to the incumbent's current or future job.
Job-related education	To be defensible, the education should be applicable to the incumbent's current or future job.

Source: U.S. Equal Employment Opportunity Commission, *Theories of Discrimination: Intentional and Unintentional Discrimination* (Washington, DC: Government Printing Office, 1995), pp. A22–A24.

Legitimate Nondiscriminatory Reasons

Presenting a **legitimate nondiscriminatory reason** means the employer is contending that the decisions to hire, fire, promote, or lay off any employee was based on sound business rationale and not the individual's protected class status. In the absence of evidence that the employer's actions were the result of purely business motives, it will be assumed that the employer acted with discriminatory intent. Because disparate treatment is intentional discrimination, the employer must provide evidence that there was no intention to discriminate. The employer does so by showing that the employment decision was based on sound business rationale. Some examples of legitimate nondiscriminatory reasons are found in Figure 3.2.

Examining the opening scenario again, the respondent (the Board of Education) deprived itself of the legitimate nondiscriminatory defense because it openly stated that its employment decision was entirely based on the race of the two employees. One teacher was laid off because of her race; the other was retained because of her race. No legitimate nondiscriminatory reason was considered in making the layoff decision. As a result, Title VII was clearly violated by the board's unlawful consideration of the employee's race. On the other hand, if the employer can show that the individual's race was not a consideration in making the final selection decision, there is no Title VII violation.

For example, consider a situation in which an African American employee brings suit alleging racial discrimination. He had been temporarily promoted to a senior operator's position and later terminated by the employer. In the respondent's rebuttal, the employer states that the employee's termination was based on violating company policies and poor job performance after assuming the responsibilities of senior operator. The company presents evidence of two instances of violating its work policies and contends that the complaining party's poor performance provided legitimate nondiscriminatory reasons for terminating him. The reason for the employment decision was not the complaining party's race but rather his workplace behavior. To add credence to this point, the employer was able to produce three written reprimands bringing the complaining party's performance deficiencies to his attention.

Perhaps the best legal reason for discharging an employee is clearly poor performance, or as one federal court put it, "poor performance is a quintessentially legitimate and nondiscriminatory reason for termination."[17] The important thing to remember is that management must provide evidence of the employee's poor performance and this means documentation.

COMPLAINING PARTY'S REBUTTAL

Even when the respondent has successfully rebutted the *prima facie* case, the complaining party is afforded one more opportunity to demonstrate that intentional discrimination has occurred. The complaining party can still win the case if he or she can prove that the employer's legitimate nondiscriminatory reason is merely a pretext. **Pretext** means that the employer has tried to hide its unlawful discrimination by fabricating an apparently legitimate justification for its actions. There are several ways by which a complaining party can demonstrate pretext.

For instance, in an employee termination case, the employer insists that the action was legitimate based on written reprimands given to the employee. After all, what could be a more nondiscriminatory reason for firing an employee than misconduct? Now suppose that the complaining party could prove that the reprimands were constructed after the fact. That is, the documents were fabricated to make the employer's action appear legitimate, but they had never been administered to the complaining party at all. Now it becomes apparent that the employer presented false information (after-the-fact documents) to mask his or her unlawful action.

An employer's legitimate nondiscriminatory reason is pretextual if it is knowingly false. A less delicate way of putting this is that the employer is caught in a lie. The complaining party may be able to establish a pretext by effectively demonstrating that similarly situated employees of a different class were treated differently than the complaining party. For example, the employer contends that the complaining party was not hired for a position in question because she did not have a college degree, yet three of the last four male candidates who were hired for the job did not have a college degree either. Pretext may be shown further by evidence of employer bias. This may come from overheard conversations in which a particular manager has openly stated that he does not believe that women can be good managers.

Though usually associated with disparate impact litigation, on rare occasions statistical evidence can be used in establishing pretext. The complaining party might be able to produce workplace statistics that show that the employer's alleged nondiscriminatory criteria have not been applied equally to all employees. Statistical evidence also might be used to indicate that an employer has an established pattern of treating other members of the complaining party's protected class unfairly.

Figure 3.3   **Traditional Remedies Under Disparate Treatment**

- Attorneys' fees
- Back pay
- Compensatory damages
- Court costs
- Front pay

- Injunctive relief
- Punitive damages
- Reinstatement
- Seniority awards

It is very important for managers to note that statistical evidence can be a double-edged sword in disparate treatment cases. If workplace statistics can be used to imply a pattern of discrimination by the complaining party, they also can be used by the employer to imply that the organization's motives are nondiscriminatory. Though statistics showing a racially balanced workforce (or even employment of a disproportionately high percentage of protected class employees) are insufficient to conclusively show that an employer's actions are not discriminatory, courts may take the organization's workforce composition into consideration.

The complaining party would likely win the case if it could be shown that employees of other races who had just as many reprimands (or more) were not terminated. In short, the complaining party would have to show that he or she was treated differently than similarly situated employees of other races. It is, therefore, important for employers to ensure that disciplinary actions are administered consistently throughout the organization.

If there were evidence that the employer had a history of racially discriminatory practices, the complaining party could make an argument that this most recent instance was racially motivated. The evidence of employer bias, in some instances, could indicate that the articulated legitimate nondiscriminatory reasons are pretextual. This would be especially true under circumstances in which a concurrent EEO investigation of another practice (i.e., hiring practices) was found to be intentional discrimination.

REMEDIES UNDER DISPARATE TREATMENT

A remedy, in a legal sense, is the means by which a court prevents the violation of a legal right, or compensates for the violation of that right. In a trial, if it has been determined that an employer has in fact failed to comply with Title VII, the court may impose a penalty on the employer for violating the complaining party's rights. As mentioned previously, the federal district courts are responsible for framing remedies for Title VII violations, and the Act provides them with a broad range of remedies (see Figure 3.3) depending on the magnitude of the offense and the nature of the employer's conduct.

At a minimum, the complaining party that wins a case may expect injunctive relief. **Injunctive relief** merely means that the court will order the employer to cease and desist unlawful practices. The court is ordering the employer to immediately stop violating Title VII. Any future discrimination on the part of the employer would not only be another Title VII violation but also becomes contempt of court.

The court may further order the employer to reinstate the complaining party. In cases of employees who were wrongfully fired, this means that they will get their jobs back. An employee who was unlawfully denied a promotion could now be promoted. An applicant who was denied employment because of discrimination could now be hired.

Reinstatement is not necessarily immediate. Sometimes the complaining party must wait for a vacancy to occur before he or she is reinstated. Trials can take a long time from initiation to conclusion. Rarely are employment law violations resolved in less than two years; often, it takes longer. Additionally, employers are not required to fire existing employees to create vacancies for aggrieved employees.

Assume that a less qualified applicant was hired and has done an exceptional job for the company as a programmer/analyst. Should that employee now be fired because his employer, not the employee, discriminated against the complaining party? A court is unlikely to require the company to fire the new hire, or any other employee for that matter, in order to create a job for the complaining party. The complaining party might have to wait until a new programmer/analyst position is created or an existing one becomes vacant.

However, this does not necessarily mean that after winning the case, the complaining party will be left out in the cold for an unspecified period of time. District courts may also award back pay or front pay. An award of **back pay** would mean that the complaining party is entitled to wages (plus interest) that accrues from the time the discrimination first occurred to the date of ordered reinstatement. To demonstrate how this award is imposed, assume a complaining party has been wrongfully terminated on January 1, 2013, and immediately files a charge on January 2, 2013. Assume that the employee is extremely lucky and the case is tried and concluded by August 29, 2013. Further assume that the court's remedies were reinstatement and back pay. Because there is a current vacancy, the employer reinstates the complaining party on September 1, 2013. The complaining party would also be entitled to eight months of back pay, plus interest, to compensate him or her for the period January 1, 2013, to September 1, 2013, or the period during which the complaining party was wrongfully unemployed.

According to the Supreme Court, "front pay is money awarded for lost compensation during the period between judgment and reinstatement, or in lieu of the reinstatement."[18] **Front pay** is technically money awarded for lost compensation during the period between judgment and reinstatement or in lieu of reinstatement. It may be used under circumstances in which the complaining party is ordered reinstated, but no position is currently vacant. The complaining party is awarded pay and benefits until reinstatement occurs. This means that the complaining party would be compensated from the date that the company initially discriminated against him or her through the time he or she is finally officially employed by the company. Paying wages and benefits to an individual who is not actually working creates a tremendous incentive to get that individual in the company's workforce to get some return from the pay. Front pay may also be imposed by a court in instances when reinstatement is believed not to be feasible. There may be irreconcilable animosity between the employer and the employee. In such an instance the court may choose to calculate payment from the date of the judgment to a specified future date.

In certain cases, one party may be required to pay the attorneys' fees for the other. Title VII permits a federal court, at its discretion, to allow the prevailing party to be awarded reasonable attorneys' and experts' fees. In practice, employers are far more likely to be required to pay these fees when the complaining party prevails than when the opposite occurs.

Some courts have ordered complaining parties to pay for their employer's attorneys' fees and court costs when it has been shown that the complaining party's allegations were false and knowingly groundless. In short, employees who make false claims about employer discrimination are susceptible to the same penalties as employers who make false claims of not discriminating against employees. At least for attorneys' fees and court costs, either party can be held liable if they are caught lying or openly trying to circumvent justice.

Compensatory and Punitive Damages

In instances where the employer's conduct has been particularly irresponsible, the court may award compensatory or punitive damages. The legal standard that the complaining party must establish is that the employer engaged in its discriminatory practices with malice or with reckless indifference to the federally protected rights of the complaining party.[19] To achieve this, the complaining party must show that the employer was aware of the obligation not to discriminate against the complaining party and engaged in the discriminating action anyway.[20] Since disparate treatment is, by definition, intentional discrimination (knowingly discriminating against any employee or applicant because of the individual's race, color, religion, or national origin), there is an inherent risk of incurring compensatory or punitive damages.

It should be further noted that compensatory and punitive damages are restricted to cases involving disparate treatment. Compensatory and punitive damages cannot be awarded in cases involving disparate impact.[21] Furthermore, even in instances of disparate treatment, compensatory and punitive damages cannot be awarded if the employer is a government agency or political subdivision.

Compensatory damages are those imposed by a court to "compensate" the complaining party for monetary and nonmonetary harm suffered as a result of the discrimination. Suppose that as a result of a wrongful termination, an employee loses not only his paycheck, but his house (which is sold at a loss) and his car. Among the damages that the court can award is money to compensate the complaining party for these losses. An attempt will be made to make the complaining party "whole" (this is legalese for returning the employee to his or her condition before the harm occurred). Usually, the employer will be required to compensate the employee for any lost principal on property. In certain instances, monetary awards may be imposed for nonmonetary harm, like emotional distress. The underlying premise is that the monetary award is imposed to compensate the victim for the employer's unlawful actions.

Punitive damages may also be awarded to the complaining party, although these remedies are not intended to compensate the complaining party but rather to punish the respondent. **Punitive damages** are imposed as a painful reminder to an employer of the consequences of blatantly violating Title VII. The rationale behind imposing puni-

Table 3.1

Maximum Awards for Compensatory and Punitive Damages

Size of Employer's Workforce	Maximum Combined Punitive and Compensatory Damages per Complaining Party
15–200	$50,000
201–300	$100,000
301–500	$200,000
>500	$300,000

tive damages under Title VII is to discourage employers from knowingly violating the statute in the future.

Whenever compensatory or punitive damages are imposed, they are limited by a ceiling established in the Civil Rights Act of 1991.[22] The ceilings (maximum amounts that can be imposed) are based on the number of workers an employer employs in four predetermined ranges (see Table 3.1). These ceilings are the maximum monetary awards that federal judges may impose for compensatory and punitive damages for each aggrieved party.

To demonstrate how this works, assume that a company employing sixty-three workers was found to have intentionally violated Title VII by terminating two employees because of their national origin. Based on the evidence, the judge has decided that the employer's actions violated Title VII and were callous enough to justify compensatory and punitive damages. The judge can award any amount up to $50,000 in damages to each of the two employees. The judge also has the discretion to award different amounts to each party (i.e., $50,000 to one worker and $25,000 to the other). The maximum penalty that the employer could face is $100,000 if the judge determined that both employees were entitled individually to the maximum penalty. If the employer had 263 employees, then the highest potential penalty would be $200,000 because each aggrieved employee could be awarded individually the $100,000 maximum by the court.

Sometimes newspaper stories report multimillion-dollar compensatory or punitive damages awarded by juries. For example, an Iowa jury awarded a Korean-American working as an employee of a warehouse $150,000 in compensatory damages and $7 million in punitive damages for unlawful discrimination on the basis of race and national origin.[23] Such awards are often misleading if the charge, as it was in this case, is exclusively a Title VII violation. The maximum amount that can be awarded by a court for such a violation has a statutory cap on punitive and compensatory damages of $300,000 for each complaining party.[24] It is an idiosyncrasy of the system that when a jury is requested to hear a Title VII case, the court is required not to inform the jury of the limitations of the compensatory and punitive damages.[25] Because of this oddity, juries may award substantial damage awards, which the judges must then reduce to the maximum limits shown in Table 3.1.[26]

For a complaining party to be eligible to receive more than the statutorily imposed cap under the Civil Rights Act of 1991, he or she would have to file a separate suit under state laws or other federal statutes.

OTHER ISSUES IN DISPARATE TREATMENT

Mixed-Motive Decisions

A variant of disparate treatment is the issue of a mixed-motive employment decision. A mixed-motive situation occurs when, during a selection process, both legitimate (i.e., job-related) and illegitimate (i.e., race-based, sex-based, etc.) reasons are used in making the final decision.[27] Since the enactment of the Civil Rights Act of 1991, it is unlawful to even consider an employee's or applicant's protected class status at any point in the process when making an employment decision, even if the decision would have been exactly the same in the absence of the protected class consideration. Therefore, if a decision maker considered a candidate's race as well as his education, prior work experience, and objective performance, the entire decision process violates Title VII. To demonstrate this, let us assume that an African American salesman has applied for a promotion to district sales manager. The promotion decision is to be made by a three-member board. While reviewing the candidate's promotion packets, one board member remarks that she is concerned that an African American district sales manager might not project a proper corporate image. This is simple consideration of the candidate's protected class status (race) and, of and by itself, would violate Title VII even if it were not the motivating factor in making the final selection decision.

Continuing our scenario, the job is eventually offered to a candidate who was objectively more qualified than the complaining party but who is not African American. However, suppose that word leaked out to the African American applicant that a board member had expressed concern that his race would affect his performance. This would be a **mixed-motive** decision, one in which both a legitimate business reason (applicant qualifications) and an unlawful reason (an applicants' membership in a protected class) were considered. As a result, the African American applicant files a complaint with the EEOC. If, during the subsequent investigation, the company produces evidence showing that the other applicant's education, experience, and performance were clearly superior to that of the African American applicant, the decision would appear to have been predicated on both legitimate (education, experience, and performance) and illegitimate (race) considerations. This would constitute a mixed-motive decision, and the complaining party could make an unlawful discrimination claim under Title VII.

If, on the other hand, the applicant can demonstrate that race was the motivating factor in not receiving the promotion, he would be eligible for all remedies under Title VII for unlawful discrimination. Should the consideration of his race cause him not to be promoted, and should the position be filled by someone of equal or fewer qualifications, his complaint would be one of simple disparate treatment.

The reason that all this hairsplitting is important is because it determines which remedies can be awarded to the complaining party by the court. If race was the sole motivating factor, the African American applicant is entitled to all of the remedies authorized for disparate treatment (those discussed later in this chapter). If race had been considered, but the employer can produce convincing evidence that the outcome would have been the same (the objectively more qualified candidate was promoted) in the absence of racial consideration, then the employer's liability is only limited to:

- Injunctive and declaratory relief,
- Attorneys' fees, and
- Court costs.[28]

In short, under mixed motive, the employer is still declared to have violated Title VII. The employer will be ordered not to consider race in future promotion decisions, and, at the discretion of the court, the employer may have to reimburse the African American applicant for his attorneys' fees and court costs. It will not, however, have to promote the African American applicant, pay him back pay, or pay him punitive or compensatory damages.

Mixed Motive and Age Discrimination

As will be discussed in greater detail in Chapter 6, mixed-motive discrimination cannot be applied in situations involving intentional discrimination based on age under the Age Discrimination in Employment Act (ADEA).[29]

The Legal Standing of Testers

Testers are individuals who apply for positions of employment for the sole purpose of determining whether the "tested" employer is engaging in discriminatory hiring practices. If offered the position in question, the tester has no intention of accepting it.[30]

Testers are normally paired: usually a protected group tester is paired with a white tester. The testers provide information on their individual employment applications that makes them appear equally qualified. There may even be several sets of testers used against a given employer to reduce the defense of an individual fluke, oversight, or personality conflict. Conventionally, the protected group tester will apply for a position first and, if rejected, be followed by a white applicant. If the white applicant is treated differently during the interview, the organization that sponsored the testers may file suit.

The EEOC has accepted charges filed by testers since November 20, 1990.[31] More recently, the EEOC has concluded that tester evidence tends to show a pattern or practice of discrimination and can establish Title VII violations. However, since testers do not intend to take the jobs for which they are applying, they are not entitled to reinstatement and back pay. They are, however, entitled to injunctive relief. That is to say, the court will order the employer who discriminated against the tester to cease the discriminatory practice.

Interestingly, the civil rights organizations that send out employment testers may be eligible for compensatory damages. To qualify for this remedy, the organization must be able to show that it diverted resources from other programs to sponsor the testers. In *Fair Employment Council v. Molovinsky,* the Fair Employment Council of Greater Washington received $79,000 in compensatory and punitive damages under such circumstances.[32]

RETALIATION

Retaliation is a charge made by an employee that he or she received some adverse employment action (demotion, termination, reassignment to a less desirable position, etc.) as a direct result of reporting an employer's willful violation of a given statute.[33] Many statutes, both federal and state, contain clauses prohibiting employers from engaging in such retaliatory action.

With regard to federal equal employment opportunity (EEO) laws, retaliation is treated as actionable under any of several statues enforced by the Equal Employment Opportunity Commission (EEOC). It is becoming increasingly invoked as demonstrated by the marked rise in retaliation complaints over the past decade and a half. In 1997, retaliation-based charges accounted for 22,768 (roughly 22.6 percent) of the 80,680 charges filed with the EEOC that year. By 2011, retaliation charges had risen to 37,334, up nearly 64 percent, while total charges rose by only 24 percent, or 99,947 during the same period.[34] This was an increase of approximately 124 percent in the actual number of charges since 1990, when retaliation constituted only 12.1 percent of total charges.[35] Retaliation-based charges accounted for over 37 percent of total EEOC receipts in 2011. The 2011 figures represent the highest number of private sector retaliation complaints to date.[36] All of this data is provided merely to demonstrate that the meteoric rise of retaliation complaints is sufficient enough to concern most employers.

The purpose of any retaliation clause is to protect the whistleblower's right to report statutory violations or actions contrary to public policy without fear of reprisal. These clauses extend protection to more than the individual whistleblowers; they also protect witnesses who come forward with their testimony by assuring them that their employers will not be permitted to take adverse action against them for having testified. Anti-retaliation provisions are designed to create a disincentive for employers to impede investigations by imposing potential litigation and penalties if they coerce or intimidate employees for filing *bona fide* charges or participating in subsequent investigations.

Title VII's Retaliation Clause

Title VII also contains its own whistleblower's clause, "it shall be an unlawful employment practice for an employer to discriminate against any of his employees or applicants for employment . . . because he has opposed any practice made an unlawful employment practice by this subchapter [§ 703], or because he has made a charge, testified, assisted, or participated in any manner in an investigation, proceeding, or hearing under this subchapter."[37] Note that five protected activities are clearly delineated in the text. Obviously directly filing, or threatening to file, a complaint is protected. This insulates the actual whistleblower, but also any employee who is indirectly involved (i.e., coworkers who testify, assist, or otherwise participate in an investigation or hearing). Even those who do not file or threaten to file complaints with an enforcement agency receive protection. Any employee who merely expresses opposition to an employer's action that is believed to be unlawfully discriminatory is protected under Title VII.

Figure 3.4   **The Three Elements of a Retaliation Claim**

1. Complaining party engaged in a protected activity
2. Adverse action
3. A causal connection between the protected activity and its adverse action

Employees are safeguarded against any retaliatory action taken by the employer regardless of whether a complaining party has filed a claim alleging the employer's disparate treatment (intentional discrimination) or disparate impact (unintentional discrimination).[38] As a Title VII issue, a simple allegation of retaliation is not sufficient to establish a viable claim of unlawful discrimination.[39] Employees must either produce direct evidence that an employer's representative retaliated against them or present circumstantial evidence of the employer's retaliation (the *McDonnell Douglas* Burden Shifting Method).[40]

Establishing a *Prima Facie* Case of Retaliation

To advance a retaliation charge it is essential that a complaining party first establish a *prima facie* case of retaliation by satisfying three criteria: (1) the complaining party engaged in a protected activity (i.e., opposition to unlawful discrimination, participation in the EEOC complaint process, etc.); or (2) suffered an adverse employment action following the protected activity; and (3) there is a causal link between engaging in the protected activity and its adverse action (see Figure 3.4).[41] All three criteria must be satisfied or the *prima facie* case fails.[42] Once the *prima facie* case has been established, there is an automatic presumption that the employer's action is unlawful discrimination.[43]

In making the argument for a causal connection between the employee's protected activity and the employer's adverse action, the third criterion, several methods are available. The easiest way to achieve this is to provide evidence that a temporal proximity exists between the protected activity and the ensuing adverse employment action.[44] This proximity must be very close,[45] as the greater the passage of time between the two, the more difficult it will be for a court to believe this is evidence of causality.[46] If an adverse employment consequence occurred within a few weeks of an employee's protected activity, it would be a sufficiently short enough period of time to assume a connection.[47] On the other hand, if it occurred after several months or a year, there would be less reason to conclude a connection.[48]

Indirect Retaliation

Retaliation is not restricted exclusively to the employee making an EEO complaint. Other individuals who are indirectly involved in the process are entitled to protection under Title VII.[49] Remember that protected activities include testifying, assisting, or otherwise participating in an investigation or hearing.

Retaliation is actionable even when an employee suffers punishment for voicing his or her opposition to what they reasonably believe was unlawful discrimination.[50] Though these employees have merely questioned the employer's motives behind a particular action or practice, they are protected from reprisal so long as they have a *bona fide* belief that the action was unlawful. It is immaterial whether it was in fact unlawful, as the law makes no distinction between perceived or actual unlawful activity, only the employer's motives.[51] The complaining parties need only prove that they opposed an unlawful employment practice which they genuinely believed had occurred or was occurring.[52]

Assume that Phil, a first-level supervisor, is at a meeting with his plant superintendent, Walter. During the meeting, Walter states that he is tired of seeing one of Phil's female workers, Tori, constantly malingering on the job. He informs Phil that, as her supervisor, Phil needs to terminate Tori's employment by week's end.

Walter's motive may be a desire to remove less productive employees from the workplace, but Phil interprets this, though perhaps erroneously, as Walter's having a bias against female workers. Phil refuses to terminate Tori because he believes that Walter is asking him to engage in an unlawful action, sex discrimination. Walter sees Phil's refusal as insubordination and demotes him from supervisor to production worker, an adverse employment action. Even though Walter's initial order to terminate Tori may have been based on a legitimate nondiscriminatory reason, if Phil can prove that his refusal to carry that order was based on a *bona fide* belief he was being asked to violate Title VII, Phil may establish actionable indirect retaliation.

Employer Practices and Retaliation

General guidance for HR professionals would be to train all management personnel on the potential pitfalls of taking any action that could be perceived as retaliatory against any employee who has made an EEO complaint, assisted another employee in making an EEO complaint, or provided testimony in an EEO investigation. This includes verbally threatening to take retaliatory action.

Managers, and especially human resource managers, should also ensure that documentation is provided (and maintained) for all adverse personnel actions, especially disciplinary actions, discharges, rehabilitative transfers, and poor performance appraisals. This documentation could be used later to establish that such undesirable employment actions are based on legitimate business reasons and not on unlawful retaliation.[53]

It is always important to remember that any action taken against an individual for voicing opposition to an employer's discriminatory practices would establish a claim of retaliation (see Figure 3.5).[54] Hence, if an employee refuses to obey an order that he or she believes would violate Title VII, and is punished for disobedience, this could be retaliation.[55] Additionally, it would be retaliatory discrimination if an employer denied an employee's transfer request to a more desirable position (provided the complaining party was qualified) because the employee had previously filed an EEOC complaint.[56] Whatever the nature of the adverse action that occurred, it is a Title VII violation if it can be linked to a protected activity (filing a claim, providing testimony for another employee who filed a claim, objecting to an employer's discriminatory actions, or refusing to engage in discriminatory action).

Figure 3.5   **Practices That Could Result in a Retaliation Claim**

- Assisting another employee in filing a charge or complaint alleging discrimination
- Complaining about or opposition to unlawful discrimination
- Filing a charge or complaint alleging discrimination
- Organizing or participating in a group that has among its objectives opposing unlawful employment discrimination
- Participation in the EEOC complaint process
- Refusing to obey a workplace order because of a "good faith" belief that it is lawfully discriminatory
- Threatening to file a charge or complaint alleging discrimination

Source: U.S. Equal Employment Opportunity Commission, *Compliance Manual Section 8: Retaliation* (Washington, DC: Government Printing Office, July 6, 2000).

It would be unrealistic to assume that all claims of retaliation are meritorious. Either through malice or ignorance, some employees may allege retaliation when none has occurred. When this happens, the employer's defense is to demonstrate that the adverse actions were based on legitimate retaliatory reasons.

For example, in *Pereira v. Schlage Electronics*, the complaining party alleged she was terminated by her employer because she had made several complaints of sexual harassment by her coworkers.[57] The employer stated she was fired because of an inability to get along with her coworkers, stealing coworkers' tools, and misappropriating other employees' work.[58] Because the complaining party could not demonstrate the employer's nonretaliatory reasons for terminating her were false (pretextual), the federal district court denied her retaliation claim. As in so many other EEO-related areas, the necessity of maintaining records to document the nondiscriminatory reasons for disciplinary action is evident.

Following the maxim, "an ounce of prevention is worth a pound of cure," avoiding retaliation complaints can best be achieved by first ensuring that all management personnel are aware that this is one of the fastest-growing EEO complaints. Perhaps the most effective training would focus on explaining to supervisory and management personnel their EEO obligations, the necessity for having clearly established discipline and discharge policies, and the need for documentation to support all adverse personnel actions. It is hoped that by exposing the legal consequences posed by retaliation for the organization, supervisors will be more conscious of their own behavior and actions when dealing with employees who have filed or are threatening to file an EEO action. This does not mean workplace discipline and order must grind to a halt—it means the rationale for such discipline should be obvious and, above all, documented.

COMMON MYTHS ABOUT TITLE VII

You Must Hire Unqualified Protected Group Members

Hiring anyone who is unqualified for the job in question is a sure sign that the decision was predicated on the individual's protected class status. The message is fairly clear that the primary reason was his or her race, color, religion, sex, or national origin. This is precisely what Title VII forbids.

You Cannot Discipline or Discharge Protected Group Members

Some managers are reluctant to discipline some employees for workplace infractions, because they are females or members of a racial or ethnic minority. This may be motivated by the fear that in imposing disciplinary sanctions, the employee may react by filing an EEO complaint. The manager, by not punishing the employee because of the employee's minority status, hopes to avoid a Title VII violation. Actually, the opposite has occurred. By not punishing the "minority" employee, but continuing to enforce work rules on "nonminority" employees, the manager is actually discriminating in the terms and conditions of employment on race, color, sex, or national origin. The race, ethnicity, or gender of an employee becomes the determining factor as to whether one is punished or not for work rule infractions. This is utterly contrary to the intent of Title VII.

You Must Give Preferential Treatment to Protected Group Members

Giving preference to individuals because of their membership in a racial, ethnic, gender, or religious group is against the basic tenet of Title VII. The only exception is permissive affirmative action to individuals who are members of a group that is underutilized (see Chapter 9).

You Must Provide Federal Equal Employment Protection to People Based on Their Sexual Orientation

Sexual orientation and/or preference is not a class protected under Title VII. "Sex," for federal EEO purposes is limited to being biologically male or female. However, sexual orientation and/or preference may be protected under state law.

White Males Under Forty Are Not Protected by Federal Law

Not so. If an employer discriminates against an applicant or employee because he is white and male, that employer violates Title VII's prohibition against discrimination based on race and sex. In the eyes of Title VII, discriminating against someone because that person is white and male is no different than discriminating against the individual for being black and female.

SUMMARY

There are two basic theories of unlawful discrimination under Title VII: disparate treatment and disparate impact. Disparate treatment results from treating individuals differently because of membership in a protected class. Disparate impact focuses on statistical imbalances in the workforce. Disparate treatment theory was discussed in detail in this chapter, and disparate impact theory will be discussed in Chapter 4.

To reduce the risk of disparate treatment claims, HR professionals must conduct a thorough job analysis of every position in the organization. Job descriptions, job specifications, and performance standards are the results of proper job analysis.

The members of the protected classes under Title VII have a reasonable expectation of fair (equal) treatment in the workplace. Employers are expected to provide a workplace that is free from unlawful discrimination, and the federal government has established sufficient disincentives for not meeting this expectation in the form of injunctions, back pay, reinstatement, attorneys' fees, court costs, compensatory damages, and punitive damages. To avoid these legal pitfalls, it is becoming increasingly important for organizations to understand what employment actions and decisions expose them to these penalties, and to develop employment policies and practices that eliminate potentially unlawful decisions. It is important that managers fully understand how disparate treatment can occur in the workplace and ensure that only legitimate nondiscriminatory reasons are ever used in justifying any employment decision.

Finally, it is important to remember that Title VII protects members of all races and ethnic categories, not just some. Note that in the opening scenario the white teacher was terminated solely because she was white. That is to say, because of her race, the white teacher received different treatment. Could she make a *prima facie* case of race discrimination under the *McDonnell-Douglas* burden-shifting method? The federal circuit court in the real case upon which the opening scenario was based concluded that she was in fact a victim of unlawful racial discrimination.[59]

KEY TERMS AND CONCEPTS

Back pay	Injunctive relief
Bona fide occupational qualification (BFOQ)	Mixed motives
Compensatory damages	Pretext
Direct retaliation	Punitive damages
Front pay	Testers
Indirect retaliation	Whistleblower
Legitimate nondiscriminatory reason	

DISCUSSION QUESTIONS

1. What are the legal proofs required to establish a *prima facie* case for disparate treatment under Title VII?
2. What must an employer prove to rebut the complaining party's *prima facie* case of disparate treatment?
3. How can a complaining party show that an employer's legitimate nondiscriminatory reasons are pretextual?
4. What are the traditional remedies that a federal court may impose for disparate treatment?

5. What are the additional remedies authorized under the Civil Rights Act of 1991? Can these remedies also be imposed in situations involving disparate impact?
6. Are legitimate nondiscriminatory reasons and BFOQs the same thing? Why or why not?
7. Why is job analysis important for managers in disparate treatment cases? How are job analysis outcomes used by HR professionals?
8. Can an employer be innocent of unlawful discrimination and still violate Title VII's prohibition on retaliation? Explain your answer.

CASES

Case 1

An assisted-care company employing over 500 employees nationwide is hiring a director of computer technology. The position advertisement stresses the need for a degree in computer engineering and at least two years' experience in computer software development.

Mark has a degree in civil engineering and has four years' experience with the Texas Department of Transportation. He is immediately rejected from consideration as not meeting the minimum qualifications.

Another applicant, Fernando, applies for the same position. He has a computer engineering degree from the University of Missouri and has worked since graduation (one year) as a computer programmer for his wife's small software applications company. Fernando interviews very well and impresses several members of the selection committee.

Finally, there is Jerri Lynn, an African American, who has a degree in computer engineering from Texas A&M and has worked for the past five years for the software development department of Pathway Computers, a large computer manufacturer on the West Coast. She interviews well enough, but several of the selection committee members express concern that she may not get along with some of her potential subordinates.

After much deliberation, the committee decides that Jerri Lynn should not be hired, but instead offers the job to Fernando.

a. Is there any indication that Title VII was violated?
b. Did Jerri Lynn meet the qualifications?
c. Was she rejected?
d. Was the position filled by someone with fewer qualifications than Jerri Lynn?
e. Was Fernando's degree appropriate for the job?
f. Is there sufficient evidence to make a *prima facie* case?

Case 2

Kelly was hired as a broker by Lone Star Mutual, an established conservative stock brokerage firm located in downtown Dallas. During her job interview, Kelly was a model of conservatism, wearing little makeup and a navy business suit. Her degree in finance from the Darden School at Virginia and prior work experience were rated as excellent. According to the interviewer, Kelly appeared to be the perfect fit for the job. She was given a job offer on the spot.

Four working days later, Kelly arrived at work in designer jeans and a tight-fitting velour halter top with a Trans AM logo on it. It was immediately obvious to everyone that she was wearing nothing underneath the top. Her immediate supervisor, Greg, told Kelly to go home immediately and change into something "more appropriate." He further informed her that all Lone Star employees were expected to wear appropriate business attire while at work, as stated in the employee handbook.

Kelly refused Greg's request, claiming this rule restricted her right to equal protection under the law and feminine self-expression. Based on this refusal, Greg promptly fired Kelly. Kelly immediately filed an EEO complaint claiming sex discrimination.

    a. Under what circumstances would Kelly win her case?
    b. Under what circumstances would she lose her case?

Case 3

Mr. Robinson, HR manager for Cover-the-Earth Trucking, advertises for the following job opening: Operations manager for a medium-size trucking company, must have a B.B.A. or B.S. in logistics or operations management, a minimum of two years' experience in the interstate transportation industry, fluency in Spanish, and be willing to relocate to Monterrey, Mexico.

Mr. Douglas, an applicant, possesses a degree in the appropriate field, operations management, from the University of Arkansas and has three years' experience as operations manager for East Texas Motor Freight, but speaks hardly any Spanish.

Ms. Flores, another applicant, applied for the job as well. She graduated magna cum laude with a B.A. in Latino Studies from the University of California, Berkeley, has four years' experience as a dispatcher for a taxi company in San Francisco, and is fluent at the diplomatic level in both Spanish and French. No other candidates apply.

Mr. Robinson decides to hire Mr. Douglas for the position. Ms. Flores files a complaint with the EEOC, alleging discrimination under Title VII.

    a. Is there any indication that Title VII was violated?
    b. Did Ms. Flores meet the qualifications for the job in question?
    c. Was she rejected?
    d. Was the position filled by someone with fewer qualifications than Ms. Flores?
    e. Was Mr. Douglas's degree appropriate for the job?
    f. Was his work experience with East Texas Motor Freight compatible with the experience requirement?

Case 4

Albert, a male mid-level manager, was aware that his supervisor, Mark, had once made a comment that he had never met a woman who was any good at being a shop foreman.

When Albert recommends Sarah, one of his female subordinates, to fill one of two vacant shop foreman positions, he is told by Mark that Sarah is not minimally qualified. Albert believes that Mark has an aversion to female shop foremen and that this is the actual animus behind Sarah's rejection, rather than her qualifications.

Following Sarah's notification that she is no longer a viable candidate for the foreman's position, Albert encourages her to file an internal EEO complaint with the HR office. Upon hearing that Albert has encouraged Sarah to make an EEO complaint against him, Mark now decides to make an example of Albert. Mark assigns Albert to less desirable projects. The following month when annual employee performance evaluations are given, Albert receives a marginal evaluation and is not recommended for a raise (previously all of his performance evaluations were well above average and he always received merit raises).

    a. Can Albert establish actionable retaliation here?
    b. Would it be direct or indirect retaliation?

NOTES

1. This scenario was developed from the findings of fact in *Taxman v. Board of Education of the Township of Piscataway*, 91 F.3d 1547 (3rd Cir. 1996).

2. 42 U.S.C. § 2000e-2(a).

3. 411 U.S. 792, 802–803 (1973).

4. *King v. Super Service, Inc.*, 68 Fed. Appx. 659 (6th Cir. 2003); *Spearman v. Ford Motor Co.*, 231 F.3d 1080 (7th Cir. 2000).

5. *Trig v. New York City Transit Authority*, 50 Fed. Appx. 458 (2nd Cir. 2002); *Kay v. Independent Blue Cross*, 142 Fed. Appx. 48 (3rd Cir. 2005); *Vickers v. Fairfield Medical Center*, 453 F.3d 757 (6th Cir. 2006); *EEOC v. Concentra Health Services, Inc.*, 2007 U.S. App. LEXIS 18487 (7th Cir. 2007); *Medina v. Income Support Div., New Mexico*, 413 F.3d 1131, 1135 (10th Cir. 2005).

6. *Steelworkers v. Weber*, 443 U.S. 193, 208 (1979).

7. *Bazemore v. Friday*, 478 U.S. 385, 395 (1986).

8. *McDonnell Douglas v. Green*, 411 U.S. at 802.

9. *McKenzie v. Milwaukee County*, 381 F.3d 619, 626 (7th Cir. 2004).

10. *Jespersen v. Harrah's Operating Co.*, 392 F.3d 1076 (9th Cir. 2004).

11. 442 F.2d 385, 388 (5th Cir. 1971).

12. 433 U.S. 321, 333 (1977).

13. *Healy v. Southwood Psychiatric Hospital*, 78 F.3d 128 (3rd Cir. 1996).

14. *Reed v. County of Casey*, 184 F.3d 597 (6th Cir. 1999).

15. 433 U.S. at 801–02.

16. 29 C.F.R. § 1625.6(b).

17. *Bryant v. Farmers Insurance Exchange*, 432 F.3d 1114, 1125 (10th Cir. 2005).

18. *Pollard v. E.I. du Pont de Nemours & Co.*, 532 U.S. 843, 846 (2001).

19. 42 U.S.C. § 1981a(b)(1) (2011).

20. *Kolstad v. ADA*, 577 U.S. 256, 535–537 (1999).

21. U.S. EEOC, "Enforcement Guidance: Compensatory and Punitive Damages Available under § 102 of the Civil Rights Act of 1991" (July 6, 2000), http://www.eeoc.gov/policy/docs/damages.html (accessed December 5, 2012).

22. 42 U.S.C. § 1981a(b)(3)(B).

23. *Jin Ku Kim v. Nash Finch Co.,* 123 F.3d 1046, 1054 (8th Cir. 1997).

24. *Peyton v. DiMario*, 287 F.3d 1121, 1126–28 (D.C. Cir. 2002).

25. 42 U.S.C. § 1981a (c) (2).

26. *Ocheltree v. Scollon Productions, Inc.,* 308 F.3d 351, 355 (4th Cir. 2003); *Madison v. IBP, Inc.,* 330 F.3d 1051, 1060 n.3 (8th Cir. 2000).

27. *Price Waterhouse v. Hopkins,* 490 U.S. 228, 244–45 (1989).

28. 42 U.S.C. § 2000e-5(g)(B).

29. *Gross v. FBL Financial Services, Inc.,* 2009 U.S. LEXIS 4535 (2009).

30. *Williams v. Staples,* 372 F.3d 662 (4th Cir. 2004).

31. U.S. EEOC, "EEOC Notice Number 915.002: Enforcement Guidance: Whether 'Testers' Can File Charges and Litigate Claims of Employment Discrimination" (1996), http://www.eeoc.gov/policy/docs/testers.html (accessed December 5, 2012).

32. 1996 D.C. App. LEXIS 194 (D.C. Cir. 1996).

33. R. Moberly, "The Supreme Court's Anti-retaliation Principle," *Case Western Reserve Law Review* 61 (2011): 375–452.

34. U.S. EEOC, *Charge Statistics FY1997 through* FY2011, and "Retaliation-Based Charges," FY1997–FY2011, www.eeoc.gov/stats/charges.html (accessed October. 25, 2012).

35. U.S. EEOC, *Annual Reports for Fiscal Year 1990* (1990), 17.

36. H. Datz. "Discrimination: Retaliation Cases-A Growing, Important Field of Employment Law." *HR Focus* 89 (2012) 12–14.

37. 42 U.S.C. § 2000e-3(a) (2011).

38. Ibid.

39. *Ghane v. West,* 148 F.3d 979, 981 (8th Cir. 1998).

40. U.S. EEOC, "Proof of Casual Connection," *Compliance Manual,* § 8, Chapter II, Part E.

41. *Nowlin v. Resolution Trust, Corportion* 33 F.3d 498, 507 (5th Cir. 1994).

42. U.S. EEOC, "Proof of Casual Connection," *Compliance Manual,* § 8-II(A).

43. *St. Mary's Honor Center v. Hicks,* 509 U.S. 502, 506 (1993).

44. *Gorman-Bakos v. Cornell Cooperative Extension,* 252 F.3d 545, 554–55 (2nd Cir. 2001).

45. *Clark County School District v. Breeden,* 532 U.S. 268, 273 (2001).

46. *Morris v. Lindau,* 196 F.3d 102, 113 (2nd Cir. 1999).

47. *Wells v. Colorado Department of Transportation,* 325 F.3d 1205, 1217 (10th Cir. 2003).

48. *Haywood v. Lucent Technologies.* 323 F.3d 524, 532 (7th Cir. 2003).

49. M. Green, "Family, Cubicle Mate and Everyone in Between: A Novel Approach to Protecting Employees from Third-Party Retaliation under Title VII and Kindred Statutes," *Quinnipiac Law Review* 30 (2012): 249–299.

50. U.S. EEOC, *Theories of Discrimination* 19 (1995).

51. *Peters v. Jenney*, 327 F.3d 307, 320 (4th Cir. 2003).

52. *Bhella v. England*, 91 Fed. Appx. 835, *847 (4th Cir. 2004).

53. *Byrd v. Ronayne*, 61 F.3d 1026 (1st Cir. 1995); *Raney v. Vinson Guard Service, Inc.,* 120 F.3d 1192 (11th Cir. 1997).

54. U.S. EEOC, *Compliance Manual* § 8–1 (2000).

55. *Moyo v. Gomez*, 40 F.3d 982 (9th Cir. 1994), cert. denied 513 U.S. 1081 (1995).

56. *McClam v. City of Norfolk Police Dept.,* 877 F. Supp. 277, 282 (E.D. Va. 1995).

57. 932 F.Supp. 1095 (N.D. Cal. 1995).

58. 932 F.Supp. at 1100.

59. *Taxman v. Board of Education of the Township of Piscataway,* 91 F.3d 1547, 1564–65.

4

UNINTENTIONAL DISCRIMINATION

Disparate Impact

LEARNING OBJECTIVES

- Describe the proofs necessary to establish a *prima facie* case of disparate impact.
- Discuss challenges to allegations of disparate impact.
- Conduct applicant flow analysis using the four-fifths criterion.
- Conduct applicant flow analysis using the two or three standard deviations method.
- Perform workforce tests of representativeness using stock analysis.

OPENING SCENARIO

Employees of a large manufacturing company bring suit against their employer as a result of complaints about the employment selection criteria the company calls the Formalized Selection Process (FSP).[1] The FSP was administered to all candidates seeking employment as production technicians at the company's newly created Metropolitan Distribution Center. The complaining parties allege that the FSP discriminated against them on the basis of their gender and age in violation of the Civil Rights Act of 1964.

The FSP was administered to 189 candidates, including internal candidates (current employees) and outside candidates (persons who never worked for the company before), as a two-phase selection device. The first phase was comprised solely of a written or "cognitive" test that focused on five subjects: (1) mechanical comprehension, (2) practical arithmetic, (3) reading comprehension, (4) forms checking, and (5) coding skills. The candidates who achieved an average-percent-correct score of 55 percent or higher passed the written test and were given the opportunity to proceed to the second phase, which consisted of both a group problem-solving exercise (GPE) and a structured interview. The group problem-solving phase tested the candidates' proficiency in five job skills: (1) work orientation, (2) ability to work with others, (3) making choices and solving problems, (4) oral communication, and (5) relevance of prior training and experience. The evaluators in the GPE phase were experienced supervisors. In order to be considered for a technician position, a candidate was required to successfully complete both the written and GPE phases of the FSP.

Of the 189 individuals (44 women, 145 men; 52 persons forty years or older, 137 persons under forty years) who participated in the FSP, 131 (31 women, 100 men; 22 persons forty years or older, 109 persons under forty years) successfully completed the first phase and were permitted to participate in the second phase.

Of the 120 candidates (29 women, 91 men; 20 persons forty years or older, 100 persons under forty years) who participated in the second phase, nineteen candidates (3 women, 16 men; one person forty years or older, 18 persons under forty years) were offered employment as technicians. Notice that not all of the candidates who passed the written phase chose to participate in the GPE phase.

In its rebuttal, the company contended that the FSP created no adverse impact on women and that the differences on the GPE were not statistically significant. The company had also hired an outside consulting firm specializing in job analysis and selection projects to evaluate the company's current and projected workforce needs and to develop the FSP.

Is the company's claim that the Formalized Selection Process does not have a disparate impact on female applicants accurate? What about those applicants over forty years old? If so, is it unlawful? By the conclusion of this chapter you should be able to answer these questions.

FROM DISPARATE TREATMENT TO DISPARATE IMPACT

From a human resource management (HRM) standpoint, Title VII compliance was relatively simple until 1971. Until that point, human resource (HR) professionals were required to ensure that none of their actions were motivated by a discriminatory intent; disparate treatment was the only actionable Title VII violation (refer to Chapter 2). Provided that the employer could prove the action was based on a legitimate, nondiscriminatory reason (and that this reason was not a pretext), the employer was usually assured of avoiding a Title VII violation.

But the view of what constituted unlawful discrimination radically changed with the advent of disparate impact, and perhaps no single statute or court decision has affected HR selection as much. From this point forward, HR professionals and federal regulatory agencies would become increasingly concerned with numbers. Organizations became preoccupied with achieving the "right numbers" in hiring and promotions. Human resource management entered an era in which planners were increasingly concerned with achieving the appropriate representation of women and ethnic minorities in their workforces.

Not only would the selection rates of various protected classes become paramount, so would knowledge of relevant labor markets and validation requirements. The complexities of the disparate impact theory of discrimination will now be examined.

Disparate Impact

The theory of discrimination known as **disparate impact** (sometimes called **adverse impact**) is responsible for the current preoccupation with proportional representation in the workplace. It is primarily the expression of the group rights view of equal employment opportunity mentioned in Chapter 3. Unlike disparate treatment, which is by its very nature intentional discrimination, disparate impact is unintentional. This is a crucial difference. Remember that under disparate treatment analysis, the respondent's rebuttal hinges on proving to a court that there was no intention to unlawfully discriminate against the complaining party because of his or her race, color, religion, sex, or national origin. The employer's defense in disparate treatment situations concentrates on demonstrating that the complaining party's protected class status had no impact on the final employment decision—there was no intent to discriminate.

Disparate impact is said to occur when a facially neutral employment practice or selection criterion has the effect of disqualifying a disproportionate number of protected class members. This is usually demonstrated by a manifest statistical imbalance. Again, the fundamental premise under disparate impact theory is that the discrimination is strictly unintentional. It is immaterial whether the employer intended to discriminate or not; only the employment outcomes are important. Perhaps the best way to explain how disparate impact works is to examine the Supreme Court decision that produced this theory of discrimination, *Griggs v. Duke Power Company* (1971).[2]

The *Griggs* Case

Duke Power Company's Dan River plant in Rockingham County, North Carolina, was organized into five operating departments: (1) labor, (2) coal handling, (3) operations, (4) maintenance, and (5) laboratory and testing. Prior to 1965, Duke Power Company required job applicants to possess at least a high school diploma for entry-level hiring for all departments with one exception, the Labor Department, for which there was no minimum education requirement. The Labor Department was also the lowest-paying unit in the company. However, a high school diploma or its equivalent was required for transfer from this department to another. This meant that any worker transferring from the company's Labor Department jobs to the higher-paying jobs in the other departments had to have a high school diploma or a GED.

Beginning in 1965, the company added an additional requirement: any employee seeking placement outside the Labor Department had to achieve a satisfactory score on two aptitude tests—the Wonderlich Personnel Test and the Bennett Mechanical Comprehension Tests. All applicants, including those requesting transfers, were required to meet these standards. Those who met the standards (high school diploma and passing aptitude test scores) were hired or transferred without regard to race, color, religion, sex, or national origin. As a result, if you were a worker in the Labor Department and wanted to get a better-paying job in Operations, you had to pass the aptitude tests, in addition to possessing a high school diploma, or you were not going anywhere.

On the surface, these new requirements appeared benign. After all, every applicant was evaluated against the same standards, and no one was given favorable or unfavorable treatment because of race, color, religion, sex, or national origin.

However, the company's African American employees challenged these requirements on the grounds that they excluded a far greater proportion of African American applicants than they did white candidates. In fact, according to the 1960 North Carolina census, the education requirements alone would guarantee an imbalance, because 34 percent of white males had completed high school, compared to only 12 percent of African American males.[3] This problem was further compounded by the fact that, of the whites who were eligible to take the aptitude tests, 58 percent would pass. The African American candidates who were eligible to take the tests (those who had a high school diploma) had a passing rate of only 6 percent. In short, the passing rate of African American applicants was a mere 10 percent of that of their white counterparts. Due to this disparity, the complaining parties argued that the education and testing requirements had the effect of denying job opportunities to capable African Americans at a far greater rate than whites.

Using the disparate treatment theory of discrimination, the employer argued the same standard had been applied to all applicants, hence no individual was treated differently because of his or her protected class status. Since there was no evidence of intentional discrimination, Title VII could not be violated. Remember that the only form of discrimination that was actionable at this time was disparate treatment, which required either direct or circumstantial evidence of intent to discriminate.

Countering this claim, the African American applicants argued that even though the same standards were administered to all applicants, the standards excluded a disproportionate number of African Americans from favorable consideration because job placement was based solely on whether an applicant met those standards. Furthermore, not only did the diploma and test requirement exclude far more African Americans from selection, the standards did not have anything to do with the jobs from which the African Americans were being excluded. There was no connection between the diploma and test results and a person's ability to perform the specific jobs in question. Moreover, there was evidence that employees who had not taken the tests (those hired before the new standards were implemented) had performed satisfactorily in the jobs.[4] The selection requirements did not appear to be connected with successful job performance in several categories in the other departments. The Supreme Court, upon hearing the case, concluded, "The [Civil Rights] Act proscribes not only discrimination but also practices that are fair in form. The touch-stone is business necessity. If an employment practice which operates to exclude Negroes cannot be shown to be related to job performance, the practice is prohibited."[5]

As a consequence of this ruling, disparate impact, a new actionable form of employment discrimination, was created. Employers could now be found in violation of Title VII when an employment practice had the effect of adversely affecting a disproportionate number of protected group members, and the practice could not be shown to be job related. Title VII was evolving from a prohibition of discrimination against individual applicants and employees to one of discrimination against groups. In order to reduce confusion, readers should note the terms **job-related** and **business necessity** are often used synonymously (as are the terms disparate impact and adverse impact). Essentially, the characterization means that the employment practice causing the disparity is viewed by the employer as directly related to the successful completion of the job in question.

Figure 4.1   **Disparate Impact Proofs**

Prima facie case:	A facially neutral employment practice has an adverse impact on a protected class (invariably demonstrated by a manifest statistical imbalance)
Respondent's rebuttal:	The challenged employment practice is shown to be a business necessity (it is job related); the complaining party's statistics are challenged
Complaining party's rebuttal:	There are other practices that would accomplish the same end but have less adverse impact on the protected class

How an employer establishes the job-relatedness of an employment practice is covered in detail in Chapter 15.

ESTABLISHING A *PRIMA FACIE* CASE

Generally, to establish a *prima facie* case under disparate impact, complaining parties must first identify the specific employment practice that has caused the exclusion of applicants because of their membership in a protected group, and then offer reliable, statistical proof that the practice contributed to the exclusion[6] (see Figure 4.1). Since the enactment of the Civil Rights Act of 1991, it is no longer enough for complaining parties to merely identify a statistical disparity; they must link the disparity to the specific practices or procedures claimed to have caused it.

This is precisely what occurred in the *Griggs* case when the test scores caused African Americans to be rejected at a rate almost ten times greater than the rejection rate of whites. Furthermore, the diploma requirement excluded nearly three times as many African Americans as whites. As a consequence, both components of the selection process (educational requirements and test scores) would have created a disparate impact. However, the question of where an actionable statistical imbalance begins would not be settled until seven years after the *Griggs* decision, and the most popular method for these determinations would be developed by a regulatory agency and not the courts.

Note that any facially neutral standard or criterion for a selection decision—a standard applied equally to all candidates—can have disparate impact if it excludes a disproportionately high number of protected class members from consideration. This places a burden on decision makers to consider the impact that any job requirement is likely to have on the demographic diversity of the applicant pool. A list of selection criteria known to have disparate impact on certain protected groups is provided in Figure 4.2. As will be explained shortly, disparate impact, in and of itself, is not a Title VII violation provided that the facially neutral selection criteria can be proven essential to performing the job in question.

DETERMINING STATISTICAL IMBALANCES

There is no one way to establish statistical imbalances. Federal courts have accepted a number of different methods that demonstrate employment practices have disparate

Figure 4.2 **Potential Selection Criteria That Create Disparate Impact**

- Arrest records
- Conviction records
- Credit checks
- Education requirements
- Height requirements
- Intelligence tests
- Language proficiency
- Nature of military service/discharge
- Tests for physical strength /endurance
- Weight requirements
- Work experience

Source: G. Jackson, *Labor and Employment Law Desk Book* (Englewood Cliffs, NJ: Prentice Hall, 2004).

Figure 4.3 **Common Statistical Measures for Establishing Disparate Impact**

- Four-fifths rule (a.k.a. 80 percent rule)
- 95 percent confidence interval
- Two standard deviations
- Three standard deviations

---

impact (see Figure 4.3). The most commonly used method was first developed by the Equal Employment Opportunity Commission (EEOC) in its 1978 *Uniform Guidelines on Employee Selection Procedures.*[7]

Under the *Uniform Guidelines,* adverse impact is assumed anytime the selection rate for any race, sex, or ethnic group is less than four-fifths (or 80 percent) of the rate for the group with the highest rate.[8] This standard for disparate impact analysis has become popularly known as the four-fifths rule. It is also known as the 80 percent rule. Because of its simplicity, it is the preferred method of disparate impact analysis by the EEOC. To make our discussion a little less cumbersome, we will refer to the group with the highest rate as the "benchmark group."

More sophisticated statistical measures have also been recognized by the courts. An employment practice can be assumed to have violated Title VII if the employment practice has a statistically significant adverse impact on members of a protected group. Adverse impact is statistically significant when the disparity between the expected result and the actual result exceeds two to three standard deviations.[9] Standard deviations are a measurement of the probability that a result is a random deviation from the predicted result. The more standard deviations, the lower the probability the result is due to chance.[10] Additionally, federal courts have judged disparate impact to have occurred when the selection rate for a protected class falls outside of a 95 percent confidence interval, essentially a selection rate falling within two standard deviations.[11]

APPLYING THE FOUR-FIFTHS RULE

Assume that ABC Manufacturing has advertised job openings in its expanding Memphis, Tennessee, plant. There are 125 new positions in entry-level manufacturing in the Production Department and 20 new positions for programmer/analysts in the Operations

Table 4.1

Applicants with Two-Year Degree in Industrial Arts

	Applied	Passed 1st Stage
African American		
Male	110	37
Female	48	18
Totals	158	55
White		
Male	146	81
Female	36	32
Totals	182	113
Total		
Male	256	118
Female	84	50
Totals	340	168

Department. The entry-level manufacturing jobs require each applicant to have at least a two-year degree in industrial arts from a two-year college and to pass a hand-eye co-ordination test. Each programmer/analyst must have a bachelor's degree in management information systems (MIS) or computer science and pass a test measuring programming skills using C++.

Of the 340 applicants applying for the entry-level positions, 48 were African American females, of whom 18 had the required degree. Of the 110 African American males applying for these positions, 37 had two-year degrees. There were 146 white males and 36 white females who applied for the entry-level manufacturing jobs, of which 81 males and 32 females had the appropriate degrees (see Table 4.1).

Of the 55 African Americans (18 females and 37 males) who passed the education requirements, 53 (16 females and 37 males) passed the hand-eye coordination test. All 53 were offered employment. Of the 113 whites (32 females and 81 males) who passed the education requirements, 103 (28 females and 75 males) passed the hand-eye coordination examination, of which 72 (28 females and 44 males) were offered jobs at the facility. Has disparate impact occurred?

The Civil Rights Act of 1991 requires that each stage of the selection process be examined separately.[12] In the case of the 125 entry-level manufacturing positions, the process consisted of possessing a two-year degree in industrial arts and passing a hand-eye coordination exam. Since this is a three-stage selection process, each stage must be analyzed separately.

In Stage I of the selection process, all candidates are screened to determine if they possess the specified education requirements, in this case a two-year degree in industrial arts. As a result, those who have two-year degrees pass Stage I and move to Stage II, and those who do not are eliminated from further consideration. Of those who pass on to the next stage, only those who pass the manual dexterity test will be considered for employment. A finding of disparate impact in either one of the two stages will be sufficient to establish a *prima facie* case. However, not even favorable hiring for the group suffering the disparate impact at the end of the selection process will absolve the employer if disparity occurs in one stage of the selection process.

Assessing disparate impact in this manner is known as **applicant flow analysis**. Applicant flow analysis examines the effect of the questioned selection criterion only on the actual candidates who applied for the position. This was the same method used to analyze the *Griggs* case. The premise is simple—the selection rate is calculated for each class of candidates (i.e., whites, blacks/African Americans, Hispanics/Latinos, Asian Americans, Hawaiian Native/Pacific Islanders, American Indians/Alaskan Natives, females, males, etc.).

This selection rate is a fairly simple calculation. The number of members of a given class who passed the criterion (i.e., the applicant had the appropriate education requirements) is divided by the total number of members of that class who applied for the job. The class that has the highest selection rate becomes the benchmark against which all other selection rates are compared.[13] To illustrate this, we can calculate the selection rate for whites for Stage I of the selection process. Remember that 146 white males and 36 white females applied for the entry-level positions, for a total of 182 white applicants (this becomes the denominator).

Selection Process, Stage I

Of those 182 qualifying white applicants, 113 (81 white males and 32 white females) met the minimum education requirements. Consequently, the selection rate for white applicants at Stage I was 0.621 (113 who met the requisite education requirement divided by the 182 whites who applied for the position). Hence, roughly 62.1 percent of all white applicants passed Stage I of the selection process (see Table 4.1).

When disparate impact (adverse impact) is investigated on the basis of race, the male and female rates for each racial group are combined. Therefore, of the 158 total African American applicants (110 African American males and 48 African American females), 55 (37 males and 18 females) had the required education and were allowed to continue in the selection process to the next stage. The other 103 were rejected because of this requirement. Put another way, the selection rate of African American applicants at Stage I was 0.348 (55 African Americans who met the requisite education requirement divided by the 158 African Americans who applied for the position). It can also be expressed by saying that the selection rate of African American applicants at Stage I is approximately 34.8 percent. This is where the four-fifths rule will be applied using the following formula:

selection rate of the protected class < 0.8 selection rate of group with the highest rate

This is the standard established by the EEOC as the preferred means of determining disparate impact in most instances.[14] There is an easier method if the selection rate of the group alleging disparate impact is divided by the selection rate of the group with the highest selection rate (the benchmark group) and the dividend of that division is less than 0.8. In that case you could conclude disparate impact. It does not matter which method is used because in either method disparate impact is considered to have occurred if the selection rate of the complaining party is less than 80 percent of the selection rate of the benchmark group.

To demonstrate this, we would conclude that disparate impact has occurred if the selection rate of the African American candidates is less than 80 percent of the selection rate of the white applicants:

$$0.348 < 0.8 \ (0.621)$$
$$0.348 < 0.497$$

or

$$0.348 < 0.621 = 0.56$$
$$0.56 < 0.8$$

Taking a look at the first method, since the selection rate of the African American applicants (34.8 percent) is less than 80 percent of the selection rate of the white candidates (49.7 percent), it can be concluded that disparate impact has occurred. Using the other method, since the selection rate of the African American applicants is only 56 percent of the selection rate of the benchmark group $(0.348/0.621 = 0.56)$, which is less than the required 80 percent, disparate impact would again be concluded.

Does this mean the company is in violation of Title VII? In other words, does this statistical imbalance alone violate Title VII? No, it only means that the complaining party has presented sufficient statistical evidence to establish a *prima facie* case. As it was with disparate treatment, a Title VII violation occurs only if the respondent is not able to carry his or her rebuttal. As will be shown in Chapter 6, when an employer can prove the criterion that caused the disparate impact is a business necessity, Title VII is not violated.

Selection Process, Stage II

Continuing the analysis of ABC Manufacturing, the second stage of the selection process, the hand-eye coordination test, must now be evaluated. Again, because we are examining alleged racial discrimination, the male and female scores for both classes (passing versus not passing) are combined (see Table 4.2).

Remember that only those candidates who met the first selection requirement, the two-year degree, are eligible to move to second-stage consideration and take the hand-eye coordination test. This means that only the 55 African Americans who had the appropriate education were permitted to take the coordination test. Of these applicants, 37 of the males and 16 of the females (a total of 53) passed the hand-eye coordination test. Of the 113 whites who moved to Stage II, 75 of the men and 28 of the women (a total of 103) passed the coordination examination. Applying the four-fifths rule to Stage II of the application process, the selection rate for African Americans of 0.964 (53 Af-

Table 4.2

Applicants Who Passed the Coordination Test

	Passed 1st Stage	Passed 2nd Stage
African American		
Male	37	37
Female	18	16
Totals	55	53
White		
Male	81	75
Female	32	28
Totals	113	103
Total		
Male	118	112
Female	50	44
Totals	168	156

rican American applicants who passed the dexterity test divided by the 55 total African American applicants who began Stage II) will be compared to the second-stage selection rate for white applicants which was 0.912 (103/113). Because the African American second stage selection rate (0.964) is higher than that of the white applicants (0.912), African Americans are the benchmark group in Stage II. As the benchmark group they cannot have suffered disparate impact at this stage in the process. There can hardly be any issue of disparate impact at Stage II for African Americans since their selection rate is nearly 106 percent that of the white selection rate ($0.964 \div 0.912 = 1.057$). Note that the *Uniform Guidelines* clearly states that the statistical comparison is made against the group with the highest selection rate.[15] If African Americans are that group, disparate impact has not affected them. What about the whites in this example—can they claim disparate impact at Stage II? Do the math:

$$0.912 < 0.8 (0.964)$$
$$0.912 < 0.771$$

or

$$0.912 \div 0.964 = 0.946$$

Even though there was no adverse impact indicated in Stage II of the selection process, the African American applicants have still established a *prima facie* case because of the adverse impact demonstrated in the first stage.

The most important fact to remember under disparate impact is that the *prima facie* case is established by a statistical imbalance at *any* stage of the selection process.[16] The second fact to remember is that this disparity, in and of itself, does not establish a Title VII violation. Statistical imbalances by themselves are not unlawful. The adverse impact violates Title VII only if the criterion that caused the imbalance (in this example, the two-year college degree) cannot be shown to be a business necessity/job related.

Selection Process Stage III

Finally the selection process culminated with offers of employment for all of the 37 African American applicants who passed both Stage I and Stage II. Hence the selection rate at this point for African Americans is 100 percent ($37 \div 37 = 1.0$). Of the 103 white applicants who passed the previous two stages, 72 were given job offers, for a selection rate of 69.9 percent ($72 \div 103 = 0.699$). As the African Americans again had the highest selection, they become the benchmark group—no disparate impact. Did the whites suffer disparate impact in Stage III?

$$0.699 < 0.8 \ (1.0)$$
$$0.699 < 0.8$$

or

$$0.699 \div 1.0 = 0.699$$

Because 0.699 is less than 0.8, according to the four-fifths rule, disparate impact has occurred for white applicants.

THE TWO OR THREE STANDARD DEVIATIONS METHOD

The basic premise behind the standard deviation method is that standard deviations are a measure of the probability that a result is a random deviation from an expected representation. Generally, the more standard deviations there are from the expected representation, the lower the probability that the actual pass rate is a random one.[17] A finding of two standard deviations corresponds to "a five percent chance that a disparity is merely a random deviation from the norm and most social scientists accept two standard deviations as a threshold level of 'statistical significance.'"[18] Generally, federal courts have held that a 0.05 level of significance is indicative that the proffered disparity occurred strictly by chance, thus disparities greater than two standard deviations from the expected outcome indicate disparate impact.[19]

As with the four-fifths rule, there is more than one way to calculate standard deviations for disparate impact analysis purposes; one of the more commonly used ones is offered below:

$$SD = \sqrt{N \times P \times (1 - P)}$$
$$z \ (z \ score) = (A - E) \div SD$$

where:

$N =$ the total number of individuals who pass a specific stage in selection

$P =$ the proportion of applicants beginning the stage who were members of the complaining party's class

$E =$ the expected number of applicants passing the stage who were members of the complaining party's class

$A =$ the actual number of applicants passing the stage who were members of the complaining party's class[20]

To demonstrate, we will analyze the data on race that we previously analyzed using the four-fifths method (see Table 4.1). In doing so, we will attempt to see if the actual number of African American applicants who passed at Stage I is within three standard deviations of their expected representation based on their proportion in the applicant pool. Remember that a total of 168 applicants passed the first stage of the selection process by having the requisite education requirements (a two-year degree in industrial arts). Initially 158 applicants who began at this stage were African American and 182 were white, for a total of 340 applicants. Another way of stating this would be that African Americans constituted approximately 46.5 percent of the applicant pool at the first stage of the selection process ($158 \div 340 = 0.465$). The standard deviation would be calculated as follows:

$$SD = \sqrt{N \times P \times (1 - P)}$$
$$SD = \sqrt{168 \times 0.465 \times (1 - 0.465)}$$
$$= \sqrt{168 \times 0.465 \times 0.535}$$
$$= \sqrt{41.784}$$
$$= 6.465$$

The assumption is that the proportion of protected group members who passed from the first to the second stage should be the same as their proportion in the applicant pool beginning at Stage I. Since African Americans represented roughly 46.5 percent of the applicants beginning at the first stage, then they should also represent approximately 46.5 percent of those who passed to the second stage. If this were true, then we would expect approximately 78 of the 168 applicants who passed to the second stage to be African American ($168 \times 0.465 = 78.12$). There were actually 55 African Americans who passed the first stage. If the actual number who passed at this stage (55) is within three standard deviations of their expected representation (78), we would conclude that no disparate impact has occurred.

Because z scores are expressed in standard deviation units, the only thing that remains for us to do is to calculate the z value or z score.[21] Z-scores tell us how many standard deviations an observation is above (a positive z score) or below (a negative z score) the mean. For disparate impact analysis purposes, z scores are applied in instances when either the two standard deviations or three standard deviations rule is used. If the two standard deviations analysis is being used, then any z score that is less than -2.0 denotes disparate impact. If three standard deviations analysis is used, then a z score less than -3.0 is indicative of disparate impact. Given our previous example, the z score would be calculated as follows:

$$z = (A - E) \div SD$$
$$z = (55 - 78) \div 6.465$$
$$= (-23) \div 6.465$$
$$= -3.558$$

In this example, the number of African Americans who actually passed (55) was -3.558 standard deviations below the expected representation of 78. Since -3.558 is less than -3.0

standard deviations, it falls outside of a range ± 3 standard deviations from the expected representation, The conclusion is that disparate impact had occurred.

Generally, if the difference between the expected value (expected representation) and the actual number of candidates who pass is outside a range of two or three standard deviations, the statistical disparities are considered to be significant.[22] It should be noted that in the event that a positive z score is calculated, this would indicate that the actual result was greater than the expected representation—hence no disparate impact for that specific group. In other words, the group claiming disparate impact is actually overrepresented in the selection process at this stage.

BOTTOM-LINE STATISTICS

Generally, bottom-line statistics cannot be used as a defense for disparate impact. In the past, some employers attempted to avoid litigation by offering the bottom-line statistics as a defense of their selection processes. **Bottom-line statistics** refers to the selection rates of protected class members at the conclusion of the selection process. In other words, bottom-line statistics focus on the final outcome of the selection process. They only compare the proportion of protected group members actually hired, or promoted, against the selection rate of the group with the highest rate. To illustrate this, think back to the ABC Manufacturing scenario. Assume that all 53 of the remaining African American applicants (those who passed both Stages I and II) were hired to fill the employer's 125 vacancies.

At the conclusion of the two-stage selection process, 53 of the original 158 African American applicants who began at Stage I were eventually given employment (see Tables 4.3 and 4.4). That would leave the remaining 72 positions to be filled by those white applicants who successfully passed the first and second stages of the selection process—the educational requirements and the hand-eye coordination test. Assume that, of the 75 white males who passed these two stages, 44 were offered employment. Of the white females who passed this second stage, all 28 were hired. In short, of the 182 total white applicants of both sexes who began the selection process at Stage I, 72 were eventually employed by the company.

Based on these bottom-line results, the company might attempt to justify its employment actions on the grounds that when the final outcome of the employment decision process is examined, African American candidates were not hired at a substantially lower rate than whites. The company could argue that the African American candidates were not unfavorably treated because their ultimate selection rate did not fall short under the four-fifths rule. The company might argue that if the final results of the selection process are examined closely, there is no adverse impact for African Americans.

The African American selection rate at the bottom line was 33.5 percent (53 of 158 initial African American applicants were hired). Though this rate is lower than the selection rate for whites (39.6 percent, or 72 of 182 applicants), it is still within the threshold of the four-fifths rule.

Table 4.3

Applicants Who Passed the Second Screening Test and Were Hired

	Passed 2nd Stage	Hired
African American		
Male	37	37
Female	16	16
Totals	53	53
White		
Male	175	44
Female	28	28
Totals	103	72
Total		
Male	112	81
Female	44	44
Totals	156	125

Table 4.4

Bottom-Line Statistics Comparing Those Who Applied and Those Who Were Hired

	Applied	Hired
African Americans		
Male	110	37
Female	48	16
Totals	158	53
Whites		
Male	146	44
Female	36	28
Totals	182	72
Total		
Male	256	81
Female	84	44
Totals	340	125

$$0.335 < 0.8 \ (0.396)$$
$$0.335 < 0.317$$

or

$$0.335 \div 0.396 = 0.846$$

Though the bottom-line statistics in our example do not reveal adverse impact against African Americans, both case law and the Civil Rights Act of 1991 are quite clear in severely limiting their use. In the 1993 decision, *Connecticut v. Teal,*[23] the Supreme Court held that as part of a multiple-stage selection process, bottom-line statistics offer no defense for an employer, although there may be some situations in which a complaining party can use them in establishing the *prima facie* case.

According to the Civil Rights Act of 1991,[24] a *prima facie* case of disparate impact is usually established when "a complaining party demonstrates that a respondent uses a particular employment practice that causes disparate impact on the basis of race, color, religion, sex, or national origin and the respondent fails to demonstrate that the challenged practice is job related for the position in question and consistent with business necessity."[25]

Essentially, this means that if one stage in a multiple-stage selection process causes adverse impact, a complaint can be made. However, it is the complaining party's responsibility to identify which stage causes the adverse impact. In most instances, the complaining party is no more allowed to use bottom-line statistics to initiate a Title VII action than the respondent is allowed to use the bottom-line to defend itself against such actions. Not surprisingly, HR professionals are continually monitoring each phase of their selection processes to ensure that they minimize adverse impact.

When bottom-line statistics are permitted by a court, they can be used only by the complaining party. If the complaining party can demonstrate that an employer's decision-making process is so complicated and its various stages or elements are so intertwined that they cannot be separated for individual analysis, the complaining party is permitted to use bottom-line statistics.[26]

Assume a university uses multifaceted teaching evaluations as part of its annual performance appraisal for assigning promotions and raises to faculty. This evaluation consists of five components:

1. Classroom teaching in degree programs
2. One-on-one/small group teaching
3. Teaching in continuing education/distance learning programs
4. Developing teaching materials/making presentations and publishing related to teaching
5. Developing courses and curricula

Further assume a group of female faculty members alleges that overall teaching evaluations have a disparate impact on women. If these five elements of a faculty member's evaluation could not be separated for analysis in the final decision process (particularly since some could be entirely or partially based on subjective assessment), bottom-line statistics for the outcome of the overall teaching evaluation could be used by the complaining parties.[27]

When a decision-making process includes particular, functionally integrated practices that are components of the same criterion (in this case, teaching) or method of administration, functionally integrated practices may be analyzed as a single employment practice.[28] The message is clear for HR professionals. When designing multifaceted evaluation instruments, the contribution of each individual component to the final decision must be readily identifiable. If a complaining party can demonstrate to a court that the elements or stages of a selection process are incapable of separation for analysis purposes, bottom-line outcomes can be used instead.[29] Once confusion arises as to how the components affected the final decision, the complaining party is afforded the opportunity to resort to bottom-line results.

Hiring by the Numbers and Disparate Treatment

As a final word on bottom-line statistics, it should be noted that they may indicate that an employer *intentionally* made job offers to successful black candidates strictly because of their race, a practice known as hiring by the numbers.[30] In the event that the employer intentionally gave preferential hiring to black applicants over more qualified nonblack applicants in order to make his or her bottom-line statistics look good, the employer has actually violated Title VII. Remember that disparate impact is unintentional discrimination, but knowingly selecting individuals because of race, gender, or ethnicity is intentional, thus it is disparate treatment.[31] In such an instance, the employer is making the final hiring decision on the applicant's race in order to make the bottom-line numbers work.

This point was illustrated in the 2009 Supreme Court decision, *Ricci v. DeStefano*.[32] In this case the City of New Haven, Connecticut, refused to certify the results of a promotion examination for lieutenant in its fire department because no African Americans passed. The result was that the white and Latino firefighters who passed would not be promoted because the city government feared that certifying the examination results would be challenged in court as causing disparate impact.

However, the Court noted that the City could be held liable for disparate-impact discrimination only if the examinations were not job related and consistent with business necessity, or if there existed an equally valid, less-discriminatory alternative that served the City's needs but that the City refused to adopt.[33] Because the examinations were shown to be job-related, the City's decision was based solely on the fact that "too many whites and not enough minorities would be promoted were the lists to be certified."[34] In other words, the City's reasons for not certifying the examination were predicated on the racial distribution of the results. Thinking that they were avoiding a disparate impact charge, the City had in fact intentionally made an employment decision based solely on the race of the successful test-takers and walked into a disparate treatment charge.

RESPONDENT'S REBUTTAL

Once the *prima facie* case has been established, the respondent (the employer) assumes the burden of rebutting the allegations of adverse impact. The defenses available to the employer most commonly consist of either demonstrating that the disparate impact does not exist or by showing that the practice causing the disparity is job related (business necessity). One means of demonstrating that the disparate impact does not exist is accomplished by challenging the complaining party's statistical analysis. Another is showing that the complaining party's data or sample are flawed.

Demonstrating That Disparate Impact Does Not Exist

The employer's best defense in any disparate impact situation is that the employment requirement is a business necessity. However, sometimes other defenses are available. One such defense is simply proving that the disparate impact does not exist. If it can be shown that there is no adverse impact, there can be no Title VII violation. The major advantage to this defense is that the respondent (the employer) does not have to establish the validity of the criterion or practice in question. As you will see in Chapter 15, validation can be a very complicated process.

The Civil Rights Act of 1991 explicitly reinforces this contention by declaring, "If the respondent demonstrates that a specific employment practice does not cause the disparate impact, the respondent shall not be required to demonstrate that such practice is required by business necessity."[35]

As an example, if, in the first stage of ABC Manufacturing's selection process, 70 African Americans (instead of 55) had possessed the requisite two-year degree in industrial arts, would a statistical imbalance have occurred? Yes, it could be argued that an imbalance did exist, since the selection rate for African Americans of 0.443 (70/158) is less than that of the white applicants, which is 0.621 (113/182). But the question remains, is it sufficiently severe to meet the four-fifths standard?

$$0.443 < 0.8 \, (0.621)$$
$$0.443 < 0.497$$

or

$$0.443 \div 0.621 = 0.713$$

Using the four-fifths rule, because the African American selection rate of 0.443 percent is less than 80 percent of the selection rate for whites (0.497 percent), the complaining party could contend that the four-fifths rule was violated.

The Supreme Court has stated that "[i]f the employer discerns fallacies or deficiencies in the data offered by the plaintiff, he is free to adduce countervailing evidence of his own."[36] Consequently, the employer can offer alternative mathematical analysis—**countervailing statistics**—to the complaining party's. To illustrate one method by which this could be accomplished, suppose that the employer took the same data and analyzed it using the two standard deviations method and arrived at the following results:

$$SD = \sqrt{N \times P \times (1 - P)}$$
$$SD = \sqrt{168 \times 0.465 \times (1 - 0.465)}$$
$$= \sqrt{168 \times 0.465 \times 0.535}$$
$$= \sqrt{41{,}784}$$
$$= 6.465$$

$$z = (A - E) \div SD$$
$$z = (70 - 78) \div 6.465$$
$$= (-8) \div 6.465$$
$$= 1.237$$

The z score would indicate that this occurrence is slightly more than one standard deviation (−1.237) less than the expected representation. This is well within the range of probability that it could be a random occurrence, since −1.237 is within our range of ± 2 standard deviations. Consequently, using the more sophisticated standard deviation method, one could conclude that disparate impact may not exist. Though federal courts have judged the significance of a statistical disparity on a case-by-case basis,[37] when confronted with the dilemma of which test for disparate impact should prevail, a court is more likely to err on the side of the more robust statistical method.[38]

However, in our original example, only 55 African American applicants passed the first criterion, and disparate impact appears to exist. This leaves the respondent with only two options: challenge the complaining party's statistics or prove that possessing a two-year degree in industrial arts is job related. The discussion now turns to other means of challenging the complaining party's statistics.

Small Sample Size

Challenging the complaining party's statistics may take several forms. First, the sample size may be too small and thus the selection or rejection of a single individual would substantially affect proportional outcomes.[39] To demonstrate the impact that a small sample size would have on the statistical or proportional outcomes, assume the number of African American applicants was 16 instead of the 168 in the ABC Manufacturing scenario. Also assume that 7 of the 16 possessed the requisite two-year degree. Further assume the numbers for the white applicants were the same—113 of the 182 white candidates held the degree. Based upon an application of the four-fifths rule, the outcome would be as follows:

$$(7 \div 16) < 0.8 \, (113 \div 182)$$
$$0.438 < 0.8 \, (0.621)$$
$$0.438 < 0.497$$

or

$$0.438 \div 0.621 = 0.7053$$

By strictly following the four-fifths rule, disparate impact would be concluded.

But look what would have happened if only one more African American applicant had possessed the appropriate two-year degree:

$$(8 \div 16) < 0.8 \, (113 \div 182)$$
$$0.50 < 0.8 \, (0.621)$$
$$0.50 < 0.497$$

or

$$0.50 \div 0.621 = 0.805$$

The number of African American applicants was so small that a single individual makes a substantial difference in the statistical outcome. In this case, each individual would affect the selection rate of African Americans by 0.0625 (or 6.25 percent), compared to 0.006

(or 0.6 percent) in the original example. The small sample size would either overstate or understate the imbalance. More importantly, the effects of variance in the sample are increasingly likely to be due to random error[40] rather than discrimination.

The general convention is that correlational studies require at least thirty subjects to establish significance. In other words, the outcome would not be statistically significant, and the results would likely occur at random. The general rule in statistical analysis is, the larger the sample size, the greater the degree of precision.[41]

Examining Relevant Labor Markets

The **relevant labor market** is the geographic area from which an employer normally recruits individuals with the requisite qualifications for a specific job. Relevant labor markets can sometimes be used to call into question the complaining party's allegations by pointing out that many of the applicants for the position in question were unqualified.

When disparate impact analysis is conducted, persons who do not possess *bona fide* job qualifications cannot be treated as legitimate candidates and should not be included in the flow statistics. To illustrate, suppose a university has posted the position of professor of business management. The job specifications for this position state that successful candidates must possess a doctorate in management from an accredited university and must demonstrate research in the field of management. Of the 400 applicants for the position, 88 are African American, of whom 12 are passed through the first stage because they possessed the requisite doctorate in management. Of the 312 white applicants, 168 are passed through Stage I, having met the appropriate degree requirement. Simple four-fifths analysis, without considering relevant qualifications, would conclude the following:

$$(12 \div 88) < 0.8 \, (168 \div 312)$$
$$0.136 < 0.8 \, (0.538)$$
$$0.136 < 0.43$$

or

$$0.136 \div 0.43 = 0.316$$

One could thus conclude disparate impact. However, is someone with a doctoral degree in a field other than management (i.e., elementary education, sociology, or history) qualified to teach undergraduate- and graduate-level courses in management? Very persuasive arguments can be made that they would not be qualified. To be an effective instructor of a college-level management course, the instructor would be expected to have a doctoral degree in that field. Hence, even though disparity exists, it exists due to job-related reasons. The individuals who do not possess the qualifications for the job (i.e., a degree in the appropriate field) are not viable candidates.

Stock Statistics as Countervailing Evidence

Finally, the respondent may attempt to challenge the complaining party's statistics by offering countervailing evidence. This can often be accomplished by analyzing the complaining party's data with either more sophisticated or more representative statistical methods. Stock analysis, or measures of representativeness (as opposed to the applicant flow analysis used in previous examples), is one such means of countering the complaining party's allegations of statistical imbalance in applicant flow. **Stock analysis** provides statistics on the composition of the employer's workforce and how that workforce compares to its relevant labor market. In order to be accurate, stock analysis begins with properly identifying the relevant labor market for the job in question. This is an extremely critical point. Too often, stock analysis is based on general population statistics and includes (or overrepresents) the portion of a protected class who actually possesses requisite job qualifications. If this has occurred, then the stock analysis is easily challenged as not truly reflecting the relevant labor market.

STOCK ANALYSIS

In the ABC Manufacturing example, the employer may have identified the relevant labor market for entry-level machine operators as all individuals with the appropriate education within a one-hour commute of the plant. Based upon data obtained from the Bureau of Labor Statistics, the employer estimates that this relevant labor market is comprised of 116,000 individuals: 13,950 African Americans, 10,000 Hispanics, 2,500 of Asian ancestry, and 89,550 non-Hispanic whites. Using these figures, the employer is able to develop proportional estimates of the relevant labor market. In this case, it is 77.2 percent white, 12 percent African American, 8.6 percent Hispanic, and 2.2 percent Asian.

The employer can now determine the proportion of its internal workforce that is African American and compare that to the proportion of African Americans in the relevant labor market. This proportional comparison is also known as a measure of representativeness. If used to bolster an employer's defense, the following formula would be desired:

(proportion of protected class in employer's internal workforce) $\geq$
(proportion of protected class in relevant labor market)

Assume the employer audits the workforce and discovers that of 5,400 current employees, 1,050 are African American (19.4 percent). Applying stock analysis, the employer would offer the following statistics:

$$0.194 > 0.12$$

The employer's argument would be that, despite the adverse impact shown by applicant flow analysis during the current hiring cycle, African Americans are actually overrepresented in the company's workforce. In fact, the proportion of African Americans in the company's internal workforce is over 60 percent greater than their representation in the relevant labor market (19.4 percent internally to 12 percent externally). If the selection requirement consistently had an adverse impact on African Americans, then one would expect them to be underrepresented in the employer's internal workforce, not over-

Table 4.5

Simpson's Paradox

Program	Male			Female			Female Selection Rate Compared to Male Selection Rate
	Admitted	Applied	Selection Rate	Admitted	Applied	Selection Rate	
A	825	825	.6206	89	108	.8241	1.328
B	520	520	.6019	17	25	.6800	1.130
C	325	325	.3692	202	593	.3406	.923
D	417	417	.3309	131	375	.3493	1.056
E	191	191	.2775	94	393	.2392	.862
F	22	373	.0590	24	341	.0704	1.193
Total	1,158	2,651	.4368	557	1,835	.3035	.695

Source: D. Freedman, R. Pisani, and R. Purves, *Statistics,* 3rd ed. (New York: W. W. Norton, 1998), 17–20.

represented. In certain instances, the EEOC and courts have accepted stock analysis as demonstrating good faith in selection.[42]

Simpson's Paradox

Simpson's Paradox (a.k.a., the Reversal Paradox)—a correlation present in different groups is reversed when the groups are combined. The paradox (the spurious correlation) disappears when causality is considered.[43] This actually occurred in a study involving the graduate admissions practices of the University of California-Berkley which were alleged to have a sex bias based on the four-fifths rule. In fall 1973, 8,442 men and 4321 women applied for admission in Berkley graduate programs.[44] *In the aggregate* of six graduate programs, 44 percent of male applicants were admitted compared to 35 percent of women. Applying the four-fifths rule to this aggregate outcome, one would technically conclude disparate impact (0.35 ÷ 0.44 = 0.795, which, though close, is still less than the requisite 0.8). However, examining Table 4.5, one realizes the selection rate of women is higher in four of the six largest programs (of 101 in the Bickel study) when each is analyzed individually. Additionally and in the other two programs, the selection rates of females are never below 86 percent of those of males.[45] Individual analysis of each program reveals no disparate impact; only when all the data is combined does a spurious disparity arise.

Age Discrimination and Disparate Impact

In 2005, the Supreme Court ruled that individuals can establish an actionable case of age discrimination by showing that certain facially neutral practices have the effect of excluding older employees/applicants.[46] Prior to that time the federal circuit courts were divided as to whether disparate impact was actionable under the Age Discrimination in Employment Act (ADEA). Some contended it was, others contended that the only claim that could be made under the ADEA was disparate treatment.[47] This issue is now resolved: facially neutral employment practices that exclude a disproportionate number of forty-years-and-older applicants or employees create disparate impact under the ADEA.

It is important to know that individuals who are forty years or older can make a disparate impact claim under the ADEA in precisely the manner as it is made under Title VII. However, under the ADEA, the employer's defense for disparate impact is legitimate nondiscriminatory reason and not business necessity/job-relatedness as it is under Title VII.[48]

To demonstrate this distinction, assume that a group of employees was able to establish that a specific selection requirement (e.g., a college degree in finance) created a manifest statistical imbalance for Hispanics/Latinos. Because this involves a Title VII issue (national origin), the employer would have to demonstrate that the education requirement creating the disparate impact was a business necessity/job-related.

Taking this example, let us now assume that the education requirement created a manifest statistical imbalance for applicants over forty. Because this time the disparity encompasses an ADEA issue, the employer would only have to demonstrate that the education requirement creating the disparate impact was based on a legitimate nondiscriminatory reason, a reason other than the applicant's age.[49]

OUTCOMES OF THE OPENING SCENARIO

In *Jones v. Pepsi-Cola Metro. Bottling Co.*, the federal case from which our opening scenario was drawn, a federal district court judge drew the following conclusions:

> [The] plaintiffs [the complaining parties] have not put forth reliable statistical proof that either procedure [the GPE and the FSP] had a statistically significant adverse impact on . . . women plaintiffs, as a matter of law, and have failed to establish a *prima facie* case of disparate impact discrimination on the basis of . . . gender. [The] defendant [the respondent/employer] is entitled to summary judgment as a matter of law. Although the statistical analysis reveals that the written test [GPE] had a statistically significant adverse impact on persons forty or older, the [FSP] was properly validated and job-related. Plaintiffs failed to show that the [FSP] was not job-related or that a viable alternative exists which would not have an adverse impact on the plaintiff class. Because plaintiffs failed to carry their burden of proof, as relates to the disparate impact age discrimination claim, summary judgment will be entered in favor of [the employer].[50]

If the four-fifths rule is applied to the FSP to analyze disparate impact on women, it will be noted that women are actually the benchmark group. Between male selection rates (0.6897) and female selection rates (0.7045), women have the higher rate.

As for the forty-years-and-older applicants, their selection rate was 0.4231 (the 22 who passed the FSP divided by the 52 over forties who took it) compared to the 0.7956 of the under-forty applicants. The forty-years-and-older applicants can make a *prima facie* case of disparate impact (0.4231 ÷ 0.7956 = 0.5316, which is less than 0.8). However, because the FSP has been validated to be a predictor of job performance, the disparate

Table 4.6

Outcomes of Opening Scenario

	Tested	Passed	Percentage Passed
FSP Phase			
Male	145	100	69.0
Female	44	31	70.5
Over 40	52	22	42.3
Under 40	137	109	79.3
GPE Phase			
Male	91	16	17.6
Female	29	3	10.3
Over 40	20	1	5.0
Under 40	100	18	18.0

impact does not violate Title VII. In essence, the employer was able to establish the business necessity/job-relatedness defense.

SUMMARY

This chapter focused on the disparate impact theory of discrimination under Title VII of the Civil Rights Act of 1964. Disparate impact, sometimes called adverse impact, is the theory responsible for the current preoccupation with proportional representation in the workplace. Unlike disparate treatment, disparate impact may be unintentional. The *Griggs v. Duke Power Company* ruling created this theory.

This chapter has shown that fairly simple statistical analyses are all that is necessary to establish imbalances sufficient to imply disparate impact. Neither the four-fifths analysis nor the two/three standard deviations analysis is a particularly robust analytic tool. Yet either one is more than sufficient to draw an employment practice into question.

If managers are to reduce their employers' exposure to charges of disparate impact, it is essential that job analysis (discussed in detail in Chapter 14) be performed on all existing and anticipated positions in the organization. This is the beginning of a sound business necessity defense. Once the essential job functions of each position have been identified, all subsequent employment practices directed toward a candidate for that position or current job incumbent must be validated based upon those essential functions. Otherwise attempts at establishing an employment requirement or practice as being job related may be a wasted effort.

KEY TERMS AND CONCEPTS

Adverse impact
Applicant flow analysis
Bottom-line statistics
Business necessity
Countervailing statistics

Disparate impact
Job-related
Relevant labor market
Stock analysis

Table 4.7

Case 1

	Number Applying	Number Receiving Passing Scores	Percentage Passed
African Americans	48	26	54.17
Hispanics/Latinos	4	3	75.00
American Indians	3	2	66.67
Whites	259	206	79.54
Unidentified	15	9	60.00
Total	329	246	74.77

DISCUSSION QUESTIONS

1. Distinguish between disparate impact and disparate treatment. How does the burden of proof differ?
2. What is the four-fifths (80 percent) rule? How is it used?
3. What is meant by the term "relevant labor market" and how is it used in EEO investigations?
4. What are the employer's rebuttals in disparate impact cases?
5. Differentiate between flow analysis and stock analysis.
6. Respond to this comment: "The only way to avoid an equal employment suit today is to hire by the numbers." Is this ethical? Is this legal?

CASES

Case 1: Hiring by the Numbers

Table 4.7 shows the passing rates of various candidate groups in an employer's promotion selection process. At the culmination of the selection process, 46 persons were promoted to permanent supervisory positions, 11 of whom were African American and 35 of whom were white. The overall result of the selection process was that, of the 48 identified African American candidates who participated in the selection process, 22.9 percent were promoted, and of the 259 identified white candidates, 13.5 percent were promoted. A white candidate alleges that disparate impact has occurred.

a. Based on the data supplied in this case, can the employee establish a *prima facie* case of disparate impact? Why or why not?
b. Are the final promotion results sufficient to be a defense to the complaining party's suit? Why or why not?

Case 2

Two cities have established a physical fitness test to evaluate candidates for the position of firefighter. City A requires candidates to deadlift a 200-pound bar bell, do 50 push-ups in

2 minutes, 50 sit-ups in 2 minutes, and run 2 miles in under 16 minutes. As a consequence of these physical fitness standards, 50 percent of male applicants pass this stage of the screening process, compared to only 12 percent of the female applicants.

City B requires candidates to pass a physical fitness test consisting of two parts—a simulation of engine company tasks and a simulation of ladder company tasks. The engine company tasks consist of taking one hose weighing 80 pounds and stretching it to 145 feet, and carrying a 2½" hose weighing 46 pounds from the entrance of a building to the fifth floor. Following a 7½ minute rest period, the candidate then performs the ladder company simulation. In this part, the candidate must:

- Raise a 20' ladder from the ground to an upright position
- Climb a 20' ladder to a second-floor window and run up the stairs of the fifth floor carrying a 16-pound pry bar
- Use an 8-pound sledge hammer to force open a door
- Simulate a rescue by dragging a 145-pound articulated dummy along a marked path on the fifth floor

All tasks must be completed within 4 minutes and 9 seconds, excluding the break period between the two parts of the test. As a result of City B's physical exam, 46 percent of male candidates passed compared to 0 percent of the female candidates.[51] Female applicants in both cities have made disparate impact claims with the EEOC.

    a. Does the City A's physical fitness standard create disparate impact for female applicants? Why or why not?

    b. Does the City B's physical fitness standard create disparate impact for female applicants? Why or why not?

    c. What is the likelihood that City A's physical fitness standard can be shown to be job related? Why?

    d. What is the likelihood that City B's physical fitness standard can be shown to be job related? Why?

Case 3

Cover-the-Earth, Inc. operates a pharmacential plant located in Mobile, AL for the across-the-counter cold remedies. Of the 2,500 production personnel currently employed at the facility, 750 are white males, 500 are Hispanic males, 150 are black males, 50 are Asian males, and 30 are American Indian males; 450 are Hispanic females, 350 are white females, 110 are black females, 90 are Asian females, and 20 are American Indian females. Cover-the-Earth traditionally has recruited its unskilled production workers from the Mobile metropolitan statistical area (MSA) as all members would possess the basic skills for production work. The Mobile MSA has a civilian labor force of 310,950 of which 106,005 are African American, 5,500 are Asian-American, 7,660 are Hispanic, 2,755 are American Indian, 4,595 are Two or More Races, and 184,435 are non-Hispanic whites.

Males account for approximately 52 percent of the total local labor market.

In 2013, 20 Asian males took a basic skills test for production jobs and 6 were hired, compared to 8 Asian female applicants, of whom 6 passed. Also, 110 Hispanic males took the test, of whom 70 passed. Additionally, 100 Hispanic females took the test for work during the same period; 45 passed. That year, 100 black males and 60 black females sat for the skills test and 25 and 20 passed, respectively. Additionally, 25 of 60 white females taking the test passed. Of the 200 white males who were tested, 110 passed. There were 10 American Indian males who took the test, of whom 5 passed compared to only 2 of 12 American Indian females who were tested. No applicants of mixed race applied during the period. Assume that all production jobs require low skills.

a. Several applicants claim that the company's basic skills test discriminates against Hispanic applicants. Using the four-fifths rule and actual applicant flow analysis, is there adverse impact on the basis of race for Hispanic applicants?

b. Similarly, an employee contends that the company's basic skills test discriminates against Black applicants. Using the four-fifths rule and actual applicant flow analysis, is there adverse impact on the basis of race for Black applicants? Is there disparate impact using the three standard deviations rule?

c. Is there any group in the employer's internal work force that does not account for 2 percent or more of the relevant labor market?

d. Does stock analysis create any concerns about the company's representation of females in its workforce?

NOTES

1. This scenario was developed from the facts in *Jones v. Pepsi-Cola Metro. Bottling Co.*, 871 F. Supp. 305 (E.D. Mich. 1994).

2. 401 U.S. 424 (1971).

3. 401 U.S. at 430 n. 6.

4. Ibid. at 431–432.

5. Ibid. at 431.

6. *Wards Cove Packing Co. v. Antonio*, 490 U.S. 642, 657 (1989).

7. 29 C.F.R. § 1607 (1997).

8. 29 C.F.R. § 1607.4D.

9. *Hazelwood School District v. U.S.*, 433 U.S. 299, 309 n. 14 (1977).

10. *Ottaviani v. State University of New York*, 875 F.2d 365, 370–71 (2d Cir. 1980).

11. *Castaneda v. Partida*, 430 U.S. 482 (1976); *EEOC v. Sears, Roebuck & Co.*, 839 F.2d 302 (7th Cir. 1988); *Payne v. Travenol Laboratories*, 673 F.2d 798 (5th Cir.), *cert. denied*, 459 U.S. 1038 (1982).

12. 42 U.S.C. § 2000e-2(K)(1)(B)(i).

13. 29 C.F.R. § 1607.4D.

14. Ibid.

15. Ibid.

16. 42 U.S.C. § 2000e-2(k)(1)(A).

17. *Castaneda v. Partida*, 430 U.S. 482, 496 n. 17 (1977).

18. *Ottaviani v. State University of New York*, 875 F.2d 365, 370–71 (2nd Cir. 1980).

19. *Segar v. Smith,* 738 F.2d 1249, 1283 (D.C. Cir. 1984) *cert. denied,* 471 U.S. 1115 (1985); *Palmer v. Schultz,* 815 F.2d 84, 96 (D.C. Cir. 1987); *Frazier v. Consolidated Rail Corp.,* 851 F.2d 1447, 1451–52 (D.C. Cir. 1988).

20. Barbara Lindemann and Paul Grossman, *Employment Discrimination Law*, Volume I, 3d ed. (Washington, DC: BNA Books, 1996), p. 93.

21. Ibid.

22. *Castaneda v. Partida,* 430 U.S. 482, 496 n. 17 (1977).

23. *Connecticut v. Teal,* 457 U.S. 440, 452.

24. 42 U.S.C. § 2000e-2(k)(1)(B)(i).

25. 42 U.S.C. at § 2000e-2(k)(1)(A)(i).

26. 42 U.S.C. § 2000e-2(k)(1)(B).

27. CCH Business Law Editors, *Civil Rights Act of 1991: Law and Explanation* (Chicago: Commerce Clearing House, 1991), pp. 21–22.

28. Ibid., citing interpretive memorandum, 137 Cong. Rec. § 15276, October 25, 1991.

29. *Stout v. Potter,* 276 F.3d 1118, 1124 (9th Cir. 2002); 42 U.S.C. § 2000e-2(k)(1)(B)(i).

30. S.R. Bagenstos, "The Structural Turn and the Limits of Antidiscrimination Law," *California Law Review* 94 (2006): 1–47.

31. *Hannon v. Chater,* 887 F.Supp. 1303 (N.D.Cal. 1995).

32. *Ricci v. DeStafano,* 2009 U.S. LEXIS 4945 (2009).

33. *Ricci,* 2009 U.S. LEXIS 4945 at *51.

34. Ibid. at *38.

35. 42 U.S.C. § 2000e-2(k)(1)(B)(ii).

36. *Dothard v. Rawlinson,* 433 U.S. 321, 331 (1977).

37. *Teamsters v. United States,* 431 U.S. 324, 340 (1977).

38. *Malave v. Potter,* 320 F.3d 321, 327 (2nd Cir. 2003).

39. 29 C.F.R. § 1607.3D.

40. L.R. Gay and P.L. Diehl, *Research Methods for Business and Management* (New York: Macmillan, 1992), pp. 140–141.

41. M. Hamburg, *Statistical Analysis for Decision Making,* 2d ed. (New York: Harcourt Brace, 1977), p. 249.

42. *Anderson v. Douglas & Lomason Co.,* 26 F.3d 1277, 1291 n. 23 (5th Cir. 1994); *Pelekai v. Raytheon Constructors, Inc.,* 74 Fed. Appx. 790 (9th Cir. 2003); *Kincade v. Firestone Tire & Rubber Co.,* 694 F.Supp. 368, 381–82 (M.D.Tenn. 1987); *Carroll v. Sears, Roebuck & Co.,* 514 F.Supp. 788, 804 (W.D.La. 1981).

43. J. Pearl, *Causality: Models, Reasoning and Inference,* 2nd ed. (New York: Cambridge University Press, 2009), pp. 128–129; 177–182.

44. P.J. Bickel, E.A. Hammel, and J.W. O'Connel, "Sex Bias in Graduate Admissions: Data from Berkley," *Science* 187 (1975): 398–404.

45. D. Freedman, R. Pisani and R. Purves, *Statistics,* 3rd ed. (New York: W.W. Norton & Co. 1998) pp. 17–20.

46. *Smith v. City of Jackson,* 544 U.S. 228, 236–237 (2005).

47. Ibid. at 242–243.

48. Ibid. at 239.

49. Ibid. at 242–243.

50. 871 F. Supp. at 309.

51. This scenario was developed from the facts in *Lanning v. SEPTA,* 181 F.3d 478 (3rd Cir. 1999).

5

DISCRIMINATION BASED ON SEX

LEARNING OBJECTIVES

- Identify the different forms of sex discrimination.
- Identify employment practices that can potentially create sex discrimination.
- Understand the circumstances under which mixed-motive sex discrimination can occur.
- Understand when sex is a *bona fide* occupational qualification (BFOQ).
- Describe the legal proofs necessary to establish sexual harassment.
- Describe in-house investigations for sexual harassment.
- Describe sexual harassment policies.

OPENING SCENARIO

Two individuals are applying for the position of production supervisor. This position requires a bachelor's degree in production management or logistics, and two years of management experience in manufacturing. Glenda McKay has a degree in production and operations management (POM) and three years' experience working as a shift supervisor for a national manufacturer of appliances. Dave Nichols has an associate's degree from Lafayette County VoTech in automotive mechanics and was a shop foreman at Robinson Brothers' Alternator Repair Shop. Ken Cyree, the plant superintendent making the hiring decision, is hesitant about hiring a woman for the position. He feels the job requires a tough, no-nonsense management style. Ken also believes women are passive leaders at best. Although Glenda's education and prior work record are impressive, Ken decides to hire Dave.

Sex discrimination, discrimination based on an individual's sex, is the second largest source of Title VII violations after race discrimination. In fiscal year 2011, discrimination on the basis of sex accounted for almost 39.7 percent of all Title VII charges handled by the Equal Employment Opportunity Commission (EEOC).[1] Because women are entering the workforce in increasing numbers, and because the vast majority of sex discrimination complaints are filed by females, special attention should be given to employment practices that can potentially discriminate on the basis of sex.

As an actionable Title VII claim, discrimination on the basis of sex can result from disparate treatment (discussed in Chapter 3) and from disparate impact (discussed in Chapter 4). Over time, other variations of sex discrimination have evolved (see Figure

Figure 5.1 **Forms of Sex Discrimination**

- Disparate impact on the basis of sex
- Mixed
- Overt (disparate treatment)
- Pay differentials motives

- Pregnancy
- Sex-plus
- Sex stereotyping
- Sexual harassment

5.1). This chapter examines each of these variations and devotes particular attention to examining the fastest-growing Title VII complaint—sexual harassment.

EMPLOYMENT-RELATED AND OTHER FORMS OF SEX DISCRIMINATION

Overt Sex Discrimination

The opening scenario provides an example of overt sex discrimination that is clearly disparate treatment. It is easily analyzed by applying the model provided by *McDonnell-Douglas Corp. v. Green* and explained in Chapter 3. To establish a *prima facie* case, Glenda must first show that she is a protected class under Title VII. "Sex" is one of the protected classes; therefore, this is easily established—she is female.

The term *sex* under Title VII refers to a biological condition and not an activity or preference. Hence, treating individuals differently because they are male (or female) is an unlawful employment practice. However, as will be discussed later in this chapter, treating an individual differently based on the individual's sexual preference (some prefer the term sexual orientation) would not be covered under Title VII. Why? Because sexual orientation does not constitute a protected class under Title VII, though some activist courts have attempted to expand this coverage, as will be discussed later in this chapter.

Only discrimination on the basis of race, color, religion, sex, and national origin is prohibited under Title VII. Discrimination on any other basis *is not* within the confines of this statute. Therefore, the very first requirement for anyone making a complaint is to show that Title VII pertains to their class (race, color, religion, sex, or national origin).

Next, Glenda must prove she applied for the position of production supervisor, which she did; that she was qualified for the position, which she was; and that she was rejected, which also occurred. The only thing left is to demonstrate that the position was eventually given to a male candidate who had equal or fewer qualifications.

On the surface, it does appear that Glenda meets the advertised job specifications and Dave does not. Dave appears to lack both the required education and industry work experience, and yet he was hired. Based on this information, there is reasonable cause to believe Glenda was not selected because of her sex.

Once Glenda has established the *prima facie* case, the burden now shifts to Ken to offer a legitimate nondiscriminatory reason for hiring Dave instead of Glenda. Should Ken fail to provide a plausible reason why he felt Dave was better qualified for the position, Glenda will have won her case. It is unlikely that Ken's theory—women are passive leaders—has the scientific foundations to establish a *bona fide* occupational qualification (BFOQ), least of all a legitimate nondiscriminatory reason.

Overt sex discrimination is not limited merely to hiring decisions, as it was in the opening scenario. It can occur in any employment decision. As with any disparate treatment situation, sex discrimination can result from decisions regarding layoffs, work assignments, or disciplinary actions. It is also important to point out that sex discrimination is not a one-way street; it applies to males as well as females. Federal courts have long held that Title VII's prohibition of discrimination "because of . . . sex" protects men as well as women.[2]

Suppose that in a revised scenario Dave has the degree in POM and the three years of appropriate work experience, while Glenda has the associate's degree and has only worked as a shop foreman. Ken decides to hire Glenda because he feels women have more nurturing leadership styles. From the decision-making standpoint, has anything really changed? This time, Dave was qualified; Glenda was not.

What was the reason Dave was rejected? His sex. Why did Ken offer Glenda the position? Her sex. Using the *McDonnell-Douglas Corp. v. Green* criteria, do you think Dave could now establish a *prima facie* case for discrimination on the basis of sex?

Employee Discipline

Another employment practice that can result in sex discrimination, and one closely watched by employees, is employee discipline. If, for example, an employer imposes stiffer penalties on male employees who are late for work than it does on tardy female employees, the employer is violating Title VII. Similarly, favoring male employees over equally qualified female employees for training, development programs, or career-enhancing work assignments also would result in unlawful sex discrimination.

Employers must be careful to ensure that their policies do not subject employees to different conditions of employment that seem to be based on sex—this invariably means *all* employment policies. For example, it is perfectly legal for employers to utilize dress codes, provided the codes are imposed on both male and female employees.[3] Businesses have the right to create policies that project the proper business image. Consequently, dress codes can be a legitimate nondiscriminatory reason provided they are applied equally to all employees. However, if such policies require female employees to dress conservatively, but men are permitted to dress casually (or vice versa), sex discrimination has occurred. The simple standard to follow on such policies is to hold male and female employees to the same neutral standards of dress and appearance.[4] It is important to remember that the underlying requirement of Title VII is to hold all employees to the same standards, not different ones. Human resource (HR) professionals must review existing policies to ensure they do indeed treat employees equally.

Sex as a BFOQ

In sex discrimination cases alleging disparate treatment, an employer is afforded the traditional defenses of nondiscriminatory reasons and *bona fide* occupational qualifications. Sex is one of the three protected classes in which BFOQ defenses are permitted (the other two are religion and national origin). However, HR professionals are reminded that sex cannot be used to disqualify a party unless it can be clearly demonstrated that all, or substantially all, members of the sex in question cannot perform the essential functions of the job. Examples of instances in which male sex has been a BFOQ include an actor,[5] a guard in a male maximum-security prison,[6] a security guard in a job requiring searches of male employees,[7] a janitor in a men's bathhouse,[8] and an attendant in a men's restroom.[9] Some examples of instances where female sex was ruled a BFOQ include an actress,[10] a salesperson in a lingerie department,[11] and a custodian in a women's dormitory.[12]

As with other BFOQs, these applications are very rare and narrowly defined. The opportunity to establish sex as a BFOQ is usually very remote. In most instances, HR professionals will need to ensure employment decisions are predicated on a legitimate nondiscriminatory rationale.

Unique to sex-based BFOQs is the issue of same-sex privacy concerns. Federal courts have permitted employers to hire employees of the same sex as that of the client or customer when the job directly involved a potential invasion of another's privacy.[13] However, such a BFOQ has been allowed only where respect of privacy is necessary to the primary purpose of the job and not a related duty that might be avoided by restructuring the job.[14] Same-sex privacy arises usually in situations germane to the job that require the invasion of another individual's personal space (i.e., strip and pat-down searches). In essence, an airport security officer whose duties include conducting body searches of female airline passengers would meet the standard for a sex-based BFOQ. Custom or convenience, however, will not justify a BFOQ exception,[15] neither will stereotypical impressions of male and female roles.[16]

Disparate Impact on the Basis of Sex

There is little need to reiterate the discussion of disparate impact covered in Chapter 4 other than to note that employment imbalances on the basis of sex *can* establish a Title VII complaint. Because of the potential for statistical disparities and the higher burden of proof placed on employers under disparate impact, HR professionals have long been encouraged to avoid certain questions on employment applications and during employment interviews (see Figure 5.2). Even the EEOC encourages employers to avoid questions about marital status as well as information about an applicant's spouse. Again, the concern for employers is not so much that they will use the information to intentionally discriminate, but it creates the impression that the information *might* be used to discriminate (see mixed-motive and sex-plus discrimination). For this same reason, HR professionals are encouraged to refrain from asking for the ages and number of dependent children. In fact, sensitivity on this matter has become so critical that even asking for information about emergency contacts is no longer recommended.

The best guidance offered regarding preemployment applications is to remember that applications and interviews have been declared "tests" by both the *Uniform Guidelines* and numerous court decisions.[17] As on any test, the questions asked on applications and

Figure 5.2   **Questions to Avoid During Pre-Employment Interviews**

- Ages of children
- Applicant's sex
- Child care requirements
- Information about spouse
- Marital status
- Number of children
- Whom to contact in an emergency

during interviews should be job related. In fact, the EEOC warns employers that "any preemployment inquiry in connection with prospective employment which expressed directly or indirectly any litigation, specification, or discrimination as to sex shall be unlawful unless based on a *bona fide* occupational qualification."[18] In the case of pre-employment questions, the operative word is "indirectly." Words that could indicate an applicant's sex could also be construed as indirectly indicating sex-based discrimination. This would place an employer in a disadvantageous position if discrimination charges were filed and there was a statistical imbalance of female employees.

Sex Stereotyping

It is impermissible under Title VII to refuse to hire an individual man or woman because of stereotypical beliefs about the characteristic of one sex or the other. As the Supreme Court has noted, "Myths and purely habitual assumptions about a woman's or a man's inability to perform certain kinds of work are no longer acceptable reasons for refusing to employ qualified individuals."[19]

The opening scenario is a straightforward example of sex stereotyping. Under **sex stereotyping**, the decision maker holds some generalized belief about behaviors or characteristics attributed to a particular gender. These conceptions (more often misconceptions) then influence subsequent employment decisions. Sex stereotyping results in actionable discrimination because it violates Title VII's basic requirement that gender must be irrelevant to employment decisions. The effect of stereotyping on the employment decision in the opening scenario is easily demonstrated by a syllogism:

Major premise: All women are passive leaders.
Minor premise: Glenda is a woman.
Conclusion: Glenda is a passive leader.

Because of Ken's preconceived opinion that women are passive leaders, Glenda will not be selected for a leadership position *because of her sex*. Since sex stereotyping is likely to influence employment decisions, and because it is contrary to Congress's intent to establish gender-neutral employment practices, it is unlawful.[20]

For managers and HR professionals, this means extreme care should be taken to ensure no candidate for hiring, promotion, or discharge is discussed in sex-based terms during evaluation. This could be accomplished through clear policy statements and training. However, it must be monitored and supported by upper-level management.

In the opening scenario, Ken's decision would have been lawful if he had observed Glenda and could substantiate she was indeed a passive leader. However, merely assuming Glenda was passive because she is female has no basis in fact. Ken had apparently never heard of former British prime minister Margaret Thatcher or any of the other women who are aggressive leaders. Making an employment decision on preferred leadership style may not create disparate treatment, but basing it on a stereotype will. Simply stated, the refusal to hire a woman because of her sex, based on assumptions of the comparative employment characteristics of women in general, will not support an employer defense.[21]

Sex Stereotyping and Dress Codes

Dress and appearance standards are usually challenged on the standpoint that they discriminate on the basis of sex because they may place a more onerous burden on one sex over the other. That is, the complaining party could demonstrate that the policy placed a significantly different burden on one of the sexes. This has become known as the "unequal burden standard" or the "unequal burden test."[22] For example, female employees are required to wear a uniform, but male employees are not.

Grooming/appearance policies inherently create a dilemma under a law like Title VII that demands equal treatment, because men dress differently from women and vice versa.[23] Societal perceptions of appropriate male and appropriate female appearance do indeed differ along gender lines. To resolve this apparent inconsistency with the basic tenets of EEO law, the federal courts have held that, though standards may be different for the sexes, Title VII is not violated when appearance standards are enforced even-handedly between male and female employees.[24] Consequently, to survive such challenges, an employer is required only to demonstrate that the policy does not place a *significantly different* burden on one of the sexes. If women are required to wear business professional attire and men are also required to wear business professional attire, there is no significant difference in the burden created by this requirement even though men and women's clothing may differ.

Mixed Motives

Sex stereotyping can lead to another variation of employment discrimination—mixed motives. As mentioned in Chapter 3, mixed motives occur when the employment decision is affected by at least two motives: a legitimate (job-related) reason and an illegitimate reason (i.e., sex stereotyping).[25]

To illustrate how mixed motives involving sex discrimination occur, let's assume a decision maker is overheard saying he would prefer to place a man in a particular middle-management position. Assume one of the applicants is a woman, and she was not selected for the position. The decision maker's remarks are relayed to the female applicant, who then files a complaint with the EEOC.

In the ensuing investigation, the employer argues that more than one reason determined the final promotion decision. Although the manager's remark indicated he was biased toward a male candidate, there is also evidence that the female applicant's job performance was mediocre and clearly inferior to that of the other candidates. The employer contends that, based on her job performance, it would not have promoted the female candidate anyway. This was precisely the case in the Supreme Court's 1989 decision, *Price Waterhouse v. Hopkins.*[26]

In this landmark Supreme Court case, a female senior manager was evaluated for partnership in a national accounting firm. During her evaluation for the promotion, several evaluators (partners in the firm) expressed negative reservations about her personality because Hopkins was a woman.[27] According to the findings of fact, she was known to be very aggressive, often to the point of abrasiveness.

Several evaluators thought this was inconsistent with what they believed was proper behavior for a woman (this was sex stereotyping). Some of the comments made included: she was "macho," "overcompensated for being a woman," and needed to take "a course in charm school," as well as objections about "a lady using foul language."[28] One evaluator went as far as to advise that she needed to "walk more femininely, talk more femininely, dress more femininely, wear makeup, have her hair styled, and wear jewelry."[29] All of these comments were sufficient to establish sex stereotyping, and had the decision been based *only* on the comments, the case would have been simple disparate treatment.

However, as is often the case, employment decisions are based on many factors. In *Price Waterhouse v. Hopkins*, the employer also claimed the eventual decision not to grant a partnership to Hopkins was predicated on legitimate business reasons. As in any disparate treatment situation, the employer's defense against the complaining party's *prima facie* case is that the employment practice is based on "legitimate nondiscriminatory reasons."[30] The respondent contended the decision not to promote Hopkins was based on her poor interpersonal skills—she was unduly harsh with her staff and was difficult to work with.[31] The problem the Court must resolve is: First, did the employer engage in an unlawful practice when it impermissibly considered sex in making an employment decision? Next, would the employer have arrived at the same conclusion had it used only legitimate nondiscriminatory criteria? Prior to 1991, if the answer to the second question was "yes," the Court would have concluded that Title VII had not been violated, even if the employer had impermissibly considered the applicant's sex in making the decision.

Today, if the answer to the first question is "yes," Title VII is judged to have been violated, regardless. According to the Civil Rights Act of 1991, an unlawful employment practice is established when the complaining party demonstrates that race, color, religion, sex, or national origin was a motivating factor for *any* employment practice, even though other factors also motivated the practice.[32] This is very clear language. It means *all* mixed-motive employment decisions automatically violate Title VII.

Before continuing, one point must be clarified regarding mixed motives. Students often get confused about the difference between mixed motive and pretextual motive. We hope to alleviate this confusion. In a true mixed-motive situation, the decision maker considered at least one legitimate criterion and one unlawful one. Let us say an employer

Figure 5.3 **Remedies Available under Mixed Motive**

Remedies, if it can *not* be shown that the same employment decision would have been reached in the absence of the discriminatory rationale:	Remedies, if it *can* be shown that the same employment decision would have been reached in the absence of the discriminatory rationale:
Back pay	Court costs
Front pay	Declaratory or injunctive relief
Reinstatement	Attorneys' fees
Promotion	
Punitive and compensatory damages	
Court costs	
Declaratory or injunctive relief	
Attorneys' fees	

had considered an employee's industrial sales experience (a legitimate reason) *and* the customer's preference for male sales representatives (an unlawful criterion) when deciding who would be hired. This would be a case of mixed motive, as both criteria were evaluated in making the decision. In contrast, in the case of **pretextual motive,** the employer intended to reject the female applicant because of her sex (it was the sole motivating factor), but is trying to hide the unlawful reason by proffering a legitimate one (alleging the other candidate is more qualified when he is not, for example).

Remedies for Mixed Motive

There is an interesting paradox in mixed-motive sex discrimination (see Figure 5.3). The moment the employer or its agent considers an applicant's sex, Title VII is violated and an unlawful practice is committed. However, there is less here than meets the eye. Even though the employment decision itself is flawed and unlawful, the employer may avoid damage awards under Title VII if it can be proved that the employer would have taken the same action in the absence of the discriminatory factor.[33]

Assume an employer can show that, given an employee's work record, the employer would still have denied him or her a promotion even though it had considered the employee's sex. Technically, when the employer considered a prohibited subject (an applicant's sex) in making the decision, Title VII was violated. However, because the same decision would have been made in the absence of considering the applicant's sex, the employer will not be required to reinstate, hire, promote, provide back pay, pay compensatory damages, or pay punitive damages to the affected applicant. The only remedies a court could impose under such circumstances would be declaratory or injunctive relief (see Chapter 1) and, perhaps, attorneys' fees and court costs.[34] Also, the employee is still afforded the opportunity to demonstrate that the employer's legitimate nondiscriminatory rationale is a pretext. As in any disparate treatment case, should the employee prove to the court that the employer's preferred reasons are pretextual, the employer becomes liable for a wide range of damages and awards. Because the employer's decision would have been the same regardless of the discriminatory motive, the employer will not be liable for reinstatement, back pay, or damages.[35] The only remedies the complaining party would be entitled to under such circumstances are injunctive relief (the employer will be ordered to cease consideration of sex in all future decisions) and, possibly, attorneys' fees and court costs.[36]

Managers should understand that if the employer fails to convince the court that the same result would have occurred without the discriminatory motive, then the employer is liable for the full remedies for sex discrimination. Since mixed motive is analyzed as a disparate treatment case, the employer is exposed to a broader range of liabilities. Consequently, the employer may be liable not only for the traditional Title VII remedies (injunctive relief, reinstatement, promotion, front pay, back pay, and/or attorneys' fees and court costs), but also for punitive and compensatory damages.

Sex-Plus Discrimination

Employers may have practices that, on the surface, appear facially neutral but may not be impartially enforced. **Sex-plus discrimination** occurs when members of one sex who possess a specific characteristic or condition are treated differently from members of the opposite sex who have the same characteristic. More succinctly, in order to make a sex-plus claim, the complaining party must show that an employer applied a requirement to one sex, but not the other, and then discriminated based on the requirement.[37]

Perhaps the best way to demonstrate how sex-plus discrimination operates in practice is to examine the findings from the landmark Supreme Court decision on the issue, *Phillips v. Martin Marietta Corp.*[38] The complaining party alleged a violation of Title VII of the Civil Rights Act of 1964 because of her sex. In the ensuing trial, the federal district court judge granted summary judgment for the respondent based on the following information:

> The employer informed the complaining party that it was not accepting job applications from women with preschool-age children.
>
> As of the time of the motion for summary judgment, the employer employed men with preschool-age children.
>
> At the time the complaining party applied, 70–75 percent of the applicants for the position she sought were women and 75–80 percent of those hired for the position in question—assembly trainee—were women; hence no question of bias against women as such was presented.[39]

In short, the respondent's defense was that there was no discrimination against women because more women than men were hired for the positions.

On appeal, the Supreme Court took particular note of the fact that during the period in question, men with preschool-age children were hired by the respondent. It is important to remember that Section 703(a) of the Civil Rights Act of 1964 requires that persons of like qualifications be given employment opportunities irrespective of their sex. Title VII was obviously violated in this instance because men were hired with a particular condition (preschool-age children), and women with the same condition were not. In essence, the respondent did not discriminate against all women, just those with preschool-age children. The Supreme Court concluded that an employment procedure permitting one hiring policy for women and another for men was clearly discrimination on the basis of sex.

The message this sends to HR staff is that all selection policies should be audited to ensure they are free from bias. Any written or de facto employment practice that excludes women with a particular characteristic but ignores the same characteristic in men (marital status, children, etc.) is a Title VII violation.

Pregnancy Discrimination

The Pregnancy Discrimination Act of 1978 amended Title VII to include discrimination on the basis of pregnancy, childbirth, or related medical conditions.[40] The intent of this statute is to ensure pregnancy is treated like any other medical-related condition in the workplace.[41] For example, denying disability benefits to a pregnant employee who is on maternity leave while providing those same benefits to male employees for other medical reasons would violate Title VII.[42]

The ironclad rule of the Pregnancy Discrimination Act is that Title VII views pregnancy as a medical condition; to treat it differently from any other medical condition that causes a temporary absence from the place of employment would be a violation. Therefore, if an employer has a medical leave policy permitting an employee to draw up to thirty days' paid leave due to injury or illness, a female employee going through childbirth is entitled to the same thirty days of paid leave (do not confuse voluntary paid medical leave with the involuntary unpaid leave mandated by the Family and Medical Leave Act—discussed in Chapter 8).

Additionally, the employer must also hold a job open for a pregnancy-related absence for the same amount of time that jobs are held open for employees on sick or disability leaves. If injured employees are allowed seven months to return to work, then so are female employees after childbirth. Similarly, an employer is required to treat a pregnant employee as it would any medically disabled employee with regard to performing the essential tasks and responsibilities of the job. If a temporarily disabled employee is given modified tasks or temporary job assignments, then a pregnant employee is entitled to the same treatment. If the employer makes no such accommodations for other employees, it is not required to make special ones for a pregnant employee.[43]

Additionally, an employer cannot refuse to hire a female applicant because of her pregnancy-related condition so long as she is able to perform the major functions of the job for which she is applying. Neither can an employer terminate a female employee for becoming pregnant. Pregnant female employees must be permitted to work at all times during their pregnancies so long as they are able to perform their jobs.[44] If, on the other hand, an individual is unable to perform the major functions necessary for the job, the employer does not have to provide an alternative job *unless* the employer has provided alternative jobs to other employees who temporarily could not perform their work. Again, the pregnant employee is entitled to all the benefits the employer has elected to provide employees for other medical contingencies. This does not mean the employer is required by law to provide pregnant workers with more or special benefits,[45] but neither is the employer permitted to provide less.

Prima facie proofs for unlawful pregnancy discrimination are only slightly different than other disparate treatment cases. In order to establish a *prima facie* case of pregnancy discrimination, the complaining party must show:

1. That she was pregnant.
2. That she was qualified for the job.
3. That she was subjected to an adverse employment decision.
4. That there was a connection between her pregnancy and the adverse employment decision.[46]

There is an interesting twist to pregnancy discrimination in regard to pregnancy medical benefits. In the case of *Newport News Shipbuilding and Dry Dock Co. v. EEOC*,[47] the Supreme Court ruled that married male employees were entitled to the same medical benefits for their spouses' pregnancies as married female employees received. The company's medical insurance plan provided for hospitalization benefits for pregnancy-related conditions for its female employees, but it provided *fewer* pregnancy benefits for the pregnant spouses of male employees. The male employees complained that they were given different medical benefits than their female counterparts, and the reason for this difference was based on sex. The Supreme Court agreed. Employers are now required to provide the same level of pregnancy-related health benefits for the spouses of male employees that they do for their female employees.

One final word of caution: because Title VII prohibits discrimination on the basis of sex, pregnancy-related benefits cannot be limited to only married female employees. These benefits must be provided to all female employees, regardless of marital status. Consequently, employers may not deny pregnancy-related medical benefits to employees who have out-of-wedlock births.[48] Those pregnancy-related accommodations covered, and those exempted, by the Pregnancy Discrimination Act are listed in Figure 5.4.

Pay Differentials

The statute making it unlawful to differentiate pay on the basis of sex for individuals in the workplace is the Equal Pay Act of 1963. Though this act is actually an amendment to the Fair Labor Standards Act of 1938, the prohibition on discrimination in compensation on the basis of sex is enforced by the EEOC. The antidiscrimination provision clearly states:

> No employer having employees subject to any provisions of this section shall discriminate, within any establishment in which such employees are employed, between employees on the basis of sex by paying wages to employees in such establishment at a rate less than the rate at which he pays wages to employees of the opposite sex in such establishment for equal work on jobs the performance

Figure 5.4   **Pregnancy Discrimination Coverage**

Conditions Covered Under Pregnancy Discrimination Act:	Conditions Exempted from Pregnancy Discrimination Act Coverage:
Disability benefits*	Job restructuring
Sick leave*	Sick leave**
Health insurance*	Health insurance**
Leave of absence*	Temporary work assignments**
Abortion (when the life of the mother would be endangered)	Elective abortions
Medical complications arising from abortion	

Source: Doe v. C.A.R.S. Protection Plus, 527 F.3d 358, 364 (4th Cir. 2008); 29 C.F.R. § 1604, Appendix; 42 U.S.C. § 2000 e(k).
*When provided for other disabilities.
**When not provided for other disabilities/medical conditions.

of which requires equal skill, effort, and responsibility, and which are performed under similar working conditions, except where such payment is made pursuant to (i) a seniority system; (ii) a merit system; (iii) a system which measures earnings by quantity or quality of production; or (iv) a differential based on any other factor other than sex: Provided, that an employer who is paying a wage rate differential in violation of this subsection shall not, in order to comply with the provisions of this subsection, reduce the wage rate of any employee.[49]

In short, the Equal Pay Act protects men and women who perform substantially equal work in the same establishment from sex-based wage discrimination. In order to establish an Equal Pay Act claim, the complaining party must first demonstrate he or she received unequal pay for "equal work on jobs the performance of which requires equal skill, effort, and responsibility, and which are performed under similar working conditions."[50] However, pay differentials are permitted on grounds other than sex.

In its most blatant form, pay discrimination would occur if two employees, one male and one female, occupy the same position, have the same essential job functions, have held their positions for the same number of years, and have equal performance evaluations, but are paid different salaries. As long as the jobs require equal skill, effort, and responsibility and are performed under similar working conditions, the rate of pay must be equal for our two individuals.

It would be an Equal Pay Act violation if a real estate agency provided one commission schedule for residential property for its female associates and another schedule for its male associates. It does not matter which sex was placed at a disadvantage if the sales were performed under similar working conditions. Only if the employer can demonstrate that the individuals differed in job performance, seniority, or some other work-related dimension will pay differentials be permitted.[51]

Another potential complaint arising from the Equal Pay Act is that it may be violated when employers replace existing job incumbents with members of the opposite sex.

For example, where an employee of one sex is assigned to a given position to replace an employee of the opposite sex but then is compensated at a lower rate of pay than the employee who was replaced, a *prima facie* violation of the Equal Pay Act occurs. The employer's only rebuttal to this *prima facie* case is to demonstrate that the wage differential is justified under one or more of the statute's four affirmative defenses. Thus, the difference between the replacement employee's and departing employee's pay is based on either seniority, merit, quantity or quality of production, or some other factor other than sex. Hence, a female senior machinist can be compensated at a higher hourly rate than a male junior machinist because the higher pay is a function of the employee's seniority and not the employee's sex. Similarly, a male technical writer whose work has fewer errors than that of a female counterpart may receive higher pay based on the accuracy, or quality, of his work and vice versa.

One final item of interest regarding pay differentials occurred in 2009. The Lilly Ledbetter Fair Pay Act was enacted to specifically overturn a Supreme Court decision which held that equal-pay complaints begin from the date that the original unlawful wage decision occurs.[52] This means that the timeliness clock begins on the date that wage discrimination began. What this act does is to set the timeliness clock from the date of the *last* paycheck.[53] In essence, even if an unlawful wage decision had occurred over a decade ago, the affected employee may still file a complaint under Title VII or the Equal Pay Act provided that he or she received his or her last paycheck from that employer within the last 180 days. If, for example, a female employee was denied a pay raise on July 1, 2004 because of her sex (both a Title VII and an Equal Pay Act violation), her complaint cannot be barred due to timeliness if it was not filed prior to December 28, 2004. Assuming that she is paid biweekly, she could file within 180 days of her last paycheck, even if she had experienced no further discrimination since July 1, 2004. Under the Lilly Ledbetter Fair Pay Act, the employee could file a complaint on July 1, 2014, a full decade after the act of discrimination occurred. However, it applies only to discrimination affecting compensation.

Differentiating Benefits on the Basis of Sex

Differences in benefits because of sex are similar to pay differentials because of sex. However, differences in benefits violate Title VII rather than the Equal Pay Act. Benefit differentials fall neatly into Title VII's proscription on discrimination "against any individual with respect to his compensation, terms, conditions, or privileges of employment, because of such individual's race, color, religion, sex, or national origin. . . ."[54] As always, any employment decision in which consideration is given to an employee's sex risks violating Title VII.

In *City of Los Angeles Department of Water & Power v. Manhart*,[55] an employer, noting that women have a greater life expectancy than men, modified its retirement plan to provide women with smaller pensions. The rationale was that such programs cost more for women, as a class, because of their greater life expectancy. Reminding the employer that Title VII protects individuals and not classes, the Supreme Court held that main-

Table 5.1

Sexual Harassment Charges Investigated by the EEOC

Year	Total Title VII Charge Receipts	Sexual Harassment Charges	Percentage of All Charges
2001	59,631	15,475	30.0
2002	61,459	14,396	23.4
2003	59,075	13,566	23.0
2004	58,328	13,136	22.5
2005	55,976	12,679	22.7
2006	56,155	12,025	21.4
2007	61,159	12,510	20.5
2008	69,064	13,867	20.1
2009	68,710	12,696	18.5
2010	73,058	11,717	16.0
2011	71,914	11,364	15.8

Source: U.S. Equal Employment Opportunity Commission, *Sexual Harassment Charges EEOC & FEPAs Combined: FY 1997–FY 2011.* http://www.eeoc.gov/eeoc/statistics/enforcement/sexual_harassment.cfm (accessed December 27, 2012).

taining different benefits based on an individual's sex did indeed constitute unlawful discrimination. After all, not *all* women live longer than men, and it is still technologically impossible to determine just how long any individual will live. Remember, Title VII prohibits discrimination against any *individual* on the basis of that *individual's* race, color, religion, *sex*, or national origin.[56]

This same standard of judicial review has also been applied when women are required to make higher contributions to an employer's deferred compensation program using sex-based actuarial tables.[57] In short, the Supreme Court has eliminated the use of sex-based actuarial tables in calculating pension contributions or retirement annuities. It does not matter that, as a group, women live longer than men; employers cannot require individual women to pay more for their benefits than individual men.

SEXUAL HARASSMENT

The EEO complaint of the 1990s was sexual harassment. Since its inception in 1976,[58] no complaint under Title VII has caused so much misunderstanding in the workplace. By fiscal year 2011 sexual harassment complaints had dropped to 37.2 percent of all harassment charges filed under Title VII (compared to 98.9 percent in 1997),[59] and accounted for 15.8 percent of all Title VII actions investigated by the EEOC (see Table 5.1).[60]

One point for the reader to remember is that what applies to one class under Title VII invariably applies to all. If sexual harassment is actionable under Title VII, so are racial harassment,[61] national origin harassment,[62] and religious harassment.[63] This also means that if *quid pro quo* and hostile environment forms are recognized under sexual harassment, they are also actionable under the other classes.

Figure 5.5 **Guidelines on Discrimination Because of Sex as Defined by the EEOC**

Harassment on the basis of sex is a violation of Section 703 of Title VII. Unwelcome sexual advances, requests for sexual favors, and other verbal or physical conduct of a sexual nature constitute sexual harassment when:

1. Submission to such conduct is made either explicitly or implicitly a term or condition of employment.
2. Submission to or rejection of such conduct by an individual is used as the basis for employment decisions affecting such individual.
3. Such conduct has the purpose or effect of unreasonably interfering with an individual's work performance or creating an intimidating, hostile, or offensive working environment.

Source: 29 C.F.R. § 1604.11(a).

Sexual harassment is a term which has very broad interpretation. It can range from an off-color remark about an individual's personal appearance to sexual assault. However, the sexual harassment that is germane to this chapter is technically actionable sexual harassment, which has a specific legal meaning. Actionable sexual harassment is a violation of Title VII of the Civil Rights Act of 1964. According to the EEOC's *Guidelines on Sex Discrimination*,[64] actionable sexual harassment is defined as unwelcome sexual advances, requests for sexual favors, and other verbal or physical conduct that result in one of three consequences: first, when submission to these sexual advances is made explicitly or implicitly a condition of the victim's employment; second, when submission to or rejection of such requests by the employee becomes the basis for future employment decisions affecting that individual; and third, when such conduct has the purpose or effect of unreasonably interfering with the employee's work performance or creating "an intimidating, hostile, or offensive working environment"[65] (see Figure 5.5).

Because the first two conditions involve the withholding or granting of tangible employment benefits in exchange for sexual favors, harassment of this nature is referred to as **quid pro quo sexual harassment**. The third consequence constitutes a slightly different sexual harassment claim, that of "hostile environment" sexual harassment. It is important to distinguish between these two general classifications because the legal proofs required to substantiate each differ. This is more than making a single offensive or tasteless comment, but is conduct sufficiently harsh or persistent as to alter the individual's working environment.

Quid Pro Quo Sexual Harassment

A party filing a complaint of *quid pro quo* sexual harassment must be able to substantiate the following:

1. The alleged victim belongs to a class or group protected under Title VII. That is to say, the object of the alleged harassment was either male or female.

Figure 5.6   **Proofs for *Quid Pro Quo* Sexual Harassment**

- The complaining party is a member of a protected class.
- The conduct of a sexual nature was *unwelcome*. The complaining party did not encourage it by word or deed.
- But for the complaining party's sex, he or she would not have been subjected to the unwelcome conduct.
- The complaining party's acceptance or rejection of the unwelcome conduct would affect tangible job benefits.
- *Respondeat superior.* The employer is liable regardless of whether he or she knew, or should have known, of the harassment and the action taken (vicarious liability).

2. The alleged victim was subjected to unwelcome sexual harassment. The alleged victim did nothing, by word or deed, to encourage the harassing behavior. Neither did the alleged victim do anything to indicate the behavior was acceptable to her (or him). If the alleged victim truly and voluntarily participated in the behavior, it could hardly have been "unwelcomed."[66]

3. Because sexual harassment is a form of sex discrimination, the sexual harassment in question must be shown to have been based on the alleged victim's sex. The alleged victim must prove that the conduct at issue was not merely tinged with offensive sexual connotations but actually constituted discrimination because of sex.[67] The critical issue here is whether the members of one sex are exposed to disadvantageous conditions of employment (in this case unwelcome behavior of a sexual nature) to which members of the other sex are not exposed.

4. Submission or rejection of these advances is made explicitly or implicitly a condition of the victim's employment.

If the alleged victim complains about the unwelcomed behavior, he or she might not be promoted, not be recommended for a raise, be denied a desired work assignment, or be discharged. On the other hand, if the employee tolerates or accedes to the unwelcomed behavior, he or she is rewarded with some tangible workplace benefit, or at a minimum is permitted to keep his or her job (see Figure 5.6).

However, the complaining party has the burden of proving there is a connection between the alleged harasser's conduct and the loss of employment benefits, as was the case in *Anderson v. University Health Center.*[68] In this case, the complaining party alleged certain remarks by a supervisor constituted sexual harassment. The complaining party failed to establish any connection between these alleged remarks and her termination. The supervisor in question was not her immediate superior or the one who made the decision to terminate her. The complaining party also failed to offer evidence to create an issue of fact that her discharge was due to her rejection of any sexual advances. The evidence provided by the employer established a legitimate nondiscriminatory reason for the complaining party's termination. The federal district court concluded there was no evidence to prove the complaining party's job was dependent upon her response to any alleged sexual advances.[69]

From the HR professional's standpoint, *quid pro quo* sexual harassment is the simpler

Figure 5.7 **Proofs for Hostile Environment Sexual Harassment**

- The complaining party is a member of a protected class.
- The conduct of a sexual nature was *unwelcome.* The complaining party did not encourage it by word or deed.
- But for the complaining party's sex, he or she would not have been subjected to the unwelcome conduct.
- The unwelcome conduct was so severe or pervasive as to create an intimidating and adverse work environment.
- *Respondeat superior.* The employer knew, or should have known, of the harassment and failed to take appropriate action (direct liability). The employer is held vicariously liable with a two-part affirmative defense if the harasser was a manager (*Faragher v. City of Boca Raton,* 524 U.S. 775 [1998]).

to monitor of the two forms of sexual harassment, because only a relatively select group of employees can be perpetrators. It is key to this form of sexual harassment that tangible employment benefits must be involved. Consequently, only those employees who can offer or withdraw these benefits can initiate this action. In other words, the pool of potential harassers is limited to supervisory personnel and other members of management. Policies and training programs focused on this relatively small class of employees would be the most likely deterrent.

The most ominous feature of this form of harassment is the fact that the EEOC's *Guidelines on Sex Discrimination* explicitly state that the employer is responsible for the acts of its supervisory personnel in *quid pro quo* situations "regardless of whether the employer knew or should have known of their occurrence."[70]

Despite this Draconian pronouncement, the employer may yet avoid even this automatically imposed liability provided that it can meet the requirements of the affirmative defense discussed in the liability section of this chapter. Potential employer liability provides an incentive for the organization to act swiftly against the alleged harassing supervisor once an allegation of sexual harassment is made. This concern for strict liability has been reinforced by two recent Supreme Court decisions, *Burlington Industries v. Ellerth*[71] and *Faragher v. City of Boca Raton.*[72]

Interestingly, nothing in the *Guidelines on Sex Discrimination* requires the employer to follow due process for the accused sexual harasser. This does not, however, relieve the HR professional of the moral obligation to conduct a thorough investigation and ensure due process to *all* parties.

Hostile Environment Sexual Harassment

Due to its peculiar characteristics, the elements, or legal proofs, necessary to substantiate a claim of hostile environment sexual harassment differ slightly from those of *quid pro quo* sexual harassment. In fact, the first three proofs for hostile environment sexual harassment are identical to those for *quid pro quo* sexual harassment. First, the employee making the complaint must belong to a protected class. Second, the conduct or behavior the employee was subjected to was unwelcomed. Third, except for the individual's sex, he or she would not have been subjected to the alleged harassment.

Table 5.2

Who Commits Sexual Harassment in the Workplace?

Position of the Alleged Offender	Percentage of Complaints
Coworker/group of coworkers	67
Manager/immediate supervisor	47
Visitor/business contact	11

Source: Percentages collected in a 1986 Bureau of National Affairs survey. Because respondents could choose more than one response, cumulative percentages total more than 100 percent. Bureau of National Affairs, *Sexual Harassment: Employer Policies and Problems* (Washington, DC: BNA 1987).

It is the fourth element, dealing with the severity or pervasiveness of the conduct, that distinguishes this type of actionable harassment from *quid pro quo*. This is also the point upon which most of these cases fail or prevail.[73] To be actionable under Title VII, the alleged harassment must have been either severe enough or pervasive enough to alter the terms or conditions of employment and create an abusive work environment.[74] If the complaining party cannot demonstrate that the harasser's conduct was serious enough[75] or of sufficient frequency[76] to have affected the complaining party's psychological well-being and work performance, then there is, legally speaking, no sexual harassment.[77]

In **hostile environment sexual harassment** claims, the unwelcomed behavior of a sexual nature must be sufficiently severe or pervasive as to alter the victim's conditions of employment,[78] or the harassment must be of a sufficient severity or frequency to create an abusive work environment. In this regard, hostile environment is very similar to **constructive discharge**, intentionally making the employee's work environment so abhorrent that a reasonable person would quit. This standard is not achieved by merely showing that the conduct in question offended the victim, but by demonstrating the alleged harassment actually affected the *terms, conditions, or privileges* of the victim's employment.[79] Examples of sufficiently severe or abusive work environments would be those that:

- Affect the psychological well-being of the victim[80]
- Detract from the employee's job performance[81]
- Create an abusive work environment[82]
- Result in a constructive discharge[83]
- Keep the employee from advancing her (his) career[84]

What is most disturbing about hostile environment claims is that the pool of potential harassers is virtually limitless. Unlike *quid pro quo* sexual harassment, in which harassers are restricted more or less to the ranks of the organization's management, almost anyone is a potential harasser under hostile environment. For example, a hostile work environment could conceivably be created by a supervisor, coworker, customer, vendor, or visitor to the employer's place of business (see Table 5.2).

Here, management's concern is that, regardless of who is engaging in the sexual harassment, it still remains the employer's responsibility to eliminate it. The courts and the EEOC hold the employer responsible for maintaining a harassment-free work environment.[85]

The employer can be held liable for hostile environment sexual harassment if it fails to remedy or prevent a hostile work environment of which it was aware or should have been aware.[86] Once the employer is made aware of the alleged sexual harassment, the *Guidelines on Sex Discrimination* recommend "immediate and appropriate corrective action"[87] be taken. When imposing corrective action, it is important to understand that employers must ensure the remedies initiated are "reasonably calculated to end the harassment"[88] and should be "assessed proportionately to the seriousness of the offense."[89] Employers are held to an even higher standard when the hostile environment was created by a member of the organization's management.

Employers who have acted expeditiously and have imposed what the courts consider appropriate action have successfully avoided liability. On the other hand, employers who have merely "slapped the wrist" of the harasser have been held liable.[90] Again, an incentive is created to insulate oneself by imposing swift punishment and sanctions on the party accused of harassment.

EMPLOYER LIABILITY FOR SEXUAL HARASSMENT

Since the perpetrator is often a supervisor who relies on actual or apparent authority to extort sexual considerations from victims, *quid pro quo* claims usually result in an automatic application of employer liability for sexual harassment.[91]

Direct versus Vicarious Liability

To appreciate the impact that indirect liability would have on employers, it is necessary to understand the conditions under which an employer is directly liable for the hostile work environment created by its agents (usually management and supervisory personnel). Under **direct liability**, an employer is liable for the hostile environment sexual harassment of its agent, only if the employer knew, or should have known, that the harassment was occurring and failed to take immediate and appropriate corrective action.[92] In essence, the employer is held responsible for failing to make a reasonable effort to prevent the harassment from recurring.

Vicarious liability, on the other hand, is so broad and inclusive in its nature that it is sometimes referred to as *strict liability* or *indirect liability*. Under **vicarious liability**, an employer can be found liable for the wrongful actions of its agent regardless of whether or not the employer knew, or should have known, of the agent's sexual harassment. It is only associated with harassment involving the loss of tangible job benefits (*quid pro quo*) or hostile environment sexual harassment perpetrated by a manager/supervisor. In a technical sense, an employer may be indirectly responsible for the sexual harassment by one of its supervisory personnel when the following conditions are met:[93]

Figure 5.8   **Liability for Actionable Sexual Harassment**

Alleged Harasser	*Quid Pro Quo*	Hostile Environment
Manager/supervisor	Vicarious (strict) liability	Vicarious (strict) liability with two-part affirmative defense
Nonmanagement (coworker, customer, and vendor)	Not applicable	Direct liability

Source: R.K. Robinson, D.D. Frink, B.J. Reithel, and G.M. Franklin, "Vicarious Liability for Hostile Environment Sexual Harassment: Examining the Implications of the *Ellerth* and *Fargaher* Decisions," *Labor Law Journal* 49 (1997): 1240.

1. *The unlawful harassment occurred within the scope of the supervisor's employment.* Essentially, the supervisor was instructed or required, as part of his job, to create a sexually hostile environment. For example, a supervisor is told by his immediate superior to make things so uncomfortable in the workplace that the newly hired female employee will quit. In the majority of instances, a supervisor's harassing conduct has been judged to be outside the scope of his employment.[94] In hostile environment, the supervisor is acting outside of his (or her) authority to hire, fire, discipline, or promote.

2. *The supervisory personnel, though acting outside the scope of their employment, were aided in accomplishing the harassment by the existence of the agency relationship.* This means that the supervisor uses the position and the authority specifically delegated to that position to pressure the employee to submit to the harassment.[95] For example, the supervisor can threaten the employee with termination, no raises, or no promotion if she (or he) refuses his advances. This is a classic example of *quid pro quo* sexual harassment.

Simply stated, in terms of sexual harassment, vicarious liability is associated with harassment involving the loss of tangible job benefits (*quid pro quo* sexual harassment) and in instances when a supervisor engages in hostile environment sexual harassment. This means that any sexual harassment involving supervisory personnel places the employer in an extremely difficult position. Even if appropriate action is taken after notification of the harassment, the employer could still be responsible for compensatory and punitive damages since it is responsible for the actions of its representatives, even when it is unaware of those actions.

The Affirmative Defense

In circumstances in which a supervisor has indeed created a hostile work environment, the employer can escape liability if two criteria have been satisfied: the employer exercised reasonable care to prevent and promptly correct any sexually harassing behavior, and the complaining party unreasonably failed to take advantage of any preventive or corrective opportunities provided by the employer, or to otherwise avoid harm.[96]

In order to demonstrate that *reasonable care* was exercised to prevent sexual harassment, it is essential that the employer have a clear sexual harassment policy and has disseminated it to *all* employees. In *Ellerth,* the Supreme Court provided guidance on this matter.

While proof that an employer had promulgated an antiharassment policy with complaint procedures is not necessary in every instance as a matter of law, the need for a stated policy suitable to employment circumstances can appropriately be addressed in any case when litigating the first element of the defense.

As a matter of practicality, firms without sexual harassment policies will find themselves hard-pressed to sustain the first criterion. Employers should further note that at a minimum, these policies should contain the following:[97]

- A statement that sexual harassment will not be tolerated.
- A definition of sexual harassment.
- Examples of conduct and behavior that could constitute sexual harassment, including both *quid pro quo* and hostile environment forms.
- A choice of channels for reporting sexual harassment, including how to report harassment during nonwork hours. This provides the employee an option if one of the company officials in the complaint procedure is the alleged harasser or has close ties to the harasser.
- Information on how the organization will handle the complaint to include conducting a thorough investigation and maintaining confidentiality.
- A statement that the organization will take appropriate corrective action to remedy any violation of the policy.
- A statement that the organization will take appropriate disciplinary action against any party making a fraudulent claim of sexual harassment.

Still, no policy by itself will insulate an employer. All members of the organization must be aware of the policy's complaint procedures; to be effective, it must be disseminated. It would perhaps be advisable to create and maintain some documentation that each employee was familiarized with the policy and how (and where) to file a complaint. A document attesting to this fact would go a long way in establishing that the employer was earnest in preventing sexual harassment and that the employees had been made fully aware of internal means of resolving misconduct.

Because these new standards of liability affect only supervisory personnel, it is recommended that these personnel be trained in their obligations under company policies regarding sexual harassment. As in documenting that rank-and-file employees were made aware of antiharassment policies, a record of supervisory training should be maintained as well. Again, this would provide evidence that the employer was exercising *reasonable care* in preventing sexual harassment.

The second criterion, the complaining party *unreasonably failed* to avail herself (or himself) of the company's preventive or corrective policies, appears to address the issue of employer notification. Unfortunately, determining what constitutes unreasonable failure to use the company's antiharassment complaint procedure is not clearly defined in either case. The problem with federal courts is that terms like "reasonable" and "unreasonable" are

Figure 5.9   **EEOC Guidance as to Who Is a Manager/Supervisor**

The Individual in Question:

- Has authority to initiate employment actions
- Has authority to recommend employment actions
- Has permanent authority to direct an employee's work activities
- Has temporary authority to direct an employee's work activities
- Is reasonably believed by the employee to have actual authority over the employee

sufficiently flexible to allow for broad interpretation in subsequent litigation. A company would hope that by providing evidence of a viable complaint/notification procedure, and proving the alleged victim was aware of the means to report the harassment, the court would recognize that failure to utilize this mechanism was done strictly at the victim's own volition. This would be particularly true if the employer's policy made provisions for filing a complaint without exposing the victim to undue risk and had a clearly delineated mechanism for investigating and resolving such complaints. Any failure on the part of the victim to use these procedures would go a long way toward satisfying the second criterion. The Supreme Court has, in effect, placed a greater burden on the complaining party to notify the employer of alleged sexual harassment when the employer has provided a viable antiharassment mechanism.

As a final word on the affirmative defense, the reader must understand that it applies exclusively to hostile environment sexual harassment attributed to supervisors.[98] The affirmative defense cannot be applied in *quid pro quo* sexual harassment. In instances where supervisory personnel threatened the employee with loss (or gain) of tangible job benefits, no affirmative defense is permitted to extenuate the employer's liability.

Who Is a Supervisor?

Since employers are exposed to a stricter level of liability when a participant in sexual harassment is a supervisor, it is important to understand just which employees qualify as supervisors. Titles are never a sufficient indicator of management status; this is determined by duties, responsibilities, and authority. Based on new EEOC guidelines, if an individual meets one of three criteria, that person is considered a supervisor (see Figure 5.9).[99] First, an individual is considered a supervisor if he or she possesses the authority to take or recommend tangible employment actions affecting the employee (i.e., raises, retention, termination, promotion, etc.).[100] Additionally, an individual who has the authority to direct an employee's daily work assignments is considered a supervisor by the EEOC. This second criterion is particularly broad because the "supervisor" need not have the authority to recommend employment actions and satisfies this requirement when given only temporary authority to direct work.[101] Finally, an individual is a supervisor—for liability purposes—if that individual is regarded by the employee filing the complaint as having actual authority over the employee, *even when no such authority (permanently or temporarily) has been granted.*[102]

The issue of who is a supervisor poses a significant threat to organizations, requiring that HR professionals take an active role. If the employer is to be insulated from vicarious liability, it is absolutely critical that all supervisory personnel be trained on their responsibilities to maintain a harassment-free work environment. Because of the broad nature of the EEOC's definitions of "supervisor," HR professionals must ensure that all potential "supervisors" (under the EEOC's definition) are included in this training. Often, employees with titles like "team leader" are not viewed as *bona fide* management personnel by their organizations, but they could be treated as such by the EEOC.

Same-Sex Sexual Harassment

In 1998, the Supreme Court of the United States unanimously ruled in *Oncale v. Sundowner Offshore Services, Inc.* that Title VII's prohibition on hostile environment sexual harassment can be violated when the harasser and the harassed are of the same sex.[103] Despite the great deal of attention this decision received from the popular media, its impact on current workplace practices may be less than initially believed.

Sexual Orientation and Title VII

With regard to sexual orientation, there is currently no Title VII recognition or protection for nonheterosexuals. Contrary to popular misconceptions, nothing in the language of Title VII implies that sexual orientation (preference) is among the list of protected classes. In fact, federal court rulings have explicitly excluded Title VII protection for homosexuals,[104] effeminate men,[105] and transsexuals.[106] Even in the previously discussed *Oncale* decision, the Supreme Court ruled that while workers are protected from unwelcome conduct of a homosexual nature, homosexuals are not protected under Title VII from harassment specifically directed toward homosexual conduct.

To illustrate this point, it would be a Title VII violation if a homosexual female manager demanded sexual favors from a homosexual female subordinate. This would satisfy the requirement to demonstrate the homosexual female employee was treated differently because of her sex. Male subordinates would not have been the objects of the homosexual female supervisor because she is not attracted to males. Consequently, the homosexual female worker's sex is what made her the object of the supervisor's unwelcome advances.

However, if the same homosexual female employee were being verbally and physically harassed by her supervisor or coworkers because of her homosexuality, this would *not be actionable under Title VII.* Title VII protects workers against discrimination based on sex (gender), not sexual preference. Some federal jurisdictions have allowed homosexuals to receive protection under Title VII based on "gender stereotyping" claims. This was the issue first raised under *Price Waterhouse v. Hopkins.* The complaining party must show that the harassment was directed against him (or her) because of his or her sex, in this instance because he or she is not conforming to accepted sex roles. The individual must demonstrate that, in the case of a man, he was not acting manly enough for men; or feminine enough in the case of a woman.[107] Here the courts split a very fine hair by

Figure 5.10   **States with Statutes Protecting Sexual Orientation/Preference in All Employment** (Private Sector and Public Sector)

California	Minnesota
Colorado	Nevada
Connecticut	New Hampshire
Delaware	New Jersey
District of Columbia	New Mexico
Hawaii	New York
Illinois	Oregon
Iowa	Rhode Island
Maine	Vermont
Maryland	Washington
Massachusetts	

Source: J. Hunt, *A State-by-State Examination of Nondiscrimination Laws and Policies* (Washington, DC: Center for American Progress, 2012): 3–4.

denying the individual protection against harassment based on sexual orientation while extending protection against sex stereotyping.[108]

Sexual Orientation and State Laws

Several states and municipalities have enacted statutes or ordinances that prohibit harassment of homosexuals and, in some instances, transsexuals. Hence, overt discrimination on the basis of sexual preference could be litigated under these laws. According to a 2012 study conducted by the Center for American Progress and Action Fund, 21 states currently have enacted legislation that protects individuals against discrimination based on sexual preference or orientation in a private sector workplace.[109] In these states (see Figure 5.10), verbal harassment of an employee because of that individual's preference or orientation becomes actionable under state law.

SUMMARY

This chapter introduced sex discrimination, the second largest source of Title VII violations after race discrimination. Discrimination based on sex can result from overt sex discrimination (disparate treatment), disparate impact, sex stereotyping, mixed motives, sex-plus, pregnancy, pay differentials, and sexual harassment.

Particular attention was devoted to the fastest-growing Title VII complaint, sexual harassment. Sexual harassment is defined as unwelcome sexual advances, requests for sexual favors, and other verbal and physical conduct of a sexual nature. Actionable sexual harassment occurs in two forms: *quid pro quo* sexual harassment and hostile environment sexual harassment. *Quid pro quo* sexual harassment involves the withholding or granting of tangible employment benefits contingent on their exchange for sexual favors. From an HR professional's standpoint, this is the simpler of the two to monitor because only a relatively select group of employees can be perpetrators. Hostile environment sexual harassment involves alleged harassment that is severe or pervasive enough to alter the terms or conditions of employment and create an abusive environment. What is most problematic about hostile environment sexual harassment is that the pool of potential harassers is limitless.

KEY TERMS AND CONCEPTS

Constructive discharge

Direct liability

Hostile environment sexual harassment

Mixed motives

Pretextual discharge

Quid pro quo sexual harassment

Sex discrimination

Sex-plus discrimination

Sex stereotyping

Vicarious liability

DISCUSSION QUESTIONS

1. Identify and briefly describe the eight forms of sex discrimination actionable under Title VII.
2. How does mixed-motive sex discrimination differ from constructive discharge issues? Give an example of each.
3. How do the remedies for mixed motives differ from the remedies for other Title VII violations?
4. Differentiate *quid pro quo* sexual harassment from hostile environment sexual harassment. Is the employer's liability for the harassment affected by the organizational position of the alleged harasser? If so, how?
5. What should be included in an employer's sexual harassment policy?
6. How does Title VII treat discrimination on the basis of sexual orientation?

CASES

Case 1

A female state government employee filed a complaint against her male supervisor for creating a hostile work environment. The charges against the supervisor were based upon four separate sexually offensive incidents that occurred over a three-year period. Three of these incidents directly involved the complaining party, and the fourth involved a comment made about a female visitor who came to the office.

Specifically, the charges involved another female employee overhearing the supervisor remarking the complaining party was the "Dolly Parton of the office" in a conversation with two visitors to the facility. On one occasion, during a private telephone conversation initiated by the complaining party, the supervisor speculated on the frequency of her sexual relations after her recent divorce. Then, the supervisor touched the complaining party's hair once and commented on how luxurious it felt. Finally, the supervisor was overheard making a joke to a male employee about a female nonemployee who had entered the office wearing very tight shorts.

During this three-year period, the complaining party never gave any indication that her supervisor ever requested sexual favors of her or any other female employee. Based on the supervisor's aforementioned comments and actions, the complaining party filed a formal complaint of sexual harassment with her agency.[110]

    a. Using the burdens of proof necessary to establish a *prima facie* case, determine if actionable sexual harassment has occurred.

    b. If so, which form of sexual harassment occurred: *quid pro quo*, hostile environment, or both?

    c. If you concluded there is actionable sexual harassment, what corrective action would you recommend?

Case 2

The complaining party was employed as a revenue agent for a state government agency in San Mateo, California, and declared she was sexually harassed by a male supervisor. The complaining party was initially assigned a workstation twenty feet in front of the supervisor's desk. One day, she accepted his invitation to join him for lunch. At this time, there was no indication of sexual harassment. Shortly afterward, the supervisor began hanging around the complaining party's desk. On several occasions, he asked her to go out with him. She declined.

Not wanting to have further social contact with him, the complaining party began avoiding the office during lunchtime. Shortly thereafter, the supervisor handed the complaining party a note that read: "I cried over you last night and I'm totally drained today. I have never been in such constant turmoil! Thank you for talking with me. I could not stand to feel your hatred for another day." The complaining party became frightened and left the room. The supervisor followed her into the hallway and asked her to talk to him. She left the building.

The note was shown to her department head, who felt it was sexual harassment. However, the complaining party requested that she be allowed to handle the situation herself. She asked a male coworker to tell her supervisor to leave her alone.

The next day, the supervisor called in sick, and the complaining party left for training in St. Louis before he returned. While in St. Louis, she received a single-spaced, three-page letter from the supervisor similar in content to the first note.

The complaining party telephoned her department head, reporting she was frightened and upset. She then requested that either she or the supervisor be transferred, because she did not feel comfortable working in the same office with him. Consequently, the department head told her that the supervisor had been demoted, that he was instructed not to contact her again, and that he was to be transferred to San Francisco. The supervisor immediately filed a grievance through his union, which resulted in his being allowed to transfer back to San Mateo one month later with a promise not to bother the complaining party. The complaining party responded by filing a formal sexual harassment complaint.[111]

a. Using the burdens of proof necessary to establish a *prima facie* case, determine if actionable sexual harassment has occurred.
b. If so, which form of sexual harassment occurred: *quid pro quo*, hostile environment, or both?
c. If you concluded there is actionable sexual harassment, what corrective action would you recommend?

Case 3

May Gilbert began working for Amalgamated Baking Company (ABC) in May 2003 as a sales supervisor at its Vernon, California, facility. In May 2005, ABC promoted her to food sales account manager and in June 2006 promoted her again to conduct training for southern California distributors. Ken Weinzimmer, ABC's senior vice president for sales and marketing and/or Dwight Carnahan, ABC's president, approved each promotion.

ABC then offered Gilbert a job in Texas. She accepted the offer and in January 2007, with Carnahan's approval, began working as the first sales supervisor at ABC's Fort Worth, Texas, facility. ABC did not then have distributors, routes, or trucks in the Dallas/Fort Worth area. No employees reported to Gilbert. In February 2007, Gilbert hired her husband to work under her supervision as a distributor.

ABC promoted Gilbert in January 2008 to the position of district sales manager for the Dallas/Fort Worth area; she received a pay raise as well. Carnahan and Gilbert's supervisor, John Davis, approved the promotion and raise. Gilbert then supervised up to eighteen distributors, of whom up to ten operated out of ABC's Dallas facility. Although ABC eventually gave her a 4 percent raise in September 2008, she received lower compensation than did male district sales managers in other areas, and ABC did not give her access to a cellular telephone. Gilbert complained about this treatment, implying she was being treated differently because she was a woman. ABC informed her that the other districts had performed better than hers during the same period.

In January 2009, several distributors whom Gilbert supervised complained she was treating them unfairly by favoring her husband in assigning the best routes, providing him advance knowledge of sales contests and other activities, and giving him other considerations. The distributors also complained of her poor supervision.

They asserted that Gilbert was one reason for the high distributor turnover in her market area. A few days later, the distributors advised Carnahan of additional complaints of favoritism they asserted Gilbert had shown to her husband. Carnahan referred these complaints to Weinzimmer.

Carnahan and Weinzimmer then met with the distributors, taking their grievances seriously because they viewed them as ABC customers. After a more detailed internal investigation, Carnahan concluded that the distributors' complaints were valid, and followed up by meeting with Gilbert.

Carnahan discussed with Gilbert the possibility of transferring her to Houston and also offered her a distributorship, both of which she refused. Carnahan then terminated Gilbert's employment. Gilbert alleges ABC fired her as an act of retaliation for her previous complaints about sex discrimination in pay and not being given a cellular phone.[112]

a.   Has Ms. Gilbert been unlawfully discriminated against because of her sex?

b.   If so, which form of sex discrimination applies?

NOTES

1. U.S. Equal Employment Opportunity Commission, *Charge Statistics FY 1997 Through FY 2011.* http://www.eeoc.gov/eeoc/statistics/enforcement/titlevii.cfm (accessed December 14, 2012); *Sex-Based Charges FY 1997–FY 2011*, http://www.eeoc.gov/eeoc/statistics/enforcement/sex.cfm (accessed December 14, 2012).

2. *Newport News Shipbuilding & Dry Dock Co. v. EEOC,* 462 U.S. 669, 682 (1983); *Oncale v. Sundowner Offshore Services,* 523 U.S. 75 (1998).

3. *Bellissimo v. Westinghouse Electric Corp.,* 764 F.2d 175 (3rd Cir. 1985).

4. *Willingham v. Macon Telegraphy Publishing Co.,* 507 F.2d 1084 (5th Cir. 1975).

5. Ibid.

6. *Dothard v. Rawlinson,* 433 U.S. 321 (1977).

7. *Sutton v. National Distillers Products Co.,* 445 F.Supp. 1319 (D.C. Ohio 1978).

8. *Brooks v. ACF Industries,* 537 F.Supp. 1112 (S.D. W.Va. 1982).

9. *Wigginess, Inc. v. Frutchman,* 482 F.Supp. 681 (S.D. N.Y. 1979).

10. 29 C.F.R. § 1604.2(a)(2).

11. Ibid.

12. *Hernandez v. University of St. Thomas,* 793 F.Supp. 214 (D. Minn. 1992).

13. *Robino v. Iranon,* 145 F.3d 1109 (9th Cir. 1998).

14. *UAW v. Johnson Controls,* 499 U.S. 187, 206, n.4 (1991).

15. *Diaz v. Pan American World Airways*, 442 F.2d 385, 388 (5th Cir.), cert. denied 404 U.S. 950 (1971).

16. *Fernandez v. Wynn Oil Company*, 653 F. 2d 1273 (9th Cir. 1981).

17. 29 C.F.R. § 1607.2 (B); *Cook v. Billington*, 59 FEP Cases 1010 (D.C. D.C. 1992); *Garland v. USAir, Inc.,* 767 F.Supp. 715 (W.D. Pa. 1991). 366.

18. 29 C.F.R. § 1604.2(a)(2).

19. *City of Los Angeles Department of Water & Power v. Manhart*, 435 U.S. 702, 707 (1978).

20. *Price Waterhouse v. Hopkins,* 490 U.S. 228, 239–240 (1989).

21. *Breiner v. Nevada Department of Corrections,* 610 F.3d 1202 (9th Cir. 2010).

22. *Gerdom v. Continental Airlines, Inc.,* 692 F.2d 602 (9th Cir. 1982).

23. K. M. Bovalino, "How the effeminate male can maximize his odds in winning Title VII litigation," *Syracuse Law Review,* 53 (2003): 1117–1139.

24. *Bellissimo v. Westinghouse Electric Corp.*, 764 F.2d 175 (3rd Cir. 1985).

25. *Miller v. CIGNA Corp.*, 47 F.3d 586 (3rd Cir. 1995).

26. 490 U.S. 228 (1989).

27. *Price Waterhouse v. Hopkins,* 490 U.S. at 235.

28. Ibid.

29. Ibid.

30. *McDonnell-Douglas Corporation v. Green*, 411 U.S. 792, 802 (1973); *Texas Dept. of Community Affairs v. Burdine*, 450 U.S. 248, 252 (1981).

31. *Hopkins v. Price Waterhouse*, 618 F.Supp. 1109, 1113 (D.C. D.C. 1985).

32. 42 U.S.C. § 2000e-2(m).

33. 42 U.S.C. § 2000e-5(g)(2)(B).

34. 42 U.S.C. § 2000e-5(g)(2)(B)(I).

35. 42 U.S.C. § 2000e-5(g)(2)(B).

36. Ibid.

37. *McBride v. Peak Wellness Center, Inc.* 688 F.3d 698 (10th Cir. 2012).

38. 400 U.S. 542 (1971).

39. *Phillips v. Martin Marietta Corp.*, 400 U.S. 542 (1971).

40. 42 U.S.C. § 2000e(K).

41. Ibid.

42. *Stansell v. Sherwin-Williams Co.*, 404 F.Supp. 696 (N.D. Ga. 1975).

43. 29 C.F.R. § 1604, Appendix.

44. 29 C.F.R. § 1604 at app. 8.

45. *Geier v. Medtronic, Inc.*, 99 F.3d 238, 242 (7th Cir. 1996); *Lang v. The Star Herald*, F.3d 1308, 1312 (8th Cir. 1997).

46. *Cline v. Catholic Archdiocese of Toledo*, 206 F.3d 651 (6th Cir. 1999); *Boyd v. Harding Academy of Memphis, Inc.*, 88 F.3d 410, 413 (6th Cir. 1996).

47. 462 U.S. 669 (1983).

48. U.S. Equal Employment Opportunity Commission, *Facts About Pregnancy Discrimination* (January, 15 2004), www.eeoc.gov/facts/fs-preg.html (accessed January 16, 2008).

49. 29 U.S.C. § 206(d).

50. *Corning Glass Works v. Brennan*, 417 U.S. 188, 195 (1974).

51. *Tomka v. The Seiler Corp.*, 66 F. 3rd 1295, 1310 (2nd Cir. 1995); *Varner v. Illinois State University*, 226 F.3d 927, 929 (7th Cir. 2000).

52. *Ledbetter v. Goodyear Tire & Rubber Co.*, 550 U.S. 618 (2007).

53. 42 U.S.C. § 2000e-5(e)(1) and (f)(1).

54. 42 U.S.C. § 2000e-2(a)(1).

55. 435 U.S. 702 (1978).

56. 42 U.S.C. § 2000e-2(a)(1).

57. *Arizona Governing Committee v. Norris*, 463 U.S. 1073 (1983).

58. *Williams v. Saxbe*, 413 F.Supp. 654 (D.C. D.C. 1976); *rev in part and vacated in part, sub. nom.*, *Williams v. Bell*, F.2d 1240 (D.C. Cir. 1978).

59. U.S. Equal Employment Opportunity Commission, *Title VII of the Civil Rights Act of 1964 Charges* (includes concurrent charges with ADEA, ADA, and EPA) *FY 1997–FY 2011.* http://www.eeoc.gov/ eeoc/statistics/enforcement/titlevii.cfm (accessed December 19, 2012); and U.S. Equal Employment Opportunity Commission, *Sexual Harassment Charges EEOC & FEPAs Combined: FY 1997–FY 2011,* http://www.eeoc.gov/eeoc/statistics/enforcement/harassment.cfm (accessed December 19, 2012).

60. U.S. Equal Employment Opportunity Commission, *Harassment Charges EEOC & FEPAs Combined: FY 1997–FY 2011,* http://www.eeoc.gov/eeoc/statistics/enforcement/harassment.cfm (accessed December 19, 2012); and U.S. Equal Employment Opportunity Commission, *Sexual Harassment Charges EEOC & FEPAs Combined: FY 1997–FY 2011,* http://www.eeoc.gov/eeoc/statistics/enforcement/harassment.cfm (accessed December 19, 2012).

61. *Jones v. UPS Ground Freight*, 683 F.3d 1283 (11th Cir. 2012).

62. *Kang v. U. Lim America, Inc.*, 296 F.3d 810 (9th Cir. 2002).

63. *EEOC v. Sunbelt Rentals, Inc.*, 521 F.3d 306 (4th Cir. 2008).

64. 29 C.F.R. § 1604.11.

65. 29 C.F.R. § 1604.11(a).

66. *Meritor Savings Banks, FSB v. Vinson*, 477 U.S. 57, 68 (1986).

67. *Oncale v. Sundowner Offshore Services, Inc.*, 523 U.S. 75, 81 (1998).

68. 623 F.Supp. 795 (W.D. Pa. 1985).

69. Ibid. at 798.

70. 29 C.F.R. § 1604.11(d).

71. 524 U.S. 742 (1998).

72. 524 U.S. 775 (1998).

73. *Fisher v. San Pedro Peninsula Hospital*, 262 Cal. Rptr. 842 (1989).

74. *Meritor*, 477 U.S. at 67 (1986).

75. *Rabidue v. Osceola Refining Co.*, 805 F.2d 611 (6th Cir. 1986).

76. *Christoforou v. Ryder Truck Rental, Inc.*, 668 F.Supp. 294 (S.D. N.Y. 1987).

77. *Vasconcelos v. Meese*, 907 F.2d 111 (9th Cir. 1990).

78. *Jones v. Flagship International*, 793 F.2d 714 (5th Cir. 1986); cert. denied 479 U.S. 1065 (1987).

79. *Doe by Doe v. City of Belleville, Il.*, 119 F.3d 563, 576 (7th Cir. 1997).

80. *Phillips v. Smalley Maintenance Service*, 711 F.2d 1524, 1529 (11th Cir. 1983).

81. *Meritor*, 477 U.S. at 63.

82. *Jones v. Flagship International*, 793 F.2d 714, 719–20 (5th Cir. 1986).

83. *Young v. Southwestern Savings and Loan Assoc.*, 509 F.2d 140, 144 (5th Cir. 1975).

84. *Harris v. Forklift Systems, Inc.*, 510 U.S. 17, 20 (1993).

85. *Meritor*, 477 U.S. at 65; 29 C.F.R. § 1604.11.

86. *EEOC v. Hacienda Hotel*, 881 F.2d 1504 (9th Cir. 1989).

87. 29 C.F.R. § 1604.11(d).

88. *Katz v. Dole*, 709 F.2d 251, 256 (4th Cir. 1983).

89. *Dornhecker v. Malibu Grand Prix Corp.*, 828 F.2d 307 (5th Cir. 1987).

90. *Katz*, 709 F.2d at 256.

91. *Davis v. Sioux City*, 115 F.3d 1365, 1367 (8th Cir. 1997); *Nichols v. Frank*, 42 F.3d 503, 513 (9th Cir. 1994); *Bouton v. BMW of North America, Inc.*, 29 F.3d 103, 106 (3rd Cir. 1994); and *Kaufman v. Allied Signal*, 970 F.2d 178, 185 (6th Cir. 1992).

92. *Katz v. Dole*, 709 F.2d 251 (1983); *Barrett v. Omaha National Bank*, 726 F. 2d 424 (8th Cir. 1984).

93. *Faragher v. City of Boca Raton*, 11 F.3d 1530, 1536 (11th Cir. 1997).

94. *Steele v. Offshore Shipping, Inc.*, 867 F.2d 1311, 1311–12 (11th Cir. 1989).

95. *Sparks v. Pilot Freight Carriers, Inc.*, 830 F.2d 1554, 1559–60 (11th Cir. 1989).

96. *Burlington Industries v. Ellerth*, 524 U.S. 742, 745; *Faragher v. City of Boca Raton*, 524 U.S. 775, 780 (1998).

97. R.K. Robinson, G.M. Franklin, and R.L. Fink, "Sexual Harassment at Work: Issues and Answers for Health Care Administrators," *Hospital and Health Services Administration* 38, no. 2 (1993): 175.

98. *Burlington Industries v. Ellerth*, 524 U.S. at 745.

99. T.S. Bland, "EEOC Issues Guidance in Effort to Clarify Harassment Rulings," *HR News* 18 (9): 7, 15.

100. *Burlington Industries v. Ellerth*, 524 U.S. at 15.

101. Ibid.

102. Ibid.

103. 523 U.S. 75 (1998).

104. *Polly v. Houston Lighting & Power Co.*, 825 F.Supp. 135 (S.D. Tex. 1993); *Ulane v. Eastern Airlines*, 742 F.2d 1081, 1087; *DeSantis v. Pacific Telephone & Telegraph Co.*, 608 F.2d 327, 329–330 (9th Cir. 1979).

105. *Smith v. Liberty Mutual Insurance, Co.*, 569 F.2d 325, 327 (5th Cir. 1978).

106. *Sommens v. Budget Marketing Inc.*, 667 F.2d 748,750 (8th Cir. 1982); *Holloway v. Arthur Andersen & Co.*, 566 F.2d 659, 662 (9th Cir. 1977); *Voles v. Ralph K. Davies Medical Center*, 403 F.Supp. 456, 457 (N.D. Cal. 1975); aff'd mem. 570 F.2d 354 (9th Cir. 1978).

107. *Prowel v. Wise Business Forms, Inc.* 579 F.3d 285, 293 (3rd Cir. 2009).

108. *Ayala-Sepulveda v. Municipality of San German*, 661 F.Supp.2d 130, 137 (D.P.R. 2009).

109. Jerome Hunt, *A State-by-State Examination of Nondiscrimination Laws and Policies* (Washington, DC: Center for American Progress Action Fund, 2012), http://www.americanprogress.org/issues/2012/06/pdf/state_nondiscrimination.pdf.

110. This scenario was developed from the facts in *Downes v. FAA*, 775 F.2d 288 (Fed. Cir. 1985).

111. Some materials for this case were drawn from *Ellison v. Brady*, 924 F.2d 872 (9th Cir. 1991).

112. This scenario was developed from the facts in *Vickers v. International Baking Company*, 2000 U.S. Dist. LEXIS 17995 (N.D. Tex. 2000).

6

DISCRIMINATION BASED ON RELIGION, AGE, AND DISABILITY

LEARNING OBJECTIVES

- Identify employment practices that violate Title VII on the basis of religion and national origin.
- Explain what an employer's duty is to reasonably accommodate an employee's religious beliefs.
- Explain the criteria for establishing actionable age discrimination.
- Understand who is protected and what constitutes a "disability" under the Vocational Rehabilitation Act of 1973 and Americans with Disabilities Act of 1990.
- Discuss employers' responsibilities to provide reasonable accommodation to applicants or employees with disabilities.
- Understand privacy and confidentiality requirements imposed on medical information.

OPENING SCENARIO

A woman who was 5′2″ tall and weighed 320 pounds applied for the position of "institutional attendant for the mentally retarded (IA-MR)" at the state Mental Health Retardation Hospital (MHRH).[1] During a pre-employment physical examination, a MHRH nurse noted that the applicant was morbidly obese, but found no limitations to her ability to perform as an IA-MR. Medically, a person is considered morbidly obese when that individual weighs more than twice his or her optimal weight, or is in excess of 100 pounds over his or her optimal weight. Based upon this information, the director of the MHRH rejected the applicant because he felt her obesity might hamper her ability to evacuate patients in the event of an emergency, placed her at a greater risk of developing serious ailments, and could increase the likelihood of the applicant filing a workers' compensation claim.[2]

The applicant filed a complaint that the MHRH had discriminated against her in violation of the Americans with Disabilities Act (ADA). In her complaint, she argued that she had applied for the position of IA-MR. She further contended that she should be protected under the ADA because she had been perceived as being disabled by her prospective employer.

The employer had excluded her from consideration for employment solely because of her perceived disability—being obese. Furthermore, she contended that she was qualified for the position despite her perceived disability based on her two previous tenures in that same position and her previous work record while performing in those positions. The applicant had, in fact, worked in this position on two previous occasions, once for two years and another for four. A review of her personnel files revealed a spotless work record.

The employer contended that the applicant did not have a disability as defined under the ADA, since she was merely overweight.

INTRODUCTION

This chapter examines the remaining classes receiving protection under Title VII (religion and national origin) as well as those protected under the Age Discrimination in Employment Act and the Americans with Disabilities Act. Because the Vocational Rehabilitation Act of 1973, which applies to holders of federal contracts and subcontracts, contains virtually the same language and requirements as the Americans with Disabilities Act, these two statutes will be discussed together.

RELIGION

Compared to complaints from other protected classes, Title VII complaints based upon religious discrimination are quite rare. In fact, it was not until 1996 that charges of religious discrimination exceeded 2 percent of the total charges handled by the Equal Employment Opportunity Commission (EEOC).[3] However, religious discrimination charges have risen steadily since 1997, when they accounted for only 2.1 percent of all Title VII charges. In actual number they have increased from 1,709 in 1997 to 4,151 in 2011, a 143 percent increase and 4.2 percent of all charges.[4]

As the American workforce becomes increasingly diverse, a growing number of religious beliefs will appear in the workplace. In addition to Christians and Jews, employers can expect to find employees who are Muslims, Hindus, and Buddhists (just to name a few). Consequently, **religious accommodations** will become more complex, and complaints can be expected to rise.

Exemptions for Religious Entities

Perhaps one of the reasons that religious discrimination charges occur so infrequently is because the religious exemption under the Civil Rights Act of 1964 permits preferential treatment to *bona fide* religious organizations. Often referred to as the Section 702 exemption because of its location in the original Act, the **religious exemption** states that the prohibition on religious discrimination:

> shall not apply . . . to a religious corporation, association, educational institution, or society with respect to the employment of individuals of a particular religion to perform work connected with the carrying on by such corporation, association, educational institution, or society of its activities.[5]

Figure 6.1   **Religious Exempted Entities Under § 702**

- Religious associations (i.e., National Council of Reformed Churches, etc.)
- Religious corporations (i.e., Presbyterian Church in America, Southern Baptist Convention, Roman Catholic Church, etc.)
- Religious societies (i.e., Knights of Columbus, Reformed University Fellowship, etc.)
- Religious educational institutions (i.e., University of Notre Dame, Emory University, etc.)

In essence, this means religious organizations are permitted to make hiring and discharge decisions based on an applicant's or employee's religious affiliation.

To be eligible for this exemption, the religious corporation, association, education institution, or society activities must show some connection between the position and the religion. If this connection is clearly visible, preferential hiring is permitted; if not, preferential hiring is prohibited (see Figure 6.1).

To illustrate this point, let's examine the case of *Killinger v. Samford University*.[6] In this case, a faculty member was hired to teach courses in religion in the School of Divinity at a Baptist university. After hiring, the faculty member was removed from the Divinity School and relegated to teaching undergraduate classes. The faculty member contended that he was being discriminated against (prohibited from teaching in the Divinity School) because his religious philosophy was incompatible with the fundamentalist theology advanced by the leadership of the Divinity School. The university contended that, as a religious institution, it was covered by Title VII's religious exemption. The Eleventh Circuit agreed with the university by concluding: "The Section 702 exemption's purpose and words easily encompass plaintiff's case; the exemption allows religious institutions to employ only persons whose beliefs are consistent with the employer's when the work is connected with carrying out the institution's activities."[7]

Clearly, religious education is at the core of a religious university, especially in its Divinity School. As a Baptist university, Samford was permitted to lawfully discriminate in favor of Baptists when making teaching assignments. The principal criterion of eligibility for a Section 702 exemption is that the organization must clearly be a religious corporation, association, education institution, or society, and it must exhibit some ministerial function. To establish this, the religious institution's primary duties must consist of teaching, spreading the faith, church governance, supervision of religious order, and participation in religious ritual or worship (see Figure 6.2).[8] It is equally important to show that the institution in question is owned in whole or in substantial part by a particular religion. Moreover, if it can be shown that a particular institution is not owned, supported, or managed by a religious entity, no exemption will be permitted.[9] In short, the organization in question would be viewed by the courts as secular, not religious.

Even if the organization in question is owned by a religious institution, it may not necessarily be eligible for the religious exemption. Any organization that claims to be religious but lacks any religious content will be considered a secular organization and not entitled to the Section 702 exemption.[10]

It is important to note that the Section 702 exemption permits religious institutions to discriminate only on the basis of religion, not gender or race.[11] However, the Title VII ban

Figure 6.2   **Criteria for Establishing a § 702 Exemption**

- Participation in church governance
- Participation in religious ritual
- Participation in worship
- Spreading the faith
- Supervision of religious order
- Teaching

Source: Little v. Wuerl, 929 F.2d 944, 947–48 (3rd Cir. 1991).

on sex discrimination does not apply in cases where a particular religion has theological prohibitions against ordaining women as ministers or priests, or bestowing positions of church leadership. For example, it is a basic tenet of faith that only men can be ordained as priests in the Roman Catholic Church. Therefore, Title VII cannot be used to require the Catholic Church to ordain women on the grounds of sex discrimination in employment. However, in other positions not connected to worship (clerical, janitorial, etc.) discrimination based on sex would be prohibited.

Religious Discrimination

Notwithstanding Section 702's religious exemption, which, as we have seen, permits preferential treatment of members of religious faiths, Section 703 makes it unlawful for secular organizations to otherwise discriminate on the basis of religion.

Here, disparate treatment and disparate impact (discussed in Chapters 3 and 4) are applicable. If an employer that is not a religious organization subjects an employee to poor treatment in the workplace because the employer, or its agent, dislikes the employee's religious beliefs, the employer has violated Title VII.[12] As in any disparate treatment situation, the complaining party establishes a *prima facie* case by proving the employer treated him or her differently from other employees because of the individual's religious beliefs.[13] Unless an applicant's religion can be shown to be a *bona fide* occupational qualification (BFOQ), a secular employer may not discriminate on the basis of religion.[14]

Religious Accommodation

Merely ensuring that an employee's religious beliefs have not affected employment decisions is not enough to avoid charges of religious discrimination. Employers may find themselves in violation of Title VII when they fail to make "reasonable accommodation" for an employee's religious practices.[15] Employers must refrain from considering an individual's religious beliefs in making decisions, and they must make accommodations for those beliefs after employment. The additional requirement to provide such accommodation comes from Section 701 of the Civil Rights Act of 1964. This is not to be confused with Section 703, which prevents discrimination on the basis of religion. Specifically, Section 701 states:

Figure 6.3 **Establishing a *Prima Facie* Case for Religious Accommodation**

- The individual has a *bona fide* belief that compliance with an employment requirement would be contrary to his or her religious beliefs or practice.
- The individual informed the employer of the conflict.
- The individual was disciplined or discharged for failing to comply with the conflicting employment requirement.

Source: Cloutier v. COSTCO Wholesale Corp., 390 F.3d 126, 133 (1st Cir. 2004).

The term "religion" includes all aspects of religious observance and practice, as well as belief, unless an employer demonstrates that he is unable to reasonably accommodate to an employee's or prospective employee's religious observance or practice without undue hardship on the conduct of the employer's business.[16]

Under this concept of religious accommodation, an individual establishes a *prima facie* case of religious discrimination by demonstrating that: (1) the individual has a *bona fide* belief that compliance with an employment requirement would be contrary to his religious beliefs or practice, (2) the individual informed the employer of the conflict, and (3) the individual was disciplined or discharged for failing to comply with the conflicting employment requirement (see Figure 6.3).[17]

Assume that Dave Leroy, a senior machinist, has recently had a religious experience and become a deacon in the First Baptist Church. Due to his recent conversion and position in the church, Dave announces that he will no longer be able to work on Sundays. This would be in keeping with his religious obligation to keep the covenant and keep the Sabbath holy.[18] In June, the plant superintendent informs all employees that they will have to work seven-day shifts for the next two weeks in order to meet a client's deadline. Leroy informs the plant superintendent that working on Sunday conflicts with his religious beliefs. The superintendent tells Leroy that if he is not at his workstation on Sunday, he will be fired. When Leroy fails to show up for work that Sunday, his employment is terminated. This series of events would be sufficient to establish Leroy's Title VII claim.

Types of Accommodation

Common methods of achieving religious accommodation include arranging for a voluntary swap of work schedules among employees, instituting flexible scheduling to allow employees to make up time lost to religious observances, or requiring employees to arrive or depart early to meet religious observances. If swaps or flexible schedule patterns cannot accommodate the employee, a transfer to a comparable job within the company may be in order. In some instances it may be that such accommodation could actually benefit an employer. Assume a delivery company offers seven-days-a-week delivery service. Some Jewish and other employees who may have religious objections to working on their Sabbaths would have little concern about working on Sundays, the Christian Sabbath. Seventh Day Adventists, Worldwide Church of God members, and Jehovah's Witnesses also hold religious tenets against working on Saturdays.

Again, because their Sabbath is a day other than Sunday, they could be scheduled to work for Christian employees on that day. Granted, this may make scheduling a little more difficult, but it can solve an accommodation dilemma. In this regard, having a religiously diverse workforce might be used to some employers' advantage.

Undue Hardship Defense

In its rebuttal, the employer must show that it met its obligation to "reasonably" accommodate the employee's religious beliefs and practices, or that the accommodation would impose an undue hardship on the employer.[19] By proving that the employee's desired accommodation would impose an undue hardship, the accommodation becomes "unreasonable." Religious accommodation, unlike the reasonable accommodation required under the Americans with Disabilities Act, does not require employers to bear more *de minimus* costs.[20] Religious accommodation is not accomplished by merely eliminating the conflict between the dress code and an employee's religious practice. This accommodation is only reasonable "provided eliminating the conflict would not impose an undue hardship."[21] What is problematic for employers is that the determination of what is or is not a reasonable religious accommodation is handled on a case-by-case basis.[22] This of course means that often the only means for resolving the reasonableness of an accommodation is through litigation.

An accommodation requiring a business employing 17 employees to hire an additional part-time employee to cover missed work due to another employee's religious observance would, most likely, be considered as imposing an undue hardship. The same requirement for a business employing 250 employees might not. Possible reasons for rejecting the requested accommodation include that it diminishes efficiency in other jobs,[23] infringes on other employees' job rights under company policies or collective bargaining agreements,[24] impairs workplace safety, or places coworkers at a greater risk.[25]

There are some circumstances under which accommodations are more likely to be judged as unduly burdensome. Normally, an accommodation becomes an undue hardship if it results in changing a *bona fide* seniority system. This occurs when, in order to accommodate the employee's religious practices, the employer must deny another employee a shift preference guaranteed by the company's seniority system.

Interestingly, even accommodations involving work schedules can quickly cross the line into undue hardship. Returning to the scenario above involving Dave Leroy, Leroy's employer could prove that accommodating his absence for religious observance would require hiring another machinist; recall that *all* employees were required to work two seven-day weeks, so this would preclude shift changes. The employer could probably establish that accommodating Leroy would cause an undue hardship, since it would involve the expense of hiring an additional employee, either permanently or temporarily.

It should be noted that employers cannot base undue hardship on theoretical fears of loss in efficiency or additional costs, but must present evidence of identifiable losses. Germane to this discussion, an employer erroneously believed that if it allowed an employee to wear a head covering at work during Ramadan, the employer could no longer enforce its uniform policy with respect to other employees. Here the employer failed to demonstrate an actual undue hardship; it merely showed that its employment decision was based on the fear that allowing the accommodation would open "the floodgates to others violating the uniform policy."[26]

The Accommodation Does Not Have to be Acceptable to an Employee

The issue of whether or not the employer's proposed accommodation is reasonable does not hinge on the employee's acceptance or approval. The complaining party cannot reject an accommodation as unreasonable merely on the grounds that it was not one that the employee desired.[27]

Neither can it be rejected because the employer did not provide the employee a choice of alternatives. There is nothing in section 701 of Title VII that requires the employer to offer the employee several accommodations from which he or she may select the one that they find most acceptable.[28] Correspondingly, the employer is not under any compulsion to accept the employee's recommended accommodation, nor is the employer required to demonstrate that the employee's rejected preferred accommodation would create an undue burden.[29] When the employer has reasonably accommodated the employee's religious needs, the statutory obligation has been met.[30]

If an accommodation is requested by an employee or applicant, the employer's only defense is that the requested accommodation would create an undue hardship.[31] Failure to do so will result in a Title VII violation, as will be discussed in the next section.

Dress and Appearance Policies

Employers often assert their right to require employees who come into contact with customers and the general public to adhere to certain grooming, hygiene, and appearance expectations. This is typically done through a clearly delineated dress code or appearance policy. Employers are aware of the importance of employee appearance to the image of their respective businesses and organizations.[32] Many employers believe that it is their prerogative to require their employees to meet minimum grooming standards, especially those employees who project the organization's image to its customers. Marketing theory has long contended that favorable customer impressions affect business outcomes.[33] Those impressions could be particularly shaped by interactions with employees who deal directly with the public (especially "potential" customers). Therefore, it is reasonable to conclude that requiring employees to conform to accepted societal expectations of dress and behavior serves the legitimate business purposes of promoting an orderly workplace and making customers comfortable.

Some federal courts have found these concerns legitimate. The District of Columbia Circuit noted in *Fagan v. National Cash Register Company* that:

> Perhaps no facet of business is more important than a company's place in public estimation. That the image created by its employees dealing with the public when on

company assignment affects its relations is so well known that we may take judicial notice of an employer's proper desire to achieve favorable acceptance.[34]

But, what if employees object to dress code regulations? Not surprisingly, employer dress and appearance standards have been challenged as contrary to employees' civil rights under Title VII of the Civil Rights Act of 1964. They are usually challenged on the standpoint that they result in disparate treatment either on the basis of religion or sex. Under religion, some employees are likely to make requests for exceptions or modifications to the employer's appearance rules in order to accommodate the employee's religious obligations.[35] For example, a Muslim female may request to wear a *hijab* as part of her religious practice,[36] or an American Indian may request exception to a hair length policy as a result of his religious practice.[37]

Federal courts have concluded that an undue hardship is established where there are identifiable costs incurred (considered in relation to the size and operating costs of the employer).[38] Whether the proposed accommodation conflicts with another law will also be considered,[39] particularly workplace safety laws. As an example, a Sikh machinist's beard (a requirement of his religious tradition) precludes his ability to wear a respirator in a job which required exposure to toxic gas. Because the beard prevents the respirator from sealing properly, his safety and health are endangered.[40]

In an instance not involving workplace safety, a female employee cashier who had direct contact with customers claimed that her body piercings were religiously significant. The company's appearance policy forbade body piercing for employees whose jobs required direct contact with customers. She was told by management to cover body piercings with flesh colored band aids when working at her cash register. She filed a lawsuit claiming the employer had failed to adequately accommodate her religious beliefs. However, the court concluded that "The temporary covering of plaintiff's facial piercings during work hours impinges on plaintiff's religious scruples no more than the wearing of a blouse which covers the plaintiff's tattoos."[41]

Implications for Employers

Employers are aware of the importance that employee appearance has on the image of their particular businesses, but there is an increasing likelihood of having appearance policies and dress codes challenged as religious discrimination. There is a balancing act that must be performed at this point.

If such policies are to be continued, the employer must be prepared to demonstrate that the appearance expectations should first be justified as serving some legitimate business purpose. These reasons must be articulated and communicated to the employees. In those cases where appearance of an applicant affects a hiring decision, it may even become necessary to empirically validate the selection criterion (appearance) with consumer and market research.[42]

Second, the appearance standard should not impose greater requirements on religious clothing and appearance than on the other individuals in other classes. Are African Americans exempted from the policy that male employees are to be clean-shaven and permitted to wear beards if they have pseudo *folliculitis barbae* (a medical reason), while Muslims are denied the same privilege for religious reasons?[43]

Once implemented, is the policy consistently enforced? Selective or haphazard enforcement invariably leads to complaints, especially if enforcement affects one group more than the other. A policy should be flexible enough to make reasonable accommodations for an employee's *bona fide* religious beliefs. It is recommended that employees seeking an exemption from the policy on religious grounds do so in writing. And if denied, a legitimate business reason should be offered for denying the request and evidence should be retained that the employee understands the reason for the policy (i.e., promoting a safe working environment, maintaining a positive public image, complying with health standards, etc.). Again, consistent enforcement indicates that the proffered reason for denying the request for accommodation is legitimate and is not a pretext to hide a discriminatory animosity toward a particular religious group.[44]

Because of the risk of potential litigation, if an appearance policy is not a component in the performance of the job, perhaps it should be avoided. To illustrate, there is hardly need for an employee appearance standard in an interstate trucking company beyond basic safety considerations. On the other hand, it can be argued that in instances where corporate image is a concern, such as a package delivery company, an employer has the right to expect employees on his or her payroll to project that image. Therefore, appearance and grooming standards should be justified and this justification communicated to all affected employees, especially for those employees responsible for making customer contact. Since appearance expectations may be as important to portraying the company to outside constituencies as polite and professional behavior, employees should be informed that appearance is to be treated as any other performance dimension for evaluation purposes.

Religious Accommodations and Union Dues

One final issue under religious accommodation is the payment of union dues. This issue not only affects unions but might also involve employers who are responsible under their collective bargaining agreements to deduct union dues from the payroll. If an employee's religious faith prohibits joining or paying dues to any organization outside of the church, can they still be required to pay the equivalent of dues to the union that represents them in the bargaining unit?

This situation occurred in *Tooley v. Martin Marietta Corp.*[45] Martin Marietta Corporation and the United Steelworkers of America had negotiated a collective bargaining agreement containing a union shop provision. Under such an arrangement, the company was obligated to discharge any employee who failed to join the union and pay union dues. Three of the employees who were Seventh Day Adventists refused to join the union. They contended that their religion prohibited them from becoming members of or paying a service fee to a union. In an attempt to achieve a compromise, the three workers offered to contribute an amount equivalent to union dues to a mutually agreed-upon charity. The union refused and held the employer to the union shop clause in the collective bargaining agreement, saying the three employees would have to join the union and pay dues or the employer would have to terminate their employment. If the employer failed to do so, it would be in violation of the collective bargaining agreement, and it would be an unfair labor practice under the National Labor Relations Act.[46]

The affected employees argued that both the union and the company were required under Title VII to make reasonable accommodations for their religious beliefs,[47] unless it caused undue hardship. The Steelworkers responded that it did create an undue hardship and was, therefore, not a reasonable accommodation.

This argument focused on the contention that substituting a charitable contribution in lieu of dues created an undue hardship on the union by denying it the funds necessary for the union's operations. The union further argued that the charity accommodation was unreasonable because it was contrary to the National Labor Relations Act's authorization of union shop agreements.

The Court concluded that Title VII was applicable in this case and that both the union and the company were obligated to make a reasonable accommodation. The Court also found that substituting a contribution to a mutually agreed-upon charity was not an undue hardship. Thus, the Court enjoined the union and the company from discharging the plaintiffs for failing to pay union dues so long as they made equivalent contributions to the mutually acceptable charity.

AGE DISCRIMINATION IN EMPLOYMENT

The Age Discrimination in Employment Act (ADEA), like the Equal Pay Act, is not an amendment to the Civil Rights Act of 1964 but an amendment to the Fair Labor Standards Act of 1938.[48] This is an important distinction because the remedies for ADEA violations are not the same as those afforded under Title VII.

The next thing that managers need to know about the ADEA is that it has resulted in one of the fastest-growing equal employment complaints. This is due in large part to the fact that the baby boomer generation is aging and constitutes a significant portion of the workforce. By 2011, age discrimination claims accounted for 23.5 percent of all charges handled by the EEOC.[49]

Additionally, there are variations as to which employers are required to comply with the ADEA's antidiscrimination provisions. Under the ADEA, the term "employer" means a person who is engaged in an industry affecting commerce and has twenty or more employees for each working day in each of twenty or more calendar weeks in the current or preceding calendar year.[50] Compare this to Title VII's application to employers with *fifteen or more* employees.[51]

The ADEA of 1967 makes it unlawful to: "fail or refuse to hire or to discharge any individual or otherwise discriminate against any individual with respect to his compensation, terms, conditions, or privileges of employment, because of such individual's age." Further, it is unlawful for an employer to even segregate or classify employees on the basis of age.[52] However, the prohibitions on age discrimination are limited to individuals

Figure 6.4 Legitimate Nondiscriminatory Factors under the ADEA

- Education
- Experience
- Output
- Productivity

who are at least forty years of age.[53] Initially, this protection on the basis of age covered only individuals who were between forty and sixty-five years old.[54] The upper limit was extended to seventy years by a 1978 amendment.[55] As of a 1986 amendment, ADEA discrimination on the basis of age encompasses all employees and applicants who are over forty; there is no upper age limit.[56]

The ADEA's ban on age discrimination means that should an employer refuse to hire an applicant for a job based solely on the premise that the employer thinks the individual is too old for the job, that employer violates the ADEA. If an employee is not promoted because the employer feels that she is too old to perform the work at the next level, the ADEA is violated. If, during a downsizing, an employer decides to lay off all employees over fifty years old, the ADEA is violated.

Like Title VII, the ADEA mandates that employment decisions must be based on factors other than the employee's age. And, like Title VII, the ADEA is not automatically violated every time an over-forty employee is not promoted or is terminated. If the employment decision is based on legitimate reasons other than age, no unlawful discrimination has occurred (see Figure 6.4).

However, if the employee's age *was* a consideration in the employment decision, the whole process is tainted, since the ADEA requires employers to evaluate employees on their merits, not their age.[57]

Establishing a *Prima Facie* Case of Age Discrimination

To establish a *prima facie* case of unlawful discrimination under the ADEA, it must be proved that:

1. The complaining party was in an age group protected by the ADEA.
2. He or she was discharged or demoted (or refused employment).
3. At the time of the discharge or demotion, the complaining party was performing his or her job at a level that met his or her employer's legitimate expectations.
4. Following the complaining party's discharge, he or she was replaced by someone of comparable qualifications who is significantly younger.[58]

The fourth proof, replacement by someone who is "significantly younger," is a relatively recent innovation. Prior to 1996, it was assumed the ADEA would be violated only when the over-forty employee (the protected class under the ADEA) was replaced by someone under forty years old. However, with the Supreme Court's decision in *O'Connor v. Consolidated Coin Caterers, Corp.*,[59] the ADEA may be violated if an older employee is replaced by an over-forty employee who is significantly younger. In the *O'Connor* case, a fifty-six-year-old employee with twelve years of service in the company was discharged and replaced with a forty-year-old employee. The employer contended that since the forty-year-old employee was also a member of the same protected class (forty years old and older), the ADEA was not violated. The Supreme Court concluded, however, that "[t]he fact that one person in the protected class has lost out to another person in the protected class is thus irrelevant, so long as he has lost out because of his age."[60] The purpose of the ADEA is quite clear: an employee's (or applicant's) age cannot be used in making any employment decision.

No Mixed Motive Under Age Discrimination

It should be noted at this juncture that, unlike Title VII, there is no mixed-motive discrimination under the ADEA. In its 2009 decision, *Gross v. FBL Financial Services, Inc.,*[61] the Supreme Court ruled that ADEA does not provide that a complaining party can establish an age discrimination claim by showing that age was simply a motivating factor (mixed motive). The complaining party must prove by a preponderance of the evidence that age was the reason that the employer decided to take the employment action in question. The ADEA does not require the burden of persuasion to shift to the employer to show that it would have taken the action regardless of age, even when a complaining party has produced some evidence that age was one motivating factor in that decision.[62]

The Employer's Rebuttal

An employer confronting an alleged ADEA violation must demonstrate convincingly that the employment decision is based on a legitimate reason, which means the employer has the burden of convincing the court that its decision was *not* based on the individual's age. If the contested matter involves promotion, the employer must demonstrate that the younger candidate was more qualified. In all cases, there must be a clear connection between the decision criteria and the job in question. This becomes particularly troublesome for the employer because the ADEA permits jury trials for all violations.[63] Remember, under Title VII, trials by a jury are also allowed, but only when a complaining party seeks compensatory or punitive damages.[64] Under the ADEA, jury trials may be requested for any violation.

For the HR staff, this means guaranteeing that education requirements, performance expectations, seniority requirements, and other skill and knowledge requirements have been clearly identified for the position in question. It is equally important to communicate these position requirements to all potential applicants before the selection process even begins. All position announcements should clearly and concisely state all of the required qualifications a successful candidate must possess. This precaution is intended to reduce unrealistic expectations among potential applicants who do not possess the necessary requirements. As always, position requirements and qualifications must be directly related to successful job performance. Consequently, it is imperative that proper job analysis has been conducted on the job in question and the criteria have been validated (see Chapter 14). As with other equal employment opportunity (EEO) matters, the presence of nonessential job requirements unnecessarily exposes an employer to litigation and undermines the organization's rebuttal in court.

In instances where the employer can prove the position was given to the more qualified candidate, the ADEA is not violated. This is a legitimate nondiscriminatory reason because the individual's qualifications determined the employment outcome, not the individual's age.

Age as a BFOQ

Some *bona fide* occupational qualifications (BFOQs) permit employers to use age as a disqualifier, but as with most BFOQs, they are very rare. In *Western Airlines v. Criswell*,[65] the Supreme Court examined an employment practice that imposed a mandatory retirement age of sixty on all flight crew members (pilots, copilots, and flight engineers). The airline's argument for the mandatory retirement was that after the age of sixty, medical research indicated that physical and mental capabilities are prone to "sudden or subtle incapacitation."[66] To strengthen its arguments, the airline cited Federal Aviation Administration regulations that prohibited any individual who had reached the age of sixty from serving as a pilot or copilot on any commercial flight.

The airline adopted this policy and merely added flight engineers. The employer contended that its mandatory retirement of flight crews was a BFOQ reasonably necessary to the safe operation of the airline. Remember, as with all BFOQs, it must be proved that the age-biased BFOQ is "reasonably necessary" for normal business operation and that the "reasonable necessity" is narrowly defined.[67]

The complaining parties provided evidence that the process of psychological and physiological deterioration caused by aging varies greatly with each individual.[68] Not surprisingly, there is evidence showing that some older workers can perform at levels equal to or even better than younger coworkers. The complaining parties argued that mandatory retirement ignores individual differences. The airline, they further argued, should determine mandatory retirements on a case-by-case basis rather than on an arbitrary age ceiling. After all, the ADEA compels employers to evaluate their employees who are forty years or older on their merits and not their age.[69] The flight engineers and several pilots who wanted to become flight engineers also pointed out that in emergency situations, the flight engineer's duties are less critical to passenger safety than the pilot's. The complaining parties then argued that Western Airlines' BFOQ defense for flight engineers was insufficient to justify its legitimate concern for passenger safety.[70]

In its ruling, the Supreme Court concluded the BFOQ exception was meant to be an *extremely* narrow exception to any general prohibition of age discrimination under the ADEA.[71] In essence, the airline had failed to show that all, or substantially all, of its flight engineers over sixty were unable to safely perform their duties. The mandatory retirement age for flight engineers (not pilots or copilots) thus violated the ADEA.

The Complaining Party's Rebuttal

If the employer offers a seemingly legitimate BFOQ, the complaining party may still win the case, provided that he or she can prove the employer's legitimate business reasons are a pretext. If the HR staff has done its job properly, this likelihood is greatly reduced. Again, good job analysis and documentation are critical.

ADEA AND DISPARATE IMPACT

As previously mentioned in Chapter 4, there was a time when the only claim under the ADEA permitted in some circuits was disparate treatment.[72] However, this changed in 2005 when the Supreme Court ruled in *Smith v. City of Jackson* that individuals can establish an actionable case of age discrimination by showing that certain facially neutral practices have the effect of excluding older employees/applicants (those forty years or older) at a disproportionately higher number than under-forty applicants.[73] The major difference between a disparate impact case under the ADEA and one under Title VII is the employer's rebuttal. Under Title VII the employer must usually show that the practice causing the adverse impact is a business necessity/job-related. This entails validation.

However, there is no employer requirement to demonstrate business necessity under the ADEA as there is under Title VII. In cases involving disparate impact because of age, the employer has only to demonstrate that the practice creating the adverse impact is not predicated on age[74]—in effect, this is a legitimate nondiscriminatory reason defense. The method of establishing the *prima facie* case under the ADEA law is the same as it is under Title VII.

Remedies for ADEA Violations

The ADEA is not an amendment to the Civil Rights Act of 1964; therefore the ADEA remedies available to a complaining party who proves age discrimination are limited to reinstatement, back pay, front pay, promotion, and/or attorneys' fees.[75] In the event that willful age discrimination has occurred, the ADEA provides for liquidated damages as well.[76]

No Protection for Those Under Forty

In its 2005 decision, *General Dynamics Land Systems, Inc. v. Cline,*[77] the Supreme Court was confronted with a case in which younger employees, those under forty years of age, claimed that the ADEA protected them from "reverse age discrimination."[78] The Court concluded that the language of the ADEA clearly establishes those who are qualified and forty years or older to be the protected class, and went on to say, "the statute [ADEA] does not mean to stop an employer from favoring an older employee over a younger one."[79] The ADEA makes it unlawful to discriminate against an individual because he or she is forty years or older; it has no such prohibition for those who are younger than forty.

PROTECTING WORKERS WITH DISABILITIES

The first law to provide federal protection for applicants and workers with disabilities was the Vocational Rehabilitation Act of 1973 (VRA).[80] This is a fairly narrow statute in that it applies only to those employers who: (1) hold a federal contract or subcontract in excess of $2,500, (2) are a depository of federal funds, and (3) receive federal grants or aid assistance.[81] Employers who did not meet these conditions had no obligations concerning employees with disabilities until the Americans with Disabilities Act of 1990 (ADA) was enacted. The VRA provided the foundation from which the ADA would arise.

When the VRA was first enacted, its definition of a *qualified handicapped* person[82] was the same as that of a *qualified individual with a disability* under the ADA.[83] Additionally, the definitions for *reasonable accommodation*, *undue hardship*, *physical or mental impairment*, *major life activities*, and *handicap/disability* in the two acts are virtually identical. To know the provisions of one of these statutes is to understand the provisions of the other. To alleviate this redundancy, the Vocational Rehabilitation Act Amendment of 1992[84] changed the term *handicapped person* to *individual with a disability* and the term *handicapped* to *disability*. Now, the two laws are almost indistinguishable, and because of these marked similarities, our discussion will focus on the ADA. The major difference between the two acts is that the VRA requires employers who hold federal contracts or subcontracts in excess of $10,000 to take affirmative action in hiring qualified individuals with a disability.[85] Beyond this affirmative action requirement, the VRA and the ADA are identical in their employment discrimination provisions.

Americans with Disabilities Act

The ADA was passed by Congress and signed into law by President George H.W. Bush on July 26, 1990. The major objectives of the law are to prevent employment discrimination against a qualified individual on the basis of a real or perceived disability (Title I), prohibit discrimination against individuals with disabilities in public transportation (Title II), and provide for public accommodation and access for persons with a disability (Title III). It is Title I's prohibition against discrimination in the terms and conditions of employment because of an individual's disability that is of particular concern to us. Perhaps the most important thing to remember is that Title I protects only *qualified individuals* with a disability from employment discrimination. It does not protect unqualified individuals with a disability any more than the other EEO laws protect unqualified individuals. It is, therefore, critical for HR professionals to understand when an individual is qualified and when he or she is not. In examining this issue, the HR professional must understand who is required to comply with the Act, who is disabled, and who is qualified.

Covered Entities

The ADA applies to all private sector employers with fifteen or more employees. It applies to all employment agencies regardless of whether they are public or private. Labor unions with fifteen or more members must comply with the ADA, as must all state and local governments. Even joint labor/management committees on apprenticeship are required to follow the provisions of the ADA's Title I. You may have already noticed that the same employers who are covered under Title VII of the Civil Rights Act of 1964 must also comply with Title I of the ADA.

Under the ADA, no covered entity shall discriminate against a qualified individual with a disability because of such individual's disability with regard to job application procedures; the hiring, advancement, or discharge of employees; employee compensation; job training; and other terms, conditions, and privileges of employment.[86]

Although the ADA is very similar to Title VII and the ADEA, there is one significant difference. Under Title VII, the protected classes are fairly easy to identify. Gender is easy to establish: the complaining party is either male or female. Race and ethnicity also can be readily established. Age under the ADEA, likewise, can easily be verified through a number of legal documents (i.e., birth certificates, medical records, etc.). All of these classifications possess an "all or nothing" nature. You are either female or you are not. You are either Hispanic or you are not. You are either over forty years of age or you are not. Disability, however, occurs in degrees. An individual may fall anywhere on the scale from marginally disabled to completely disabled. The extent to which an individual is disabled often determines whether or not he or she is *qualified* to perform a particular job in question and the length to which employers must go to accommodate the individual. The ADA adds further confusion through its definition of *disability*.

Who Is Disabled?

When assessing whether an individual candidate or employee is protected under the ADA, a two-part standard must be met. In achieving this end, two questions must be answered: is the applicant disabled, and is the individual qualified? From the ADA's inception, some critics have contended that it casts an overly broad net on this matter.[87] Under the ADA (and VRA), the term **disability** means a physical or mental impairment that substantially limits one or more of the major life activities of an individual, a record of such impairment, or regarding an individual as having such an impairment. This means that those who currently are disabled are protected under the ADA. Additionally, those who were disabled but have since recovered or have been rehabilitated are covered. Surprisingly, applicants or employees who are not now, nor have they ever been, afflicted with a mental or physical disability covered under the ADA may still be protected if the employer *thought* they had a disability and discriminated against them because of the imagined disability. As strange as this may sound, an employer can violate the ADA by erroneously assuming that a nondisabled individual is disabled.

This situation occurred in the opening scenario. The director of the MHRH rejected the applicant because he *assumed* she could not perform some of the essential job functions (i.e., patient evacuation). It was merely his *perception* that she would not be able to evacuate her patients in a timely manner and that she was a workers' compensation risk. He could offer no basis in fact for this presumption.

Figure 6.5   Major Life Activities Under EEOC Regulations

1. Caring for one's self
2. Performing manual tasks
3. Seeing
4. Hearing
5. Eating
6. Sleeping
7. Walking
8. Standing
9. Sitting
10. Reaching
11. Lifting
12. Bending
13. Speaking
14. Breathing
15. Learning
16. Reading
17. Concentrating
18. Thinking
19. Communicating
20. Interacting with Others
21. Working

Source: U.S. EEOC, *Regulations to Implement the Equal Employment Opportunity Provisions of the Americans with Disabilities Act*, 29 C.F.R. § 1630.2(i).

Figure 6.6   Body Systems Whose Dysfunction Constitutes Physical Impairment Under the ADA

Bladder
Bowel
Brain
Cardiovascular
Circulatory
Digestive
Endocrine
Genito-urinary
Hemic and lymphatic
Immune system
Neurological
Normal cell growth
Reproductive
Respiratory
Skin
Special sense organs
Speech organs

Source: Americans with Disabilities Amendment Act of 2008, 29 C.F.R. § 1630.3(h).

An employer runs the risk of triggering an ADA claim any time an employment decision is based on an individual's perceived disability. In one case, an employer refused to hire an applicant for the position of electrician because a drug test indicated his blood sugar was high and the employer assumed he was diabetic.

The employer's action was based on the assumption that the applicant had an impairment that would substantially restrict his ability to perform the essential functions of the job. However, this was a false assumption, and the applicant, who was not disabled as defined under the ADA, was able to perform all the essential functions of an electrician. Because the employer perceived the applicant to be disabled and based the decision not to hire him on that perception, the employer violated the ADA.[88]

The meaning of *disability* under the ADA entails having a physical or mental impairment that substantially limits one or more of the *major life activities*. Unless we know what these major life activities are, this definition is not going to be very helpful. The EEOC, the agency responsible for enforcing the ADA, defines **major life activities** as caring for oneself, performing manual tasks, and so forth (see Figure 6.5).[89] As for *physical impairment*, this can be any physiological condition, disfigurement, or loss of one of seventeen body systems (see Figure 6.6).

Figure 6.7   **Major Life Functions as Expanded under the ADAA**

Old Standards	New Standards
Breathing	Bending
Caring for one's self	Breathing
Hearing	Caring for oneself
Learning	Communicating
Performing manual tasks	Concentrating
Seeing	Eating
Speaking	Hearing
Walking	Learning
Working	Lifting
	Performing manual tasks
	Reading
	Seeing
	Sleeping
	Speaking
	Standing
	Thinking
	Walking
	Working

Source: The Americans with Disabilities Amendment Act of 2008, 42 U.S.C. § 12102(2)(A) (2012).

Mental impairment encompasses any mental or psychological disorder that results in mental retardation, organic brain syndrome, emotional illness, mental illness, or specific learning disabilities. These are very broad areas and encompass an extremely wide range of conditions.

The Americans with Disabilities Amendment Act of 2008

The Americans with Disabilities Amendment Act (ADAA) was signed into law by President George W. Bush on September 25, 2008, and became effective on January 1, 2009. The ADAA expanded the number and scope of *limitations on major life activities* that could constitute a disability. Previously, there had been only nine limitations on major life activities, there are now eighteen (see Figure 6.7).[90] It should be further noted that the EEOC has added interacting with others, reaching, and sitting, to the list of limitations in their regulations (see Figure 6.5 above).

Additionally, the ADAA lowers the bar for establishing a disability, as well as eliminating the consideration of mitigating measures in making disability determinations. For example, an employee who suffered from epilepsy that was in remission due to medication was previously not considered to be disabled, because the medication mitigated the condition.[91] Under the new amendments, mitigated conditions like epilepsy, diabetes, and high blood pressure would now constitute disabilities under the ADAA. This is to say that they could be used to establish the first part of the two-part standard previously mentioned, "Is the applicant disabled?" However, the ADAA does note that wearing ordinary glasses or contact lens would mitigate an individual's disability. An individual with diabetes, even though it is controlled by insulin, would meet the requirements as an individual with a disability, while an individual with 20/80 vision, corrected to 20/20 with glasses, would not.[92]

Qualified Individual with a Disability

If you have at least a general idea of what qualifies as a disability, then it is easier to determine that any person who has a physical or mental impairment based on these criteria would be an "individual with a disability." In employment situations, the ADA does not protect "individuals with a disability." It only protects "*qualified* individuals with a disability."[93] The next step is to ascertain when a candidate with a disability is qualified.

A **qualified individual with a disability** is one who can perform the essential functions of the job in question with reasonable accommodation; therefore the principal concern is whether or not an individual with a disability can perform the essential functions of a particular job with or without reasonable accommodation.[94]

The essential functions, according to the EEOC, can be ascertained by examining three criteria.[95] First, a function is essential if the position in question exists for the purpose of performing that function. For example, driving a truck is the purpose of the job position of long-distance truck driver. Therefore, this is the essential function of that job. The next issue deals with the number of other employees available to perform the function or among whom the performance of the function can be distributed. If a task associated with the job can be assigned to another employee without disrupting the primary purpose of the job in question, that task would not be essential. Suppose one of the duties of a long-distance truck driver included changing the motor oil every 3,000 miles. Since this task could easily be assigned to company maintenance personnel, it would not be an essential function. However, driving the truck safely from destination to destination could not be assigned to another employee—it would be an essential function. The final factor considered by the EEOC involves the degree or skill required to perform the function. Returning to our previous example, changing oil requires little skill and expertise compared to actually driving, maneuvering, and backing up a tractor trailer. The more skill required to perform a task, the more difficult it is to assign to an employee in a different job category. Additionally, requisite expertise makes the task more essential to the job in question.

All of this means that basic job analysis for each position in an organization is absolutely critical. It further means that job analysis, and the resulting job descriptions and job specifications, must be continually monitored and reviewed to ensure they provide *current* and *accurate* information about each specific job. If the essential tasks, duties, and responsibilities associated with any given job are flawed, it is unlikely that reasonable accommodation can be ascertained. This is why job analysis is so critical when dealing with ADA accommodations (see Chapter 14).

Having clearly established what the essential functions of the job are, the HR professional can then concentrate on the individual's qualifications. If the candidate can presently perform the essential functions without any assistance from the employer, that candidate is a qualified individual with a disability. To deny such an individual employment based on a physical disability (when he or she has previously proved able to perform the essential job tasks) would be an obvious violation of Title I of the ADA.

Had the director of the MHRH in the opening scenario tested the applicant's ability to evacuate patients (an essential job function), there might have been a different outcome. She could have been tested by participating in a fire drill involving real patients. If the applicant could not adequately evacuate her patients within a prescribed time frame (determined by job analysis and local fire codes), she would be unqualified for the position in question. Since the ADA protects only "qualified" individuals with a disability (either real or perceived), the applicant would lack cause to file under the ADA.

Interestingly, not all candidates can demonstrate work performance so clearly. Some candidates may require reasonable accommodation.

Reasonable Accommodation

Reasonable accommodation refers to modifications that would permit the individual with a disability to perform the essential functions of the job in question, provided these modifications do not create an undue hardship for the employer. The first thing a manager or HR professional should do when any individual requests reasonable accommodation under the ADA is to clarify the individual's degree of impairment. The actual physical or mental impairment must "substantially limit" a major life activity. Since the enactment of the ADAA in 2008, any determination as to whether an individual is "substantially limited" in performing a major life activity must consider the individual's impairment as compared to most people in the general population.[96] This a very low bar, and many impairments, such as diabetes, are still considered to be disabilities even when ameliorated with medication. However, not every impairment will constitute a disability within the meaning of the Act.[97] For example, if a person with astigmatism (the inability of the eyes to focus properly) can function perfectly normally as long as she wears corrective lens (contact lens or eyeglasses), she would not be considered to have a disability under the ADA.[98] While she is wearing her glasses, her major life activities are not "substantially limited." On the other hand, an employee who was confined to a wheelchair, even though he is capable of mobility, would not be capable of the same mobility of a person without disabilities. He would meet the ADA's requirement for "disability" because he would be "substantially limited" in his ability to walk. The one employee's corrective measures (eyeglasses) overcame her limitations in performing daily activities in light of the general population; hence, she would not have met the ADA's definition of being "disabled."[99]

In the case of a person who is paraplegic, he is limited in his ability to go about his daily activities despite his corrective measure, the wheelchair. His mobility is improved by the wheelchair, but it is still short of that of a nonparaplegic.

Managers and HR professionals must always remember that assessment of whether or not an individual is disabled under the ADA must be done on an individualized basis. Also, remember that the final determination of whether an individual has a disability is not necessarily based on a diagnosis of the individual's impairment, but on whether if the impairment is corrected, it still substantially limits a major life activity.[100]

Once it is determined an applicant or employee is considered disabled under the ADA, the decision maker may now move to the next question: Can the individual perform the essential job functions with or without reasonable accommodation? Again, if the individual can perform the essential job functions without any accommodation, he or she is qualified. If not, what is the appropriate reasonable accommodation that would permit performance of these functions?

In determining reasonable accommodation, the employer might ask the individual for reasonable documentation about the disability and functional limitations. But employers should be careful. The ADA prohibits the employer from requesting medical information that is not pertinent to the accommodation.[101] This usually precludes employers from requesting complete medical records on the individual in question, because such records would include a good deal of information not related to the accommodation.[102] The EEOC recommends that when requesting medical information, employers should specify what types of information they need regarding the disability and the functional limitations it imposes. Remember, once this information is obtained, the employer is responsible for keeping it confidential.

Making accommodations under the ADA is far more complex and complicated than religious accommodation under Title VII. The EEOC has developed three categories of "reasonable accommodation" under the ADA. Under the EEOC's guidance, when attempting to accommodate an applicant or employee, an employer should consider modifying the job application process, modifying the work environment, or modifying the benefits and privileges of employment.[103]

Modifying the Job Application Process

Modifying the job application process entails avoiding anything in the selection process that could be construed as discriminating against applicants because of disability. First and foremost, an employer cannot ask an applicant if he or she has a disability. In fact, the EEOC contends that an employer may not even ask an applicant if he or she needs reasonable accommodation before a conditional job offer is made.[104] The only exception to this is under circumstances in which the applicant's disability is apparent, or the applicant has voluntarily disclosed information about his or her disability. In most instances, the employer is permitted to inquire if reasonable accommodation is necessary only after an offer of employment has been made.

Employers may also be required to modify tests or testing methods to accommodate applicants. A deaf applicant might require a sign language interpreter for an interview. An applicant with attention deficit disorder may require someone to read a written examination.

If the accommodation requested by the applicant causes the employer an *undue hardship*, the applicant would not be a *qualified individual with a disability*. The accommodation would not be reasonable, and the employer would not be compelled to hire the applicant. For example, a person who is paraplegic applies for the position of truck driver at a small delivery company. But technology is not available that would permit the applicant to perform the essential functions of the job. Therefore the accommodation needed would indeed cause undue hardship.

Modifying the Work Environment

In the second category of accommodation—physical modifications to the work environment—a number of actions may be taken. First, the employer's existing workplace can be made more accessible. This includes reconfiguring work areas to make them wheelchair accessible.

Physical modifications may require manuals and work procedures to be provided in Braille. Making other physical modifications to work areas might be as simple as lowering a worktable so it can be reached by an employee in a wheelchair. But it could also be as elaborate as acquiring a state-of-the-art TTY keyboard telephone system to allow a deaf and mute employee to make and receive telephone calls.[105]

Another work environment accommodation is *job restructuring*. This involves identifying the essential job functions (see Chapter 14) and eliminating or reassigning nonessential job functions that the disabled employee cannot perform. A paraplegic secretary confined to a wheelchair has the job description in Figure 6.8. Noting that it accounts for only 2 percent of her job, assume that she is expected to stock printer paper in the supply room. Although the door is sufficiently wide to allow her easy entry and exit from the supply room, boxes of copy paper weigh 25 pounds each and must be stored on shelves that are as high as 6 feet from the floor. The employer could lower the shelves (and double the size of the storage area), or this one aspect of the job could be assigned to another employee. Since the stocking duties are a marginal portion of the secretary's duties, assigning these tasks to another employee would be the more reasonable action to take.

Often, permitting an employee to work in a *flexible or part-time schedule* would be sufficient accommodation. This is particularly effective for those employees who have become disabled since hiring.

Suppose an employee requests that her workday be reduced to six hours per day to allow her to attend physical therapy sessions in the afternoon. Usually, the employer would be required to adjust the employee's schedule, if it does not significantly disrupt the employer's operations (cause undue hardship).

Modifying the Benefits and Privileges of Employment

When job restructuring, workplace modification, and flexible scheduling will not accommodate the employee with a disability, the employer may want to consider reassignment.

It is important to note that the employer is not required to create a position for the employee. The employer is only required to consider reassignment to a vacant position for which the employee is qualified. In addition, the employer is not required to promote the employee to a higher position. Under most circumstances, the employee must be

Figure 6.8   **Job Description for a Word-Processing Secretary**

JOB DESCRIPTION

Job Title: Word-Processing Secretary
Department: Administrative Services
Position of Immediate Supervisor: Director of Administrative Services

I. GENERAL SUMMARY OF RESPONSIBILITIES

Types, edits, and distributes various correspondence to clients and internal staff.
Transmits and proofs various essential status reports for day-to-day operations.

II. SPECIFIC DUTIES AND RESPONSIBILITIES

1. Types daily correspondence and reports (50%)
2. Proofs and prints out final copies for distribution (10%)
3. Receives handwritten copies and places them in priority files (2%)
4. Types special projects, such as proposals, quotations, system analysis, and customer and client surveys (20%)
5. Transmits documents through the use of electronic mail (10%)
6. Logs updates, volume, and turnaround time records of completed work (2%)
7. Receives and places priority on rush requests and special projects (2%)
8. Serves as a backup for the receptionist (2%)
9. Stocks the office supply closet (2%)
10. Performs other duties as directed

III. JOB SPECIFICATIONS

1. High school diploma or GED, 1–2 years of college helpful
2. Knowledge of Microsoft Word, Corel WordPerfect, Microsoft Excel, and Corel Quattro Pro
3. Must have a good eye for neatness and attention to detail.
4. Must lift 25-pound containers to a shelf of 72″
5. Ability to work well with others in developing proposals and projects

Source: Modified from E.H. Burack and N.J. Mathys, *Human Resource Planning: A Pragmatic Approach to Manpower Staffing and Development* (2d ed.). Lake Forest, IL: Brace-Park Publishing, 1987.

---

reassigned to a vacant job that is equivalent in terms of pay, status, benefits, and other relevant factors as the job the employee is leaving.[106]

The final accommodation available to employers is use of accrued paid leave and/or unpaid leave. Situations that could require leave as an accommodation include medical therapy, recuperation time, training for prosthetic devices, repair time for wheelchair-accessible vans, training for sign language, acquiring a seeing-eye dog, or avoiding temporary workplace conditions that adversely affect the disabled person.[107] Normally, the employer will allow the employee to exhaust any accrued paid leave and then permit a certain amount of unpaid leave.

Suppose an employee is scheduled to receive a new prosthetic leg. The installation, therapy, and training on the artificial limb are projected to take two weeks (ten work-days). The employee has accrued four days of paid leave. The employer could reasonably expect to permit the employee to use the four days of paid leave and then six days of unpaid leave.

Figure 6.9 **Considerations When Establishing Undue Hardship Under the ADA**

- Cost of the accommodation
- Size (number of employees)
- Number and type of facilities
- Composition and structure of workforce
- Essential job functions

The use of employee leave has become complicated with the enactment of the Family and Medical Leave Act (FMLA) of 1993, which mandates that covered employees are entitled to twelve weeks of unpaid leave in the event of specified emergency situations and are allowed to return to their jobs (the FMLA is addressed in greater detail in Chapter 10). Employers now must decide which law is more applicable to a given situation, the ADA or the FMLA. There may be some instances in which both could apply.

Undue Hardship

Any accommodation demanded of the employer is reasonable only as long as it does not create an undue hardship on the employer. Unfortunately for managers and HR professionals, this is determined too often on a case-by-case basis.[108]

In determining **undue hardship**, the ADA requires that five factors be considered (see Figure 6.9).[109] First, the overall cost of the accommodation must be compared to the overall financial resources of the facility, number of persons employed by the facility, and its projected effect on the operating expenses of the facility. Second, the overall financial resources, number of employees, and number and location of all the facilities owned by the employer are considered with regard to the cost of the accommodation. Third, the accommodation must be considered in light of the type of operation in which the employer is engaged—this includes considering the organizational structure, the functions of the workforce, the geographic separateness of facilities, and the degree of administrative or fiscal interdependence between the facility and other operations of the employer. Fourth, the impact that the accommodation will have on the operation of the facility in question must be considered. All of these considerations are extremely broad and make developing viable HR policies difficult. Finally, provided proper job analysis was performed on the job in question, the employer is *not* required to change the *essential job functions*.

To illustrate the impact of these considerations, let's assume that an employee of a small grocery store has been diagnosed with non-Hodgkin's lymphoma. The grocery store currently assigns four clerks and one assistant manager per shift; three of the clerks restock the shelves. The employer has determined that there are just enough clerks per shift to efficiently serve its customers, keep shelves restocked, maintain cleanliness, and reduce shoplifting. In order to receive chemotherapy and adjust to its debilitating effects, the employee requests three weeks' leave, a reduced work schedule, and fewer duties. The employer insists that accommodation will require hiring another employee and redistributing work responsibilities on the shift during which the disabled employee works.

Based on the small size, lack of fiscal resources, functions of the workforce, and impact on daily operations at the grocery store, the requested accommodations might be judged

Figure 6.10   **Pre-Employment Medical Inquiries Under the ADA**

In making pre-employment inquiries, employers may not ask:

- Whether the candidate has (or ever had) a disability, how he/she became disabled or about the nature or severity of a disability;
- To provide medical documentation regarding his/her disability;
- Coworker's, family member, doctor, or another person about the candidate's disability;
- About genetic information;
- About prior workers' compensation history;
- Whether he/she is currently taking or has taken any prescription drugs or medications, nor can they monitor the taking of such drugs or medications if the candidate is accepted for employment; and,
- Questions about impairments that are likely to elicit information about a disability (e.g., What impairments do you have?).

In making pre-employment inquiries employers may ask:

- About an applicant's ability to perform specific job functions. For example, an employer may state the physical requirements of a job (such as the ability to lift a certain amount of weight or the ability to climb ladders), and ask if an applicant can satisfy these requirements;
- About an applicant's non-medical qualifications and skills, such as the applicant's education, work history, and required certifications and licenses;
- Applicants to describe or demonstrate how they would perform job tasks.

Source: U.S. EEOC, *EEOC Enforcement Guidance on Disability-Related Inquiries and Medical Examinations of Employees under the Americans with Disabilities Act* (ADA). http://www.eeoc.gov/policy/docs/guidance-inquiries.html (accessed November 4, 2013).

---

to create an undue hardship. However, the same circumstances in a large regional chain of grocery stores might not create an undue hardship and, therefore, an accommodation would be reasonable.

In one instance, a hearing impaired applicant was given $200,000 in compensatory damages and back pay for the company's failing to make a "reasonable accommodation." The individual in question had been denied employment as "loader/scanner" at a distribution center because he was unable to hear the beep that would notify him that a product's bar code had been read by the scanner. The EEOC contended that the individual should have been provided adaptive equipment or given a position in another part of the facility.[110]

Pre-Employment Medical Inquiries

The ADA has greatly restricted the use of pre-employment medical examinations and inquiries (see Figure 6.10). It has also created a very fine line between permissible inquiries and prohibited ones during interviews. For example, it is unlawful to ask applicants if they have a disability or to inquire into the nature or severity of any perceivable disability.[111] However, it is permissible to ask applicants if they can perform job-related functions.[112] At the same time, pre-employment medical examinations are unlawful, but under certain circumstances, an employer may require an applicant to take a medical examination *after* a job offer is made and *before* the applicant begins working.[113] One of the certain circumstances previously mentioned would be cases in which *all* new hires, regardless of disability, are required to take a post-hiring medical examination.

In *EEOC v. Wal-Mart Stores, Inc.,* the nation's largest retailing firm agreed to pay a settlement of $6.8 million arising out of charges that its employment practices discriminated against applicants with disabilities.[114] The EEOC alleged that the company's "Matrix of Essential Job Functions" asked applicants about medical conditions and disabilities prior to a job offer. Because this was considered to be a pre-employment medical inquiry, the company was, in essence, engaging in an unlawful practice in violation of the ADA.

In a later case, the EEOC alleged that Wal-Mart discriminated against an applicant with cerebral palsy when it failed to give him a job as a cashier. Unlike the previous situation, Wal-Mart had evaluated the individual's work-related ability and lack of retailing work experience before concluding that he could not perform the essential tasks.[115] This time, the company prevailed.

Direct Threat to Others/Threat to Self

In the event that post-offer medical examinations indicate the medical condition of the individual would pose a threat to his or her health or that of others, the employer is not required to hire or retain the individual.[116] For example, assume that a post-offer medical examination reveals that an individual has a respiratory condition that would become significantly worse if the employee were exposed to certain chemical agents and the essential functions of the job require such exposure. Hiring the employee would result in either the employee's exacerbating the disability or, perhaps, even death, thus the employer could legitimately refuse to hire the individual in question.

According to EEOC regulations governing enforcement of the ADA, **direct threat** means a significant risk of substantial harm to the health or safety of the individual or others that cannot be eliminated or reduced by reasonable accommodation.[117]

For example, a bulldozer operator on a pipeline project complains that several times in the previous three weeks he has become dizzy for a time and has blacked out while operating his dozer. The employer may require the operator to have a medical examination in order to determine whether or not these symptoms prevent him from safely performing his job. In all cases, it is the employer's obligation to establish that he or she had a reasonable belief, based on objective evidence (observations, medical examinations, etc.) that the employee would pose a direct threat to others as a result of his or her medical condition.[118]

Determining direct threat, either to self or others, is not to be taken lightly. The EEOC requires that the following four factors must first be considered by the employer:

1. the duration of the risk;
2. the nature and severity of the potential harm;
3. the likelihood that the potential harm will occur; and
4. the imminence of the potential harm.[119]

Confidentiality of Medical Information

The other restriction is that once the medical information has been collected, the employer is responsible for keeping it confidential. Generally, it is unlawful for an employer to even ask a job applicant if he or she is an individual with a disability, or about the nature or severity of such disability.[120] Often, this responsibility is delegated to the HR department, which in most organizations is responsible for maintaining employee medical records. In the case of employee medical records, the key words have now become "extremely limited access."[121] The only circumstances under which these files can be accessed by anyone are clearly detailed by the ADA and limited to only three.[122] First, management personnel may be informed of medical conditions requiring work restrictions or other reasonable accommodations. Second, company first aid and safety personnel may be informed if the employee's disability might require emergency treatment. Finally, the medical records may be made available to government officials investigating ADA compliance. Other than those instances, the medical records should be kept safeguarded. Most disclosures of employee medical records are likely to result in ADA violations.

Drug Testing Rehabilitation and the ADA

The term "qualified individual with a disability" also includes any individual who is participating in a supervised drug rehabilitation program and no longer using illegal drugs, has completed a supervised drug rehabilitation program and is no longer using illegal drugs, or is erroneously regarded as engaging in using illegal drugs and is no longer engaging in such use.[123] Note that in each instance the phrase "is no longer engaging in the use of illegal drugs" is essential to remaining a qualified individual with a disability. The ADA does not protect current substance abusers. In fact, the Act specifically authorizes covered employers to prohibit the use of drugs and alcohol in the workplace, requires that employees not be under the influence of drugs and/or alcohol during work hours, and holds drug and alcohol users to the same employment and performance standards as other employees.[124]

The ADA clearly states that employers have the right to require their employees to conform to the requirements established under the Drug-Free Workplace Act.[125] Although the ADA has placed severe restrictions on the use of medical examinations by employers, "tests to determine the illegal use of drugs shall not be considered a medical examination."[126] This exemption permits employers to conduct pre-employment drug screening and drug testing following an employment offer.

SUMMARY

This chapter identifies unlawful employment practices that result from discrimination on the basis of religion, national origin, age, and disability. Discrimination in employment based on religion and national origin is prohibited under Title VII of the Civil Rights Act of 1964. Applicants and employees are protected from discrimination based on age under the Age Discrimination in Employment Act. The Vocational Rehabilitation Act of 1973 and the Americans with Disabilities Act of 1990 protect applicants and employees from discrimination based on a disability.

The ADA presents even more concerns for managers and HR professionals, especially in the area of job analysis. As noted, determination as to whether an applicant is qualified hinges on assessing two important factors: What is the extent of the applicant's disability and, in light of the disability, can the applicant perform the essential functions of the job with or without reasonable accommodation?

To make these determinations and assess the degree of accommodation, the essential job functions must be identified and understood. The ADA has further increased the HR professional's responsibility for maintaining the confidentiality of personnel records, particularly medical records.

Because many of these policies will eventually result in written policy statements or in employee handbooks, employers are placed in an awkward predicament. Compliance with these federal statutes and regulations requires dissemination to employees. However, formal dissemination often requires documentation, and this documentation takes the form of employee handbooks. As will be explained in Chapter 13, handbooks and written policies can create implied or explicit employment contracts.

KEY TERMS AND CONCEPTS

Disability	Reasonable accommodation
Direct threat	Religious accommodation
Major life activities	Religious exemption
Qualified individual with a disability	Undue hardship

DISCUSSION QUESTIONS

1. What organizations are afforded religious exemptions under Section 702 of the Civil Rights Act of 1964?
2. Under what circumstances may employers who are not exempted under Section 702 engage in preferential treatment on the basis of religion? Provide an example.
3. In terms of disability, what three covered entities does Title I of the Americans with Disabilities Act of 1990 protect from unlawful discrimination?
4. What is "reasonable accommodation" under both the Vocational Rehabilitation Act of 1973 and the Americans with Disabilities Act of 1990?
5. How is "undue hardship" determined under both the Vocational Rehabilitation Act of 1973 and the Americans with Disabilities Act of 1990?

CASES

Case 1

Dave Phillips had been employed by an independent contractor at Cover-the-Earth Oil, an oil refinery that employs 350 permanent employees in League City, TX. There were another 69 personnel on the facility who worked for contractors on the site. In

2008 the oil refinery decided that, for better operational control, it would replace all contractors with permanent employees effective January 1, 2009. Employees of former contractors were permitted to apply for their old positions as employees of Cover-the-Earth. On March 1, 2013, Dave applied for a job with Cover-the-Earth and was told that the job was his if he passed the physical exam required of all Cover-the-Earth new hires.

Unfortunately for Dave, the medical exam revealed that he suffered from liver damage, a result of the hepatitis C virus. Company physicians concluded that this condition would be aggravated by continued exposure to toxins at Cover-the-Earth's refinery. As a consequence, Dave's offer of employment was retracted.

After the retraction of Dave's job offer, the corporation asked the contractor to either reassign Dave to jobs without exposure to harmful chemicals until the contract expired at the end of the year or remove him from the plant entirely—he was subsequently laid off. Dave contended that he had worked in the same job for the contractor for ten years and was, therefore, qualified to fill it. The company contended that if they hired him, his condition would only get worse, maybe even kill him.

Not satisfied, Dave filed suit, claiming that he was discriminated against in violation of the Americans with Disabilities Act.[127]

    a. Can Dave establish actionable discrimination on the basis of disability? Why or why not?
    b. Can the employer base a hiring decision on the outcome of a medical exam? If so, how?

Case 2

Basma (formerly Patricia), a recent convert to Islam, alleges that she was terminated from her job as a metal punch operator in a metal fabrication plant because of her religion (Islam). Shortly after her conversion, she notified her supervisor, Ken, that her new faith required her to dress according to *hijab*, "the correct standard of modesty." She also stated that this meant she could no longer wear pants, as required by the factory's dress code. She further requested religious accommodation by being permitted to wear the *jibaab*, a loose-fitting floor-length garment, while at work.

Ken responded that this could not be done as OHSA and other safety regulations precluded anyone from working around the machinery in loose clothing. Ken then said that he could transfer her to another job. He told her that the only other jobs in the plant were interstate truck driver and office worker. Ken informed her that since she possessed no clerical skills, she was not qualified for the office. He then asked her if she could drive a tractor trailer, to which she responded that she could not. When Basma showed up for work the next day in a *jibaab,* Ken told her to go home and return in the appropriate work attire. When she refused, she was terminated.

Management contends that the dress code is essential to the safe and efficient operation of the mill, and has evidence that it was imposed following several accidents in which skirts worn by employees were caught in the same type of mill machinery that Basma operates. Because the evidence establishes that wearing pants is truly necessary for safety reasons, the accommodation requested by Basma poses an undue hardship and a legitimate nondiscriminatory reason for treating her differently.[128]

    a. Is Ken engaging in religious discrimination? Why or why not?
    b. Is there a reasonable religious accommodation for Basma?

Case 3

Phil is a marketing employee who works for a medium sized firm employing 120 full-time and 46 part-time employees. Phil was diagnosed as having a severe learning disability when he was an adolescent. As part of his job duties, he is required to attend weekly departmental meetings to plan marketing strategies. In order to remember what is being discussed at these meetings Phil must take detailed notes. However, he contends, due to his disability, he has great difficulty writing. After being reprimanded by Mindy, his supervisor, Phil tells Mindy about his disability and requests a laptop computer to use in the meetings.[129]

    a. Is Phil asking for a reasonable accommodation?
    b. Can his supervisor ask Phil for reasonable documentation about his impairment?
    c. Can his employer also ask why the disability necessitates use of a laptop computer (or any other type of reasonable accommodation, such as a tape recorder) to help the employee retain the information from the meetings?

NOTES

1. This scenario is based on the findings of fact in *Cook v. Rhode Island,* 10 F.3d 17 (1st Cir. 1993).
2. *Cook,* 10 F.3d at 34, n. 13.
3. U.S. Equal Employment Opportunity Commission, *Charge Statistics FY 1997 Through FY 2011,* http://www.eeoc.gov/eeoc/statistics/enforcement/charges.cfm (accessed December 4, 2012).
4. Ibid.
5. 42 U.S.C. § 2000e-1(a).
6. 113 F.3d 196 (11th Cir. 1997).
7. *Killinger v. Samford University,* 113 F.3d at 200.
8. *Little v. Wuerl,* 929 F.2d 944, 947–48 (3rd Cir. 1991).
9. *EEOC v. Kamehameha School,* 990 F.2d 458 (9th Cir. 1993).
10. *Fike v. United Methodist Children's Home of Virginia, Inc.,* 547 F.Supp. 286 (E.D. Vir. 1982).
11. *EEOC v. Mississippi College,* 626 F.2d 477 (5th Cir. 1980).
12. *Shapolia v. Los Alamos National Laboratory,* 773 F.Supp. 304, 305 (D. N.M. 1991); aff'd without comment, 13 F.3d 406 (10th Cir. 1993).
13. *Breech v. Alabama Power Company,* 962 F.Supp. 1447, 1456 (S.D. Ala. 1997).
14. *Kern v. Dynalectron Corp.,* 577 F.Supp. 1196 (N.D. Tex. 1983).
15. 29 C.F.R. § 1605 (2011).
16. 42 U.S.C. § 2000e (j) (2011).

17. *Beadle v. City of Tampa*, 42 F.3d 633, 636 n.4 (11th Cir. 1995); *Bhatia v. Chevron U.S.A., Inc.*, 734 F.2d 1382,1383 (9th Cir. 1984).

18. Exodus 20:8; Deuteronomy 5:12.

19. *Chalmer v. Tulon Company of Richmond*, 101 F.3d 1012, 1019 (4th Cir. 1996).

20. *TWA v. Hardison*, 432 U.S. 63, 84 (1977); *Endres v. Indiana State Police*, 334 F.d 618, 623 (7th Cir. 2003).

21. *EEOC v. Ilona of Hungary, Inc.*, 108 F.3d 1569 (7th Cir. 1997).

22. *Smith v. Pyro Mining Co.*, 827 F.2d 1081, 1085 (6th Cir. 1987).

23. *Protos v. Volkswagen of Am., Inc.*, 797 F.2d 129, 134–35 (3d Cir. 1986); *Webb v. City of Philadelphia*, 562 F.3d 256 (3d Cir. 2009).

24. *Virts v. Consolidated Freightways Corp. of Delaware*, 285 F.3d 508 (6th Cir. 2002).

25. *Balint v. Carson City*, 180 F.3d 1047, 1054 (9th Cir. 1999).

26. *EEOC v. Alamo Rent-A-Car, LLC*, 432 F. Supp.2d 1006 (D. Ariz. 2006).

27. *Lee v. ABF Freight System, Inc.*, 22 F. 3d 1019 (10th Cir. 1994).

28. *Wilshin v. Allstate Insurance Co.*, 212 F. Supp. 2d 1369, 1373 (M.D. Ga. 2002).

29. *Ansonia Board of Education v. Phillbrook*, 479 U.S. 60, 68 (1986).

30. Ibid.

31. *EEOC v. Firestone Fibers & Textiles Co.*, 515 F.3d 307, 312-13 (4th Cir. 2008).

32. P. Sheehan, "Dressed to Impress," *Lodging Hospitality* 59 (2003): 48, 50.

33. T. Adcock, "Casualties of Casual Dress Code," *New York Law Journal ONLINE*, (2002). http://www.law.com; S. Cline, "Office Attire Swinging Back to Professional from Casual," *Colorado Springs Business Journal*, March 11, 2005; P. Sheehan, "Dressed to Impress," *Lodging Hospitality* 59 (2003): 48, 50.

34. 481 F.2d 1115, 1124–25 (D.C. Cir. 1973).

35. *Booth v. Maryland*, 327 F.3d 377, 382–383 (4th Cir. 2003); *Brown v. Johnson*, 116 Fed. Appx. 342, 343 (3d Cir. 2004); *Cloutier v. Costco Wholesale Corp.*, 390 F.3d 126 (1st Cir. 2004).

36. *Holmes v. Marion Community Office of Family and Children*, 349 F.3d 914 (7th Cir. 2003).

37. *Hussein v. Waldorf Astoria Hotel*, 31 Fed. Appx. 740 (2d Cir. 2002); *Vargas v. Sears & Roebuck Co.*, 1998 U.S. Dist. LEXIS 21148 (E.D. Mich. 1998).

38. 29 C.F.R. § 1605.2(e)(1).

39. *Sutton v. Providence St. Joseph Medical Center*, 192 F.3d 826 (9th Cir. 1999).

40. *Bhatia v. Chevron USA, Inc.*, 734 F.2d 1382 (9th Cir. 1984).

41. *Cloutier v. Costco Wholesale Corp.*, 390 F.3d 126 (1st Cir. 2005).

42. G. Panaro, "Is Hiring on the Basis of Appearance Illegal?" *Fair Employment Practices Guidelines* 581 (October 2003), http://www.bankersonline.com/operations/gp_appearance.html (accessed December 6, 2012).

43. *Fraternal Order of Police v. City of Newark*, 170 F.3d 359 (3d Cir. 1999).

44. *EEOC v. United Parcel Service, Inc.*, 587 F.3d 136 (2nd Cir. 2009).

45. 648 F.2d 1239 (9th Cir. 1981).

46. 29 C.F.R. § 158(a)(5) (2011).

47. *Wilson v. National Labor Relations Board*, 920 F.2d 1282, 1287 (6th Cir. 1990).

48. Pub. L. 90–202, 81 Stat. 602 (Dec. 15, 1967).

49. U.S. Equal Employment Opportunity Commission, "Enforcement Statistics and Litigation," http://www.eeoc.gov/eeoc/statistics/enforcement/adea.cfm and http://www.eeoc.gov/eeoc/statistics/enforcement/all.cfm (accessed December 6, 2012).

50. 29 U.S.C. § 630 (2011).

51. 42 U.S.C. § 2000e (b).

52. 29 U.S.C. § 621.

53. 29 U.S.C. § 623.

54. Pub. L. 90–202, § 2 (1967).

55. Pub. L. 95–256, § 3a (1978).

56. Pub. L. 99–592, § 2(c)(1) (1986).

57. *Western Air Lines, Inc. v. Criswell*, 472 U.S. 400, 422 (1985).

58. *O'Connor v. Consolidated Coin Caterers Corp.*, 517 U.S. 308 (1996).

59. 517 U.S. 308.

60. *O'Connor v. Consolidated Coin Caterers Corp.*, 517 U.S. at 312.

61. *Gross v. FBL Financial Services, Inc.*, 557 U.S. 167 (2009).

62. Ibid. 178.

63. 29 U.S.C. § 626(c)(2).

64. 42 U.S.C. § 1981a(c).

65. 472 U.S. 400 (1985).

66. *Western Airlines v. Criswell*, 472 U.S. at 404.

67. *Dothard v. Rawlinson*, 433 U.S. 321, 334 (1977).

68. *Criswell*, 472 U.S. at 409.

69. Ibid. at 422.

70. Ibid. at 408.

71. Ibid. at 412.

72. A.N. Bitter, "*Smith v. City of Jackson*: Solving an Old-Age Problem," *The Catholic University Law Review* (56): 647–682.

73. *Smith v. City of Jackson*, 544 U.S. 228, 236 (2005).

74. Ibid. at 239.

75. *Cancellier v. Federated Department Stores*, 672 F. 2d 1312 (9th Cir.), cert, denied 459 U.S. 859 (1982).

76. *Skalka v. Fernald Environmental Restoration Management Corp.*, 178 F.3d 414 (6th Cir. 1999).

77. 540 U.S. 581 (2004).

78. *Cline*, 540 U.S. at 585.

79. Ibid. at 600.

80. 29 U.S.C. § 791 *et. seq.* (2011).

81. 29 U.S.C. § 794.

82. Pub. L. 93–112, §. 7 (1973).

83. 42 U.S.C. § 12 111(8) (2011).

84. Pub. L. 102–569, 106 Stat. 4346 (Oct. 29, 1992).

85. 29 U.S.C. § 793.

86. 42 U.S.C. § 12 112(a).

87. G.S. Becker, "How the Disabilities Act Will Cripple Business," *BusinessWeek*, September 14, 1992, p. 14.

88. *EEOC v. Chrysler Corp.*, 917 F.Supp. 1164 (E.D. Mich. 1996).

89. 29 C.F.R. § 1630.2(I).

90. 42 U.S.C. 12102(4)

91. 42 U.S.C. 12102(4)(E)(i).

92. U.S. Equal Employment Opportunity Commission, *Notice Concerning the Americans with Disabilities Act (ADA) Amendments Act of 2008* (March 25, 2011). http://www.eeoc.gov/laws/statutes/adaaa_notice.cfm (accessed January 2, 2013).

93. 42 U.S.C. § 12112.

94. 42 U.S.C. § 12111(8).

95. U.S. Equal Employment Opportunity Commission, *The Americans with Disabilities Act: Your Responsibilities as an Employer* (Washington, DC: Government Printing Office, 2005), pp. 3–4.

96. 29 C.F.R. § 1630.2(j).

97. Ibid. at 483.

98. U.S. Office of Federal Contract Compliance Programs, *The ADA Amendments Act of 2008: Frequently Asked Questions*, http://www.dol.gov/ofccp/regs/compliance/faqs/ADAfaqs.htm#Q4 (accessed February 11, 2013).

99. Ibid.

100. *Bragdon v. Abbott,* 524 U.S. 624 (1998).

101. U.S. Equal Employment Opportunity Commission, *Enforcement Guidance: Reasonable Accommodation and Undue Hardship under the Americans with Disabilities Act* (October 17, 2002), http://www.eeoc.gov/policy/docs/accommodation.html (accessed January 2, 2013).

102. Ibid.

103. Ibid.

104. Ibid.

105. *Davis v. Frank,* 711 F. Supp. 447 (N.D. Ill. 1989).

106. 29 C.F.R. part 1630, appendix 1630.2(o) (2007).

107. U.S. Employment Standards Administration, *Compliance Guide to the Family and Medical Leave Act* (2008), www.dol.gov/dol/esa/public/regs/compliance/whd/1421.htm (accessed January 23, 2008).

108. *Stone v. City of Mount Vernon,* 118 F. 3d 92, 101 (2nd Cir. 1996).

109. 42 U.S.C. § 12111(10)(B) (2007).

110. U.S. Equal Employment Opportunity Commission, *Annual Report Fiscal Year 2002* (Washington, DC: U.S. Government Printing Office, 2003).

111. 42 U.S.C. § 12112(d)(2)(A).

112. U.S. Equal Employment Opportunity Commission, *Notice Concerning the Americans with Disabilities Act (ADA) Amendments Act of 2008* (March 25, 2011), http://www.eeoc.gov/laws/statutes/adaaa_notice.cfm (accessed January 2, 2013).

113. 42 U.S.C. § 12112(d)(2)(B).

114. U.S. Equal Employment Opportunity Commission, *Annual Report Fiscal Year 2002.*

115. *EEOC v. Wal-Mart Stores, Inc.,* 2005 U.S. Dist. Lexis 40868 (W.D. Mo. 2005).

116. *Chevron U.S.A., Inc. v. Eschazabal,* 536 U.S. 73, 86–86 (2002).

117. 29 C.F.R. §§ 1630.2(r).

118. U.S. Equal Employment Opportunity Commission, *Enforcement Guidance: Disability-Related Inquiries and Medical Examinations of Employees under the Americans with Disabilities Act (ADA),* http://www.eeoc.gov/policy/docs/guidance-inquiries.html (accessed January 2, 2013).

119. 29 C.F.R. §§ 1630.2(r).

120. 42 U.S.C. § 12112(d)(2)(A).

121. 42 U.S.C. § 12112(d)(2)(B).

122. 42 U.S.C. § 12112(d)(3)(B).

123. 42 U.S.C. § § 12114(a) & (b).

124. 42 U.S.C. § 12114(c).

125. 42 U.S.C. § 12114 (c)(3).

126. 42 U.S.C. § 12114(d).

127. Some materials for this case were drawn from *Chevron U.S.A. v. Echazabal,* 536 U.S, 73 (2002).

128. Some materials for this case were drawn from *EEOC v. Oak Rite Manufacturing,* 2001 U.S. Dist. LEXIS 15621 (S.D. Ind. 2001).

129. Some materials for this case were drawn from U.S. Equal Employment Opportunity Commission, *Enforcement Guidance: Reasonable Accommodation and Undue Hardship under the Americans with Disabilities Act,* http://www.eeoc.gov/policy/docs/accommodation.html (accessed January 2, 2013).

7

NATIONAL ORIGIN DISCRIMINATION AND IMMIGRATION ISSUES

LEARNING OBJECTIVES

- Identify employment practices that potentially discriminate on the basis of national origin.
- Know which individuals are protected against discrimination based on national origin.
- Understand the circumstances under which employers may establish language proficiency requirements.
- Identify the conditions under which English-only work rules are permissible.
- Understand an employer's obligations under the Immigration Reform and Control Act (IRCA).
- Know what the employment verification requirements are under the Immigration Reform and Control Act.
- Understand the circumstances under which an employer can commit an unfair immigration-related employment practice under IRCA.
- Understand when a U.S. citizen working overseas is covered under Title VII.

OPENING SCENARIO

Primo Operator Services, Inc., was a telemarketing company operating in a large metropolitan area in the southwestern United States and employing approximately 50 employees. The recruitment and hiring of the operators was based on the applicant's bilingual ability, and in particular, oral fluency in Spanish, because of a need for the employer's business to service Spanish-speaking customers when connecting long-distance telephone calls. The ability to speak Spanish was viewed by the employer as essential to conducting business. Fluency in Spanish was considered to be so important to the business that applicants were tested at the time of hiring to verify their ability to speak and understand Spanish.

In January 2012 Primo enacted an "English-only" policy specifically prohibiting the speaking of Spanish on the company premises, except in dealing with customers. The policy was posted on the door at the entrance of the office building in which Primo was located. The same sign conspicuously coupled the policy with a warning about weapons. Specifically, the sign read:

> Absolutely No Guns, Knives, or Weapons of any kind are allowed on these Prem-
> ises at any time! English is the official language of Primo Operator Services, Inc.
> All conversations on these premises are to be in English. Other languages may be
> spoken to customers who cannot speak English.

In effect, this policy prohibited Primo employees from speaking Spanish to each other
at all times, including during free moments operators had between calls, during lunch, in
the employee break room, when making personal telephone calls, and before and after
work if inside the building. Under the employer's policy, the only time it was acceptable
to speak Spanish was when assisting a Spanish-speaking customer.

Before Primo began hiring non-Hispanic operators in mid-January 2013, everyone
spoke Spanish. Once the policy was instated, Spanish-speaking employees working in the
close quarters of a small work area were required to speak to their Hispanic colleagues
in English or face discipline or dismissal. Lunchroom conversations, even between a
Hispanic husband and wife, could not include Spanish words or phrases. The employer
later admitted that it went as far as to plan the installation of a public telephone outside
of the building so that Hispanic employees would have to go outside to make personal
phone calls during which they might speak Spanish.

On January 16, 2014, the employer required its employees to sign an agreement de-
tailing the employer's English-only policy as a prerequisite to continued employment.
Vice President of Operations Bill Robinson admitted that it was understood that if the
employees did not agree to the prohibitions imposed by the policy, their employment
would be terminated. Six employees who refused to sign the memo were immediately
terminated.[1]

Does Primo's English-only policy violate Title VII? Why or why not? What standards
must any English-only policy meet in order to avoid a Title VII violation? These and
other questions will be answered by the end of this chapter.

NATIONAL ORIGIN

National origin (sometimes called ethnicity) is the last protected class under Title VII
to be discussed. Like the preceding protected classes (race, color, sex, and religion),
employers cannot consider a candidate's national origin when making any employment
decision. In a similar vein, employees are protected against any consideration of their
ethnicity that could result in disparate treatment, harassment, or mixed motives. Furthermore, disparate impact on the basis of national origin is actionable under Title VII, just
as it is for sex and race.

Because members of many ethnic groups often display nationality-specific characteristics (i.e., particular religious affiliations, speech patterns, languages, surnames, etc.),
Title VII can be violated when a connection is made between unfavorable treatment in
the workplace and such ethnic characteristics (see Figure 7.1). For example, a parishioner
from St. Basil's Greek Orthodox Church might be assumed to be of Greek ancestry by
an employer who happens to be predisposed against Greeks. Conversely, an applicant

Figure 7.1   **Employment Consideration That May Trigger National Origin Discrimination**

- Marriage to a person of a national origin group
- Association with persons of a national origin group
- Membership in, or association with, an organization identified with or seeking to promote the interests of national origin groups
- Attendance or participation in schools, churches, temples, or mosques generally used by persons of a national origin group
- An individual's name is associated with a national origin group
- A spouse's name is associated with a national origin group

Source: 29 C.F.R. §1606.1 (2012).

with the name Mustapha Kamal may be assumed to be of Turkish descent by a potential employer who dislikes Turks and consequently treats Mustapha differently than other candidates with non-Turkish surnames. Whether the employee is actually of Turkish descent is immaterial. If he is *assumed* by the employer to be Turkish and is treated differently because of this assumption, Title VII is violated.[2] In addition, a potential violation may result when an employee is a member of an organization associated with specific ethnic groups and, therefore, is assumed to be a member of such ethnic groups. For example, a member of the Ancient Order of Hibernians might be assumed to be of Irish ancestry, just as a member of La Raza might be assumed to be a Latino.

Another interesting facet of national origin discrimination is that it is not limited to the actual members of an ethnic group against whom discrimination is directed. If an employer punishes nonethnic employees for associating or fraternizing with members of an ethnic group whom the employer finds distasteful, Title VII has been violated. Suppose that Bill, a German-American, is fired because his supervisor feels that he is "too friendly" with his Mexican-American coworkers. Bill can file a complaint under Title VII as a result of this action.

Similarly, if an employee is subjected to adverse employment outcomes because he or she is married to a member of an ethnic group the employer finds offensive, Title VII is again violated on the basis of national origin. Assume that Patrick, an individual of Irish ancestry, is married to Maria, a Puerto Rican. Assume also that his employer disapproves of mixed marriages between "Anglos" and Hispanics. As a result of this attitude, the employee is continually passed over for promotion and receives no merit pay raises. Patrick would not have suffered the adverse action had it not been for his wife's nationality. In this case Patrick, the husband, can initiate a complaint of unlawful discrimination under Title VII on the basis of national origin.[3] As the U.S.'s ethnic diversity continues to grow and so-called mixed marriages increase, managers must be aware of the possibility of claims of adverse employment actions.

If an employee does not receive a merit pay raise, the employer should have appropriate documentation (i.e., performance appraisals, counseling statements, etc.) to demonstrate that he or she did not deserve the raise. All employment decisions should be predicated on legitimate nondiscriminatory reasons.

Language

A substantial proportion of the American workforce's projected growth is from immigration.[4] Many first-generation legal immigrants to the United States often have limited language proficiency. There are some parts of the nation in which languages other than English are spoken. The language of preference for the local population may be Spanish, Russian, Vietnamese, or a combination thereof. There may even be circumstances in which employers see the necessity of requiring managers in facilities located within these enclaves to be multilingual.

English is still the language used by the vast majority of Americans.[5] It is the de facto, though not the official, language of the United States, and failure to achieve proficiency in English would likely limit an individual's social and career mobility.[6] The ability to communicate with superiors, peers, subordinates, and a firm's customer base is important in many jobs.

Fluency in English

The question confronting many managers is just how language proficiency (especially English proficiency) can be used in making employment decisions before one crosses the line into unlawful discrimination based on national origin. The line of demarcation is simple: language proficiency is a lawful requirement if the applicant's language abilities preclude his or her ability to perform the job in question.[7] This standard applies not only to English fluency, it also applies to accents.[8]

It should be noted that language proficiency is not merely limited to oral communication; it can be based on written communication skills as well. In a particular instance, an individual was removed from a position that required him to produce written scientific reports and related information.[9] Unfortunately, his written English skills were insufficient for him to perform these duties adequately. If the position requires the job incumbent to prepare written reports, correspondence, and other written communication, requiring successful candidates to demonstrate written English communication skills is a legitimate nondiscriminatory reason for making the employment decision.

Conversely, when the essential job tasks do *not* involve either oral or written English proficiency, then the individual's linguistic deficiencies cannot be used to disqualify him or her from employment or promotion. To deny employment as a dishwasher, a position which has no contact with customers, to an individual with marginal English language skills is likely to trigger a national origin discrimination claim, whereas denying the individual a position as waiter would not. Proper job analysis is the best means of determining what level of English language proficiency is important to job accomplishment (see Chapter 14).

Accents

A person may be fluent in English, but may have an accent that interferes with oral communications. If oral communication skills are critical to the job in question, and an applicant's ability to express herself is impeded by a heavy accent, the heavy accent may be a legitimate nondiscriminatory reason for disqualifying the candidate.[10] To illustrate this point, assume a person is applying for a position as a driver for a parcel delivery service. She speaks conversational English but with a thick French accent. Can she be denied the job based on her accent? Recalling Chapters 3 and 4, what information would you have to possess to make that call? How critical is speaking English without an accent to the performance of the essential job functions of a parcel delivery person? If your job analysis shows it has little, if any, impact on job performance, then rejecting the applicant based on her accent could be unlawful discrimination based on national origin.

Now assume the position for which the heavily accented candidate has applied is that of an air traffic controller. Job analysis should indicate that clearly enunciated and understandable communication between the air traffic controller and aircraft pilots is an essential component of the job. If the individual's accent is such that understanding her instructions is hampered, the employer may classify the applicant as unqualified for the position.[11] The burden for the employer is to demonstrate that the applicant's accent is so heavy that it affects comprehension. This then demonstrates her employment was denied based on a legitimate job-related reason rather than on her nationality.

Proficiency in Languages Other than English

Employers who base employment decisions on language proficiency (whether it is Spanish, Russian, Mandarin, etc.) must be able to justify such preferences as related to job performance.[12] Again, this is a lawful employment criterion provided that it can be shown to be related to successful job performance. The burden is on the employer to demonstrate that the foreign language skills used in making the selection decision are tied to successful job performance.

Misconceptions of English as an Official Language

At the time of publication, over half of the states in the union have passed laws declaring English the official language in their state.[13] As a consequence, some employers believe that these laws grant them the authority to declare that their employees can speak only English in the workplace. This is certainly not the case, and this misconception arises from a mistaken belief of what English as an official language mandates.

English as the official language statutes mandate that all official government business must be conducted in the English language.[14] This means that all government documents (driver's licenses, deeds, records, legislative enactments, court decisions and orders, etc.) must be recorded in English. Additionally all public meetings and hearings must also be in English. It imposes no such requirement for private employers nor does it afford them any protection from EEO laws if they require their employees to speak only English while on their premises. Private sector employers and employees should not confuse English as the official language laws with English-only work rules.

ENGLISH-ONLY WORK RULES

English-only work rules require employees to speak English in certain work situations as a condition of employment. This creates a problem for employers because the *EEOC Guidelines on Discrimination Because of National Origin* currently declares that employer policies prohibiting employees from speaking their primary language at all times may create an "atmosphere of inferiority, isolation, and intimidation *which could result in a discriminatory working environment.*"[15] Consequently, any language policy that creates a complete bar to speaking languages other than English is likely to be interpreted by the EEOC as a potential Title VII violation and, therefore, is subject to strict scrutiny.

However, this policy creates a paradox. On one hand, the EEOC has created disincentives to encourage employers not to adopt English-only policies (except where business necessity can be demonstrated). On the other hand, the EEOC expects employers to maintain a working environment free from harassment on the basis of race,[16] sex,[17] and national origin.[18] This is where the employer's dilemma arises—an employer might implement an English-only rule in response to racial or sexual harassment complaints. Will the federal government conclude the employer is merely meeting its obligation to maintain a harassment-free workplace? Or will it conclude the employer is discriminating against non-English speakers on the basis of nationality?

The apparent solution to this dilemma was offered in the Ninth Circuit case *Garcia v. Spun Steak Company.*[19] Spun Steak Company, a California poultry and meat processor, implemented an English-only rule with the expressed purpose of promoting racial harmony in the workplace. The company's policy was initiated in response to complaints that some Hispanic workers were using their bilingual capabilities to make "derogatory, racist" comments in Spanish about an African-American coworker. As a repercussion of perceived racial harassment, the employer imposed a new policy that only English would be spoken in the company during work periods. It is important to note that this policy was not an all-inclusive prohibition; Spanish could still be spoken during lunch breaks and on the employees' own time. However, no language other than English could be spoken in work areas during work times.

The Spanish-speaking employees then argued the language policy was discriminatory because it denied them a privilege enjoyed by English-only speakers (the ability to speak in the language with which they felt most comfortable) and it created an atmosphere of inferiority and intimidation.[20] The Ninth Circuit observed that Title VII is not intended to protect employees from policies that "merely inconvenience" them; rather it exists to protect them only against practices that have a *significant* impact.[21] Because the employees in this case were bilingual, the Ninth Circuit concluded that the English-only rule did not preclude conversation on the job, merely Spanish conversation while engaged in normal work activities. All employees could still converse in English.

The policy was a business necessity—it was in place in order to prevent certain employees from using their fluency in a language other than English to intimidate monolingual coworkers who were members of other ethnic groups. Thus, the Ninth Circuit concluded that the policy did not violate Title VII. Other business-related rationales justifying English-only

Figure 7.2 **Guidelines for English-Only Rules**

1. The English-only rule must be justified.
2. The English-only rule cannot create a universal prohibition.
3. The English-only rule must describe consequences for noncompliance.
4. The English-only rule must be communicated to all employees.

Source: Garcia v. Spun Steak Company, 13 F.3d 296 (9th Cir. 1993).

rules would include communication with customers, communication with coworkers, and communication with supervisors in order to promote efficiency or safety.[22]

When language restrictions are necessary in the workplace, it becomes incumbent upon managers and HR administrators to guarantee that the following general guidelines are observed (see Figure 7.2). First, and foremost, is there any alternative to resolving the problem that does not resort to limiting the use of a given language?[23] If not, then the employer must ensure the English-only policy serves a legitimate business necessity (i.e., safety, clear communications, etc.). The EEOC has included in its regulations that English-only policies are permissible when they are (1) applied only at certain times, and (2) the employer can show that the requirement to speak only English at these times is justified by business necessity.[24] This justification must therefore be documented, and the policy should be implemented with the expectation that it will be challenged by the offended employees. If it cannot be readily and reasonably justified, the employer should not have an English-only policy.

Care must also be taken to ensure that the policy does not create a universal prohibition throughout the place of employment. Rather, the English-only provisions should be limited to those activities and times mandated by the previously established business necessity.[25] Invariably, this means limiting the language restrictions to work-related communications and work settings. Employers should avoid requiring employees to speak only English in conversations in nonwork areas during nonwork times.[26] Finally, before any English-only policy is enforced, it is absolutely imperative that the employer first make the affected employees aware of the policy and the consequences for not obeying it. In its *Guidelines on Discrimination Because of National Origin*, the EEOC asserts that any employer's failure to notify its employees of the consequences of violating the English-only requirement would result in the commission's including "the employer's application of the [English-only] rule as evidence of discrimination" if it then took disciplinary action.[27] As always, documentation of both the business justification for the policy and the specific notification process is highly recommended.

IMMIGRATION ISSUES AND NATIONAL ORIGIN

There are many employment issues arising from both legal and illegal immigration. Do foreign employers operating facilities in the United States have to obey our employment laws? What are the employer's obligations in hiring foreign nationals? What employment rights do U.S. citizens have when working overseas, and what employment rights do foreign nationals have working in the United States? These questions will be answered in this section of this chapter.

Foreign Employers in the United States

Generally, foreign employers operating in the United States are covered by U.S. employment laws and regulations. For example, Title VII applies to Daimler Benz's treatment of its employees working in its Tuscaloosa, Alabama, assembly facility just as it does to General Motors' treatment of its employees working in its Toledo, Ohio, plant. Foreign employers who operate on U.S. soil are expected to follow U.S. law.

There are some very rare instances under which a foreign employer may discriminate in favor of its own national laws if this is specifically permitted by a Treaty of Friendship, Commerce and Navigation.[28] This usually entails giving preference to staffing executive positions in the U.S. facility with individuals who are nationals of the employer's home country.[29] For example, if a U.S./Korean friendship, navigation, and commerce treaty existed, a Korean firm operating in the United States might be permitted to staff the key executive positions in its U.S. operation with Korean nationals. Bear in mind that such treaties also convey a reciprocal right for U.S. companies operating in Korea to give similar preferences to U.S. citizens working there.

Foreign Employees Working in the United States

When addressing national origin discrimination, it is important to remember that Title VII applies just as much to foreign nationals residing in the United States as it does to U.S. citizens. Individuals who are employed in the United States are protected by Title VII and other EEO statutes regardless of citizenship or immigration status.[30] A resident alien who is a Jamaican national working in the United States is protected against national origin discrimination just as much as a U.S. citizen of Cuban ancestry born in Miami, Florida. What managers must also be aware of is that the legal status of the foreign national does not diminish his or her Title VII protection.

It should be noted, however, that even an illegal alien is protected under Title VII against being treated differently in a work setting because of his or her national origin. Unfortunately, many employers and managers assume that because an individual is in the United States unlawfully, he or she is not covered under U.S. employment laws; nothing could be further from the truth. However, courts have ruled that though illegal aliens cannot be discriminated against under Title VII, they are not entitled to the remedies of reinstatement and/or back pay.[31]

American Employers Overseas

The Civil Rights Act of 1991, mentioned in Chapter 2, expanded the jurisdiction of Title VII to the overseas plants, offices, and facilities of American-owned companies.[32] Previously, Title VII was enforced only within the United States and its territories. Since 1991,

U.S. citizens working in the overseas facilities and offices of U.S.-controlled companies are protected against discrimination under Title VII, unless the host country has laws that supersede Title VII. This protection applies only to U.S. citizens working for U.S. companies or U.S.-controlled companies and not the citizens of other nations working at the same overseas facility.

The extraterritorial application of Title VII does not apply to foreign nationals working in the overseas facilities.[33] **Extraterritorial application** is a term which indicates that a U.S. law is being applied beyond the boundaries of the United States. Most U.S. statutes are enforceable only within the confines of the fifty states, the District of Columbia, and the U.S. territories (e.g., U.S. Virgin Islands and Guam). Laws that are extraterritorially applied affect American companies operating on foreign soil.

Assume that a U.S. company operating in Saudi Arabia has two female employees (one an American, the other a Saudi national) who both claim to have been sexually harassed in their respective workstations. The Saudi woman, who is not a U.S. citizen, can make no Title VII claim against the employer. The U.S. woman can make a Title VII claim, but only if there is no Saudi law governing sexual harassment. Since Saudi Arabia has no such laws, she may pursue her sexual harassment issue in a U.S. federal district court.

If the same incident had occurred in New Delhi, India, the outcomes for the two women would be as follows. Again, the woman who is not a U.S. citizen is precluded from invoking Title VII. However, the U.S. woman also is barred from making a Title VII claim, because India does have statutes governing sex discrimination. Consequently, she would have to litigate her case in the Indian court system.

Since the Civil Rights Act of 1991 extended extraterritorial protection only to U.S. citizens working overseas for U.S.-controlled companies, those who work overseas for foreign employers are not protected under Title VII. A U.S. citizen employed by BASF Aktiengesellschaft, the German chemical company, working at its Shreveport, Louisiana, facility is fully protected under U.S. law. If the U.S. citizen is transferred to Mannheim, Germany, he or she is now covered under the employment laws of Germany. Since BASF is not an American company or an American-controlled company, the extraterritorial provisions do not apply in any of its operations outside of the United States.

It should also be noted that the Civil Rights Act of 1991 made similar extraterritorial provisions for the Americans with Disabilities Act (ADA).[34]

THE IMMIGRATION REFORM AND CONTROL ACT OF 1986

One final issue closely related to national origin discrimination comes from the Immigration Reform and Control Act of 1986 (IRCA). The IRCA was enacted to address two very divergent immigration problems. Section 1324a of IRCA makes it unlawful for employers to knowingly hire, or to continue to employ, illegal aliens.[35] Additionally, Section 1324b of the Act prohibits the employer from discriminating in employment on the basis of citizenship status.[36]

To achieve its primary purpose, preventing the hiring of illegal aliens (i.e., undocumented workers), employers are required to verify that all employees are legally authorized to work in the United States. Parties legally authorized to work in the United States include American citizens, resident aliens, and aliens with the express permission of the attorney general to work in the United States.[37] Employers are required to show proof of this verification by having every employee hired after November 6, 1986, complete a **Form I-9** (see Figure 7.3) and provide documentation establishing two critical conditions: the applicant's identity and his or her authorization to work in the United States (see Figure 7.4). This verification must be completed within "three business days of the hire."[38] The most common documents used to establish employment authorization and applicant identity are a social security card and a state driver's license. In order to clearly demonstrate that the employer has verified the applicant's identity, photocopies of the two sources of documentation should be filed with the Form I-9.

One question that often arises is, if the applicant submits fraudulent documents at the time he or she fills out the Form I-9, is the employer liable? Provided that the documents used in the verification process are not overt forgeries (i.e., bogus license formats, eight-digit social security numbers, etc.), the employer will not be considered guilty of knowingly hiring illegal aliens. The employer's obligation to verify the employment status of the applicant is satisfied by examining documents that reasonably appear to be genuine.[39]

E-Verification

The Department of Homeland Security (DHS) and the Social Security Administration (SSA) encourage state workforce agencies and private sector employers to voluntarily electronically verify (**E-verify**) the employment eligibility status of all newly hired employees.[40] Since the 2011 Supreme Court decision, *Chamber of Commerce v. Whiting*,[41] the number of states mandating E-verify has more than tripled. In this case, the Supreme Court upheld the constitutionality of Arizona's law requiring every employer to verify the employment eligibility for each employee using E-verify.[42] As of January 2013, six states (Alabama, Arizona, Georgia, Mississippi, North Carolina, and South Carolina) currently require all employers within their respective boundaries to E-verify.[43] Five other states (Indiana, Missouri, Nebraska, Oklahoma, and Virginia require employers holding state and/or federal contracts to use the E-Verify program.[44] Three states (Louisiana, Minnesota, and Pennsylvania) require public sector employers to e-verify all new hires.[45]

One of the purposes of the E-Verify program is to provide the employer with instant verification of the authenticity of the applicant's employment documents, in particular, his or her social security account number (SSAN). Under this system, the employer would E-verify a new hire's SSAN within three business days of his or her hiring. There are some constraints in this process. Only individuals receiving job offers can have their SSANs verified. The employee has to have completed the Form I-9. The employer *cannot* use the e-verification system as a pre-employment screening tool.[46] Employers are also prohibited from using E-Verify to screen their current workforces.[47]

Figure 7.3 **Form I-9**

OMB No. 1615-0047; Expires 06/30/09

**Form I-9, Employment
Eligibility Verification**

Department of Homeland Security
U.S. Citizenship and Immigration Services

Please read instructions carefully before completing this form. The instructions must be available during completion of this form.

ANTI-DISCRIMINATION NOTICE: It is illegal to discriminate against work eligible individuals. Employers **CANNOT** specify which document(s) they will accept from an employee. **The refusal to hire an individual because the documents have a future expiration date may also constitute illegal discrimination.**

Section 1. Employee Information and Verification. To be completed and signed by employee at the time employment begins.

Print Name: Last	First	Middle Initial	Maiden Name

Address *(Street Name and Number)*	Apt. #	Date of Birth *(month/day/year)*

City	State	Zip Code	Social Security #

I am aware that federal law provides for imprisonment and/or fines for false statements or use of false documents in connection with the completion of this form.

I attest, under penalty of perjury, that I am (check one of the following):
☐ A citizen or national of the United States
☐ A lawful permanent resident (Alien #) A _____
☐ An alien authorized to work until _____
(Alien # or Admission #) _____

Employee's Signature	Date *(month/day/year)*

Preparer and/or Translator Certification. *(To be completed and signed if Section 1 is prepared by a person other than the employee.)* I attest, under penalty of perjury, that I have assisted in the completion of this form and that to the best of my knowledge the information is true and correct.

Preparer's/Translator's Signature	Print Name

Address *(Street Name and Number, City, State, Zip Code)*	Date *(month/day/year)*

Section 2. Employer Review and Verification. To be completed and signed by employer. Examine one document from List A OR examine one document from List B and one from List C, as listed on the reverse of this form, and record the title, number and expiration date, if any, of the document(s).

List A	OR	List B	AND	List C
Document title:				
Issuing authority:				
Document #:				
Expiration Date *(if any)*:				
Document #:				
Expiration Date *(if any)*:				

CERTIFICATION - I attest, under penalty of perjury, that I have examined the document(s) presented by the above-named employee, that the above-listed document(s) appear to be genuine and to relate to the employee named, that the employee began employment on *(month/day/year)* _____ and that to the best of my knowledge the employee is eligible to work in the United States. (State employment agencies may omit the date the employee began employment.)

Signature of Employer or Authorized Representative	Print Name	Title

Business or Organization Name and Address *(Street Name and Number, City, State, Zip Code)*	Date *(month/day/year)*

Section 3. Updating and Reverification. To be completed and signed by employer.

A. New Name *(if applicable)*	B. Date of Rehire *(month/day/year) (if applicable)*

C. If employee's previous grant of work authorization has expired, provide the information below for the document that establishes current employment eligibility.

Document Title:	Document #:	Expiration Date (if any):

I attest, under penalty of perjury, that to the best of my knowledge, this employee is eligible to work in the United States, and if the employee presented document(s), the document(s) I have examined appear to be genuine and to relate to the individual.

Signature of Employer or Authorized Representative	Date *(month/day/year)*

Form I-9 (Rev. 06/05/07) N

Source: Form I-9 Compliance. https://www.formi9.com/.

Figure 7.4   **Verification Requirements under IRCA**

Documents Establishing Both Employment Identity and Authorization to Work in U.S.:	Documents Establishing Only Identity:	Employment Documents Establishing Authorization to Work in U.S Only:
U.S. passport	State driver's license	Social security card
Unexpired Temporary Resident Card (I-688, I-688A, I-688B)	State identification for those under age 16	U.S. birth certificate
Foreign passport with the authorization of the attorney general to work in the U.S. (Unexpired Employment Authorization Document I-766)		Other documentation authorizing employment in the U.S. approved by the attorney general

Source: 8 U.S.C. § 1324a(b)(1)(B).

In the event that the new hire's SSAN does not match the Social Security Administration's database, the employee must be immediately notified and afforded the opportunity to challenge and resolve the discrepancy. If the employee does not contest the initial "tentative nonconfirmation" notice, that employee may be terminated.

If the employee chooses to contest the "tentative nonconfirmation" notice, he or she is afforded several appellate opportunities with both the Social Security Administration and the Department of Homeland Security. Only when these appeals have been exhausted and DHS renders a decision of "employment unauthorized" or "no show" can the employer terminate the individual's employment.[48]

Penalties for Failure to Verify

Failure to maintain IRCA's documentation in either the electronic or paper form can subject the employer to civil fines ranging from a minimum of $110 per each individual worker without a Form I-9 to a maximum of $1,100 per individual worker (see Figure 7.5).[49]

In addition to prohibiting the hiring of illegal aliens, IRCA also prohibits discrimination in hiring and discharge based on national origin (as does Title VII) and citizenship status.[50] Specifically, Section 1324b prohibits discrimination based on citizenship status, a prohibition not encompassed by other antidiscrimination statutes.[51] Violations of IRCA's antidiscrimination provisions are referred to as **unfair immigration-related employment practices**. These antidiscrimination provisions are intended to prevent employers from attempting to comply with the Act's work authorization requirements by discriminating against foreign-looking or foreign-sounding job applicants. Of particular concern for smaller organizations is that IRCA's antidiscrimination provisions apply to smaller employers than those covered by EEOC enforceable laws. IRCA's national origin discrimination provisions also apply to those employers who would not be covered by Title VII—those falling within the range of having between four and fourteen employees.[52] IRCA's citizenship discrimination provisions effectively extend protection against discrimination based on national origin to all workplaces with at least four employees.

Figure 7.5   **Employer Penalties Under IRCA since March 27, 2008**

	Knowingly Recruiting and Hiring Undocumented Workers	Failure to Comply with Documentation/Verification Requirements
1st Offense	$375–$3,200	$110–$1,100
2nd Offense	$2,200–$6,500	
3rd Offense	$4,300–$16,000	
Pattern of Offenses	$3,000 and 6 months' imprisonment	

Because lawmakers were concerned that the verification process and penalties for hiring undocumented workers might cause employers to be reluctant to hire applicants of Hispanic origin, IRCA contains provisions making it an unfair immigration-related employment practice for:

> a person or other entity to discriminate against any individual (other than an unauthorized alien) with respect to the hiring, or recruitment or referral for a fee, of the individual employment or the discharging of the individual from employment—(a) because of such individual's national origin, or (b) in the case of a citizen or intending citizen (as defined in paragraph [3]) because of such individual's citizenship status.[53]

As a further concern, Title VII may be violated during the verification process if individuals of one national origin group (e.g., Hispanics) are subjected to greater scrutiny than individuals from other groups. For example, an applicant with a Hispanic surname is given a thorough background investigation while a candidate with a non-Spanish Western European surname only has her driver's license and social security card photocopied. This would be a Title VII violation because the individual with the Hispanic surname was subjected to different treatment (a more rigorous application process) because of his national origin.

In complying with IRCA's verification requirements, it is important to treat *all* employees the same. If thorough background checks are initiated, they must be initiated on all applicants, not just those of one particular national origin. It should be noted that IRCA does permit employers to give preference in hiring and recruiting of U.S. citizens over foreign nationals if the two individuals are *equally qualified*.[54]

Inpatriation and Temporary Immigrants

Inpatriation is the recruiting and selection of foreign employees to work in facilities in the United States. Perhaps the most publicized incident of inpatriation occurred in the 1970s when Filipino registered nurses were being actively recruited in response to the nationwide shortage of nursing professionals.[55] By 2000, foreign nurses represented over 4 percent of the total registered nurse population in the United States.[56] Since that time other understaffed industries (such as engineering, medicine, physical sciences, business specialties, etc.) have sought scarce skills in the global labor market.

To facilitate inpatriation, the Immigration and Nationality Act permits the temporary hiring of alien workers in certain specialty occupations.[57] To initiate this process, the U.S. employer (not the individual alien) must petition the U.S. Citizenship and Immigration Services (USCIS). By filing a labor certification request the employer enters the annual lottery to get an **H-1B visa** for the alien in question The H-1B is a nonimmigrant visa, and it only permits the holder to temporarily work in the United States. It is not a permanent resident's card (I-551, a.k.a. the green card), which, as the name implies, permits the holder to permanently remain in this country and to work in jobs that do not raise security concerns. Under current law, an alien can maintain his or her H-1B status for a maximum of six years. There is a cap of 65,000 such visas for each fiscal year.[58] However, the number of exceptions granted each year invariably exceed this number. For example in FY2012, there were 129,134 H-1B visas issued.[59]

Generally, temporary immigrants may only stay in the United States for a maximum of six years,[60] at which time, they must return to their home country upon the H-1B's expiration. There is an exception under the American Competitiveness in the Twenty-first Century Act of 2000[61] that permits extension of the temporary status in one-year increments for H-1B holders who have filed an Adjustment of Status petition with the outcome still pending.[62]

SUMMARY

It is always important to remember that national origin discrimination under Title VII applies to foreign nationals residing in the United States just as it does to U.S. citizens. National origin discrimination also encompasses language ability and proficiency, therefore it is important to ensure that all language requirements be related to successful job performance.

Once again, knowledge of an employer's compliance responsibilities must be translated into policies and practices to preclude potential litigation. In the case of English-only rules, managers must walk the fine line between meeting the organization's business-related needs and avoiding discrimination based on national origin.

Employers are also responsible for ensuring that their workforces include only those individuals who are lawfully authorized to work in the United States—U.S. citizens and resident aliens. Knowingly hiring illegal aliens exposes the employer to penalties under the Immigration Reform and Control Act. Even if managers have not knowingly hired illegal workers, employers could still be liable for penalties under IRCA if they fail to properly document that they verified an applicant's identity and authorization to work in the United States.

KEY TERMS AND CONCEPTS

English-only work rules

Extraterritorial application

E-Verify

Form I-9

H-1B visa

Inpatriation

Unfair immigration-related
  employment practices

DISCUSSION QUESTIONS

1. Are foreign nationals excluded from Title VII protection? Are illegal aliens?
2. When can employers impose English proficiency requirements for employment selection purposes?
3. To avoid a Title VII violation, English-only work rules must satisfy what four criteria?
4. What are an employer's verification responsibilities under the Immigration Reform and Control Act? Is there a time limit in which verification must be documented?
5. Does Title VII prohibit discrimination in employment based on U.S. citizenship? The Immigration Reform and Control Act?
6. What is an unfair immigration-related employment practice?
7. What is the E-Verify program and how does it work?
8. Under what circumstances is Title VII extraterritorially applied?

CASES

Case 1

Blackheart Enterprises is a small landscaping business employing 14 full-time and 10 part-time employees in the midwestern United States. Among Blackheart's employees were four Nicaraguan nationals who entered the United States illegally: Manuel Ortega, Felipe Sanchez, Fernando Montenegro, and Luis Vaca.

The four undocumented employees were worked harder than the U.S. citizens and were paid less. Manuel Ortega and his coworkers had grown weary of working long hours without being paid overtime. But each time Manuel and his friends complained, they were always told the same thing by their supervisor: "You are undocumented workers and in this country illegally. You have no right to overtime compensation if you have no right to work here. Now get back to work before you are fired or turned over to the immigration people and you get your [expletive deleted] hauled back to Mexico."

Several months later, Manuel met an organizer for the International Brotherhood of Teamsters (IBT). The organizer promised that if his coworkers vote in the union, all the workers would be treated better and get paid the same. The following day Manuel began handing out IBT organizing pamphlets in the break area during break time to all his fellow employees. His activities did not go unnoticed by his supervisor, who approached him and said, "I thought I told you that you 'illegals' don't have the same rights as real American citizens. I guess you're hard of hearing. Now you and the rest of your undocumented buddies can get off the company's property, and get off now! You're all fired!"

a. Is Manuel's supervisor correct?
b. If Manuel and his friends are undocumented workers, what U.S. employment laws discussed in this and previous chapters have been violated by the employer, if any?

Case 2

Rebecca was a resident alien working as a structural engineer for Cover-the-Earth International Construction, a U.S.-based company headquartered in Dallas, Texas, that engages in commercial construction projects worldwide. She is a native of Canada and a permanent resident of the United States, and worked for Cover-the-Earth for three years on its Minot, North Dakota, project. She liked her coworkers and the Minot project, and it was conveniently located near her home in Manitoba, Canada. When that project was completed, Rebecca was transferred to a new project in Riyadh, Saudi Arabia.

Within days of her transfer, Rebecca finds that Riyadh is a very different working environment from North Dakota. Many of the local workers refuse to respond to her instructions. Additionally, the two coworkers with whom she has been assigned are constantly berating her for trying to work in a place where women are not wanted. One coworker constantly refers to her, often in her presence, as the "Canadian b__h with the can't-do attitude," and tells the Saudi workers to just ignore her and she will go away.

Despondent, Rebecca complains that she is being sexually harassed and demands that Cover-the-Earth transfer her to their project in the U.S. Virgin Islands. When the company refuses to do so, Rebecca threatens to file a sex discrimination complaint with the EEOC.

   a. Does Rebecca have a viable Title VII claim? Why or why not?
   b. If this happened to Rebecca in the U.S. Virgin Islands, would she have a viable Title VII claim? Why or why not?
   c. If Rebecca had been a U.S. citizen in Saudi Arabia would she have a viable Title VII claim? Why or why not?

Case 3

Kaizen Automotive, a Japanese automaker, has a production facility in Ohio that employees over 600 workers. In December 2013, it announces an executive position has opened at the facility and solicits applications. Among the finalists for the position is June, a Japanese citizen and graduate of MIT with four year's experience in automotive production. Another candidate is John, an African American who is also an MIT graduate and holds an MBA from Harvard. John has over ten year's automotive manufacturing experience. In very short order, Kaizen announces that June is the successful candidate and offers her the position.

John files a charge with the EEOC alleging that he was not selected for the position because of his race and national origin.

Kaizen states that it lawfully considered June's Japanese citizenship pursuant to a treaty permitting it to favor Japanese applicants. The subsequent EEOC investigation reveals that a Treaty of Friendship, Commerce and Navigation exists and that Kaizen has never promoted an American citizen to an executive level position in its U.S. operations.

   a. Does John have a viable Title VII complaint? Why or why not?

b. If June had been a U.S. citizen of Japanese ancestry, would the outcome be changed?

c. If June had been a Chinese citizen, would the outcome be changed?

NOTES

1. Scenario was developed from the facts in *EEOC v. Premier Operator Services*, 113 C. Supp.2d 1066 (N.D. Tex. 2000).

2. 29 C.F.R. § 1606 (2012).

3. 29 C.F.R. § 1606.1.

4. C. Bowman, "BLS projections to 2006—a summary," *Monthly Labor Review* 120, no. 11 (1997): 3–5.

5. H. Shin and R. Bruno, *Language Use and English-Speaking Ability: 2000* (Washington, DC: U.S. Bureau of the Census, 2003).

6. G. Bhattacharya and S. Schoppelrey, "Preimmigration beliefs of life success, postimmigration experiences, and acculturative stress: South Asian immigrants in the United States," *Journal of Immigrant Health* 6, no. 2 (2004): 83–92.

7. *De La Cruz v. New York City Human Resources Administration*, 82 F.3d 16, 22 (2nd Cir. 1996); *Fragante v. City & County of Honolulu*, 888 F.2d 591, 598 (9th Cir. 1989), cert. denied, 494 U.S. 1081 (1990).

8. *Ghirmai v. Northwest Airlines, Inc.,* 131 Fed. Appx. 609 (9th Cir. 2005).

9. *Shieh v. Ling*, 710 F.Supp. 1024 (E.D. Penn. 1989).

10. *Baltazar v. Shinseki*, 2012 U.S. App. LEXIS 12931, *14 (10th Cir. 2012).

11. *Church v. Kare Distribution*, Inc., 211 Fed. Appx. 278 (5th Cir. 2006).

12. *Morales v. Human Rights Division,* 878 F. Supp. 653, 659 (S.D.N.Y. 1995).

13. U.S. English, Inc., States with Official English Laws, http://www.us-english.org/inc/official/states.asp (accessed January 13, 2013).

14. J. Hill, D. Ross, B. Serafine, and R.E. Levy, "Survey: Watch Your Language! The Kansas Law Review Survey of Official English and English-Only Laws and Policies," *Kansas Law Review* 57 (2009): 699–737.

15. 29 C.F.R. § 1606.7(a).

16. 29 C.F.R. § 1603.

17. 29 C.F.R. § 1604.11.

18. 29 C.F.R. § 1606.8(a).

19. 998 F.2d 1480 (9th Cir. 1993).

20. *Garcia v. Spun Steak Company*, 998 F.2d at 1487.

21. Ibid., at 1488.

22. *EEOC v. Sephora USA, LLC*, 419 F.Supp.2d 408, 417 (S.D.N.Y. 2005).

23. B. Piatt, *Language on the Job: Balancing Business Needs and Employee Rights* (Albuquerque: University of New Mexico Press, 1993).

24. 29 C.F.R. §§ 1606.7(a) & (b).

25. 29 C.F.R. § 1606.7(b).

26. *Maldonado v. City of Altus,* 433 F.3d 1294 (10th Cir. 2006).

27. 29 C.F.R. § 1606.7(b).

28. *Wallace v. SMC Pneumatics, Inc.*, 103 F.3d 1394 (7th Cir. 1997).

29. *Sumitomo Shoji America, Inc., v. Avigliano*, 457 U.S. 176, 180 (1982).

30. EEOC, *EEOC Compliance Manual* §2-III(A)(4) (July 21, 2005).

31. *Rivera v. NIBCO, Inc.*, 284 F.3d 882 (9th Cir. 2004).

32. 42 U.S.C. § 2000e-1(b).

33. *Sheykoyan v. Sibley International Corp.*, 409 F.3d 414, 421 (D.C. Cir. 2005).

34. 42 U.S.C. §§ 12101–12213 (Supp. V 1993).

35. 8 U.S.C. § 1324a(a).

36. 8 U.S.C. § 1324b(a).

37. 8 U.S.C. § 1324a(b).

38. 8 C.F.R. § 274a.2(b)(ii).

39. *Collins Foods International, Inc. v. INS*, 948 F.2d 549, 553 (9th Cir. 1991).

40. USCIS "Statement for the Record: E-Verify" (May 2008), www.uscis.gov/portal/site/uscis/menuitem.5af9bb95919f35e66f614176543f6d1a/?vgnextoid=bca6fa693660a110VgnVCM100000 4718190aRCRD&vgnextchannel=68439c7755cb9010VgnVCM10000045f3d6a1RCRD (accessed January 3, 2013).

41. 131 S. Ct. 1968 (2011).

42. 131 S. Ct. at 1976.

43. J. Feere, *An Overview of E-Verify Policies at the State Level*. Center for Immigration Studies. (July 2012). http://cis.org/e-verify-at-the-state-level (accessed January 3, 2013).

44. Ibid.

45. Ibid.

46. US Citizenship and Immigration Services, *E-Verify User Manual for Employers* (Washington, DC: USCIS, (September 2012).

47. Ibid.

48. Ibid.

49. 8 U.S.C. § 1324a(e)(5).

50. 8 U.S.C. § 1324a.

51. *General Dynamics Corp. v. United States*, 49 F.3d 1384 (9th Cir. 1995).

52. 8 U.S.C. § 1324(a)(2)(B).

53. 8 U.S.C. § 1324b(a).

54. 8 U.S.C. § 1324(a)(4).

55. M. Harvey, M.R. Buckley, and M. Novicevic, "Addressing ethical issues associated with in-patriation of nursing professionals," *Journal of Applied Management and Entrepreneurship* 11, no. 4 (2006).

56. E. Spratley, A. Johnson, J. Sochalski, M. Fritz, and W. Spenser, *The Registered Nurse Population: Findings from the National Sample Survey of Registered Nurses* (Washington, DC: Division of Nursing, Bureau of Health Professions, Health Resources and Services Administration, U.S. Department of Human Services, March 2000).

57. 8 CFR § 214.2(o)(1)(i) & (ii).

58. U.S. Citizenship and Immigration Services, *Fact Sheet: Changes to the FY2009 H-1B Program* (Washington, DC: USCIS, March 19, 2008).

59. U.S. Department of State, *Report of the Visa Office 2011: Table XVI(B) Nonimmigrant Visas Issued by Classification (Including Crewlist Visas and Border Crossing Cards) Fiscal Years 2007–2011*. http://www.travel.state.gov/pdf/FY11AnnualReport-Table%20XVI%28B%29.pdf (accessed January 3, 2013).

60. 114 Stat. 1251.

61. 8 U.S.C. §1184(g)(4).

62. U.S. Citizenship and Immigration Services, Interim Guidance for Processing Form I-140 Employment-Based Immigrant Petitions and Form I-485 and H-1B Petitions Affected by the American Competitiveness in the Twenty-First Century Act of 2000 (AC21) (Public Law 106-313) (May 12, 2005). http://www.uscis.gov/USCIS/Laws/Memoranda/Static_Files_Memoranda/Archives%201998-2008/2005/ac21intrm051205.pdf (accessed January 13, 2013).

8

AFFIRMATIVE ACTION

LEARNING OBJECTIVES

- Recognize the difference between affirmative action and equal employment opportunity.
- Describe the difference between involuntary and voluntary affirmative action programs.
- Understand the arguments for preserving or eliminating affirmative action.
- Identify the conditions under which affirmative action is permissible under Title VII.
- Identify the conditions under which public sector employers may engage in affirmative action.
- Describe the major components of an affirmative action plan.
- Develop a permissible affirmative action plan.
- Identify employment practices that could create reverse discrimination complaints.

OPENING SCENARIO

A small private college is trying to fill the position vacancy for its director of equal opportunity and regulatory compliance. A search committee has been formed, and during its first meeting, the following position announcement has been presented for committee approval:

POSITION: Director of Equal Opportunity and Regulatory Compliance

QUALIFICATIONS: Bachelor's degree from an accredited institution required; graduate degree preferred. Demonstrated supervisory skills, ability to work in positive relationships and to communicate with all segments of the university community, experience with computer-based applications, and ability to interpret and manage data used in preparation of reports submitted to federal and state regulatory agencies required for effective performance of the job.

RESPONSIBILITIES: Administer the Office of Equal Opportunity and Regulatory Compliance; prepare university's affirmative action plan and related compliance reports to federal and state regulatory agencies; conduct educational training sessions for university community on issues pertaining to equal opportunity and affirmative action; prepare and maintain statistical information for regulatory reports; supervise support staff and student workers; investigate complaints of equal opportunity violations; maintain affirmative action job classification files and ensure the files are in compliance with federal and state regulations; serve as university's Sections 503/504, ADA, and Title IX Coordinator; prepare university responses to Equal Employment Opportunity Commission (EEOC), Office of Civil Rights of the Department of Education (OCR), and Office of Federal Contract Compliance Programs (OFCCP) charges; and perform related duties as required. Reporting line for the Director of Equal Opportunity and Regulatory Compliance is to the provost of the university.

APPLICATION PROCEDURE: Submit letter of application that addresses the advertised qualifications, comprehensive resume, and names, addresses, and telephone numbers of three current references.

One of the committee members, Charles Silvey, expressed concern that the job responsibilities and qualifications did not seem to be consistent with one another. It appeared to Charles that anyone with a bachelor's degree in any field could apply for the job. Should not the candidate at least have training in human resource management or business management?

Elizabeth Day responded that the field was immaterial, since the candidate could easily learn on the job. Besides, requiring a professional degree could result in more minority candidates being excluded from the applicant pool. However, Elizabeth did have a problem with the minimum requirement being only a bachelor's degree. After all, she contended, the faculty had little respect for anyone who did not possess a doctorate. Elizabeth then recommended that the candidate should have a terminal degree (a doctorate).

William Eaton next suggested that whatever criteria were chosen, they must be framed to ensure that either a minority or a female candidate was chosen for the position. After all, he contended, white males lack the empathy to understand affirmative action issues. The committee then began discussing the merits of these proposals.

THE HISTORY OF AFFIRMATIVE ACTION

No topic in employee relations has generated as much controversy and emotion as affirmative action. When one looks at the preferential treatment component of affirmative action programs, one is immediately confronted with a practice that has not only polarized American society but has the potential of disrupting the workplace as well. Not surprisingly, no other employment practice is more misunderstood or abused than affirmative action.

On July 2, 1965, the Civil Rights Act of 1964 provisions mandating color-blind employment practices became effective.[1] Within 114 days, President Lyndon Johnson signed Executive Order 11246, which provided the motivation for race-conscious recruiting and hiring under affirmative action.[2]

The term "affirmative action" can be traced to the earlier Executive Order 10925. In this order, President John F. Kennedy urged federal contractors to take "affirmative action" to ensure individuals, during employment, were treated without regard to their race, color, religion, sex, or national origin.[3] However, under Executive Order 11246, each contractor or subcontractor was required to file a compliance report with the contracting federal agency or secretary of labor.

It was this requirement to monitor applicants and selection outcomes that led to race-conscious employment practices. These compliance reports required contractors to provide information on practices, policies, programs, and *employment statistics*. Over time, these requirements would evolve into more elaborate reporting formats such as the EEO-1 through EEO-6 reports and the very sophisticated formalized affirmative action programs delineated in **Revised Order No. 4**.[4] *Revised Order No. 4* contains the OFCCP's guidance for constructing programs that would meet their standards of review.

In theory, affirmative action was intended to "level the playing field," or allow groups that had previously been discriminated against to catch up with those who faced no such barriers. Proponents of affirmative action still make this argument. Opponents often argue there have been nearly four decades of such programs. Many proponents insist there can be no equality of opportunity until affirmative action has leveled the field.

Affirmative action plans eventually received limited statutory recognition with the enactment of the Vocational Rehabilitation Act of 1973. This statute requires certain federal contractors and grant recipients to take affirmative action in employing *qualified handicapped individuals*. One year later, the Vietnam Era Veteran's Readjustment Assistance Act of 1974 contained language requiring specified federal aid recipients and contractors to provide similar affirmative action in employing Vietnam-era veterans.

By 1978, affirmative action programs were becoming common enough in both the public and private sectors that the Equal Employment Opportunity Commission issued its *Uniform Guidelines on Employee Selection Procedures*. These guidelines contained provisions covering affirmative action obligations and encouraged the adoption of voluntary affirmative action programs.[5] The EEOC maintains that affirmative action is a legitimate means to achieve equal employment opportunity and is not only permitted but encouraged.[6]

In practice, affirmative action focuses employers' attention on the racial, ethnic, and gender composition of their internal workforces compared with the relevant external labor market. Employers then must determine whether given protected groups are represented in proportion to their percentage of the relevant labor market. Under specific circumstances, employers are permitted to make race-, ethnic-, or gender-conscious decisions to achieve (but not maintain) proportional representation. Both federal courts and regulatory agencies have established guidelines where protected classes may receive preferential treatment under an affirmative action plan and not violate Title VII or the Equal Protection Clause of the Fourteenth Amendment. However, failure to comply with these guidelines will expose organizations to reverse discrimination.

Affirmative action has many different meanings and can be applied to at least four general employment practices. First, affirmative action can be the intentional recruitment of applicants or the utilization of training programs to impart necessary job skills for current employees who are members of underutilized protected groups.[7] An **underutilized protected group** is a protected group under Title VII that is underrepresented in the workforce in proportion to the relevant external market. Second, affirmative action can be the implementation of measures to eliminate any prejudices that managers and supervisors have toward underutilized protected groups in the employer's workforce.[8] Third, affirmative action can imply the identification of existing employment practices that work to foster and promote underutilization of a particular protected group and the removal of such practices.[9] Fourth, affirmative action can involve the preferential hiring and promoting of protected group members in order to remedy underutilization.[10]

Because of the potential legal liability for employers, the remainder of this chapter will examine the preferential component of affirmative action and its consequences for employers. Any further reference to "affirmative action" will mean the preferential treatment element.

The preferential treatment of protected group members is often initiated by an employer (or a court) to correct some past discrimination in the selection, promotion, or employment of women and minorities. This is particularly true when it can be proved the underutilization of the protected group is a present effect of the employer's past discriminatory practices. The preferential treatment form of affirmative action is also the component that has led many critics to assert that such actions constitute reverse discrimination. It is the least popular form of affirmative action and is responsible for much of the opposition to such programs. In fact, public opinion polls conducted during the past 25 years reveal that between 70 to 80 percent of the respondents oppose granting preferential treatment to individuals based on racial or ethnic classifications[11] (see Table 8.1).

Most Americans do not seem to be opposed to the more benign forms of affirmative action, the three forms other than preferential treatment. Polls show majority support for special training or education programs for underrepresented protected group members to enhance their qualifications for better jobs, particularly when the term, "Affirmative action" is used.[12] However, in the context of competition for a position or benefit (such as promotions or choice assignments), most survey respondents indicate that the concept of extending preferences is distasteful and the benefit should ultimately go to the *most qualified* applicant, regardless of the group to which the applicant belongs.[13] By the late 1990s, public dislike of preferences culminated in increased organized support for the elimination of the fourth form of affirmative action through such measures as the California Civil Rights Initiative (i.e., Proposition 209),[14] Washington State Civil Rights Act (i.e., I-200),[15] and an increase in reverse discrimination litigation.

Table 8.1

Public Opinion Polls Showing Percentage of Americans Who Do NOT Favor Preferential Treatment

Demographic Category	Year of Survey					
	1977	1980	1984	1989	1995‡	2001‡
Ethnicity:	89	90	90	90	87	92*
Nonwhites	70	71	73	86	83	86*
Whites	91	93	92	93	89	92*
Gender:						
Men	88	89	89	90	87	92*
Women	90	91	91	90	87	92*
Political Party:						
Democrats	89	86	87	83	81	87*
Republicans	93	94	95	95	92	97*

Sources: Statistics for the years 1977, 1980, 1984, and 1989 were drawn from G. Gallup, Jr., *The Gallup Poll*, for the respective year of the survey: 1977: 1057–1060; 1980: 106–107; 1984: 141–143; and 1989: 231. The statistics for 1995 were drawn from the CNN, *USA Today*, and Gallup Organization surveys of February 24–26, 1995, and March 17–19, 1995.

*Percentages of respondents not identifying with the former viewpoint in the question, "Some people say that, to make up for past discrimination, women and minority groups should be given preferential treatment in getting jobs and places in colleges. Others say that their ability, as determined in test scores, should be the main consideration. Which point of view comes closer to how you feel on the subject?"

‡Phrasing of question was somewhat different for survey taken in 1995.

Arguments Supporting Affirmative Action

Both proponents and opponents of preferential treatment offer powerful arguments for retaining or eliminating such programs[16] (see Figure 8.1). As the United States becomes an increasingly diverse society, this debate is likely to intensify. The following is a brief overview of the principal arguments offered by *both* sides of the debate.

Corrects Past Wrongs

Many advocates of preferential treatment view it as a means of providing reparations for groups that have been discriminated against historically—ethnic minorities and women. From this retributive perspective, preferential treatment is a means to repay groups for historical discrimination. An argument popularly offered is that African Americans do poorly in American society in terms of income and education due to the vestiges of "three hundred years of slavery." [17] Thus, since they have been historically victimized, society owes them the opportunity to catch up. Although this view is widely held by the proponents of affirmative action, it has not been accepted by the courts. Practitioners are warned that the Supreme Court has held that *societal discrimination* does not come under the domain of either Title VII or the Equal Protection Clause.[18] As the Supreme

Figure 8.1   **The Affirmative Action Debate**

Arguments For:	Arguments Against:
Corrects past wrongs	Fights discrimination with discrimination
Achieves economic and occupational equity	Group rights versus individual rights
Breaks down stereotypes	Reinforces stereotypes
Creates role models	Punishes the innocent

Court noted in the 1989 *Croson* decision, if courts permitted preferences based on the harm that various minorities suffer at the hands of general society, personal opportunity and achievement would be lost in a mosaic of shifting preferences based inherently on immeasurable claims of past wrongs.[19] This bluntly means employers cannot use *societal discrimination* to justify their preferential programs.

However, the courts have long held that employers *are* responsible for the present effects of any discrimination in which they engaged.[20] Consequently, any injury caused by the employer's actions must be remedied or corrected. Affirmative action has been accepted as one of those remedies. Therefore, employers are justified (if not compelled) to correct their own discriminatory actions but precluded from correcting society's past discrimination.

Achieves Economic and Occupational Equality

Due to centuries of oppression, many proponents of affirmative action contend that some ethnic groups are ill prepared to take full advantage of equal opportunities. One analogy often used is that these groups got to the starting line after the race had begun. Under this perspective, affirmative action is seen as a temporary device designed to make "the race" fair. Without this help, ethnic minorities would be doomed to being left behind, never being able to quite catch up to the income levels of those groups that got a head start. Under this line of reasoning, preferential treatment becomes the means of correcting these societal inequities and ensures ethnic minorities can achieve the American dream.

Breaks Down Stereotypes

Affirmative action, it is theorized, is also necessary in order to break down stereotypes about women and ethnic minorities. By ensuring these groups are appropriately represented at all levels of the organization, other employees will, in theory, learn to respect and appreciate female and minority employees. The basic benefit of this inclusion is that superiors, peers, and subordinates alike will see, through daily contact, that women and ethnic minorities are as technically competent as any other employee. By achieving a balanced workforce, other employees may see that the negative attitudes they held against these groups were unfounded. Through education, contact, and example, all employees of an organization will develop a new respect and understanding for the preferred classes.

Provides Role Models

Affirmative action is necessary in order to provide role models for successive generations. By observing members of their own ethnic groups as successful business leaders, physicians, attorneys, and other professionals, children from these groups will be encouraged to succeed as well. As more members from these groups succeed, even more will be encouraged to try. In the long run, this process would eventually eliminate the economic and educational inequities that currently exist along ethnic lines. Proponents contend these anticipated results will take decades to achieve, but by maintaining affirmative action programs, they will eventually be attained. The underlying belief is that in the absence of discrimination, all occupations will be representative of the ethnic composition of the population.[21] However, the Supreme Court ruled in *Wygant v. Jackson Board of Education* that role models cannot be used to justify preferences.[22]

Arguments Against Affirmative Action

Opponents have long contended that the use of preferential programs clearly violates Title VII's prohibition of basing *any* employment decision on *any* individual's race, color, religion, sex, or national origin. Although the stated goal of affirmative action is the elimination of race and gender inequity in employment practices, preferential treatment attempts to accomplish this goal by practicing race and gender consciousness.[23] This contradiction—creating a racially neutral society through the use of race-conscious actions and decisions—is at the very heart of the current affirmative action debate.

The situation creates an interesting paradox. On one hand, employers are required by the Civil Rights Act of 1964 to make racially neutral decisions. On the other hand, affirmative action requires them to make racially conscious decisions. However, the federal courts have been reluctant to satisfactorily resolve this dilemma. Beyond expressing concern that "[r]acial and ethnic distinctions of any sort are inherently suspect and thus call for the most exacting judicial examination,"[24] the judiciary has resorted to constructing complicated rules and procedures to perpetuate the distinctions.

Fights Discrimination with Discrimination

One of the most common arguments against these programs asks the question, how can Americans move to a color-blind society by encouraging race-conscious programs like affirmative action? In other words, can you eradicate discrimination with discrimination?

In practice, it is argued, preferential treatment actually creates racial barriers rather than removing them. Tension is likely to result in situations like the following. Suppose that a white male applicant (who has never discriminated against anyone) is denied an employment opportunity in favor of an applicant who is Hispanic and who has never experienced tangible employment discrimination.[25] If the white applicant is the more qualified, he is likely to perceive this outcome as being unfair.

Group Rights versus Individual Rights

Affirmative action shifts the premise of equal opportunity from individual rights to group rights. Title VII was intended to protect any *individual* from discrimination because of "such *individual's* race, color, religion, sex, or national origin."[26] Instead of focusing on individual outcomes, affirmative action concentrates on group outcomes. How a *group* is proportionately represented in a workplace supersedes *individual* interests.

Reinforces Stereotypes

Opponents of affirmative action have long contended that when minimally qualified preferred group members are selected for hiring or promotion over more qualified non-preferred group candidates, notions of inferiority and hostility will naturally follow.[27] The conclusion is often drawn that had it not been for an applicant's ethnicity or gender, he or she would not possess the qualifications to compete *fairly* for the job. Opponents offer the adage that when affirmative action talks, merit walks. Proponents of affirmative action too frequently conclude that if employment outcomes were truly left to merit, there would be very few preferred group members in the organization at all, and that protected groups cannot compete in a workplace based on equal opportunity.

Punishes the Innocent

If affirmative action is a device designed to repay one group for the evils of past discrimination, who pays whom? There exists a very real fear that persons who have not actually been discriminated against will be advanced at the expense of persons who have neither practiced nor benefited from discrimination.[28] The argument is as follows: Suppose the granddaughter of a man who benefited from the preferential promotion of whites in the late 1950s is applying for a promotion in a major marketing firm today. Is it fair for her to bear the burden of her grandfather's benefiting from discrimination by now being passed over for promotion in favor of the less qualified grandson of an African American man who was discriminated against in the 1950s?

Regardless of your personal feelings about affirmative action, the cold hard fact of the matter is that it is a legal practice common to many businesses and organizations. In its legal form, it does not please many proponents, who believe it does not go far enough. Nor does it please opponents, who believe it should not exist at all. The outcome of this highly political debate is better left to the ballot box. As a human resource manager, your primary obligation to your employer is to guarantee compliance with the laws and regulations that cover affirmative action. Your task will be to walk the very fine line between permissible affirmative action and reverse discrimination.

INVOLUNTARY VERSUS VOLUNTARY AFFIRMATIVE ACTION

The two broad categories of affirmative action programs are involuntary affirmative action and voluntary affirmative action (see Figure 8.2). The significant difference between the two is that **involuntary affirmative action** is a remedy imposed by a court when an employer

Figure 8.2 **Types of Affirmative Action**

Involuntary
- Court imposed

Voluntary
- Consent arrangements
- Eligibility for federal contracts or grants
- Voluntarily initiated programs

has been found in violation of Title VII or the Equal Protection Clause. For example, a state agency may have engaged in blatant and continuous racial discrimination in its hiring practices. The court may then order preferential hiring of qualified applicants of the race against whom the agency had discriminated. The action, provided it is narrowly tailored to do so, is intended to correct the present effects (the underrepresentation of members of the race against which unlawful discrimination had occurred) of past discriminatory hiring practices.

Voluntary affirmative action is applied to all other programs *not* imposed by a court, including consent agreements, programs developed for eligibility in certain federal programs, and programs created by an employer for the express purpose of eliminating the effects of past discriminatory policies and practices.

On some occasions, an employer may be required to establish an **affirmative action plan** (AAP) as the result of a court order. Under such circumstances, the court compels the employer to engage in affirmative action, particularly in its preferential treatment aspect, to remedy some past discriminatory practices. Involuntary affirmative action has been recognized as a remedial tool to alleviate discriminatory employment practices since 1965, when the Supreme Court ruled in *U.S. v. Louisiana* that "[a] district court not merely has the power but the *duty* to render a decree which will, so far as possible, eliminate the discriminatory effects of the past, as well as bar like discrimination in the future."[29] This perspective was reinforced in the 1987 case, *U.S. v. Paradise*, in which the Supreme Court ruled that court-imposed race-conscious relief is justified so long as the nonfavored group candidates are qualified.[30]

The authority to require involuntary affirmative action is drawn from Title VII of the Civil Rights Act of 1964. Title VII empowered federal courts to impose affirmative action where the employer is engaging in unlawful employment practices, either intentionally *or* unintentionally. Specifically, Section 706(g) of Title VII empowers the court to "[e]njoin the respondent from engaging in unlawful employment practices, and order such affirmative action as may be appropriate, which may include, but is not limited to, reinstatement of hiring of employees, with or without back pay or any other equitable remedy as the court deems appropriate."[31] Based on the interpretation of this clause, federal courts have ordered AAPs to rectify racial and gender imbalances that are present in an employer's workforce as a result of prior discriminatory practices.

VOLUNTARY AFFIRMATIVE ACTION

There are three general categories into which voluntary affirmative action programs may fall: consent arrangements, eligibility requirements, and voluntarily initiated plans.

Consent Arrangements

Closely associated with involuntary AAPs are consent arrangements. Under a consent decree, the employer and the complaining party or parties enter into an agreement creating an AAP *prior* to a judgment (an involuntary remedy) being rendered by the court. In these instances, the employer has been found guilty of some discriminatory employment practice. Rather than depending on the court to impose an AAP of its design, the employer opts for a solution that would be mutually acceptable to all involved parties. Once the parties to the suit have agreed to a formal plan, it is presented to the court for approval. Barring any obvious flaw in the plan developed by the employer and the aggrieved party (parties), the court will approve the implementation of the consent decree.

To illustrate this practice, suppose an employer was found to have discriminated against female employees in its promotion practices and a court-ordered remedy was pending. The employer instead chooses to meet with the affected female employees and develop an AAP acceptable to them. Such an arrangement may be more realistic than one fashioned by a federal judge unfamiliar with the employer's business. It could also improve relations with the aggrieved employees by demonstrating that the employer is sincere in its desire to make amends for its previous actions.

Let's assume the solution mutually agreed to was to set aside 50 percent of all promotions for *qualified* women. The employer may be agreeable to this, and likewise, the female employees may find it acceptable. However, one group of employees—males—might see this arrangement as detrimental to their interests. If the plan were implemented as stated, men could feasibly see 50 percent of their advancement opportunities disappear during the life of the AAP. Since it is a well-held principle in American jurisprudence that individuals cannot be held to a contract to which they are not a party,[32] the Civil Rights Act of 1991 now provides a degree of protection to third parties of consent decrees. If a group of employees will be adversely affected by the consent arrangement, they should be notified of its contents and given the opportunity to have their arguments heard.

Thus, the Civil Rights Act of 1991 requires that all parties affected by a consent agreement must be notified of the actual terms of the agreement and afforded the opportunity to present objections to provisions that would adversely affect their interests.[33] Failure to include a representative for the other applicants or employees affected by the consent agreement could expose the company to legal challenges in the future.

Because the AAP is developed outside of the courtroom and submitted to the court for approval before the court provides a plan of its own, such plans are treated as voluntary programs. Even though they are court approved, these AAPs are subject to the same scrutiny as any other voluntary plan when reverse discrimination is alleged.[34]

The Civil Rights Act of 1991 imposes limitations on challenges to such AAPs to preclude third parties from initiating an indefinite number of litigations. The law contains language that strengthens the finality of consent decrees. The Act modifies accepted contract theory by declaring "an employment practice that implements and is within a consent judgment or order that resolves a claim of employment discrimination under the United States Constitution or federal civil rights laws may not be challenged under the circumstances described in subparagraph (B)."[35] Among the circumstances mentioned in the Act that limit challenges to consent decrees are those persons who, prior to the entry of the decree, had notice of the pending arrangement and had a *reasonable opportunity* to voice their objections to its contents. If "a reasonable opportunity to present objections to such judgment" was provided to affected parties, no party may challenge the judgment at a later date.[36] Once they have been notified of the decree's contents and given the opportunity to express their dissent, the affected parties cannot challenge the consent arrangement in the future if they chose not to exercise their dissent. Additionally, no current or future employees can challenge a decree later if their interests or views were reasonably represented by another party, or parties, who challenged the judgment prior to its entry (or chose not to). In essence, if any employee or group of employees with similar interests to the aggrieved party either presented or *had the opportunity to present objections to the initial decree*, then an aggrieved party is prevented from raising the issue at a future date.

From the employer's standpoint, the Civil Rights Act of 1991 provides a good degree of insulation against future reverse discrimination suits. Since the Act bars all after-the-decree challenges by adversely affected parties, provided that they were given sufficient notification of the consent agreement and given an opportunity to intervene before it was adopted, employers need only ensure these accommodations are made.[37] The concept is quite simple. If the employees are provided the opportunity to voice their concerns initially, they may not raise them at a later date.

Eligibility for Federal Contracts

The next form of voluntary affirmative action involves establishing eligibility for federal contracts. It is "voluntary" to the extent the employer has the choice of establishing an AAP or being disqualified from federal contract consideration. Therefore, any organization wishing to do business with the federal government must adopt such programs and assume affirmative action obligations.[38]

Employers and entities affected by this form of voluntary affirmative action include:

1. Prime contractors and subcontractors with fifty or more employees and a federal contract of $50,000 or more.
2. Organizations with government bills of lading that total $50,000 or more. A bill of lading is a document used by a transportation company that verifies the receipt of goods.
3. Depositories for federal funds in any amount.
4. Firms that serve as issuing or paying agents for United States savings bonds.[39]

Any employer meeting these conditions must develop a written affirmative action compliance program for each of its establishments or have its contracts or deposits removed. If an employer receives government money, he or she must comply with the government's regulations.

The classes of employees entitled to preferential selection under federally mandated AAPs are more extensive than those under Title VII. Certain federal statutes require affirmative action be taken for qualified individuals with a disability[40] and Vietnam-era veterans,[41] in addition to women and ethnic minorities.

Thus, the list of classes to which utilization analysis applies includes race, sex, national origin, disability, and veteran status. Remember, the need to establish a formal AAP with goals and timetables is dependent upon the size of the government contract or subcontract the employer holds.

Voluntarily Initiated Programs

In addition to those employers who "voluntarily" initiate AAPs in order to maintain federal contracts, some employers may be motivated to adopt affirmative action as a result of social or ethical responsibility. The employer may also be acting out of a desire to create corporate legitimacy or may be attempting to avoid potential unlawful discrimination charges. Regardless of employer motives, care should be taken to ensure the voluntary AAP criteria are met. Courts will expect such plans to be based on some "manifest imbalance" in the employer's workforce—an imbalance best supported by good utilization analysis. Always remember that in order to be permissible under Title VII, a voluntary plan must be remedial in nature.[42]

Although the EEOC contends it does not require employers to follow mandatory methods and formats, the agency does state that an acceptable AAP should contain three elements: a reasonable self-analysis, a reasonable basis for concluding affirmative action is appropriate, and reasonable action.[43] However, the EEOC also encourages employers to follow the more exacting guidelines presented by the Office of Federal Contract Compliance Programs' *Revised Order No. 4*.[44] As a consequence, the reasonable self-analysis could be accomplished through the utilization analysis described in *Revised Order No. 4*.

Recall from Chapter 2 that Title VII prohibits discrimination in employment against *any individual* on the basis of that *individual's* race, color, religion, sex, or national origin. It applies to:

- Private employers with fifteen or more employees
- Labor unions with fifteen or more members
- Public and private employment agencies
- Educational institutions (public and private)
- State and local governments

Even the Congress of the United States is covered, although the rest of the federal government is not. Therefore, these employers and organizations must construct any AAP very carefully to avoid a Title VII violation.

How can you develop a racially or ethnically conscious preferential AAP that *does not* violate Title VII's prohibitions against treating individuals differently because of race, color, religion, sex, or national origin[45] or even classifying them in that manner?[46] Critics of affirmative action have long argued that Section 703(j) of Title VII makes it unlawful. This subsection states:

> Nothing contained in this subchapter shall be interpreted to require any employer, employment agency, labor organization, or joint labor-management committee subject to this subchapter to grant preferential treatment to any individual or group because of race, color, religion, sex, or national origin of such individual or group on account of an imbalance which may exist with respect to the percentage of persons of any race, color, religion, sex, or national origin . . . in the available workforce in any community, state, section or other area.[47]

Although this language appears fairly straightforward, in *Steelworkers v. Weber* (1979), the Supreme Court interpreted this passage to actually *permit* preferential treatment. In the opinion for the Court, Justice William Brennan wrote that had Congress truly intended to prohibit all race-conscious affirmative action, it would have substituted the word *permit* for *require* in the first clause of Section 703(j).[48] Because the clause did *not* read, "[n]othing contained in this subchapter shall be interpreted to *permit* any employer. . . ." voluntary preferential programs could be permitted. Whether or not you agree with the Court's ruling in this matter, it is now the law of the land and the precedent for subsequent cases. Therefore, affirmative action does not, of and by itself, violate Title VII.

PERMISSIBLE AFFIRMATIVE ACTION PLAN CRITERIA

In overcoming the hurdle of Section 703(j), the Supreme Court had to impose restrictions on AAPs to avoid undoing Title VII entirely. For any preferential program to be permissible under Title VII, four criteria must be satisfied (Figure 8.3). The plan: (1) must be *justified* by mirroring the purposes of Title VII, (2) must not *unnecessarily trammel the interests* of employees belonging to nonpreferred groups, (3) must not create an *absolute bar* to the advancement of employees belonging to nonpreferred groups, and (4) must be a *temporary measure* designed to attain, but not maintain, a racial balance.[49]

In a purely legal sense, if any one of these conditions is not satisfied, then the AAP is unlawful, and reverse discrimination has occurred. Because these criteria are so important to the development of programs permissible under Title VII, each criterion will be examined in more detail. To initiate a reverse discrimination complaint, the complaining party must first make a clear connection between the affirmative action plan and the resulting employment decision.[50] Then the plan will be evaluated on the aforementioned criteria.

Justifying the Affirmative Action

The first condition is that any affirmative action pursued by an employer must be *justified*. Under voluntary programs, affirmative action is a remedial action. Thus, the preferential treatment is pursued for the purpose of eliminating any traces of previous discrimination.

Figure 8.3 **Standards for Affirmative Action to Be Permissible Under Title VII**

- The plan must be *justified.*
- The plan must not *unnecessarily trammel the interests* of employees belonging to nonpreferred groups.
- The plan must not create an *absolute bar.*
- The plan must be a *temporary measure.*

Source: Steelworkers v. Weber, 443 U.S. 193, 208 (1979).

The easiest means of satisfying this requirement is to produce documentation that the organization had, at one time, implemented policies that specifically denied or limited the employment opportunities available to members of specific protected classes. For example, a company may have excluded African Americans from outside sales jobs, or a fire department may have denied women access to firefighter positions. Any evidence of policies or practices that segregated certain jobs by race, color, religion, sex, or national origin would provide the foundation for justifying a program.

Interestingly, mere historical knowledge that an employer had discriminatory policies is insufficient, by itself, to justify preferential treatment. The employer must show there is still some remaining effect from these past policies, which is often demonstrated by a gross statistical imbalance in the employer's internal workforce.[51] The underlying rationale is that because of the employer's past discriminatory hiring or promoting practices, individuals were denied access to positions due to their race, color, religion, sex, or national origin. As a consequence of years of engaging in such practices, the members of the affected protected classes became **underrepresented** (or what we call "underutilized" when referring to AAPs) in the workplace. Federal courts have accepted underrepresentation (statistical imbalance) as an indication of the present effects of previous discrimination.[52]

From a practical standpoint, the absence of underrepresentation jeopardizes the employer's contention that preferential affirmative action is necessary (justified). It is, therefore, imperative that before any organization embarks on an AAP, it must first conduct *utilization analysis* to assess whether underrepresentation exists. The absence of this justification removes the permissibility of any AAP under Title VII and exposes the employer to reverse discrimination litigation.[53]

Unnecessarily Trammeling Interests

If the program is justified, the AAP must determine whether it **unnecessarily trammels** the interests of individuals who are not members of the "preferred group." *Trammel* means to confine or hinder—and in this case, it means the AAP cannot unnecessarily restrict the rights of individuals who are members of nonpreferred groups.

The problem with affirmative action is that not *all* members of protected classes are entitled to preferential treatment. As ethnic diversity continues to increase in the United States, more and more of the parties filing reverse discrimination complaints are themselves members of protected classes. In such instances, they may find themselves not being the protected class receiving preferential treatment under the AAP in question because their ethnic group was not "underrepresented" in their workplace. For instance, a Hispanic student filed suit against a university's race-based scholarship program that favored only African Americans.[54] Likewise, a female applicant who was denied admission to a professional school filed a reverse discrimination suit against race-based admissions programs.[55] Therefore, in order to avoid confusion between those groups designated to benefit from affirmative action and those not designated, the terms *preferred group* and *nonpreferred group* will be used (other sources may use the terms, "favored" and "non-favored" groups).

The term **preferred group** includes all employees or applicants entitled to preferential treatment under an AAP. As will be seen later in this chapter, only groups that are *underutilized* are entitled to preferences. The term **nonpreferred group** includes all employees or applicants *not* entitled to preferential treatment under an AAP, including those who are members of protected classes. For example, if an AAP permits preferential hiring of African Americans and Hispanics, all other ethnic classifications would be placed in the single category of *nonpreferred group*. Not only would whites be in this category, but so would Asian Americans, Puerto Ricans, Cubans, American Indians, and so on.

To avoid unnecessarily trammeling the interests of nonpreferred employees, employers must walk a very fine line. The major problem imposed by this standard lies in the word "unnecessarily." As stated explicitly in the Supreme Court's decision in *Weber*, "[a]t the same time, the plan does not unnecessarily trammel the interests of the white employees."[56] This has been widely interpreted to imply that there are circumstances under which it may be *necessary* to trammel the rights of nonpreferred groups. Or, in the words of Chief Justice Warren Berger, "[W]hen effectuating a limited and properly tailored remedy to cure the effects of prior discrimination, such a 'sharing of the burden' by innocent parties is not impermissible."[57]

In other words, the interests of employees from nonpreferred groups can be restricted, but only within very narrow limitations and only in order to eliminate a manifest imbalance. Just what those limitations are is hard to determine and could vary on a case-by-case basis. However, some employment actions are readily recognized as unnecessarily trammeling nonpreferred employee interests. For example, terminating or demoting an individual who is a member of a nonpreferred group in order to create a vacancy for an applicant from a preferred group would violate this standard.[58] In some instances, federal courts have determined that the rights of nonpreferred employees have been unnecessarily trammeled when their promotion and advancement opportunities have been unduly restricted by affirmative action.[59] Unfortunately for employers, the line between what would constitute necessary and unnecessary trammeling is not always easily discerned.

Absolute Bars

Determining whether a given program creates an absolute bar is much easier. An affirmative action program creates an **absolute bar** when it excludes from consideration for any position *all* parties who *are not* members of the preferred group.

By setting aside specific positions to be filled only by individuals who belong to specific ethnic or racial groups, the plan creates an inflexible quota. Although federal courts have long permitted employers to consider race and ethnicity under formal AAPs, they have not permitted such consideration to be the *sole* decision criterion.[60] When an applicant's race, sex, or ethnicity becomes the *only* factor in determining eligibility for a position, Title VII is violated.[61]

In an attempt to meet affirmative action goals, employers, or their well-meaning HR managers, unintentionally create absolute bars in recruiting and selecting practices. Take, for example, the affirmative action officer who once told a department head that she would not approve any more employment recommendations from his department unless the candidate was either African American or female. In essence, *all* male non–African American candidates were barred from consideration for any position in that department based solely on their sex and race, which needlessly exposes the employer to reverse discrimination. Even under affirmative action goals, if a *qualified* member of the *preferred* group cannot be found, the position must be offered to the most qualified *nonpreferred* group member. The position need not remain vacant until filled by a member of the preferred group. If the position remains unfilled, an unacceptable absolute bar is maintained.

Affirmative Action Must Be Temporary

The courts further acknowledge that permitting preferential treatment under affirmative action to continue in perpetuity would undermine the purpose of Title VII. Instead of eliminating racially conscious hiring, the program would instead institutionalize it. To avoid this, all AAPs must demonstrate that they are temporary measures. Recall that affirmative action, in theory, was intended to be a remedial device to "even the playing field," or, in legalese, "to eliminate the present effects of past discrimination."[62] Once the affirmative action goals are attained, the program should be terminated. As a consequence, any plan that continues to operate after achieving its goals does so in violation of Title VII.

In practice, however, some "temporary" plans have operated for over forty years. It is not uncommon for preferential hiring to become so ingrained in an organization's selection criteria that it becomes the standard operating procedure.

Even the EEOC, the agency that oversees many AAPs and even publishes guidelines for such programs,[63] was successfully sued for reverse discrimination because its own plan had become a permanent fixture. The EEOC continued operating its preferential hiring and promotions for members of preferred groups long after statistical imbalances were eliminated. By continuing hiring practices that favored ethnic minorities and women when no statistical disparity existed between the numbers of these employees in the EEOC's internal workforce and the external labor force, Title VII was violated.[64] The EEOC's own case illustrates how easy it is for an organization to overemphasize the importance of preferential selection and lose sight of the stated goal of such programs (making the transition from affirmative action to equal employment opportunity). The advice for employers is simple: Once you have eliminated the statistical imbalance, document it and cease all affirmative action.

Figure 8.4 **Three General Components of a Formal Affirmative Action Plan**

1. Utilization analysis
2. Goals and timetables
3. Action plan

PERMISSIBLE AFFIRMATIVE ACTION IN THE PUBLIC SECTOR

Public sector employers (i.e., governments, public schools, public universities, public hospitals, law enforcement, fire departments, etc.) not only have to avoid violating Title VII when they implement affirmative action initiatives but are also constrained by the Fourteenth Amendment's Equal Protection Clause. The **Equal Protection Clause** specifically states that: "No State shall make or enforce any law which shall abridge the privileges or immunities of citizens of the United States; nor shall any State deprive any person of life, liberty, or property without due process of law, or deny to any person within its jurisdiction the equal protection of the laws." Therefore, state and local governments are forbidden from treating individuals differently because of some characteristic the individual cannot change, like race or ethnicity. The Equal Protection Clause renders race and ethnicity irrelevant in governmental decision making.[65]

As with Title VII, federal courts have been confronted with the dilemma of remedying the effects of past discrimination through preferential treatment programs while, at the same time, maintaining equal treatment. Again, there is no satisfactory solution, and the courts have concluded that there are some instances in which the necessity to address past state-imposed discrimination may place a burden on innocent third parties. It is not our intent or purpose to discuss either the morality or efficacy of this course of action, only to present its consequences for public sector employers. Racial or ethnic preferences have increasingly been seen as facially suspect when initiated by a government agency.[66] Compared to their private sector counterparts, government employers are held to a higher standard of judicial review.[67]

DEVELOPING AN AFFIRMATIVE ACTION PLAN

A formal AAP is comprised of utilization analysis, goals and timetables, and an action plan. The utilization analysis determines the degree to which any protected class is underutilized in the workplace. An underutilized group would then become the preferred group under the plan for preferential hiring or selection (see Figure 8.4).

Once the extent of the underutilization is known, the employer will establish specific and measurable goals for eliminating the imbalance and a timetable for achieving the goals. Finally, the action plan identifies the steps and actions to be implemented by the employer to accomplish the stated goals.

Utilization Analysis

The purpose of **utilization analysis** is to determine the extent to which ethnic minorities and/or women are being "underutilized" by the organization in question. "Underutilization" is defined as having fewer ethnic minorities or women in a particular job group than would reasonably be expected by their availability.[68]

A "job group" means one or more jobs that have similar content, wage rates, and opportunities. For example, a metal press operator, a sheet metal cutter, and an assembler, all of whom work on a small assembly line under similar working conditions and for similar wages, could be covered by the same job group. On the surface, utilization appears to be very similar to stock analysis as discussed in Chapter 4. Its calculations are in fact essentially the same, but the factors considered when determining the relevant minority population make it far more cumbersome.

In December 2000 the OFCCP replaced the eight-factor analysis used to determine the availability of minorities and women with a more simplified two-factor analysis.[69] This change now requires that contractors use the following two factors when determining availability of underutilized groups: (1) the percentage of minorities or women with requisite skills in the reasonable recruitment area, which is defined as the geographical area from which the contractor usually seeks or reasonably could seek workers to fill the positions in question; (2) the percentage of minorities or women among those promotable, transferable, and trainable within the contractor's organization.

The new rule defines the contractor's "reasonable recruitment area" as "the geographic area from which the contractor usually seeks or reasonably could seek workers to fill the positions in question."[70] This is not a very specific definition, and no doubt it will be subject to broad interpretation. Also under the rule, the term "trainable" refers to those workers currently employed by the contractor who "could, with appropriate training which the contractor is reasonably able to provide, become promotable or transferable during the AAP year."[71] Again, the definition is sufficiently broad to be open to a wide range of interpretations. Ultimately, it is likely that the OFCCP itself will make the determination as to what the contractor is "reasonably able to provide." Not only must the employer identify those members of the underutilized group that currently possess the requisite skills, knowledge, and ability for the job group in question, it must also estimate those that have the potential to acquire those requisite skills.

As with any analysis of representativeness, utilization analysis is absolutely dependent upon accurate job analysis and validated selection criteria. Flawed job descriptions and job specifications will improperly specify the requisite skills, knowledge, and abilities that a job incumbent must possess. As a consequence, the affirmative action goals predicated on utilization analysis will be bogus.

The 1989 case of *City of Richmond v. J.A. Croson Co.* demonstrates how public organizations may be vulnerable to litigation when they initiate an AAP without first conducting adequate utilization analysis. The City of Richmond, through its Minority Business Utilization Plan, issued the requirement that primary contractors of construction projects had to subcontract *at least* 30 percent of the dollar amount of every municipal contract

Table 8.2

Distribution of Business Management Faculty by Demographic Class in the College of Business

EEO Classifications	Number of Faculty
Male	55
Female	21
Total	76
White (not Hispanic or Latino)	64
Black or African American (not Hispanic or Latino)	2
Hispanic or Latino	3
Asian (not Hispanic or Latino)	7
Native Hawaiian or Other Pacific Islander (not Hispanic or Latino)	*
American Indian or Alaska Native (not Hispanic or Latino)	0
Two or more races (not Hispanic or Latino)	*
Total	76

*This EEO classification did not exist at the time of data collection.

to minority businesses.[72] Under this plan, the City of Richmond defined a "minority business" to be a business from anywhere in the country with at least 51 percent of that business being owned and controlled by African American, Spanish-speaking, Oriental, Indian, Eskimo, or Aleut citizens. The Supreme Court affirmed the Fourth Circuit Court of Appeals' judgment that the 30 percent figure was chosen arbitrarily and was not tied to the number of minority subcontractors in Richmond or to any other relevant number.[73]

In fact, if the City of Richmond had conducted proper utilization analysis, it would have discovered that only 4.7 percent of the contractor firms in the United States are owned by minorities, and the actual percentage of minority contractors in Richmond is somewhat less. The City of Richmond failed to identify the relevant labor market—those members of ethnic minorities with the requisite qualifications to be subcontractors—and then determine whether contract awards indicated that they were being underutilized.

In the absence of utilization analysis, proving a "manifest imbalance" in awarding contracts existed (as a result of past discrimination), the Supreme Court concluded that the City of Richmond had established an affirmative action goal with no basis in fact. In short, the City of Richmond had not established a compelling government interest to justify its preferential treatment of minority subcontractors. This led the Court to rule that Richmond had discriminated against the white plaintiff because of race, an action that is prohibited under the Equal Protection Clause.

To further illustrate the importance of accurately specifying relevant labor markets, let's assume a particular state university is conducting utilization analysis to develop its AAP. The affirmative action officer of the university has decided to examine the utilization of minorities and women for faculty teaching positions within the College of Business and has developed the faculty distribution found in Table 8.2. By converting the current staffing table to a percentage of the college's faculty, the results in Table 8.3 are available for comparison with national statistics.

Table 8.3

Percentage of Business Faculty by Demographic in the College of Business

EEO Classifications	Percentage of Business Faculty
Male	72.4
Female	27.6
White (not Hispanic or Latino)	84.2
Black or African American (not Hispanic or Latino)	2.6
Hispanic or Latino	3.9
Asian (not Hispanic or Latino)	9.2
Native Hawaiian or Other Pacific Islander (not Hispanic or Latino)	*
American Indian or Alaska Native (not Hispanic or Latino)	0
Two or more races (not Hispanic or Latino)	*

*This EEO classification did not exist at the time of data collection.

Examining the university's position announcement, the affirmative action officer attempts to identify the relevant qualifications of a successful candidate.

> Assistant Professor. State University seeks a full-time, tenure-track assistant professor of management to begin fall semester, 2014. Responsibilities include: teaching (6–9 credit hours per semester, including occasional distance education classes), advising (at the graduate and undergraduate levels), research (resulting in scholarly publications), and service to the profession and university. Qualifications include: (1) graduate course work and teaching experience in one of the following fields: (a) international business/international management, or (b) strategic management; (2) a record of refereed, scholarly publications; and (3) an earned doctorate in management.
>
> Experience in distance education is desirable. Preference will be given to candidates who excel in the above areas. To apply, please submit a letter of application, curriculum vitae, three letters of recommendation, and copies of undergraduate and graduate transcripts to Professor Carol Smith, chair, Search Committee, College of Business, State University. Review of applications will begin October 20, 2013, and continue until the position is filled. AA/EEO.

In performing utilization analysis for this position, the affirmative action officer initially decided to compare its faculty to the population of all full-time college and university faculty in the United States. After all, the College of Business traditionally has had to conduct nationwide searches to fill faculty positions. Therefore, national statistics are appropriate for making its workforce comparisons. Based on figures from the U.S. Department of Education, the national proportion of full-time faculty members with teaching duties, by race/ethnicity and sex, is shown in Table 8.4.

As a result, the affirmative action officer announces that women are underrepresented in the College of Business. Internally, 2.6 percent of the college's faculty is African American, while the education statistics selected for comparison indicate that 5.4 percent of all full-time faculty are African American.

Table 8.4

Percentage of Full-Time Faculty in All Fields (with and without doctorates, and excluding nonresident aliens)

	Male	Female	Total
White (not Hispanic or Latino)	.484	.331	.815
Black or African American (not Hispanic or Latino)	.026	.028	.054
Hispanic or Latino	.019	.016	.035
Native Hawaiian or Other Pacific Islander (not Hispanic or Latino)	**	**	**
Asian (not Hispanic or Latino)	.049	.026	.075
American Indian or Alaska Native (not Hispanic or Latino)	.003	.001	.004*
Two or more races (not Hispanic or Latino)	**	**	**
Total	581	402	

Source: U.S. Department of Education, "Full-Time Instructional Faculty in Degree-Granting Institutions, by Race/Ethnicity and Residency Status, Sex, and Academic Rank," *Digest of Educational Statistics: 2007*, Table 239. Note that excluding nonresident aliens reduced total full-time instructional staff from 675,624 to 647,567.

*Goals are not established for groups with a representation of less than .02.

**This EEO classification did not exist at the time of data collection.

Problems with Utilization Analysis

Using the national statistics for all university instructors, one would expect 40.2 percent (see Table 8.4) of the faculty to be female when in fact only 28 percent of the faculty positions in the College of Business are held by women. The next step would be to develop action plans and timetables to eliminate the underutilization (the statistical imbalance).

Unfortunately, the utilization analysis is terribly flawed. The figures upon which the affirmative action officer based the conclusions do not reflect the skills necessary to be an effective *management* professor. The figures used to make the comparison between the proportion of women in the College of Business faculty and the national labor market included terminal degrees in *all* fields, everything from agriculture to zoology. However, to be an effective professor of international management, one must have at least a degree in *management* or *international business*. An applicant with a doctorate (Ed.D.) in education leadership will not perform well teaching international management or publishing

Table 8.5

National Faculty Demographics for Business Schools

EEO Classifications	Percentage of Business Faculty
Male	68.5
Female	31.5
White (not Hispanic or Latino)	79.5
Black or African American (not Hispanic or Latino)	4.5
Hispanic or Latino	2.3
Asian (not Hispanic or Latino)	12.2
Native Hawaiian or Other Pacific Islander (not Hispanic or Latino)	*
American Indian or Alaska Native (not Hispanic or Latino)	1.6
Two or more races (not Hispanic or Latino	*

Source: U.S. Department of Education, "Full-Time and Part-Time Faculty and Instructional Staff in Degree-Granting Institutions, by Field and Faculty Characteristics," *Digest of Educational Statistics: 2011*, Table 269.

*This EEO classification did not exist at the time of data collection.

in that field. Hence, the appropriate comparisons must be with applicants who possess terminal degrees in business. Those percentages are provided in Table 8.5.

After reviewing these figures, underutilization still exists, but the more accurate goal (the one based on more relevant qualifications) is 31.5 percent—not 40.2 percent. To ignore the relevant labor market (business professors) would result in overrepresentation of female professors and possible reverse discrimination charges because the university failed to base its plan on persons who were truly qualified to fill the business faculty positions. This would not only expose the employer to a reverse discrimination complaint being brought under Title VII,[74] but because the university is a public institution (a state university), this could have resulted in an Equal Protection Clause complaint as well.[75]

Too often AAPs are initiated without proper consideration of the skills a job incumbent truly needs. Failure to consider the relevant labor market for applicants is a frequent problem. Thus, it is critical to be mindful of these issues before embarking on any preferential treatment program. If utilization analysis is not properly conducted, all actions that follow are superfluous, and could expose the organization to litigation.

Goals and Timetables

Assuming the utilization analysis was properly conducted, the next step in developing an AAP is to create goals and timetables. In the event of substantial disparities in the utilization of specific groups, it is unreasonable to expect an immediate resolution. In such instances, the organization must eliminate the imbalances incrementally over time.

In some cases, underrepresented groups may not be underutilized in lower-skilled entry positions, but they are absent in management and supervisory ranks. In order to generate a sufficient number of qualified minority applicants for the supervisory positions, it may be necessary to allow such individuals time to gain supervisory experience over time. An individual who does not fully understand a job can hardly be expected to supervise workers performing it, and this may require additional time for training and on-the-job experience.

Additional time may be warranted for supervisory education and training programs as well. If the employer is recruiting from an area that is a significant distance from its facility, the recruiting process will take longer to complete. When jobs require specific and technical skills, recruiting may be even more complicated.

Suppose a company is trying to fill an industrial engineering position. It is likely that the employer would have to recruit nationally. Compare this to recruiting for day laborers, where the recruiting effort would not go too far beyond an hour's commute of the plant. It is reasonable to expect most nationwide recruiting drives to last six to twelve months, while local recruiting efforts last only a few days or weeks. Because of the difficulty in locating underrepresented group members with requisite skills, it is also possible that affirmative action goals will not be attained.

Provided the employer has shown a good faith effort to attain them, the OFCCP and the EEOC are unlikely to take adverse action against the employer. Failure to attain goals may be traced to unrealistic goals based on faulty utilization analysis. In such instances, a new, proper analysis should be conducted and the goals adjusted accordingly. Overly ambitious timetables could be the culprit. If so, an employer should seriously reexamine the underlying assumptions for identifying minority and female applicant goals and then modify the timetable to reflect the more realistic expectations.

Developing an Action Plan

The **action plan** is the nuts and bolts of an AAP. This plan, as the name implies, consists of action-oriented programs designed to eliminate problems and attain previously established goals and objectives.[76] Some techniques suggested by the OFCCP to increase the flow of minority and female applicants are:[77]

- Recruit through organizations that serve as advocates for minority and female rights such as the Urban League, National Organization for Women, welfare rights organizations, and state employment services.
- Include minorities and females in the company's Personnel Relations Staff.
- Actively participate in "job fairs," particularly those held in areas with large minority populations.
- Establish internship and cooperative programs with historically black universities and women's colleges.
- Provide "after school" and work-study jobs for minority youths.
- Provide "summer jobs" for the underprivileged.
- Put pictures of minority and female workers in recruiting brochures.
- Advertise position vacancies in minority news media.
- Brief current minority and female employees on current and future job openings.
- Establish active recruiting programs at secondary schools, vocational technical schools, and junior colleges with predominantly minority or female enrollments.

One critical point to remember when implementing any AAP is never to select an *unqualified* candidate to fill a position. Note that there is a fine line between *permissible* affirmative action and *unlawful* discrimination. Hiring an unqualified individual crosses that line.

ADDITIONAL REPORTING REQUIREMENTS

In addition to performing utilization analysis, federal contractors and subcontractors (and other entities that come under Executive Order 11246) must submit an annual Equal Opportunity (EO) Survey to the OFCCP. The EO Survey requires the employer to provide most of the information that is already contained in the EEO-1 Report and then some. The employer must not only furnish the ethnic and gender composition of his or her current workforce in the nine job categories, but must also provide the same information regarding applicants, hires, promotions, and terminations during the previous affirmative action program year. Unlike the EEO-1 Report, the EO Survey further requires the employer to break down Hispanic employees and applicants into three distinct categories: Hispanic or Latino (all races), Hispanic or Latino (white race only), and Hispanic or Latino (all other races)—this last category tallies all Hispanics/Latinos who are not white.

Under the Equal Protection Clause, "No State shall make or enforce any law which shall abridge the privileges or immunities of citizens of the United States; nor shall any State deprive any person of life, liberty, or property, without due process of law; *nor deny to any person within its jurisdiction the equal protection of the laws*."[78] From its inception, the Fourteenth Amendment's Equal Protection Clause clearly forbade states and their respective subunits from creating any law, regulation, or policy that treated a citizen differently because of race.

Beginning in 1971, the Supreme Court embarked on a series of decisions that interpreted the Fourteenth Amendment in a manner that would allow the Equal Protection Clause to permit limited preferential treatment under specific circumstances—rejecting the notion that Congress must *always* act in a "color-blind fashion."[79]

First, only state and local governments and their agencies can violate the Equal Protection Clause. Private sector employers are not covered under the Fourteenth Amendment. Because the concept that making distinctions among citizens based on their ancestry is contradictory in a society that claims equality under the laws, the courts have been willing to permit government-initiated affirmative action only under extreme circumstances. In recent years, federal courts have become even stricter in their analysis of those circumstances.

Under the principle of *strict scrutiny*, any preferences pursued by a state or local government must pass a two-part test (see Figure 8.5). The landmark case establishing this two-part test is the 1986 *Wygant v. Jackson Board of Education*.[80] *Wygant* establishes the standard by which AAPs are permissible under the Equal Protection Clause in the same manner that *Weber* sets the standard under Title VII. Remember, state and local governments must pass *both* of these standards if they are to operate *any* program that grants *preferential employment practices*.

Figure 8.5   **The Two-Part Test Under Strict Scrutiny**

The preferential treatment serves a **compelling government interest**:
- The need to eliminate the present effects of past discrimination
- Must be remedial in nature

The preferences are **narrowly tailored** to achieve the compelling government interest:
- The efficacy of alternative race-neutral policies
- The planned duration of the policy
- The relationship between the numerical goal and the relevant population or relevant workforce
- The flexibility of the policy
- The burden that the program places on third parties

Sources: Wygant v. Jackson Board of Education, 476 U.S. 267, 274 (1986); *Regents of University of California v. Bakke*, 438 U.S. 265, 307 (1978); *City of Richmond v. J.A. Croson Co.*, 488 U.S. 469, 486 (1989).

The first part of this test is to establish that there exists a *compelling government interest* to be served by the affirmative action.[81] If this criterion is satisfied, then the courts will examine the AAP to ascertain if it is *narrowly tailored* enough to accomplish the compelling government interest. Just as under Title VII, the program must be justified. The state or local government must have a strong basis in evidence that its classification of citizens along racial, ethnic, or gender lines is absolutely necessary. For governments and their agencies, this is an even more difficult burden because the expressed purpose of the Equal Protection Clause of the Fourteenth Amendment is to prohibit government decision making from using such irrelevant factors as a person's race.[82]

COMPELLING GOVERNMENT INTEREST

Essentially, the only government interest that is sufficiently compelling to justify preferential treatment of one group of citizens over another is the need to eliminate the present effects of past discrimination.[83] In establishing this justification, the state or local government has two issues to prove. First, it must clearly identify present effects that can be traced to some previously discriminatory practices.

Next, it must show that it actually implemented the discriminatory policy or practice. As in Title VII, statistical imbalances in given job groups are used as evidence of the present effects. However, imbalances, in and of themselves, are not sufficient to justify the preferential treatment. There must be a direct link between the previous discriminatory practices and the current imbalance.

Additionally, courts are becoming more rigorous in requiring governments to clearly demonstrate this connection. Mere knowledge that a government or one of its agencies engaged in de jure discrimination is no longer sufficient to establish a compelling government interest in several circuits.[84] De jure discrimination refers to discriminatory practices that were enacted into law or published as written regulations or policies.

Diversity as a Compelling Government Interest

"Diversity," like "affirmative action," has become a much used, but ill-defined term. It encompasses a wide array of employment ideas ranging from being aware of the demographic changes in the labor market to achieving and maintaining an internal workforce that proportionally reflects the "diversity" of the surrounding population.[85] The last definition of diversity, proportional representation, is being subjected to increased scrutiny by federal courts and is the focal point here. Although diversity consultants stress that diversity is more than affirmative action,[86] if achieving a diversity goal involves giving preferences to applicants based on their race, ethnicity, or sex, the courts will treat the diversity initiative as affirmative action.

This is consistent with over four decades of employment law. Federal courts have long viewed any employment practice that openly encourages (or even implies) differential treatment of employees based upon their ethnic, racial, or gender characteristics as a potential violation of Title VII or the Equal Protection Clause.

This is a very real concern as many organizations have adopted diversity as an organizational goal. In some cases, organizations have implemented employment practices to increase the representation of individuals of different gender, ethnic, and cultural backgrounds within their organizations.[87] What is more, the concept of proportional representation is becoming increasingly institutionalized as an accepted business practice.[88] The Society for Human Resource Management (SHRM) and the American Society for Training and Development (ASTD), two business-based professional associations, have given formal recognition to diversity programs. In fact, SHRM not only certifies diversity consultants, it also produces a diversity newsletter, *Mosaics*, which it has published since 1995. More convincing evidence of diversity's widespread acceptance can be inferred from the fact that most business management and human resource management textbooks now contain chapters or sections devoted to managing diversity.[89] It is important to note that the legality of a goal to achieve diversity is not the question here, but the means of attaining it is.

One very significant aspect of diversity goals differentiates them from affirmative action goals. Specifically, diversity goals are permanent whereas affirmative action goals are temporary. However, when challenged, diversity programs are challenged as affirmative action and reviewed under the same standards. This means that any diversity program predicated on proportional representation potentially violates Title VII of the Civil Rights Act of 1964 and/or the Equal Protection Clause.

Since the 1990s federal circuit courts have held any race- or ethnicity-based preferential treatment to ever increasingly rigorous standards of judicial scrutiny. In at least five instances, public sector employers who either directly or indirectly attempted to advance the argument that achieving diversity was a compelling government interest for their preferences lost. In three instances, federal circuit courts explicitly declared that diversity does not establish a compelling interest that would justify preferences.[90] In one case, a circuit court indirectly overturned diversity justifications by holding that decisions based on retaining minorities strictly because of underrepresentation would not withstand a constitutional challenge.[91] The most interesting case, *Taxman v. Board of Education of Piscataway*,[92] not only held that a goal of maintaining racial diversity could violate the Equal Protection Clause, but it could also violate Title VII. In this decision, the Court of Appeals for the Third Circuit was emphatic that it could not accept the premise that a "nonremedial diversity goal is a permissible basis for affirmative action under Title VII."[93] The goal of maintaining a racially diverse workforce, in the absence of any remedial justification, would unnecessarily trammel the interests of employees who were members of nonpreferred racial groups, and it would equally fail to be a temporary measure by maintaining a racial balance.[94]

Narrowly Tailored Programs

Once the government agency or department has justified its use of affirmative action through the demonstration that the program serves a compelling government interest, the program must then clear the second hurdle: show that it is **narrowly tailored** to achieve its ends. In other words, is the preferential treatment designed in such a way as to minimize the harm to innocent third parties? There appears to be an emerging consensus that in determining whether a plan is sufficiently narrowly tailored, the courts should consider five key factors:[95]

- The efficacy of alternative race-neutral practices
- The planned duration of the policy
- The relationship between the numerical goal and the percentage of preferred group members in the relevant population or relevant workforce
- The flexibility of the policy, including waivers if the goal cannot be met
- The burden that the program places on innocent third parties

Efficacy of Alternative Race-Neutral Practices

By the mid-1990s, federal courts began to require governments to demonstrate they have considered and exhausted race-neutral alternatives before being allowed to resort to racial preferences.[96] Unless the government can demonstrate that an individual suffered direct harm from the agency's practices, neutral alternatives must have been examined first. For example, assume a municipal fire department refused to consider three female applicants for the position of firefighter. Two years later, the department decides to make amends for its past discriminatory policies by implementing a new AAP. Because the three female applicants, provided they were at least minimally qualified for the position, suffered actual injury from the previous policy, the department could engage in preferential hiring. As identified victims of, in this case, gender-based discrimination, the three women would be entitled to remedial affirmative action. This action would correct the effect of the discrimination they had suffered.

But what about situations in which there are no identified victims of discrimination? What occurs when there is underrepresentation of a protected group that has historically been discriminated against? In this situation, the department must demonstrate it considered gender-neutral alternatives, but none of these alternatives would have adequately eliminated the statistical imbalances caused by the past discrimination. An example of a race-neutral alternative would be replacing a selection criterion (such as written test) with another that would have less disparate impact on the group in question (actual performance of a task). Remember that whatever selection criterion is substituted, it must still be validated.

Regardless of its justification for initiating any preferential program, the initiators must be prepared to show that explicit racial or gender preferences were pursued as a "last resort" option.[97]

Duration of the Program

Just like their private sector counterparts, AAPs initiated by public sector organizations are expected to be *temporary* measures. Any use of racial or gender preferences by a government or its subdivisions must be limited to ensure they do not outlast their need. They may not take on a life of their own.[98] As under Title VII, public sector affirmative action should cease once the goals of the plan have been attained. Public sector programs can no more be used to maintain a balanced workforce than private sector ones.[99]

Goals and Relevant Markets

Another striking similarity between factors affecting narrowly tailored programs and the Equal Protection Clause and programs permissible under Title VII is the necessity to develop goals based on the relevant labor market. Once again, any affirmative action goal must be based upon the proportion of underrepresented group members who possess the requisite skills, knowledge, and abilities to perform the job in question. Hence, the appropriate percentage to determine underutilization of Hispanic teaching staff in a given school district is not the population of Hispanics in that school district. The appropriate percentage for comparison is Hispanic composition of the qualified public school teacher population in the relevant labor market.[100]

The Flexibility of the Plan

This standard of scrutiny in the public sector bears a good deal of similarity to the absolute bar provisions under *Weber*. In the event that there are not enough of the preferred group applicants possessing the minimum requirements for the benefit in question (i.e., promotion, hiring, etc.), the positions may be filled with qualified applicants of nonpreferred groups.

Assume a law enforcement agency is operating an AAP with a goal stating that 25 percent of all promotions to sergeant should go to African Americans. To be eligible for promotion, *all* candidates must pass the civil service test, have a minimum of four years' experience as a patrolman, and have at least satisfactory ratings on annual performance evaluations during the three years prior to applying for promotion. Also, assume these criteria have been properly validated. This year there are eight vacancies for sergeant. Under ideal circumstances, this means that possibly two promotions could be assigned to African American applicants who meet or exceed the minimum qualifications.

However, through no fault of the department, only one African American candidate met the prerequisites for eligibility. The employer would create an inflexible quota if it promoted an *un*qualified African American candidate or *did not* fill the vacancy when qualified candidates from nonpreferred groups were available.

The appropriate course of action would be to promote the qualified African American candidate to one position and fill the remaining seven positions with the most qualified candidates from other ethnic backgrounds. Employers get into trouble with their AAP when they operate under the assumption that minority set-asides are reserved *exclusively* for minority candidates. There must be no absolute exclusions; to do so creates hard-and-fast racial quotas.

Impact on Third Parties

The final factor to consider when determining whether or not a plan is sufficiently narrowly tailored is the burden that it places on innocent third parties. In practice, this appears to be very similar to avoiding trammeling the interests of nonpreferred group members. Consequently, laying off or firing individuals to create opportunities for applicants from preferred groups would naturally impose too heavy a burden.[101]

The problem confronting public sector employers is just *where* the line is drawn between a preferential goal that imposes an unacceptable burden on third parties. Remember that federal courts have "permitted" innocent persons to shoulder the burden of redressing grievances not of their making.[102]

Until 1995, the federal government enjoyed a far more lenient judicial review of its AAPs than either private sector organizations or state and local governments. Up until that time, federally mandated programs only had to meet standards of "intermediate scrutiny" (as opposed to strict scrutiny). Although the exact legal differences between *intermediate* and *strict* scrutiny are tedious, intermediate scrutiny would permit the federal government to engage in preferential treatment as long as the government could prove the program met some legitimate government end. For example, if the federal government concluded that increased minority representation in the broadcast industry was necessary for the sake of achieving sufficient diversity, such a goal would be considered an "important government objective."[103] Just as with state governments, strict scrutiny places a more onerous burden on federal government agencies to establish the necessity of imposing preferential practices. And, just as with the Fourteenth Amendment for state and local governments, **strict scrutiny** under the Fifth Amendment requires a federal government employer to first establish that any preferences serve a "compelling government interest" and, second, that the preferences are "narrowly tailored" to achieve that interest. Under strict scrutiny, increasing minority representation would not establish a "compelling government interest," and the preferential treatment would not be allowed.

Today, intermediate scrutiny is no longer available to the federal government. Since June 12, 1995, federal programs are now evaluated under the same level of strict scrutiny under which state and local programs are examined. The standards discussed in the previous section now apply to the federal government.

In *Adarand Constructors v. Pena*,[104] the Supreme Court, in a 5–4 decision, ruled that there is an implied Equal Protection Clause in the Fifth Amendment. In this ruling, the Supreme Court held that the two-part test of the *Wygant v. Jackson Board of Education* (the standard for testing state and local preferential programs) would be applied to federal programs mandating race-based preferences. Hence, all federal classifications must now serve a compelling government interest and must be narrowly tailored to achieve that interest.[105]

AVOIDING REVERSE DISCRIMINATION

Developing and implementing AAPs is increasingly placing employers between a rock and a hard place. On one hand, failure to have a plan places the employer in jeopardy of losing eligibility for government contracts. The employer is further deprived of a legal means by which he or she can hire-by-the-numbers to reduce its exposure to disparate impact claims. On the other hand, race- and gender-based preferences are being increasingly challenged as reverse discrimination. Consequently, the employer must walk a legal tightrope between disparate impact litigation and reverse discrimination. With reverse discrimination on the rise, an interesting phenomenon has occurred.

In the past, it was thought the complaining parties in such suits were restricted to being white males. As American society has become more ethnically diverse, more reverse discrimination suits are being initiated by the so-called protected groups. Technically, preferential treatment is extended only to members of the protected group or groups that are underrepresented. This, of course, means members of protected groups that are *not* underrepresented are not entitled to preferential treatment. Hence, these nonpreferred group members are initiating suits when they feel they are being denied employment opportunities and benefits.

In California, the number of employment lawsuits pitting members of one ethnic group against those of another is on the rise. Furthermore, this trend can be expected to increase as American demographics continue to diversify. The following practices invariably result in reverse discrimination and, therefore, should be avoided:

- Barring all nonpreferred group members from consideration for the position or benefit in question. This could occur by refusing to hire, or to approve the hiring of, any individual except from the preferred group.
- Selecting unqualified members of the preferred group.
- Establishing inflexible quotas or setting aside a specific percentage of positions for reserved members of the preferred group.
- Not establishing affirmative action goals on the relevant labor market for the job in question. Too often, this occurs when goals are predicated on national or regional ethnic proportions of the population rather than the proportion of ethnic minorities possessing the requisite job skills.

- Terminating, laying off, or demoting members of nonpreferred groups to ensure employment opportunities for members of the preferred groups.

RECENT DEVELOPMENTS AND CONFUSION

There has been a confusing development as a result of the 2003 U.S. Supreme Court decision, *Grutter v. Bollinger*.[106] In a 5-to-1 decision, the Supreme Court made an exception to precedent regarding "diversity" as serving a compelling government interest by declaring that a diverse student body could serve such an interest.[107] However, this precedent is restricted only to university admissions. Diversity currently does not justify preferential treatment for employment and contract awards.[108]

In 2007, in *Parents Involved in Community Schools v. Seattle School District No. 1*,[109] an attempt was made to expand "diversity" as a compelling government interest in student assignments to public primary and secondary schools. In this instance, the Supreme Court chose not to permit racial diversity as a justification for school assignments in primary and secondary education.

From an employment standpoint, "diversity, because of its nonremedial nature," does not serve a compelling government interest—at least, not at the time of this writing. Even in *Grutter*, this diversity justification was not extended to either employment or contract awards.[110] However, the *Grutter* case continues to cause confusion as some do not understand its narrow application. For employers it is simple, affirmative action plans predicated on the desire to create or maintain racial, gender, or ethnic diversity in the workplace will not be permitted under either Title VII or the Equal Protection Clause.

On October 10, 2012, the Supreme Court sent a college submission case back to the U.S. Court of Appeals for the Fifth Circuit. In *Fisher v. University of Texas*, the Supreme Court held that the Fifth Circuit had failed to apply strict scrutiny when it failed to require the University of Texas to prove that its admission program to "obtain the educational benefits of diversity" was narrowly tailored.[111] Though this decision did not overturn *Gruttner*, it does increase the burden placed on universities to justify preferences in admission based on diversity goals.

PRACTICAL APPLICATION

Let us return to the opening scenario. It should be apparent that position announcements must reflect the minimum knowledge, skills, and ability the applicant must possess in order to perform the essential tasks, duties, and responsibilities of the job. The first thing the committee should have done was to ensure a proper job analysis had been conducted. This would not only delineate the essential tasks, duties, and responsibilities that the Director of Equal Opportunity and Regulatory Compliance had to perform, but also the skills, knowledge, and abilities needed to perform the job.

Assume the responsibilities in the position announcement are accurate. A great deal of the job involves submitting reports to regulatory agencies, investigating alleged violations of numerous laws, developing AAPs, and ensuring university practices do not violate federal and state civil rights laws. If the candidate is not familiar with these laws and regulations, he or she will not be able to perform the job adequately. If the candidate is not knowledgeable of *Revised Order No. 4*, he or she can hardly be expected to develop a legally permissible AAP.

In light of this, do you believe someone with a bachelor's degree in social work or elementary education would have the proper training and knowledge of the governing laws to be an effective Director of Equal Opportunity and Regulatory Compliance? Do you believe a candidate with a Ph.D. in oriental philosophy would be any better qualified? Does Charles Silvey's suggestion that the candidate possess at least a bachelor's degree in HRM or business management seem reasonable? The committee may even wish to go further and require experience in related positions.

Does Elizabeth Day's recommendation that the candidate have a doctorate have any merit? Focusing on the job's tasks, duties, and responsibilities, would not having a doctorate prevent a candidate from fulfilling the job functions?

Finally, is William Eaton's insistence that the committee select either a female or member of an ethnic minority a valid argument? Why or why not?

SUMMARY

This chapter provided a detailed look at affirmative action. No other topic in employee relations has generated as much controversy, and no other employment practice is more misunderstood or abused. Simply stated, affirmative action was intended to ensure individuals are treated without regard to their race, color, religion, sex, or national origin during employment. There are two types of affirmative action programs: voluntary and involuntary.

The preferential nature of affirmative action programs runs the risk of violating either Title VII or the Equal Protection Clause if they are not properly constructed or implemented. Such programs are permissible under Title VII only if they are justified, do not unnecessarily restrict the rights of other employees, do not create an absolute bar, and are temporary in duration.

For public sector employers, it is essential to comply with Title VII, but it is also necessary not to violate the Equal Protection Clause of the Fourteenth Amendment. To have a permissible affirmative action program under the Equal Protection Clause, government employers must ensure the programs serve a *compelling government interest* and are *narrowly tailored* to achieve that interest.

To guarantee that affirmative action programs do not violate either Title VII or the Fourteenth Amendment, HR professionals should properly construct the plans. No affirmative action program can be initiated until utilization analysis has been conducted, and utilization analysis cannot begin until proper job analysis has been performed on all positions in the organization. Only after proper utilization analysis has been completed can affirmative action goals and timetables be developed.

Finally, existing affirmative action programs must be periodically reviewed to ensure they are current and to preclude potential reverse discrimination challenges.

KEY TERMS AND CONCEPTS

Absolute bar
Action plan
Affirmative action plan (AAP)
Equal Protection Clause
Involuntary affirmative action
Narrowly tailored
Nonpreferred group
Preferred group

Revised Order No. 4
Strict scrutiny
Underrepresented
Underutilized protected group
Unnecessarily trammels
Utilization analysis
Voluntary affirmative action

DISCUSSION QUESTIONS

1. What is affirmative action? How is affirmative action distinguished from equal employment opportunity?
2. What are some arguments supporting affirmative action? What are some arguments against affirmative action?
3. Distinguish between involuntary and voluntary affirmative action.
4. What are the three components of an affirmative action plan under the OFCCP's *Revised Order No. 4*? Which is the most important?
5. What are the four circumstances under which affirmative action can be implemented?
6. How does the two-part test determine if an affirmative action program is permissible under the Equal Protection Clause? Which Supreme Court decision imposed these requirements on state and local governments? Which Supreme Court decision imposed these requirements on the federal government?
7. You have been asked by your employer to review the current affirmative action program. What is the very first thing that you will either do or ensure has been done before reviewing the plan? In developing your plan, what three basic components must that plan contain? Provide four conditions that your plan must meet in order to be "permissible." Hint: *Steelworkers v. Weber*, 433 U.S. 193, 208 (1979).

CASES

Case 1

An eastern city had been under a court-ordered affirmative program since 1974, which required preferential hiring and promotions of minority candidates.[112] By 2000, minority firefighters accounted for approximately 40 percent of the fire department. The census of 2000 reveals the city population is roughly 38 percent minority.

Under the court order, white male candidates had to identify themselves as nonminority applicants. Five of the white applicants who took the firefighter entrance examination (our complaining parties) scored 99 out of a possible 100 points.

These scores easily satisfied the threshold criterion for employment. Along with all other qualifying applicants, the five white candidates were placed on a civil service eligibility list in rank order. This ranking made allowance for various statutory preferences (e.g., veterans, residents, children of firefighters killed or disabled in the line of duty), ceding pride of place to the holders of such preferences in accordance with state law (even if those persons had earned lower test scores than other qualified candidates). None of these statutory preferences involved race or ethnicity.

In preparing to hire fifty new firefighters, the city fire department requested a certified list of eligible applicants from the state civil service commission. The civil service commission selected individuals in rank order (based on statutory preferences and test scores) and grouped them into a recognized "hiring class." After screening out those individuals who stumbled over a variety of race-neutral preconditions (such as drug tests and physical examinations), the civil service commission composed a slate of "hiring pairs" by placing the highest-ranking minority member and the highest ranking nonminority member into a group of two and then repeating the process until the hiring class had been exhausted.

In November the city fire department, following this rank order, chose twenty-five pairs from the eligibility list and appointed those fifty individuals as entry-level firefighters. The complaining parties were not among those selected. Each received a letter from the city fire department stating that the vacancies had been filled by persons who outranked him on the certification list. However, the record suggests that, had the city fire department followed a strict rank-order selection process (without any consideration of race or ethnicity), the complaining parties (or some of them) likely would have been in the top fifty.

    a. Under Title VII, has the city impermissibly used race in its selection procedure? Why or why not?

    b. Under the Fourteenth Amendment, has the city impermissibly used race in its selection procedure? Why or why not?

Case 2

The transportation agency of a California county unilaterally created a voluntary affirmative action plan for the hiring and promotion of employees. One provision of the plan provided that, in making promotions to positions within a traditionally segregated job classification in which women have been significantly underrepresented, the agency was authorized to consider as one factor the sex of a qualified applicant. The agency noted in its affirmative action plan that women were represented in numbers far lower than their proportion of the county labor force in five of seven job categories.

The stated goal of the affirmative action plan was to achieve a statistically measurable yearly improvement in the hiring, training, and promotion of minorities and women in all major job classifications where they were underrepresented. The long-term goal was to attain a work force whose composition reflected the proportion of minorities and women in the area relevant labor market.

When a vacancy arose in the agency for promotion to road dispatcher, twelve county employees applied, and nine of them were deemed qualified and were interviewed. At the conclusion of the interviews, seven employees were certified as eligible for selection by the appointing authority. Two of the seven scored 75 and were tied for second, and a female applicant scored 73 and was ranked third. The director of the agency, who was authorized to choose any of the seven candidates, chose not to follow a second interviewing board's recommendation to promote one of the second-ranked applicants, a male, but instead opted to select the only female candidate, who was the third-ranked applicant. In doing so, the director had taken into account the candidates' qualifications, their test scores, their expertise, and their backgrounds, as well as the affirmative action goal.

Upon hearing that the female candidate had been selected over him, the male applicant who had been recommended by the board filed a complaint with the EEOC, claiming that he had been denied promotion in violation of Title VII on the basis of his sex.

a. Under Title VII was the county impermissibly using sex in its selection procedure? Why or why not?
b. Under the Fourteenth Amendment was the county impermissibly using sex in its selection procedure? Why or why not?

Case 3

Ken Cyree, the complaining party, is a law enforcement officer for the city of New Orleans, LA. He alleges that he was subjected to gender discrimination when he was not selected for a Special Agent-in-Charge position. The law enforcement agency acknowledged that a female candidate was selected to appease a management official's desire for diversity candidates and to meet the department's goals under a *permissible* affirmative action program.

Further investigation by the EEOC found, by clear and convincing evidence, that the female candidate was qualified for the position, but she also had the fewest qualifications of any of the six candidates for the position. Specifically, her efficiency reports, though good, were lower than any other candidate's and her interview did not go well; however, she still met minimum job standards.

a. Can Ken establish a *reverse discrimination* case? Why or why not?
b. Will the police department be held liable for a Title VII violation? Why or why not?

NOTES

1. Pub. L. 88–352, Title VII, § 716(b), July 2, 1964, 78 Stat. 266.
2. Exec. Order 11246, 30 Fed. Reg. 12319 (1965), reprinted as amended in 42 U.S.C. § 2000e (2007).

3. Exec. Order 10925, 3 C.F.R. 448 (1959–1963).

4. 41 C.F.R. § 60–2.1(a) (2012).

5. 29 C.F.R. § 1607.13 (2012).

6. 29 C.F.R. § 1608.1 (2012).

7. 29 C.F.R. §§ 1608.2(1) & (2).

8. 41 C.F.R. § 60–2.21.

9. 41 C.F.R. § 60–2.23(e).

10. 29 C.F.R. § 1608.4(c).

11. G. Gallup, Jr., *The Gallup Poll* (1997): 1057–1060; (1980): 106–107; (1984): 141–143; (1989): 231; K. Johnson and A. Stone, "Affirmative Action: Four Groups' Views," *USA Today*, March 24, 1995, p. 1.

12. Johnson and Stone, "Affirmative Action: Four Groups' Views," p. 1.

13. P. Schmidt, "Poll Finds Most Americans Oppose Affirmative Action When Defined as 'Preferences,'" *The Chronicle of Higher Education* (June 3, 2009), http://chronicle.com/article/Poll-Finds-Most-Americans/47684 (accessed March 31, 2013); CNN, *USA Today*, Gallup Organization, "Attitudes Toward Affirmative Action: A Nationwide Survey," (February 24–26 and March 17–19, 1995); D.W. Moore, "Americans Today are Dubious about Affirmative Action," *The Gallup Poll Monthly*, March 1995: 36–38.

14. Cal. Const. Art 1 § 31(a).

15. Rev. Code Wash. (ARCW) § 49.60.400 (1999).

16. B.R. Bergmann, *In Defense of Affirmative Action* (New York: Basic Books, 1996); L.A. Graglia, "Affirmative Action: Have Race and Gender Conscious Remedies Outlived Their Usefulness?" *American Bar Association Journal* 81 (1995): 40; T. Eastland, *Ending Affirmative Action: The Case for Colorblind Justice* (New York: Basic Books, 1996); B.M. Roth, *Prescription for Failure: Race Relations in the Age of Social Science* (New Brunswick, NJ: Transaction, 1994); R. Nieli, ed., *Racial Preference and Racial Justice: The New Affirmative Action Controversy* (Washington, DC: Ethics and Public Policy Center, 1991); M. Rosenfeld, *Affirmative Action and Justice* (New Haven, CT: Yale University Press, 1991); R.R. Thomas, *Beyond Race and Gender: Unleashing the Power of Your Total Workforce* (New York: AMACOM Press, 1991); S. Steele, *The Content of Our Character: A New Vision of Race in America* (New York: St. Martin's Press, 1990).

17. R.D. Kahlenberg, *The Remedy: Race, Class and Affirmative Action* (New York: Basic Books, 1997), p. 112; M. Salvador and P.M. Sias, *The Public Voice in a Democracy at Risk* (Westport, CT: Greenwood Publishing Group, 1998), p. 166; S. Better, *Institutional Racism: A Primer on Theory and Strategies for Social Change* (Lanham, MD: Rowman & Littlefield Publishers, 2007), p. 34.

18. *Taxman v. Board of Education of Piscataway*, 91 F.3d 1547, 1560 (3rd Cir. 1996); *Wygant v. Jackson Board of Education*, 476 U.S. 267, 274 (1986); *Regents of University of California v. Bakke*, 438 U.S. 265, 310 (1978).

19. *City of Richmond v. J.A. Croson Co.*, 488 U.S. 469, 505–506 (1989).

20. *Croson*, 488 U.S. at 493.

21. *Teamsters v. U.S.*, 431 U.S. 324, 340 n. 20 (1977).

22. *Wygant*, 476 U.S. at 276.

23. H. Belz, *Equality Transformed: A Quarter-Century of Affirmative Action* (New Brunswick, NJ: Transaction, 1991).

24. *Bakke*, 438 U.S. at 291.

25. R.H. Bork, *Slouching Towards Gomorrah* (New York: Regan Books, 1996), p. 242.

26. 42 U.S.C. § 2000e-2(a)(1).

27. *Croson*, 488 U.S. at 493.

28. *Billish v. City of Chicago*, 989 F.2d 890, 897 (7th Cir. 1993).

29. 380 U.S. 145 (1965).

30. 480 U.S. 149, 183 (1987).

31. 42 U.S.C. § 2000e-5(g)(1)(2012).

32. See *Martin v. Wilks*, 490 U.S. 755 (1989).

33. 42 U.S.C. § 2000e-2(n)(1) (2012).

34. *Martin*, 490 U.S. at 765.n.6.

35. Pub. L. No. 102–166, § 108.

36. Ibid.

37. R.K. Robinson, B.M. Allen, D.E. Terpstra, and E.G. Nasif, "Equal Employment Opportunity Requirements for Employers: A Closer View of the Civil Rights Act of 1991," *Labor Law Journal* 43, no. 11 (1992): 725–734.

38. *United States v. Mississippi Power and Light Company*, 638 F.2d 899 (5th Cir. 1981).

39. 41 C.F.R. § 60–2.1(a) (2007).

40. Rehabilitation Act of 1973, 29 U.S.C. § 794 (2007).

41. Vietnam Era Veteran's Readjustment Act, 38 U.S.C. § 2021 (2007).

42. *Cunico v. Pueblo School Dist. No. 60*, 917 F.2d 431, 437 (10th Cir. 1990) (citing, inter alia, *United Steelworkers v. Weber*, 443 U.S. 193 [1979]); *Wygant v. Jackson Board of Education*, 476 U.S. 267 (1986).

43. 29 C.F.R. § 1608.4.

44. 29 C.F.R. § 1608.4(a).

45. 42 U.S.C. § 2000e-2(a)(1).

46. 42 U.S.C. § 2000e-2(a)(2).

47. 42 U.S.C. § 2000e-2(j).

48. *Steelworkers v. Weber*, 443, U.S. 193, 208 (1979).

49. Ibid. at 205.

50. *Mlynczak v. Bodman*, 442 F.3d 1050 (7th Cir. 2006).

51. *Johnson v. Transportation Agency, Santa Clara County*, 480 U.S. 616, 632 (1987).

52. *Cunico*, 917 F.2d 431; *Bennett v. Alexander* (In re Birmingham Reverse Discrimination Employment Litigation), 20 F.3d 1525, 1539 (11th Cir. 1994).

53. *Taxman*, 91 F.3d at 1560.

54. *Podberesky v. Kirwan*, 38 F.3d 147 (4th Cir. 1994).

55. *Hopwood v. State of Texas*, 78 F.3d 932 (5th Cir. 1996).

56. *Weber*, 443 U.S. at 208.

57. *Fullilove v. Klutznick*, 448 U.S. 448, 484 (1980).

58. *Teamsters*, 431 U.S. at 371–379; *Firefighters Local Union No. 1784 v. Stotts*, 467 U.S. 561, 579 (1984).

59. *Bennett*, 20 F.3d at 1542; *San Francisco Police Officers Association v. San Francisco*, 812 F.2d 1125, 1132 (9th Cir. 1987).

60. Ibid. at 1541.

61. Ibid.

62. *Johnson*, 480 U.S. at 620.

63. Affirmative Action Appropriate Under Title VII of the Civil Rights Act of 1964, As Amended, 29 C.F.R. § 1608 (2007).

64. *Jurgens v. Thomas*, 1982 U.S. Dist. LEXIS 15480, *67 (N.D. Tex. 1982).

65. *Shaw v. Reno*, 509 U.S. 630 (1993); *Palmore v. Sidoti*, 466 U.S. 429, 432 (1984); *Bakke*, 438 U.S. at 307.

66. *Bakke*, 438 U.S. at 291.

67. *Adarand Constructors, Inc. v. Pena*, 515 U.S. 200 (1995).

68. 41 C.F.R. § 60–2.11(b).

69. 165 Fed. Reg. 68031 (November 13, 2000).

70. 41 C.F.R. § 60–2.14(c).

71. Ibid.

72. *Croson*, 488 U.S. at 477.

73. Ibid., at 480–481.

74. *Hazelwood School District v. United States*, 433 U.S. 299, 308 (1977).

75. *Wygant*, 433 U.S. at 274; *Croson*, 488 U.S. at 492.

76. 41 C.F.R. § 60–2.13(f).

77. 41 C.F.R. § 60–2.24(e).

78. U.S. Const. amend. XIV, § 1.

79. *Swan v. Charlotte-Mecklenburg Board of Education*, 402 U.S. 1, 18–21 (1971); *McDaniel v. Barresi*, 402 U.S. 39, 41 (1971); *Franks v. Bowman Transportation, Co.*, 424 U.S. 747, 763 (1976); *Bakke*, 438 U.S. at 378–379.

80. 476 U.S. 267 (1986).

81. *Palmore v. Sidoti*, 466 U.S. 429, 432 (1984).

82. *Croson*, 488 U.S. at 495; see also, *Loving v. Virginia*, 388 U.S. 1, 11 (1967); *Hirabayashi v. United States*, 320 U.S. 81, 100 (1943).

83. *Bakke*, 438 U.S. at 307; *Wygant*, 476 U.S. at 274; *Croson*, 488 U.S. at 486.

84. *Lutheran Church-Missouri Synod v. FCC*, 141 F.3d 344 (D.C. Cir. 1998): *Quinn v. City of Boston*, 325 F.3d 18 (1st Cir. 2007); *Biondo v. City of Chicago*, 383 F.3d 680 (7th Cir. 2004).

85. R.K. Robinson, G.M. Franklin, and D.E. Terpstra, "Diversity in the '90s," *HR Focus* 71, no. 1 (1994): 9.

86. P. Arredondo, *Successful Diversity Management Initiatives: A Blue Print for Planning and Implementation* (Thousand Oaks, CA: Sage, 1996), p. 15.

87. M. Loden, *Implementing Diversity* (Chicago: Irwin, 1996); Thomas, *Beyond Race and Gender*; M. Loden and J.B. Rosener, *Workplace America! Managing Employee Diversity as a Vital Resource* (Homewood, IL: Business One Irwin, 1991).

88. F. Lynch, *The Diversity Machine* (New York: The Free Press, 1997), p. 177.

89. F. Cascio, *Managing Human Resources*, 9th ed. (New York: McGraw-Hill, 2012); R. Noe, J. Hollenbeck, B. Gerhart, and P. Wright, *Human Resource*, 8th ed. (New York: McGraw-Hill, 2012); L. Gomez-Mejia, D. Balkin, and D.L. Cardy, *Managing Human Resources*, 7th ed. (Englewood Cliffs, NJ: Prentice-Hall, 2011); R.L. Mathis and J.H. Jackson, *Human Resource Management*, 13th ed. (Cincinnati, OH: South-Western Cengage Learning, 2010).

90. *Hunter v. The Regents of the University of California*, 190 F.3d 1061, 1074 (9th Cir. 1999); *Wessmann v. Gittens*, 160 F.3d 790, 800 (1st Cir. 1998) (the concept of "diversity" implemented by BLS does not justify a race-based classification); *Lutheran Church-Missouri Synod v. FCC*, 141 F.3d 344, 354 (D.C. Cir. 1998); *Hopwood v. State of Texas*, 78 F.3d 932, 944–945 (5th Cir. 1996).

91. *Cunico*, 917 F.2d at 439.

92. 91 F.3d 1547.

93. *Taxman v. Board of Education of Piscataway*, 91 F.3d at 1561.

94. Ibid.

95. *U.S. v. Paradise*, 480 U.S. 149, 171 (1987) (plurality opinion).

96. *Podberesky*, 38 F.3d at 160–161; *Bennett*, 20 F.3d at 1545–1546.

97. *Alexander v. Estepp*, 95 F.3d 312, 315 (4th Cir. 1996).

98. *Hayes v. North State Law Enforcement Officers Association*, 10 F.3d 207, 216 (4th Cir. 1993).

99. *Johnson*, 480 U.S. at 639–640.

100. *Hazelwood School District v. U.S.*, 433 U.S. 299, 308 (1977).

101. *Peightal v. Metropolitan Dade County*, 26 F.3d 1545, 1561 (11th Cir. 1994).

102. *Bakke*, 438 U.S. at 298.

103. *Metro Broadcasting, Inc. v. FCC*, 467 U.S. 547, 600 (1990).

104. 515 U.S. 200 (1995).

105. *Adarand Constructors v. Pena*, 515 U.S. at 240–241.

106. 539 U.S. 306 (2003).

107. Ibid. at 328–329.

108. Ibid. at 341.

109. 551 U.S. 701 (2007).

110. 539 U.S. at 342.

111. 133 S. Ct. 2411, 2421 (2012).

112. This case is based on the findings of fact in *Quinn v. City of Boston*, 325 F.3d 18 (1st Cir. 2003).

PART III

REGULATION OF EMPLOYEE RELATIONS

9

COMPENSATION

Wage, Hour, and Related Statutes

LEARNING OBJECTIVES

- Describe the basic provisions of the Fair Labor Standards Act.
- Explain the federal limitations on the use of child labor.
- Distinguish between exempt and nonexempt employees under the Fair Labor Standards Act.
- Explain the impact of the Lilly Ledbetter Fair Pay Act of 2009 on the timeliness requirements of Title VII and the Equal Pay Act.
- Describe who is required to pay the prevailing wage under the Davis-Bacon, Walsh-Healy, and McNamara-O'Hara Service Contract Acts.
- Explain the circumstances under which an employer has a legal obligation to inform employees of plant closings or major layoffs.
- Discuss the conditions under which employers are prohibited from using polygraph testing in employment.

OPENING SCENARIO

Bob DeWright had worked in the blueprinting department at Swartzwelder's Engineering and Architectural Supply for several years. Bob's principal duties involved taking customer orders, producing blueprints to customers' specifications, performing routine maintenance on the machines, and keeping the work area clean. As a blueprint machine operator, Bob worked five days per week from 8:00 a.m. to 5:00 p.m. with one hour off for lunch.

Bob's rate of pay was $10 per hour.

In December, the owner, Mr. Swartzwelder, informed Bob that in recognition of his hard work and loyalty, he was to be promoted. Effective immediately, Bob was the executive vice president of reprographic services with a monthly salary of $1,900.

Bob quickly discovered that his new duties as executive vice president included taking customer orders, producing blueprints to customers' specifications, performing routine maintenance on the machines, and keeping the work area clean. However, Bob now worked six days per week and usually ten hours per day.

Bob realized that if he worked by his old hourly rate, he would be making roughly $2,800 per month before taxes (taking overtime into account) instead of the $1,900 he currently made. Armed with this knowledge, Bob confronted Mr. Swartzwelder and asked to be paid overtime. Mr. Swartzwelder was quick to inform Bob that since he was promoted to management, he was not entitled to overtime payments. Upset by this response, Bob threatened to file a complaint with the Wage and Hour Division (WHD) of the Department of Labor. Shortly thereafter, Mr. Swartzwelder fired Bob for his poor attitude and lack of loyalty. In a moment of anger, Mr. Swartzwelder told Bob, "Go ahead and whine to the Wage people. I know the law and it's on my side in this matter!"

Is Mr. Swartzwelder correct? Is the law on his side or Bob's? It depends on whether Bob is an exempt employee under the Fair Labor Standards Act. This is a determination you should be able to make by the end of this chapter.

THE FAIR LABOR STANDARDS ACT

The Fair Labor Standards Act (FLSA) is one of the oldest statutes regulating the private sector workplace. Enacted in 1938 as part of President Franklin Roosevelt's New Deal, the FLSA was intended to lessen the effects of the Great Depression by creating an incentive for businesses to hire more employees. This was to be accomplished by creating a minimum wage, imposing a penalty for working any employee beyond forty hours per week, and placing limitations on the use of child labor (see Figure 9.1). The Act's method for encouraging employers to hire more workers was quite simple. For each hour worked in excess of forty during a 168-consecutive-hour workweek, the employer would have to pay the employee his hourly wage plus an additional 50 percent of the base pay rate for overtime (time-and-a-half). **Overtime** is legally defined as any hours worked in excess of forty during a 168-consecutive-hour workweek.[1] Additionally, the FLSA contained provisions entitling workers to receive a minimum hourly wage set by the federal government. In 1938, the first minimum wage was $0.25. As of July 24, 2009, the minimum wage had risen to $7.25.[2]

To demonstrate how the FLSA was intended to increase employment, we will examine its effect on payroll at the time of its enactment in 1938. Assume, on average, an employer with 20 employees has been working them 60 hours per week at an hourly rate of pay of $0.25. Prior to the FLSA, this hourly rate of pay would remain constant regardless of the number of hours worked. So, at the end of the week, the employer would pay the employees $15 (60 hours × $0.25/hour) each, for a total payroll of $300 ($15 weekly wage × 20 employees).

Beginning in 1938 when the FLSA went into effect, the employer would have to pay each employee $17.50 for a 60-hour week ($0.25 × 40 hours plus $0.375 × 20 hours of overtime), for a total payroll of $350. Thus, as a result of the FLSA, payroll expenses increased by nearly 17 percent with no change in productivity.

One objective behind the FLSA was to create an incentive for the employer to avoid

Figure 9.1 **Major Provisions of the Fair Labor Standards Act**

Minimum Wage
- $7.25 as of July 24, 2009
- 90-calendar-day $4.25 youth minimum wage

Overtime
- Time and one-half for each hour worked in excess of 40 during a 168-consecutive-hour workweek
- Certain professions in the health care industry time and one-half for each hour worked in excess of 80 during a 336-consecutive-hour workweek

Child Labor
- 16- and 17-year-old workers prohibited from working hazardous jobs as defined by the Secretary of Labor, but unlimited hours
- 14- and 15-year-old workers prohibited from working in hazardous jobs as defined by the Secretary of Labor and limited in the number of hours they may work per day and per week

Source: U.S. Employment Standards Administration, Fair Labor Standards Act Advisor, "What does the Fair Labor Standards Act require?" http://www.dol.gov/elaws/esa/flsa/screen5.asp.

this penalty by hiring more employees. It was hoped that it would stimulate employment. This is, in theory, how it was to work. To avoid the overtime penalty, the employer was limited to two options. He or she could reduce the hours worked by his or her current employees. The option presents the obvious downside of there being not enough man-hours to complete the scheduled work. By reducing the current 20 employees to 40-hour workweeks, production would be reduced by 33 percent (800 hours compared to the 1,200 hours previously worked).

The other option offered an economically sound way to avoid the overtime penalty by increasing the size of the workforce by hiring more employees. If, in our example, the employer hired 10 more workers, then he or she would be able to accomplish 1,200 man-hours of work and reduce payroll costs at the same time. The cost of operating 30 workers at straight time is $300 ($0.25 × 40 hours × 30 employees) as opposed to $350 if 20 employees had to work 20 hours of overtime each week ($0.25 × 40 hours plus $0.375 × 20 hours of overtime × 20). This generates nearly a 17 percent savings over maintaining a workforce of 20 and working them 60 hours in a week. The idea was that this would create more employment for Americans during the Great Depression when over one-third of all workers were without jobs.

However, this simple solution to Depression-era unemployment may no longer be applicable in the twenty-first century. One must remember that the 1930s were simpler times, and workers did not have the mandated or voluntary benefits as they do today. The American worker has come to expect benefits as one of the conditions of employment (i.e., pensions, health insurance, life insurance, paid vacations, paid sick leave, the Affordable Care Act, etc.). The FLSA's incentive to hire more employees is presently diminished because the cost of providing mandatory and voluntary benefits to new hires (which can range between 60 and 67 percent of base pay),[3] is greater than the overtime penalty (50 percent of the base pay rate). To illustrate, in a firm in which benefit costs account for 38 percent of payroll expenses, an individual hired at $10.00 per hour would also be receiving an additional $6.13 per hour in benefit costs, for a total of $16.13. Having a current employee work overtime would cost $15.00 per hour.

Covered Employers and Employees

Though the FLSA set different sales/revenue thresholds for firms in different industries, for practical purposes, private sector enterprises with two or more employees and an annual gross volume of sales of $500,000 or more are covered under the FLSA.[4] However, even when the employer is not covered under the FLSA, individual employees may be covered. Such covered employees include those who produce, receive, ship, transport, or load goods that are moving in interstate commerce.[5] Additionally, individual employees may be protected under the Act if their work entails preparing, handling, or transmitting information or documents in interstate trade.[6] Under such broad coverage, it would be difficult to find an employee who is not entitled to protection under the FLSA, and consequently an employer who is not required to comply with its provisions. As with all federal laws, immediate family members (parents, spouse, and children) are exempted.

Minimum Wage

Since July 24, 2009, the FLSA has required covered employers to pay a minimum wage of at least $7.25 per hour.[7] This hourly rate is the base on which all wage and hour claims are made. To determine whether an employer is in compliance, the employee's weekly gross pay is divided by the number of hours worked. Considering overtime compensation in the calculations, the hourly rate must equal at least the federal minimum wage. For example, if a nonexempt employee, one who is covered by the FLSA, is receiving a flat salary of $350 per week, for a 50-hour workweek, compliance would be based on this $7.25 per hour minimum wage rate.

Suppose our employee worked consistently fifty hours per week. Would the employer be in compliance with the FLSA? The determination would be based on forty hours at $7.25 ($290.00) and ten hours of overtime at $10.875 (1.5 × $7.25), for a total of $398.75 ($290.00 + 108.75). Since the employee received only $350 per week, but was entitled to $398.75 per week, the employer is not in compliance. The employer is responsible for making up the difference of $48.75 per week.

A unique feature of the FLSA is that it permits state minimum wage laws and municipal minimum wage ordinances to supersede the mandatory federal minimum wage when they are higher. In essence, when state minimum wage requirements exceed the federal minimum wage, the higher wage must be paid (refer to Table 9.1). For example, in California, the state minimum wage is $8.00.[8] Consequently, all California employers must pay employees at least $8.00 rather than the $7.25 federal hourly minimum wage. If our employee in the previous example was working in California, the employer would be responsible for compensating the employee at a rate of $440.00 for a fifty-hour workweek, forty hours at $8.00, or $320.00, plus ten hours at $12.00 (1.5 × $8.00), or $120.00.

Some states have minimum wages below the federal standard primarily because the state legislatures have not chosen to update them. Some states, like Missouri, merely

Table 9.1

State and District of Columbia Minimum Wages as of January 1, 2013

States with Minimum Wages Higher than FLSA		States with Minimum Wages Lower than FLSA		States with No Minimum Wage
Arkansas	$7.75	Arkansas	$6.24	Alabama
Arizona	$7.80	Georgia	$5.15	Louisiana
California	$8.00	Minnesota	$6.15	Mississippi
Colorado	$7.78	Wyoming	$5.15	South Carolina
Connecticut	$8.25			Tennessee
Dist. of Columbia	$8.25			
Florida	$7.79			
Illinois	$8.25			
Maine	$7.50			
Massachusetts	$8.00			
Michigan	$7.40			
Missouri	$7.35			
Montana	$7.80			
Nevada	$8.25			
New Mexico	$7.50			
Ohio	$7.85			
Oregon	$8.95			
Rhode Island	$7.75			
Vermont	$8.06			
Washington	$9.19			

Source: U.S. Department of Labor, "Minimum Wage Laws in the States—January 1, 2013," http://www.dol.gov/whd/minwage/america.htm.

grew weary of adjusting the state minimum wage laws to meet changes in the federal rate and allowed their state laws to fall into abeyance. Other states like Mississippi, merely abolished theirs, defaulting to the federal minimum. Because the FLSA stipulates that the higher of the two minimum wages (state or federal) will prevail, there is little incentive for states desiring only to conform with FLSA minimum standards to amend their existing statutes.

Nonexempt Employees

Having discussed the FLSA's general minimum wage and overtime requirements, it is necessary to identify those employees to whom the FLSA applies and those for whom it does not. When dealing with the FLSA, the two important classifications of employees are *exempt employees* and *nonexempt employees.* A **nonexempt employee** is any employee who is entitled to protection under the FLSA's minimum wage and overtime provisions. Failure to provide minimum wages and overtime payments for nonexempt employees will result in a FLSA violation. Nonexempt employees can be either hourly employees or salaried employees.

Because the FLSA is an all-encompassing act intended by Congress to cast the broadest coverage possible, it is easier to identify the employee classifications that it

Figure 9.2 Employees Exempt from Minimum Wage and Overtime under the FLSA

Administrative personnel
Babysitters on a casual basis
Bona fide executives
Commissioned sales employees
Companions for the elderly
Computer professionals paid at least $27.63 per hour
Farm workers
Federal criminal investigators
Fishing employees
Home workers making wreaths
Newspaper delivery employees
Newspaper employees of limited circulation newspapers
Professionals (including academic or administrative personnel and teachers in elementary or
    secondary schools)
Salesmen, parts men, and mechanics employed by automobile dealerships
Seamen on other than American vessels
Employees of seasonal and recreational establishments
Switchboard operators

Source: 29 U.S.C. § 213(a) (2012).

---

does not cover than to list all those that it does cover. Therefore, the FLSA does not list those occupational classifications that are nonexempt; it specifies only the exempt classifications.

Exempt Employees

Exempt employees are those employees specifically excluded from the FLSA's protection for minimum wage and overtime. Among those employees who are automatically excluded from the FLSA's protection are those who work for statutorily exempted employers. Individuals employed by the federal government are excluded, as are individuals employed by the U.S. Postal Service.[9] State employees *not* subject to state civil service laws, public elected officials, or members of an elected official's personal staff are not covered by the FLSA.[10]

Beyond the exemption of certain government employees, the FLSA provides exemptions from minimum wage *and* overtime payments as well as partial exemptions from overtime only. Although a comprehensive list of these exemptions is provided in Figures 9.2 and 9.3, our discussion will focus on the five most common exemptions: *bona fide* executives, *bona fide* administrative employees, *bona fide* professionals, outside sales personnel, and computer professionals.

Bona Fide Executives

It is important to note that an employee's title is meaningless when establishing *bona fide* executive status or any other exemption category. The determination of the employee's

Figure 9.3 **Partial List of Employees Exempt from Overtime under the FLSA**

Aircraft salespeople
Airline employees
Amusement/recreational employees in national parks/forests/ Wildlife Refuge System
Boat salespeople
Buyers of agricultural products
Country elevator workers (rural)
Domestic live-in employees
Farm implement salespeople
Firefighters working in small (fewer than 5 firefighters) public fire departments
Forestry employees of small (fewer than 9 employees) firms
Fruit and vegetable transportation employees
House parents in nonprofit educational institutions
Livestock auction workers
Local delivery drivers and drivers' helpers
Lumber operations employees of small (fewer than 9 employees) firms
Motion picture theater employees
Police officers working in small (fewer than 5 officers) public police departments
Radio station employees in small markets
Railroad employees
Seamen on American vessels
Sugar processing employees
Taxicab drivers
Television station employees in small markets
Truck and trailer salespeople

Source: 29 U.S.C. § 213(b) (2012).

status is based on explicit conditions outlined in the *Code of Federal Regulations.*[11] To be an executive/manager, the individual's primary duties must consist of the management of his or her area of the organization. This entails planning, organizing, directing, and controlling the work activities in his or her administrative unit. In fact, the manager cannot spend more than 20 percent of work time in nonmanagement activities. In retail or service organizations, managers may not spend more than 40 percent of work time in nonmanagement activities. Additionally, the manager must regularly direct the work of two or more employees and have the authority to hire, promote, or fire (or recommend such actions for) these employees. The manager must also receive a salary of at least $455 per week.[12]

To demonstrate why these requirements are important when assessing "exempt" employee status, let's return to our opening scenario. If Bob is a *bona fide* executive, as his new title implies, he is not entitled to minimum wage and overtime payments. However, the Wage and Hour Division (WHD) does not rely on titles; it relies on the criteria mentioned previously. In order to determine whether Bob is an exempt employee, the WHD investigator will have to analyze his work duties according to the stated standard. What percentage of Bob's time is spent in nonmanagement activities? Actually, 100 percent; he performs no management duties. This alone would be sufficient to establish that Bob is not a *bona fide* executive. How many employees does Bob supervise? The answer is none, less than the minimum of two required. Having no employees under his charge would preclude further evaluation on whether Bob had the authority to hire, fire, or promote his subordinates (or at least make such recommendations).

Only Bob's salary would be in compliance with the stated requirements. Therefore, based on this analysis and even though his job title is executive vice president of reprographic services, Bob is *not* a *bona fide* executive/manager under the FLSA. As a direct consequence of this determination, Bob *is not* exempt from the FLSA's minimum wage and overtime requirements. Thus, Mr. Swartzwelder would have to pay the overtime compensation that Bob had accrued.

Bona Fide Administrative Employees

The WHD has established standards for determining which employees are legitimately exempted from the FLSA as *bona fide* administrators. To be classified as a *bona fide* administrator, an employee must perform work related to the management policies or general business operations of the employer or the employer's customers. In the case of educational institutions, the employee's duties must be tied to the administration of the educational establishment or institution. Whether in an educational institution or other organization, the "administrator" must customarily and regularly exercise discretion and independent judgment.[13] Similar to *bona fide* executives, *bona fide* administrators cannot spend more than 20 percent of work hours in nonadminstrative activities. Administrative personnel in retail or service establishments may not spend more than 40 percent of their time in nonadminstrative activities.

Administrative employees must be compensated on a salary or fee basis at a rate of not less than $455 per week.

Bona Fide Professionals

The term "employee employed in a *bona fide* profession" applies to any employee whose primary job responsibilities are tied to performing work:

1. Requiring knowledge of an advance type in a field of science or learning customarily acquired by a prolonged course of specialized intellectual instruction and study, as distinguished from a general academic education and from an apprenticeship, and from training in the performance of routine mental, manual, or physical processes.
2. That is original and creative in character in a recognized field of artistic endeavor (as opposed to work that can be produced by a person endowed with general manual or intellectual ability and training), and the result of which depends primarily on the invention, imagination, or talent of the employee.
3. Teaching, tutoring, instructing, or lecturing in the activity of imparting knowledge and who is employed and engaged in this activity as a teacher in the school system or educational establishment or institution by which he is employed.

4. That requires theoretical and practical application of highly specialized knowledge in computer systems analysis, programming, and software engineering, and who is employed and engaged in these activities as a computer systems analyst, computer programmer, software engineer, or other similarly skilled worker in the computer software field.[14]

Not surprisingly, the work professionals do requires the consistent exercise of discretion and judgment in its performance. Primary job duties of *bona fide* professionals also tend to be intellectual in nature. A *bona fide* professional under the FSLA cannot devote more than 20 percent of work time to nonprofessional activities (nonintellectual or creative work), and these professionals must be compensated on a salary or fee basis at a rate of not less than $455 per week.[15]

Outside Sales Personnel

Outside sales personnel are employees who are employed for the purpose of customarily making sales away from the employer's place of employment.[16] As with the other exempted classifications, persons engaged in outside sales cannot spend more than 20 percent of work hours in nonsales activities.[17]

Computer Professionals

A computer professional is any employee who is employed as a computer systems analyst, computer programmer, software engineer, or other similarly computer-skilled worker.[18] As in the previous categories, the employee's title is not sufficient to establish this. The employee's primary duties must involve the application of systems analysis techniques and procedures including consulting with users to determine hardware, software, or system functional specifications. Additionally, an employee who designs, develops, documents, tests, or modifies computer systems or programs would most likely be a computer professional under the FLSA.[19] A person hired for the simple task of data entry on a computer would not be a computer professional regardless of the title possessed.

In addition to performing the previously mentioned job duties, the employee must be compensated at a rate of at least $27.63 an hour in order to be a *bona fide* computer professional.[20]

Independent Contractors

It is important to note that the distinction between an individual's status as an "employee" or "independent contractor" is not a matter of his or her title but the substance of his or her relationship to the employer.[21] The substance of this relationship is determined through a twenty-factor test developed by the IRS (see Figure 9.4). As an example, this twenty-factor test was applied to determine whether certain persons employed by Microsoft Corporation were employees of the company or independent contractors.[22] Microsoft had classi-

Figure 9.4 The Internal Revenue Service's Twenty-Factor Control Test to Determine Independent Contractor Status

The Internal Revenue Service, building on the common law test, has set forth a more detailed test for determining whether an individual is an independent contractor for purposes of paying employment tax and withholding. These factors and their applications are as follows:

1. An individual who is required to follow instructions is more likely to be considered an employee.
2. The greater the amount of training needed for the individual to complete an assigned task, the greater the likelihood that the individual will be considered an employee.
3. Where an individual is integrated into the employer's business to a great extent, the individual is more likely to be considered an employee.
4. The fact that an individual personally renders services will weigh in favor of employee status.
5. The fact that the individual hires, fires, and pays assistants, and the employer has no right to do so, indicates independent contractor status.
6. The existence of a continuing relationship is indicative of employee status.
7. The establishment of a set amount of work hours suggests employee status.
8. An individual whose time is substantially devoted to the job is more likely to be considered an employee.
9. The fact that an individual works on the employer's premises suggests employee status.
10. An individual who works according to a sequence set by the employer will more likely be deemed an employee.
11. The fact that an individual submits regular or written reports to the employer will weigh in favor of employee status.
12. An individual who is paid by the project, rather than by the hours, or other period of time, will more likely be considered an independent contractor.
13. An individual who is reimbursed for expenses is more likely an employee.
14. An individual who furnishes the necessary tools and materials for the job is more likely an independent contractor.
15. That an individual makes an investment in the facilities in which he or she works weighs in favor of independent contractor status.
16. The fact that an individual's work results in the possible realization of a profit or the risk of a loss suggests independent contractor status.
17. An individual who works for more than one firm at a time is more likely to be an independent contractor.
18. An individual who makes his or her services available to the general public is more likely to be considered an independent contractor.
19. The fact that the employer has the right to discharge the individual suggests an employment relationship (independent contractor relationships are more likely to be contractual).
20. The fact that the individual has the right to terminate the relationship also suggests an employment relationship because independent contractors are usually bound by a contract.

Source: U.S. Chamber of Commerce, "The IRS's 20-Factor Analysis." http://www.uschambers-mallbusinessnation.com/toolkits/guide/P07_1115 (accessed March 3, 2013); IRS Code Section 1706 (Section 1706 of the Tax Reform Act of 1986).

fied many employees as "freelancers," essentially independent contractors, even though they often participated on the same work teams, performed the same tasks, and worked under the same supervisors as "regular employees." Despite these specific similarities, the freelancers were not entitled to the same benefits enjoyed by the regular employees. In 1989, the IRS had previously applied the twenty-factor test to these "freelancers" and had declared them to be common law employees for tax purposes; Microsoft was now responsible for withholding the freelancers' income taxes, social security taxes, Medicare, and unemployment taxes. The U.S. Court of Appeals for the Ninth Circuit took this one step further. Using the same twenty-factor test, the Ninth Circuit now applied it to an employer's obligation to provide voluntary benefits.[23]

Other Minimum Wage Issues

Although the FLSA is primarily known for establishing the federal minimum wage, it also includes other important minimum wage–related provisions. Most notable are provisions related to youth subminimum wage, full-time student workers' subminimum wage, tipped employee minimum wage, and compensatory time.

Youth Subminimum Wage

Newly hired employees who are less than twenty years old may be paid a subminimum wage during their first ninety consecutive calendar days of employment. This subminimum wage is established at a rate not less than $4.25 an hour. As a safeguard against potential abuse, employers are prohibited from terminating employees at the conclusion of the ninety-day period for the purpose of hiring another subminimum wage employee to keep wages at the $4.25 level. An employer cannot fire an employee who has completed the ninety-day subminimum wage period to avoid paying him or her standard federal minimum wage ($7.25 per hour).

The question has been raised; did the youth wage go up when the FLSA minimum wage goes up? No. An eligible youth may still be paid a minimum of $4.25 an hour during the ninety calendar days after initial employment by his/her employer, but at the end of that period the individual's pay must be raised to the $7.25 minimum.

Full-Time Students' Subminimum Wage

Full-time student workers are another category of workers that can be paid a subminimum wage. A full-time student worker is anyone, regardless of age, who meets the requirements of a full-time student at the institution of higher education that employs him or her.[24] The subminimum wage authorized by the secretary of labor for full-time students is an amount not less than 85 percent of the current national minimum wage. Currently, this amount is $6.17 per hour ($7.25 × 0.85).[25]

In order to obtain authorization to pay the subminimum wage to full-time student workers, the college or university must apply for a certificate with the appropriate regional office of the Wage and Hour Division (WHD) of the Department of Labor. The purpose of the application is to ensure that the institution of higher education is not using student workers for the purpose of reducing full-time employment opportunities for other (nonsubminimum wage) workers.[26] For example, the WHD is unlikely to issue a college a certificate if the purpose of the application is to replace two full-time secretaries with four part-time student workers.

One final, and somewhat peculiar, stipulation is attached to the use of full-time student workers. There are specific restrictions on the amount of time they are authorized to work per week. Odd as it may sound, the WHD has interpreted the FLSA restrictions on the employment of full-time students of institutions of higher education to be the same as those for full-time students who are at least fourteen years of age.[27] Therefore, full-time college students are held to the same total weekly worker hours as fourteen- to sixteen-year-olds in the FLSA's child labor provisions. Full-time students will not be permitted to work at subminimum wages for more than eight hours per day nor more than forty hours per week when school is not in session.[28] When school is in session, full-time students are limited to only twenty hours per week at the subminimum wage.[29] The twenty-hours-per-week limitation does not apply on days that are full-day school holidays, although the eight-hour-per-day restriction still applies.[30]

Tipped Employee's Minimum Wage

Some employees are treated differently under the FLSA because of the peculiar nature of compensation within their industries, such as tipped employees. Employers who employ tipped employees (e.g., waiters and waitresses), particularly those in the hotel and restaurant industries, may credit a certain amount of the tips received against the employer's minimum wage obligation when certain conditions are met. The FLSA requires an employer to pay not less than $2.13 an hour in wages to tipped employees, who are defined under the Act as those who regularly receive more than $30.00 per month in tips.[31] In the event an employee's tips combined with the employer's cash payment of $2.13 an hour does not equal the minimum hourly wage, the employer must make up the difference.[32] It is important to note that some states have state laws placing higher minimum wages on tipped employees. For example, the state of Colorado requires a minimum of $4.00 per hour for tipped employees.[33]

To illustrate this point, assume a waiter works for a restaurant forty hours per week. The employer pays the waiter the $2.13-an-hour wages prescribed by the FLSA, for a total of $85.20. If the employee makes only $100 in tips for the week, the employer must make up the difference between the sum of what the employee actually made in tips plus the employer's $2.13-per-hour contribution ($85.20) and the $290 per week the waiter would have received had he been paid at the $7.25 minimum hourly rate. In this example, the waiter was actually compensated $185.20 ($100 in tips and $85.20 by the employer). Had he been paid the minimum wage, he would have received $290. Therefore, the employer must make up the difference of $104.80 ($290.00–$185.20).

Compensatory Time

Employees of a public sector (governmental) employer may receive compensatory time. **Compensatory time**, not to be confused with "compensable time," is time off in lieu of overtime compensation. However, this compensatory time off must be calculated at a rate not less than one-and-one-half hours for each hour of employment for which overtime compensation would have been paid.[34] For example, if a government employee had worked 46 hours in a 168-consecutive-hour workweek, that employee would be entitled to 9 hours of compensatory time (6 hours over 40 times 1.5).

Private sector employers may also use compensatory time to compensate employees for overtime, with one important catch. Whereas public sector employees may accrue compensatory time throughout the year and use it, more or less, at the employer's convenience, private sector employees may not. In the private sector, the compensatory time must be used within the pay period it was accrued. Specifically, public employees may carry compensatory time over from one period to another, but private employees may not. For employees who are private sector employees and are paid on a weekly basis, compensatory time is not a viable option as it would have to be used in the same week in which it was accrued. If the employee was paid on a bi-weekly basis, compensatory time accrued in week 1 would have to be used in week 2.

Compensable Time

Compensable time refers to the difference between situations in which employees are entitled to be paid for their time and when they are not. The FLSA requires that nonexempt employees be paid for all hours worked; but what about hours in which the employee is required to be at the place of work although not actually performing work? Employees are not required to be compensated during meal breaks when they are not performing work-related services for their employers,[35] but if they have to remain at their work stations and perform work-related tasks, they must be compensated. For example, a receptionist who eats lunch at her desk while answering the company's telephones is entitled to compensation.

Arriving to Work Early

When employees are required to report to work prior to the shift period or scheduled work period in order to prepare for the day's activities, that is considered compensable time. Assume an employer requires employees to be present at the workplace fifteen minutes prior to "clocking in" for the purpose of performing preventive maintenance checks on equipment. Because such activity is an integral part of the job to which the employee is assigned, the employees must be compensated for those fifteen minutes.[36] The employer may even be responsible for work that is not required of the employee but is performed voluntarily. If an employee arrives early and begins performing normal work-related duties before "clocking in," that time is compensable time.[37] For HR professionals the solution to the dilemma is simple. Either have the employees clock in when performing job-related work, or do not permit them to perform such work until the scheduled time period.

Break and Rest Periods

There is still considerable debate over whether or not break and rest periods are compensable time. The Wage and Hour Division of the Department of Labor contends that only break periods of twenty minutes or longer are noncompensable.[38] For any period less than twenty minutes, the employee must be paid. The circuit courts are split on this matter. As a matter of convention, most employers pay employees while they are on break or rest periods.

Arguably, employees are serving their own interests while on break and not those of employers. Making such periods technically nonwork times would make them noncompensable.[39]

Training Periods

Mandated or compulsory training is any training the employee must attend or else risk termination. Naturally, all mandatory training periods are compensable time. The employee has no choice in being present.

Additionally, time spent in compulsory training can be accrued when calculating overtime. For example, an employer requires employees to attend safety training for one hour after the conclusion of their scheduled eight-hour shifts for the next five days. Assuming the training is initiated at the beginning of each employee's 168-consecutive-hour workweek, each employee would be entitled to five hours of overtime (the five eight-hour shifts plus five one-hour training sessions total forty-five compensable hours).

Training in which the employee voluntarily engages is usually not compensable. As an example, as part of an employee's career planning, she is told she must earn an M.B.A. degree in order to advance in the organization. Because the employee enrolls in night courses, she is pursuing additional training for her own interests or personal advancement. Time spent in the M.B.A. program would not be compensable time.

Portal-to-Portal Time

Under normal circumstances, travel time to and from the place of employment is not compensable.[40] Under the 1947 amendment to the FLSA, the so-called Portal-to-Portal Act, unless the travel time is specifically related to company business, the employer is not required to pay the employee. To help differentiate compensable travel time from noncompensable travel time, examine the following two examples involving a nonexempt employee. Assume the employee in question has a one-hour commute to work each morning and a one-hour commute home each evening. This travel to and from work is noncompensable as it is not work related. After all, the employee chooses where he or she lives, not the employer.

Now, assume that one morning after arriving at his place of employment, a generator repair business, the employee is dispatched to a customer located one hour away from the employer's office. This time, the travel is in the line of duty, it is work related, and consequently, the one-hour travel time to the customer and the one-hour travel time back to the employer's office are compensable. Any travel on company business is compensable time for nonexempt employees.

Child Labor Limitations

Another provision of the FLSA places limitations on an employer's use of child labor. Employers may assign employees eighteen years of age or older to any position in the

Figure 9.5 **Hazardous Jobs Identified by the Secretary of Labor That Are Prohibited to Minors 16 to 17 Years of Age**

- Manufacturing or storing explosives
- Driving a motor vehicle and being an outside helper on a motor vehicle
- Coal mining
- Forest fire fighting
- Operating power-driven wood-working machines
- Exposure to radioactive substances and to ionizing radiations
- Operating power-driven hoisting equipment
- Mining, other than coal mining
- Operating power-driven metal-forming, punching, and shearing machines
- Operation of power-driven meat-processing machines
- Operating power-driven bakery machines
- Operating power-driven balers, compactors, or paper-products machines
- Manufacturing brick, tile, and related products
- Ship wrecking, demolition, and ship-breaking operations
- Operating power-driven circular saws, band saws, and guillotine shears
- Roofing operations
- Excavation operations

Sources: 29 C.F.R. §§ 570.50–68 (2012).

Figure 9.6 **Hazardous Jobs Identified by the Secretary of Labor That Are Prohibited to Minors 14 to 15 Years of Age**

- Manufacturing, mining, or processing occupations
- Operating, tending, setting up, adjusting, cleaning, oiling, or repairing hoisting apparatus
- Work performed on or about a boiler or engine room
- Operating, tending, setting up, adjusting, cleaning, oiling, or repairing power-driven machinery
- Operation of motor vehicles
- Outside window washing involving ladders, scaffolds, or other substitutes
- All baking and cooking activities
- Working in freezers and meat coolers
- Youth peddling
- Loading and unloading goods or property onto or from a motor vehicle
- Catching and cooping poultry for transportation to market
- Occupations with connection to transportation of persons or property by rail, highway, air, pipeline, or other means
- Occupations with connection to warehousing and storage
- Occupations with connection to communications and public utilities
- Occupations with connection to construction

Sources: 29 C.F.R. § 570.33 (2012).

workplace, to work at any time, and in virtually any context (provided the working conditions are in compliance with the Occupational Safety and Health Act; refer to Chapter 11). However, for applicants or employees under age eighteen, the FLSA imposes restrictions on work times and working conditions. Workers sixteen and seventeen years old may work for unlimited hours but only in nonhazardous jobs.[41] Hazardous jobs are listed in Figure 9.5 and cannot be assigned to any individual younger than eighteen years of age.[42]

Workers between fourteen and fifteen years of age have further restrictions on both the hours that can be worked and the time of day that such work may occur (see Figure 9.6).

Figure 9.7   Record Keeping Requirements Under the FLSA

Address, including zip code
All additions to or deductions from the employee's wages
Basis on which employee's wages are paid (e.g., "$6 an hour," "$220 a week," "piecework")
Birthdate, if younger than 19
Date of payment and the pay period covered by the payment
Employee's full name and social security number
Hours worked each day
Regular hourly pay rate
Sex and occupation
Time and day of week when employee's workweek begins
Total daily or weekly straight-time earnings
Total hours worked each workweek
Total overtime earnings for the workweek
Total wages paid each pay period

Source: 29 C.F.R. Part 516.

These allowable working times are also tied to the school year. Workers in the fourteen- to fifteen-year-old age bracket are permitted to work outside school in nonmanufacturing, nonmining, and nonhazardous jobs within specific hourly and time limits depending upon when schools are in session. For example, on school days, fourteen- and fifteen-year-olds are limited to working no more than three hours per day and may work only during a time frame between 7:00 a.m. and 7:00 p.m.[43] Furthermore, the total number of hours that can be worked in a school week is capped at eighteen.[44]

During nonschool days, the fourteen- or fifteen-year-old employees may work up to eight hours per day, and during a nonschool week, they may accrue up to forty total hours.[45] During the period from June 1 to Labor Day, the time frame during which fourteen- and fifteen-year-olds may work is expanded to the period 7 a.m. to 9 p.m.[46] Again, fourteen- and fifteen-year-olds are excluded from hazardous jobs even during the summer months.

Record Keeping

The most important function of the HR department, with regard to the FLSA, is keeping the necessary documentation to substantiate the employer's good faith effort to comply with the Act's provisions. In the event of an investigation by the WHD, the employer is responsible for making payroll records available within seventy-two hours.[47] In the event of such a request, the employer must make all records stipulated in Figure 9.7 available for inspection and transcription by the WHD administrator investigating the complaint.[48] Employers are required to keep payroll records on each employee for three years.[49]

Remedies and Penalties

When an employer has failed to pay employees the minimum wage or overtime due under the FLSA, the employer is liable for paying *all affected employees* the amount of unpaid minimum wages or unpaid overtime compensation.[50] Returning to our opening scenario, Bob is due the overtime that Mr. Swartzwelder failed to pay him. If Bob worked sixty hours per week for three months at $1,900 per month, Mr. Swartzwelder would have to pay him approximately $2,700.

This is the difference between his monthly salary of $1,900 and his projected monthly wage at his old hourly rate ($10 per hour) and overtime rate ($15 per hour for every hour worked in excess of forty during the workweek). If Bob had indeed worked sixty hours per week for a twelve-week period (three months) he would have earned a total of $8,400 instead of the $5,700 paid him by Mr. Swartzwelder.

The employer would also be responsible for compensating all employees (even the ones who are no longer current employees) for all unpaid minimum wages or overtime that they were not paid, even though they did not file a complaint.

When investigating FSLA complaints, the WHD will examine all of the employer's payroll records, and any employee who was not paid overtime or minimum wage is entitled to the difference. The critical point to remember is that the WHD inspects all payroll records of the employer, not just those of the complaining party.

The FLSA, like most federal legislation, contains a whistleblower clause.[51] Therefore, the employer may not take retaliatory action against an employee who has filed an FSLA complaint. In the event that an employer has taken retaliatory action against an employee, as Bob's employer did, the employee may be entitled to reinstatement, in addition to the payment of wages lost and an additional equal amount as liquidated damages.[52]

In situations in which the employer has been judged to have willfully and knowingly violated the FLSA's minimum wage and overtime provisions, additional penalties may be imposed. In circumstances involving repeated and willful violations, an employer may be assessed a fine of up to $1,000 per violation.[53]

Among the factors used by the WHD when determining whether the employer has willfully violated the FLSA are:

1. Good faith efforts to comply with the Act
2. The employer's explanation for the violations
3. The employer's previous history of violations
4. The employer's commitment to future compliance
5. The interval between violations
6. The number of employees affected by the violation
7. Whether there is any pattern to the violations[54]

Myths about the FLSA

Although the FLSA provides very real compensation requirements, there are limitations to its coverage that are often misunderstood. And, over the years, many misconceptions have developed, particularly among employees. Beyond the minimum wage, overtime, and child labor limitations previously discussed, the FLSA imposes no other requirements on covered employers. Because there is so much misunderstanding of the requirements

Figure 9.8 **What the FLSA Does Not Require**

- A discharge notice, reason for discharge, or immediate payment of final wages to terminated employees
- Meal or rest periods, holidays off, or vacations
- Pay raises or fringe benefits
- Premium pay for weekend or holiday work
- Vacation, holiday, severance, or sick pay

mandated by the FLSA, some compensation-related benefits or prohibitions that the Act *does not* require are listed in Figure 9.8.

Interestingly, the FLSA does not place any obligation on employers to provide vacation, holiday, severance, or sick pay. These are strictly at the discretion of the employer, unless mandated by state law. Nor does the FLSA contain any provision requiring an employer to furnish employees with meal or rest periods, holidays off, or vacations, whether paid or unpaid. Additionally, employers are not obligated under the FLSA to provide premium pay for weekend, night, or holiday work. No portion of the Act compels employers to offer pay raises or fringe benefits. Finally, the FLSA does not mandate any obligation to provide terminated employees with a discharge notice, reason for discharge, or immediate payment of final wages. Many employees believe they must be paid in full all accrued wages immediately upon discharge. This is not true, unless required under state law or local ordinance. In most instances involving employee termination, final payment may be made at the next normally scheduled pay period.

OTHER FEDERAL COMPENSATION LAWS

Other federal laws require certain employers to provide either specific levels of compensation, dictate particular overtime requirements, or both. However, these statutes apply only to a select group of employers—those who hold federal contracts or subcontracts. As a condition for eligibility for the contract in question, the employer agrees to pay the compensation stipulated under the applicable statute.

Davis-Bacon Act of 1931

The Davis-Bacon Act covers any employer who holds a federal construction contract in excess of $2,000.[55] This would apply to any employer contracted to assist in the construction of public buildings or public works of the U.S. government or any employer who is subcontracted by a prime contractor performing similar work. It also covers employers who are contracted or subcontracted to provide alterations and/or repairs (including painting and decorating) to existing federal buildings.

The primary requirement under the Davis-Bacon Act is that covered employers must pay their employees the prevailing wage for the geographic area in which the work is being performed. The **prevailing wage** is the minimum wage established for each class of workers as determined by the secretary of labor. This prevailing, or minimum, wage is invariably the union scale for the geographic area in question.

Walsh-Healy Act of 1936

Originally entitled the Public Contracts Act, the Walsh-Healy Act applies to contractors and subcontractors who hold federal contracts or subcontracts for the manufacture or furnishing of materials, supplies, articles, and equipment in any amount exceeding $10,000.[56] Like the Davis-Bacon Act, the Walsh-Healy Act requires its covered employers to pay employees the prevailing minimum wage as determined by the secretary of labor. At one time, this statute even required affected employers to pay overtime for any hours worked in excess of eight in any twenty-four-hour period. However, a 1985 amendment[57] eliminated this requirement.

McNamara-O'Hara Service Contract Act of 1965

The McNamara-O'Hara Service Contract Act, commonly referred to as the Service Contract Act, applies to contractors or subcontractors who provide services in excess of $2,500 to the U.S. government. Like the preceding statutes, the Service Contract Act requires covered employers to pay the prevailing wage for service employees for the geographic area in which the services are provided.[58] As with the previous acts, this prevailing wage is determined by the secretary of labor and is usually based on the union scale for service workers in the area where the services are contracted.

Unlike the Davis-Bacon and Walsh-Healy Acts, the Service Contract Act contains two additional requirements. First, this statute contains a provision specifying that the covered employers must provide fringe benefits to service employees comparable to the prevailing benefits for that class of workers in the geographic region. Again, these benefits are usually derived from the benefits typical in the collective bargaining agreements of union service workers in the area. Second, there is a provision that no part of the services covered under the statute will be performed in buildings or surroundings or under working conditions that are unsanitary or hazardous to the health or safety of service employees engaged in furnishing the services.[59]

The Wage and Hour Division is the enforcement agency for at least two other statutes that may have an impact on the HR department: the Worker Adjustment and Retraining Notification Act (WARN) and the Employee Polygraph Protection Act (EPPA), both of which were enacted in 1988. WARN imposes notification requirements on employers in the event of plant closings or mass layoffs. The EPPA places restrictions on the use of lie detectors in pre-employment screening for certain organizations. The Family Medical Leave Act of 1993, which the WHD also enforces, will be discussed in Chapter 10.

Worker Adjustment and Retraining Notification Act of 1988

The Worker Adjustment and Retraining Notification Act applies to any business enterprise that employs 100 or more employees, excluding part-time employees, or 100 or more employees who in the aggregate work at least 4,000 hours per week, exclusive of hours of overtime.[60] Covered employers are required to provide a sixty-day written notice to employees in the event of a plant closing or mass layoff. No employees may be laid off until the end of this sixty-day period following the written notice. In addition to this employee notification requirement, the employer must notify the state dislocated worker unit (designated under Title III of the Job Training Partnership Act).[61] A written sixty-day notice must also be given to the chief elected official of the unit of local government to which the employer pays the highest taxes.[62]

For the purpose of WARN, the term **plant closing** means the permanent or temporary shutdown of a single site of employment or one or more facilities or operating units within a single site of employment, provided that the shutdown results in an employment loss of fifty or more employees (excluding part-time employees) at the single site during any thirty-day period.[63]

Assume a company employs 200 workers at two plants. Due to financial demands, one plant employing seventy workers will be closed permanently. Since the closing involved fifty or more full-time employees, the written sixty-day notification would have to be given. If, on the other hand, the closing plant employed only thirty-five workers, WARN's notification provisions would not apply. Be cautious, as there may be state laws that would impose additional requirements to provide notification. HR professionals are responsible for knowing state laws that relate to plant closings as well.

A **mass layoff** occurs when a reduction in force is not the result of a plant closing but involves (1) at least one-third (33 percent) of the employees (excluding part-time employees), and (2) *at least fifty* employees are laid off for at least a thirty-day period. Under this provision, if an employer with 120 full-time employees had laid off one-third of its employees, it would not be required to provide the sixty-day notification. The employer would be covered under WARN (more than 100 workers were employed), and at least one-third of the workforce was laid off. However if only forty employees were laid off, the employer would be ten laid off workers short of the minimum fifty established in the Act to meet the definition of *mass layoff*.

There is one more circumstance under which a *mass layoff* would be established. In any instance in which at least 500 employees (excluding any part-time employees) are laid off, regardless of the percentage of the workforce, a mass layoff is considered to have occurred, and the employer is required to provide a sixty-day notice. Therefore, a plant employing 2,000 workers would be required to provide notice if it laid off 500 employees within a thirty-day period, even though this would result in only a 25 percent reduction in force (a proportion less than the 33 percent specified for smaller employers). An exception to the sixty-day notification is permitted when the closing or layoff is the result of the relocation or consolidation of part or all of the business.

However, prior to the closing or layoff, the employer must offer to transfer the affected employees to a different site of employment within a reasonable commuting distance. Furthermore, such transfers cannot result in more than a six-month break in employment.[64] The employer is not required to give notice when it offers to transfer employees to any other site of employment regardless of distance provided that there is no more than a six-month break in employment and that the employee accepts within thirty days of the offer or by the date of the closing or layoff, whichever is later.[65]

To illustrate this point, assume a plant was to be closed on April 1, 2001, and an employee was given the option to transfer to another plant on March 15, 2001. That employee would have until April 14, 2001, to accept or reject the transfer offer. Regardless of the employee's decision, the employer would not have to give a sixty-day notice of the plant closure.

The sixty-day notification period may also be reduced under circumstances that necessitate a plant closing or mass layoff resulting from business circumstances that were not reasonably foreseeable to afford the sixty-day notification. For example, no notice would be required if the plant closing or mass layoff resulted from a natural disaster such as a flood, earthquake, or drought.[66]

Employee Polygraph Protection Act of 1988

The WHD is also responsible for enforcing the Employee Polygraph Protection Act. The EPPA prohibits most private employers from using lie-detector tests either for pre-employment screening or during the course of employment. Specifically, an employer or prospective employer cannot require, request, suggest, or cause an employee or applicant to take or submit to any lie-detector test.[67] Nor can an employer discharge, discipline, discriminate against, deny employment or promotion, or threaten to take any such action against an employee or applicant for refusing to take a lie-detector test. Neither can such adverse employment action be based on the results of a test, for filing a complaint under the EPPA, or for testifying in any proceeding investigating a violation of the EPPA.[68]

It is important to note the EPPA does not provide an absolute prohibition against polygraph testing. There are some exceptions to the Act's ban on the use of polygraph testing in the workplace. Polygraph tests, but no other types of lie-detector tests, may be permitted under limited circumstances. First, federal, state, and local government employers are exempted from the EPPA. Government employees may be required to take polygraph tests as part of their pre-employment screening.[69] Second, employers authorized to manufacture, distribute, or dispense controlled substances (i.e., pharmaceutical companies) can use polygraph testing on employees.[70] Private sector employers who provide security services are also permitted to use polygraph testing on employees.[71] Polygraph testing can also be used by private sector employers as part of an investigation of economic loss or injury.[72] In circumstances involving theft, embezzlement, misappropriation, industrial espionage, or industrial sabotage, an employer would be allowed to use a polygraph test as part of an investigation.

Managers and HR professionals need to be aware that the EPPA does not allow indiscriminate use of polygraphs in investigations. The employer must have a reasonable suspicion that a particular employee was involved in the activity under investigation. Therefore, the employer cannot require all employees to submit to a polygraph test as part of an investigation of property theft. Only those employees whom there is a reasonable cause to suspect can be tested.

In regard to the EPPA, HR professionals and managers should remember that unless a practice in question meets the specified exemptions, the use of polygraph testing should be avoided. In the event that polygraph testing is necessitated (i.e., as part of an accident investigation), HR professionals and managers should ensure the justification for the testing is appropriately documented. It is also advisable that the organization's employee handbook contain a warning to employees that polygraph testing may be used in certain investigations.

The EPPA empowers the secretary of labor to bring injunctive actions in U.S. district courts to halt polygraph testing that violates the Act. It also provides for civil money penalties up to $10,000 against employers who violate any provision of the Act.[73] Finally, the EPPA requires all employers to post notices summarizing the protections of the Act in their places of employment.

Lilly Ledbetter Fair Pay Act of 2009

The Lilly Ledbetter Fair Pay Act[74] was signed into law by President Obama on January 29, 2009. It was passed to specifically overturn a U.S. Supreme Court decision, *Ledbetter v. Goodyear Tire & Rubber Company*[75] in which the Supreme Court denied the complaining party's 1998 lawsuit alleging discrimination in compensation on the basis of sex on the grounds that it was not filed in a timely manner. As it occurred in the state of Alabama (a nondeferral state, see Chapter 2), she had to file her claim within 180 days of the discrimination.[76] Since the actual discrimination had occurred between 1979 and 1981, seventeen years before her lawsuit, the claim had not been filed in a timely manner.

The Lilly Ledbetter Fair Pay Act changes the calculating of timeliness requirements as they relate to compensation discrimination and affects such provisions in five federal statutes: The Equal Pay Act of 1963, Title VII of the Civil Rights Act of 1964, the Age Discrimination in Employment Act of 1967, the Rehabilitation Act of 1973, and the Americans with Disabilities Act of 1990. The Fair Pay Act amends the timeliness requirements under the five previously mentioned statutes through the following:

> For purposes of this section, an unlawful employment practice occurs, with respect to discrimination in compensation in violation of this title, when a discriminatory compensation decision or other practice is adopted, when an individual becomes subject to a discriminatory compensation decision or other practice, or *when an individual is affected by application of a discriminatory compensation decision or other practice, including each time wages, benefits, or other compensation is paid*, resulting in whole or in part from such a decision or other practice.

What the Lilly Ledbetter Fair Pay Act has done is make the timeliness of the charge counted from the date of the employee's last pay check. As an example, an employee was discriminated against in her salary in March 1993 by being paid $8.75 per hour for the same work that a male worker with the same skills and seniority was getting paid $9.75 per hour. Over the years she has received both cost-of-living and merit pay increases so that when she retires in 2013 she is making $22.50 per hour, while the male counterpart is making $21.55. She may still bring a charge against her employer for the discrimination that occurred in 1993, because the 180- or 300-day filing period (depending on the State) after the alleged unlawful employment practice occurred is now calculated from her last pay check, not the date in 1993. The new law basically makes the timeliness requirement for compensation discrimination based on sex, age, or disability open-ended.

SUMMARY

The Fair Labor Standards Act was enacted in 1938 as part of the New Deal. The Act created the minimum wage (currently $7.25 per hour), established a forty-hour workweek with time-and-one-half to be paid for hours worked in excess of forty during a 168-consecutive-hour workweek, and placed limitations on the use of child labor.

The Davis-Bacon, Walsh-Healy, and McNamara-O'Hara Service Contract Acts require government contractors and subcontractors to provide specific levels of compensation, certain overtime requirements, or both.

The FSLA, Davis-Bacon Act, Walsh-Healy Act, and McNamara-O'Hara Service Contract Act are all regulated in whole or part by the Department of Labor. The Worker Adjustment and Retraining Notification Act and Employee Polygraph Protection Act are also enforced by the Department of Labor. WARN requires notification requirements by employers in the event of plant closings or mass layoffs.

The EPPA restricts the use of polygraph tests in pre-employment screening. It should be apparent that ensuring regulatory compliance with equal employment opportunity laws is not the only concern confronting HR professionals.

Compensation laws and regulations also cover a significant portion of HR activities and require the constant attention of HR professionals. In dealing with many of the compensation laws, the obligation for HR professionals is not merely knowing the provisions of these statutes, but understanding to which employees they apply. The requirements imposed by many of these statutes apply only to specific classes of workers, nonexempt employees.

For example, under the FLSA, it is essential to know under what circumstances the employee is entitled to overtime and how to calculate these overtime obligations. But, it is equally important to know which employees are entitled to overtime compensation (nonexempt employees) and which are not (exempt employees).

KEY TERMS AND CONCEPTS

Compensable time

Compensatory time

Exempt employees

Mass layoff

Nonexempt employee

Overtime

Plant closing

Prevailing wage

DISCUSSION QUESTIONS

1. What three general employment practices are regulated under the FLSA of 1938? Describe the specific requirements of each.
2. What are the three age categories under the FLSA regarding child labor? What are the restrictions for each category?
3. Provide examples of five classes of employees who would be *exempt* employees under the FLSA's minimum wage and overtime provisions. Why are they *exempt*?
4. How is compensatory time calculated?
5. What employers are required to pay the prevailing wage under the Davis-Bacon, Walsh-Healy, and McNamara-O'Hara Service Contract Acts?
6. Who is covered under WARN? What are the main provisions?
7. Under what circumstances can an employer use lie detectors in making employment decisions? What employers are not bound by these restrictions?
8. What effect has the Lilly Ledbetter Fair Pay Act had on claims of compensation discrimination? What laws are affected?

CASES

Case 1

Following a short stint as a waitress, Donde Arnold "tried out" for a position as an exotic dancer at Babe's. Arnold began dancing at Babe's in December of 1993. She had started working as a waitress in October of 1993. While a waitress, Arnold was paid at a rate of one-half the minimum wage plus tips. As a dancer, Arnold's sole source of income was the tips, or "dance fees," she extracted from customers for the performance of "stage dances" and "table dances." A "stage dance," as the term implies, is a dance performed on a raised platform for the customers at large. A "table dance" is a dance performed off-stage in a relatively smaller space, such as the space immediately in front of a seated customer, or on a couch or tabletop, for one paying customer. In general, a customer paid a "set fee" of $5 or $10 for a table dance.

The relationship between a dancer and Babe's, a Diamond A club, is structured as a licensing arrangement. The dancer and Diamond A enter into a "License to Use Business Premises," which grants the dancer a nonexclusive license to dance and entertain customers at certain specified nightclubs. In exchange for the license, the dancer pays the club a licensing fee, called "shift pay," of $10 per day shift and $15 per night shift. The dancer retains all tips or "dance fees" that she receives from customers for stage dances and table dances and does not report, or otherwise account for, any of her earnings to the club; the club does not pay the dancer any wages or other form of stipend.[77]

a. Is the dancer an exempt employee under the FLSA? Why or why not?
b. Under what circumstances could the dancer be a nonexempt employee?

Case 2

Troy Barnett worked for a property management company that employed over 2,000 full-time employees nationwide. The property manager at Barnett's worksite gave him his daily work assignments.

When Barnett was initially hired, the property manager informed him that the job would require overtime for which he would be compensated. Barnett's duties were generally performed during a 9:00 A.M. to 5:00 P.M. shift, which included daily preventative maintenance of the building's boilers and air-conditioning system. There were also some seasonal responsibilities regarding the pool and snow removal. He performed garbage removal as well as responding to mechanical or plumbing problems reported by residents. He was further required to restore newly vacated rental units to their original condition in order that they could be rented to new tenants.

Barnett was also required to be "on call" every other week to handle any after-hours emergencies. During the week that he was on call, Barnett was automatically paid two hours' overtime pay. If he worked more than two hours, he was paid additional overtime compensation. If he performed no work at all, he still received a minimum of two hours overtime pay that week.[78]

In fall 2009, Barnett was informed by the property management that due to financial exigencies, he would no longer receive overtime for being on call; he would receive overtime compensation only for actual hours worked in excess of forty in his workweek. Distraught over this loss of income, Barnett filed a complaint with the Wage and Hour Division of the Department of Labor.

a. Is the complaining party a nonexempt employee under the FLSA?
b. Does the complaining party have a legitimate FLSA complaint? Why or why not?
c. Could he be compensated with compensatory time?

NOTES

1. 29 U.S.C. § 207 (2012).
2. 29 U.S.C. § 206.
3. Society for Human Resource Management, *2011 Employee Benefits: Examining Employee Benefits Amidst Uncertainty* (Alexandria, VA 2011): 12; U.S. Chamber of Commerce, *U.S. Chamber Study Finds Employee Benefit Costs Consume 40 Percent of Payroll Expenses*, http://www.uschamber.com/press/releases/2006/april/us-chamber-study-finds-employee-benefit-costs-consume-40-percent-payroll-e (accessed March 22, 2013).
4. U.S. Department of Labor, Wage and Hour Division, *Fact Sheet # 27: New Businesses Under Fair Labor Standards Act (FLSA)*, July 2008, http://www.dol.gov/whd/regs/compliance/whdfs27.pdf (accessed March 24, 2013).
5. Ibid.
6. Ibid.
7. 29 U.S.C. § 206(a)(1).
8. U.S. Department of Labor Wage and Hour Division, *Minimum Wage Laws in the States*, January 1, 2013, http://www.dol.gov/whd/minwage/america.htm (accessed March 24, 2013).

9. 29 U.S.C. § 203e(2)(B).

10. 29 U.S.C. § 203e(2)(C).

11. 29 C.F.R. § 541.1.

12. 29 C.F.R. § 541.100(a)(1).

13. Ibid.

14. 29 C.F.R. § 541.300.

15. 29 C.F.R. § 541.300 (a)(1).

16. 29 C.F.R. § 541.500.

17. 29 C.F.R. § 541.500(b).

18. 29 U.S.C. § 514.400.

19. 29 U.S.C. § § 514. 400(a)(1)-(4).

20. 29 U.S.C. § 541.400(a).

21. U.S. Department of the Treasury, Internal Revenue Service, *Employer's Supplement Tax Guide, Publication 15-A* (Washington, DC: Government Printing Office, 2013), pp. 7–8.

22. *Vizcaino v. United States District Court*, 173 F.2d at 713 (9th Cir. 1999), cert denied 528 U.S. 1105 (2000).

23. *Vizcaino*, 173 F.2d at 717.

24. 29 C.F.R. § 519.12.

25. Ibid.

26. 29 C.F.R. § 519.13.

27. 29 C.F.R. 519.12.

28. 29 C.F.R. § 519.16.

29. Ibid.

30. Ibid.

31. U.S. Department of Labor, Wage and Hour Division, *Fact Sheet #15: Tipped Employees Under the Fair Labor Standards Act (FLSA)*, March 2011, http://www.dol.gov/whd/regs/compliance/whdfs15. htm (accessed March 24, 2013).

32. U.S. Department of Labor, Wage and Hour Division, *Fact Sheet # 2: Restaurants and Fast Food Establishments Under the Fair Labor Standards Act (FLSA)*, July 2009, http://www.dol.gov/whd/regs/ compliance/whdfs2.pdf (accessed March 24, 2013).

33. Department of Labor and Employment, *Colorado Minimum Wage Fact Sheet* (Denver, CO: Division of Labor, November 2007).

34. 29 U.S.C. § 207(o)(1).

35. 29 C.F.R. § 553.223(c).

36. *Mitchell v. King Packing Co.*, 350 U.S. 260 (1956).

37. Ibid., at 263.

38. 29 C.F.R. § 785.18.

39. *Owens v. IT T Rayonier, Inc.*, 971 F.2d 347 (9th Cir. 1992).

40. 29 U.S.C. §§ 251–262.

41. 29 U.S.C. § 212.

42. Ibid.

43. 29 C.F.R. § 570.35.

44. Ibid.

45. Ibid.

46. Ibid.

47. 29 C.F.R. § 516.7.

48. U.S. Department of Labor, Wage and Hour Division, *Fact Sheet #21: Recordkeeping Requirements under the Fair Labor Standards Act (FLSA)* (July 2008), http://www.dol.gov/whd/regs/compliance/ whdfs21.pdf (accessed March 24, 2013).

49. 29 C.F.R. § 516.7.

50. 29 U.S.C. § 216(b).

51. 29 U.S.C. § 215(a)(3).

52. 29 U.S.C. § 216(b).

53. 29 C.F.R. § 578.3.

54. 29 C.F.R. § 578.4.

55. 40 U.S.C. § 276a.

56. 41 U.S.C. § 3.

57. Pub. L. 99–145, § 1241(b) (November 8, 1985).

58. 41 U.S.C. § 351(b).

59. 41 U.S.C. § 351 (a)(3).

60. 29 U.S.C. § 2101(a)(1).

61. 29 U.S.C. § 1651 *et seq.*

62. 29 U.S.C. § 2102(a).

63. 29 U.S.C. § 2101(a)(2).

64. 29 U.S.C. § 2101(b)(2).

65. Ibid.

66. 29 U.S.C. § 2102(b).

67. U.S. Department of Labor, Wage and Hour Division, *Fact Sheet #36: Employee Polygraph Protection Act of 1988*, July 2008, http://www.dol.gov/whd/regs/compliance/whdfs36.htm (accessed March 24, 2013).

68. Ibid.

69. 29 C.F.R. § 801.10.

70. 29 C.F.R. § 801.13.

71. 29 C.F.R. § 801.14.

72. 29 C.F.R. § 801.12.

73. 29 C.F.R. § 801.42(a).

74. 42 U.S.C. 2000e-5

75. 550 U.S. 618 (2007).

76. 550 U.S. at 632–33.

77. Scenario was developed from the facts in *Harrell v. Diamond A Entertainment*, 992 F. Supp. 1343 (M.D. Fla. 1997).

78. Scenario was developed, in part, from the facts in *Wood v. Mid-American Management Corp.*, 2006 U.S. Dist. LEXIS 37016 (N.D. Ohio).

10

COMPENSATION

Benefits

LEARNING OBJECTIVES

- Understand the reasons for the growth of employee benefits.
- Discuss the evolution of government regulation of employee benefits and the costs associated with such regulation.
- Describe the two major types of employee benefits and major provisions of federal and state laws dealing with employee benefits.
- Describe the conditions under which an employee is ineligible for unemployment benefits.
- Describe the circumstances under which an employee is entitled to unpaid leave under the Family and Medical Leave Act of 1993.
- Describe an employer's obligations under the Employee Retirement Income Security Act of 1974.
- Understand the general provisions for employers under the Affordable Care Act of 2010.

OPENING SCENARIO

Jerri Lynn McClure has been working as full-time quality inspector for Frink & Rose Septic Tank, Inc., for two-and-a-half years. Frink & Rose employs 162 employees at its single production facility in Tulsa, Oklahoma. The majority of the employees live within a thirty-minute commute of the plant.

In March, Jerri Lynn's husband, Kenny, was severely injured in a hunting accident. As a result, Kenny is immobilized and will require home nursing for two months. Jerri Lynn asks her immediate supervisor, Bob Johnson, if she can have the next two months off to care for her husband.

Although sympathetic to her plight, Bob informs Jerri Lynn that if she takes her accrued vacation time and he lets her take her accrued sick leave, the most she can have off is one month. Bob further tells her that right now is peak production time, and the company is trying to build up its finished goods inventory to satisfy the expected surge in demand at the beginning of the construction season. Bob adds that even if he is able to allow her the one month off to care for Kenny, he really cannot guarantee that her old job will be waiting when she returns to work.

Distraught, Jerri Lynn begins discussing the issue with a coworker, Dave Nickles. Dave tells her that Bob does not know what he is talking about. He says he has heard about a law called the Family and Medical Leave Act that allows anyone with a sick relative to take up to twelve weeks of paid leave from the employer.

Who is right, Bob or Dave? As we will soon see, neither is right. Yes, there is a Family and Medical Leave Act, but it does not apply to all sick relatives, and it does not mandate paid leave. Although the Act is somewhat complicated, it will solve several of Jerri Lynn's problems.

HISTORICAL PERSPECTIVE ON EMPLOYEE BENEFITS

The number and types of employee benefits offered by employers have grown over the years to now represent a major component in the total compensation program. According to the U.S. Chamber of Commerce, employee benefits account for roughly 44 percent of all payroll costs.[1] Employee benefits programs have developed to meet important needs of both the employer and the employee. Employers view benefits as a means to achieve organizational goals and objectives by attracting and retaining qualified employees, improving morale, providing a sense of security for employees, and increasing productivity. Employees, on the other hand, view them as an important part of their compensation packages when considering employment opportunities and making choices.

Around the turn of the twentieth century, very few employers offered benefits, and the few that were offered were designed to attract and retain employees with the required education and skills. By the 1920s, an era of "welfare capitalism" emerged in the United States.[2] Welfare capitalism was a system in which employers voluntarily and intentionally improved the living conditions of employees through various supplements to direct money pay. These employers offered employees what became known as "fringe benefits," such as paid vacations and holidays, insurance benefits, and pension plans. Some employers were motivated to provide these benefits due to a paternalistic attitude toward employees. Others provided benefit packages as a pragmatic means of keeping employees from organizing unions. Regardless of the rationale for providing the benefit packages, fringe benefits became a fixture in American business organizations.

Although the mix of benefit packages offered varied from employer to employer, all of the early welfare programs involved components that could be systematized and classified. Arnold Tolles identified eight broad groups or classes of early welfare programs, many of which are still in use today:[3]

1. *Recreational plans* included athletic teams, glee clubs, and drama clubs. Many employers provided facilities such as clubhouses, recreation rooms, gymnasiums, bowling alleys, and game rooms to bring employees relief from boredom, provide relaxation, and generate group spirit.

2. *Health and safety plans* provided employer-paid physical examinations, first aid, guards on machines, safety instructions, and medical advice and treatment in cases of accidents and sickness on the job.

3. *Education and information plans* included services such as company-sponsored educational programs, company-financed scholarship funds, the provision of technical libraries for employees, and the sponsorship of a variety of seminars.

4. *Economic security plans* are now one of the most costly types of welfare benefits. These provisions included thrift clubs, credit unions, stock purchase plans, paid vacations, paid sick leave plans, and group life, accident, and health insurance plans.

5. *Convenience plans* for employees included a wide variety of effects, the most elemental of which were adequate toilets and washrooms. Other examples included locker rooms, lunchrooms, and lunch wagons.

6. *Personal and family problems plans* consisted of emergency financial assistance to the employee, vocational guidance, and advice on problems of health and family finances.

7. *Community interests programs* included such activities as paying for time not worked while the employee is voting, serving on a jury, appearing as a witness, or conducting union duties. If the employer's facilities were located in isolated areas, they often provided housing for employees and their families.

8. *Employee representation plans,* endorsed by some larger companies, provided collective representation of employees as an alternative to labor unions. These plans were initially called "work councils" during the 1920s and were later known as "shop committees." Today they are known as employee empowerment programs, quality circles, or employee participation programs (see Table 10.1).

OVERVIEW OF THE REGULATION OF EMPLOYEE BENEFITS

Not surprisingly, as soon as employee benefits became widespread, government regulation was not far behind (see Figure 10.1 for a complete list of laws regulating benefits). Beginning as early as 1921, the Internal Revenue Code was amended to regulate interest income on profit-sharing programs and certain incentive programs offered by employers. By the time of the Great Depression, the era of socialism had begun, and the first federally mandated employee benefits emerged with the passage of the Social Security Act of 1935.

By the early 1970s, most employers and employees viewed employee benefits as an integral part of the total compensation program, and the majority of employees felt they were entitled to receive them as part of the employment relationship. Despite the expansion of benefits outside of collective bargaining agreements, there was little federal regulatory control over the management of private voluntary employee benefit programs until the Employee Retirement Income Security Act of 1974 (ERISA) was passed. This statute would be to employee benefits what the Civil Rights Act of 1964 was to equal employment opportunity.

Table 10.1

Employee Benefits by Type of Benefit (Employers' Share Only)

Type of Benefit	1947	1965	1983	1995	2005
Total employee benefits as a percentage of payroll	16.1%	28.1%	36.6%	40.7%	40.2%
Mandatory payments	2.6%	4.2 %	9.0%	8.9%	—
Pension, insurance, other agreed-upon payments	5.0%	9.9%	13.6%	17.2%	—
Paid rest periods, breaks, lunch periods, wash-up time, travel time, etc.	1.6%	2.4%	2.3%	2.2%	—
Payments for time not worked (vacations, holidays, etc.)	5.6%	9.6%	9.4%	9.7%	10.5%
Profit-sharing payments and other items	1.3%	2.0%	2.3%	2.7%	—
Total employee benefits in cents per hour	$0.221	$0.888	$3.691	$7.157	—
Total employee benefits as dollars per employee per year	$450	$1,874	$7,582	$14,678	$20,158

Source: Adapted from surveys in U.S. Chamber of Commerce editions of *Employee Benefits.*

In the 1980s and continuing into the present, federal and state governments have actively increased their roles regulating existing employee benefit programs. Government has also legislated tax reforms in order to provide incentives for private employers to create additional benefits as well as improve existing benefit plans. Benefits administration and management of employee benefits programs have become much more complex due to the extensive tax implications.

Mandatory and Voluntary Benefits

The benefits provided to employees fall into one of two broad categories: mandatory and voluntary. **Mandatory benefits**, quite simply, are those mandated or required by law. Employers have no choice but to provide the benefits. Examples of mandatory benefits include social security, unemployment compensation, workers' compensation, and family and medical leave.

Voluntary benefits are benefits that are not required by law. Thus, the employer may provide them, but no statute or regulation is violated if such benefits are not provided to employees. In reality, failing to provide certain benefits could be disastrous for an organization's recruitment and retention of qualified employees. After all, voluntary benefits have become so commonplace that employees have come to expect them as a normal part of the compensation package. How many people do you know would work for an employer who does not provide medical insurance, paid vacation time, and a retirement program? Even though employees may expect these benefits, they are still voluntary benefits that employers are not required by law to provide. However, any employer who

Figure 10.1 **Major Legislation Governing Employment Benefits**

Legislation	Provisions
Revenue Acts of 1921, 1926, and 1928	Exempts interest income on profit-sharing plans, bonus plans, and pension trusts from current taxation.
Social Security Act of 1935, as amended	Provides for such benefits as retirement, disability payments, health payments, and survivor income.
Labor-Management Relations Act of 1947	Provides fundamental guidelines for the establishment and operation of pension plans administered jointly by an employer and a labor union in Section 302.
Welfare and Pension Plans Disclosure Act of 1958	Requires plan administrators for collectively bargained plans to provide annual financial reports of plans.
Revenue Act of 1961	Amends § 403(b) to defer taxes of annuity purchases to employees of public educational institutions.
Welfare and Pension Plans Disclosure Act Amendments of 1962	Shifts responsibility for protection of plan assets to the federal government.
Self-Employed Individual Retirement Act of 1962 (Keogh Act)	Allows self-employed individuals a limited deduction of earnings for their own pension contributions.
Tax Reform Act of 1969	Provides guidelines for implementation and application of employer and union jointly administered pension plans.
Employee Retirement Income Security Act of 1974 (ERISA)	Protects private pension plan benefits for participants and establishes the Pension Benefit Guaranty Corporation (PBGC).
Revenue Act of 1978	Introduces qualified deferred taxation compensation plans in Section 401(k).
Economic Recovery Tax Act of 1981 (ERTA)	Extends IRA eligibility to employees covered by employer pension plans and authorizes qualified, voluntary employee contributions, increases contribution limits for IRA and Keogh Plans, and creates incentive stock options (ISO).
Tax Equity and Fiscal Responsibility Act of 1982 (TEFRA)	Establishes alternative minimum tax provisions, restricts qualified retirement benefits for highly paid employees, restricts top-heavy plans, modifies Keogh plans and Social Security integration rules, and establishes requirements for group term life insurance.
Deficit Reduction Act of 1984 (DEFRA)	Imposes various restrictions on benefit plans in an effort to reduce a budget deficit and makes changes affecting 401(k) plans.
Retirement Equity Act of 1984 (REA)	Amends ERISA pension plan provisions to expand employee benefit rights and protections regarding enrollment, vesting, breaks in service, and survivor provisions.
Consolidated Omnibus Budget Reconciliation Act of 1985 (COBRA)	Requires employers to offer extended group health insurance coverage for up to 36 months to employees and dependents whose coverage would otherwise terminate due to qualifying events.

Legislation	Provisions
Tax Reform Act of 1986	Establishes major changes in several benefit plans for vesting schedules, Social Security integration, pension plan standards, and tax penalties as well as controlling discrimination in favor of highly paid employees.
Age Discrimination in Employment Act amendment of 1986 (ADEA)	Prohibits mandatory retirement based upon age for most employees.
Omnibus Budget Reconciliation Act of 1986 (OBRA 1986)	Requires that employers allow accrual and participation in established pension plans for employees who continue working beyond age 64 and for employees who are hired within 5 years of the plan's normal retirement age.
Omnibus Budget Reconciliation Act of 1987 (OBRA 1987)	Increases and extends the PBGC pension insurance premium provisions for participants employed beyond a pension plan's normal retirement age.
Omnibus Budget Reconciliation Act of 1989 (OBRA 1989)	Expands health care continuation under COBRA (1985) and includes some forms of deferred compensation in determining average compensation and Social Security taxable base.
Omnibus Budget Reconciliation Act of 1990 (OBRA 1990)	Increases the excise tax for pension asset reversions, the taxable base for Medicare payroll tax, and the PBGC premium rates.
Older Workers Benefit Protection Act of 1990 (OWBPA)	Amends the Age Discrimination in Employment Act (ADEA) to be applicable to employee benefit eligibility and participation.
Omnibus Budget Reconciliation Act of 1993 (OBRA 1993)	Reduces compensation limit for 401(k) plans, increases amount of Social Security benefits subject to taxation from 50 percent to 85 percent for individuals earning more than $34,000 and married persons filing jointly earning above $44,000, and enacts a cap on deduction of executive compensation in excess of $1 million not linked to performance.
Family and Medical Leave Act of 1993 (FMLA)	Grants employees up to 12 weeks of unpaid leave for various family and employee reasons including an employee's own illness, serious health conditions of an employee's spouse, children, or parents, and to care for a newborn child or a child placed by adoption or foster care.
Health Insurance Portability and Accountability Act of 1996 (HIPAA)	Prohibits group health insurance plans from establishing eligibility rules based on health status, limits duration and extent of excluding preexisting conditions, requires group health insurance plans to track a person's coverage upon leaving the plan to allow that person to gain access to another plan with reduced or no preexisting conditions restrictions, requires special enrollment periods for persons losing other coverage under qualifying circumstances, extends COBRA provisions, and expands ERISA's disclosure requirements.
Patient Protection and Affordable Care Act of 2010 (PPACA)	Children are permitted to remain on parent's health insurance plans until age 26. Companies cannot charge higher premiums for pre-existing conditions. Employers are required to report the value of health care benefits on the employee's annual form W-2. Pre-tax employee contributions to flexible spending accounts are limited to $2,500. Beginning January 1, 2014, employer sponsored health insurance plans are limited to $2,000 annual deductibles for single individuals.
Health Care and Education Reconciliation Act of 2010	An amendment to the PPACA, imposes a $2,000 fine, for each full-time worker over the first 30 workers, on employers who employ 50 or more employees who do not offer health coverage.

does not "voluntarily" offer these benefits will have a difficult time attracting and retaining qualified employees.

Although the majority of the benefits employers offer are voluntary, many (especially pension and health care benefits) are regulated by federal and/or state authorities. In certain cases, where there is no law requiring employers to provide the benefit, once employers elect to provide it, the benefit must be administered according to law.

REGULATION OF MANDATORY BENEFITS

From an employee relations perspective, the most relevant mandatory benefits are unemployment compensation, workers' compensation, and family and medical leave. The regulations related to unemployment compensation and family and medical leave will be discussed next. Because of its relationship to workplace safety and health issues, *workers' compensation* is addressed in Chapter 11. Before the Affordable Care Act, the cost of mandatory benefits accounted for approximately 19 percent of an employee's average annual salary.[4]

Unemployment Compensation

Although unemployment compensation programs are administered by individual states, these programs were established by the Social Security Act of 1935.[5] This New Deal legislation was enacted to provide **unemployment compensation** in order to offset workers' lost income during periods of involuntary unemployment and to help unemployed workers locate new employment. Because the employer's contribution to the unemployment fund is based on the number of unemployment claims filed against it, there is a very real incentive for the employer to maintain a stable workforce.

Unemployment compensation is actually an unemployment insurance program. Like all insurance programs, the amount of premium an employer pays varies based upon the number of former employees who file unemployment claims.[6] As automobile insurance premiums increase with the number of traffic accidents a policyholder has, so too do unemployment compensation premiums increase with the number of employees laid off by an employer. The connection is clear: employers with few layoffs pay low state unemployment taxes; those organizations that lay off many employees will pay higher taxes.

Covered Employers

The Unemployment Tax Act defines an "employer" as any entity who paid wages of $1,500 or more in any quarter in the current or preceding calendar year and employed at least one individual on at least one day during twenty weeks in the current or previous year.[7] This includes virtually all employers nationwide. However, various state laws have exempted specific categories of employers from unemployment eligibility. Because exemptions vary from state to state, readers are cautioned to consult the respective state unemployment commission for specific information on exempted employers.

Employee Eligibility

As a rule, certain classes of employees are not entitled to coverage under state unemployment compensation laws. In all states, railroad workers are not entitled to draw unemployment compensation because railroad workers and their families are covered under separate social insurance legislation, the Railroad Retirement Act of 1935,[8] and not the Social Security Act.

Additionally, all states exclude persons who are self-employed from unemployment compensation. Persons who are employed by their immediate family members (parent, spouse, or child) cannot draw unemployment benefits.[9] Full-time students and the spouses of full-time students who provide employment services for schools, colleges, and universities are not provided unemployment insurance coverage.[10] Finally, persons who are currently drawing pensions, retirement pay, or other annuities are disqualified automatically from collecting unemployment compensation.[11] Although all of these classes of individuals are universally denied unemployment benefits, states, individually, have excluded other classes of employees (see Figure 10.2).

Even if an employee is not in one of the exempted classes, that employee is not eligible automatically for unemployment compensation upon termination. To receive unemployment compensation, the terminated employee must meet three conditions. First, the employee must have been involuntarily terminated. Thus, if the employee voluntarily terminates employment (resigns), he or she may be ineligible to draw unemployment benefits, depending on the state regulations.[12] If the employee has been discharged for either misconduct (i.e., violating a work rule, insubordination, theft, etc.) or failure to meet minimum performance standards, he or she is disqualified from unemployment compensation eligibility.

Second, the terminated employee must be able and willing to work. This means the terminated employee is entitled to unemployment compensation as long as he or she is unemployed and has not refused suitable work. Unemployment claimants are required to make regular visits to the state unemployment commission for the purpose of locating another job. If the claimant fails to actively seek new employment (i.e., does not check with the employment commission regularly) or refuses to accept a comparable position through the employment commission, unemployment benefits may be terminated.

Third, in order to be eligible for unemployment compensation, the terminated employee must have met the state's minimum income and contribution levels. Before a claimant can draw the state's unemployment benefits, he or she must have first earned a certain base wage amount and worked for a minimum period of time (usually at least three months in the previous year prior to the unemployment claim).

Interestingly, in all states, except New York, an individual is ineligible for unemployment compensation if the unemployment is due to a labor strike or work stoppage.[13] See Figure 10.3 for a list of reasons for ineligibility for unemployment compensation.

Figure 10.2 **Individuals Specifically Disqualified from Receiving Unemployment Benefits by State Law**

State	Casual Employees	Commercial Fishing Vessels	Hospital Interns	Insurance Agents	Minor Newspaper Carriers	Patients Employed by Hospitals	Real Estate Agents[1]	Undocumented Workers
Alabama		x	x	x	x	x		
Alaska		x	x	x	x	x	x	x
Arizona	x		x	x	x	x	x	
Arkansas	x	x	x	x	x	x	x	
California	x		x	x	x	x	x	
Colorado	x		x	x	x	x	x	
Connecticut	x			x		x	x	
Delaware			x	x	x	x	x	
Florida	x	x	x	x	x		x	
Georgia	x	x	x	x	x	x	x	
Hawaii	x	x	x	x	x	x		
Idaho		x^2	x	x	x	x	x	
Illinois		x^2	x	x	x	x	x	
Indiana		x^2	x		x		x	
Iowa		x						
Kansas		x^2		x			x	
Kentucky		x^2	x	x	x		x	
Louisiana		x^2	x	x	x		x	
Maine		x	x	x	x	x	x	
Maryland		x	x	x		x	x	
Massachusetts		x	x	x		x	x	
Michigan				x	x	x	x	
Minnesota	x		x	x	x	x	x	
Mississippi	x	x^2	x	x	x		x	
Missouri				x	x		x	
Montana				x	x	x	x	

State							
Nebraska					X	X	X
Nevada						X	X
New Hampshire				X	X	X	X
New Jersey				X		X	X
New Mexico				X	X	X	X
New York	X						X
North Carolina	X	X		X	X	X	X
North Dakota	X			X	X	X	X
Ohio		X		X	X	X	X
Oklahoma		X		X	X	X	X
Oregon	X			X	X	X	X
Pennsylvania	X			X	X	X	X
Rhode Island	X		X	X	X	X	X
South Carolina	X		X	X	X	X	X
South Dakota	X		X	X	X	X	X
Tennessee		X		X	X	X	X
Texas			X	X	X	X	X
Utah			X	X	X	X	X
Vermont				X	X	X	X
Virginia	X	X		X	X	X	X
Washington	X	X		X		X	X
West Virginia				X	X	X	X
Wisconsin	X			X	X	X	X
Wyoming					X	X	X

Source: G.E. Jackson, *Labor and Employment Law Desk Book*, 2d ed. (Paramus, NJ: Prentice Hall, 1999 Cumulative Supplement).

[1] Insurance and real estate agents who work for commission only are ineligible for unemployment compensation.

[2] Commercial fishing vessel employees are excluded except those that work for employers with operating offices in that state.

Figure 10.3 **Reasons for Ineligibility for Unemployment Compensation**

- Failure to seek suitable employment
- Involuntary termination for misconduct
- Unemployment resulting from labor strike
- Voluntary termination without good cause
- Failure to meet the State requirements for wages earned or time worked

Unemployment Benefits

If an individual is laid off by a covered employer, that individual is entitled to receive unemployment compensation for up to twenty-six weeks. Keep in mind that during this twenty-six-week period, the claimant must be actively seeking suitable employment. The amount of unemployment compensation the individual may draw per week is established by the individual state. In all states, this amount is based on a percentage of the employee's average weekly pay (usually 50 percent) and a maximum ceiling, whichever amount is smaller.

Family Medical Leave

Family and medical leave is provided under the Family and Medical Leave Act of 1993 (FMLA). Effective as of August 5, 1993, the FMLA requires that eligible employees receive up to twelve weeks of *unpaid* leave for the birth of a child, adoption of a child, care of an immediate family member (spouse, child, or parent) suffering from a "serious health condition," or recovery from a personal "serious health condition."[14] In determining an employee's entitlement to FMLA's mandatory leave, two questions must be addressed:

- Is the employer a covered entity (required to comply with the provisions of the Act)?
- Has the employee in question met the FMLA's eligibility requirement?

Covered Employers

Private sector employers must comply with the FMLA when they employ fifty or more employees for at least twenty workweeks in the current or previous year, including joint employers and successor employers. The term **joint employers** refers to two or more employers who employ the same individual. Think of a situation in which the employee is paid by an employment service (i.e., Kelly or Manpower) and contracted to work for yet a second employer (i.e., Western Corporation or Lockheed Martin).[15] Even though the employee receives his or her pay check and benefits from Manpower, if Lockheed Martin controls and supervises the employee's work activities, Lockheed Martin is a joint employer. If the leased employee brings the joint employer's workforce to the fifty-employee threshold, the joint employer is covered under the FMLA.[16]

Figure 10.4 **Basic Eligibility Provisions for the FMLA**

- Employee must work for a covered employer.
- Employee must have worked for the employer for at least twelve months (can be nonconsecutive).
- Employee must have worked in excess of 1,250 hours during the twelve-month period.
- Employee must work at facility with 50 or more employees who live within 75 miles of the facility.

Source: 29 U.S.C. §§ 2611 and 2612.

A **successor employer**, as the name implies, is an employer who replaces another employer. If one company was acquired by another company, the acquiring company is the successor employer. If Company X (employing thirty-five employees) acquires Company Y (employing sixty employees), Company X, as the successor employer, has also acquired Company Y's FMLA obligations. If as a result of the acquisition the total employee threshold of fifty or more is met, the successor employer (Company X) is now required to follow the FMLA.[17]

When there are separate buildings/operations within a *reasonable* geographic proximity, and they are used for the same business purposes, sharing the same staff and equipment, they are treated as a single worksite.[18] For example, an employer operates five ministorage facilities in the St. Louis, Missouri, metropolitan area, each employing twelve workers. The employees can be shifted from facility to facility on an as-needed basis. Because they are all engaged in the same business activities and because they can share staff, the employer's five locations are treated as a single work site. Individually, none would attain the fifty-employee threshold, but treated as a single site, they easily meet it.

One additional feature of the FMLA, and somewhat unusual for a federal statute, is that all public sector entities are "employers" covered by the Act.[19] The federal government is included as a covered employer under the Act, as are state and local governments.[20]

Employee Eligibility

Determining employee eligibility can become a little more complicated than determining employer coverage. Just because an individual is working for a covered employer does not, of and by itself, mean the particular employee is eligible for FMLA leave. The employee is not automatically eligible if the employer is a covered entity. There are four conditions that must be satisfied before any individual is classed as an eligible employee under the FMLA. First, the employee must work for an employer who is covered under the Act, and then the employee must meet all three of the additional conditions (see Figure 10.4).

Fifty Employees Within 75 Miles

The second eligibility requirement is that only those employees who work at a facility where at least 50 employees reside within 75 miles of that location are eligible employees.[21]

To demonstrate the effect this requirement has, assume an employer operates a business from two locations—one in Flagstaff, Arizona, with 100 employees, and another in Shreveport, Louisiana, with 35 employees.

The employer is a covered entity, but what about the company's unit in Shreveport? Are its employees covered? It has only 35 employees of whom only 28 live within the 75-mile radius. Does the company have to grant them FMLA leave? The answer is no. Though the corporation is clearly covered under the FMLA,[22] the Shreveport employees cannot receive FMLA leave because they do not meet all of the criteria necessary for eligibility. They are not employed at a worksite with a sufficient number of employees to qualify to draw the benefit.[23]

If the company consisted only of the Shreveport facility, it would not be covered under the FMLA at all. However, all of the Flagstaff employees who meet the individual 12-month and 1,250 hours service requirements are eligible for FMLA leave.

What if the employer has a reduction in force due to downsizing and drops the number of employees at a facility below 50? Assume that a company employed 60 people in August, but expects that the number of employees will drop to 40 in December. It does not matter. The employer must grant FMLA benefits to an otherwise eligible employee who gives notice of the need for leave in August for a period of leave to begin in December. If the threshold had been met for 20 weeks during the previous 12 months, the leave applies.

Length of Service Requirements

The next eligibility requirement is that the individual requesting the FMLA must have worked for the covered employer for a minimum of twelve months prior to the date on which the requested leave begins. This twelve-month period does not have to be continuous service.[24]

In addition to meeting the 12 months of service requirement, the employee must also have worked for at least 1,250 hours during the 12 months preceding the beginning of the FMLA leave.[25] Again, these 1,250 hours do not have to be continuous. The 1,250 hours are equivalent to working roughly 24 hours in each of the 52 weeks of the year, more than 104 hours worked in each of the 12 months of the year, or 40 hours worked per week for more than 31 weeks (more than 7 months) of the year.[26]

Are employees who have accrued 1,250 hours but not yet worked for the organization for 12 months entitled to FMLA? No. The requirement expressly states that employees must have worked for the employer for at least 12 months. How the 12 months are tolled is up to the employer.

Qualifying Events for FMLA Leave

Assuming the employer and employee are both covered under the FMLA, what are the circumstances by which an employee may request leave? There are two broad categories of leave: parental leave and leave related to a serious health condition.

Parental Leave Under the FMLA

An employee is entitled to FMLA leave for the birth or adoption of a child.[27] This "parental leave" applies to either parent (fathers as well as mothers). The FMLA also permits leave for foster care. The parental leave provisions are more restrictive than the serious health condition leave permitted under the Act. For example, parental leave cannot be taken intermittently; it must be taken in a single increment. Therefore, the employee cannot take off four weeks now, four more weeks later, and four more weeks further in the future. If the employee takes four weeks of parental leave now, there will be no future parental leave.

The second major difference regarding parental leave is that it *must* be taken within twelve months of the birth or adoption. If the father or mother wishes to take FMLA parental leave twelve months and one day after the child's birth, it is too late. The employee's right to the leave has already expired.[28]

Finally, if both parents work for the same organization, they are collectively limited to only twelve weeks of leave.[29] Both the father and the mother cannot separately request twelve weeks of parental leave (a total of twenty-four weeks' leave between the two employees). If they wanted to split the parental leave evenly, then each would be limited to requesting only six weeks. They may choose any combination of leave provided it does not exceed the twelve-week maximum. If the father and mother work for different employers, *each* is entitled to request the entire twelve-week leave period.

Serious Health Condition Leave Under the FMLA

Covered employees are entitled to up to twelve weeks unpaid leave to care for themselves or family members in the event of a "serious health condition." Serious health conditions will be discussed in the next section, but for now our discussion will focus on who is a family member according to the FMLA.

Under the Act, employees are entitled to take *unpaid* leave to care for a "spouse, son, daughter, or parent who has a serious health condition."[30] A spouse is a husband or wife recognized as married under state law. This includes common law marriages in those states recognizing such forms of marriage.[31] It does not include couples that are merely cohabitating. This means that domestic partners whose relationship is not legally recognized in their respective states are not entitled to FMLA leave. In order to be eligible for spousal leave, there must be a legally recognized relationship.

Sons and daughters include minor children (those under eighteen years of age) and children who have reached their majority (eighteen years or older) but are incapable of caring for themselves due to a physical or mental disability. Sons or daughters may be biological offspring, foster children, adopted children, stepchildren (if legally adopted), or a legal ward.[32] As with spouses, there must be a legally recognized relationship.

An employee may request FMLA leave in order to care for a parent. However, that employee has no FMLA entitlement to care for in-laws. A serious health condition affecting either a father-in-law or mother-in-law would not be a qualifying event. For example, a covered employer must authorize a female employee to take up to twelve weeks of unpaid leave to care for her seriously ill mother, but the employer is not required under the FMLA to permit her a single minute of unpaid leave to take care of her seriously ill mother-in-law.

Interestingly, as in parental leave situations, married couples are permitted only a total of twelve weeks leave between them to handle serious health conditions of family members when they work for the same employer.[33] If the wife, for example, has already exhausted eight weeks leave during the current twelve-month period to care for her ailing father, her husband could only take a maximum of four weeks if his mother needed assistance. If the husband and wife work for separate employers, each is entitled to the full twelve-week unpaid leave.

One major difference between serious health condition leave and parental leave is that any FMLA leave used to care for ill family members can be taken intermittently.[34] Where parental leave can be taken only in a single period of time, serious health condition leave can be taken incrementally—a few days now, a few days later.

The employer has the right to require the employee to provide documentation when requesting family leave. Employees seeking FMLA leave for the serious health condition of a family member may be required to verify the relationship of the family member.[35] In addition, the employer may demand verification of the family member's serious health condition.[36]

Regardless of the reason for the FMLA leave—parental leave or serious illness leave—the employee is guaranteed the right to return to his or her job or a comparable position at the leave's conclusion. In the opening scenario, Jerri Lynn likely would be able to return to her old job at the conclusion of her requested two months' leave.

Employees with Serious Health Conditions

When it comes to establishing serious conditions of either the individual employee or a family member, it is important to understand what criteria the FMLA designates as demonstrating a serious health condition. Such conclusions are not left to either the employer or the employee, but are strictly defined in the Act.

The FMLA defines serious health conditions as "an illness, injury, impairment, or physical or mental condition that involves inpatient care in a hospital, hospice, or residential medical care facility; or continuing treatment by a health care provider."[37] The critical point to make about serious health conditions is that they are *not* minor illnesses or injuries that last only a few days. Maladies like minor food poisoning,[38] earaches, influenza, colds, or cosmetic treatments (e.g., for acne) do not qualify as serious health conditions.[39] Instead, conditions requiring at a minimum an overnight stay in a hospital are more likely to rise to the level of a serious health condition. Other maladies or conditions that would meet this standard of severity would be broken bones, chronic illnesses (such as asthma and diabetes), surgery, medical conditions requiring prolonged episodic treatment (such as chemotherapy or radiation treatment for cancer), or any permanent long-term conditions that require monitoring (such as stroke or terminal illness).[40]

Unfortunately, the definition offered in the FMLA is unduly broad. In an attempt to clarify what constitutes a "serious health condition," the Employment Standards Administration developed specific regulations. Under these regulations, a "serious health condition," for the purposes of the FMLA, is established when one or more of the following conditions is met:

1. A period of incapacity (i.e., inability to work, attend school, or perform other regular daily activities due to the serious health condition, treatment therefore, or recovery therefrom) of more than three consecutive calendar days, and any subsequent treatment or period of incapacity relating to the same condition.
2. Any period of incapacity due to pregnancy, or for prenatal care.
3. Any period of incapacity or treatment for such incapacity due to a chronic serious health condition.
4. A period of incapacity that is permanent or long-term due to a condition for which treatment may not be effective. Examples include Alzheimer's, a severe stroke, or the terminal stages of a disease.
5. Any period of absence to receive multiple treatments (including any period of recovery therefrom) by a health care provider or that would likely result in a period of incapacity of more than three consecutive calendar days in the absence of medical intervention or treatment, such as cancer (chemotherapy or radiation), severe arthritis (physical therapy), or kidney disease (dialysis).[41]

Based on these regulations, some federal courts have concluded that for an employee to prove he or she has a serious health condition and is entitled to FMLA leave, two facts must be established.[42] First, the employee must demonstrate that he or she was unable to work for at least three consecutive days. Second, the employee must show that he or she received subsequent treatment in which he or she was either seen at least twice by a health care provider or obtained a regimen of treatment under a health care provider.[43]

Despite the Employment Standards Administration's narrowing of the definition of a serious health condition, there is still room for abuse since conditions such as the common cold, flu, and nonmigraine headaches would meet at least one of the aforementioned two conditions.[44] Interestingly, the Society for Human Resource Management's December 1996 *Work and Family Survey* found that approximately 60 percent of responding firms had experienced significant costs due to FMLA implementation and enforcement; most of the costs incurred resulted from hiring temporary employees to cover the FMLA employee's work or assigning the work to coworkers, thus creating overtime costs.[45] In 2007, approximately 63 percent of the respondents in a SHRM survey on the FMLA reported that compliance had a negative impact on absenteeism, 55 percent that it adversely affected employee productivity, and 53 percent reported it negatively affected business productivity.[46]

Advance Notification for FMLA Leave

The FMLA requires that employees give employers at least thirty days' notice when the reason for the leave is "foreseeable." However, the thirty-day requirement does not apply in situations when the serious health condition requiring the leave was sudden. Under such circumstances, the employee is merely required to provide employer notification as soon as possible. This exception makes the thirty-day notification requirement virtually pointless except in instances where scheduled medical treatments are known well in advance. Employees who have advance knowledge of a scheduled medical service or treatment must always provide timely notification. It is important that employers make employees aware of their responsibilities in this area and of the consequences of failing to provide proper notification when the date of the treatment was known.

For example, if on September 15, an employee knows that he is scheduled for in-patient surgery on October 16, he is required by the FMLA to notify the employer of this fact within twenty-four hours. Yet the employee neglected to provide the company with this timely notification and waited until October 1 to request the leave. Provided the employee has no reasonable excuse for this oversight, the employer can delay the leave up to *thirty days after the employee gives notification.*[47] The employee could be required to reschedule the surgery. However, it is recommended that human resource managers avoid using this rule in instances when delaying the treatment could adversely affect the employee's health. It is one thing to make a point, and it is quite another to cause harm.

Determining Unpaid Leave

If an employer already offers employees paid leave (i.e., vacation, sick leave, personal leave), the unpaid leave mandated by the FMLA may run concurrently with the paid leave, provided the employer has identified such leave as being taken for a FMLA reason. For example, assume an employer provides employees with two weeks' paid sick leave as a benefit. Now assume an employee requests the full twelve weeks' under the FMLA for a medical emergency. The employee cannot demand two weeks' paid leave in addition to the twelve weeks unpaid leave (a total of fourteen weeks). The FMLA authorizes the employer to require the employee to substitute any of the accrued paid vacation leave, personal leave, or family leave.[48] Using the previous example, the employer may include the two weeks' paid sick leave as part of the FMLA required leave, for a total of twelve weeks (two paid and ten unpaid weeks).

In our opening scenario, Jerri Lynn could draw her paid vacation to run concurrently with her FMLA leave. If she had one month's leave accrued, this would guarantee her a stream of income for the first of the two months' FMLA leave requested. However, during the second month, Jerri Lynn would have no income from her employer.

Calculating the Twelve-Month Period Under FMLA

The FMLA provides several options when establishing from which date the twelve-month eligibility period is calculated. Employers may select one of four options for determining this twelve-month period:

1. The calendar year.
2. Any fixed twelve-month "leave year" such as a fiscal year.
3. A year required by state law.
4. A year starting on the employee's "anniversary" date.[49]

The twelve-month period is measured forward from the date an employee's first FMLA leave begins, or a "rolling" twelve-month period is measured backward from the date the employee uses FMLA leave.[50]

Looking at this chapter's opening scenario, is Jerri Lynn eligible for FMLA? First, with 162 employees, Frink & Rose is a covered employer. Obviously Jerri Lynn satisfies the first criterion for eligibility by working for a covered employer. She satisfies the second, working at a facility with 50 or more employees working within 75 miles, because over half of Frink & Rose's employees live within 30 minutes of the plant (obviously less than 75 miles). The third requirement of having worked at least 12 months is assumed to be satisfied because Jerri Lynn has been employed by Frink & Rose for over two-and-a-half years. Finally, the 1,250-hour requirement can be assumed to have been met because she is a full-time employee. A full-time employee is defined as one who works 35 hours per week or more (usually 40 or more). Even using the lower figure, Jerri Lynn would have accrued at least 1,750 hours during the previous 12-month period.

Now that her eligibility for FMLA leave has been established, does Jerri Lynn have a qualifying event? Yes she does, as her husband, Kenny, has a serious health condition as defined in the Act. Because it was unforeseeable, Jerri Lynn does not have to give the thirty-day notice. So Bob was wrong about her having the time off and losing her job. However, Dave was also wrong when he told Jerri Lynn that the company had to pay her while she was on leave. FMLA only mandates up to twelve weeks of *unpaid* leave.

REGULATION OF VOLUNTARY HEALTH BENEFITS

Prior to the Affordable Care Act of 2010, medical and health-related benefits (i.e., group health insurance, dental insurance, prescription drug coverage, etc.) accounted for roughly 19 percent of an employee's total annual salary.[51] Although currently there is no federal law requiring private sector employers to provide health care coverage, employers are required to provide continued coverage to former employees under certain circumstances. Typical of most voluntary benefit programs, once an employer implements a group health insurance program for employees, that program is subject to federal regulation. Interestingly, the statutes that regulate health care benefits are actually amendments to the Employee Retirement Income Security Act, an Act more commonly associated with retirement benefits and discussed in greater detail at the end of this chapter.

Consolidated Omnibus Reconciliation Act of 1985, as Amended

The Consolidated Omnibus Reconciliation Act (COBRA) regulates group health insurance programs. Specifically, COBRA directs covered employers to offer continuation of group health care protection to participants and certain dependents for eighteen or thirty-six months, where coverage would otherwise cease upon termination of employment. COBRA further requires employers to continue health insurance coverage to separated employees due to voluntary or involuntary termination of employment at the group insurance rate plus a 2 percent administrative charge. Additionally, employers must provide the continued coverage when there is a reduction of work. Employers also are required to extend this coverage to the spouse of an employee in the event of the death of the employee or divorce.

Covered Employers and Plans

COBRA covers all employers engaged in interstate trade but exempts certain employers and specific plans. For one, employers with fewer than twenty employees are exempt from COBRA's provisions. In addition, government health plans or health plans administered by religious organizations are not covered by the Act.

Qualifying Events for COBRA

Certain conditions, referred to as **qualifying events** (see Figure 10.5), require continued coverage under COBRA if the employee, dependents, or divorced spouse elect to be covered within a sixty-day period from occurrence of the qualifying event. Qualifying events for COBRA eligibility would include a reduction in an employee's work hours to part-time status resulting in no coverage under the existing plan or termination of employment for any reason other than gross misconduct.[52] If an employee loses his or her job because of an economic downturn, the employer must continue coverage, but if the employee is terminated because of documented insubordination, the employer does not have to provide continued coverage.

There are also qualifying events that entitle the dependents of a covered employee to continued health benefit coverage. The spouse and minor children of an employee are entitled to continued coverage in the event of the employee's death.[53] Additionally, these dependents are entitled to continued coverage in the event of a divorce or legal separation from the employee.[54] Also, the dependent child of the employee may request continued health coverage if he or she has lost dependent child status under the employer's group health insurance plan (this typically occurs when the child marries or reaches age twenty-three).

Employees who are protected under the Uniformed Services Employment and Re-employment Rights Act (USERRA) are entitled to a maximum of twenty-four months COBRA coverage.[55]

Duration of Continued Coverage

The period of COBRA coverage varies based on the particular circumstances of the qualifying event. In the event of an employee's termination, the employee is usually entitled to continued group health coverage for 18 months.[56] If the terminated employee

Figure 10.5 **Qualifying Events Under COBRA**

Qualifying Events	Beneficiaries	Maximum Period of Coverage
Termination for other than gross misconduct or reduction in hours to part-time status	Employee Spouse Dependent child	18 months
Termination or reduction in hours to part-time status when disability is involved	Employee Spouse Dependent child	29 months
Divorce or legal separation	Spouse Dependent child	36 months
Death of employee	Spouse Dependent child	36 months
Loss of dependent child status under existing plan	Spouse Dependent child	36 months

Source: 29 U.S.C. § 1163.

is disabled, the coverage period is extended by an additional 11 months, making the total coverage period 29 months.[57] If the qualifying event is the employee's death or divorce (including legal separation), the employee's former spouse and dependents are entitled to group health insurance coverage for 36 months.[58]

There are other conditions that can shorten the continued coverage period. For example, continued coverage may be terminated if the employer no longer offers group health coverage to employees.[59] To illustrate this, assume an employee is laid off on July 1, 2013, and is not disabled. Under typical circumstances, he or she would be entitled to eighteen months of continued coverage—that employee could expect coverage under COBRA until December 31, 2014. However, if the employer decided to discontinue *all* group health coverage for employees effective April 30, 2014, the laid-off employee's continued health coverage would end on that date as well.

Another justification for terminating continued coverage is the failure of the former employee or the beneficiary to make timely premium payments. The former employee (or his or her dependents in the case of death or divorce) is responsible for making the premium payments for health coverage, not the employer. As with any other insurance policy, should the former employee fail to pay premiums on time, the policy could be canceled.

When a qualifying event occurs, the terminated employee has sixty days from the day coverage would otherwise end to elect continuation of coverage under COBRA. The terminated employee then has up to forty-five days from the date of coverage election to pay the initial premium. The premium for continuation of coverage under COBRA may be as high as 102 percent of the group health insurance rate. If the employee had been participating in a contributory program (while employed) in which he or she paid 50 percent of the benefit cost, the employee will now pay the full cost of the insurance premium plus an additional 2 percent. This 2 percent is paid to offset the employer's administrative costs. For disabled former employees, the premium may be as much as 150 percent of the group rate.[60]

Much like the FLSA in the previous chapter, COBRA's provisions can be subordinate to state laws. State laws mandating health insurance continuation after termination of employment may preempt COBRA when the state law is more strict. If the state law is not as strict as COBRA, the federal law applies.

Paying for the Coverage

Employers must give the employee (or dependents in the event of death, divorce, or legal separation) notice of the option for continued health care within thirty days of the qualifying event.[61] Most of the legal problems arising from COBRA result from employers either failing to give notice of continuation of medical insurance coverage or doing so in an untimely manner.[62] Once terminated, the employee is still covered under the employer's group health care plan, but he or she must pay the full premium plus 2 present, as previously mentioned.

Health Insurance Portability and Accountability Act of 1996

In 1996, President Bill Clinton signed into law the Health Insurance Portability and Accountability Act (HIPAA). HIPAA places certain restrictions on the rights of employers and insurers to deny or limit coverage for preexisting conditions. HIPAA also amended COBRA to extend maximum coverage to twenty-nine months for any former employee or beneficiary with qualifying disabilities and amended COBRA's definition of "qualified beneficiary" to include any child born to or placed for adoption with the former employee during the covered period.[63]

The regulations under HIPAA allow employees who change jobs or lose jobs to maintain health coverage by requiring later employers to admit them into the group health plan. HIPAA also imposes requirements on the application of preexisting condition exclusions in group health plans. As defined in HIPAA, a preexisting condition exclusion comprises any limitation or exclusion of benefits because the condition was present before the first day of coverage.[64] The preexisting condition must be disclosed through diagnosis or medical records before the first day of coverage. Group health plans may impose a preexisting condition exclusion only if it is related to a physical or mental condition for which diagnosis was made and care or treatment was recommended or received during a six-month period ending on the enrollment date.[65] The exclusions must be limited to a twelve-month period after the enrollment date or a nineteen-month period in the case of a late enrollment. The period of preexisting condition exclusion must be reduced by the length of any periods of creditable coverage under other group health plans, Medicare, or other similar types of coverage as of the enrollment date. Preexisting condition exclusions do not apply to pregnancy. In certain circumstances, preexisting condition exclusions may not apply to newborns or adopted children.

Figure 10.6 **Mandates under the Patient Protection and Affordable Care Act**

Year	Mandate
2010	No denial of health coverage due to pre-existing conditions. Effective for the children, 18 years old or younger, of employees in 2010, and for employees in 2014.
2010	Children of employees can be covered under group health insurance until age 26.
2011	Employers must report group benefits information to the IRS.
2012	A new excise tax of 2.3% is levied on the sale of any taxable medical device.
2013	The Medicare tax rate on wages is increased by 0.9% (from 1.45% to 2.35%) on individuals earning over $200,000 per annum, and for married couples earning over $250,000 who file jointly.
2014	New excise tax is levied on pharmaceutical companies based on market share.
2014	New excise tax is levied on health insurance companies based on market share.
2015	A premium tax of $2,000 will be assessed per full-time employee (excluding the first 30 employees) for employers with 50 or more employees who do not offer coverage and have at least one full-time employee who receives a premium tax credit.
2014	There are no caps on annual or lifetime health care benefits.
2018	A new excise tax of 40% will be levied on "Cadillac" health care plans.

Sources: 75 Fed. Reg. 37,190 (June 28, 2010); 42 U.S.C. § 300gg-14; 26 U.S.C. § 6051(a)(14); 77 Fed. Reg. 72,931 (December 7, 2012); Internal Revenue Service, Publication 926 (January 4, 2013); Patient Protection and Affordable Care Act, Pub. Law 111–148 § 9008–10; Pub. Law 111–148 § 9010(f)(2); 26 U.S.C. § 4980H (2013); 42 U.S.C. § 300gg-11; Pub. Law 111–148 § 9001; IRS notice 2013–4 (July 18, 2003).

Patient Protection and Affordable Care Act of 2010

On March 23, 2010, President Barack Obama signed the Patient Protection and Affordable Care Act into law. For simplicity sake and in line with convention, this Act will be referred to as the "Affordable Care Act" for the rest of our discussion. The Affordable Care Act consisted of 906 pages of text when enacted [66] and this does not include the 55 pages in the subsequent Health Care and Education Reconciliation Act of 2010[67] which was signed into law one week later to amend some of the flaws in the Affordable Care Act. This is to illustrate the complexity of these two pieces of legislation that are mandating the most sweeping changes to the healthcare system in the nation's history.

These radical changes in the way healthcare is delivered will be incrementally introduced over an eight year period (2010–2018). Its effects will be directly felt by employers in the form of government mandates (see Figure 10.6), and indirectly by adding to the cost of current healthcare coverage (i.e., requiring insurance programs to cover pre-existing conditions, not permitting higher premiums for individuals presenting higher risks, etc.)[68]

The most significant changes affecting employers, were to become effective on January 1, 2014, but have been extended until 2015. These include penalties imposed on large employers, defined as organizations with 50 or more full-time employees.[69] For the purpose of the Affordable Care Act, a full-time employee is defined as ". . . an employee who is employed on the average at least 30 hours of service per week."[70] This standard would also be used to calculate full-time equivalencies for the 50 or more full-time employee threshold necessary to classify a company as a large employer under the Act.

The Affordable Care Act imposes two different penalties depending on the health coverage of the employer. One penalty is imposed on large employers who offer no insurance coverage to their employees and another for large employers who offer insurance plans to employees which do not meet new government minimum standards. At the time of this book was in press, these minimum standards had yet to be determined.

Large employers who do not offer health coverage, will be assessed a $2,000 per employee per year tax penalty. In practice the monthly penalty is calculated by subtracting 30 from the total number of actual full-time employees (excluding full-time equivalents) and multiplying the difference by one-twelfth of $2,000.[71] At the end of the tax year, monthly penalties would be aggregated for payment to the Internal Revenue Service.

To illustrate, Bill is not offered insurance when he is hired in January. Prior to Bill's hiring, the employer had only 49 employees. The month of January is calculated as: ((50-30)($2,000))/12 = $3,333.33. In July, Mary is hired and the monthly tax is calculated as: ((51–30)($2,000))/12 = $3,500.00. If no other applicants are hired and no current employees are terminated, the annul tax for the employer would be $40,999.98 (Six months at $3,333.33 (January–June), or $19,999.98, plus six months at $3,500 (July–December), or $21,000).

The $3,000 penalty is imposed on large employers only if they offer health coverage that does not conform to what the Department of Health and Human Services (HHS) determines to be affordable and providing minimum value,[72] and at least one of its full-time employees obtains coverage through a state or federal insurance exchange and receives a premium credit.[73] The monthly penalty is calculated monthly on the base amount of one-twelfth of $3,000 times the number of full-time employees receiving tax credits from the health insurance exchange.

To illustrate the effect, Bill is not happy with the employer's health package and goes to the health insurance exchange. Assuming that Bill's employer has a work force of 50 full-time employees, the tax for January is calculated as: ((1)($3,000))/12 = $250. The following month, February, 12 more employees decide to use the exchange (now there is a total of 13 employees in the exchange), the monthly tax is calculated as: ((13)($3,000))/12 = $3,250.00. Assuming that no other employees go to the exchange, the annual tax for the employer would be $36,000—one month (January) at $250 plus eleven months at $3,250 (February–December), or $35,750. One final note on the large employer penalties, the $2,000 and $3,000 penalties discussed above will increase annually by the percentage growth in insurance premiums.

In 2018, employers will be assessed an additional penalty—an excise tax on high-cost employer-sponsored health coverage, the so-called "Cadillac" insurance plans. A "Cadillac" plan is generally defined as a high-cost insurance policy in terms of its premiums. Under the Affordable Care Act, a "Cadillac" plan is statutorily defined as a plan with annual premiums exceeding $10,200 for individuals or $27,500 for families, and is taxed at a rate of 40 percent.[74] The unintended consequence is that this tax ignores the fact that sometimes high premiums are necessitated by the nature of the work of the employees. Highly dangerous occupations entail high premiums in order to mitigate the risk. Commercial fishermen, logging workers, and pilots are perennially listed by the Bureau of Labor Statistics as occupations with high fatal work injury rates.[75] The Act currently makes no allowances for these.

REGULATION OF VOLUNTARY RETIREMENT BENEFITS

Retirement benefit plans are of two basic types: defined benefit and defined contribution plans. **Defined benefit plans** are ones in which the employer develops a program that identifies how much a retiring employee will receive each month for the remainder of his or her life. Such plans commonly utilize a benefit formula combining the years of employment with the employer, the employee's age, and the employee's ending salary to compute the amount of the individual's monthly retirement payment.

Defined contribution plans, on the other hand, are based on a prescribed amount invested periodically into an individual account for each employee. Such plans do not have to identify how much is to be placed into the account each year, but they must spell out the process by which it is done. These defined contribution plans are sometimes referred to as individual account plans. Defined contribution plans are exempt from the funding requirements and the plan termination insurance provisions of ERISA. As a consequence, more employers prefer defined benefit plans.

Employee Retirement Income Security Act of 1974

Probably the most comprehensive employee benefit regulation statute is the Employee Retirement Income Security Act. ERISA does not require employers to offer employee benefit plans; however, once an employer has established a plan, the Act protects the interests of participants and their beneficiaries. Because COBRA and HIPAA are merely amendments to ERISA's provisions governing health care benefits (ERISA's comprehensive nature includes a broad range of employee "welfare benefits"),[76] the remaining discussion will focus only on the Act's pension plan requirements.

ERISA establishes standards of conduct, responsibility, and obligations for fiduciaries of employee benefit plans. It provides for remedies, sanctions, and ready access to the federal courts as well. ERISA is a cumbersome and complicated statute that increases its inherent confusion by dividing enforcement responsibilities between three government agencies: the Pension and Welfare Benefits Administration of the Department of Labor, the Internal Revenue Service of the Department of the Treasury, and the Pension Benefit Guaranty Corporation.

Title I of ERISA was created to protect the interests of employee benefit plan participants and their beneficiaries. First, ERISA requires that sponsors of private employee benefit plans provide participants and beneficiaries with adequate information regarding the plans. This includes a summary plan description and any modifications and changes to the plan.[77] ERISA specifies that the employer must provide each employee with a summary plan description that consists of:

1. The name and type of administration of the plan
2. The names and addresses of the plan administrator and trustee
3. The plan's requirements respecting eligibility for participation and benefits
4. The description of the provisions providing for nonforfeitable pension benefits

5. Circumstances that could result in disqualification, ineligibility, or denial or loss of benefits
6. The source of financing of the plan and the identity of organizations through which benefits are provided
7. The date of the end of the plan year and whether the records of the plan are kept on a calendar, policy, or fiscal-year basis
8. The procedures to be followed in presenting claims for benefits under the plan, including the office at the Department of Labor through which participants and beneficiaries may seek assistance or information regarding their rights under ERISA[78]

Protecting Participants

ERISA ensures that plan participants and beneficiaries are protected from discrimination when exercising specific rights in qualified pension plans. In the event that unlawful discrimination occurs, plan participants and beneficiaries may bring a civil action to enforce their rights to their retirement or benefits.

In *Fleming v. Ayers,* the Sixth Circuit Court of Appeals upheld the lower court's finding that the plaintiff, Fleming, was discharged in order to avoid her employer incurring what were foreseen to be high future medical expenses for her infant child.[79] The court held that the plaintiff was a participant in the defendant's benefit plan and that ERISA prohibits the discharge of "a participant or beneficiary for exercising any right to which he is entitled under the provisions of an employee benefit plan . . . or for the purpose of interfering with the attainment of any right to which such participant may become entitled under the plan. . . ."[80]

Fiduciary Responsibility

ERISA also imposes stricter accountability on those individuals who have the fiduciary responsibility of managing employee retirement plans. A **fiduciary** is a person who is placed in a position of trust and confidence to exercise a standard of care in the administration or management of an activity.[81] ERISA generally identifies a fiduciary as anyone who exercises discretionary authority or control over a pension plan's management or assets, including anyone who provides investment advice to the plan.[82] Fiduciaries who do not follow the principles of conduct outlined in the Act may be held responsible for restoring losses to the plan resulting from their actions.[83] ERISA also gives the pension plan's participants the right to sue for benefits and breaches of fiduciary duty.

Vesting

The Act provides for minimum standards governing participation, vesting, benefit accrual, and funding of pension plans. **Vesting** means an individual has a nonforfeitable right to pension benefits. ERISA establishes the time frame in which an individual must

Figure 10.7 **Basic Vesting Provisions Under ERISA**

7-Year Graduated Vesting Schedule, Years of Vesting Service, Percentage of Accrued Benefit Vested:

Less than 3 years' service	0%
At least 3, but less than 4 years	20%
At least 4, but less than 5 years	40%
At least 5, but less than 6 years	60%
At least 6, but less than 7 years	80%
At least 7 years' service	100%

5-Year Cliff Vesting Schedule, Years of Vesting Service, Percentage of Accrued Benefit Vested:

Less than 5 years' service	0%
At least 5 years' service	100%

Source: 29 U.S.C. § 1053(a).

be employed before becoming eligible to participate in a pension plan and accumulate benefits. The Act provides two methods for becoming vested. One method affords the employer the option of allowing employees to become 100 percent vested after five years of service. For the employee, it means that in the event he or she quits or is terminated before five full years of employment, the employee is not entitled to any pension benefit. The other option permits employers to offer employees partial vesting beginning at the conclusion of the employee's third year of employment and becoming fully vested by the conclusion of the seventh year (see Figure 10.7).

ERISA also establishes detailed funding rules that require plan sponsors to provide adequate funding for pension plans. ERISA requires employers to insure all defined benefit programs through the Pension Benefit Guaranty Corporation, a federally chartered corporation.

Retirement Plans Not Covered by ERISA

Federal, state, or local government employee plans are not covered by ERISA. Certain church or church association plans are also exempted. Retirement plans that are maintained under state workers' compensation, unemployment compensation, or disability insurance laws are further excluded from coverage under the Act.

Multinational corporations are not required to comply with ERISA for the retirement plans that they have created for foreign nationals at overseas sites. However, the pension plans of U.S. citizens working for these companies in overseas locations are protected.

Summary of ERISA's Major Provisions

ERISA's most significant impact has been in four areas:

1. *Vesting rights.* Vesting is the process by which employees may earn a nonforfeitable right to retirement benefits provided by a plan. Retirement plans can use a participant vesting schedule of either two years, five years, or three to seven years.

Vested employees who terminate employment may either have to wait until they reach the plan's early retirement age or normal retirement age before receiving any benefit payments, or they may be required to take a lump-sum payment if the accumulated vested benefits are $3,500 or less.

2. *Termination insurance.* ERISA established the Pension Benefits Guaranty Corporation (PBGC) to administer an insurance fund to which all covered employers with qualified retirement plans must contribute. When a plan terminates leaving unpaid obligations, the PBGC may recover from the employer the cost of paying benefits to vested participants.

3. *Reporting and disclosure requirements.* The Act requires periodic filing of detailed information with both the Department of Labor and the Internal Revenue Service as well as a detailed disclosure to plan participants.

4. *Fiduciary standards.* The Act establishes federal standards of conduct for fiduciaries involved in administering all covered benefit plans. Plan fiduciaries are the individuals who control and manage retirement benefit plans and their assets. The Act requires fiduciaries to act in a prudent manner and make decisions with the benefit of participants in mind. Fiduciaries are personally responsible for breaches of responsibilities. Plan participants are allowed to sue in federal courts to recover losses.

Older Workers Benefit Protection Act of 1990

The Older Workers Benefit Protection Act (OWBPA) was enacted to protect older workers from discrimination in benefits based on age. The OWBPA requires employers to provide workers who are over forty years of age with benefits that are equal to those offered to younger employees unless it can be demonstrated that there is a greater cost for providing the benefits to older employees.[84]

The OWBPA also provides a three-week waiting period for older employees who are offered early retirement options. This provision of the Act gives any older employee a period of not less than three weeks from the date that an early retirement offer is made to consider the option before signing any agreement.[85] In addition, the employee can elect to revoke the early retirement agreement within one week of signing the agreement.[86] The OWBPA further requires the employer to advise the employee of his or her right to consult with an attorney prior to signing any agreement.

The Age Discrimination in Employment Act of 1967 (ADEA), which prohibits discrimination based on age, did not address situations under which protected rights or disputed claims could be waived or released. As a result, age discrimination waivers were subject to the same rules as releases of other types of employment discrimination claims. Consequently, there was no statutory, administrative, or court direction for waivers of claims under the ADEA. Most **waivers** were simply private agreements between the employer and the former employee, and the parties were free to decide the terms of the waiver.

The OWBPA applies to four different waiver instances: a waiver by an employee who is involuntarily terminated and who has not filed an EEOC charge or lawsuit; a waiver by an employee who is involuntarily terminated pursuant to reductions in force or layoff and who has not filed an age discrimination claim; a waiver in settlement of a disputed claim, either pending EEOC charges or civil actions; and a waiver by an employee who has voluntarily terminated employment pursuant to an incentive program to reduce the workforce. Many of the requirements under the OWBPA are the same in all four instances. Therefore, an employee may not waive any right or claim under the ADEA unless the waiver is knowing and voluntary. The OWBPA, amending the ADEA, asserts that a waiver may not be considered "knowing and voluntary" unless, at a minimum, the following conditions have been satisfied:[87]

1. The waiver is part of an agreement between the employee and the employer that is written in a manner calculated to be understood by such employee, or by the average employee eligible to participate.
2. The waiver specifically refers to rights or claims arising under the ADEA.
3. The employee does not waive rights or claims that may arise after the date the waiver is executed.
4. The employee waives rights or claims only in exchange for consideration in addition to anything of value to which the employee already is entitled.
5. The employee is advised in writing to consult with an attorney prior to executing the agreement.
6. The employee is given a period of at least twenty-one days within which to consider the agreement, or if a waiver is requested in connection with an exit incentive or other employment termination program offered to a group or class of employees, the employee is given a period of at least forty-five days within which to consider the agreement.
7. The agreement provides that for a period of at least seven days following the execution of such agreement, the employee may revoke the agreement, and the agreement shall not become effective or enforceable until the revocation period has expired.
8. If a waiver is requested in connection with an exit incentive or other employment termination program offered to a group or class of employees, an employee is given a period of at least forty-five days to consider the agreement.

In the 1998 case, *Oubre v. Entergy,* the U.S. Supreme Court held that a release signed by the petitioner for receipt of severance pay under an employment termination agreement did not comply with the OWBPA's requirements.[88] Consequently, the terminated employee was permitted to pursue a claim under the ADEA.

The Uniformed Services Employment and Reemployment Rights Act

The Uniformed Services Employment and Reemployment Rights Act (USERRA)[89] was enacted in 1994 for the express purpose of protecting the civilian jobs and employment benefits of veterans and members of reserve armed forces components (i.e., National Guard, U.S. Army Reserve, U.S. Air Force Reserve, etc.) when called to active duty.

Returning veterans are entitled to be reemployed in their old civilian jobs, or a comparable job, upon release from active duty under honorable conditions. To be eligible for reemployment, the individuals cannot have been absent from their civilian jobs in excess of five years while in uniformed service,[90] and they have informed the employer in writing before departure on active duty.[91] The individuals must return to work in a timely manner upon release from active duty.

In 2004 an amendment to USERRA called the Veterans' Benefits Improvement Act (VBIA) imposed a new requirement on employers to provide written notice to all individuals eligible under USERRA of their rights, benefits, and obligations under USERRA.[92] Additionally, qualifying employees may elect to continue their employer-based health plan for up to twenty-four months while on active duty.[93]

USERRA also makes it unlawful for any employer to discriminate against any employee or applicants because the individual is a past or present member of the uniformed services, has applied for membership in the uniformed services, or is obligated to serve in the uniformed services.[94]

Independent Contractors and Employee Benefits

Whether or not an individual is entitled to an employer's mandatory benefits is a function of whether the individual is or is not an "employee" of the employer. There are some individuals who perform work for an employer but are not technically employees. They are instead independent contractors as discussed in Chapter 9. **Independent contractors**, as their name implies, are independent individuals who contract with employers to perform specific duties and jobs for a set rate of compensation (refer to Figure 9.4 on page 248).

Independent contractors are not employees and therefore are not entitled to benefits available to employees of a specific employer. Not only are independent contractors not eligible for the employer's voluntary benefits, the employer does not have to provide them with the mandatory benefits (i.e., unemployment compensation, workers' compensation, social security, overtime, etc.). In fact, independent contractors are completely responsible for their own benefits and are even required to withhold their own federal income taxes and FICA taxes (both the employer's and employee's portions).[95]

An employer is not required to provide voluntary benefits (i.e., paid holidays, paid vacations, stock options, etc.), but once the employer decides to offer a specific benefit, it must be offered to all eligible employees. The employer cannot arbitrarily declare some individuals to be employees and others to be independent contractors. If an individual is classified as an independent contractor, it must be demonstrated that he or she truly is one.

SUMMARY

This chapter has discussed the reasons for the growth of employee benefits, the major legislation governing employee benefits, and the impact of regulation on benefit plans. Employee benefits are either mandatory or voluntary.

From an employee relations viewpoint, the most relevant mandatory benefits are unemployment compensation, workers' compensation, and family medical leave. Unemployment compensation is administered by the individual states, but such programs were established under the Social Security Act of 1935. Family and medical leave is covered under the Family and Medical Leave Act of 1993.

All other benefits are voluntary. The most common of these are health insurance and retirement plans. COBRA does not require employers to provide health benefits, but once an employer chooses to offer such benefits, COBRA's continuation policies for former employees must be followed. Similarly, ERISA does not require employers to provide pension benefits for employees, but once an employer elects to provide a retirement benefit, the Act's fiduciary requirements apply.

Regulations regarding both mandatory and voluntary employee benefits make it essential for benefits administrators to understand their employers' statutory responsibilities. There is more to benefits administration than ensuring that the employer has the appropriate mix of benefits to attract and retain employees. Administrators must also ensure that the implementation of the benefits programs does not violate the law.

There are some individuals who perform work for an employer but are not technically employees. They are instead independent contractors, and as their name implies, they are independent individuals who contract with employers to perform specific jobs. Independent contractors are not employees and are not entitled to benefits that are available to employees of a specific employer. The IRS has established a twenty-factor test to determine employee versus independent contractor status.

KEY TERMS AND CONCEPTS

Defined benefit plans

Defined contribution plans

Family and medical leave

Fiduciary

Independent contractors

Joint employers

Mandatory benefits

Qualifying events

Successor employer

Unemployment compensation

Vesting

Voluntary benefits

Waivers

DISCUSSION QUESTIONS

1. Why have employee benefits increased?
2. What are the two types of employee benefits? Provide examples of each.
3. Why was unemployment compensation established? Who is typically entitled to unemployment compensation?
4. What conditions must an employee attain in order to be eligible for mandatory benefits under the FMLA? What are those benefits?
5. What does COBRA regulate? What are the main provisions under COBRA?
6. Why was HIPAA passed?

7. Discuss employer penalties imposed under the Patient Protection and Affordable Care Act.
8. Discuss ERISA's major provisions.
9. How does the OWBPA protect workers?
10. What are the major provisions of USERRA?

CASES

Case 1

Leora Nichols is an assistant manager of the Dayton office of Ohio Wholesale Florists (OWF). She began working at OWF in 1990. In February 2013, Lenora suffered a severe back injury during a skiing trip to Aspen. Receiving a disability certificate from the state of Ohio, Leora notified her employer that as a result of her injuries she would no longer be able to perform her duties and would terminate her employment. She also announced that she was divorcing her husband of thirty-five years in order to marry her childhood sweetheart.

Upon receiving her COBRA notification, Leora elects to continue her group health plan for as long as she is permitted.

a. How long can Leora enjoy COBRA continuation of her health coverage?
b. Is her husband entitled to COBRA continuation? If so, for how long?
c. Is Leora's thirty-three-year-old son entitled to COBRA continuation? If so, for how long?

Case 2

Frances Atwater performed services as a computer programmer/analyst for Bob & Dave Bottling beginning in February 2011 until she was terminated in March 2013. Atwater originally heard of the position after answering an advertisement placed by HR Solutions, Inc. Generally, HR Solutions places advertisements seeking individuals to fill certain positions. If HR Solutions determines that an applicant meets the criteria established by a client, the applicant is then called in to be interviewed by the client, who makes the ultimate decision as to whether the applicant will be used. Before Atwater commenced work, she met with Bob & Dave Bottling employees Mildred Mero and Dave Nickles. Bob & Dave Bottling provided Atwater with a desk, office space, computer, and other materials needed to perform her work.

Atwater did not meet with a representative from HR Solutions until after she had been working at Bob & Dave Bottling for a few days. Russell Cochet, an HR Solutions representative, met with her and asked her to sign the one and only agreement she ever signed with HR Solutions. In the agreement, Atwater was referred to as an "independent contractor." HR Solutions never promised Atwater that she would be employed by HR Solutions for any period of time, nor that her services could not be terminated except for cause. Furthermore, Atwater had no agreement, written or oral, with Bob & Dave Bottling regarding her status.

Atwater's employment was governed by a series of annual agreements between HR Solutions and Bob & Dave Bottling known as Statements of Work (SOWs). The SOWs provided rates of compensation and lengths of employment for Atwater's work at Bob & Dave Bottling.

Regarding payment, Atwater recorded her hours on a weekly basis and submitted them to Bob & Dave Bottling for confirmation. Atwater contends that Bob & Dave Bottling would make payments to HR Solutions, who in turn remitted payments to her. Bob & Dave Bottling claims that Atwater was paid directly by HR Solutions, who then invoiced Bob & Dave Bottling for the payment.

Sometime in 2011, Atwater was assigned to the ICS project. ICS is a group of computer programs that run on the AS/400 computer, a mid-sized computer system. According to defendants, the ICS project began in 2010 and was originally intended to provide a short-term computerized solution to Bob & Dave Bottling's need to track the whereabouts and status of fountain equipment. Around that same time, Bob & Dave Bottling began development of the Fountain Equipment Tracking System (FET). FET, which is much more complex than ICS, was designed to be the long-term computerized solution to the need to track fountain equipment. Sometime in 2012, Bob & Dave Bottling decided to integrate ICS and FET, which meant that ICS had to be upgraded and converted to a permanent system.

Atwater's duties with ICS included analyzing and programming system enhancements and assisting ICS users in resolving day-to-day problems with the system. She also assisted in screening new employees for Bob & Dave Bottling. While working on the ICS project, she was supervised by Rush O' Riley and Robert Harper. O'Riley reported to Dave Nickles, who reported to Mildred Mero, Bob & Dave Bottling's director of application development.

In February 2012, Bob & Dave Bottling's audit department conducted an audit of the AS/400 environment at Bob & Dave Bottling. The audit turned up numerous operational and security deficiencies. Application Development Department (ADD) was directed to correct these deficiencies in order to secure the AS/400 environment. As a result, ADD took steps to limit the authority that applications support personnel, such as Atwater, had to affect the internal operations of the AS/400s. ADD's efforts to secure the AS/400 environment created tension with non-ADD support personnel. Atwater alleges that ADD's actions were intended to harass and interfere with her performance. She resisted the ADD's efforts to restrict her strictly to the AS/400 system.

On January 28, 2013, Atwater contacted Computer Solutions in Florida, a company that provides contract workers to other companies. Atwater also sent her resume and applied for a job. She informed Computer Solutions that it would be possible for her to relocate in three weeks.

On February 28, 2013, Atwater met with Jennifer Edwards, human resources director of Bob & Dave Bottling, and Jefferson Blythe, Bob & Dave Bottling's senior counsel for labor relations. Atwater's counsel requested the meeting on her own behalf. During the meeting, there was a discussion concerning the efforts of Harper and O'Riley to sabotage the ICS application. Atwater claims they also discussed how ADD was harassing her. Atwater asserted that she was a Bob & Dave Bottling employee during this meeting.

Sometime after the meeting, Atwater spoke with O'Riley, the ICS project manager, and told him about the meeting. It is undisputed that Atwater did not tell O'Riley that she intended to file a lawsuit concerning possible employee benefits. O'Riley immediately informed his supervisor, Nickles, about his conversation with Atwater. At that point, Nickles, who had authority to do so, decided to terminate Atwater.

Soon thereafter, Edwards, Blythe, Cochet, and Nickles met to discuss Atwater. At that meeting, Nickles informed Cochet, the HR Solutions representative, that Atwater's services would no longer be needed. On March 7, 2013, Cochet informed Atwater that her services were no longer needed. Atwater moved to Florida on March 30, 2013, and began working for Computer Solutions.

Bob & Dave Bottling provides its regular employees with benefits that are set forth in a book entitled, "Your World of Benefits Handbook." Benefits, which are provided to "permanent" employees of Bob & Dave Bottling, include health, dental, dependent life, life insurance, business travel accident insurance, dependent care account, flexible spending account, long-term disability, employee retirement plan, employee assistance program, survivor's counseling program, severance pay, survivor's benefit program, and a thrift plan.[96] Atwater insists that she was wrongfully denied these benefits while an "employee" of Bob & Dave Bottling.

    a. Is Atwater an employee or an independent contractor? Explain your reasoning.
    b. What criteria must be met in order to demonstrate that a party is a *bona fide* independent contractor?

NOTES

1. U.S. Chamber of Commerce, *2007 Employee Benefits Study,* 44th ed. (Washington, DC: U.S. Chamber of Commerce, April 2008).

2. A. Tolles, *Origins of Modern Wage Theories* (Englewood Cliffs, NJ: Prentice Hall, 1964), p. 97.

3. Ibid., pp. 93–97.

4. Society for Human Resource Management, *2011 Employee Benefits: Examining Employee Benefits Amidst Uncertainty* (Alexandria, VA: Society for Human Resource Management, 2012).

5. 42 U.S.C. Chapter 7.

6. 42 U.S.C. § 503.

7. 26 U.S.C. § 3306(a).

8. 45 U.S.C. Chapter 11.

9. G.E. Jackson, *Labor and Employment Law Desk Book,* 2d ed. (Paramus, NJ: Prentice Hall, 1999 Cumulative Supplement).

10. Ibid.

11. Ibid.

12. Ibid.

13. Consolidated Laws of New York, § 592 (103).

14. 29 C.F.R. § 825.

15. 29 C.F.R. § 825.106.

16. 29 C.F.R. § 825.106(d).

17. 29 C.F.R. § 825.111.

18. 29 C.F.R. § 825.111(a)(1).

19. 29 C.F.R. § 825.104(a).

20. 29 C.F.R. § 825.104.

21. 29 C.F.R. § 825.110.

22. 29 C.F.R. § 825.104(a).

23. 29 C.F.R. § 825.110(a)(3).

24. 29 C.F.R. § 825.110.

25. 29 C.F.R. § 825.110(c).

26. U.S. Department of Labor, Office of the Assistant Secretary for Policy Health Benefits, *Retirement Standards, and Workers' Compensation: Family and Medical Leave*, http://www.dol.gov/compliance/guide/fmla.htm (accessed March 29, 2013).

27. 29 U.S.C. § 2612.

28. *Bocalbos v. National Western Life Insurance,* 162 F.3d 379 (5th Cir. 1998).

29. 29 C.F.R. § 825.202.

30. 29 U.S.C. § 2612.

31. 29 C.F.R. § 825.113(a).

32. 29 C.F.R. § 825.800(c)(6)(ii).

33. 29 C.F.R. § 825.202.

34. 29 C.F.R. § 825.116.

35. 29 C.F.R. § 825.113.

36. 29 C.F.R. § 825.307.

37. 29 U.S.C. § 2611(11).

38. *Oswalt v. Sara Lee Corp.,* 74 F.3d 91 (5th Cir. 1996).

39. 29 C.F.R. § 825.114.

40. U.S. Department of Labor, *Fact Sheet #28: The Family and Medical Leave Act* (revised 2012). http://www.dol.gov/whd/regs/compliance/whdfs28.pdf (accessed March 29, 2013).

41. 29 C.F.R. § 825.114(a)(2).

42. *Murray v. Red Kap Industries, Inc.,* 124 F.3d 695, 698 (5th Cir. 1997).

43. 29 C.F.R. § 825.114(a)(2)(i)(B).

44. Society for Human Resource Management, *Legislative Fact Sheets: Family and Medical Leave Act* (July 2000), www.shrm.org/government/factsheets/factfmla00.asp.

45. Ibid.

46. Society for Human Resource Management, *SHRM Summary Brief: An Overview of the 2007 FMLA Survey* (Alexandria, VA: SHRM, March 2007).

47. 29 C.F.R. § 825.304.

48. 29 U.S.C. § 2612(d)(2)(A).

49. 29 C.F.R. § § 825.110; 825.200; 825.201; 825.202; 825.500; and 825.800.

50. 29 C.F.R. § 825.200(b)(4)(2012).

51. Society for Human Resource Management, *2011 Employee Benefits: Examining Employee Benefits Amidst Uncertainty* (Alexandria, VA: Society for Human Resource Management, 2012).

52. 29 U.S.C. § 1163(2).

53. 29 U.S.C. § 1163(1).

54. 29 U.S.C. § 1163(3).

55. 20 C.F.R. § 164.

56. 29 U.S.C. § 1162(2)(A).

57. 29 U.S.C. § 1162(2)(A)(v).

58. 29 U.S.C. § 1162(2)(A)(iii).

59. 29 U.S.C. § 1162(2).

60. U.S. Department of Labor, Employee Benefits Security Administration, *An Employer's Guide to Health Benefits Under the Consolidated Omnibus Reconciliation Act (COBRA)* (September 2010), http://www.dol.gov/ebsa/pdf/cobraemployee.pdf (accessed March 29, 2013).

61. 29 U.S.C. § 1163(2).

62. *Vincent v. Wells Fargo Guard Services, Inc.,* 44 F.Supp. 2d 1302 (S.D. Fla. 1999); *Mlsna v. Untel Communications, Inc.,* 91 F.3d 876 (7th Cir. 1996); *Switzer v. Wal-Mart Stores, Inc.,* 52 F.3d 1294 (5th Cir. 1995).

63. 29 U.S.C. § 1169.

64. U.S. Pension and Welfare Benefits Administration, *Questions and Answers: Recent Changes in Health Care Law* (Washington, DC: Government Printing Office, June 1999), p. 4.

65. Ibid.

66. Public Law 111–148 (March 23, 2010).

67. Public Law 111–152 (March 30, 2010).

68. J. Sherk, "Obamacare will Price Less Skilled Workers out of the Full-time Jobs," *Heritage Foundation WebMemo No. 3390* (October 11, 2011).

69. 26 U.S.C. § 4980H(c)(2)(A).

70. 26 U.S.C. § 4980H(c)(4)(A).

71. H. Chaikind and C.L. Peterson, *Summary of Potential Employer Penalties under the Patient Protection and Affordable Care Act (PPACA)* (Alexandria VA: Society for Human Resource Management Congressional Research Service, May 14, 2010).

72. 42 U.S.C. § 300gg-13.

73. 26 U.S.C. §§ 4980H(a)(2) ans (b)(1)(B).

74. 26 U.S.C. § 4980I(b)(3)(B)(i).

75. U.S. Department of Labor, Bureau of Labor Statistics, *National Census of Occupational Injuries in 2011: Preliminary Results* (September 20, 2012) http://www.bls.gov/news.release/pdf/cfoi.pdf (accessed March 30, 2013).

76. 29 U.S.C. § 1002(i).

77. 29 U.S.C. § 1022.

78. 29 U.S.C. § 1024(b).

79. *Fleming v. Ayers & Associates,* 948 F.2d 993 (6th Cir. 1991).

80. Ibid. at 997.

81. H.C. Black, *Black's Law Dictionary,* 9th ed. (St. Paul, MN: West Publishing, 2009).

82. 29 C.F.R. § 2584.8477(e)-6.

83. 29 U.S.C. § 1109.

84. 29 U.S.C. § 623.

85. 29 C.F.R. § 1625.22.

86. Ibid.

87. 29 U.S.C. § 626(f).

88. *Oubre v. Entergy Operations, Inc.,* 522 U.S. 422 (1998).

89. 38 U.S.C. §§ 4301–4333.

90. 38 U.S.C. § 4312(c).

91. 38 U.S.C. § 4312(a)(1).

92. 38 U.S.C. § 4334(a).

93. 38 U.S.C. § 4317(a)(1)(A).

94. 38 U.S.C. § 4311.

95. U.S. Department of the Treasury, Internal Revenue Service, Publication 15-A, *Employer's Supplemental Tax Guide* (Washington, DC: Government Printing Office, 2013), pp. 7–10.

96. This scenario was developed from the facts in *Wolf v. Coca-Cola Co.,* 82 F.Supp. 2d 1366 (N.D. Ga. 1998).

LAWS AFFECTING WORKPLACE
HEALTH AND SAFETY

LEARNING OBJECTIVES

- Understand the reasons for government regulation of workplace safety and health.
- Discuss the evolution of government regulation of workplace safety and health.
- Describe the major provisions of federal and state laws related to workplace safety and health.
- Discuss the development of workers' compensation legislation.
- Explain the benefits of and problems associated with workers' compensation.
- Understand the basic provisions of the Occupational Safety and Health Act of 1970.
- Describe the five types of citations issued by the Occupational Safety and Health Administration.

OPENING SCENARIO

On his way to investigate a complaint at a worksite, Occupational Safety and Health Administration Compliance Officer Scott Douglas drove past a construction site and observed, on the side of the road, two men excavating a trench. The Compliance Officer drove by the trench, parked his car, and called his supervisor. The Occupational Safety and Health Administration (OSHA) has a nationwide program that requires any compliance officer, upon viewing an excavation, to inspect it.

Douglas then walked to the trench, announced that he was an OSHA compliance officer and why he was there, and he asked the two workers to exit the trench. The compliance officer learned the two employees were Sam Cousley, the foreman at the site, and Bart Garner, a laborer, and that both men worked for Cyree Excavation Co. He also learned the employees had been setting up a "cutter" on a preexisting 12-inch-diameter pipe in the trench in order to cut the pipe and add a fitting; the cutter sat on top of the pipe, and a chain went around the pipe and was attached to the cutter on the other side. Douglas then took photographs of the employees working in the trench and how the trench looked after they got out, as well as the cutter on the pipe.

Douglas then took various measurements of the trench and found it to be 27 feet long, 4 feet 3 inches wide at the top and the bottom, and 4 feet deep in the middle. At one end, however, where the employees had been working, it was 5 feet 6 inches deep, and the sides of the trench were vertical. Excavations over 5 feet require a "trench box" under OSHA regulations.

According to the compliance officer, the soil at the site was granular, sandy, and crumbly; in addition, the pipe was preexisting and was thus in previously disturbed soil, making the soil "Type C," and the trench was adjacent to a road with heavy traffic, which would create vibrations. The compliance officer concluded that all of these factors, combined with the trench's depth and vertical sidewalls, could have resulted in a cave-in and serious injuries or even death.

Mr. Cousley, the foreman, testified he had worked for the company for eleven years, that he was trained in excavation safety, and that he had an "OSHA 10-hour card." He said the job in question had started in July 2008, and that by the time of the inspection he had laid about 3,000 feet of pipe for the job. He further stated that he had used a trench box for the entire 3,000 feet of the job. He also said it was his practice to measure the trench "every time we went in." In fact, Mr. Cousley claimed that he had measured it the day of the inspection in about the same area that Douglas later measured it, and that, because the depth was 4 feet 9 to 4 feet 10 inches, he had concluded he did not need to use the trench box.[1]

Who is right? Will Cyree Excavation Co. be cited for an OSHA violation, and if so, which one? Because Sam Cousley was a member of management (a foreman), does this mean the employer knew or should have known of a potential violation?

HISTORICAL OVERVIEW OF WORKPLACE SAFETY

Prior to the Industrial Revolution, most nonagricultural workers were independent craftsmen. In the event that a craftsman lost work as a result of an occupational accident or illness, he suffered the full economic loss. This was solely the individual's responsibility, as was personal safety while in the workplace. The independent craftsman was expected to assume all personal financial consequences of a workplace injury. If the craftsman did not have sufficient savings to get through the recovery period, he and his family would be destitute.

This predicament continued throughout most of the nineteenth century. As the United States became more industrialized, unsafe and unhealthy working conditions spread. Not surprisingly, the resulting surge of workplace injuries, diseases, and deaths from industrial accidents began to draw society's attention to workplace safety and health.

During this same period, employers continued to operate under the assumption that their employees were completely responsible for occupational accidents and illnesses. As in the past, industrial employees were expected to assume the inherent risks of the job. As had been the case with their independent craftsmen predecessors, when an industrial worker was injured on the job or suffered an illness brought on by prolonged exposure to a harmful work environment, his or her only recourses for compensation were personal savings or the courts. Deaths and disabling injuries due to occupational accidents were frequent, but relief was rare.

By the latter part of the nineteenth century, a number of mine disasters prompted the American public to pressure governments to regulate industries in order to reduce industrial accidents. One of the earliest attempts to regulate hazardous workplace conditions occurred in the Commonwealth of Massachusetts. Massachusetts passed legislation providing for industrial inspectors. Under this statute, inspectors were given authority to enter factories and could require employers to safeguard employees from dangerous industrial equipment.[2]

A number of states passed laws providing for workers' compensation in the opening years of the twentieth century. **Workers' compensation** laws provided workers with cash benefits for work-related injuries and deaths. Because workers' compensation was established as insurance, the premiums levied on employers increased as the number of claims against employers increased. This created an economic incentive to enhance workplace safety. As a result of employer concern for improving workplace safety and health, work-related accidents and injuries declined steadily from the early 1930s until the late 1950s.[3]

The concept of providing financial relief for workers injured or killed in industrial accidents originated in Europe as early as the 1880s. Switzerland passed a limited no-fault workers' compensation law in 1881, and Germany enacted a similar workers' compensation act in 1884. The German law would become a model for similar laws in the United States.[4] By 1903, most industrialized nations in Western Europe had some form of workers' compensation legislation.[5]

In 1908, the Federal Employees' Compensation Act was enacted in the United States.[6] This Act allowed federal employees injured in certain hazardous jobs to receive limited compensation. In 1916, this legislation was amended to provide coverage to all federal employees.[7] In addition, some federal workers were covered under the Longshore and Harbor Workers' Compensation Act.[8]

On May 3, 1911, Wisconsin became the first state to enact a workers' compensation law (that was not repealed or found to be unconstitutional) for private sector employees.[9] Two other states, Washington and Kansas, had passed permanent workers' compensation laws on March 14, 1911, but they did not become effective until after the Wisconsin law.[10] During the next ten years, forty-three other states would enact similar workers' compensation laws. Currently, there are workers' compensation laws in all fifty states, the District of Columbia, Puerto Rico, and the Virgin Islands.

In the early 1930s, it was estimated that work-related accidents, each year, resulted in as many as 20,000 employee deaths, 80,000 employees becoming totally or partially disabled, and more than 2 million employees losing work time due to injuries.[11] Much of the annual death rate among wage earners during this period was considered to be directly or indirectly due to the nature of workers' employment. The data in Table 11.1 reflect the higher annual death rate for unskilled, semiskilled, and skilled workers than employees in less hazardous occupations from a survey of ten industrialized states conducted in 1930 for a congressional committee.

In the late 1960s, the annual rate of work-related accidents and injuries began to reverse the previous four decades' decline, and there was spreading support for establishing federal

Table 11.1

Annual Deaths per 1,000, Ages 15–64 in Ten States, 1930

Type of Worker	Tuberculosis	Pneumonia	Accidents	All Causes
Unskilled	1.85	1.36	0.52	14.48
Semiskilled	1.02	0.72	0.34	10.09
Skilled	0.72	0.60	0.34	8.29
Proprietors and managers	0.43	0.52	0.22	7.93
Clerks/Kindreds	0.66	0.51	0.19	7.75
Professionals	0.26	0.39	0.15	6.71
Agricultural	0.47	0.43	0.15	6.23
All gainfully employed	0.88	0.69	0.30	9.10

Source: U.S. Senate, 75th Congress, Third Session, *Hearings Before a Special Committee to Investigate Unemployment and Relief,* 1938, vol. 2, p. 1491.

standards of occupational safety and health in the workplace. The Occupational Safety and Health Act of 1970 became the first comprehensive federal legislation enacted to apply safety and health standards to practically every employer and employee in the United States. Although federal safety and health standards had been mandated previously in the Walsh-Healey Act of 1936[12] and the Service Contract Act of 1963,[13] those requirements applied only to those employers who held federal construction and service contracts.

The National Safety Council estimates that the work-injury death rate in 1933 was 37 deaths per 100,000 employees.[14] In 1970, the year the Occupational Safety and Health Act was passed, 18 out of 100,000 employees died from work-related injuries.[15] By 2009, the work-injury death rate had declined to 2.8 deaths per 100,000 employees.[16] The improvements in accident prevention and reduced work-related death rates have been attributed to the combined efforts of industrial management, organized labor, and government.

It is important to remember that prior to the enactment of workers' compensation statutes, the only recourse for injured workers was to sue their employers for damages under state tort laws. However, injured workers were unlikely to win such suits because of two obstacles to pursuing such litigation. One obstacle arose from the worker's burden of proving negligence on the part of the employer. The second obstacle stemmed from the workers' difficulty in overcoming the three common law defenses (discussed in more detail later) available to employers in negligence suits: assumption of risk, fellow-servant rule, and contributory negligence.

As many workers learned, courts held that when workers knew of the risks inherent in the work before accepting employment, they assumed responsibility for their injuries. In many instances, it also could be shown that injuries were in some part the result of the worker's own negligence.[17]

Workers' compensation laws evolved to guarantee that benefits would be paid to workers injured on the job and that they would be paid promptly with a minimum of legal formality. This may have been the intention when such laws were originally enacted; however, in most states, claims resolution has become a cumbersome and time-consuming process. Although claims are paid promptly (within one week under most state laws), worker claims are often challenged. Typically, worker claims are contested in quasi-judicial workers' compensation appeal board hearings presided over by administrative law judges.

EXCLUSIVITY PRINCIPLE

As part of the fundamental rationale for workers' compensation legislation, an employee injured in the course of employment receives fixed compensation that is described statutorily as the employee's "exclusive remedy" against the employer.

This concept is popularly known as the exclusivity principle. Under the **exclusivity principle**, an employee receiving workers' compensation benefits is barred from bringing a common-law suit against the employer for a work-related injury. Yet there are several exceptions to this general rule. For example, the exclusivity principle will not apply to cases where injuries are found to be caused by intentional acts of the employer. If an employee can prove an accident arose out of an employer's specific intent to injure the employee, then the employee is not barred from bringing a common-law claim.[18] Therefore, if an employer or his or her agent purposely placed an employee in harm's way (i.e., told the employee to ignore a safety procedure), the exclusivity principle would no longer apply.

In certain instances, some states permit litigation when it can be shown that an employer was grossly negligent regarding a work-related accident or illness. For example, if the conditions causing the accident were so obvious and the resulting injury so apparent that a reasonable person would have easily anticipated the employee's injury, then the employer's failure to eliminate or reduce the hazard was clearly the major factor contributing to the employee's injury.

Even when challenged in court, the employer is still often able to prevail in litigation using any of three previously mentioned defenses (assumption of risk, the fellow-servant rule, and contributory negligence). Even though the employer incurs the additional cost of paying the workers' compensation premiums, this expense is offset by avoiding, or at least reducing, the likelihood of resolving the claim through the courts.

The advantages offered by workers' compensation laws are that in return for assuming liability, not only was the employer's monetary liability fixed to specific statutory amounts, but employees also, by statute, had to forgo any further attempts to recover compensation through common law. In short, when workers' compensation is the employee's exclusive remedy, this relieves the employer of unpredictable, and potentially costly, common-law litigation.

COMPENSABLE INJURIES AND ILLNESSES

One characteristic of all workers' compensation systems is that the employee is required only to demonstrate that the injury or illness was work related. The employee does not have to show that the employer's actions are responsible for the injury. The basic premise of workers' compensation laws is that the cost of work-related injuries should be assumed by the employer; consequently, providing for such coverage is considered part of the cost of doing business. Workers' compensation quickly evolved into a mandatory benefit program with the expenses associated with the insurance coverage borne by the employer.

Workers' Compensation

Workers' compensation is not paid to an individual merely because he or she is injured or ill. The injury or illness must arise from employment; either the injury or illness must be related to work.

Work-related Injuries

Naturally, an injury sustained while at work is covered. For example, a warehouse employee who is struck and injured by a delivery truck while at work would be entitled to workers' compensation. If the same employee was struck and injured by a delivery truck in front of his home during nonwork time, he would not be eligible for the benefit. Usually, workers' compensation does not apply to injuries sustained during nonwork hours, at a location off the employer's premises, when work duties are not being performed, or while performing activities that are not in the course of employment.[19]

What about employees who engage in work activities off the employer's premises? Any injuries would be covered, provided the employees were engaged in the employer's work, or as some courts have noted, the employer derives substantial direct benefit from the employee's activity.[20] If the activity is not for the employer's benefit, workers' compensation benefits can be denied. Such was the case in *Koger v. Greyhound Lines, Inc.*[21] A striking employee was struck by a company bus while he was picketing the employer. The Ohio State Court of Appeals ruled that he was not eligible for workers' compensation because his injury was "not received in the course of, and arising out of, the injured employee's employment."[22]

The same is true for injuries that occur during company outings or company-sponsored events, including sporting events. Injuries to an employee would be covered only if the employee were engaged in the employer's work. Therefore, if attendance at a company party or event is mandatory, any resulting injury is likely to be compensable. On the other hand, if the employee is not required to attend or participate, is not paid to do so, and the event was not sponsored by the employer, the injury is not covered under workers' compensation.[23] Unfortunately, this is not as simple as it sounds.

Assume a company is holding an annual company picnic on company property. Attendance is strictly voluntary. While at the picnic, Craig Billings, an accountant, decides to join a football game. While playing football, Billings fractures his leg. Recall that attendance at the picnic was not mandatory, and the decision to participate in the football game was made by Billings. In most states, this would not be a compensable workers' compensation injury.

Now, consider that Faye Gilbert, assistant HR manager, is at the same company picnic. Gilbert's job at the picnic is to oversee the refreshments and provide enough food and drinks for all employees who attend. While delivering ice, Gilbert slips and breaks her ankle. Although this is the same picnic on company grounds where Billings was injured and not entitled to workers' compensation for his injury, Gilbert is entitled to workers' compensation for her injury.

While the football injury was the result of voluntary participation, Gilbert's injury arose from her employment; she was at the picnic for direct benefit for her employer.[24]

Work-related Illnesses

As with injuries, illnesses must be shown to arise out of employment; this includes mental illnesses.[25] Whether for physical or mental illnesses, the employee must establish a causal connection between the disability and the nature of his or her employment. This causal link invariably requires substantial medical evidence to support any claim that occupational exposure to some factor resulted in the illness.[26]

Worker Benefits

Workers' compensation benefits are distributed in three major categories; medical, temporary disability, and permanent disability. *Medical benefits* pay for 100 percent of the medical costs for the injured employee.

Temporary disability payments are made in those instances in which the employee is, as its name implies, temporarily unable to return to the pre-injury job or one for which he or she is otherwise qualified, due to injury or health problems. Temporary disability benefits are the most common category of cash benefit. Temporary disability payments are designed to replace two-thirds of an employee's average weekly wage, up to a maximum dollar amount, which ever amount is less. The cap on maximum weekly temporary disability benefits in January 2012 ranged from $37 per week in Mississippi to $ 1,427 in Iowa.[27]

Permanent disability benefits are paid to workers whose injury or illness has so severely impaired them that they are unable to ever return to work. The method of determining the appropriate payment varies from state to state. Most operate within ranges in which benefits are paid for specific losses. For, example the Pennsylvania Workers' Compensation Act provides, "For the loss of a forearm, sixty-six and two-thirds per centum of wages during three hundred seventy weeks."[28]

Controlling Workers' Compensation Costs

Workers' compensation costs were approximately $57.5 billion in 2010.[29] The obvious solution to controlling costs is to control the incidents of injury or illness in the workplace. This means creating safety programs and providing employee training to promote safe working behavior. The more emphasis that management places on safety awareness, the more safety conscious employees are likely to become.

When injuries or illnesses do occur, the employer should get a medical assessment as quickly as possible. This information will be essential in determining whether the employee is no longer fit for employment. It can also be used to determine whether the injured employee can be reassigned to less strenuous work.

If the employee can continue employment in another position, he or she would not be entitled to disability benefits. Similarly, the employer should attempt to get a rehabilitation assessment of the injured or ill employee. Again, this could be used to assist in determining the probability of the employee returning to work and/or being reassigned to other work. It is recommended that this assessment be performed within thirty days after the injury if it is to be successful.[30]

One major problem with workers' compensation is its potential for fraud. Some employees will misrepresent the facts surrounding an injury in order to gain benefits for which they would otherwise be ineligible. For example, a worker injures his knee dirtbike racing, but later claims that it was incurred at work in order to draw workers' comp payments during his rehabilitation. Some employees may suffer from no injury or illness and intentionally defraud the system.[31]

Because there is so much abuse in the system—perhaps as many as 10 percent of all workers' compensation claims[32]—employers should investigate all employees who are suspected of submitting false claims and take action against those found to have submitted false claims. Since such employees are engaging in an unlawful activity (fraud), some courts have upheld surveillance of employees off company premises.

Employer Common Law Defenses

The **assumption of risk defense** is based on the philosophy that a person accepts the inherent risks involved in the job, thus absolving the employer of responsibility for injuries or illnesses incurred as a result of the normal risks of a job. The employer must be able to show that the employee was aware of, or should have been aware of, the hazards pertaining to a particular job. Safety briefings and training would provide means of establishing knowledge. Good job analysis and thorough job descriptions of working conditions would be another means of establishing this, provided that the job descriptions were disseminated to the affected employees.

The **fellow-servant rule defense** involves an employer's assertion that injuries or illnesses were derived from the actions, whether accidental or intentional, of another employee. The injury or illness to one employee stemming from the negligent act of a fellow employee could be remedied by suing the other employee rather than the employer. Properly conducted accident investigations would be a viable method for making such an assertion.

Under the **contributory negligence defense**, an employer claims that the damages for injuries were due, at least in part, to the negligence of the affected employee. Injured workers cannot recover awards for damages for which they were primarily responsible. However, if judges or juries determine that responsibility for injuries or illnesses is mutually shared by both the employee and the employer, the liability for damages may be distributed proportionally. Again, well-constructed work rules, proof that the employee was aware of safety procedures, and thorough investigations (documentation) would be helpful in establishing the defense.

As enacted by each of the fifty states and the territories, workers' compensation laws represent the most prevalent and comprehensive no-fault insurance program in the United States. However, there is no uniform national program. State workers' compensation provisions differ from state to state with regard to procedural aspects, compensation provisions, and jobs covered (see Table 11.2). State laws also differ with regard to specific types of coverage, insurance funding requirements, and the extent and types of costs and benefits paid. In some states, the insurance company is a single state agency; in others, employers may choose between several private companies. There is even some variance between the states as to what specifically constitutes a work-related, compensable injury.

Despite these and other differences, state workers' compensation laws have several characteristics in common. In all states, only work-related injuries are compensated. Other injuries, illnesses, or preexisting disabilities (unless aggravated by work-related factors) are not covered under workers' compensation. Neither are injuries that are self-inflicted or caused by the employee's willful misconduct.[33] The bottom line is that there must be some causal connection between the employee's injury or illness and work.

All programs provide prompt (compared to litigation) income payments (usually one-half to two-thirds of the affected employee's average pay up to a maximum cap), medical benefits to injured workers, and lump sum survivors' benefits regardless of who is at fault. As mentioned earlier, because these programs are experience rated, they still continue to provide an incentive for employers to develop and maintain safe work programs (a pre-injury objective) and an incentive to get the employee back to work (a post-injury objective).[34] Rehabilitative services provided under workers' compensation reduce overall cases of such programs by returning the employee to work as quickly as possible.

Mandatory Versus Voluntary Participation

State workers' compensation laws are either mandatory or voluntary. The vast majority of states have mandatory laws in which *all* employers must carry workers' compensation insurance and comply with the state law by providing specific benefits. Covered employers are afforded no choice, and failure to participate in the program is a violation of the law. Covered employers are typically public and private employers either in certain hazardous industries or in the type of businesses that experience the highest rates of job-related injuries.

States with voluntary, or elective, workers' compensation laws allow employers to accept or reject insurance coverage of their own volition, but employers choosing not to participate can be sued by workers who are injured or become ill due to a work-related incident. Only three states (New Jersey, Texas, and Wyoming) permit some level of voluntary choice in workers' compensation insurance participation.[35] However, if employers in these particular states elect to reject insurance coverage, they also waive their rights to use the three common-law defenses mentioned earlier when sued by injured employees.

Table 11.2

Summary of State and Territory Workers' Compensation Legislation

State	Compulsory or Elective	State-funded or Private Insurance Carrier	Exemption for Employer with Fewer Than __ Employees	Method of Payment
Alabama	Compulsory	Private carrier	5	Direct
Alaska	Compulsory	Private carrier	No exemption	Direct
Arizona	Compulsory	Private carrier	No exemption	Direct
Arkansas	Compulsory	Private carrier	3	Direct
California	Compulsory	Private carrier	1	Direct
Colorado	Compulsory	Private carrier	No exemption	Direct
Connecticut	Compulsory	Private carrier	No exemption	Agreement
Delaware	Compulsory	Private carrier	No exemption	Agreement
Florida	Compulsory	Private carrier	4	Agreement
Georgia	Compulsory	Private carrier	3	Direct
Hawaii	Compulsory	Private carrier	No exemption	Direct
Idaho	Compulsory	Private carrier	No exemption	Direct
Illinois	Compulsory	Private carrier	No exemption	Direct
Indiana	Compulsory	Private carrier	No exemption	Agreement
Iowa	Compulsory	Private carrier	No exemption	Direct
Kansas	Compulsory	Private carrier	No exemption	Direct
Kentucky	Compulsory	Private carrier	No exemption	Direct
Louisiana	Compulsory	Private carrier	No exemption	Direct
Maine	Compulsory	Private carrier	No exemption	Direct
Maryland	Compulsory	Private carrier	No exemption	Direct
Massachusetts	Compulsory	Private carrier	No exemption	Agreement
Michigan	Compulsory	Private carrier	3	Direct
Minnesota	Compulsory	Private carrier	No exemption	Direct
Mississippi	Compulsory	Private carrier	5	Direct
Missouri	Compulsory	Private carrier	5	Direct
Montana	Compulsory	Private carrier	No exemption	Direct
Nebraska	Compulsory	Private carrier	No exemption	Direct
Nevada	Compulsory	Private carrier	No exemption	Direct
New Hampshire	Compulsory	Private carrier	No exemption	Direct
New Jersey	Elective	Private carrier	No exemption	Direct
New Mexico	Compulsory	Private carrier	3	Direct
New York	Compulsory	Private carrier	No exemption	Direct
North Carolina	Compulsory	Private carrier	3	Agreement
North Dakota	Compulsory	State funded	No exemption	Direct
Ohio	Compulsory	State funded	No exemption	Direct
Oklahoma	Compulsory	Private carrier	No exemption	Direct
Oregon	Compulsory	Private carrier	No exemption	Direct
Pennsylvania	Compulsory	Private carrier	No exemption	Direct
Puerto Rico	Compulsory	State funded	No exemption	Direct
Rhode Island	Compulsory	Private carrier	No exemption	Agreement
South Carolina	Compulsory	Private carrier	4	Agreement
South Dakota	Compulsory	Private carrier	No exemption	Direct
Tennessee	Compulsory	Private carrier	5	Direct
Texas	Elective	Private carrier	No exemption	Direct
Utah	Compulsory	Private carrier	No exemption	Direct
Vermont	Compulsory	Private carrier	No exemption	Agreement
Virginia	Compulsory	Private carrier	3	Agreement
Virgin Islands	Compulsory	State funded	No exemption	Direct
Washington	Compulsory	State funded	No exemption	Direct
West Virginia	Compulsory	State funded	No exemption	Direct
Wisconsin	Compulsory	Private carrier	3	Direct
Wyoming	Elective	State funded	No exemption	Direct

Source: The Office of Workers' Compensation Programs, Employment Standards Administration (revision), *State Workers' Compensation Laws Tables 1, 2, and 16 from OWCP* (Washington, DC: U.S. Department of Labor, August 15, 2006).

Yes, the participation is elective, but it is very risky for any employer to choose not to participate.

State requirements for employers to finance workers' compensation insurance may vary from state to state but usually fall into one of these models. Financing workers' compensation insurance in compliance with state laws may be through paying for a policy with a private insurance company, self-insuring by employers themselves, or paying into either a monopolistic or a competitive state insurance fund. Most states require employers to pay insurance premiums in advance, although some permit employers to avoid such payments through self-insurance, provided they have proof of financial ability to assume their risks.[36] Some degree of self-insurance is allowed in the workers' compensation laws of forty-eight states.[37]

Workers' Compensation Benefits

State workers' compensation laws generally provide payments for lost income while the worker is disabled, payment of medical expenses for work-related injuries or illnesses, lump-sum payments or lifetime compensation for disfigurement, benefits for dependent survivors, and rehabilitative assistance (see Figure 11.1). State laws ordinarily set minimum and maximum rates for indemnity benefits based on a designated proportion or percentage of an injured employee's weekly wage and the degree of disability. For most states the maximum proportion is based on two-thirds of the state's average weekly wage.

To illustrate how benefits are determined, assume an employee working in Texas has an average weekly pay rate of $1,500 (based the thirteen weeks prior to the injury). The employee is injured at work and clearly eligible to draw workers' compensation temporary disability benefits for the first twenty-six weeks following that injury.[38]

Texas workers' compensation legislation provides for a weekly payment of up to 70 percent of the employee's average weekly pay, or $817.94, whichever amount is smaller.[39] If the worker is eligible for the maximum benefit and 70 percent of $1,500 (approximately $1050 per week) is more than the $817.94 cap on the benefit, the injured employee will receive the smaller amount, or $817.94 per week.

Additionally, an employee's weekly benefit is based on the degree to which he or she is disabled. The degree of disability used in determining the weekly benefit amount is based on one of the four following classifications: temporary total disability, permanent total disability, temporary partial disability, or permanent partial disability. Benefits for disability income are generally payable based upon the disabled worker satisfying a waiting period, typically from three to seven days. Each program has a schedule of benefits to determine what percentage of the benefit the disabled employee is eligible to draw.

Under some state laws, dependent survivors are eligible for lump-sum payments in the event that the employee is killed in a work-related incident. In addition, burial allowances are also paid up to a specific maximum amount.

Rehabilitative assistance is generally available to employees disabled as a result of a work-related injury or illness. This particular benefit provides an expedient means of helping disabled employees return to work. Thirty-four states have second-injury funds,

Figure 11.1   **Benefits Afforded Individuals with Compensable Injuries/Illnesses Under Worker's Compensation**

- Dependent survivors' death benefits
- Payment for disability (temporary or permanent)
- Payment for lost income
- Payment for medical expenses
- Rehabilitative assistance

which serve as an incentive for employers to hire employees with disabilities.[40] The intent of the second-injury fund is to equalize the compensation costs that an employer and the insurance company pay for disabled and nondisabled workers alike. Should the permanently disabled worker incur additional disability due to a work-related accident, the employer's compensation costs are limited to the incremental disability and not the total disability (the preexisting permanent disability plus the newly incurred disability).[41]

Criticisms of Workers' Compensation

Workers' compensation laws are considered to generally provide minimal levels of compensation; the emphasis here is on *minimal*. Benefits have failed to keep pace with inflation in many cases, and are frequently regarded as inadequate compensation for employees' injuries and disabilities. Increasingly, injured employees are bringing actions in the courts instead of filing claims under workers' compensation statutes, thus undermining the exclusivity principle. In some instances, workers are filing workers' compensation claims *and* filing suits against their employers.

Contesting Questionable Claims

Since workers' compensation premiums are experience rated (the more claims against an employer, the higher the premium), employers have a very real incentive to contest or challenge dubious claims. After all, if an employee is truly not eligible for the benefit, it is the employer who will be penalized.

   Remember, the injury for which the worker is seeking compensation must be work related. If there is no clear connection between the worker's injury and his or her employment, the worker is not entitled to draw the benefit. Recall the example in which an Ohio court held that an employee who was injured when hit by a company bus while picketing his employer during a strike did not suffer a work-related injury.[42] Injuries arising from off-duty conduct during nonwork hours will usually fail to make the critical connection to employment. However, the off-duty injuries exception usually does not apply to injuries resulting from "mandatory" company functions such as banquets, parties, and picnics.[43] In these cases, the injury is usually treated as work related.

   In the case of *bona fide* work-related injuries, an employer may challenge the claim on the grounds that the injury was the result of a preexisting condition. For example, an employee with a medical history of heart problems suffers a heart attack at work while

Figure 11.2   **Employer Challenges to Worker's Compensation Claims**

- Employee willfully violated safety rules
- Fraud
- Injury or illness is due to employee misconduct
- Injury or illness is due to preexisting condition
- Injury or illness is due to substance abuse
- Injury or illness is not work related

engaging in nonstrenuous activities.[44] Here, there is serious doubt as to whether the employee's work caused or aggravated the health condition. If the preexisting condition does not completely negate the employee's eligibility for workers' compensation, it may mitigate the benefit and permit the employer to utilize the state's second-injury fund.

Ultimately, an employer may challenge the workers' compensation claim on the grounds that the injury is the result of misconduct on the part of the employee. This could include fraud (the employee is faking the injury),[45] or it could even include a self-inflicted injury (the employee purposely drops a heavy box on her foot in order to draw the benefit). Employees may also lose eligibility for flagrant violations of work or safety rules, especially those prohibiting substance abuse. In most jurisdictions, employees who are injured while intoxicated are not eligible to draw benefits unless they can show by the preponderance of evidence that their substance abuse did not contribute to the injury (see Figure 11.2).[46]

THE OCCUPATIONAL SAFETY AND HEALTH ACT

The Occupational Safety and Health Act[47] was passed in 1970 amid much controversy. Proponents contended the government had to take drastic measures to reduce the number of workplace deaths and injuries occurring each year and to lessen workers' exposure to health hazards. Because the Occupational Safety and Health Act and its enforcement agency, the Occupational Safety and Health Administration, have the same acronym, OSHA, some sources distinguish between the legislation and the agency by referring to the Occupational Safety and Health Act as *OSH Act*. To avoid confusion with OSHA, NIOSH, and OSHRC, the authors of this text have chosen to spell the Act out (Occupational Safety and Health Act).

The Bureau of Labor Statistics of the U.S. Department of Labor estimated that, in 1968, slightly more than 2.2 million workers were injured in their jobs.[48] Opponents to the Occupational Safety and Health Act contended it was an unwarranted intrusion into the workplace. By 2011 there were nearly 3.0 million workplace injuries and illnesses reported by private industry employers.[49]

One peculiar characteristic of the Occupational Safety and Health Act is that it created three federal agencies: one to enforce its provisions, one to review these enforcement actions, and one to conduct studies and research for developing standards. These agencies span two executive departments, the Department of Labor and the Department of Health and Human Services.

The primary agency given the responsibility for administering and enforcing the Occupational Safety and Health Act is the Occupational Safety and Health Administration (OSHA). This agency was organized as a new division within the Department of Labor. It has the authority, through the secretary of labor, to promulgate standards, conduct inspections, and seek enforcement action (fines and/or injunctions) where there has been noncompliance.

The Occupational Safety and Health Act also created the National Institute of Occupational Safety and Health (NIOSH), an occupational health research center. Through an unusual twist, this agency is actually organized as part of the Department of Health and Human Services rather than the Department of Labor. NIOSH studies various safety and health problems, conducts research for recommending safety and health standards to be adopted by OSHA, provides technical assistance to OSHA, and conducts training programs.

The third agency provided by the passage of the Occupational Safety and Health Act is the Occupational Safety and Health Review Commission (OSHRC), a quasi-judicial body that serves to adjudicate challenged enforcement actions undertaken by OSHA. Like OSHA, the OSHRC is part of the Department of Labor. The OSHRC consists of three members appointed by the president of the United States for staggered six-year terms and is completely independent from OSHA. Penalties for violations based on OSHA recommendations are assessed by OSHRC. As with other federal agencies exercising quasi-judicial functions (such as the National Labor Relations Board), OSHRC decisions are appealed directly to the appropriate Federal Circuit Court of Appeals.

The Occupational Safety and Health Administration (OSHA)

The Occupational Safety and Health Administration primarily establishes safety standards and conducts workplace inspections. The standards set by OSHA generally require that employers adopt certain practices, means, methods, or processes deemed to be reasonably necessary to protect workers on the job.

The Occupational Safety and Health Act places an obligation on employers to become familiar with standards applicable to their organizations, to eliminate hazardous conditions to the extent possible, and to comply with the standards. The employees have the responsibility, under the Act, to comply with all rules and regulations that are applicable to their own actions and conduct in the workplace.

Additionally, OSHA requires employers to post notices furnished by the agency in the employers' establishments and keep the notices current.[50] The required notices inform employees of the protections and obligations provided for in the Act as well as provide contact information for assistance and information on specific safety and health standards. Notices are required to be posted in conspicuous places where other organization-related policies and communication to employees are customarily posted. Employers are expected to take reasonable steps to assure the notices are not altered, defaced, or covered by other material. Failure to comply with these posting requirements can result in a $7,000 fine.[51]

OSHA Inspections and Outcomes

In its capacity to conduct inspections and investigations, OSHA is authorized to issue citations and propose fines and penalties for Occupational Safety and Health Act violations.[52] Although the Act authorizes unannounced random inspections, most inspections result either from employee complaints[53] or OSHA injury and illness incident reports filed by employers.[54] As a result of such inspections, OSHA inspectors may issue one of five citations for any violation of the Occupational Safety and Health Act: imminent danger, serious, other-than-serious, *de minimus*, and willful and repeated.

An **imminent danger violation** occurs when, as the name implies, death or serious physical harm to an employee is imminent (i.e., an open flame in a fireworks factory). The organization must stop the activity immediately, and work may not be resumed until the specified danger has been eliminated or corrected.[55]

A **serious violation** occurs where there is substantial probability that death or serious physical harm could result and that the employer knew, or should have known, of the hazard (i.e., a stairway without a guard rail). An **other-than-serious violation** is one involving a situation in which the most serious illness or injury would probably not result in death or serious physical harm (i.e., an extension cord coiled on the floor but not in a pathway).

A *de minimus* **violation** arises from a nonserious condition that has "no direct or immediate relationship to safety or health"[56] (i.e., not having partitions between toilets in the restroom). No citations are issued, only a *de minimus* notice.

Finally, a **willful and repeated violation** occurs when an employer is notified of a violation by a compliance officer and refuses or fails to take corrective action. Essentially, any of the citations mentioned earlier, except *de minimus* violations, can become a willful violation.

The Occupational Safety and Health Act prescribes that citations be in writing and explain the particular nature of the alleged violation, including a reference to the provision(s) of the Act, standard, rule, regulation, or order stated to have been violated.[57] The citation will also provide a reasonable time for the abatement of the purported violation.

As used by OSHA, the term "abatement" merely means that the condition causing the violation has been corrected. The secretary of labor, under Section 658(a) of the Occupational Safety and Health Act, may decide to issue either a citation or a *de minimus* notice for a certain setting of nonserious violations (i.e., those *de minimus* violations that do not have a direct or immediate impact on employee health or safety).

Employers are required to post a copy of any citation and notice of any proposed penalty in an appropriate location at the facility where the citation occurred.[58] Failure to post the citation could result in a fine not to exceed $7,000.[59] If an employer decides to contest a citation, a notice of such intention to contest must be posted in the same location where the citation is posted.

Challenging OSHA Citations

Should an employer decide to challenge either the citation, the time set for abatement, or the proposed penalty, he or she must do so within fifteen working days from the time the citation and proposed penalty are received.[60] The employer is required to notify the director of the area OSHA office in writing. This written notification is called a "Notice of Contest." If the written Notice of Contest has been filed within the required fifteen working days, the OSHA area director forwards the challenged case to the OSHRC, who then assigns the case to an administrative law judge for hearing. Employer representatives and the affected employees have the right to participate in the hearings. The administrative law judge's determination may be submitted for further review by OSHRC upon the request of any party to the case. If the employer is still dissatisfied with the outcome, the OSHRC ruling may be appealed to the appropriate U.S. Court of Appeals.

An employer may challenge the OSHA citation on a number of grounds. For one, the employer may not be an entity that the Occupational Safety and Health Act covers. The Act applies to all employers engaging in interstate commerce regardless of size.[61] However, there are specific entities that have been excluded from the Occupational Safety and Health Act's definition of "employer." For example, federal (except the U.S. Postal Service), state, and local governments are specifically exempted from coverage.[62] Businesses operating on an Indian reservation are also exempted.[63]

Barring an exemption claim, the employer may challenge the citation on the basis of the OSHA standard itself. In essence, the citation is not being challenged, but the standard upon which it is based is not appropriate. Challenges to OSHA standards will be discussed later in this chapter.

OSHA Standards

The OSH Act gave OSHA broad authority in establishing workplace safety and health standards. The Act provides for the issuance of three categories of standards: interim, permanent, and emergency. **Interim** (or temporary) **standards** are those that the secretary of labor was given the power to establish for two years following the effective date of the Act. These were generally taken from preexisting national consensus standards. The two-year authority under Section 29 U.S.C. § 655(a) to promulgate "national consensus standards" as occupational safety and health standards expired on April 29, 1973.

The second type, **permanent standards**, are either newly created or revised from the original interim standards. An advisory committee may be appointed periodically to assist in the issuance of permanent standards. Permanent standards are issued on an as-needed basis or evolve from emergency standards. In either case, permanent standards must follow one process before becoming effective.

Once OSHA has developed a proposed or amended standard, it must publish its recommendation in the *Federal Register*. Upon its publication, the public (particularly employers in the affected industries) is given at least thirty days in which to respond to the recommendation. If any interested party requests a public hearing, OSHA must schedule such a hearing and publicize it to the general population. Within sixty days after the close of the public comment and hearing phase, OSHA is required to publish the new standard and the date it will become effective. The secretary of labor has the authority to delay its effective date, for any sufficient cause. In *Industrial Union Dept., AFL-CIO v. Hodgson*, a delay of four years for a standard on asbestos dust was considered to be within the scope of the secretary of labor's authority.[64]

The third type of standards that can be imposed by the secretary of labor are emergency standards.[65] The key to the issuance of an **emergency standard** is the necessity to protect employees from a grave danger. After issuing an emergency temporary standard, the secretary of labor must set in motion the procedures for the transition of the emergency standard to a permanent standard, which must occur within six months of the emergency standard's publication.[66] The secretary may bypass most of the established formalities and create temporary emergency standards when it is believed that workers are in grave danger from exposure to toxic substances or other newly discovered hazards.

In a Fifth Circuit case concerning an emergency standard set for a specific type of pesticide, *Florida Peach Growers Association, Inc. v. Department of Labor*, the court held that death or injury need not occur before an emergency standard is declared, but there must be assurance that a truly serious emergency exists before such a standard is dispensed.[67] All emergency standards are essentially temporary measures because they are effective for only six months. They then either become permanent or expire.

The General Duty Clause

OSHA citations can be issued only for violations of safety standards established under the OSH Act. Because it would be both cumbersome and virtually impossible for OSHA to establish safety standards to cover all situations applicable to all processes in all industries, the general duty clause is also a source for violations. The general duty clause simply requires that "[e]ach employer shall furnish to each of his employees employment and a place of employment which are free from recognized hazards that are causing or likely to cause death or serious physical harm to his employees."[68] This creates a sufficiently broad interpretation to permit its application to any situation not covered by existing OSHA standards.

Although OSHA has promulgated many safety standards, and these standards are notorious for their attention to detail (see Figure 11.3), not all unsafe conditions can be foreseen. Thus, the intent of the general duty clause is to make the employer ultimately responsible for those unforeseen or newly created workplace hazards. The general duty clause, in requiring that the workplace be free of "recognized" hazards, concedes that the employer's liability may be limited to hazards that are detectable. In theory, hazards due to careless acts of an employee of which the employer was unaware are not the responsibility of the employer. An example would include an employee who rashly disregards the safety policies and training of an employer. The burden falls on the employer, however, to show that any employee accident was the result of an employee's negligence and not the employer's negligence. However, the general duty clause also places a great deal of

Figure 11.3 **OSHA Standards for Portable Wood Ladders**

§ 1910.25(a) "Application of requirements." This section is intended to prescribe rules and establish minimum requirements for the construction, care, and use of the common types of portable wood ladders, in order to insure safety under normal conditions of usage. Other types of special ladders, fruit-picker's ladders, combination step and extension ladders, stockroom step ladders, aisle-way step ladders, shelf ladders, and library ladders are not specifically covered by this section.

§ 1910.25(b)(1)(i) All wood parts shall be free from sharp edges and splinters; sound and free from accepted visual inspection from shake, wane, compression failures, decay, or other irregularities. Low density wood shall not be used.

§ 1910.25(c)(2) "Portable stepladders." Stepladders longer than 20 feet shall not be supplied. Stepladders as hereinafter specified shall be of three types:

> Type I—Industrial stepladder, 3 to 20 feet for heavy duty, such as utilities, contractors, and industrial use.
>
> Type II—Commercial stepladder, 3 to 12 feet for medium duty, such as painters, offices, and light industrial use.
>
> Type III—Household stepladder, 3 to 6 feet for light duty, such as light household use.

§ 1910.25(c)(2)(i)(b) A uniform step spacing shall be employed which shall be not more than 12 inches. Steps shall be parallel and level when the ladder is in position for use.

§ 1910.25(c)(2)(i)(c) The minimum width between side rails at the top, inside to inside, shall be not less than 11 1/2 inches. From top to bottom, the side rails shall spread at least 1 inch for each foot of length of stepladder.

§ 1910.25(c)(2)(i)(f) A metal spreader or locking device of sufficient size and strength to securely hold the front and back sections in open positions shall be a component of each stepladder. The spreader shall have all sharp points covered or removed to protect the user. For Type III ladder, the pail shelf and spreader may be combined in one unit (the so-called shelf-lock ladder).

§ 1910.25(c)(3)(ii)(a) Single ladders longer than 30 feet shall not be supplied.

§ 1910.25(c)(3)(iii)(a) Two-section extension ladders longer than 60 feet shall not be supplied. All ladders of this type shall consist of two sections, one to fit within the side rails of the other, and arranged in such a manner that the upper section can be raised and lowered.

§ 1910.25(c)(3)(iv)(a) Assembled combinations of sectional ladders longer than lengths specified in this subdivision shall not be used.

§ 1910.25(c)(3)(v)(a) Trestle ladders, or extension sections or base sections of extension trestle ladders longer than 20 feet shall not be supplied.

§ 1910.25(c)(4)(ii)(a) Painter's stepladders longer than 12 feet shall not be supplied.

§ 1910.25(c)(4)(iii) "Mason's ladder." A mason's ladder is a special type of single ladder intended for use in heavy construction work.

§ 1910.25(c)(4)(iii)(a) Mason's ladders longer than 40 feet shall not be supplied.

§ 1910.25(c)(5)(i) "Length." Trolley ladders and side-rolling ladders longer than 20 feet should not be supplied.

§ 1910.25(d)(1) "Care." To insure safety and serviceability the following precautions on the care of ladders shall be observed:

§ 1910.25(d)(1)(i) Ladders shall be maintained in good condition at all times, the joint between the steps and side rails shall be tight, all hardware and fittings securely attached, and the movable parts shall operate freely without binding or undue play.

§ 1910.25(d)(1)(ii) Metal bearings of locks, wheels, pulleys, etc., shall be frequently lubricated.

§ 1910.25(d)(1)(iii) Frayed or badly worn rope shall be replaced.

§ 1910.25(d)(1)(iv) Safety feet and other auxiliary equipment shall be kept in good condition to insure proper performance.

§ 1910.25(d)(1)(x) Ladders shall be inspected frequently and those which have developed defects shall be withdrawn from service for repair or destruction and tagged or marked as "Dangerous, Do Not Use."

§ 1910.25 (d)(1)(xi) Rungs should be kept free of grease and oil.

§ 1910.25(d)(2) "Use." The following safety precautions shall be observed in connection with the use of ladders:

§ 1910.25(d)(2)(i) Portable rung and cleat ladders shall, where possible, be used at such a pitch that the horizontal distance from the top support to the foot of the ladder is one-quarter of the working length of the ladder (the length along the ladder between the foot and the top support). The ladder shall be so placed as to prevent slipping, or it shall be lashed, or held in position. Ladders shall not be used in a horizontal position as platforms, runways, or scaffolds;

§ 1910.25(d)(2)(ii) Ladders for which dimensions are specified should not be used by more than one man at a time nor with ladder jacks and scaffold planks where use by more than one man is anticipated. In such cases, specially designed ladders with larger dimensions of the parts should be procured;

§ 1910.25(d)(2)(iii) Portable ladders shall be so placed that the side rails have a secure footing. The top rest for portable rung and cleat ladders shall be reasonably rigid and shall have ample strength to support the applied load;

§ 1910.25(d)(2)(iv) Ladders shall not be placed in front of doors opening toward the ladder unless the door is blocked upon, locked, or guarded;

§ 1910.25(d)(2)(v) Ladders shall not be placed on boxes, barrels, or other unstable bases to obtain additional height;

§ 1910.25(d)(2)(viii) Ladders with broken or missing steps, rungs, or cleats, broken side rails, or other faulty equipment shall not be used; improvised repairs shall not be made;

§ 1910.25(d)(2)(ix) Short ladders shall not be spliced together to provide long sections;

§ 1910.25(d)(2)(x) Ladders made by fastening cleats across a single rail shall not be used;

§ 1910.25(d)(2)(xi) Ladders shall not be used as guys, braces, or skids, or for other than their intended purposes;

§ 1910.25(d)(2)(xii) Tops of the ordinary types of stepladders shall not be used as steps;

§ 1910.25(d)(2)(xiii) On two-section extension ladders the minimum overlap for the two sections in use shall be as follows:

Size of ladder (feet)	Overlap (feet)
Up to and including 36	3
Over 36 up to and including 48	4
Over 48 up to and including 60	5

§ 1910.25(d)(2)(xiv) Portable rung ladders with reinforced rails (see paragraphs (c)(3) (ii)(c) and (iii)(d) this section) shall be used only with the metal reinforcement on the under side;

§ 1910.25(d)(2)(xv) No ladder should be used to gain access to a roof unless the top of the ladder shall extend at least 3 feet above the point of support, at eave, gutter, or roofline;

§ 1910.25(d)(2)(xvii) Middle and top sections of sectional or window cleaner's ladders should not be used for bottom section unless the user equips them with safety shoes;

§ 1910.25(d)(2)(xix) The user should equip all portable rung ladders with nonslip bases when there is a hazard of slipping. Nonslip bases are not intended as a substitute for care in safely placing, lashing, or holding a ladder that is being used upon oily, metal, concrete, or slippery surfaces;

§ 1910.25(d)(2)(xx) The bracing on the back legs of stepladders is designed solely for increasing stability and not for climbing.

Source: 29 C.F.R. § 1910.25 *et seq.* (2012).

discretion with compliance officers in determining what is and what is not a violation of the OSH Act. Conflict often arises when a compliance officer "recognizes" a hazard that the employer does not.

There is a real potential for differences of opinion over what is and what is not a safe situation. Still, according to the OSHA *Field Inspection Reference Manual*, a general duty clause citation will only be issued when there is a serious and recognized hazard in the workplace that can feasibly be abated.[69]

Challenging OSHA Standards

In the event that employers believe OSHA has developed and implemented an unrealistic standard, that standard may be challenged in the U.S. Court of Appeals during a sixty-day period following issuance of the standard. The Supreme Court, in a case involving standards established for exposure to benzene, affirmed that a standard must address a "significant risk" of material health impairment to be sustained by the courts. In *Industrial Union Department v. American Petroleum Institute*,[70] the producers and users of benzene challenged the validity of one part benzene per million parts of air exposure level standard as being unreasonable. The Supreme Court found that the near zero-tolerance-level standard established by OSHA was not reasonable when the secretary of labor failed to prove that a standard of ten parts per million did not present a significant risk to health impairment.[71] Consequently, the OSHA standard was successfully challenged and overturned.

When standards are challenged, federal courts have to consider two major questions in deciding their efficacy: Is the standard technologically feasible? And is the standard economically feasible? Technological feasibility is usually easier to determine than economic feasibility. A Second Circuit Court decision held that OSHA may set standards "which require improvements in existing technologies or which require the development of new technology, and the secretary of labor is not limited to issuing standards based on devices already developed."[72] But they must be capable of being developed within the limits of existing technology.

This principle, called "technology forcing," has been reaffirmed in other cases. In *United Steelworkers of America v. Marshall*,[73] the D.C. Circuit Court held that, in setting standards, OSHA must demonstrate that the protections the standards demand are capable of being put into place by the affected industries. In short, it is unreasonable to hold employers to standards that cannot be technologically achieved. A challenged standard would be considered technologically feasible only if OSHA can demonstrate that "modern technology has at least conceived some industrial strategies or devices which are likely to be capable of meeting . . . [the standard] and which industries are generally capable of adopting."[74]

As for the second question, the Supreme Court defines an economically infeasible standard as one that would make "financial viability generally impossible" for an industry.[75] In *American Textile Manufacturers Institute v. Donovan*, the Supreme Court concluded that OSHA must determine "that the industry will maintain long-term profitability and competitiveness" when establishing the economic feasibility of a standard.[76] This appears to indicate that compliance should not bankrupt the affected employer. However, the employer must provide convincing evidence that compliance with the new standard would indeed threaten the firm's long-term survival. It is always important to remember that most bureaucrats and judges do not have business backgrounds or education.

Requesting Variances from OSHA Standards

An alternative to challenging a standard in the judicial system is requesting a variance. The secretary of labor may grant employers an exemption from a standard, under Section 16 of the Act, if it is inappropriate to the employer's particular situation. This is known as a variance and is classified as either temporary or permanent.[77] A **temporary variance** may be granted when an employer cannot meet the requirements to comply with a standard by its effective date. In essence, the employer is asking for an extension.

The firm cannot be in compliance by the effective date, but it will, eventually, be in compliance. However, to qualify for a temporary variance, the employer must demonstrate that all possible measures are being taken to protect employees and that all steps necessary for compliance are also being taken. Additionally, all employees must be informed by the employer of the variance request. Temporary variances may be granted for the time needed to comply, not to exceed a period of one year. The employer may renew temporary variances up to two times, each of these for a period not to exceed six months.[78]

A **permanent variance** may be granted to an employer who can prove that current conditions or particular methods provide as safe a worksite as those that would exist through compliance with the OSHA standard.[79] The Occupational Safety and Health Agency ordinarily inspects the premises before granting a permanent variance. Again, all employees must be informed of the application for the variance, and of their right to request a hearing on the matter necessitating a variance. Within six months after a permanent variance has been granted, either the employer or the firm's employees may petition OSHA to modify or revoke the variance.[80] The secretary of labor may take similar steps to modify or revoke the variance regardless of employer initiatives.

Record-keeping Requirements

Although all employers engaged in interstate commerce are covered by OSH Act, those who have more than ten employees are required to maintain specific records of job-related injuries and illnesses.[81] Some employers may be selected to be part of a national survey of workplace injuries and illnesses conducted by the Department of Labor's Bureau of Labor Statistics (BLS), in which case the employer will be notified before the end of the year to keep records during the coming year. This is not a voluntary program, as any employer selected for the BLS survey must maintain the records. Unless an employer has been selected in a particular year to be part of a national survey of workplace injuries and illnesses conducted by the BLS, employers with fewer than ten employees or employers in traditionally low-hazard industries are exempt from maintaining these records.[82]

An example of industries that typically are designated as traditionally low hazard include: automobile dealers; apparel and accessory stores; furniture and home furnishing stores; eating and drinking places; finance, insurance, and real estate industries; and service industries such as personal and business services, legal, educational, social, and cultural services, and membership organizations.[83]

The OSHA Injury and Illness Log and Summary, OSHA Form 300 (see Figure 11.4) and the OSHA Injury and Illness Incident Record, OSHA Form 301 (see Figure 11.5) are the two primary recording and reporting forms established by OSHA. Both forms are for the employers' records and are not submitted to OSHA, but they must be available for inspections. The OSHA Form 300 provides a log for recording and reporting injuries and illnesses with a separate line entry for each recordable injury or illness. A recordable injury or illness consists of "work-related deaths, injuries, and illnesses other than minor injuries that require only first aid treatment and which do not involve medical treatment, loss of consciousness, restriction of work or motion, or transfer to another job."[84] There is a summary section of OSHA Form 300 for annual totals of the year's injury and illness experience.

The OSHA Form 101 is a supplementary record to be used as an individual incident record and report form providing more details about each individual recordable injury or illness. This form must be completed and available for reporting purposes no more than six work days after experiencing and receiving information of a recordable incident.

An employer with an employee exposed to toxic materials or potentially harmful physical agents in the workplace is required to provide access to exposure and medical records for the employee and the appropriate safety agency.[85] Remember, the Americans with Disabilities Act (ADA) requires an employer to keep employee records confidential and limit access to them.[86] Additionally, any employee who is exposed to toxic materials or potentially harmful physical agents has a right to access monitoring records kept by the employer, material safety data sheets, and any other exposure records available.

Employees who believe that an OSHA violation has or may imminently occur have certain rights granted under the Act that include: filing a complaint with the appropriate safety and health agency, bringing action in the appropriate district court to order an inspection, taking part in the inspection tour and conference, having the employer post copies of all citations, and inspecting the log of occupational injuries and illnesses.[87]

OSHA Inspections

The Occupational Safety and Health Act allows assigned OSHA compliance safety and health officers (CSHOs) to enter, inspect, and investigate an employer's workplace to

Figure 11.4   OSHA Form 300

Source: U.S. Department of Labor, Occupational Safety and Health Administration, "OSHA Forms for Recording Work-Related Injuries and Illnesses," p. 7. http://www.osha.gov/recordkeeping/new-osha300form1–1-04.pdf.

Figure 11.5　OSHA Form 301

OSHA's *Form 301*

Injury and Illness Incident Report

U.S. Department of Labor
Occupational Safety and Health Administration

Form approved OMB no. 1218-0176

Attention: This form contains information relating to employee health and must be used in a manner that protects the confidentiality of employees to the extent possible while the information is being used for occupational safety and health purposes.

This *Injury and Illness Incident Report* is one of the first forms you must fill out when a recordable work-related injury or illness has occurred. Together with the *Log of Work-Related Injuries and Illnesses* and the accompanying *Summary*, these forms help the employer and OSHA develop a picture of the extent and severity of work-related incidents.

Within 7 calendar days after you receive information that a recordable work-related injury or illness has occurred, you must fill out this form or an equivalent. Some state workers' compensation, insurance, or other reports may be acceptable substitutes. To be considered an equivalent form, any substitute must contain all the information asked for on this form.

According to Public Law 91-596 and 29 CFR 1904, OSHA's recordkeeping rule, you must keep this form on file for 5 years following the year to which it pertains.

If you need additional copies of this form, you may photocopy and use as many as you need.

Information about the employee

1) Full name

2) Street

City　　　State　　　ZIP

3) Date of birth 　/　/

4) Date hired 　/　/

5) ☐ Male
☐ Female

Information about the physician or other health care professional

6) Name of physician or other health care professional

7) If treatment was given away from the worksite, where was it given?

Facility

Street

City　　　State　　　ZIP

8) Was employee treated in an emergency room?
☐ Yes
☐ No

9) Was employee hospitalized overnight as an in-patient?
☐ Yes
☐ No

Completed by

Title

Phone (　)　—　　　Date 　/　/

Information about the case

10) Case number from the Log 　　　 *(Transfer the case number from the Log after you record the case.)*

11) Date of injury or illness 　/　/

12) Time employee began work 　　　 AM / PM

13) Time of event 　　　 AM / PM ☐ Check if time cannot be determined

14) **What was the employee doing just before the incident occurred?** Describe the activity, as well as the tools, equipment, or material the employee was using. Be specific. *Examples:* "climbing a ladder while carrying roofing materials"; "spraying chlorine from hand sprayer"; "daily computer key-entry."

15) **What happened?** Tell us how the injury occurred. *Examples:* "When ladder slipped on wet floor, worker fell 20 feet"; "Worker was sprayed with chlorine when gasket broke during replacement"; "Worker developed soreness in wrist over time."

16) **What was the injury or illness?** Tell us the part of the body that was affected and how it was affected; be more specific than "hurt," "pain," or sore." *Examples:* "strained back"; "chemical burn, hand"; "carpal tunnel syndrome."

17) **What object or substance directly harmed the employee?** *Examples:* "concrete floor"; "chlorine"; "radial arm saw." *If this question does not apply to the incident, leave it blank.*

18) **If the employee died, when did death occur?** Date of death 　/　/

Public reporting burden for this collection of information is estimated to average 22 minutes per response, including time for reviewing instructions, searching existing data sources, gathering and maintaining the data needed, and completing and reviewing the collection of information. Persons are not required to respond to the collection of information unless it displays a current valid OMB control number. If you have any comments about this estimate or any other aspects of this data collection, including suggestions for reducing this burden, contact: US Department of Labor, OSHA, Office of Statistical Analysis, Room N-3644, 200 Constitution Avenue, NW, Washington, DC 20210. Do not send the completed forms to this office.

Source: U.S. Department of Labor, Occupational Safety and Health Administration, "OSHA Forms for Recording Work-Related Injuries and Illnesses," p. 10. http://www.osha.gov/recordkeeping/new-osha300form1-1-04.pdf.

determine compliance with the standards.[88] The Act requires the CSHOs to conduct inspections during either regular working hours or other reasonable times. Compliance officers may question any employee, agent, employer, or owner privately during an inspection. All establishments covered by the Act are subject to inspections by OSHA compliance safety and health officers. States with their own occupational safety and health programs may conduct separate workplace inspections using their own qualified state compliance officers.[89]

The OSH Act does provide some rights to employers during a workplace inspection. The OSH Act states that a CSHO must grant an employer the right to accompany a walk-around inspection.[90] This was reinforced in *Chicago Bridge v. OSHRC* in which the Seventh Circuit Court of Appeals held that managers and other designated employer representatives may accompany OSHA compliance officers on workplace inspection tours.[91] The Seventh Circuit ruled that by upholding the employer's right to accompany the CSHO, any mere procedural or technical violation noted by the employer would not automatically void a citation.

This was a concession to the CSHOs who may have felt that their citations might be overturned on a technicality rather than on merit. Employers do not have to admit CSHOs on their premises automatically, although such a refusal is hardly recommended. As representatives of the government, CSHOs are constrained by the Fourth Amendment's restriction on unlawful search and seizure. However, should an employer refuse to permit a compliance officer access to his or her workplace, the compliance officer may petition the appropriate district court to issue a search warrant. The 1978 Supreme Court ruling on *Marshall v. Barlow's, Inc.*, held that the Department of Labor must prove probable cause exists in order to issue a search warrant.[92] The Court held that the constitutional protection provided in the Fourth Amendment against unreasonable search of private homes applies to commercial establishments as well. However, any workplace accident or employee complaint would be sufficient to establish probable cause that the OSHA violations are occurring at the employer's place of business.

Though a relatively small agency, OSHA when partnered with state workplace safety agencies, can field approximately 2,200 inspectors. Despite these human resource limitations OSHA inspections netted over 202,651 violations in 2012, of which nearly 5,000 were repeated (refer to Table 11.3).[93]

Furthermore, OSHA may impose penalties for employer violations of the OSH Act. Monetary penalties and fines may be assessed for serious violations, nonserious violations, or willful violations. In fiscal year 2012 OSHA collected $198,152,349.25 in penalties and fines (refer to Table 11.4).[94] It is important to note that these penalties are normally based on the gravity of each violation.

An employer who has been cited for a serious violation is assessed a penalty of up to $7,000 for each violation.[95] A penalty for a serious violation may be adjusted downward based on the employer's good faith, the history of rectifying previous violations, the gravity of the alleged violation, and the size of the business. When an employer willfully violates the Act, that employer may be assessed a penalty of not more than $70,000 but not less than $5,000 for each violation (see Table 11.5).

Table 11.3

OSHA Inspections in FY 2012

Violations	Percent	Type
445	0.2	Willful
126,585	70.01	Serious
4,986	2.4	Repeat
70,628	34.8	Other
7	0.0	Unclassified
202,651		Total

Source: U.S. Department of Labor, Occupational Safety and Health Administration, DOL Enforcement Website, OSHA for FY 2012, http://ogesdw.dol.gov/searchExplorer/searchExplorer.php (accessed February 13, 2013).

Table 11.4

OSHA Inspections and Penalties, 2003–2012

Year	Inspections	Violations	Penalties
2012	94,436	203,616	$198,152,349.25
2011	103,402	243,588	$257,324,693.91
2010	109,282	262,624	$200,685,544.88
2009	111,277	269,918	$174,843,771.45
2008	106,189	263,604	$147,359,963.49
2007	103,716	263,569	$138,704,738.76
2006	107,246	269,228	$133,176,442.06
2005	104,976	266,976	$148,350,413.14
2004	107,176	274,124	$125,844,538.90
2003	108,895	277,692	$126,526,642.70
Total	1,056,595	2,594,939	$1,650,969,098.54

Source: U.S. Department of Labor, Occupational Safety and Health Administration, DOL Enforcement Website, OSHA for FY 2012, http://ogesdw.dol.gov/searchExplorer/searchExplorer.php (accessed February 13, 2013).

If an employer is convicted of a willful violation that has resulted in the death of an employee, the offense is punishable by a court-imposed fine or by imprisonment for up to six months, or both. A fine of up to $250,000 for an individual or $500,000 for a corporation may be imposed under the Comprehensive Crime Control Act of 1984 for a criminal conviction involving an employee's death.[96]

Employers

The OSH Act protects employees who refuse to work in unsafe conditions under Section 11(c)(1).[97] This provision of the Act further prohibits an employer from discharging, or in any manner discriminating against, any employee because the employee files a complaint or institutes any proceeding under the Act. Just as with the Civil Rights Act of 1964, employers cannot retaliate against an employee for cooperating with investigators or testifying in any proceeding under the OSH Act.

Table 11.5

Monetary Penalties by OSHA Citation Type and Other Offenses

Citation	Minimum fine of not less than for each violation	Maximum fine of not more than for each violation	Imprisonment of no more than
Willful and/or repeated (levied against the company)	$5,000	$70,000	N/A
Willful and/or repeated resulting in death (levied against the individual responsible)	N/A	$10,000 $20,000*	6 months 1 year*
Serious	N/A	$7,000	N/A
Other than serious	N/A	$7,000	N/A
False statement	N/A	$10,000	6 months
Violation of posting requirements	N/A	$7,000	N/A
Assaulting or interfering with a compliance officer	N/A	$5,000	3 years

Source: 29 U.S.C. § 666 *et seq.;* OSHA, OSH Act, OSHA Standards, Inspections, Citations and Penalties, http://www.osha.gov/doc/outreachtraining/htmlfiles/introsha.html (accessed February 13, 2013).

*When the conviction of such person is for a subsequent violation committed after a first conviction for willful and/or repeated resulting in death.

This right to refuse to work in unsafe conditions (not connected with the normal nature of the work) was established in *Whirlpool Corp. v. Marshall*. In this decision, the Supreme Court held that an employee's refusal to perform an assigned task due to a reasonable fear of death or serious injury is a valid right afforded by Occupational Safety and Health Act.[98] The key word here is *reasonable*. An employee working in an office where the temperature is 50°F because the heating system is not working would be hard-pressed to prove that he or she had a reasonable fear of death or serious injury. On the other hand, an employee doing strenuous work on an assembly line where the temperature is 120°F may easily prove a reasonable fear for personal safety or health.

Employee Protection Against Retaliation

Like any of the other statutes previously discussed in this textbook, whistleblowers are protected against retaliation for filing an OSHA complaint. Therefore, any adverse action taken against an employee who requests an OSHA inspection or participates in an accident investigation violates the OSH Act. Managers should ensure that any disciplinary actions, terminations, or transfers of employees who have filed OSHA complaints can be clearly shown not to be connected to the OSHA complaint.[99]

STATE REGULATION OF WORKPLACE SAFETY

Like the Civil Rights Act of 1964, the OSH Act permits individual states to establish and manage their own safety and health programs for the private sector. Under the OSH

Act, OSHA may transfer authority to approved states to cover their own occupational safety and health matters. This is very similar in principle to the Equal Employment Opportunity Commission's (EEOC's) deferring EEO matters to state fair employment practice agencies (FEPAs).

Currently, the OSH Act certifies twenty-five states and two territories that manage their own safety and health programs covering private sector and public sector employees (see Figure 11.6).[100] There are two other states operating programs that cover only state and local government employees. In order to receive certification from OSHA, a state must demonstrate that it will conduct inspections to enforce those standards and conduct occupational safety and health training and education programs.

Workplace safety and health issues are continually evolving in response to real or perceived threats. Among the safety and health issues that have received increasing attention in the popular media and, consequently, have garnered growing public concern are: secondhand smoke in the workplace, workplace violence, carpal tunnel syndrome and other musculoskeletal disorders, and work-related stress and emotional disorders.

Secondhand Smoke in the Workplace

Most companies in the United States have adopted workplace smoking policies, although they vary from company to company. These policies typically differ in degree of stringency, but they generally serve one primary goal in the workplace: to protect employees from exposure to the chemicals found in environmental tobacco smoke, commonly called "secondhand smoke." Since the Environmental Protection Agency (EPA) first classified tobacco smoke as a group A carcinogen (similar to asbestos, benzene, and radon), safety officers have become concerned about its connection to workplace illness. One report links secondhand smoke to inducing asthma and increasing the incidence of respiratory infections; it is also blamed for 3,000 lung cancer deaths per year.[101]

In its *Guide to Workplace Smoking Policies*, the EPA recommends that employers build enclosed, ventilated smoking lounges if they allow employees to smoke on the companies' premises. The EPA has strongly endorsed indoor air quality legislation that would require employers to take steps to avoid employee exposure to secondhand smoke.[102] Employers respond to such initiatives by developing internal policies in anticipation of future compliance requirements.

Many companies have taken the simplest approach to meeting indoor air quality recommendations by banning all indoor smoking. Currently, 80 percent of all employees work for companies that have a smoking policy.[103] At least twenty-one states have preempted voluntary employer efforts by enacting laws regulating smoking in private workplaces.[104] Other companies are implementing restrictions on smoking in anticipation of a proposed OSHA standard that would ban smoking in the workplace except in separately ventilated areas (much like the EPA has previously recommended).

Remember that under the OSH Act, the "general duty" provision requires an employer to provide places of employment "free of recognized hazards that are causing or likely to cause death or serious physical harm to his employee."[105]

Figure 11.6   **States and Territories with Approved OSHA Programs**

Alaska	New Mexico
Arizona	New York
California	North Carolina
Connecticut	Oregon
Hawaii	Puerto Rico
Illinois	South Carolina
Indiana	Tennessee
Iowa	Utah
Kentucky	Vermont
Maryland	Virgin Islands
Michigan	Virginia
Minnesota	Washington
Nevada	Wyoming
New Jersey	

Source: U.S. Department of Labor, Occupational Safety and Health Administration, State Occupational Safety and Health Plans. www.osha.gov/dcsp/osp/index.htm (accessed February 13, 2013).

Note: Connecticut, Illinois, New Jersey, New York, and the Virgin Islands only cover public sector employers.

Under this broad umbrella, secondhand smoke from cigarettes could easily be covered. Not surprisingly, many employers are opting for smoke-free work environments, rather than contesting the proposed standards and laws.

Workplace Violence

Media emphasis on shootings in places of employment has highlighted concerns about workplace violence. Workplace violence is generally defined as violent acts committed by an employee against other persons at work or while on duty. A report on workplace violence published by the Department of Justice in 1998 and based on Federal Bureau of Investigation statistics revealed that approximately 1,000 employees were murdered each year while performing their work duties.[106] Another extensive report shows that more than 2 million incidences of workplace violence were reported each year during the survey period between 1993 and 1999.[107] This sounds especially worrisome, particularly in light of the media exposure that such cases attract. However, compare the 518 workplace homicides that occurred in 2010[108] to the 14,748 murders that occur in places other than work each year and the over 1.2 million incidents of violence outside of the workplace.[109] In a workforce of 143,492,000 employed workers,[110] workplace deaths due to coworker violence are extremely rare, and the workplace is generally safer than the home. Nonetheless, HR professionals and managers need to be concerned about violence in the workplace, but they should not exaggerate its likelihood.

While many organizations now have some formal workplace violence policy, a joint survey conducted by the Risk and Insurance Management Society and the American Society of Safety Engineers finds that most have not conducted assessments of the risks for actual workplace violence incidents.[111] Some HR responses to reducing workplace violence include limiting access to facilities, workplace surveillance, employee background checks, and open-door policies.

Carpal Tunnel Syndrome and Other Musculoskeletal Disorders

In the 1990s, as more and more personal computers were being utilized in the workplace, a new work-related disorder, carpal tunnel syndrome, emerged. Managers immediately began devoting attention to the health needs of computer operators and users. Since then, scientific and medical literature has concentrated on identifying occupations that subject employees to high biomechanical stress, such as heavy lifting and repetitive motion. All of the work-related conditions are covered under the general term "work-related musculoskeletal disorder" (WMSD). This generalization also includes repetitive stress injuries, also called cumulative trauma disorders, ergonomic injuries, and musculoskeletal disorders, which affect muscles, tendons, ligaments, nerves, bones, cartilage, and blood vessels in the upper and lower extremities, and in the back. Some examples of WMSD include such problems as back injuries, tendonitis, and the previously mentioned carpal tunnel syndrome. There is a cost incentive for reducing WMSD, as the estimated economic impact associated with lost days and compensation claims have been estimated to be as high as $54 billion annually.[112]

Perhaps the most significant employer response to WMSD is the implementation of effective ergonomics programs. **Ergonomics** is the science of adapting the job to the biomechanical needs of the worker. It is a human engineering process of matching the physical requirements of the job and the physical capacity of the worker. This naturally affects not only job design but the design of the worker's equipment as well.

In some cases, WMSD can be prevented by easy and inexpensive modifications to the workplace. Typical adjustments include changing the height of working surfaces, varying tasks for workers, encouraging short rest breaks with physical exercise, and decreasing the number and weight of items workers must lift—job design issues. Furnishing equipment to assist workers with lifting, and providing specially designed equipment, such as ergonomically developed computer keyboards, are two simple examples of how employers may reduce risks.

Work-related Emotional Stress Disorders

Work-related stress is considered a growing problem for workers in today's highly competitive work environment. For a number of reasons (lack of personal autonomy, poor leadership, budgetary constraints, reduced staffing, and so on), many employees have concluded that their jobs do not meet their expectations, and this may cause stress. Some of the factors inherent to jobs that contribute to high levels of work-related stress are workload, control over one's work, extrinsic and intrinsic rewards of work, coworker and supervisor relationships, sense of community in the workplace, perception of fairness and equity in the workplace, and compatibility of a person's roles to personal and organizational values. Stress may be exacerbated as workers become increasingly concerned about achieving and maintaining a balance between family and work obligations.

Women, particularly, are torn between workplace and family responsibilities. HR

Figure 11.7 **Sick Building Syndrome Symptoms**

- Coughing
- Dermatitis
- Difficulty concentrating
- Dizziness
- Eye, nose, throat, and respiratory
  irritation

- Fatigue
- Headache
- Muscle pain
- Nausea
- Sensitivity to odors

Source: U.S. Occupational Safety and Health Administration, *OSHA Technical Manual*, Section III, Chapter 2 (II) (A) (1), http://www.osha.gov/dts/osta/otm/otm_iii/otm_iii_2.html (accessed February 13, 2013).

strategies related to reducing stress involve job design (emphasizing employee control) and developing reward and incentive programs that not only satisfy employee needs but are equitably administered as well. Managerial training programs may be used to ensure that managerial personnel fully understand their leadership roles and the adverse consequences for poor leadership. Clearly communicated expectations and criteria for benefit and incentive eligibility can reduce exaggerated and unrealistic expectations among employees. Flexible work schedules may be developed to accommodate employees' family obligations. Finally, stress management courses can be offered to help employees develop strategies to deal with stress.

Sick Building Syndrome

Sick building syndrome (SBS) is a term used to encompass a number of medical ailments associated with physical workplace settings.[113] These are most often attributed to indoor air pollution, molds in ventilation systems, poor lighting, poor acoustics, poor ergonomics, and chemicals leaching from construction materials or furniture.[114]

The symptoms from such exposure fall into a broad range, from headaches to respiratory problems (see Figure 11.7). SBS has real implications for businesses as research has linked it to higher employee absenteeism and turnover, lower productivity, and lower job satisfaction.[115] It is also a potential source of ADA complaints requesting accommodations,[116] workers' compensation claims,[117] and may result in litigation under state tort statues.[118]

SUMMARY

Managers and HR professionals have a very real responsibility for overseeing safety in the workplace. There exist tangible economic incentives to afford workers safe workplaces. An unsafe work environment may cost the employer by increasing workers' compensation program costs and exposing the organization to increased litigation. Conversely, safe work environments may actually reduce expenses.

Workers' compensation laws were among the earliest attempts to address safety and health issues in the workplace. Although workers' compensation laws were originally designed as a system to provide benefits, not necessarily safe worksites, employers who experienced fewer accidents on the job paid lower premiums. Even now, employers who are ambivalent to workers' safety will experience more accidents and incur larger premiums.

The most significant guidance on safety and health from the federal government came with the passage of the Occupational Safety and Health Act in 1970. The OSH Act has extended federal safety and health standards to almost every workplace. The basic goal of the OSH Act was to assure safe and healthy conditions for workers on the job by encouraging employers and employees to reduce workplace hazards, but it has also imposed reporting and record-keeping requirements.

Employers should endeavor to maintain a safe working environment for employees because it is the right thing to do. However, there is sufficient regulation in this area to compel compliance.

KEY TERMS AND CONCEPTS

Assumption of risk defense	Other-than-serious violation
Contributory negligence defense	Permanent standards
De minimus violation	Permanent variance
Emergency standard	Serious violation
Ergonomics	Sick building syndrome
Exclusivity principle	Temporary variance
Fellow-servant rule defense	Willful and repeated violations
Imminent danger violation	Workers' compensation
Interim standards	

DISCUSSION QUESTIONS

1. What events led to regulation of safety and health in the workplace?
2. What is workers' compensation?
3. Describe the exclusivity principle of workers' compensation as a legal remedy.
4. Explain the compulsory or elective options regarding employer acceptance under state workers' compensation laws.
5. What are the grounds for challenging an employee's workers' compensation claim?
6. What three federal agencies were established under the OSH Act of 1970? What are the specific functions of each of these three federal agencies?
7. What are the specific requirements for employers under the "general duty clause" of the OSH Act?
8. What are the employees' rights to refuse to work in unsafe work conditions established by the *Supreme Court in Whirlpool Corp. v. Marshall*?

CASES

Case 1

Technotics, Inc., a small electronics components manufacturing firm, began operations several months ago. The firm is owned and operated by two young entrepreneurs who know very little about occupational safety and health issues. The company has fifty employees, several of whom operate the heavy equipment needed to package, warehouse, and ship the products.

The firm's owners hired a safety manager, Jim Strong, to develop and administer an industrial safety program. Unfortunately, before Strong could implement a formal safety program, the state Occupational Safety and Health Agency compliance officer entered the facility and conducted a tour, unaccompanied by either management or employees. At the end of the compliance officer's tour, Technotics was cited with one serious violation and two other-than-serious violations. The serious violation involved a forklift operator who was not wearing a seat belt, which is considered life threatening, and the employer should have known of the hazard.

The owners want to contest the citations, claiming they have made a good faith effort to establish a safety and health program but have not been able to implement such a program. They ask Strong for his suggested course of action.

What steps would you recommend if you were the safety manager for this firm? Why?

Case 2

Jeannette Krappels is a former employee of PersonPower, Inc. Krappels has brought suit against PersonPower, alleging that PersonPower terminated her employment in retaliation for her filing a workers' compensation claim under the Illinois Workers' Compensation Act.

Krappels worked for PersonPower from approximately January of 2001 to July 28, 2008, as a customer service specialist. On January 9, 2008, Krappels suffered a severe work-related injury. The injury prevented her from working at PersonPower until January 15. On that date, Krappels began to work at home with physician's restrictions on her activities. On January 30, PersonPower required Krappels to return to working from the office, rather than from home.

After Krappels returned to work, several PersonPower employees, including her immediate supervisors, became concerned with her repeated absences and poor performance. Several e-mails between Chuck Taylor, her supervisor; Bud Busch, a regional director; and Mark Walker, a regional human resources manager, reflected these concerns. In July of 2008, Krappels apparently began to worry that she might be fired because of her injury and because of the "way she was being treated by PersonPower after her injury."

In that same month, Krappels's coworker Monica Lemmon reported to Taylor and

Busch that Krappels had asked her to testify in her favor for the workers' compensation case. Lemmon alleges that Krappels offered to pay her $1,000 in exchange for testimony that would back Krappels's claim.

On July 28, 2008, Albert Busch, the vice president of human resources at Person-Power, sent Krappels a letter notifying her that she was terminated. The parties dispute the reason for her termination. PersonPower claims that Busch's decision to terminate Krappels was based only on information about the alleged bribe Krappels made to Lemmon, while Krappels contends that her termination was in retaliation for her decision to file a workers' compensation claim.[119]

    a. Does Krappels have a legitimate workers' compensation claim?

    b. What must PersonPower demonstrate in order to prove they did not retaliate against Krappels?

NOTES

1. This scenario was developed from the findings of fact in D'Allesandro Corporation, OSHARC No. 07–0533 (2008).

2. U.S. Department of Labor, *Growth of Labor Law in the United States* (Washington, DC: Government Printing Office, 1967), p. 182.

3. T.J. Anton, *Occupational Safety and Health Management* (New York: McGraw-Hill, 1979), pp. 189–190.

4. U.S. Department of Labor, *Growth of Labor Law in the United States,* pp. 139–140.

5. Ibid.

6. 35 Stat. 556 (May 30, 1908), codified as amended at 5 U.S.C. § 8101 *et seq.* in 1916.

7. U.S. Department of Labor, *Growth of Labor Law in the United States,* p. 140.

8. 33 U.S.C. § 901 *et seq.*

9. U.S. Department of Labor, *Growth of Labor Law in the United States,* p. 141.

10. Ibid.

11. R.A. Lester, *Economics of Labor* (New York: Macmillan, 1949), pp. 490–491.

12. 41 U.S.C. § 35 *et seq.*

13. 41 U.S.C. § 351 *et seq.*

14. National Safety Council, *Injury Facts* (Itasca, IL: National Safety Council, 1999).

15. Ibid.

16. National Safety Council, *Injury Facts* (Itasca, IL: National Safety Council, 2011), p. 52.

17. R.A. Epstein, "The Historical Origins and the Economic Structure of Workers' Compensation Law," *Georgia Law Review* 16 (1982): 775–779; Anton, *Occupational Safety and Health Management,* pp. 53–56.

18. R.B. Ulrich, "Survey of Illinois Law: Workers' Compensation." *Southern Illinois University Law Journal* 19 (1995): 999.

19. *Stivison v. Goodyear Tire & Rubber Co.,* 687 N.E.2d 458 (Ohio 1997).

20. *Shade v. Ayars & Ayars, Inc.,* 525 N.W.2d 32 (Neb. 1994).

21. 629 N.E.2d 492 (Ohio App. 1993).

22. *Koger v. Greyhound Lines, Inc.,* 629 N.E.2d at 389–390.

23. *Dorosz v. Green & Seifter,* 708 N.E.2d 162 (N.Y. 1999).

24. *Ludwinski v. National Courier,* 873 S.W.2d 890 (Mo. App. 1994).

25. *Frantz v. Campbell County Memorial Hospital,* 932 P.2d 750 (Wyo. 1997).

26. *Rosas v. Workers' Compensation Appeals Board,* 20 Cal. Rptr.2d 778 (Cal. App. 1993); *Davis v. Dyncorp,* 647 A.2d 446 (Md. App. 1994).

27. I. Sengupta, V. Reno, J.F. Burton, and M. Baldwin. *Workers' Compensation: Benefits, Coverage, and Costs* (Washington DC: National Academy of Social Insurance, 2012).

28. Pennsylvania Workers' Compensation Act § 306(c)(1) (2009).

29. I. Sengupta, V. Reno, J.F. Burton, and M. Baldwin. *Workers' Compensation: Benefits, Coverage, and Costs* (Washington DC: National Academy of Social Insurance, 2012).

30. J. Kilgour, "A Primer on Workers' Compensation Laws and Programs," *SHRM White Paper* (Arlington, VA: Society for Human Resource Management, January 2000).

31. T. Moore, "Maintenance and Cure: A Seaman's Misrepresentation of His Health History Excuses His Employer. *Brown v. Parker Drilling Offshore Corp.*," *Journal of Maritime Law & Commerce* 36 (2005): 545–561.

32. J.M. Williams, P.L. Dunn, S. Bast, and J. Giesen. "Factors Considered by Vocational Rehabilitation Professionals in Employability and Earning Capacity Assessment," *Rehabilitation Counseling Bulletin* 50, no. 1 (2006): 24–34.

33. *Stivison v. Goodyear Tire and Rubber Co.,* 687 N.E.2d 458 (Ohio 1997).

34. Commonwealth of Massachusetts, Department of Industrial Accidents, *Employer's Guide to Workers' Compensation* (Springfield, MA: Department of Industrial Accidents, 1999).

35. Office of Workers' Compensation Programs, Employment Standards Administration, *State Workers' Compensation Laws* (Washington, DC: U.S. Department of Labor, January 1999).

36. U.S. Chamber of Commerce, *1997 Analysis of Workers' Compensation Laws* (Washington, DC: U.S. Chamber of Commerce, 2007).

37. Ibid.

38. Texas Workers' Compensation Act § 408.061. Maximum Weekly Benefit. http://www.statutes.legis.state.tx.us/Docs/LA/htm/LA.408.htm#408.061 (accessed march 20, 2013).

39. Division of Worker's Compensation, Maximum and Minimum Weekly Benefits, Texas Department of Insurance (2008), www.tdi.state.tx.us/wc/employee/maxminbens.html (accessed March 20, 2013).

40. Legislative Audit Council, *A review of the South Carolina Second Injury Fund* (State of South Carolina, March 2007) www.lac.sc.gov/NR/rdonlyres/E646C435-2B65-43DC-BABB-8861DA1D52E4/0/SIF_Summary.pdf.

41. Alaska Statutes 23.30.205.

42. *Koger v. Greyhound Lines, Inc.*, 629 N.E.2d 492 (Ohio App. 1993).

43. *Ludwinski v. National Courier*, 873 S.W.2d 890 (Mo. App. 1994).

44. *Roberts v. Estep*, 845 S.W.2d 544 (Ky. 1993).

45. *Reswelser v. Havoil Construction Co.*, 660 S0.2d 7 (La. 1995).

46. *Recchi America Inc. v. Hall*, 692 S0.2d 153 (Fla. 1997).

47. 29 U.S.C. § 651 *et seq.* (2007).

48. Lyndon Johnson, "President's Message to Congress on Manpower and Occupational Safety and Health Programs," *Weekly Compilation of Presidential Documents,* January 23, 1968, vol. 4, no. 4, pp. 110–111.

49. U.S. Bureau of Labor Statistics, *Workplace Injury and Illness Summary* (October 25, 2012) http://www.bls.gov/news.release/osh.nr0.htm (accessed March 22, 2013).

50. 29 C.F.R. § 1903.2 (2012).

51. 29 U.S.S. § 666(i).

52. 29 U.S.C. § 654(a).

53. 29 U.S.C. § § 2200.70–2200.77.

54. Ibid.

55. U.S. Occupational Safety and Health Administration, *Imminent Danger* (2013), http://www.osha.gov/as/opa/worker/danger.html (accessed March 20, 2013).

56. 29 U.S.C. § 658(a).

57. 29 C.F.R. § 1903.14(b).

58. 29 U.S.C. § 658(b).

59. 29 U.S.C. § 666(I).

60. 29 C.F.R. § 1903.17.

61. 29 U.S.C. § 652(5).

62. *Donovan v. Coeur d'Alene Tribal Farm*, 751 F.2d 1113, 1116 (9th Cir. 1985).

63. Ibid.

64. 499 F.2d 467 (D.C. Cir. 1974).

65. 29 U.S.C. § 655(c)(1) (2012).

66. 29 U.S.C. § 655(c)(3).

67. 489 F.2d 120, 132 (5th. Cir. 1974).

68. 29 U.S.C. 654(a)(1).

69. U.S. Occupational Safety and Health Administration, *Field Inspection Reference Manual* (Washington, DC: Government Printing Office, 2000), § 7C.2.c.1.d.

70. 448 U.S. 607 (1980).

71. *Industrial Union Department v. American Petroleum Institute*, 448 U.S. at 632.

72. *Society of Plastics Industry v. OSHA*, 509 F.2d 1301 (2nd Cir. 1975).

73. 647 F.2d 1189 (D.C. Cir. 1980), cert. denied, 453 U.S. 913 (1981).

74. *United Steelworkers of America v. Marshall*, 647 F.2d at 1277.

75. *Industrial Union Department v. American Petroleum Institute*, 448 U.S. 607 (1980).

76. 452 U.S, 490, 531 n.55 (1981), citing *United Steelworkers of America v. Marshall*, 647 F.2d 1189, 1265 (D.C. Cir. 1981).

77. 29 U.S.C. § 655(b)(6)(a).

78. Ibid.

79. 29 U.S.C. § 655(d).

80. Ibid.

81. 29 C.F.R. § 1904 *et seq.*

82. 29 C.F.R. § 1904.17.

83. 29 C.F.R. § 1904.16.

84. 29 C.F.R. § 1904.12(c).

85. 29 C.F.R. § 1904.12(d).

86. U.S. Equal Employment Opportunity Commission, "Enforcement Guidance: Reasonable Accommodation Under the Americans with Disabilities Act" (October 17, 2002), www.eeoc.gov/policy/docs/accommodation.html (accessed January 30, 2008).

87. 29 U.S.C. § 657(f)(1) and (2).

88. 29 U.S.C. § 657(a) and 29 C.F.R. § 1903.7(a).

89. 29 C.F.R. § 1903.7.

90. 29 U.S.C. § 657(e).

91. 535 F.2d 371 (7th Cir. 1976).

92. 436 U.S. 307, 323–24 (1978).

93. Source: U.S. Department of Labor, Occupational Safety and Health Administration, *DOL Enforcement Website, OSHA for FY 2012*. http://ogesdw.dol.gov/searchExplorer/searchExplorer.php (accessed February 13, 2013).

94. Ibid.

95. 29 U.S.C. § 666(b).

96. Comprehensive Crime Control Act of 1984, Pub. L. 98–473, Tit. II, 98 Stat. 1976.

97. 29 U.S.C. § 660(c)(1).

98. 445 U.S. 1 (1980).

99. 29 U.S.C. § 653.

100. U.S. Department of Labor, *2007 OSHSPA Report: State Plan Activities of the Occupational Safety and Health State Plan Association* (Washington, DC: Government Printing Office, 2007), pp. 13–15.

101. Anonymous, "What Cigarettes Do to American Business" *Business and Health* (August 1997), pp. 10–13.

102. Respiratory Health Effects of Passive Smoking: Lung Cancer and Other Disorders, EPA/600/6–90/006F.

103. Ibid.

104. Ibid.

105. 29 U.S.C. § 651, 654(a).

106. G. Warchol, *Workplace Violence, 1992–96* (Washington, DC: Bureau of Justice Statistics, U.S. Department of Justice, 1998).

107. D.T. Duhart, *Violence in the Workplace, 1993–99* (Washington, DC: Bureau of Justice Statistics, U.S. Department of Justice, December 2001).

108. U.S. Bureau of Labor Statistics, *Fact Sheet: Workplace Homicides from Shootings* (January 2013) Workplace Homicides from Shootings, http://www.bls.gov/iif/oshwc/cfoi/osar0016.htm (accessed March 22, 2013).

109. U.S. Bureau of Federal Investigation, *Uniform Crime Report:Crime in the United States, 2010*, http://www.fbi.gov/about-us/cjis/ucr/crime-in-the-u.s/2010/crime-in-the-u.s.-2010/violent-crime/violentcrimemain.pdf (accessed February 14, 2013).

110. U.S. Bureau of Labor Statistics, The Employment Situation—February 2013 (March 8, 2013), http://www.bls.gov/news.release/pdf/empsit.pdf (accessed March 10, 2013).

111. D.M. Katz, "Study Finds Lag in Violence Prevention," *National Underwriter* 104 (3).

112. S. Ferguson, B. Silverstein, M. Chemiack, A. Garg, and S. Lavender, Prevention of Work-related Musculoskeletal Disorders, *Proceedings of the Human Factors and Ergonomics Society 50th Annual Meeting* (2006): 1299–1302.

113. U.S. Environmental Protection Agency, *Indoor Air Facts No. 4* (revised) February 1991.

114. U.S. Occupational Safety & Health Administration, *OSHA Technical Manual*. Section III, Chapter 2 (2013), http://www.osha.gov/dts/osta/otm/otm_iii/otm_iii_2.html (accessed March 15, 2013).

115. J.P. Hewitt, *Sick Building Syndrome: Fact or Fiction?* (Morrisville, SC: Lulu Press, 2007); J.O. Crawford and S.M. Bolas, "Sick Building Syndrome, Work Factors and Occupational Stress," *Scandinavian Journal of Work, Environment & Health* 22, no. 4 (1996): 243–250.

116. S.J. Henning and D.A. Berman, "Mold Contamination: Liability and Coverage Issues," *West-Northwest Law Review* 8 (2001): 73–93.

117. W.D. Sheldon, "Worker's Compensation: Office Workers and Sick Building Syndrome," *Arizona Attorney* 33 (1996): 20–37.

118. A.W. Reitze, Jr., and S.L. Carof, "The Legal Control of Indoor Pollution," *Boston College Environmental Affairs Law Review* 25 (1998): 247–345.

119. This scenario was developed from the facts in *Hobbs v. Peoplesoft, Inc.*, 2000 U.S. Dist. Lexis 17087 (N.D. Ill. 2000).

EMPLOYMENT-AT-WILL, EMPLOYEE DISCIPLINE, AND NEGLIGENT HIRING ISSUES

LEARNING OBJECTIVES

- Understand and explain an employer's prerogatives under the employment-at-will doctrine.
- Understand the situations that erode an employer's ability to exercise employment-at-will.
- Explain the advantages and disadvantages of having an employee handbook.
- Explain how an employee handbook can create an implied contract.
- Explain an employer's responsibilities for ensuring due process in the workplace.
- Understand the primary concerns when conducting in-house investigations.
- Distinguish between negligent hiring and negligent retention and understand the implications of each.

OPENING SCENARIO

The following letter was sent to a job applicant by the senior vice president of marketing for D.L. Nichols & Sons, Inc.[1]:

Dear Mr. Frederick Schwartz:

The purpose of this letter is to confirm D.L. Nichols & Sons' offer of employment. It is our hope that you will take advantage of this offer.

We are offering you employment as our Sales Director for Southeastern Operations with a salary of $100,000 per year.

Your work responsibilities will be throughout the twelve states of our Southeastern Region, but your office will be located in our corporate headquarters in Atlanta. We realize that this will necessitate you and your family to move to Atlanta; however, D.L. Nichols & Sons will reimburse you for all moving and relocation expenses.

Should you accept our offer, your employment will begin immediately. You and your family will be afforded free accommodations in our corporate condominium for up to one year. The corporate condominium is conveniently located within walking distance from our headquarters complex.

Upon hiring, you will immediately become eligible for full insurance coverage and the other benefits and executive prerequisites we discussed during our last interview. To refresh your memory, I have taken the liberty of enclosing all the relevant benefit brochures.

Please give serious consideration to this offer and let me know of your decision no later than 4 p.m. (EST) next Friday, the 25th. We are confident that you are well qualified for this position and are relying on you to raise sales in our Southeastern Region to $25 million within a year's time.

Sincerely,
Gregory Rose
Sr. Vice President, Marketing

Fred accepted D.L. Nichols & Sons' job offer and began his employment in May. However, after several heated discussions with Mr. Rose over the allocation of promotion and advertising budgets, Fred was fired in September. When Fred protested his termination, Mr. Rose reminded him that he never signed a written employment contract with the corporation. Mr. Rose stated, "Since there was no formal contract and Georgia is an employment-at-will state, D.L. Nichols & Sons has the legal right to terminate your employment at any time and without notice. The company is exercising its employment-at-will rights, and there is nothing that you can do about it. Have a nice day."

EMPLOYMENT-AT-WILL

Employment-at-will (EAW) is actually an old common law concept based on the premise that if the employee can terminate his or her employment relationship with an employer anytime he or she sees fit, and for any reason, the employer is entitled to do the same. Say, for example, that, while working her way through college, an individual has taken a job at a local fast-food restaurant. After working there one week, the student concludes that the job is interfering too much with her studies and she decides to quit. Can the employer force the student to keep working against her will? In the absence of a written employment contract, the answer is "no." In fact, she is not even legally required to give two weeks' notice, though this is the customary and ethical thing to do.

The employment-at-will doctrine holds that if the employee has the freedom to quit at his or her own volition, then the employer has an equal right to fire the employee at his or her own volition. Or, put another way, if under the employment-at-will doctrine an employee can terminate an employment relationship for a good reason, a bad reason, or no reason at all, then the employer may terminate the employment relationship for a good reason, a bad reason, or no reason at all.[2] Again, this concept merely mirrors the employee's right to voluntarily quit for any reason. It does not give any manager license to engage in arbitrary or capricious behavior.

A good manager should never terminate a subordinate for any reason other than a good reason, and the vast majority of employee terminations are done for good reasons (i.e.,

Figure 12.1 **Situations That Erode Employment-at-Will**

- Contracts (explicit and implied)
- Whistleblower clauses (anti-retaliation clauses)
- Equal employment opportunity laws
- Just cause statutes
- Public policy
- Good faith and fair dealing (called "outrage" in some states)

poor performance, violating work rules, excessive absences, theft, etc.). There is no ethical justification for discharging an employee for a bad reason, or for no reason at all. Yet if this is true, then why are employers so concerned with protecting their employment-at-will rights? The answer is simple: documentation.

If an employer does not enjoy employment-at-will, then each termination must be for just cause, which then places the burden on the employer to provide evidence that the firing was justified; this requires additional documentation. For example, the employer must provide tangible evidence that the employee is being terminated for a behavioral problem (i.e., insubordination, fighting, theft, threats, harassment, etc.), performance deficiencies (i.e., inability to perform essential job functions, violation of policies or rules, etc.), or a financial exigency (i.e., plant closings, reductions in force, reengineering, etc.). If such documentation can be produced (and is factual), the discharge is likely to be judged as being for a "just cause." In the absence of such documentation, the termination will be suspect.

Naturally, all of the previously mentioned rationales are good reasons not to keep an employee on the payroll; however, in the absence of employment-at-will, an employer may be required to substantiate them. Loss of employment-at-will status, therefore, increases the administrative and record-keeping duties of the employee's immediate supervisor and the human resource (HR) department. Additionally, it increases the potential for litigation. As will be further disclosed in this chapter, there are no jurisdictions in which employment-at-will is absolute, and there are many factors that already erode employment-at-will doctrine (see Figure 12.1).

CONTRACTUAL EXCEPTIONS TO EAW

Two situations can arise creating a contractual obligation to terminate an employee for only just cause reasons. There may be an explicit contract that creates such a guarantee, or the guarantee may be derived from an implicit contract. Employees and employers are aware of explicit contracts, having both agreed to the terms and conditions of employment and having expressed them in a written manner.

Employers may be unaware of the existence of implied contracts. As we shall see shortly, implied contracts often occur because of a verbal or written statement made by the employer that the employee interpreted as a guarantee of continued employment. The employer may not have intended to make such a guarantee, but some state courts have ruled that such statements do prevent employee discharges except for just cause.

Explicit Contracts

There is no employment-at-will when an explicit contract exists. An **explicit contract** is a written document (in most instances) that exists between the two parties (the employer and the employee) establishing the terms of employment. Usually, a period of employment is specified, as well as other terms and conditions of that employment. To terminate an employee who is formally contracted to perform specific work for a specific period of time for either an invalid reason or no reason at all would be a breach of the contract. This also applies to employees covered under collective bargaining agreements negotiated by a labor union, which are in effect labor contracts. Consequently, all contractual employees may be terminated only for just cause.

From business law courses you probably know that a contract consists of two important parts: mutual assent and a consideration.[3] *Mutual assent* is founded upon the offer (sometimes called "promise") and acceptance.[4] The offer is communicated by one party (in our case, the employer) to the other (the prospective employee).

Essentially, the employer must communicate an offer to the prospective employee to perform in a particular manner in exchange for the prospective employee's agreeing to reciprocate by acting as requested. In a business setting, a seller advertises or communicates that he or she is willing to perform in a particular manner by providing a product or service to a buyer (the second party), provided that the buyer agrees to act as requested (i.e., pay the asking price for the product or service initially offered). It is important to note that no offer becomes effective until it has been communicated to the second party.[5] In an employment situation, the employer invariably communicates an offer to pay a particular salary for a specified period of time if the prospective employee agrees to perform as requested (i.e., perform specific work activities).

In either case, mutual assent does not occur until the second party accepts the offer by willingly agreeing to be bound by the terms of the offer. Acceptance occurs when the buyer pays the requested purchasing price for a good or service, thus obligating the first party to provide that good or service. In the instance of employment contracts, acceptance occurs when the prospective employee signs the written contract, obligating the employer to pay the agreed-upon salary for the agreed-upon period. The prospective employee also obligates himself or herself to perform the agreed-upon work activities for the agreed-upon period.

Still, we do not have a binding contract until the offer and acceptance have been validated by consideration. *Consideration* is defined as a bargained-for exchange and is based on the premise that one promise (i.e., providing a product or service) is consideration for another promise (i.e., receiving the payment). Consideration is the price paid for the offer or promise. There is no contract when the second party refuses to pay the first party's asking price. Nor is there a contract if the seller refuses to provide the product when the buyer offers to buy only at a lower price. Or in an employment situation, no contract exists if the employee refuses to work for the employer's initial salary offer, or the employer refuses to meet the employee's counteroffer.

During contract negotiations in employment, an employee may refuse to sign a contract because he or she feels that either the salary is too low or the period of obligated employment is too long. Conversely, the employer may feel that the employee's wage demands are too high or the contract duration is too short. In either instance, there is no contract because there is no agreed-to or bargained-for exchange.

There are two other elements that must be present for a contract to be legally enforceable. First, no contract is legally enforceable if it requires either party to perform an unlawful act. The so-called contracts in Mafia genre films for "hit men" to execute various and sundry people are not contracts in the true legal sense. In a more serious view, an employment contract with a certified public accountant requiring him or her to create knowingly false financial records is not an enforceable contract. Any contract, employment or otherwise, must be legally consistent with existing law and sound public policy.[6]

Second, the parties to the contract must be legally competent, which means all parties must be legally capable of entering into a contract. In most cases, the parties must be adults (check individual state statutes to determine the legal age of adulthood, also called "age of majority"). Minors enjoy the legal right to avoid contracts. Insanity or impaired mental state may also be used as a means to void a contract. Even circumstances involving a temporarily impaired mental state (i.e., intoxication) can be used as a defense in breach-of-contract litigation.

Breach of contract is the real concern in contractual employment relationships. Once a contract becomes legally enforceable, the party that fails to provide the previously discussed consideration is legally liable for breaching the contract. Not only is an employer liable for breaching the contract when terminating an employee for any reason other than just cause, but the employee breaches the contract as well if he or she attempts to sever the employment relationship before the contract expires.

Just Cause Statutes

In 1987, Montana passed the only just cause discharge statute in the United States, the Montana Wrongful Discharge from Employment Act.[7] Under a **just cause statute**, employers are limited to discharging non-probationary employees (not to exceed six months) only for broadly and statutorily defined reasons. Specifically, the Montana statute declares a discharge to be wrongful if "the discharge was not for a good reason and the employee had completed the employer's probationary period of employment. . . ."[8] Just cause reasons for terminating an employee usually include misconduct, poor performance, or reductions in an employer's workforce due to financial reasons. Failure to provide, and document, the justifications for the employee's termination under such a statute opens the discharge action to potential litigation. As previously mentioned, the problem for employers is that they have the burden of providing evidence to demonstrate that the termination was indeed predicated on just cause reasons.[9]

The Montana statute further makes it unlawful for any covered employer to "violate the expressed provisions of its own written personnel policy."[10] If the employee handbook clearly delineates progressive discipline, then progressive discipline will be meticulously followed.

Many states, while not enacting just cause statutes, have passed laws that prohibit the termination of employees for several specific reasons. For example, eighteen states have passed legislation that forbids employers from discharging any employee who refuses to take a polygraph test or based on the results of a polygraph test.[11] These restrictions are in addition to those imposed by the Federal Employee Polygraph Protection Act.[12]

There are several states that, though not providing statutory protection for all employees, require just cause terminations for specific classes of employees. At least fifteen states have their own state labor laws (in addition to the National Labor Relations Act)[13] that protect employees engaged in organizing activities from employment-at-will. There are also forty-five states with state equal employment opportunity laws that can be more inclusive (in terms of classes of workers they protect) than federal laws. Furthermore, thirty-two states provide varying degrees of protection from termination for employees who are performing duties in the National Guard or the U.S. Army, Navy, Air Force, or Marine Corps Reserves.[14] Also, numerous states provide statutory recognition for other employee activities that would be considered public policy issues (e.g., jury duty, reporting unlawful activities, political activities, etc.). Connecticut even guarantees employees First Amendment rights in the workplace. This means, at least in Connecticut, that an employer may not terminate an employee for stating his or her opinion on a matter of public concern.

Equal Employment Opportunity and Other Employment Laws

Employment-at-will is stopped in its tracks by the equal employment opportunity statutes at federal, state, and local levels. Although employment-at-will permits an employer to fire employees for bad reasons, unlawful discrimination is not among any of them. Any employer automatically loses its employment-at-will status when it impermissibly uses the race, color, religion, sex, national origin, or disabilities of qualified individuals in its termination decisions (see Chapters 2–7).

Protection against Retaliation (Whistleblower Clauses)

Another statutory limitation on employment-at-will arises from anti-retaliation or whistleblower clauses. Employment-at-will cannot be used as a justification for termination when the employee has reported the employer's violation of any law that contains a whistleblower clause. You will recall that **whistleblower clauses** protect employees from employer retaliation for reporting violations of a given law. Most federal statutes (i.e., the National Labor Relations Act, Occupational Safety and Health Act, Fair Labor Standards Act, Civil Rights Act of 1964, etc.)[15] contain these clauses. Usually, if the employee is terminated for "blowing the whistle," he or she is entitled, at least under federal laws, to reinstatement, back pay, and attorneys' fees.[16]

Finally, many state laws make it unlawful to retaliate against employees who file workers' compensation complaints, report unsafe working conditions under state workplace safety laws, or report violations of state minimum wage laws.

Figure 12.2 **Public Policy Issues**

- Engaging in a legal duty
- Engaging in a legal right
- Refusing to perform an illegal act
- Encouraging immoral acts or behavior
- Assisting another party to break the law

It is essential for managers and HR professionals to know that any action taken against a whistleblower must be consistent with the treatment initiated against other employees under similar situations. If, for example, a whistleblower has been discharged for excessive tardiness, while other employees with the same record remain on the payroll, a wrongful discharge could be easily deduced. Again, documentation is key to demonstrating that any adverse employment action is based on the employee's performance or conduct.

Most agencies that enforce federal statutes are very sensitive to constructive discharges and are more likely to initially believe an employee who alleges that he or she is being retaliated against. This does not imply whistleblowing employees cannot be disciplined for breaking work rules, only that they cannot be singled out for harsher punishment than other employees. Managers and HR professionals, because of the likelihood that retaliation will be alleged, have the additional burden of providing the necessary evidence to prove that any disciplinary action was justified. This means not only proving that the whistleblower violated a rule or policy but also that he or she was not treated differently from other violators. Showing consistency with previous disciplinary actions is extremely important.

Public Policy

A termination violates **public policy** when an employee is discharged for refusing to violate a law or ordinance, fired for refusing to avoid a civic duty or obligation (i.e., jury duty or when summoned as a witness), or terminated for engaging in a legally protected activity (see Figure 12.2). Take, for example, the case of *Peterman v. International Brotherhood of Teamsters*,[17] in which an employee was fired for refusing to submit false and untrue statements to a California legislative committee. The employee lost his job for refusing to commit perjury. A manager who assists another manager in committing perjury is also in violation. The employee was forced to choose between breaking the law and securing his continued employment. Demanding that an employee lie under oath or refuse to provide testimony clearly requires the employee to violate a legal obligation and, therefore, is an unequivocal public policy violation. Also, public policy can be violated if an employee is pressured into committing immoral acts such as requiring an employee to sleep with a client in order to keep an important account.

Public policy can also be violated when an employer retaliates against an employee for enjoying a legal right or entitlement. For example, even in the absence of a whistleblower clause, discharging an employee for filing a workers' compensation claim resulting from a work-related injury would be in violation of public policy.[18] Furthermore, discharging an employee for even threatening or indicating that he or she will file for workers' compensation violates public policy.[19]

Not surprisingly, there may be instances in which an employee makes a false allegation against an employer. When allegations of public policy violations arise, the employer's only defense is to offer a job-related reason (a just cause reason) for the employee's termination. Legitimate business reasons that typically substantiate just cause terminations include poor job performance, low quality of work (it is advisable to show that the employee received repeated warnings), tardiness, or increased absenteeism (in the event of workers' compensation claims, the employer must ensure these absences are not injury related).

It is a manager's duty to maintain specific documentation that substantiates the employer's legitimate business reason for terminating the employee in question. However, managers should also supply this proper documentation to HR. More than just good record keeping (although that is important too), documentation entails having good disciplinary policies in effect and ensuring management personnel are aware of their responsibilities under these policies and are trained in the initiation and recording of disciplinary actions.

Covenant of Good Faith and Fair Dealing

Some states (currently eleven of them)[20] permit an employee to bring suit when an employer's termination is intended to either intentionally cause the employee injury or to deprive the employee of some benefit or compensation to which he or she is entitled.[21] In essence, the employer has behaved in an outrageous or patently unfair manner toward an employee. Perhaps the most often cited case used to demonstrate wrongful discharge under good faith and fair dealing is *Fortune v. National Cash Register Co.*[22] In this case, a salesman who had made $5,000,000 in sales for his employer was terminated to avoid paying him over $92,000 in sales commissions that the sales had earned him.[23] In a jurisdiction recognizing good faith and fair dealing, any attempt to deprive an employee of an earned wage or benefit would be a violation.[24]

Implied Contracts

Finally, there are many states that recognize implied contracts as a means of eroding an employer's EAW rights. In these jurisdictions, courts hold that not all contracts are explicit; some may be implied. An **implied contract** results when a contract can be inferred by the actions or conduct of the parties rather than stated in an expressed offer and acceptance. This is also called an implied-in-fact contract. Three conditions will establish an implied-in-fact contract: a party furnished some service or property; that party had an expectation to be compensated for the service or property furnished, and the other party knew, or should have known, that compensation was expected; and the other party had an opportunity to decline the service or property, and did not.[25] In employment environments, implied contracts are often alleged to hold that some assurance was made by the employer that the employee would enjoy continued employment so long as he or she did a good job. These implied contracts often arise when an employee can prove he or she received some assurance of employment for a specific period of time. In essence, the employee offers good job performance with the expectation, based on the employer's oral statements or written policies, that such performance will be compensated by continued employment and job security.

Because state laws vary, it is important for managers to know how their individual state defines the circumstances under which an implied contract exists. Some states, like Mississippi, do not recognize implied contracts in any form.[26] In other states, like California and Indiana, courts have required that the employer make clearly expressed promises of termination only for cause, not vague assurances, before an implied contract can be established.[27] Such assurances of permanent employment may be verbal or in writing, but they must be expressed by the employer. Yet in other states, no expressed assurance is required.[28] Unfortunately, a broad spectrum of interpretation exists among the various state jurisdictions as to what constitutes an actionable assurance of job security.

In most employment situations, implied contracts can arise when an employee receives written or oral assurances (other than in a formal contract) about job security or continued employment. These assurances can take many forms. For example, Michigan state courts have held that an oral statement to the effect that an employee will be employed by the company as long as he or she continues to perform the job satisfactorily is an implied contract.[29] In other states, there must be an unequivocal guarantee of continued employment in writing.[30] For example, a handbook with the following statement would be necessary to establish this unequivocal guarantee: *The employees of XYZ Company are guaranteed continued employment provided that they obey the work rules contained herein.* In the absence of such language, the relationship is assumed to be at-will.

Our opening scenario is an example of a statement (one that was in writing) that established an implied contract. Note that Mr. Rose's letter to Mr. Schwartz contained three references to a definite one-year period of time. The salary was for one year, the free condominium was available for "up to one year," and the sales performance expectations were for "within a year's time." This would appear to promise Mr. Schwartz employment for a specific period of time—one year.

Additionally, any written personnel policies or guidelines that imply employment guarantees may constitute an implied contract.[31] Perhaps the most widely accepted means (at least from a state court standpoint) of establishing implied employment contracts are employee handbooks. In the landmark case *Toussaint v. Blue Cross and Blue Shield*, the complaining party successfully argued that he was wrongfully discharged because his employer had not terminated him in accordance with the progressive discipline procedures promised in the employee handbook.[32] Employee handbooks will be examined in greater detail later in this chapter, but they do present a perplexing dilemma for employers. In most state jurisdictions, employee handbooks often establish implied contracts, thus eroding the employer's employment-at-will rights. However, failure to have written policies and procedures to ensure fair and consistent handling of HR decisions may unnecessarily expose the employer to litigation under state and federal employment laws. This is especially true for laws and regulations regarding sexual harassment (Chapter 5) and harassment based on national origin (Chapter 7).[33] Herein is the dilemma confronting HR professionals: Failure to state the policies in a handbook may expose the employer to litigation under a

Figure 12.3   **A Sample of Policies Typically Included in Employee Handbooks**

- Welcoming statement
- Purpose of the handbook
- Disclaimers (to maintain employment-at-will status)
- Definitions of terms
- Antiharrassment policy
- Dress code
- Attendance/tardiness policy
- Disciplinary policies
  Progressive discipline
  Offenses resulting in immediate discharge
  Penalties/disciplinary outcomes
- Behavioral expectations
  Prohibited workplace conduct
- Workplace safety policies
- Limitations on outside employment
- Dating policies
- Nepotism/employment of family members policy
- Telephone use policy

- Employee surveillance/monitoring policy
- E-mail/Internet access policy
- Substance abuse policy
- Disclosure of confidential information policy
- Restrictions on solicitation on company property policy
- Explanation of employee benefits
  Health insurance
  Dental insurance
  Other insurance
  Employee discounts
  Educational reimbursements
  Credit unions
  Paid sick leave
  Family and Medical Leave Act issues
  Jury duty leave
  Military service leave
- Wage/salary policies
- Travel reimbursement policy

myriad of equal employment laws, while having a handbook may expose the employer to litigation for wrongful discharge under breach of an implied contract.

The solution is for HR professionals to properly develop and implement employee handbooks. An employer must guarantee the employee handbook is properly worded, and, once it is developed and implemented, must follow its procedures. This situation means more work for HR professionals and line managers; they must enforce these provisions and policies. This will, in the long run, offset the liability and remedies that could result from Title VII and state tort lawsuits.

Employee Handbooks

Employee handbooks often present a double-edged sword for employers. On one hand, they provide a valuable means for disseminating important work-related information and policies to employees. On the other hand, an employee handbook may be viewed as an implied contract by many courts, thus eroding an employer's employment-at-will prerogatives. This can create a "you can't live with them and you can't live without them" situation. In truth, it is far more likely that employers "can't live without them" because properly constructed employee handbooks provide far more benefits than costs (see Figure 12.3).

One important benefit of a handbook is that it provides proof of antiharassment policies (this issue has already been addressed in detail in Chapter 5). What better means of demonstrating an employer's good faith effort to maintain a harassment-free workplace than to have the antiharassment policy statement (and reporting procedures) prominently displayed in the organization's employee handbook? The federal courts' increased emphasis on employers' policies and procedures in establishing an affirmative defense makes publication of such policies crucial. In the absence of proof that an employer has a policy and the employee was aware of the policy, there is no affirmative defense.[34]

Practical Guidance on Handbook Language

There are other considerations when developing an employee handbook. Because of the concern over potential litigation, there is a tendency for the HR professionals who write the handbooks to use overly legalistic terminology. This usually results in handbooks that are written well above the reading comprehension levels of the employees for whom they were intended. The cardinal rule when writing an employee handbook is: If the employees cannot read and understand the contents, it is a waste of time and paper. A good employee handbook is readable and conveys the employer's policies and behavioral expectations to the employees. Several authorities on employee handbooks suggest that initial drafts of the handbook should be tested on a sample of employees before it is published and disseminated.[35] The ultimate purpose of any employee handbook or organizational policy is communication. If the employer's message is not effectively communicated, then one can hardly expect compliance.

Some employers operate in multilingual work environments. Such employers should be aware that this may necessitate multilingual handbooks and written policies. For example, an employer may have a number of workers whose verbal English skills are marginal and whose written English skills are even more limited. However, their oral and written Spanish skills might be good. As a result, it would make sense for the employer to provide a Spanish version of the employee handbook for these employees.

In other work environments there may be a problem with employees' written language skills in general. According to the National Institute for Literacy, approximately 20 percent of the U.S. workforce reads at or below the fifth-grade level.[36] The National Assessment of Adult Literacy (NAAL) reported that in excess of 40 million Americans over the age of sixteen had significant literacy needs.[37] One should specify the length of any probationary period. It can be a period from one month to one year. Typically, the common probationary period for most new hires is 90 days.[38] An employer with a workforce that reads at this level might have to consider additional methods for communicating company policies. One means of assuring this is to conduct classes on the handbook's contents during new employee orientations. Providing training sessions when new policies are implemented is another method. Because of the importance of documenting each employee's awareness of the material, it becomes necessary to maintain records of these training sessions or classes. In some instances employers may even administer examinations at the conclusion of such classes to verify that employees are aware of company policies.

Reducing Exposure to Implied Contract

When writing an employee handbook, employers should make every effort to reduce their implied contract exposure. There are several ways to do this, but keep in mind that the legalities of these suggestions vary significantly from state to state.

First, review handbooks and organizational policies for any phrases such as "permanent employee," "probationary employee," or "regular employee."[39] Such language could be construed to mean the employer is giving up employment-at-will rights at the conclusion of the probationary period. Further, it could be inferred that at the end of the probationary period, the employee moves to a "just cause" status as a "permanent employee." As demonstrated in the opening scenario, any written statements should be void of references of employment for specified periods of time, which is especially true for handbooks. If an employer explicitly stipulates employment for a definite time period, the employee can only be terminated for just cause.[40]

Second, the handbook should contain a written statement that the handbook or policy is not a guarantee of job security or permanent employment. However, in some states these disclaimers are not recognized, and virtually all handbooks constitute implied contracts.[41] Most states will allow employers to preserve their employment-at-will rights provided that the disclaimer is not contradicted or compromised by some other provision contained elsewhere in the handbook.

Suppose an employer has inserted the following disclaimer at the beginning of the employee handbook:

> This handbook is not, nor is it intended to be, a contract of employment. All employees are employed at will. No agent of this company has the authority to alter this relationship, and no employee should interpret any remarks by such agents as a guarantee of continued employment. The management of XYZ Company reserves the right to terminate your employment at any time.

Now assume that in the employee discipline portion of the employee handbook, the following policy is provided:

> Employees who have completed one or more years of service with XYZ Company are expected to give two weeks' notice of their intention to terminate their employment. The company will only terminate without notice any employee, probationary or permanent, for the following reasons:
>
> 1. Fighting;
> 2. Furnishing confidential information to unauthorized persons;
> 3. Reporting to work under the influence of drugs or alcohol;
> 4. Illegal possession of alcohol or drugs on company property;
> 5. Falsifying any employment records;
> 6. Possession of firearms or other weapons on company property;
> 7. Willful damage of company property;
> 8. Insubordination.
>
> For other offenses, to include unsatisfactory performance, excessive absenteeism, or tardiness, no permanent employee will be terminated without first being afforded the progressive disciplinary procedures afforded in Section IV (Disciplinary Procedures) of this handbook.

The confusion should be apparent. The employer, in the disclaimer, states that the company is reserving the employment-at-will prerogative. However, in the employee discipline policy, the employer appears to tell employees that they will be terminated only for "just cause." In instances where employers make statements in writing that employees will be terminated only for just cause, some courts have held that the employee can then be discharged only for just cause, even though the employee had no guarantee of employment for a definitive period.[42]

The lesson for managers and HR professionals is quite simple. Employers should audit employee handbooks and remove any language that contradicts employment-at-will disclaimers. In the event of contradictions, courts are more likely to interpret the implied contract's terms in favor of the employee.

ENSURING DUE PROCESS

Due process refers here to an employee's right to fair and consistent treatment in regard to terms and conditions of employment.[43] Simply stated, due process is the employee's guarantee against arbitrary and capricious treatment in the workplace.

Public sector (or government) employees enjoy far stronger due process protection than their private sector counterparts. Public sector employees have a significant amount of workplace protection because of their unique position as citizen-employees. The Fifth and Fourteenth Amendments, guaranteeing due process and protecting citizens from arbitrary actions by the government, carry over into public sector work environments. The Fourth Amendment protects them from unreasonable searches in their workplaces, in most instances. In its employee relations, the government must walk a fine line between its rights as an employer and its employees' rights as citizens.

In the private workplace, due process is not quite the same as due process of law and is, in most instances, not a statutory right—particularly in an employment-at-will environment. This does not imply that private sector workplaces are without due process protection. Providing for due process (even in the absence of a legal requirement to do so) is the ethical approach to follow: it is simply the right thing to do. Furthermore, it is a sound management practice that benefits the organization by creating positive employee-management relations.

At times, private sector employers may find themselves legally obligated to provide for due process through collective bargaining agreements, explicit contracts, or implicit contracts. Since most employee handbooks cover such matters as disciplinary actions and terminations, it is not surprising that they often provide procedures by which such determinations are made. Once an employer has committed to these procedures in writing, then he or she is expected to follow them.

One of the ways in which employers can ensure that they are providing for adequate due process is through proper in-house investigations. A properly conducted in-house investigation not only helps employers document that steps were taken to find the facts surrounding work rule violations, it further ensures any discipline taken by the employer was justified and fairly imposed. When offering employees due process, it is important

Figure 12.4 Douglas McGregor's Hot Stove Principle

- Like a hot stove, which burns immediately, disciplinary actions should be administered quickly.
- Like a hot stove, which gives a warning, so too should discipline.
- Like a hot stove, which consistently burns everyone who touches it, discipline should be applied to all employees who violate the rule.
- Like a hot stove, which burns everyone in the same manner, regardless of who they are, discipline must be impartially imposed.

Source: D. McGregor, "Hot Stove Rules of Discipline," in *Personnel: The Human Problems of Management*, ed. G. Strauss and L. Sayles (Englewood Cliffs, NJ: Prentice Hall, 1967).

to note that you are not only guaranteeing them fair treatment, you are also promising them two forms of due process: substantive and procedural.

Substantive Versus Procedural Due Process

Substantive due process focuses on the purpose or the reason for employment practices so as to ensure that an employee has not been arbitrarily disciplined or terminated.[44] Substantive due process assures employees that no disciplinary action shall be taken against any employee unless there is clear and convincing evidence that the employee committed a disciplinary offense.

Another element of substantive due process is ensuring the disciplinary action imposed on the offender is appropriate for the offense committed. This is sometimes referred to as "distributive justice."[45] In a more simplistic way, it answers the question, "Does the punishment fit the crime?" If the employer's disciplinary actions are judged by the employees to be too harsh (or too lenient in some cases), the employer will have failed to provide adequate substantive due process. For example, a policy that calls for immediate termination the first time an employee returns late from a break might appear arbitrary and unduly harsh to many employees.

A final element of substantive due process involves the consistent application of an organization's disciplinary policies to all employees. That is to say, disciplinary actions are imposed equally on all offenders. A good gauge to follow is that of Douglas McGregor's well-known Hot Stove Principle.

According to McGregor, discipline operates like a hot stove in four basic ways (see Figure 12.4). First, discipline should be immediate. It should be administered as soon after the offense is committed as is practical, which does not mean managers should rush to judge. Rather, as soon as the investigation results confirm that a disciplinary offense occurred, the disciplinary consequences should be imposed. This strengthens the cause-and-effect relationship between the offense and the disciplinary action.

Second, like a hot stove, the organization's disciplinary policies should give a warning. As one gets closer to a hot stove, the warmer or hotter it becomes. Similarly, the closer an individual's action gets to violating a work rule or company policy, the more averse attention that employee should draw. There is an old axiom in employee discipline that no disciplinary action should come as a surprise. The employee should be told of the rule and informed that he or she is violating or close to violating the rule. As the employee comes closer to a violation, the warnings should become stronger.

Third, discipline must be consistent. Like the hot stove that burns anyone and everyone who touches it, disciplinary actions should be imposed on every employee who violates the policy. It does not matter who the employee is or whether he or she has a good or poor work record; the individual is held accountable for the action.

Finally, discipline must be impartial. Disciplinary actions are based on the magnitude of the offense, just like the severity of the burn increases the longer you touch the hot stove. This is really the distributive justice concept all over again. An employee who commits a major offense (i.e., theft of company property) should be subjected to greater punishment than an employee who commits a lesser offense (i.e., tardiness as a first offense).

Procedural due process refers here to the fairness of the procedure used by the organization in determining whether its work rules or policies have been violated. Procedural due process focuses on such factors as notifying the accused party of the allegations against him or her. It also includes affording the accused a hearing with an opportunity to respond to the allegations and present witnesses and evidence to support his or her position before an impartial party or parties. Thus, procedural due process is provided when any accused party is permitted to respond to charges in an impartial forum.

In-house investigations will provide procedural due process if they are pursued from a fact-finding standpoint. Any internal process that is pursued strictly from the standpoint of "building a case" against one party or the other provides neither substantive nor procedural justice and may open an employer to further litigation. When investigations are embarked upon to prove guilt and not find the facts, the organization has set itself up to be accused of constructive discharge.

Conducting In-House Investigations

Whether confronted with establishing a just cause discharge or a complaint of unlawful discrimination, it is absolutely essential that HR professionals have policies and procedures in place to investigate such allegations. No organization should take an adverse action against any employee before it has gathered sufficient information to substantiate that such action is necessary. In short, an employee should not be held accountable for a work rule violation until you have enough information to indicate that he or she did indeed violate the rule. Employers and their representatives often get themselves into trouble when they react before finding enough facts or hearing the accused employee's side of the story (see Figure 12.5).

Take, for example, an incident that involved a hospital administrator who was charged with sexual harassment by three of his female subordinates. The hospital's sexual harassment policy had been disseminated to its employees. The policy contained a process for filing complaints as well as an alternative process in the event that a direct supervisor

Figure 12.5   **Errors to Avoid When Conducting Investigations**

- Failing to investigate
- Excessive delays in starting the investigation
- Inconsistency
- Retaliation
- Lack of thoroughness in the investigation
- Inappropriate disclosure of confidential information
- Losing objectivity
- Strong-arm interview tactics
- Invasion of employee's privacy
- Inadequate feedback to the parties during the investigation process

Source: L. Guerin, *The Essential Guide to Workplace Investigations: How to Handle Complaints & Problems,* 2d ed. (Berkeley, CA: Nolo, 2010).

was involved in the alleged harassment. The hospital was also aware of the potential liability it faced in the event of *quid pro quo* sexual harassment (see Chapter 5). Realizing the administrator had placed the hospital in jeopardy by engaging in the sexual harassment of three female subordinates, the administrator's superiors confronted him. Immediately after being informed of the charges made against him, the administrator was fired. The hospital believed it had taken immediate and prompt corrective action that would then guarantee the harassment would not recur. However, in its rush to judgment, the hospital failed to verify that any sexual harassment had actually occurred. The administrator was terminated merely on the unsubstantiated accusation that he had harassed the three women. No investigation had been launched by the hospital, nor had the administrator been afforded any opportunity to defend himself against the allegations.

Fortunately for the administrator, he was a contractual employee and could not be fired except for just cause. In the absence of an investigation, this was difficult for the hospital to establish. During the protracted litigation that ensued (breach of contract), two of the women eventually came forward with a confession that their sexual harassment complaint had been a fabrication. It seems the administrator was a very demanding boss. The women thought that if they made a sexual harassment complaint against him, the administrator would back off from the demanding management style. They had never intended for him to lose his job, only for him to stop supervising them so closely. Things had quickly gotten out of hand, however. In the end, the hospital paid a sizable damage award for breaching the contract and defaming the administrator's good name—all because it acted without first investigating.

What follows is a description of a generic investigation. Think of it as the bare-bones essentials that any investigation should possess. Remember, the more complicated the allegations, the greater the amount of detail that must be examined in the investigation. Still, the process of fact-finding is essentially the same. Whether for sexual harassment or for willful destruction of company property, appropriate organizational responses follow the same general process:

1. A complaint or allegation is received.
2. An investigation is conducted.
3. Appropriate corrective action is implemented.
4. Management monitors affected employees to ensure that desired results occur.

Receiving a Complaint

The first thing HR professionals must remember about any complaint or reported violation is that it may not be truthful or factual. It goes without saying that the complaint should be documented. It is also imperative that whoever is assigned the task of investigating the allegation approach this task in an impartial manner. If the investigation is not conducted in an impartial manner, it will not be a proper investigation and could be subject to later legal challenges.

It is important to keep the complaint and the proceedings as confidential *as possible*.[46] We say *as possible* because, in the event of litigation or intervention by a government agency (i.e., Equal Employment Opportunity Commission [EEOC], Office of Federal Contract Compliance Programs [OFCCP], National Labor Relations Board [NLRB], etc.), the employer may be compelled to disclose all materials to the government. This fact should be conveyed to the parties involved in the investigation. However, barring a subpoena from a court or agency, it is advisable to avoid disclosure, because of potential defamation allegations.

It is important to let both parties know that the organization cannot guarantee that the matter under investigation can be kept confidential permanently. To promise absolute confidentiality could actually expose the employer to litigation. However, making the parties aware that no permanent offer of confidentiality exists may reduce the employer's exposure to potential breach of contract litigation by eliminating the employee's argument that he or she justifiably relied on defendant's alleged promise of permanent confidentiality in cooperating in the investigation.[47]

The Investigation

Investigations are exercises in fact-finding. Generally, investigations should be structured to answer questions that will establish either that an organizational policy or work rule was violated or that it was not. Some of the typical questions that should be asked are listed in Figure 12.6.

In the event of an incident in which witnesses were present, written statements regarding what they saw should be collected as soon as possible. Witnesses should put their observations in their own words. Avoid having supervisors or any other company representative "coach" the witnesses on their responses. Also avoid questions that support the answer you are looking for or want to hear[48]—so-called *leading questions*. These actions could be construed as the organization's trying to coerce the witnesses into fabricating testimony to support the company's interests. HR professionals must go to great lengths to ensure that facts (not just collaborating evidence) are gathered and that the investigation is systematic and fair throughout.

Figure 12.6   **Questions to Answer When Conducting Investigations**

- What happened?
- When did it happen?
- What did you do or observe?
- What is the background of the incident?
- What documentation or physical evidence is present?
- Who else witnessed the incident?
- What were their observations?

Figure 12.7   **Findings from Investigations**

- Is the alleged perpetrator innocent or guilty?
- If innocent, what should be done to maintain or restore his or her credibility?
- If guilty, how serious was the infraction of organizational rules?
- What other policies were violated?
- Was the violation intentional or unintentional?
- Was the violator aware of the organizational policy or work rule?
- Was the violator cooperative in the investigation?
- Were there other violators?
- What corrective action is appropriate?
- What corrective action has the organization imposed for similar violations in the past?

Sources: Bureau of National Affairs, *Sexual Harassment: Employer Policies and Problems* (Washington, DC: Bureau of National Affairs, 1987); W.S. Hubbartt, *Personnel Policy Handbook: How to Develop a Manual That Works* (New York: McGraw-Hill, 1993).

Taking Appropriate Corrective Action

In the event that the facts indicate a violation has indeed occurred, the next step is to determine the appropriate corrective action that must be taken. When an organization takes any corrective action, including disciplinary action, the punishment should always fit the violation (see Figure 12.7). After any corrective action has been administered, it is incumbent upon managers to monitor the employee to see if the desired behavioral changes have occurred.

Negligent Hiring and Misrepresentation

Negligent hiring has become a significant source of employment litigation. This is a tort arising from state law and varies to some degree from state to state.[49] In general, **negligent hiring** becomes actionable when an employer fails to exercise ordinary care in hiring or retaining an employee and that employee creates a foreseeable risk of harm to a third party.[50] For example, assume an employer hires a programmer analyst who is known to have been terminated from her previous place of employment for threatening a coworker with physical violence.

Shortly after the programmer analyst was employed, she physically assaults an auditor from the accounting department following an argument over a program's output. The employer could be held liable for the injuries sustained by the auditor if the following can be established: The employer knew or reasonably should have known of the employee's tendency toward violence (or even incompetence), the employee in question committed a tortuous act against the third party, and the employer owes a duty of care to third parties within the zone of foreseeable risks created by the employment relationship.[51] In this example, the employer knew the new programmer analyst had a record of violent behavior.

The programmer analyst assaulted and injured a coworker, a third party. The employer owes its employees a safe work environment and jeopardized that safety interest by knowingly hiring a volatile programmer analyst. Therefore, the company has committed negligent hiring.

Negligent retention, sometimes called **negligent supervision**, is very similar to negligent hiring. Negligent retention is a cause of action under tort law by which an employer is liable for the damages caused by an employee when the employer knew that the employee posed a danger to others and failed to remove the employee from his/her position of responsibility.[52] Knowingly retaining a dangerous employee thus increases the employer's exposure to liability in the event that a coworker or third party suffers harm.[53] Here, the knowledge that an employee presents a danger to coworkers or other third parties (through violent behavior, sexual harassment, or incompetence) is based on the employee's demonstrated performance or behavior.[54] To illustrate this slight distinction, consider the scenario concerning negligent hiring. Expanding the scenario to include the following situation will provide a good example of negligent retention. Since beginning employment, the programmer analyst has repeatedly been counseled about her violent outbursts when contradicted by coworkers. She has, on at least four occasions, verbally assaulted and physically threatened coworkers, as demonstrated by formal complaints made against her.

Despite the employer's knowledge of the programmer analyst's ongoing violent behavior, she has not been terminated, or even disciplined, for her actions. When the programmer analyst finally physically assaults a coworker, the employer may be held liable for the coworker's injuries. Although aware of the programmer analyst's violent behavior, the employer failed to make reasonable efforts to prevent injury to others.[55]

Not only may employers be held liable for injuries to third parties caused by current employees, they may be held liable for injuries caused by former employees.

Under **negligent misrepresentation**, sometimes called negligent referral, an employer can be held responsible for acts of workplace violence or incompetence at a former employee's new place of employment. This is only an issue when the former employer provides a positive recommendation or evaluation of the former employee's performance and knowingly conceals incidents of workplace violence,[56] inability to perform critical work tasks, fraudulent/criminal activities, or sexual harassment that may place others at risk.

In order to establish an employer's negligent misrepresentation, the complaining party must demonstrate that the former employer knowingly provided false information to the new employer, the new employer relied on that false information in making an employment decision, and the new employer was exposed to liability for injuries to a third party because of the reliance on false information.[57] Assume that an employer gives a positive recommendation regarding a former employee to his or her new employer, but fails to mention that the employee had been disciplined on a number of occasions for workplace violence. Later, the former employee becomes violent at his or her new place of employment and injures a coworker. The former employer may be liable for his or her misrepresentation.[58] Even if the previous employer is asked about a former employee (one with a record of violence or fraud) and makes no comment, that employer could be liable for the former employee's misconduct.[59]

The lesson for HR professionals is simple. To prevent negligent hiring, thorough background investigations should be conducted, and applicants with potential liability problems should be screened. To avoid negligent retention charges, employees who pose a threat to the safety and health of others, even with training and counseling, and those who cannot perform their duties should be removed from the workplace. Finally, when giving reference information to potential employers on former employees, employers should provide only factual information in order to avoid negligent misrepresentation. To avoid potential defamation, there should be documentation on hand to substantiate the former employee's performance or misconduct. There is no law that requires an employer to provide a recommendation, good or bad, for a former employee. However, if a recommendation is provided, it must be honest.

SUMMARY

This chapter examined employment-at-will, employee handbooks, and employee discipline issues. Employment-at-will is based on the notion that if the employee can terminate the employment relationship at any time, the employer is free to do the same. It should be clear that when it comes to an employer's employment-at-will rights, there is less there than meets the eye. In reality, there appear to be very few situations under which an employer may actually terminate employees for bad reasons or no reasons at all, and the erosion of employment-at-will has placed an ever-increasing burden on employers to demonstrate that terminations are justified.

Although employee handbooks have contributed to the erosion of employment-at-will terminations, they provide far more benefit as a means for justifying legitimate employer actions. It is important that employee handbooks be thorough. However, they should be easy to read and understood by all of the company's employees.

Whatever employment practices or policies an employer creates and enforces, these must be perceived as justified and fair by the employees if they are to be effective. This means ensuring employees are aware of the policies, the rationale behind them, and the consequences for violating them. A burden is therefore placed on all managers to not only be familiar with the employer's workplace rules but also to make efforts to ensure that they are fairly enforced. And, as a final word of caution, employers should never take disciplinary action unless there is evidence (as the result of a proper investigation) that the individual employee did indeed commit the disciplinary offense.

Thus, it is a good idea to provide due process to all employees. Due process is the employee's guarantee against arbitrary and capricious treatment. Unfortunately, only public sector employees enjoy significant due process protection in the workplace.

Employers may also be held liable for negligent hiring, negligent retention, or negligent misrepresentation. It is imperative that employers protect themselves from negligent hiring claims through the pre-employment screening process, from negligent retention actions by acting swiftly to terminate employees who cause a threat to coworkers and other third parties, and from negligent misrepresentation situations by providing only factual information on past employees when it is requested.

KEY TERMS AND CONCEPTS

Due process	Negligent retention
Employment-at-will	Negligent supervision
Explicit contract	Procedural due process
Implied contract	Public policy
Just cause statute	Substantive due process
Negligent hiring	Whistleblower clauses
Negligent misrepresentation	

DISCUSSION QUESTIONS

1. Under the employment-at-will doctrine, an employee may be terminated for what three reasons (*Payne v. Western and Atlantic Railroad Co.*)?
2. What are four limitations to the employment-at-will doctrine? Provide an example of each.
3. Why would some HR professionals call employee handbooks a double-edged sword? Why would an employer need to have an employee handbook?
4. What is due process? Distinguish between substantive and procedural due process.
5. When conducting an in-house investigation, what are the primary concerns of the investigator?
6. Distinguish between negligent hiring, negligent retention, and negligent misrepresentation.

CASES

Case 1

On March 17, 2014, Bonnie Van Ness was injured when the car that she was driving was struck by a Millstone Enterprises delivery truck driven by David LeRoi, who had run a red light.[60] David LeRoi's blood alcohol level was found to be .20 following the accident. At the time of the accident, David LeRoi was acting in the course and scope of his employment with Millstone Enterprises.

In October 2012, David had been stopped in a state police roadblock checking driver's licenses and at that time was found to have been driving under the influence of alcohol (with a blood alcohol level of .10). Since David was in a company vehicle, he was reprimanded and given an adverse counseling statement.

In May 2013, David's driver's license was suspended for six months due to his second DUI conviction. As this involved his personal car during nonwork time, his supervisor decided to assign him to work on the loading dock until his driver's license would be returned. On October 12, 2013, David returned to his duties as a delivery driver.

However, David appeared disoriented on January 16, 2014. He had trouble standing and his speech was slurred. His supervisor smelled bourbon on his breath and asked him to submit to a blood test. When David refused, he was suspended for three days without pay. Upon returning to work, David was informed that if he ever reported to work in that condition again, he would be fired on the spot. There were no further incidents until the accident of March 17.

Can Bonnie Van Ness sue David LeRoi's employer for negligent retention? Why?

Case 2

Marvin was employed as a teacher for a privately owned school in Katy, TX which employs 7 full-time and 7 part-time staff. On June 21, 2013, his acting immediate supervisor, Margaret, asked him to drive a van of preschool children to the Children's Museum for a scheduled field trip. Marvin informed Margaret that he did not have the requisite Class C Texas Commercial Driver's license necessary to drive a school bus or van. Margaret asked Marvin if he knew how to drive a van. He replied yes. She then told Marvin that he had a choice, he could either drive the kids to the museum or he could drive himself home and not come back.

When Marvin told her that it was against the law for him to drive the students to the museum, Margaret repeated her demand. When he still refused, Margaret said, "It looks like somebody is going home."

When Marvin appeared at work the following day, a new teacher was in his classroom. When he approached the owner, Lynn, he was told he did not work there anymore. Marvin claimed he was wrongfully terminated, to which Lynn replied he was terminated for insubordination. "Besides," she said, "you are an at-will employee." On June 26, 2013, after filing an internal complaint, the complaining party resigned from his employment and went directly to the EEOC.

    a. Does Marvin have a Title VII complaint? Why?
    b. Does Marvin have any legal recourses against his employment-at-will status?

NOTES

1. This scenario was developed from the facts in *Rosen v. Gulf Shores, Inc.*, 610 S0.2d 366 (Miss. 1992).

2. *Payne v. Western & Atlantic Railroad Co.*, 81 Tenn. 507, 518 (1884).

3. F.B. Cross and R.L. Miller, *West's Legal Environment of Business*, 6th ed. (St. Paul, MN: South-Western College/West Publishing, 2006).

4. R.L. Miller and G.A. Jentz, *Fundamentals of Business Law*, 6th ed. (Mason, OH: Thomson; South-Western, 2005).

5. Ibid.

6. Ibid.

7. Montana Code Annotated § 39–2-901 *et seq.* (2012).

8. Montana Code Annotated § 39–2-904(b).

9. *Bourdelais v. Semitool, Inc.*, 77 P.3d 555 (Mon. Sup Ct. 2003).

10. Montana Code § 39-2-904.

11. J.J. Fitzpatrick, Jr., and J.L. Perine, "State Labor Legislation Enacted in 2007," *Monthly Labor Review* 131, no. 1 (2008): 3–31.

12. 20 U.S.C. § 2001 *et seq.* (2012).

13. J.J. Fitzpatrick, Jr., and J.L. Perine, "State Labor Legislation Enacted in 2007."

14. USERRA Project.org, State Reemployment Rights and Laws for Service Members, www.user-raproject.org (accessed August 5, 2008).

15. 29 U.S.C. 1001 *et seq.*; 29 U.S.C. § 651 *et seq.*; 29 U.S.C. § 201 *et seq.*; 42 U.S.C. § 2000e *et seq.*

16. 42 U.S.C. § 2000e-5.

17. 29 Cal. Rptr. 399 (1963).

18. *Boyd v. Winton Hills Medical & Health Center, Inc.*, 711 N.E. 2d 1014 (Ohio 1999).

19. *Abels v. Renfro Corp.*, 436 S.E. 2d 822, 826 (N.C. 1993).

20. C. Muhl, "The Employment At Will Doctrine: Three Major Exceptions," *Monthly Labor Review* 124, no. 1 (2001): 3–11.

21. Bureau of National Affairs, *Employment Guide* (Washington, DC: Bureau of National Affairs, 1991), volume 10, pp. 87–88.

22. 364 N.E. 2d 1251 (Mass. 1977).

23. Ibid. at 1254.

24. *Firgeleski v. Hubbell, Inc.*, 1999 Conn. Super. LEXIS 397; *Raffaele v. Ryder Dedicated Logistics, Inc.*, 931 F. Supp. 76 (D. Mass. 1996); *Gupta v. New Britain General Hospital*, 687 A.2d 111 (Conn. 1996).

25. Cross and Miller, *West's Legal Environment of Business*, pp. 181–185.

26. *Nuwer v. Mariner Post-Acute Network*, 332 F.3d 310, 314 (5th Cir. 2003). *HeartSouth PLLC v. Boyd*, 865 S0.2d 1095, 1108 (Miss. 2003).

27. *Foley v. Interactive Data Corp.*, 765 P.2d 373, 385 (Cal. 1988); *Ryan v. Upchurch*, 474 F.Supp. 211, 213 (S.D. Ind. 1979).

28. *Toussaint v. Blue Cross and Blue Shield*, 408 Mich. 579 (Mich. 1980).

29. *Ebling v. Masco Corp.*, 292 N.W. 2d 880 (Mich. 1980).

30. *Dubard v. Biloxi H.M.A., Inc.*, 1999 Miss. App. LEXIS 468 (October 19, 1999).

31. *Toussaint v. Blue Cross and Blue Shield*, at 610.

32. Ibid. at 614.

33. 29 C.F.R. § 1604.11 App. A and 29 C.F.R. § 1606 App. A.

34. *Faragher v. City of Boca Raton*, 524 U.S. 775, 804 (1998); *Burlington Industries v. Ellerth*, 524 U.S. 742, 764 (1998); *Kolstad v. American Dental Association*, 527 U.S. 526 (1999).

35. W.S. Hubbartt, *Personnel Policy Handbook: How to Develop a Manual That Works* (New York: McGraw-Hill, 1993); J. Luna, "Case Studies," *CCH Ideas and Trends* (Chicago: Commerce Clearing House, August 30, 1995).

36. National Institute for Literacy, Fast Facts on Adult Literacy (2007), http://nces.ed.gov/fastfacts/display.asp?id=69 (accessed January 30, 2008).

37. National Institute for Literacy, Facts on Literacy. http://literacy.kent.edu/NEABLE/facts.html (accessed January 30, 2008).

38. P. Falcone, *101 Tough Conversations to Have with Employees: A Manager's Guide to Addressing Performance, Conduct, and Discipline* (New York: AMACOM Books, 2009).

39. *Fox v. T-H Continental, Ltd.*, 78 F.3d 409 (8th Cir. 1996).

40. *Ridenhour v. IBM Corp.*, 512 S.E. 2d 774 (N.C. App. 1999).

41. *Leikvold v. Valley View Community Hosp.*, 688 P.2d 170, 174 (Ariz. 1984).

42. *Goodyear Tire and Rubber Company v. Portilla*, 879 S.W.2d 47, 52 (Tex. 1994).

43. Y.T. Abraham and E.B. Flippo, *Managing a Changing Workforce* (Chicago: Commerce Clearing House, 1991).

44. W.H. Holley and K.M. Jennings, *The Labor Relations Process*, 5th ed. (Fort Worth, TX: The Dryden Press, 1994).

45. D. McGregor, "Hot Stove Rules of Discipline." In *Personnel: The Human Problems of Management*, ed. G. Strauss and L. Sayles (Englewood Cliffs, NJ: Prentice Hall, 1967).

46. P.R. Garber, *Conducting Workplace Investigations (HR Skills Series)* (Amherst, MA: HRD Press, Inc., 2009).

47. *Lau's Corp. v. Haskins*, 405 S.E.2d 474, 476 (Ga. 1991).

48. L. Guerin, *The Essential Guide to Workplace Investigations: How to Handle Employee Complaints and Problems* (Berkley, CA: Nolo, 2010).

49. A. Long, "Addressing the Cloud over Employee References: A Survey of Recently Enacted State Legislation," *William and Mary Law Review* 39 (1997): 177–183.

50. *Pennington v. Dollar Tree Stores, Inc.*, 104 F.Supp.2d 710, 715 (E.D. Ky. 2000).

51. G. Befort, "Pre-Employment Screening and Investigation: Navigating Between a Rock and a Hard Place," *Hofstra Labor Law Journal* 14 (1997): 365, 376.

52. J. Levashina and M.A. Campion, "Expected Practices in Background Checking: Review of the Human Resource Management Literature," *Employee Responsibilities and Rights Journal*, 21 no. 3 (2009): 231–249.

53. *Campbell v. Humphries*, 353 Fed. Appx. 334 (11th Cir. 2009).

54. K.L. Stone, "License to Harass: Holding Defendants Accountable for Retaining Recidivist Harassers," *Akron Law Review* 41, no. 4 (2008): 1059–1090; T.M. Winn, "Labor and Employment Law," *University of Richmond Law Review* 35 (2001): 725–740.

55. *Ponticas v. K.M.S. Investment*, 331 N.W.2d 907, 915 (Minn. 1983).

56. *Randi W. v. Muroc Joint Unified School Dist.*, 929 P.2d 582, 595 (Cal. 1997).

57. J. Davis, "Survey of Developments in North Carolina and the Fourth Circuit, 1999: Potential Violence to the Bottom Line—Expanding Employer Liability for Acts of Workplace Violence," *North Carolina Law Review* 78 (2000): 2067.

58. *Davis v. Board of County Commissioners*, 987 P.2d 1172 (N.M. Ct. App. 1999).

59. J.W. Belknap, "Defamation, Negligent Referral, and the World of Employment References," *Journal of Small and Emerging Business Law* 5 (2001): 113–134.

60. Parts of this scenario were developed from the findings of fact in *Marquis v. State Farm Fire & Casualty Insurance*, 961 P.2d 1213 (Sup.Ct. Kan. 1998).

13

PRIVACY AND RECENT DEVELOPMENTS IN EMPLOYMENT REGULATION

LEARNING OBJECTIVES

- Identify those circumstances in which an employer may violate an employee's privacy interests.
- Describe how absolute privilege and qualified privilege may reduce an employer's exposure to litigation.
- Explain the circumstances under which an employer might lawfully monitor employee e-mail.
- Identify the conditions under which an employer may enforce employee weight and no-smoking policies in the workplace.
- Explain the circumstances under which an employer might lawfully implement and enforce an employee appearance policy/dress code.

OPENING SCENARIO

CTE Telecommunication Company, a private, for-profit company operating in the Rocky Mountain states, runs the CTE Communications Center located on the top floor of the Van Ness Building in Clear Water Springs, CO. The center maintains communication between the company's various operating units and the senior executive on duty, but it does not have primary corporate responsibility for security and it does not house communication switching centers, cables, transmission lines, or related equipment. However, for security reasons, access to the center is restricted; both the elevator foyer on the top floor and the doors to the center itself are inaccessible without a control card.

CTE employs John Daniel, Ray Juergens, and others as attendants (known colloquially as "security operators") in the center. They monitor computer banks to detect signals emanating from alarm systems at CTE facilities throughout the Mountain region, and they alert the appropriate authorities if an alarm sounds. Although individual employees work eight-hour shifts, the center is staffed around the clock.

The workspace inside the center consists of a large L-shaped area that contains the computers, the monitors, and assorted furniture (e.g., desks, chairs, consoles). The workspace is completely open, and no individual employee has an assigned office, cubicle, workstation, or desk.

CTE installed a video surveillance system at the center in 2005 but abandoned the project when employees complained. In June of 2009, the company reinstated video surveillance. Three cameras survey the workspace and a fourth tracks all traffic passing through the main entrance to the center. None of them covers the rest area. The surveillance is exclusively visual; the cameras have no microphones or other immediate eavesdropping capability. Video surveillance operates all day, every day; the cameras implacably record every act undertaken in the work area. A video monitor, a switcher unit, and a video recorder are located in the office of the center's general manager, Dave Nichols, and the videotapes are stored there. CTE has no written policy regulating any aspect of the video surveillance, but it is undisputed that no one can view either the monitor or the completed tapes without Nichols's express permission.

Soon after CTE installed the surveillance system (claiming that it was desirable for security reasons), Daniel and Juergens and several fellow employees protested. They asserted, among other things, that the system had no purpose other than to pry into employees' behavior. When management turned a deaf ear, the appellants filed suit in the federal district court. They contended that the ongoing surveillance constitutes an unreasonable search prohibited by the Fourth Amendment, violating a constitutionally conferred entitlement to privacy.[1]

PRIVACY ISSUES

Privacy expectations of employees in both the public and private sectors have increased with the expansion of employee rights in the workplace. However, there is still a good deal of misconception about what privacy might truly exist in workplace settings. As will soon be shown, the degree to which employees are afforded privacy protection hinges on whether the employee works for a public or private sector employer. Employee privacy protection will be divided into three general categories for discussion in this chapter: public disclosure of employee information, defamation, and invasion of privacy.

Disclosure of Employee Information

Most Americans are aware that, as citizens of the United States, they are endowed with certain rights to privacy that are protected by the Constitution.[2] However, many individuals do not understand that these constitutional protections are limited only to intrusion into their privacy by governments (federal, state, or local).[3] Although some states (most notably Michigan and California) have enacted laws specifically protecting individual privacy rights in the private sector, the majority have not.[4] On the whole, there are very few statutory prohibitions on nongovernmental employers that cover invasion of privacy other than the state tort laws previously mentioned. Simply stated, employees in the public sector enjoy far greater privacy protection than their private sector counterparts because their employers are governmental entities.[5]

Since the privacy statutes do not differentiate between intrusion from the government as an information seeker or as an employer, the result is that the personnel records of government employees are entitled to far greater protection from public access. For example, a government employee, as a citizen, has certain rights to privacy protection from the government, which is also his employer. In the private sector, there are far fewer prohibitions on public disclosure of personnel documents. State tort statutes may, however, provide some recourse and protection against disclosure of certain private sector personnel records.

Disclosure of Personnel Records

Disclosure of information about employees is a major privacy concern for HR professionals. Although few laws regulate private sector employers' personnel records, tort action under slander and libel create a substantial incentive to safeguard employee information. Both terms relate to injury to the employee that results from public disclosure of information about that employee. If the information is disclosed orally, it may be slander; if in writing, it is potentially libelous. To be either one, the comments must challenge the employee's reputation in the community.

Because personal records are required to document employer's claims that personnel decisions are based on business reasons, most employment records are kept on file for a period of years.

Disclosure of Medical Records and Information

Two federal statutes, the Health Insurance Portability and Accountability Act (HIPPA) and the Americans with Disability Act (ADA), require employers to take particular precautions regarding the disclosure of employee medical information. When employees bring privacy-related legal action against their employers, it is often for invasion of privacy. State tort law governs employees' right to privacy in the private sector workplace. A "tort" is merely a wrong or injury that is actionable in court. There are four torts that cover an individual's right to privacy: unreasonable intrusion upon the seclusion of another, publicity that unreasonably places another in a false light before the community, unreasonable publicity given to another's private life, and misappropriation of another's name or likeness.[6] Most employer surveillance and monitoring activities are likely to be challenged on the grounds that such activities are an unreasonable intrusion into the employee's private affairs. Employer disclosure of employee information or records is either litigated as an unreasonable publication of the employee's private life or as placing the employee in a false light in the community.

Employee Polygraph Protection Act

The Employee Polygraph Protection Act of 1988 (EPPA) makes it unlawful for most private sector employers to require applicants to submit to a lie detector test as a condition of employment.[7] Nor can an employer discharge or discipline an employee for refusing to take a lie detector test except under circumstances involving theft if, "during

Figure 13.1 **Firms Exempted Under the Employee Polygraph Protection Act**

- Armored car companies
- Banking institutions
- Federal contractors in intelligence and counterintelligence work
- Federal government
- Local governments
- Pharmaceutical companies
- Security alarm services
- Security companies
- State governments

the normal course of a subsequent investigation, [law enforcement] authorities deem it necessary to administer a polygraph test to an employee(s) suspected of involvement in the reported incident."[8] This means that an employee reasonably suspected of committing the Act may be required to submit to a polygraph test. However, to require all employees in a department or section to undergo polygraph testing in hopes of finding the culprit (so-called fishing expeditions) would violate the Act.

The EPPA uses the terms "polygraph" and "lie detector" interchangeably. As defined in the Act, a "lie detector" includes "a polygraph, deceptograph, voice stress analyzer, psychological stress evaluator, or other similar device (whether mechanical or electrical) that is used, or the results of which are used, for the purpose of rendering a diagnostic opinion regarding the honesty or dishonesty of an individual."[9]

Not all employers are covered under the EPPA—there are specific exemptions (see Figure 13.1). For one, all governmental agencies at the local, state, and federal level can use lie detector/polygraph testing in their pre-employment screening.[10] This government exemption also applies to federal contractors engaged in security intelligence or counterintelligence work.[11] Applicants for jobs with security firms (armored car services, security alarm providers, or security guards) can also be required to submit to polygraph tests.[12] Banks and similar financial institutions may also use polygraphs in pre-employment screening[13] as may pharmaceutical companies.[14]

Invasion of Privacy and Defamation

By disclosing an employee's performance appraisal results, a company may run afoul of the common law torts of invasion of privacy and defamation. These state tort laws would also apply to private organizations not explicitly covered by state privacy legislation.

Invasion of privacy and defamation claims address the manner and scope of disclosing highly personal matters such as an employee's qualifications and performance.[15] **Defamation** is distinguished from invasion of privacy in that defamation focuses on injury to the employee's reputation, while privacy torts are tied to the resulting emotional injury. Defamation laws may vary in their specific provisions from state to state, but they all possess some generic elements.[16] In defamation, the aggrieved party must demonstrate that:

1. *A statement was made concerning the individual.* In the case of performance information, this statement could involve whether the employee adequately performed assigned tasks, failed to follow instructions, missed deadlines, and so forth.
2. *The statement was presented as fact and is substantially false.* This may be very susceptible to the reliability and validity of the performance appraisal instrument. If the instrument is flawed, a strong argument could be made that its inferences about an employee's work performance are false. This would be particularly true if an instrument purporting to measure performance was overly subjective or measured nonwork-related behaviors.
3. *The statement impugned the employee's character or abilities and caused actual injury to his or her reputation.* This element is particularly worrisome to HR professionals as any poor evaluation of an employee that is publicized would undoubtedly have disastrous effects on his or her reputation at that organization, or even within the industry, as in the case of higher-level employees.
4. *In order to be actionable, the defamatory statement must be "published."* Making public statements about the employee in question is an example.

Employer Defenses against Defamation

When confronted with a defamation charge, the employer would have three general defenses on which to rely. The first defense would be to demonstrate that the statement was true. The truth is proof against defamation.[17] In cases involving the disclosure of performance information, a validated performance appraisal becomes indispensable. The statement made by the organization would not be "substantially false," and the complaining party would be unable to establish defamation if the performance appraisal is valid and substantiated.

Failing to establish this, the employer may resort to two other defenses based on either an *absolute privilege* or *qualified privilege* regarding the dissemination of any employee information. The term "privilege" in a legal context refers to an organization's exemption from liability for speaking or publishing defamatory words concerning an individual. Qualified privilege (also called conditional privilege) may also be asserted as a defamation defense in an employment context. In the instance of **qualified privilege**, immunity is based on the fact that the statement was made in the performance of some judicial, social, or personal duty.[18] Under this doctrine, the employer would have to demonstrate that the published communication (e.g., teaching evaluation scores for a university instructor) was made in good faith between the concerned parties with a common interest in the subject matter addressed.[19] Unlike absolute privilege, qualified privilege may be lost or exceeded.[20]

To illustrate this point, the employer could attempt to justify its disclosure of an instructor's teaching evaluations as relevant to students' matriculation as it ensures that students can select the more effective instructors. This is assuming, of course, that the teaching evaluations accurately measure teaching effectiveness and course knowledge.

However, even if this is substantiated to the satisfaction of a court, the employer could still lose its qualified privilege based on "abuse" through excessive publication of the defamatory information. Abuse of privilege can occur when the information in question is accessible to parties to whom the privilege does not apply, in this case, nonstudents.[21] An illustrative example of how this could occur may be an instance where a faculty member is applying for a position at another institution and the published teaching evaluations fall into the hands of the prospective employer. This would be a particular problem if the faculty member's recent scores were much lower than usually received (perhaps due to a new preparation, unfamiliar subject material, etc.) and considered by the prospective employer to reflect the instructor's overall ability.

Privilege is said to be absolute when the employer is protected from liability regardless of the motive for publishing information about the individual in question and regardless of the truth or falsity of the information. **Absolute privilege** in regard to disclosing personnel information, to include performance evaluation scores, could be attained merely by having the individual faculty member's written permission to do so.[22] This would provide the best and surest insulation against future litigation, but it must be clearly understood that such consent cannot be obtained under duress.

EMPLOYEE PRIVACY IN A WORK SETTING

Employers have been monitoring employees on the job since there were jobs. Before the technology boom, such monitoring was usually accomplished by supervisors directly observing the employees. Later, employers would install one-way mirrors in manager's offices in order to observe employees and ensure they were properly working, but also to keep employees from knowing when they were being watched. Now technology permits managers to monitor employees' telephone conversations (including text messaging and voicemail), e-mail, and computer activities. Technology has even enhanced management's abilities to observe employee activities and behavior through video monitoring. In a 2007 electronic monitoring survey, 28 percent of respondents indicated that they had terminated employees for inappropriate use of the Internet (see Figure 13.2).[23] Another 28 percent reported having terminated employees for e-mail misconduct.[24] Not surprisingly, when and how to apply electronic monitoring in a work setting is generating a good deal of discussion among employer advocacy and employee rights groups.

Telephone Monitoring

Because some jurisdictions have held that the improper interception of employees' phone calls may constitute a tortuous invasion of privacy,[25] monitoring company telephones must be done very carefully. For one, the employer should have a legitimate business reason for monitoring its employees' telephone conversations.[26] For example, an employer who monitors telephone calls in an effort to ensure quality control would be doing so for a work-related purpose. An employer's asserted interest in recording phone calls "must be balanced against the degree of intrusion resulting from the employer's methods to

Figure 13.2 **Employer Monitoring Practices**

66%	Monitor employee Internet usage
45%	Track content, keystrokes, time online
65%	Use software to block connections to inappropriate websites
45%	Store and review employee computer files
43%	Monitor employee e-mails
28%	Fired workers for misusing the Internet
28%	Terminated employees for e-mail misuse
6%	Fired employees for misusing office phones
48%	Use video monitoring

Source: American Management Association, "2007 Electronic Monitoring and Surveillance Survey: Over Half of All Employers Combined Fire Workers for E-Mail & Internet Abuse," Press release, February 28, 2008, http://press.amanet.org/press-releases/177/2007-electronic-monitoring-surveillance-survey/ (accessed March 20, 2013).

obtain the information."[27] If the nature of the employee's job entails using the telephone to conduct company business, and the quality of the employee's communications affects those transactions, the employer may monitor the job-related conversations. In this case, the employer's need to know how well the employee is communicating with customers outweighs the employee's expectation of privacy.

The second consideration involves employee awareness that calls are being monitored. Not only must the monitoring activities be considered reasonable, the employees must know the employer is monitoring incoming and outgoing calls.[28] If employees are aware that calls on the company phone are subject to monitoring by the employer, they can hardly claim later that they enjoyed an expectation of privacy. The point, quite simply, is that if you are going to monitor company telephones, make certain you let your employees know.

Assume a computer manufacturer has several employees who operate the company's "help line." Customers who are having difficulty installing computers or having trouble operating software can call the "help line" for technical assistance. The employer expects "help line" employees to communicate solutions to the customers effectively and understandably. This is particularly important because most customers are not technocrats, and have trouble understanding instructions with technical terminology. Additionally, the employer knows that customers become easily frustrated when assistance is delayed as a result of busy telephone lines. Consequently, the employer has a policy of no personal telephone calls during work hours on the "help line" telephones. A separate line is available for employees to make personal calls during breaks or to receive emergency calls. Additionally, during new employee orientation and in the employee handbook, the employer has informed all employees that in order to make service quality control checks, the employer will monitor "help line" calls. The employer has also informed workers of the penalties that may be incurred for using "help line" telephones for personal calls. By taking these actions, the employer has removed the employee's expectation of privacy on the "help line" telephones. As with any monitoring or surveillance activity, employee notification is crucial. The purpose behind the monitoring is not to fire employees, but to curb abuse by employees. Employees should be informed that their telephone conversations are subject to being monitored, why, and the consequences for violating the policy.

Computer and E-mail Monitoring

Generally speaking, there is no reasonable expectation of privacy in e-mail communications made on an employer's equipment. In the case *Smyth v. The Pillsbury Co.*, one federal district court even held that an employee had no expectation of privacy for e-mail messages sent to his supervisor over a companywide e-mail system, even though the employer had previously promised the plaintiff that the e-mail messages would not be intercepted by management.[29]

The best rule to follow regarding e-mail is: never put into an e-mail what you would not write on a piece of paper, sign your name to, and then throw on the ground. E-mails can be forwarded to anyone, and often are. They are by no means confidential.[30]

Video Monitoring

Employers have even applied video surveillance to off-the-job circumstances. This type of surveillance most frequently occurs when an employer is investigating workers' compensation claims. In some instances, when the employer has reason to suspect that an employee's injury is not legitimate, a private investigator may be hired to acquire evidence to prove the employee's claim is fraudulent. In *Saldana v. Kelsey-Hayes Co.*, the Michigan Supreme Court concluded that an employer's legitimate business interest in investigating an employee's claim of work-related injury outweighed the employee's privacy interest in not being monitored in his home.[31]

One area receiving a good deal of attention is video monitoring. Employers may use video surveillance in the workplace for a number of legitimate purposes (e.g., security, pilferage reduction, employee safety, performance monitoring). However, employers should avoid placing surveillance cameras in locations where employees may have strong privacy expectations. Unless there is an overriding business concern, it is suggested that cameras not be installed in employee lounges or restrooms. At least five states (California, Connecticut, Illinois, New York, and Rhode Island) have enacted state privacy laws expressly forbidding the use of electronic surveillance devices (voice as well as video devices) in employee restrooms, lounges, and locker rooms.[32] As with all workplace monitoring, employers should endeavor to inform their employees that they are under surveillance and give the reasons such surveillance is necessary.

Workplace Search and Seizure

Perhaps no privacy issue is as misunderstood as searches in the workplace. Searches not only include such matters as physical searches of desks, lockers, vehicles, and other items on the employer's premises but employee surveillance, telephone monitoring, and computer monitoring as well. Private sector employers enjoy far greater latitude in conducting searches and surveillance of their workplaces than government employers. As one court noted, requiring an employer to obtain a warrant whenever the employer wishes to access an employee's office, desk, or file cabinets for a work-related purpose would seriously disrupt the routine conduct of business and would be unreasonable.[33]

This does not mean employers enjoy unrestrained liberty to monitor or search their employees with impunity. Searches are usually restricted to the employer's property, and the scope of such searches varies from state to state. In some jurisdictions there are restrictions imposed by state invasion of privacy laws.

Physical Searches

Employers generally have access to company-owned property when searching for work-related materials. In one case, *O'Bryan v. KTIV Television*, a federal district court held that an employee failed to establish a common law invasion of privacy claim as a result of a search of his desk.[34] The court ruled that searching an employee's desk did not establish a common law invasion of privacy claim under state law. In this particular situation, it was concluded that the employee did not have a reasonable expectation of privacy in the contents of his desk since it was not locked and contained work-related information needed by coworkers.[35]

Such is not the case, however, when searches are conducted for the purpose of acquiring nonwork-related items or information. The method by which an employer carries out any inquiry into an employee's private concerns may constitute an intrusion upon the employee's right to privacy. If that inquiry fails to give due regard to the employee's privacy or reveals personal matters unrelated to the workplace, the employer can be sued under state tort laws. Several courts have ruled that searching an employee's workspace may constitute a tortuous invasion of privacy if the search is conducted in such a way as to reveal information unrelated to the workplace.[36] A tortuous invasion of privacy is merely one that creates an injury to the employee that is actionable under state law. For example, an employer is not authorized to open mail addressed to a person at the workplace that appears to be personal.[37] Mail addressed to an employee from company clients, suppliers, or vendors may be assumed to contain work-related material, but mail from the employee's mother or mail marked "personal" or "confidential" is far more likely to contain nonwork-related information.[38]

Drug Testing

Many employees view drug testing as an issue of search and seizure and may erroneously assume that employers cannot require them to be tested because the Fourth Amendment protects citizens against unreasonable search and seizure. Their error is one of confusing public sector constitutional limitations with private sector employment. The Fourth Amendment does indeed protect citizens from unreasonable search, but this constitutional prohibition only applies to "unreasonable" searches conducted by the government.[39] Even government employers can conduct drug testing provided they can show that such searches are "reasonable."[40]

Figure 13.3   **Obligations Under the Drug-Free Workplace Act**

- Disseminate the policy.
- Establish a drug-free awareness program.
- Make a good faith effort to continue to maintain a drug-free workplace.
- Publish a statement notifying employees that the unlawful manufacture, distribution, dispensation, possession, or use of a controlled substance is prohibited.

Source: 41 U.S.C § 701.

Figure 13.4   **Legitimate Business Justifications for Drug Testing**

• Absenteeism	• Illness rates
• Accident rates	• Turnover rates
• Compliance with Drug-Free Workplace Act of 1988	• Worker's compensation rates

In fact, the Drug-Free Workplace Act of 1988 provides employers with a great deal of insulation by actually requiring holders of government contracts or subcontracts to maintain a drug-free workplace as a condition for continued contract eligibility (see Figure 13.3).[41] But even private sector employers without contracts can initiate drug testing programs provided they are uniformly applied to all employees. Private sector employers can require drug testing as part of their pre-employment screening procedures as long as all applicants are tested.[42] Employers can also require random drug testing and alcohol testing throughout an individual's employment, again, provided that all employees are subject to the random testing.[43]

Additionally, drug testing can be implemented under circumstances in which the employer has a reasonable basis for suspecting that an employee is under the influence of drugs during work hours and when an employer has a legitimate business interest in having the work performed by employees who are not impaired by drugs or alcohol use (see Figure 13.4).[44] As an example, a school bus driver who shows up for work intoxicated or under the influence of cocaine would pose a far more serious threat to an employer's legitimate business interest than a stock boy similarly incapacitated.

Perhaps the simplest means to eliminate privacy issues arising from drug testing is to get employees to consent to drug testing and waive related statutory rights.[45] In addition, informing employees that they may be subject to unannounced random drug and alcohol testing might serve as a deterrent to substance abuse. Not only are such warnings ethical, they may have a practical effect as well.

A final word of caution about drug testing in the workplace: Since the results of the actual drug test can ultimately result in an employee's work record being blackened, or even the employee's termination for just cause, it is important to ensure that the test is accurate. HR professionals should make certain that the testing is conducted by a licensed and approved laboratory. It is also recommended that first-time offenders be enrolled in employee assistance programs (EAPs).

Figure 13.5 **States with Indoor Smoking Bans**

State	Statute
Arizona	Ariz. Rev. Stat § 36–601.01
California	Cal. Lab. Code § 6404.5
Colorado	Colo. Rev. Stat. § 25–14–204 through 207
Connecticut	Conn. Gen. Stat. § 19a-342
Delaware	Del. Code Ann. tit. 16, §§ 2901 through 2908
Hawaii	Haw. Rev. Stat. § 328J-3 through 12
Illinois	Illinois Public Act 095–0017
Iowa	Iowa Code § 142D.3
Kansas	Kan. Rev.Stat. 61.165
Maine	Me. Rev. Stat. tit. 22, § 1542
Maryland	Md. Clean Indoor Air Act of 2007 (House Bill 359)
Massachusetts	Mass. Gen. Law Ch. 70, § 22
Michigan	Mich. Compiled Laws 333.12603
Minnesota	Minn. Rev. Stat. § 144.414
Montana	Mont. Code Ann. § 50–40–104
Nebraska	Neb. Rev. Stat. § 71–5729
New Jersey	N.J. Stat. § 26:3D-58
New Mexico	N.M. Stat. Ann. § 24–16–4
New York	N.Y. Pub. Health Law § 1399-O
North Dakota	N.D. Code § 23–12–09
Ohio	Ohio Rev. Code Ch. 3794
Oregon	Ore. Rev. Stat. § 433.845
Rhode Island	R.I. Gen. Laws § 23–20.10–3
South Dakota	S.D. Codified Laws § 34–46–14
Utah	Utah Code 1953 § 26–38–2
Vermont	Ver. Stat. Title 28, § 1421
Washington	Wash. Rev. Code § 70.160.030
Wisconsin	Wisc. Laws § 101.123

No Smoking Policies

There are many reasons that employers might consider no smoking policies. There are economic incentives, for example, one study estimated that $4,430 was lost annually in productivity per each employee who smoked due to unproductive time at work and absenteeism.[46] Another study ascribed $12,000 annual health and disability related costs to the average smoker.[47]

Some employers may have no choice about maintaining a smoke-free work environment. As of January 2013, twenty-eight states have enacted statutes prohibiting smoking in all enclosed public places, including enclosed workplaces (see Figure 13.5). In these states, covered employers have no choice but to establish no smoking policies and enforce them, but these prohibitions are normally limited to the employer's premises.

This is where confusion comes into play, as many states that have mandated smoke-free workplaces have also enacted smoker protection laws. Smoker protection laws, or smoker's rights laws, are state statutes that prohibit employers from discriminating against employees for merely using tobacco products. Employers are generally prohibited from either refusing to hire or firing an employee for using any type of tobacco product during non-working hours and off of the employer's property. Currently twenty-nine states

Figure 13.6   **States with No Smoker Protection Laws**

Alabama	Maryland
Alaska	Massachusetts
Arizona	Michigan
Arkansas	Nebraska
Delaware	Ohio
Florida	Pennsylvania
Georgia	Texas
Hawaii	Utah
Idaho	Vermont
Iowa	Washington
Kansas	

and the District of Columbia have such laws. This means that twenty-one states do not have smoker protection laws (see Figure 13.6). In the absence of smoker protection laws, employers may be able to refuse to hire any applicants who smoke or could force current employees to quit smoking entirely, not just while at work, or could charge smokers more for their health insurance.[48]

Overweight Employees and Applicants

American employers are concerned about rising health care costs, and one costly health condition is worker obesity. Among the health-related consequences of being overweight are high blood pressure, heart disease, type 2 diabetes, depression, osteoarthritis, sleep apnea, respiratory problems, and acid reflux disease. Obesity is even more costly to employers than smoking. A Mayo Clinic study reported that mean health costs of obese employees annually ranged from $5,467 to $5,530 during a seven-year period compared to $1,274 to $ 1,401 for smokers.[49]

When combined with an estimated $73.1 billion per year loss of productivity due to obesity, employers have a great financial incentive to reduce obesity in the workplace.[50] As a physical impairment, only morbidly obese workers are protected under the Americans with Disabilities Act (ADA) and Americans with Disabilities Act Amendments Act (ADAA). Morbid obesity is medically defined as an individual with a Body Mass Index (BMI) of 35 or more kilograms of weight per cubic meter (kg/m).[51] Typically, a morbidly obese individual is usually 100 pounds over the ideal weight for his or her height. However, if an overweight employee who is not morbidly obese is regarded by an employer as being physically impaired because of his or her weight, that employee would then be protected under the ADA (see Chapter 6).[52]

Currently only the state of Michigan protects such workers, as it makes it an unlawful employment practice to:

> Limit, segregate, or classify an employee or applicant for employment in a way that deprives or tends to deprive the employee or applicant of an employment opportunity, or otherwise adversely affects the status of an employee or applicant because of religion, race, color, national origin, age, sex, height, weight, or marital status.[53]

Barring running afoul of the ADA, Michigan's state law, or local ordinances, there is little to preclude employers from denying employment to overweight applicants or charging additional premiums to offset the additional health care costs.

To illustrate this point, on March 19, 2013, it was reported that Rhode Island-based CVS Caremark was requiring its employees to report their weight, body fat, and glucose levels. The company would pay for the doctor's visit to get the requested health information. Those employees who did not provide the requested information would pay an extra $50 per month on their company group health insurance ($600 per year more).[54] Additionally, CVS also warned employees that they must be tobacco-free by May 1, 2014, or participate in a company-sponsored tobacco cessation program.

DNA Testing

On May 21, 2008, the **Genetic Information Nondiscrimination Act (GINA)** of 2008 was signed into law.[55] The purpose of GINA is to prohibit the use of genetic information in either health insurance eligibility issues or employment.

Under GINA, group health plans cannot deny coverage or charge higher premiums to individuals based solely on a genetic predisposition for a specific disease or medical condition. Any genetic information that the employer possesses should be viewed as a confidential medical record and be treated accordingly.[56] The employer is authorized to disclose this information only under the following circumstances:

- The employee requests the information
- To an occupational or other health researcher
- In response to a court order
- To a government official investigating compliance with GINA
- In connection with the employer's certification provisions of the Family Medical Leave Act (FMLA)
- To a public health agency[57]

Employers are prohibited from basing any employment decision (hiring, termination, promotion, etc.) on genetic information.[58] Employers may not even collect genetic information about an applicant for employment unless it is for a health or genetic service offered as part of a wellness program, and then only with the voluntary written permission of the employee.[59] Genetic information and family medical history can be requested to support an employee's certification of eligibility for FMLA leave.[60] Employers can even collect genetic data where the information involved is to be used for genetic monitoring of the biological effects of toxic substances in the workplace, but only with the employee's voluntary written consent, and in this case the individual is informed of the results of the genetic monitoring.[61]

Dress Codes

Employers may require employees who come into contact with customers and the general public to adhere to certain grooming, hygiene, and appearance expectations. Employers are aware of the importance of employee appearance to the image of their respective businesses and organizations.[62] Many employers therefore create dress codes or appearance policies requiring their employees to meet minimum grooming standards, especially those employees who project the organization's image to its customers. Marketing theory has long contended that favorable customer impressions affect business outcomes.[63] Those impressions could be particularly shaped by interactions with employees who deal directly with the public (especially "potential" customers). Therefore, it is reasonable to conclude that requiring employees to conform to accepted societal expectations of dress and behavior serves the legitimate business purposes of promoting an orderly workplace and making customers comfortable.

Some federal courts have found these concerns legitimate. The District of Columbia Circuit noted in *Fagan v. National Cash Register Company* that:

> Perhaps no facet of business is more important than a company's place in public estimation. That the image created by its employees dealing with the public when on company assignment affects its relations is so well known that we may take judicial notice of an employer's proper desire to achieve favorable acceptance.[64]

But, what if employees object to dress code regulations? Some employer dress codes have been challenged as contrary to employees' civil rights under Title VII of the Civil Rights Act of 1964.

When a challenge under Title VII of the Civil Rights Act of 1964 is made, it is always important to have an understanding of what the law actually prohibits. As noted in Chapter 3, Title VII makes it unlawful for a covered employer to discriminate against any individual on the basis of that individual's race, color, religion, sex, or national origin.[65] What Title VII prohibits is not necessarily undesirable treatment, or bad treatment, but rather it prohibits different treatment because of an individual's protected class. If, in terms of religious discrimination, all religious beliefs are treated equally, there is no Title VII violation. Generally, only when one individual in the workplace is treated differently than the others because of his or her faith does an actionable Title VII violation occur. This form of discrimination is referred to as disparate treatment or intentional discrimination.

Dress and appearance standards are usually challenged on the standpoint that they result in disparate treatment either on the basis of religion or sex. Until recently, if a dress code was alleged to create sex discrimination, it was invariably because the policy placed an undue burden on one sex over the other. That is, the complaining party could demonstrate that the policy placed a significantly different burden on one of the sexes. For example, female employees are required to wear a uniform, but male employees are not. The key issue in dress codes is to ensure that they impose similar requirements on both sexes and not focus merely on one.

As for religion, Chapter 6 discussed the requirement for an employer to provide reasonable accommodation for religious beliefs unless they imposed an undue hardship. In addition to identifiable costs associated with the accommodation, federal courts have accepted as adequate reasons for rejecting the requested accommodation that it diminishes efficiency in other jobs,[66] infringes on other employees' job rights under company policies or collective bargaining agreements,[67] impairs workplace safety, or places coworkers at a greater risk.[68]

Whether the proposed accommodation conflicts with another law will also be considered.[69] As an example, a Sikh machinist's beard (part of his religious observance) precluded his wearing a respirator in a job which required exposure to toxic gas, thus endangering his safety and health.[70] In another instance, an employee who claimed that her body piercings were religiously significant was merely told that she had to cover them with flesh-colored bandages when working at her cash register. "The temporary covering of the plaintiff's facial piercings during work hours impinges on the plaintiff's religious scruples no more than the wearing of a blouse which covers the plaintiff's tattoos."[71]

SUMMARY

Workplace privacy is far less developed than many of the other employment regulations previously discussed. It is very much an evolving issue in the current regulatory environment. In the private sector, employees enjoy very few privacy protections. Though federal law prohibits the disclosure of an employee or applicant's medical information, it affords little else. In most states, employees can only seek redress through defamation laws when employers knowingly disseminate false information about the employee.

As for surveillance while at work, private sector employees enjoy far fewer privacy rights than their public sector counterparts. Too many employees operate under the misconception that they have an inviolate constitutional right to privacy in the workplace. This is the assumption held by John and Ray, the employees in the opening scenario who felt that their employer could not legally use video cameras to monitor their activities at work. They would find out that the Constitution protects citizens' privacy only from infringement by a government entity, and that their private sector employer was not bound by the Constitution.[72]

Employers, nonetheless, should endeavor to engage in employee monitoring only when it serves a legitimate business purpose and, in all instances, should inform employees that they are being monitored. After all, the true purpose of employee monitoring is to ensure that employees are performing the jobs for which they are being paid, not to serve as an excuse to discipline them.

KEY TERMS AND CONCEPTS

Absolute privilege	Genetic Information Nondiscrimination Act
Defamation	Qualified privilege

DISCUSSION QUESTIONS

1. What are the main privacy concerns of American employees? Discuss each.
2. Which employers are exempted from the provisions of Employee Polygraph Protection Act?

3. What federal laws impose nondisclosure obligations on employees' medical information?
4. Discuss the following statement: "I have a constitutional right protecting me from surveillance in the workplace."
5. Discuss the business reasons for drug-testing employees.

CASES

Case 1

Dan Martinez was employed as a sales representative by B.J. Rothman, Inc., a telemarketing company. Martinez's immediate supervisor was Greg Rose, and Rose's supervisor was Victoria Bush. Rothman, Inc., was under contract with Consolidated Telephone to solicit advertising for its telephone directories from present and prospective advertisers. All such solicitation was done by telephone, and Martinez was hired and trained to make these calls.

Rothman, Inc. has an established policy, of which all employees are informed, that monitoring solicitation calls is part of its regular training program. The monitored calls are reviewed with employees to improve sales techniques. This monitoring is accomplished through a standard extension telephone located in the supervisor's office, which shares lines with the telephones in the employees' offices. Employees are permitted to make personal calls on company telephones, and they are told that personal calls will not be monitored except to the extent necessary to determine whether a particular call is of a personal or business nature.

In May 2013, during his lunch break, Martinez received a call in his office from a friend. At or near the beginning of the call (there are conflicting indications), the friend asked Martinez about an employment interview Martinez had had with Banjoville Sales Company, a competitor of Rothman, Inc., the evening before. Martinez responded that the interview had gone well and expressed a strong interest in taking the Banjoville Sales job.

Unbeknownst to Martinez, Rose was monitoring the call from his office and heard the discussion of the interview. After hearing the conversation (how much is unclear), Rose told Bush about it. Later that afternoon, Martinez was called into Bush's office and was told that the company did not want him to leave. Martinez responded by asking whether he was being fired. Upon discovering that his supervisor's questions were prompted by Rose's interception of his call, Martinez became upset and tempers flared. The upshot was that Bush did fire Martinez the next day. However, Martinez complained to Bush's supervisor and was reinstated with apologies from Bush and Rose. Within a week, Martinez left Rothman, Inc., to work for Banjoville Sales. Two weeks later, he filed suit against Rothman, Inc., claiming that monitoring his personal phone call was an invasion of his privacy.[73]

a. Will Martinez prevail in his lawsuit? Why or why not?
b. Under what circumstances can a private sector employer monitor the phone conversations of its employees?

Case 2

Bob and Dave had been coworkers at the Cheatam Consulting Group for over ten years. The two were the best of friends and often socialized outside of work; on several occasions the men and their families took vacations together. Both men had sterling work records and were highly praised by Cheatam's clients.

In 2009, Linda Faybert was hired to head Bob and Dave's department. Linda was viewed by most of the department personnel (both male and female) as being aloof and lacking a sense of humor. On more than one occasion she had publicly reprimanded Bob and Dave (as well as some other employees) for making snide comments during departmental meetings and not setting a serious tone about their work.

On June 13, 2009, Linda gave Dave a written counseling statement for being too familiar with a client because he had been overheard making fun of a politician. When Dave explained that he had known the client in question for years and knew that he intensely disliked the political figure in question, Linda replied that she found such conduct unprofessional. She further stated that she had voted for the politician against whom the joke was made and thought it was disrespectful of Dave to make those comments.

Upon returning to his office, Dave sat down at his computer and sent a long, expletive-laced e-mail to Bob expressing his loathing for Linda and how she was undoubtedly the most "pathetic excuse for a manager I've ever had to work under."

Bob responded, with "You've hit the nail on the head. That social arthritic couldn't lead a boatload of sailors to a house of ill-repute if she paid their way. I've seen more leadership skills in an empty beer can."

The following morning both Bob and Dave were called into Linda's office, where she handed them copies of their respective e-mails. She then replied, "I have had enough of you two, and the rest of the department needs an example of how not to keep their jobs. I am firing you both for insubordination in accordance with the employee handbook."

Bob responded, "You can't do that. Those are private conversations between me and my buddy. You have no right to stick your nose in our private e-mails."

    a. Is Bob right? Why?
    b. Can Linda fire Bob and Dave?
    c. Would it be different if Bob and Dave had an explicit contract?

NOTES

1. This scenario was developed from the facts in *Vega-Rodriguez v. Puerto Rico Tel. Co.*, 110 F.3d 174 (1st Cir. 1997).

2. *Griswold v. Connecticut*, 381 U.S. 479, 483–484 (1965).

3. D.S. Hames and N. Diersen, "The Common Law Right to Privacy: Another Incursion into Employers' Right to Manage their Employees?" *Labor Law Journal* 42, no. 11 (1991): 757–765.

4. B.A. Harstein, "Rules of the Road in Dealing with Personnel Records," *Employee Relations Law Journal* 17, no. 4 (1992): 673–692.

5. L.B. Pincus and C. Trotter, "The Disparity Between Public and Private Sector Employee Privacy Protections: A Call for Legitimate Privacy Rights for Private Sector Workers," *American Business Law Review* 33, no. 1 (1995): 51–90.

6. Restatement (Second) of Torts § 652A.

7. 29 U.S.C. § 2002 (2012).

8. 29 C.F.R. § 801.3(b) (2013).

9. 29 C.F.R. § 801.2(d).

10. 29 U.S.C. § 2006(a) (2012).

11. 29 U.S.C. § 2006(b)(2).

12. 29 U.S.C. § 2006(e).

13. 29 U.S.C. § 2006(e)(1)(B).

14. 29 U.S.C. § 2006(f).

15. B.W. Sanford, *Libel and Privacy: The Prevention and Defense of Litigation* (Clifton, NJ: Prentice Hall Law & Business, 1987).

16. D.M. O'Brien, *Privacy, Law, and Public Policy* (New York: Praeger, 1979).

17. *Brady v. Ottaway Newspapers, Inc.*, 445 N.Y.S.2d 786 (N.Y. App. 1981).

18. B.A. Garner, *Black's Law Dictionary*, 8th ed. (St. Paul, MN: Thomson West Publishing, 2004).

19. Restatement (Second) of Torts § 596.

20. J.J. Balenovich, "Defeating Qualified Privilege with a Showing of Negligence: A Solution to an Educator's Libelous Intra-Office Memo Dilemma," *Journal of Law and Education* 33, no. 4 (2004): 565–572.

21. *Abofreka v. Alston Tobacco, Co.*, 341 S.E.2d 622 (S.C. 1986).

22. Restatement (Second) of Torts § 583.

23. American Management Association, "2007 Electronic Monitoring and Surveillance Survey: Over Half of All Employers Combined Fire Workers for E-Mail & Internet Abuse." Press release, February 28, 2008, http://press.amanet.org/press-releases/177/2007-electronic-monitoring-surveillance-survey/ (accessed March 20, 2013).

24. Ibid.

25. *Awbrey v. Great Atlantic & Pacific Tea Co., Inc.*, 505 F. Supp. 604, 608–10 (N.D. Ga. 1980); *Jackson v. Nationwide Credit, Inc.*, 426 S.E.2d 630 (Ga. App. 1992), cert. denied, 206 Ga. App. 900 (1993); *Benoit v. Roche*, 657 So. 2d 574 (La. App. 1995); *Oliver v. Pacific Northwest Bell Telephone Co.*, 632 P.2d 1295, 1298 (Or. App.), rev. denied, 642 P.2d 310 (Or. 1981); *Walker v. Darby*, 911 F.2d 1573 (11th Cir. 1990).

26. *Simmons v. Southwestern Bell Tel. Co.*, 452 F. Supp. 392, 394 (W.D. Okla. 1978), aff'd 611 F.2d 342 (10th Cir. 1979).

27. *Pulla v. Amoco Oil Co.*, 882 F. Supp. 836, 867 (S.D. Iowa 1994), aff'd in part and rev'd in part on other grounds, 72 F.3d 648 (8th Cir. 1995).

28. *Ali v. Douglas Cable Communications*, 929 F. Supp. 1362, 1382 (D.C. Kan. 1996).

29. 914 F. Supp. 97 (E.D. Pa. 1996).

30. M.S. Hornung, "Think Before You Type: A Look at Email Privacy in the Workplace," *Fordham Journal of Corporate & Financial Law* 11 (2005): 115–159.

31. 443 N.W.2d 382, 384 (Mich. Ct. App. 1989).

32. California Labor Code § 435 (2012); Connecticut General Statutes § 31–48b (2011); 720 Illinois Compiled Statutes 5/26-4 (2012); New York Labor Law § 203-c (2011); and Rhode Island General Laws 28-6.12-1 (2012).

33. *O'Connor v. Ortega*, 480 U.S. 709 (1987).

34. *O'Bryan v. KTIV Television*, 868 F. Supp. 1146 (N.D. Iowa 1994), aff'd in part, 64 F.3d 1188 (8th Cir. 1995).

35. Ibid. at 1159.

36. *Doe v. Kohn, Nast and Graf*, 862 F. Supp. 1310 (E.D. Pa. 1994).

37. *Vernars v. Young*, 539 F.2d 966 (3d Cir. 1976).

38. *Borse v. Piece Goods Shop, Inc.*, 963 F.2d 611, 621 (3d Cir. 1992).

39. *Stein v. Davidson Hotel Co.*, 945 S.W.2d 714 (Tenn. 1997).

40. *Lyons v. Norfolk & Western Railway Co.*, 163 F.3d 466 (7th Cir. 1999).

41. 41 U.S.C. §§ 701 & 702 (2012).

42. *Pilkington Barnes Hind v. Superior Court*, 77 Cal.Rptr.2d 596 (Cal. App. 1998).

43. 41 U.S.C. § 701.

44. *Kraslawsky v. Upper Deck Co.*, 65 Cal.Rptr.2d 297 (Cal. App. 1997).

45. *Poulos v. Pfizer, Inc.*, 711 A.2d 688 (Conn. 1998); *Adams v. Kaiser Aluminum*, 685 S0.2d 269 (La. App. 1996).

46. W.B. Bunn III, G.M. Stave, K.E. Downs, J.M.J. Alvir, and R. Dirani, "Effect of Smoking on Productivity Loss," *Journal of Occupational and Environmental Medicine,* 48 no. 10 (2006): 1009–1108.

47. J. Deschenaux, "Is a 'Smoker-Free' Workplace Right for You? Employers May Refuse to Hire Smokers, but Beware of Legal Hurdles in Many States," *HR Magazine*, 56 no. 7 (2011): 43–45.

48. C. Valleau, "If You're Smoking You're Fired: How Tobacco Could be Dangerous to More Than Just Your Health," *DePaul Journal of Health Care Law*, 10 (2007): 457–492.

49. J.P. Moriarty, M.E. Branda, K.D.Olsen, N.D. Shah, B.J. Borah, A.E. Wagie, J.S. Egginton, and J.M. Naessens, "The Effects of Incremental Costs of Smoking and Obesity on Health Care Costs Among Adults: A 7-Year Longitudinal Study," *Journal of Occupational and Environmental Medicine,* 54 no. 3 (2012): 286–291.

50. E.A Finkelstein, M.C. DiBonaventura, S.M. Burgess, and B.C. Hale, "The Costs of Obesity in the Workplace," *Journal of Occupational and Environmental Medicine*, 52 no. 10 (2010): 971–976.

51. National Institutes of Health conference, "Gastrointestinal Surgery for Severe Obesity. Consensus Development Conference Panel," *Annals of Internal Medicine,* 115 no. 12 (1991): 956–961.

52. *Lowe v. American Eurocopter, LLC,* 2010 U.S. Dist. Lexis 133343 (N.D. Miss. 2010).

53. Michigan Compiled Laws § 37.2202(1)(a) (2012).

54. M. Malamut, "CVS Asking Employees for Weight, Fat, and Glucose Levels," *Boston Magazine* (March 19, 2013). http://www.bostonmagazine.com/health/blog/2013/03/19/cvs-asking-employees-for-weight-fat-and-glucose-levels (accessed March 19, 2013).

55. 122 Stat. 881 (May 21, 2008).

56. 42 U.S.C. § 2000ff-5 (2012).

57. Ibid.

58. 42 U.S.C. § 2000ff-1.

59. 42 U.S.C. § 2000ff-1(b).

60. 42 U.S.C. § 2000ff-1(b)(4) and 29 U.S.C. § 2613(a).

61. 42 U.S.C. § 2000ff-1(b)(5).

62. P. Sheehan, "Dressed to Impress," *Lodging Hospitality*, 59 no. 14 (2003): 48–50.

63. T. Adcock, "Casualties of Casual Dress Code," *New York Law Journal Online* (2002), http://www.newyorklawjournal.com/PubArticleNY.jsp?id=900005376013&Casualties_Of_Casual_Dress_Code&slreturn=20130225112133 (accessed March 13, 2013).

64. 481 F.2d 1115, 1124-25 (D.C. Cir. 1973).

65. 42 U.S.C. § 2000e-2 (2012).

66. *Protos v. Volkswagen of America., Inc.*, 797 F.2d 129, 134-35 (3d Cir. 1986); *Webb v. City of Philadelphia*, 562 F.3d 256 (3d Cir. 2009).

67. *Virts v. Consoidated Freightways Corp. of Delaware*, 285 F.3d 508 (6th Cir. 2002).

68. *Balint v. Carson City*, 180 F.3d 1047, 1054 (9th Cir. 1999).

69. *Sutton v. Providence St. Joseph Medical Center,* 192 F.3d 826 (9th Cir. 1999).

70. *Bhatia v. Chevron USA, Inc.* 734 F.2d 1382 (9th Cir. 1984).

71. *Cloutier v. Costco Wholesale Corp.*, 390 F.3d 126 (1st Cir. 2005).

72. *Vega-Rodriguez v. Puerto Rico Tel. Co.*, 110 F.3d at 182–183.

73. This scenario was developed from the facts in *Watkins v. L.M. Berry & Company*, 704 F.2d 577 (11th Cir. 1983).

PART IV

REGULATORY MECHANICS

14

JOB ANALYSIS

The Foundation of Employment Decision Making

LEARNING OBJECTIVES

- Know the three major components of systematic job analysis and what information they provide.
- Describe how organizations use job analysis as the basis for employment decisions and how it can reduce exposure to specific allegations of unlawful discrimination.
- Explain how job analysis is used in affirmative action.
- Identify the circumstances under which job analysis would be weakened as a defense in employment litigation.
- Describe the traditional approach to job analysis.
- Explain the uses of competency-based job analysis.
- Know the eight legal standards required of job analysis.

OPENING SCENARIO

Dee Dee Taylor is the summer intern for Dragon Breath Mouthwash. Dee Dee just completed her junior year at State University and is excited about her internship in the human resource (HR) department. Though an HR major, Dee Dee has completed only two human resource management (HRM) courses (Principles of Human Resource Management, and Compensation and Benefits).

During the second week of her internship, Dee Dee is called into the office of the HR manager, Doug Van Ness. Doug tells Dee Dee that he is pleased with her can-do attitude and is giving her an assignment by which she can gain great practical experience. Dee Dee is informed that she is going to write the job descriptions for the positions of Quality Assurance Technician and Distribution Associate. When asked how to do the task, Doug gives Dee Dee a job description of a Marketing Representative to use as a template and tells her to ask the appropriate supervisor about the job tasks and what kind of qualifications a job incumbent in each position should possess.

Dee Dee does as she is instructed and by week's end she delivers the two job descriptions to Doug. Because she did such a good job, she is assigned the task of updating all of the firm's job descriptions, which she finishes by the end of her internship. At her farewell party, Dee Dee is again commended on her work and told by the permanent HR staff that they were happy she was there to do it. After all, no one in the department enjoyed doing job analysis.

Eight months later a complaint is filed against Dragon Breath through the Equal Employment Opportunity Commission (EEOC) alleging that the education requirement (an MBA) for four new Quality Assurance Technician positions creates disparate impact for Hispanic applicants. In response to these charges, Doug tells the company not to worry, as the job specifications for the Quality Assurance Technician positions were derived from systematic job analysis.

Is Doug correct in his assertion? Was the job analysis properly done and can it be defended against a legal challenge? By the end of this chapter the answers should be apparent.

Information Provided by Job Analysis

Systematic job analysis is the planned collection of information about a job in order to establish how the work in question is performed (the tasks, duties, and responsibilities) and what particular traits or characteristics (the knowledge, skills, and abilities) a person must possess in order to perform the work properly. When done properly, job analysis should also establish the minimum level of output expected from the individual assigned to the job—the minimum expected level of performance.

For many students, and many HR professionals for that matter, few things are as mundane and boring as conducting job analysis. It can be an arduous, time-consuming task. Having said this, however, there is nothing as important to effective HR planning and practice as job analysis. When done properly, it not only ensures that organizations will obtain an accurate profile of successful job incumbents, it further provides an accurate benchmark against which managers can compare employee qualifications and performance. However, when job analysis is done improperly, it makes HR decisions little more than a matter of chance and exposes the employer to potential EEO litigation.

When conducted correctly, systematic job analysis produces three highly useful components: job descriptions, job specifications, and performance standards. The **job description** component focuses on gathering information relating to the actual performance of the work associated with the job. This component identifies specific work activities, such as the tasks to be accomplished, the duties to be performed, and the responsibilities of the worker assigned to that job. The tasks, duties, and responsibilities developed in the job description are conventionally referred to by the acronym TDR. In addition to the TDR, the job description also identifies the conditions under which the work is typically performed. This is often referred to as work context. For example, the work context of a chemical engineer at a refinery might include inspections of outside facilities under all types of inclement weather (rain, snow, heat), exposure to toxic substances, and so on. The job description may also include any specific tools and equipment used in the performance of the job's TDR. The position of heavy equipment operator for a pipeline construction company may entail the operation of a D-10 bulldozer or a Kubota L48 backhoe.

The next component arising from job analysis is the **job specification**, which identifies the knowledge, skills, and abilities (KSA) that a job incumbent must possess in order to adequately perform the essential tasks, duties, and responsibilities of the job in question. The job specifications are, in most cases, drawn from the job description, and they are crucial to sound employment decisions. What they do is delineate the traits and characteristics that an applicant or employee should possess if the job is to be performed correctly. In other words, an applicant or employee who lacks the requisite KSA is unlikely to successfully perform that specific job. Putting legal concerns in selection and assignment decisions aside, it is inconceivable that a manager could make an informed, rational employment decision in the absence of such information. It is simply a sound management practice to base such decisions on whether candidates possess sufficient KSA to get the job done. In the absence of job analysis linking KSA to job descriptions, there are no criteria for selecting a qualified candidate, because you have no means of determining what those job-relevant qualifications may be. When prospective applicants look at an employer's job vacancy announcement, they are looking at the job specification for that particular job.

Most often, job specifications are expressed in advertisements for job vacancies. They often address such issues as education, experience, skills certification, and demonstrated proficiency. Sound job analysis should ensure that job specifications match the job descriptions. After all, it would make no more sense to require a forklift operator to have a B.S. in transportation management than to expect a candidate with a GED to be qualified as a programmer/analyst. Improperly formulated job specifications expose the employer to challenges as to which candidate was truly qualified for the job. The accuracy of job specifications is essential to disparate impact analysis because they are used to establish the degree of qualification of each candidate. As will be seen in the next chapter, disparate impact analysis concentrates heavily on minimum job qualifications.

Finally, there is the third component of job analysis—the performance standards. In many instances, organizations fail to establish these during the job analysis process.[1] This makes little business sense as the data can, and should, be collected. Furthermore, it is very important that performance standards be shown to be work related.[2] **Performance standards** are the minimum levels of activity and output that a job incumbent must attain if the essential tasks and duties of the job are to be accomplished. Any level of performance that falls below the performance standard simply means that the job is not being done properly.[3] Performance standards establish the basis for any organization's performance appraisal system. Individual employee performance evaluations form the basis for many employment decisions such as promotions, work assignments, layoffs, transfers, discipline, and discharge. If performance standards have been properly constructed, they can be used to defend employment decisions as being based on legitimate nondiscriminatory rationale. However, arbitrary or inconsistently imposed performance standards offer the employer no protection at all.

Ideally these standards should be objective and measurable. For example, minimum outcomes can be expressed in units of production, dollar value of sales, number of claims processed, etc. Standards should also include behaviors that facilitate appropriate job conduct such as being polite and courteous to customers, being respectful toward coworkers, and obeying work rules. When it is appropriate to the work in question, the performance expectations should include timeliness expectations such as meeting deadlines, being punctual, attending meetings on time, and adhering to work schedules.

Determining Essential and Nonessential Job Functions

One of the major issues regarding work performance in a regulatory compliance context is whether the task, duty, or responsibility in question is essential to the job. A given job must be examined to determine its essential functions. Why is this important? Recall that in Chapter 6, an individual with a disability was qualified only if he or she could perform the *essential job functions* with or without reasonable accommodation. Most job descriptions include many nonessential functions in the list of tasks, duties, and responsibilities. It is the manager's task to eliminate the nonessential functions associated with a specific job and focus only on the essential duties when making any employment decisions.

To illustrate how this is done, review the job description in Figure 14.1. Assume that it is accurate and has been validated. Be aware that this is a fairly simple job; more complex job descriptions will require more analysis. The job of secretary will at least demonstrate the process.

What are the Word-Processing Secretary's essential job functions? Assuming that the job description is correct in terms of the estimated time the employee devotes to the primary duties, what activity consumes most of the employee's time? Note that many job descriptions do not provide this information. When they do not, the HR professional must collect that information. In this example, 50 percent of the Word-Processing Secretary's time is devoted to word processing; therefore this is an essential job function. Types special projects occupies another 20 percent of the employee's time and could be judged essential. Transmitting correspondence through e-mail also demands a sufficient amount of time (10 percent). If any of these three tasks is not adequately performed by the Word-Processing Secretary, the primary tasks of this position have not been accomplished.

What about some of the other functions? They all occur infrequently or account for a very small percentage of the employee's job activities and do not affect health, safety, or security.

Note the requirement to stock the secretarial supply cabinet. This would require the secretary to be able to lift 25 pounds (the weight of a box of copy paper) at least to the highest shelf in the storage room. If the highest shelf is 72 inches above the ground, the employee must be physically able to lift 25 pounds to a height of 72 inches.

Assume among the lesser duties (performs other duties as directed), the secretary is responsible for watering the plants in the company reception area and for ensuring the reception area is maintained in a neat, clean, and professional manner. This implies some general housekeeping duties. If an applicant in a wheelchair applied for this position, would the employer be lawful in refusing her the job based on her inability to perform

Figure 14.1 **Job Description for a Word-Processing Secretary**

JOB DESCRIPTION
Job Title:	Word-Processing Secretary
Department:	Administrative Services
Position of Immediate Supervisor:	Director of Administrative Services

I. GENERAL SUMMARY OF RESPONSIBILITIES
- Types, edits, and distributes various correspondence to clients and internal staff.
- Transmits and proofs various essential status reports for day-to-day operations.

II. SPECIFIC DUTIES AND RESPONSIBILITIES
1. Types daily correspondence and reports. (50%)
2. Proofs and prints out final copies for distribution. (10%)
3. Receives handwritten copies and places them in priority files. (2%)
4. Types special projects, such as proposals, quotations, system analysis, and customer and client surveys. (20%)
5. Transmits documents through the use of electronic mail. (10%)
6. Logs and updates volume and turnaround time records of completed work. (2%)
7. Receives and places priority on rush requests and special projects. (2%)
8. Serves as a backup for the receptionist. (2%)
9. Stocks the secretarial supply cabinet. (2%)
10. Performs other duties as directed.

III. JOB SPECIFICATIONS
1. High school diploma or GED, 1–2 years of college helpful.
2. Knowledge of Microsoft Word, Excel, and Power Point, OneNote, Outlook.
3. Must have a good eye for neatness and quality typed documents.
4. Must lift 25-pound containers to a shelf of 72".
5. Ability to work well with others in developing proposals and projects.

Source: Modified from E.H. Burack and N.J. Mathys, *Human Resource Planning: A Pragmatic Approach to Manpower Staffing and Development*, 2d ed. (Lake Forest, IL: Brace-Park Publishing, 1987).

---

essential job functions, or is stocking the supply closet likely to be a nonessential job function? In an ADA situation, the answer to this question becomes very important.

Employment-related Uses of Job Analysis

Of the three components of job analysis (or JA), the one that has the greatest effect on most management–employee relations is the job specification. Since the job specifications describe the KSA necessary for successful job accomplishments, they can be said to create a profile of a qualified applicant or employee. This profile becomes the template for many HR functions and activities: planning, staffing, training/development, compensation, and so forth (see Figure 14.2).

This profile is at the heart of all human resource planning (HRP). The purpose of HRP is to ensure that an organization has the appropriate number of employees who possess the appropriate skills at the time they are needed. When conducting human resource planning, it is absolutely necessary to know what critical KSA are needed at a specific future time. HRP, when done properly, prevents there being too many or too few *quali-*

Figure 14.2   **Employment-Related Uses of Job Analysis**

- Basis for human resource planning (HRP)
- Basis for recruiting and selections
- Benchmark for compensation systems
- Determines appropriateness of bargaining units
- Establishes the minimum requirement for affirmative action programs
- Foundation for job redesign and productivity improvements
- Foundation of performance appraisal
- Identifies health, safety, and security problems
- Identifies training and development needs (through training and development needs analysis)
- Legal foundation for job-relatedness/business necessity
- Performance standards developed in JA become the basis for performance appraisal
- Sets the path for individual career planning

fied employees where needed. If the job specifications were not specific enough, the HR plan would require the wrong mix of KSA needed to accomplish organizational tasks and objectives. A manufacture's HR plan might have called for five machine operators (semiskilled individuals) on a particular date when, in actuality, it needed five machinists (highly skilled individuals).

Job specifications are at the very core of HR sufficiency. When a firm recruits to fill new or vacated positions it does so on the basis of KSA. When the recruiters have provided a pool of qualified applicants, the selection process is then predicated on evaluating candidates based on individual "qualifications." Those "qualifications" are based on the relevant KSA for the job they seek. In the absence of a systematic job analysis that produces accurate job specifications, an employer is likely to recruit and/or select either underqualified or overqualified candidates. The former cannot adequately perform the job in question, and the latter are expensive to employ and bring probable turnover risks.

In the area of training and development, job analysis is used in assessing organizational and individual training needs. The task approach to training needs analysis is predicated on identifying deficiencies between the KSA required in the job specification and the KSA actually possessed by the individual.[4] Training interventions are then developed to eliminate the skill deficiencies.

Job specifications are also used in compensation. Often compensation systems are benchmarked based upon the KSA requirements for specific jobs.[5] Additionally, organizations that offer skill-based pay in order to enhance their human capital will use job specifications to identify the significant knowledge and skill acquisitions to be rewarded.[6]

Job specifications obviously have substantial application in both equal employment opportunity and affirmative action programs. Remember that, as explained in Chapter 3, Title VII makes it an unlawful employment practice to base any employment decision on the individual's race, color, religion, sex, or national origin. Employment decisions predicated on job specifications drawn from job analysis ensure that the employee's qualifications, not his or her protected class status, motivate the final outcome.

Figure 14.3   **Employment Practices That Can Result in Unlawful Discrimination Complaints**

- Affirmative action programs
- Compensation and benefits
- Human resource development
- Human resource staffing
- Performance evaluation

- Recruiting
- Selection
- Terminations
- Training
- Transfers
- Work assignments

When confronted with an allegation of unlawful discrimination under Title VII, the most frequently used employer defense is that there was a legitimate nondiscriminatory reason for the employment decision—that is, it was based on selecting the more qualified candidate.[7] Proper job analysis is essential to demonstrating that the qualifications upon which this decision was made were truly related to successful job performance.[8] If there was no job analysis conducted on the job in question, then there are no job specifications. If there are no valid job specifications, then there is no way of showing that the decision was truly based on work-related qualifications. Employment practices that can result in potential unlawful discrimination complaints, but can be defended by systematic job analysis, are enumerated in Figure 14.3.

In the case of affirmative action, as was explained in Chapter 8, preferential treatment can be granted only to individuals who are members of underutilized groups (as established by utilization analysis) and who meet the *minimum qualifications* for the specific job. Hiring or promoting a member of an underutilized group who is not minimally qualified is unlawful.[9] Since job specifications articulate minimal qualifications for the job, without them there are no means of objectively demonstrating who is qualified.

Performance standards play a very important role in ensuring that employers can document all performance-based employment actions. Recall that in Chapter 2 it was noted that employee terminations result in more complaints of unlawful discrimination than all other employment practices combined.[10] Also remember that no federal or state EEO law requires an employer to continue to employ any individual who is not adequately performing his or her job. Any employee who does not perform the job to minimum expectations can be terminated for just cause.[11] However, in the absence of performance standards it is difficult to prove that the individual was not performing the job. Courts have held that performance standards must be job-related, and the preferred means of showing this relationship is through job analysis.[12]

Other Uses of Job Descriptions

There are also benefits to be drawn from job descriptions. Knowledge of the TDR of a job is essential in both the job's design and its eventual redesign to gain productivity improvements. Reengineering is a process by which organizations make a concerted effort to improve organizational efficiency and productivity, often by redesigning work to eliminate redundancy and wasted resources.[13] It would be difficult, if not impossible, to

Figure 14.4   **Common Reasons Why Job Analysis Does Not Provide Adequate Defense**

- Job descriptions and specification become outdated
- Job descriptions are either too broad or too narrow
- Job specifications often fail to reflect the true qualifications

accomplish this without first knowing how work is currently being performed (information available in the job description).

Because the job description also contains information regarding the work context, potential threats to the job incumbent's health and safety can be ascertained. The working conditions of certain jobs (i.e., outside on a construction site in all kinds of weather) by their very nature mean that the employee is exposed to injury or illness. This translates to special training, protective clothing and/or equipment, or other precautions to mitigate the risk. Again, improper job analysis could result in the employer being oblivious to these dangers.

Why Job Analysis Does Not Provide an Adequate Defense

The reason why an employer's job analysis might fail to provide an adequate defense in legitimizing employment decisions is simple—it was not done properly (see Figure 14.4). Sometimes job descriptions, job specifications, and performance standards are allowed to become outdated. New processes or technologies will invariably change the tasks and duties that are part of a given job. For example, an organization has replaced most of its paper forms and reports with a new electronic submission system. The travel clerk in the payroll department previously received paper requests for travel authorization, entered them into a log, re-verified the justification for travel, checked travel funding availability for the specific department, verified the supervisory approvals, and issued a travel authorization number in writing (if approved) within two weeks of receipt. Under the new system, the individual's supervisor submits the request for travel authorization electronically (eliminating the necessity for verification of supervisory approval), and the travel authorization is submitted to the individual requesting the travel within seventy-two hours of receiving the request from the individual's supervisor.

Obviously, since the manner in which the travel clerk performs his or her duties has changed, the job description will have to change to reflect this. If operating the new electronic system requires special training (which is very likely the case), then the job specifications will have to be changed in order to reflect the up-to-date knowledge that the clerk must now possess. Finally, because the response time to the initial submission of the travel authorization request has changed from two weeks to seventy-two hours, the performance standards must be modified to reflect this.

Sometimes job analysis fails because the job specifications do not reflect the true qualifications a job incumbent needs to possess in order to perform the essential TDR referenced in the job description. The qualifications can be understated or overstated. Assume, for example, that an organization has the following job specifications for a computer data entry specialist:

- Education: BBA in management information systems or equivalent
- Experience with Excel spreadsheets
- Ability to take instructions
- Ability to pay attention to detail in data entry

The job description for the position reads as follows:

- Controls console of computer workstation while entering data in Excel spreadsheet software.
- Takes instructions prepared by programmers, users, or operation managers
- Operates peripheral laser jet printers for work output
- Prepares printouts and other computer output for distribution to programmers, users, or operation managers
- Loads equipment with disks and paper as needed
- Responds to operating and computer messages
- Performs routine operator preventative maintenance on equipment
- Maintains a log on each job that is run and on events, such as machine malfunctions
- Performs other duties as directed

Though the most of the KSA listed in the job specifications appear to be consistent with the TDR list in the job description, there is one questionable requirement—education. If the job specification is supposed to identify the minimum qualifications for this job, is it reasonable to conclude that a BBA in management information systems (MIS) is necessary to perform it properly? What is implied is that any candidate who did not have the requisite BBA would be unlikely to adequately perform the essential TDR. Is this plausible? Probably it is not. The TDR are relatively simple to perform and would not be dependent on the skill sets possessed by a MIS graduate.

The result of overstating the education requirements in our example is to either (1) hire an individual who is overqualified for the job, or (2) not hire an individual who is sufficiently skilled to perform it. In the case of hiring the overqualified individual, the employer would likely have to pay a higher salary in order to attract an individual with a college degree. This is not to imply that someone with a BBA in MIS could not do this work, but the employer is going to pay a higher salary for KSA that will not be used on the job. That is inefficient and a waste of human, as well as, financial resources.

On another front, one even more germane to this book, the BBA requirement denied an employment opportunity to many individuals who realistically have sufficient KSA to perform the essential. This is not only a bad employment decision (as they would do the work for a reasonable wage), but it could be unlawful should disparate impact result. There is a very strong likelihood of this occurring.

Yet another problem arises when job descriptions are written and are either too broad or far too detailed. Take, for example, the two job descriptions in Figure 14.5. The first description for the position of secretary says, "[P]erforms word processing in a professional manner," which conveys no meaningful information about the TDR. On the other

Figure 14.5 **Two Examples of Poor Job Descriptions**

Too broad:	Performs word processing in a professional manner
Too narrow:	Must possess knowledge of Microsoft Office 365 macro files to save to current document, to save document and clear screen, to insert italic codes, to transpose words, to select font, to select boldface print, to select underline, to select outline, to select double underline, to select shadow, to select small capitalize, to change font, to superscript, to subscript, to insert table, to insert footnotes, to insert endnotes, to insert columns, to delete columns, to insert rows, to delete rows, to change font size, to increase indent, to decrease indent, to align text left, to align text center, to align text right, to fully justify text, to inset page break . . .

hand, the second job description (which, by the way, is over fifteen pages in length) is so minutely specified that an understanding of the essential TDR is lost in the detail. If job descriptions, job specifications, and performance standards do not convey meaningful job information, they are worthless as a management tool and will not help insulate the employer during employment-related litigation.

Why Organizations Do a Poor Job of Job Analysis

There are several reasons why job analysis is not properly conducted by organizations (see Figure 14.6). First, there is the cost involved in conducting the analysis. This would include direct costs associated with salaries for the individuals who actually collect the data and write the descriptions, specifications, and performance standards. This can either be accomplished by permanent employees or contract consultants. There are also indirect costs incurred when supervisors and job incumbents are pulled away from their daily activities to provide job-related information through questionnaires and interviews.

Job analysis also consumes time. Time is expended in planning, preparing interviews and questionnaires, data collection, collating information, analyzing the data, and writing the initial descriptions and specifications. It will also require time to review the initial drafts of the job description and specification, review them for completeness and accuracy, and put them into their final form.

In some cases, the organization may not have personnel in their HR department who possess the expertise and training to collect meaningful job data and then construct accurate descriptions, specifications, and performance standards. Many graduates with degrees in HRM have been exposed to only superficial training in job analysis techniques and thus lack the skill to perform job analysis on anything but the simplest of jobs. Classification (the HR activity dealing with job analysis) is underemphasized in many programs in favor of compensation and benefits administration, human resource development, employment law, labor relations, and performance management, although in some instances it is addressed in human resource staffing courses. As a result, internal expertise is frequently unavailable and financial resource limitations preclude hiring outside constituents. The result may be that job analysis is conducted internally as an on-the-job training exercise (without an experienced coach).

Finally, as previously mentioned, most people see job analysis as being very boring.

Figure 14.6   **Why Organizations Allow Job Analysis to Fail**

- Cost
- It's time consuming
- Staff lacks experience or expertise
- It's boring!

This does not mean that it is not important! Job analysis is an extremely important component to virtually every HR activity in the organization. But to say that it is a fun and exciting activity would be disingenuous. In a similar vein, a good number of college business majors may find accounting to be boring, but no businessperson would ever discount its absolute importance to conducting organizational business. So it is for job analysis as well.

Unfortunately, because it is boring, many people conducting the job analysis and those who are providing job information do not put forth the effort and attention to detail that is necessary to ensure the accuracy of its results. It is, therefore, imperative to "sell" all individuals involved in the process on the importance of job analysis and the benefits that they and their organization will derive from it.

The Job Analysis Process

If job analysis is to truly benefit an organization, it must be done in a systematic manner. Systematic job analysis typically proceeds through five phases (see Figure 14.7).[14] As in any organizational endeavor, the most important phase is the first—the planning phase. Job analysis has a purpose. It is going to consume organizational resources, so it cannot be conducted in a half-hearted way.

Planning for Job Analysis

The organization and its management team must clearly delineate what benefits they hope to gain *before* these resources are expended. We have previously discussed how job analysis impacts on every personnel action in an organization, from compensation system design to setting affirmative action. It enhances staffing by setting the qualifications for hiring individuals with the appropriate KSA necessary for the organization to achieve a competitive advantage.[15] In the absence of accurate job specifications all HR planning is a matter of guessing, and if HR planning is flawed, so is the organization's strategic plan.[16]

All of the benefits must be articulated if the top management at the organization is going to support the job analysis. This is not only important in order to ensure that sufficient financial and human resources are allocated to the effort, but also to ensure middle-level and first-level managers are encouraged to support it. Managers in the lower levels of the organizations are already under enough pressure to perform their jobs. It would be unrealistic to assume that they would not view the time diverted to that data collection as an additional burden. When a project manager is trying to deal with meeting tight

Figure 14.7 **The Job Analysis Process**

Phase I. Planning
  Identify the objectives of the job analysis
  Obtain top-level management support

Phase II. Preparation Analysis
  Review existing job documents
  Identify jobs to be analyzed
  Select the appropriate methodology

Phase III. Conduct the Job Analysis
  Collect job data
  Review and compile collected data

Phase IV. Develop Job Descriptions, Specifications, and Performance Standards
  Prepare the draft job descriptions, specifications, and performance standards
  Review the drafts with managers and job incumbents
  Make amendments based on recommendations/corrections
  Prepare the finalized job descriptions, specifications, and performance standards

Phase V. Monitor and Update Job Descriptions, Specifications, and Performance Standards
  Update when organization changes occur
  Update when new technologies are introduced
  Update when work processes are changed or modified
  Schedule periodic reviews of all job descriptions, specifications, and performance standards

completion deadlines, handle client complaints about quality, and meet a cost reduction quota, it is understandable that he or she might be less than enthusiastic about diverting attention to the job analysis effort. The consequence may be a half-hearted effort to provide relevant data and to quickly finish the job analysis questionnaire or interview in order to get back to "more important things." If the project manager's boss emphasizes the necessity for accurate information collection, however, job analysis becomes a "more important thing."

This is why it is also important to educate all affected managers on the benefit they will receive if the job descriptions, specifications, and performance standards are accurate. Show them that they can get better-qualified employees who will be able to better perform their jobs, assure better product quality, and reduce costs. The quality of the analysis will be greatly enhanced if the managers are willing (as opposed to coerced) participants.

Preparing for Job Analysis

The second phase of job analysis focuses on preparation, assuring that the process itself is performed in an efficient manner. If not properly implemented, job analysis wastes time and resources, giving ammunition to those in the organization who are opposing job analysis efforts.

No improvements are likely to be made unless you establish where your organization is currently. This means a review of existing job descriptions, specifications, and performance standards. There may be documents on jobs that no longer exist within the organization; remove them. There may be jobs that have not been realistically changed; make the necessary modifications. There may also be jobs that have gone through substantial changes and jobs for which there is no documentation at all. These will require a good deal of attention later.

Next, each job identified in the review for major overhaul or analysis from scratch should next be evaluated to determine which job analysis methodology would be more effective in correcting its deficiencies. Fairly simple jobs with readily observable TDR and work outcomes can be analyzed using simpler techniques. Conversely, more complex technical jobs and management jobs are likely to require more sophisticated methodology, such as a Position Analysis Questionnaire.

The decision made at this phase is not just restricted to how data will be collected (questionnaire, interviews, observations) but also from what source data will be drawn (job incumbents, supervisors, job market). It is recommended that data be collected from several sources. Managers are more likely to provide information about how a job *should be* done, while job incumbents tend to tell the classification specialist how the job is *actually* done.

Conducting the Job Analysis

In this third phase, the actual task of data collection occurs, whether it is done by observation, interview, survey questionnaire, or a combination thereof. The appropriate collection methodology was selected in the previous two preceding phases. It is important to ensure that the person collecting the data is a person with expertise in doing so. It does not matter if this person is an employee of the organization for which the job analysis is being conducted (an internal expert) or is a consultant hired from outside of the organization (an external expert).

In data collection, two or more sources should be tapped. At a minimum, job data should be collected from supervisors/managers, as they will explain how the job *should* be performed, and from the job incumbents, who will explain how the job is *actually* performed. For example, supervisors of drivers for transportation companies are likely to emphasize pre-operation safety and preventive maintenance (PM) inspections of the vehicle, trailer, and load. Vehicle operators rarely mention these and focus more on actual vehicle operation. Data collected from supervisors would likely omit details associated with highway operation of the vehicle while data collected solely from vehicle operators is likely to omit safety and PM responsibilities.

Developing Job Descriptions, Specifications, and Performance Standards

After the data have been collected and compiled, the information will be converted into a job description document. Here the terminology can be confusing because the phrase "job description" can mean two things. First, the job description is that part of job analysis which identifies the TDR necessary to perform the job, as well as the context under which that job is performed. In its other sense, a "job description" is the document that serves as a written explanation of the job's essential functions (TDR), the equipment (if any) needed to perform these functions, and the conditions under which they are performed.

The job description also provides the minimum qualifications (KSA) that the employee needs in order to perform the job adequately. This information is drawn from the job specification. This part of the job description document is consulted when determining whether or not one individual is more, less, or equally qualified in EEO complaints. It is also consulted when determining whether an individual can meet the minimum qualifications for a job under the ADA, with or without reasonable accommodation.

Finally, the job description document should indicate the minimum performance expectations of the job incumbent. If an employer is trying to demonstrate that an employee was terminated for performance reasons, this document provides evidence as to the veracity of this claim. From a very practical standpoint, an employer's performance appraisals should be tied to this component to assure that employees' evaluations are being benchmarked against actual work-related behaviors and outcomes.

Preparing the Finalized Job Descriptions, Specifications, and Performance Standards

After the job descriptions have been drafted, there is still one more task to conduct before they can be finalized: The draft job descriptions should be circulated among the job incumbents and the supervisors to ensure that no important aspects of the job have been omitted. This is also an opportunity to ensure that no irrelevant or marginal activities have been incorporated in the description.

Once the relevant TDR, RSA, and performance expectations have undergone this final review, the new job description document can be adopted. As with all workplace documents, the old job description should be destroyed and the new document should clearly state that it supersedes and replaces all earlier versions.

Monitoring and Keeping Job Descriptions, Specifications, and Performance Standards Current

After ensuring that job descriptions, job specifications, and performance standards are all based on sound job analysis, managers and HR professionals should then develop policies to ensure that all future employment decisions are predicated on sound business reasons. This not only involves establishing uniform organizational selection procedures but also encompasses informing every decision maker of the policy or procedure. It does not benefit an organization to have a well-crafted personnel policy if that policy is thrown in a file cabinet or desk drawer and never put into practice. For any company policy to be effective, it must be fully disseminated to all affected personnel. Furthermore, such policies should have the support of upper-level management, and this support should be advertised through the organization.

Finally, after all employment practices have been implemented, HR professionals and managers should continually review these policies. Here, there are two concerns—one internal and the other external. Internally, managers and HR professionals should constantly review all actions and decisions arising from the company policies to ensure that those policies are being followed. Some companies get into trouble not because they did not have a policy to cover a particular Title VII issue (i.e., sexual harassment), but because they ignored their own policy. Internal monitoring would reduce the likelihood of such occurrences.

External concerns involve the ever-changing nature of employment discrimination laws. Either through the enactment of new civil rights legislation, or, as is more often the case, through federal court decisions or new EEOC regulations, company policies and practices can become obsolete. It is the responsibility of both managers and HR professionals to become aware of these changes and their impact on company operations. When necessary, new policies must be formulated and old ones updated. Again, disseminating these changes becomes critical if the organization is to avoid unnecessary complaints and disruptions.

TRADITIONAL APPROACHES TO JOB ANALYSIS

Observation

For fairly simple jobs that are primarily comprised of observable physical activities, the classification specialist can gather relevant information about essential job tasks by merely observing the work being performed. For example, a cashier in a retail store performs a series of repetitive activities during his or her shift.

Interviews

For jobs comprised of more complex and/or varied work activities, job information may be collected by interviewing the job incumbents, their supervisors, or both. In the planning phase, the organization should decide on which interview format is appropriate for collecting the relevant job information.

Unstructured interviews begin with a general question such as, "Tell me about your current job." This allows the individual to tell the interviewer all of the aspects of his or her job. The downside is that the information is limited by the individual's communication skills and ability to organize a description of the job into a coherent narrative.

Structured interviews ask a series of questions that are narrowly focused and designed to gather specific information from the individual. Some typically focused questions asked in structured interviews include:

- Describe the primary duties of your job.
- Describe the routine duties you perform.
- What physical activities do you perform?
- What are the special duties?

- How much time is spent on these duties?
- What types of equipment are you required to use?
- Is there any specific training required to perform your work?
- Do you have to work with any other person in order to do the duties? If so, who?
- In performing your job, what decisions do you regularly make?
- What special knowledge or skill do you have to use in performing your work?
- Describe your working conditions.
- Are there any hazards connected with your job?

Questionnaires

As with interviews, the initial decision regarding the selection of a questionnaire format is whether it should be structured or unstructured. Questionnaires offer an advantage over interviews in that they are less costly and require less time to collect data. Assume that a company has designed a structured interview that takes roughly one hour to administer. There are forty job incumbents to be interviewed and there is one interviewer, a classification specialist. Obviously it will take forty hours to interview all forty applicants. Even if the poor interviewer interviews eight incumbents per day, it would take a full workweek to just collect the work-related information. The company is out forty hours of wages (the forty individuals will be "on the clock" while they are being interviewed for one hour) plus forty hours for the interviewer who is conducting the forty one-hour interviews. If the organization can develop a questionnaire that takes one hour to complete and can administer it to all forty applicants simultaneously, the classification specialist can collect the bulk of the data in one hour as opposed to forty. In general, questionnaires speed the data-gathering process. When they can be administered in an electronic setting, not only is data collection expedited but so is the process of collating and organizing the information.

Questionnaires are not a panacea; they have shortcomings, such as individuals not fully understanding what is being asked of them. Poorly constructed questions may inadvertently ask for two separate responses. These are sometimes referred to as "double-barreled questions" because they address two issues.[17] For example, "What specific training do you need to do your job and be eligible for promotion?" The training the individual needs to perform her current job may not be the training they need in order qualify for promotion to another job. Two job incumbents holding the same job may give different responses based on their individual interpretations of the question.

A question might ask about a factor that does not pertain to the job in question. For example, a clerical employee in a hospital billing department whose job does not entail providing medical treatment might be asked, "Describe how you last handled a potential bio-hazard."

It is always important to write questions that take into account the reading and understanding level of your targeted respondents. Schmidt and Klimoski have offered the following sound advice: "Make sure all words are simple, direct, and familiar to potential respondents."[18]

Figure 14.8 **Traditional Approaches to Job Analysis**

- Examination of previous job analysis*
- Questionnaires completed by the job incumbent*
- Questionnaires completed by the supervisor*
- Observation of the actual work
- Interview of the job incumbent
- Interview of supervisor
- Job log**
- VCR/film studies (modern version of time/motion studies)
- Panel of experts
- A combination of the above

  *Least costly and least reliable
**Accepted by the EEOC

Competency-based Job Analysis

Not all jobs lend themselves to tradition approaches. Some jobs, because they do not have easily identifiable work outcomes, are instead dependent on the attributes and behaviors of the job incumbent.[19] Typically, technical, professional, and managerial positions, positions with vague duties and responsibilities, are more likely to be dependent on the personal technical and behavioral competencies of the job incumbent than jobs with clearly defined TDR.

    Competency-based job analysis (e.g., worker-based or behaviorally based) focuses on those individual skills, abilities, and characteristics that can be linked to successful job performance (i.e., ability to adapt to changing conditions, decisiveness, ability to work in ambiguous situations, ability to take initiative in the absence of instructions, etc.). It is the antithesis of traditional job analysis method (e.g., task- or work-based), which first identifies the TDR of a given job (see Figure 14.8) and then proceeds to identify the KSA. Competency-based job analysis *begins* with identifying the KSA.

LEGAL CHALLENGES TO JOB ANALYSIS

Despite the method used, the end result must be able to withstand challenges in court (see Figure 14.9). For openers, the job analysis must have been performed on the exact job in question. One cannot, for example, use the job specifications developed for a maintenance technician for an assembly line and then apply them to a maintenance technician for a shipping operation. Too many tasks would be specific to equipment in the one job that are not germane to the other.

    The results of the job analysis (description, specifications, and performance standards) must be presented in written form. This ensures consistency in their application and documentation of their existence.

    In the event of a legal challenge, someone representing the organization must be required to describe the procedures used in conducting the job analysis. This person must be knowledgeable about the techniques used in conducting the analysis and should also be able to explain the process in a comprehensible manner.

Figure 14.9   **Nine Legal Standards for Job Analysis**

1. Job analysis must be performed on the exact job for which the selection criteria are used.

2. It must be in written form.

3. The organization must be able to describe the procedures used.

4. Data must come from several up-to-date sources and should have been collected by an expert (either internal or external).

5. Data should be collected from a sufficiently large sample.

6. The analysis should describe the job in question and its relevant tasks, duties, and activities.

7. Tasks, duties, and responsibilities must be clearly identified.

8. Amount of competency required at the entry level must be clearly defined.

9. KSA must be shown to be essential for job accomplishment.

Source: D.E. Thompson and T.A. Thompson, "Court Standards for Job Analysis in Test Validation," *Personnel Psychology* 35, 4 (Winter 1982): 865–878.

The data must come from several up-to-date sources, which is why both supervisors and job incumbents should be tapped. Additionally, the person collecting the data should have training in collecting, collating, and analyzing the data. This implies expertise, and this expert can either be a permanent employee of the organization (internal) or can be a consultant/independent contractor (external).[20] Note that in the opening scenario, the company had the summer intern conduct the job analysis. Do you think that she would be regarded as an expert by a court? The data should also have been drawn from a large sample of respondents (sometimes referred to as "subject matter experts"). This ensures that there is sufficient input to avoid the omission of critical job functions. The end result of the analysis should clearly identify and describe the job in question and its relevant tasks, duties, and activities, as well as laying out the knowledge, skills, and abilities necessary for job accomplishment. It should further clearly describe the amount of competency required at the entry level (the performance standard).

SUMMARY

To reduce the risk of disparate treatment claims against employers, HR professionals have a great deal of preparation ahead of them. It is imperative that a complete and thorough job analysis be conducted on every position in the organization. Job analysis is a time-consuming and often tedious task. However, no single HR function is as critical as job analysis when it comes to justifying and defending a firm's hiring, promotion, and discharge practices.

Job descriptions outline the tasks, duties, and responsibilities of the job in question. Job analysis will identify those tasks and duties that are essential to the job and those that are peripheral to it. These distinctions will be particularly important if managers and HR professionals have to establish a bona fide occupational qualification (BFOQ), determine job relatedness under disparate impact analysis, or assess employee/applicant qualifications under the Americans with Disabilities Act.

KEY TERMS AND CONCEPTS

Competency-based job analysis   Performance standards
Job description   Systematic job analysis
Job specification

DISCUSSION QUESTIONS

1. What are the three major components of systematic job analysis and what general information does each provide?
2. Provide examples of employment decisions for which job analysis is the basis.
3. Why is job analysis important in setting affirmative action goals?
4. Identify and describe two traditional approaches to job analysis.
5. What is competency-based job analysis and how is it different from the traditional approach to job analysis?
6. What are the nine legal standards required of job analysis?

CASE

TGF operates a single production facility in Peoria, Illinois, employing between 450 to 500 full-time and part-time employees at any given time. The company manufactures a variety of custom molded plastic products for its customers. A good deal of TGF's business consists of large, heavy plastic parts (pallets and doors, e.g.). The larger products (those weighing up to 200 pounds) are produced in Departments 1 and 2, while the lighter products (those weighing up to 65 pounds) are produced in Department 3. The Department 3 work handles smaller runs with short production times, requiring workers with greater manual dexterity and the ability to clip small parts from the molds.

Martha Johnston began working for TGF Enterprises in 2009 as a press operator in Department 3. On June 13, 2013, she injured her left hand on the job. Following surgery on her left thumb, she attempted to return to her old job in Department 3, but could not perform the work because it required the use of both hands.

Martha requested that she be accommodated under the Americans with Disabilities Act (ADA). However, she could not perform her old job and she could not be assigned to Departments 1 and 2 because her work release documents from her doctor restricted her work activities to light duty with no lifting over 7 pounds. As a consequence, Martha was placed on Family Medical Leave Act (FMLA) leave and began receiving worker's compensation until her condition improved or her benefits ran out. TGF informed her as follows:

> As previously communicated to you, due to your situation we will not be able to accommodate your work restrictions at this time. TGF will continue to monitor your medical progress and asks you to contact us in the event your physical abilities improve. At the time we will review what job opportunities exist for you.

Rather than responding to TGF's letter, Martha filed a complaint with the Equal Employment Opportunity Commission (EEOC) alleging that she had been discriminated against under the provisions of the ADA.[21]

   a. Explain why job analysis is important to this case.
   b. How would you conduct the job analysis for this company? Traditional or competency based? Why? Which method would you use for a job like Martha's?

NOTES

1. R.L. Heneman, *Strategic Reward Management: Design, Implementation, and Evaluation* (Charlotte, NC: Information Age, 2002), p. 400.

2. *Albemarle Paper Co. v. Moody,* 422 U.S. 402 (1975).

3. E.J. Feeney, "Performance Standards, Feedback and Rewards: A Performance Improvement System," *National Productivity Review* 2, no. 1 (1982): 36–42.

4. J. Lui and A. Mackinnon, "Comparative Management Practices and Training: China and Europe," *Journal of Management Development* 21, no. 2 (2002): 118–132.

5. J. Senger, *Designing a Not-for-Profit Compensation System* (San Francisco, John Wiley & Sons, 2005).

6. J.D. Shaw, N. Gupta, A. Mitra, and G.E. Ledford, Jr. "Success and Survival of Skill-based Pay Plans," *Journal of Management* 31, no. 1 (2005): 28–49.

7. U.S. EEOC, EEOC Compliance Manual: Compensation Discrimination. § 10-III (2000).

8. *Contreras v. City of Los Angeles,* 656 F.2d 1267, 1281–82 (9th Cir. 1981).

9. *U.S. v. Paradise,* 480 U.S. 149, 183 (1987); *Wygant v. Jackson Board of Education* 476 U.S. 267 (1986).

10. U.S. EEOC, *Theories of Discrimination: Intentional and Unintentional Discrimination* (Washington, DC: Government Printing Office, 1995).

11. *City of Minneapolis v. Johnson,* 420 N.W.2d 156, 160–61 (Ct. App. Minn. 1990).

12. *Albemarle Paper Co. v. Moody,* 422 U.S. 402 (1975).

13. K. Grint, "Reengineering History: Social Resonances and Business Process Reengineering," *Organization* 1, no. 1 (1994): 179–201.

14. R.L. Mathis and J.H. Jackson, *Human Resource Management,* 12th ed. (Mason, OH: Thomson/South-Western, 2008), pp. 178–179.

15. R.S. Schuler and I.C. MacMillan, "Gaining Competitive Advantage Through Human Resource Practices," *Human Resource Management* 23, no. 3 (1984): 241–255.

16. B. Feller, "Death by Assumption: Why Great Planning Strategies Fail (Reducing Failures in Strategic Planning)," *Supervision* 69, no. 2 (2008): 18–19.

17. N. Schmidt and R.J. Klimoski, *Research Methods in Human Resources Management* (Cincinnati, OH: South-Western Publishing, 1991).

18. Ibid., p. 347.

19. N. Schaper, "Theoretical Substantiation of Human Resource Management from the Perspective of Work and Organizational Psychology," *Management Review* 15, no. 2 (2004): 192–200; P.R. Jeanneret, E.L. D'Egidio, and M.A. Hanson, "Assessment and Development Opportunities Using the Occupational Information Network (O*NET)." In *Comprehensive Handbook of Psychological Assessment,* vol. 4, ed. M. Herson (San Francisco, CA: John Wiley & Sons, 2004).

20. D.E. Thompson and T.A. Thompson, "Court Standards for Job Analysis in Test Validation," *Personnel Psychology* 35, no. 4 (1982): 865–874.

21. This scenario was developed from the facts in *Ciszewski v. Engineered Polymers Corp.,* 179 F.Supp.2d 1072 (D. Minn. 2001).

15

ESTABLISHING JOB-RELATEDNESS: VALIDATION

LEARNING OBJECTIVES

- Understand the why job-relatedness/business necessity is important for employers in making selection decisions from a legal and human resources (HR) selection perspective.
- Know what constitutes a "test" for validation purposes.
- Discuss the three methods of validating employment practices.
- Conduct criterion-related validation using the Pearson's product-moment correlation coefficient.
- Know the legal standards that employee performance appraisals must meet in order to be used in employment decision making.

OPENING SCENARIO

Atrophy Manufacturing, a company employing 430 full-time and 42 part-time employees, has advertised job openings in its expanding Salt Lake City plant. There are twenty new positions for programmer/analysts in the Operations Department.

Each programmer/analyst must have a bachelor's degree in Management Information Systems (MIS) or computer science from an accredited university and pass a test measuring programming skills using object-oriented programming, HTML, Unix Shell Scripting, VBScript, and JavaScript. Of the 140 applicants applying for the entry-level positions, 48 were Hispanic, of whom 18 possessed the required degree and were eligible to take the test measuring programming skills. The remaining 92 applicants consisted of 1 Asian and 91 whites. The single Asian candidate possessed the appropriate degree and passed on to the next stage of the selection process, as did 57 of the white applicants. Asians constituted less than 2 percent of the relevant labor market.

A legal representative for a group of Hispanic applicants contends that the degree requirement has the effect of disqualifying a disproportionate number of otherwise qualified Latinos for these jobs. As a consequence, she wants Atrophy to stop using the MIS degree as a screening device. Additionally, she would like Atrophy to allow the "otherwise qualified" Hispanics to pass to the next stage of the selection process. Atrophy feels successful computer analysts should have a computer degree. Note that the employer "feels" the degree is important to successful job performance, but it really does not know if this is so.

First of all, can the affected applicants establish a *prima facie* case that disparate impact occurred? If they can, what can the employer do in order to show that this requirement is related to the positions in question? By the end of this chapter the answer will become clear.

JOB-RELATEDNESS/BUSINESS NECESSITY

The *Uniform Guidelines on Employee Selection Procedures* define "adverse impact" (i.e., disparate impact), in part, in this way:

> [A] selection rate for any race, sex, or ethnic group which is less than four-fifths (4/5) (or eighty percent) of the rate for the group with the highest rate will generally be regarded . . . as evidence of adverse impact, while a greater than four-fifths rate will generally not be regarded . . . as evidence of adverse impact.[1]

Assume that the initial hiring statistics are true in the Atrophy Manufacturing example, and only eighteen Hispanics possessed the MIS degree and successfully passed at Stage I. Using the four-fifths method discussed in Chapter 4, the selection rate for Hispanics is 0.375 (18/48), compared to the selection rate for whites, which was 0.626 (57/91). The four-fifths rule would be applied as follows:

$$0.375/0.626 = 0.599, \text{ which is less than } 0.8$$

The MIS/Computer Science degree does indeed have an adverse impact on Hispanic populations.

The burden of proof (as we also learned in Chapter 4) would now shift to the company to demonstrate that this educational requirement for entry-level programmer/analysts is a business necessity. In order for an employer to prove that any employment practice is a business necessity, it must be validated as job-related. The term "business necessity" is synonymous with "job-related." The specific guidance on validation is found in the *Uniform Guidelines on Employee Selection Procedures.*[2] The premise behind job-relatedness is that even though the requirement may cause adverse impact, it is essential to performing the job in question. This is why good job analysis (see Chapter 14) is absolutely critical. If the knowledge, skills, and abilities needed to perform the job's essential tasks and duties have not been identified, the employer has no way of knowing if the requirements in the position vacancy announcement are tied to actual job performance.

As we found out in the previous chapter, job analysis is an essential part of virtually all HR practices. It is the central factor in establishing the job-relatedness of a selection criterion. In the absence of job analysis, the employer is unlikely to succeed with the validation of the selection requirement, and certainly cannot defend the validation results in court.[3]

A good starting point for establishing job-relatedness of any employment requirement is to review the job description, which outlines the activities the specific job entails. This means identifying the essential tasks, duties, and responsibilities (TDR) associated with the job in question. Assuming a proper job analysis was used, review the job description for a computer programmer/analyst in Figure 15.1.

Next, the job specifications would be consulted to determine what knowledge, skills, and abilities (KSA) a job incumbent must possess in order to perform the essential tasks, duties, and responsibilities contained in the job description. Note that in the job description of the computer programmer/analyst, the duties primarily consist of consulting with computer users and then writing computer programs to solve their needs. The programmer/analyst also has the duty of monitoring current software and making changes in it to enhance the efficiency of its use. The job of computer programmer, according to the job description, encompasses a broad range of complex tasks, duties, and responsibilities requiring specific knowledge, skills, and abilities to perform them adequately (e.g., knowledge of specific programming languages).

In the opening scenario, the question that must now be answered is whether the education requirement is commensurate to the TDR of the job. If the employer can prove that a candidate who lacks the requisite education is unlikely to be able to successfully perform these essential TDRs, then the requirement is a business necessity. If, conversely, a substantial number of candidates who do not possess the college degree can still perform these programming duties adequately, then the degree requirement is not job-related. The rest of this chapter will examine the means by which this relationship between candidate qualifications and successful job performance is evaluated—that is, job validation.

EMPLOYMENT TESTING

Before discussing how validation is accomplished, it is beneficial to identify the typical selection requirements likely to require validation. Employers have long used employment testing in aiding employment-related decisions. Such devices are commonly used in hiring, promotion, and work assignment decisions. The EEOC considers all criteria used in making employment decisions to be "tests."[4] It is therefore important to distinguish among particular types of tests used for selection decision purposes (see Figure 15.2).[5]

Cognitive tests (also known as cognitive ability tests) are designed to measure the test-taker's reasoning, mathematical, and reading comprehension skills. They are useful in assessing the individual's ability to process information quickly and accurately. They may also assess the individual's knowledge of certain processes or applications (i.e., knowledge of EEO laws and regulations, how to apply computer technology to solving engineering problems, how to calculate net present value in financial analysis, etc.). Cognitive tests should be used to assess these skills only if they are germane to the successful accomplishment of the job for which the test is being used.[6] For example, requiring a candidate for an entry-level management position in a warehouse to pass a test with quadratic equations when the job itself requires no such skills serves only to eliminate individuals who could otherwise perform the job. In this instance, the ability

Figure 15.1 **Job Description for a Programmer/Analyst**

Job Title: Programmer/Analyst   **Reports To:** Head Data Systems Department
Department: Data Systems Department   **FLSA Status:** Exempt

Job Functions
- Programmer is responsible for analyzing systems specifications to determine whether all required elements have been included.

- Programmer consults with departments regarding program needs, objectives, functions, features, and input and output requirements.

- Programmer uses C++ and Visual Basic programming languages to code computer instructions and makes use of any special programming techniques necessary to complete the program.

- Programmer makes modifications in existing software to conform to system changes or to make improvements in the existing program.

- Programmer is responsible for testing and debugging programs.

- Programmer trains departmental personnel in the use of any specific procedures necessary to enter data into terminals.

- Programmer monitors the performance of all software programmers upon implementation and makes adjustments and corrections as necessary.

- Programmer advises departments in how to make software and other computer applications more efficient.

- Programmer maintains a good working relationship with departments and users.

- Programmer performs other duties as directed.

Qualifications

Education:	Bachelor's degree in management information system (MIS), computer information systems (CIS), computer science (CS), or a related field.
Language Skills:	Ability to read and interpret documents such as operating and equipment maintenance instructions and procedure manuals. Ability to write routine reports and correspondence. Ability to speak effectively before employees of the organization.
Mathematical Skills:	Ability to calculate figures and amounts such as discounts, interest, commissions, proportions, percentages, area, circumference, and volume. Ability to apply concepts of basic algebra and geometry.
Reasoning Skills:	Ability to solve practical problems and deal with a variety of concrete variables in situations where only limited standardization exists. Ability to interpret a variety of instructions furnished in written, oral, diagram, or schedule form.
Technical Skills:	Ability to apply programming procedures and programming languages. Ability to write programming code in C++ and Visual Basic. Knowledge of computer flow charts and of programming logic and codes. Ability to write technical instructions in the use of programs and/or program modifications. Ability to investigate and analyze information and to draw conclusions. Ability to learn and support new systems and applications.
Interpersonal Skills:	Ability to work well with others in a cooperative environment. Ability to produce required results under minimal supervision.

Job Context
Working conditions are normal for an office environment. Work requires extensive use of a computer. Responsibilities may require evening and weekend work in response to needs of the systems being supported.

Figure 15.2 **Types of Employment Tests**

- Cognitive tests assessing reasoning, memory, perceptual speed and accuracy, and skills in arithmetic and reading comprehension, as well as knowledge of a particular function or job
- Physical ability tests measuring the physical ability to perform a particular task or the strength of specific muscle groups, as well as strength and stamina in general
- Sample job tasks (e.g., performance tests, simulations, work samples, and realistic job previews)
- Medical inquiries and physical examinations, including psychological tests
- Personality tests and integrity tests that assess the degree to which a person has certain traits or dispositions (e.g., dependability, cooperativeness, safety) or that aim to predict the likelihood that a person will engage in certain conduct (e.g., theft, absenteeism)
- Criminal background checks
- Credit checks
- Performance appraisals
- English proficiency tests to determine English fluency

Source: U.S. EEOC, Fact Sheet on Employment Tests and Selection Procedures, September 23, 2010, http://www.eeoc.gov/policy/docs/factemployment_procedures.html (accessed March 20, 2013).

to solve quadratic equations is no better an indicator of future job performance than a candidate's knowledge of the Peloponnesian Wars.

Personality tests attempt to assess traits that predict the candidate's predisposition to react in a given way to environmental stimuli. When selecting an individual for a position as a sales representative or a loan counselor it may be important to ascertain whether the person is extroverted or introverted. Obviously, an individual with a marked propensity for introversion (a desire to be alone, away from other people) would hardly be a likely candidate for a position as a sales representative. The problem with personality tests is that they can be faked by a reasonably clever applicant.[7]

Closely tied to personality tests are honesty and integrity tests. These tests attempt to predict whether the individual is likely to engage in particular undesirable types of conduct such as theft, misappropriation, and voluntary absenteeism. Again, the problem with these tests is their vulnerability to manipulation by the test-taker.[8]

Physical ability tests, as the name implies, deal with the individual's ability to physically perform certain tasks. Such tests measure the individual's physical strength, endurance, and stamina. They may also measure such things as hand-eye coordination or the ability to carry particular loads. When a specific job requires that certain physical feats be performed, it is always advisable that the candidates perform the physical tasks under conditions similar to those experienced on the job.

Language proficiency tests are used to determine how well the individual can speak or write in a specific language. They are a benchmark of linguistic fluency. Many jobs require the incumbents to master verbal and/or written communication tests. It should be noted that language tests are not just limited to English. If an employer needs a bilingual employee fluent in both English and Spanish, proficiency tests could be given in both languages. However, there must be a clearly demonstrated need for the language proficiency. Here job analysts likely play a crucial role.

Criminal background checks are conducted to see if an applicant has an arrest or conviction record. These tests generally have a disparate impact on several ethnic groups. As a consequence, they should only be used when they can be shown to be connected to the specific position.[9] For example, an individual with several convictions as a house burglar would hardly be a rational choice as an upscale apartment security officer. On the other hand, such an individual would not pose a threat as a sanitation worker. A candidate with DUI convictions would justifiably be barred from positions involving vehicle operation, but would be eligible for a position as a retail salesperson in a florist shop.

The same can be said for **credit checks**. These background checks focus on the applicant's financial and credit history. If they are connected to the job in question they may be used despite adverse impact. For example, it would be appropriate to deny employment as a bank teller to an applicant who had bad credit and financial problems. However, to deny the same individual employment as a construction worker might be inappropriate. Both credit and background checks, despite their potential for disparate impact, are also important in avoiding negligent hiring charges as discussed in Chapter 12. Finally, performance appraisals (discussed later in this chapter) are treated as tests by the EEOC.[10]

VALIDATION STUDIES

The use of any selection device (even though it appears neutral at face value) that has a disparate impact on members of protected classes and that has not been properly validated by the employer constitutes a discriminatory act.[11] In fact, the *Uniform Guidelines* require an employer to conduct a "validity study" when a particular selection procedure has an adverse impact on a minority group; otherwise, the selection procedure will be deemed discriminatory.[12]

For many students, and many professionals for that matter, few tasks are as mundane and tedious as validation. It can be an arduous, time-consuming task. Yet although validation may be underappreciated, nothing is more critical to an organization's disparate impact defense than a properly conducted validation. Without validating a challenged employment practice (whether it is a hiring criterion like a professional certification, or promotion criteria like good performance evaluations), an employer will lack the documentation necessary to prove that a questioned employment practice is job-related.

In performing validation, the EEOC recognizes three general types of studies:

1. Content validity
2. Criterion-related validity
3. Construct validity[13]

Though criterion-related validation is the preferred method, not all jobs lend themselves to such studies. A brief discussion of each method follows.

Content Validity

Content validity involves having the applicant perform a "fair sample" of the work required to be performed in the job in question.[14] In other words, the applicant is required to execute tasks or duties from the actual job for which he or she is applying. Requiring a secretary to type a letter on a personal computer using a specific word-processing package would be a selection criterion with content validity. It is important to remember that content validation is appropriate where the selection procedure measures tasks constituting a relatively complete sample of those required by the job, that is, for jobs requiring only a few simple tasks.[15]

The important factor in content validation is that the employment test in question must be based on thorough job analysis to ensure that the skills and abilities being tested are truly necessary for successful job performance.[16] In the case of physical abilities tests, it is often necessary to ensure that the test is performed under realistic working conditions. Physical tests for firefighters, such as dragging 200-pound dummies 70 feet in a self-contained breathing apparatus have been ruled to have content validity.[17] Similarly, having an applicant for a welder's position perform a series of welds would be demonstrating necessary on-the-job skills.

Content validation tends to be more appropriate for selection criteria, especially those of a physical nature, that measure the abilities and skills that are prerequisites for entry-level job performance.[18] It is also the employer's responsibility to prove that the selection criterion itself is an important part of the job.[19] In order to have content validity, the test must measure important attributes of the job, not merely inconsequential ones. However, not every trait being validated has to be proportional to frequency of its use in the job.[20] Nonroutine tasks critical to safety or emergency operations can be assessed through content validation. The shutting down of a nuclear reactor under emergency conditions (hopefully not a routine function) would be an absolutely critical task for a nuclear control technician in the rare event that it is needed. It would, therefore, be an appropriate ability to measure in applicants for the job.

If, on the other hand, the validation measures only duties and tasks that are peripheral and nonessential to the job in question, there is no content validity. Assume that an entrance examination has been developed for firefighters to measure their cooking skills. It could be argued that since meals must be prepared and eaten at the station during shifts, this is an important skill. Poor meals are not conducive to good morale. But would it be reasonable to conclude that this skill is an essential job function for a firefighter? Would job analysis show that cooking was among the critical responsibilities of the position? Is a cooking proficiency necessarily needed in a good firefighter? Imagine how ineffective the selection process for firefighters would be if it consisted only of a pen-and-paper examination on basic fire safety, followed by a cooking exercise. Doubtless, the cooking exercise could accurately rate the candidate's culinary skills, but because it ignores far more critical job functions, it would be a poor predictor of successful firefighting abilities. In contrast, carrying heavy firefighting equipment up and down ladders or demonstrating the ability to evacuate unconscious people from burning buildings would be critical. The guidance is relatively simple—the abilities being tested by content validation must be essential to the successful performance of the job and must not be marginal activities.

Content validation is not efficacious in all situations. It affords the employer no insulation against disparate impact when the knowledge, skills, or abilities it measures can be acquired quickly or after a brief training period.[21] To illustrate this point, an employer in a sheet metal plant is hiring machine operators and requires candidates to operate a metal punch as part of the selection process. Assume that this practical application has adverse impact on Asian Americans. The employer may argue that this "test" encompassed virtually all of the essential job functions of the position of machine operator. On this point the employer may be correct. To anyone who has never operated a metal punch, turning it on and then operating the machine seems to be a daunting request. Yet, after a relatively short training session (perhaps no more than thirty to sixty minutes), the task is readily achievable. Since the skills needed to operate the punch are acquired very easily after a short period of training, claiming that the operation test requirement is content validated in accordance with the *Uniform Guidelines* is simply not true.

In evaluating the sufficiency of an employer's content validation, federal courts usually rely on the following standards:

- The criteria are based on job analysis.
- The personnel who developed the criteria used reasonable competence in constructing the test itself.
- The content of the selection criteria must be related to the job in question.
- The evaluation of candidates against the selection criteria must identify those candidates who are better able to perform the job.[22]

Criterion-related Validation

Most jobs are based on traits or behaviors that are difficult to observe (knowledge skills and abilities). Since inferences about mental processes cannot be supported solely on the basis of content validity, such jobs must, therefore, be validated using criterion-related[23] or construct validation techniques. **Criterion-related validity** is more commonly used than either content or construct validation, and it is demonstrated by empirical data proving a selection procedure is predictive of the important elements of the job in question. If, in our opening scenario, an ability test is administered to individuals applying for the job of programmer/analyst, and if the test scores are significantly correlated with successful performance of the key elements of the job, then the test has criterion-related validity. In short, test scores have criterion-related validity if they are an accurate predictor of job performance.

To illustrate this point, consider in the opening scenario Atrophy Manufacturing's second selection criterion. Job analysis previously indicated that the primary functions of the job include working on multiple projects in a team environment involving object-oriented programming, HTML, Unix Shell Scripting, VBScript, and JavaScript. Assume that the employer has developed a programming proficiency test to ensure each applicant's knowledge of these.

As part of the selection process, all applicants are required to take a written examination to assess their knowledge of the requisite programming languages. Any candidate who fails to attain a score of 60 percent on the written examination is removed from further consideration for employment. If the written examination causes disparate impact among women but can be validated as an accurate predictor of job success as a programmer, the employer will be able to establish a job-relatedness/business necessity defense. The employer may do this in two ways. First, high scores on written tests evaluating programming proficiency are correlated with satisfactory work performance on those actual work assignments requiring objective-oriented programming, HTML, Unix Shell Scripting, and so on. Second, low scores (particularly those below 60 percent) on written tests evaluating programming proficiency are correlated with poor or unacceptable job performance.

In establishing a relationship between the predictor of performance (in this case the test) and the actual performance, concurrent validation and predictive validation are the two methods available to HR professionals. Under **concurrent validation**, the correlation coefficients between test and performance are determined by administering the test to current employees and correlating the test scores to their individual performance evaluations. This allows for the performance data and test scores to be collected and analyzed "concurrently." This points to a major advantage of concurrent validation—it can be done quickly. Because it can be done in a timely manner, it is also less expensive for the company.

However, the results of the concurrent validation may be somewhat biased because the sample (the current employees who take the test) overrepresents successful workers. It can be assumed that poor-performing employees are removed from the workforce over time, leaving mostly competent employees. Since primarily good performers take the test, there is no way to determine if poor performers would have scored equally well. Therefore, it can be argued that if poor performers could score just as well as good performers, then the test is not an accurate predictor of job performance. If the test then has a disparate impact on a protected class but does not accurately predict job performance, the employer has no business-necessity defense for the disparate impact and will likely be found in violation of Title VII. Fortunately, studies have demonstrated that there are no significant differences in the validity estimates of those using concurrent validation and those using predictive validation.[24]

Predictive validation is another means of establishing criterion-related validity. When predictive validation is used, the test is given to applicants rather than current employees. The results are then archived for future use. After an appropriate passage of time (usually the end of the probationary period or the conclusion of a performance evaluation cycle), performance data on each new employee is gathered. Correlations between test scores and actual performance are then determined and analyzed.

If it can be statistically demonstrated that there is a moderate to strong relationship between the test and job performance, the test will be job-related. Predictive validity, because it tests both good and poor performers, is the preferred validation method of the EEOC.[25]

Predictive Versus Concurrent Validation

A question arises as to which of the two means of conducting criterion-related validation (predictive validation or concurrent validation) is the better technique to use. In both, the method of analyzing data is the same. They differ only in how the data are collected. Predictive validation uses job applicants to provide data while concurrent validation uses current employees to provide data, but the results do not appear to differ significantly regardless of the validation strategy used.[26]

If an employer was going to evaluate the criterion-related validity of a specific selection requirement and decided to do so using predictive validation, the process would be conducted generally as follows: First, the "test" would be given to applicants who were hired. Next, at the conclusion of a period of time (usually the probationary period or evaluation cycle) the individual employee's performance would be evaluated. Test scores and work performance would then be correlated. Finally the "test" would be considered validated if a moderate to strong correlation was produced. The downside of this choice is that the results are delayed. The employer must wait until a sufficient period has elapsed in order to collect the job performance data. Typically, 90 to 180 days (longer depending on the size of the sample) could pass between the date of the "test" data to the date of the performance data.

On the other hand, if the employer used concurrent validation to establish criterion-related validity, the data collection time is substantially reduced. The "test" would be given to employees holding the particular job for which the selection criterion is being validated, and these employees already have performance data on file. This permits the test scores and work performance data to be correlated immediately. Regardless of the method the employer chose, the "test" would be considered to be validated if a moderate to strong correlation were produced.

Correlation of Predictor and Criterion Variables

The Pearson product-moment correlation coefficient (also called Pearson's r), named for Karl Pearson, is a parametric statistic. As such, it assumes that the variables being assessed are normally distributed. This coefficient r is the most commonly used measure of how well linearly related variables co-vary. The relationship is represented between two variables, X and Y. X is called the predictor variable and in our examples, it will represent the "test" or selection requirement (i.e., a cognitive ability test, physical ability test, etc.). Variable Y is called the criterion variable and will represent the performance criterion (i.e., performance evaluation scores, ability to perform a particular procedure, job-related knowledge, job tenure, etc.). The correlation coefficient r is determined by dividing the covariance of X and $Y(\Sigma(X-\bar{X})(Y-\bar{Y}))$ by the square root of the product of the sum of the squares of variable X times the sum of the squares of variable $Y(\Sigma(X-\bar{X})^2\Sigma(Y-\bar{Y})^2)$. The correlation coefficient r will range from –1.0 to 1.0, with –1.0 indicating a strong negative correlation and 1.0 indicating a strong positive correlation. A correlation coefficient outside of this range is an indicator that it was incorrectly calculated. The square of r

is conventionally used as a measure of the strength of the association between X and Y. Therefore, if r is .90, then 81 percent of the variance of Y is said to be explained by the changes in X and the linear relation between X and Y.

$$r = \frac{\sum_{i=1}^{n}(X_i - \overline{X})(Y_i - \overline{Y})}{\sqrt{\sum_{i=1}^{n}(X_i - \overline{X})^2 \sum_{i=1}^{n}(Y - \overline{Y})^2}}$$

A strong negative correlation means that a change in the score of the predictor variable X indicates commensurate change in the score of criterion variable Y in the opposite direction. For example, a high score on a cognitive ability test (if that was the predictor variable) would predict a low score on job tenure (if that was the criterion variable).

A strong positive correlation means that a change in the score of the predictor variable X indicates commensurate change in the score of criterion variable Y in the same direction. This time, a high score on a cognitive ability test (provided it was the predictor variable) would predict a high score on job tenure (the criterion variable).

Note that these correlations do not imply causality, that is, the predictor variable does not cause the change in the criterion variable, it merely indicates the change. It may be that the variables are accidentally related. They might both be related to yet a third variable that actually causes the change. It may be that both variables actually influence each other. Pearson's r only tells us that the presence of one variable indicates that the other will move in the same direction (a positive relationship), in the opposite direction (a negative relationship), or that there is no relationship at all.

How well the independent variable predicts a change in the dependent variable is a matter of magnitude. Magnitude is a measure of the strength of the relationship. The closer the correlation coefficient approaches -1.0 or 1.0, the stronger the relationship. The closer the correlation coefficient approaches 0, the weaker the relationship. If the correlation coefficient is 0, there is no relationship at all.

If larger values of X tend to be paired with larger values of Y, and smaller values of X would be paired with smaller values of Y, then the correlation would be a strong positive. It would be close to 1.0.[27] On the other hand, if the larger value of X tended to be paired with smaller values of Y (and smaller values of X with larger values of Y), then the correlation would be a strong negative one. The correlation coefficient r would be closer to -1.0.[28] If the values of X and Y appear to randomly pair (some larger X are paired with larger Y, but some larger X are paired with smaller Y and vice versa), then there is little correlation and the coefficient r will be closer to 0 indicating that X and Y are uncorrelated.[29]

Rules of Thumb for Correlations

What is considered a strong, moderate, or weak relationship is a function of the type of test being administered. As a rule of thumb, for "tests" involving reasoning abilities, mathematical skills, cognitive abilities, a weak relationship occurs when r is below

.3 or above −.3. A very strong relationship would occur if the *r* is above .7 or below −.7. A moderate relationship would be any *r* falling between a weak or strong relationship.

Again, it is very important to remember that these rules should always be qualified by the circumstances. For example, when studying human behavior, weak is usually .0 to .2, moderate is .21 to .5, and strong ≥.51.[30]

A Scenario to Demonstrate Validation

To help understand this process, it is best to walk through a practice scenario. Please note: this simulation has been simplified in order to help the reader understand the process. The authors do not wish to imply that validation is always this easy. Because the purpose of the scenario is instructional, the number of observations is limited to only five (this number is far too small to perform a test of significance on the results). That being said, assume that a large employer is going to begin recruiting for an EEO compliance specialist for the corporate HR department. Job analysis is performed for the position to identify critical job tasks, duties, and responsibilities. Then job specifications are developed in order to identify the relevant knowledge, skills, and abilities an applicant should possess in order to perform satisfactorily in that position. As a result of the job analysis it is discovered that knowledge of compliance requirements constitutes 60 percent of the job. Particularly, successful job performance is dependent on knowledge of Title VII, Title I of the ADA, the ADEA, the *Uniform Guidelines,* and the ability to conduct investigations. Together these become our selection criterion, or dependent variable.

The employer is looking at two "tests" to measure (predict) the aforementioned job-related knowledge: individual PHR certification scores and an internally developed test. Before adopting either "test," the employer wants to ensure that each really predicts the trait that is being sought in a candidate. This is very important: The primary reason that selection requirements should be validated is not because they help protect the employer from disparate impact allegation (though this is significant), but because they help identify the best-qualified candidates. Without validation, the employer has no way of knowing if the test really predicts future performance or not—he or she is merely assuming that a high test score indicates a better-performing employee without any evidence to support that conclusion. Does a high IQ score indicate that the individual is going to be a great janitor? There is no way of knowing unless you can show that a high IQ score is correlated with better janitorial performance.

The employer in our example decides to conduct concurrent criterion-related validation of the two "tests." Remember that the process began with job analysis on the position. This identified both the job's critical TDR and the relevant KSA required to perform those TDRs. Next, the employer selected the experimental predictors, the PHR certification scores, and an internally developed test. Then criteria for job success would have to be selected (in this example, the employer has chosen individual employee performance evaluation scores). The predictors will then be administered to existing employees. PHR scores will be gathered on each employee and the employees will take the internally developed examination. Finally, the employer will then analyze the predictor and criterion

Table 15.1

PHR and Internal Exam Scores Compared to Employee Performance Appraisal Scores

Employee	PHR Score	Internal Exam Score	Mean Performance Appraisal Score
Selber	461	72	92
Franklin	588	31	65
Nichols	624	56	91
Vitello	506	63	85
Grado	548	56	70

Table 15.2

Variance Between PHR Scores and Performance

PHR Scores Employee	X (PHR Score)	$X - \overline{X}$	Y (Appraisal)	$Y - \overline{Y}$
Selber	461	−84.4	92	11.4
Franklin	588	42.6	65	−15.6
Nichols	624	78.6	91	10.4
Vitello	506	−39.4	85	4.4
Grado	548	2.6	70	−10.6
	2,727		403	

$\overline{X} = 545.4$
$\overline{Y} = 80.6$

relationships of the two "tests" using the Pearson product-moment correlation coefficient. Table 15.1 shows the information gathered on the five EEO specialists working in the HR department.

The next step is to calculate the variance between individual PHR score X_i and the mean of the PHR scores $\overline{X}$. Then calculate the variance of individual performance appraisal scores Y and their mean $\overline{Y}$ (see Table 15.2).

In the next stage the variance of X will be squared $(X-\overline{X})^2$ and totaled $\Sigma(X-\overline{X})^2$, as will the variance of Y be squared $(Y-\overline{Y})^2$ and summed $\Sigma(Y-\overline{Y})^2$. When the products of the covariance of X and $Y(X-\overline{X})(Y-\overline{Y})$ have been summed $(\Sigma(X-\overline{X})\Sigma(Y-\overline{Y}))$, the correlation coefficient r can be calculated using our formula (see Table 15.3). Since $r = -0.3159$, one would conclude that the PHR scores are negatively inversely related to performance and that this relationship is very weak (-0.3159 is close to 0). The PHR scores would not be valid predictors of future applicant performance.

The process can now be repeated to calculate the correlation coefficient for the internally developed test (refer to Table 15.1). Note that since the correlation coefficient of the internally developed test is 0.7991 (a strong positive relationship), the internal test has been validated (see Table 15.4). Because the PHR scores produced a correlation coefficient of -0.3159 (a weak negative relationship), it should be rejected as a selection tool.

Table 15.3

Pearson's Coefficient for PHR Scores and Performance

Employee	PHR Score X	Y	$(X-\bar{X})$	$(X-\bar{X})^2$	$(Y-\bar{Y})$	$(Y-\bar{Y})^2$	$(X-\bar{X})(Y-\bar{Y})$
A. Selber	461	92	−84.4	7,123.36	11.4	129.96	−962.16
B. Franklin	588	65	42.6	1,814.76	−15.6	243.36	−664.56
C. Nichols	624	91	78.6	6,177.96	10.4	108.16	817.44
D. Vitello	506	85	−39.4	1,552.36	4.4	19.36	−173.36
E. Grado	548	70	−2.6	6.76	−10.6	112.36	27.56
Total	2,727	403		16,675.2		613.2	−1,010.2

$$\sum(X-\bar{X})(Y-\bar{Y})$$

$$\sum(X-\bar{X})^2 \ \text{-------▶} \ r = \frac{-1,010.2}{\sqrt{(16,675.2)(613.2)}} \ \text{◀-----} \ \sum(X-\bar{X})^2$$

$$= -0.3159$$

Tests of Significance

A test of significance is a means by which one can assess the probability of a type I error—the error of rejecting the null hypothesis when it is true.[31] The null hypothesis would be that the "test" did not predict performance appraised scores. Hence, a type I error under these circumstances would be concluding that the "test" predicted future performance when it did not.

Interestingly, the EEOC does not advocate the use of tests of significance, or, in its own words:

> Question #18. Q: Is it usually necessary to calculate the statistical significance of differences in selection rates when investigating the existence of adverse impact?

> A: No. Adverse impact is normally indicated when one selection rate is less than 80 percent of the other. The federal enforcement agencies normally will use only the 80 percent (4/5ths) rule of thumb, except where large numbers of selections are made.[32]

Are employers required to calculate the statistical significance of differences in selection rates in disparate impact analysis? According to the EEOC, the answer is no. Specifically, the EEOC is on record stating:

> Where the sample of persons selected is not large, even a large real difference between groups is likely not to be confirmed by a test of statistical significance (at the usual .05 level of significance). For this reason, the *Guidelines* do not rely

Table 15.4

Pearson's Coefficient for PHR Scores and Internal Test Score

Internal Test Score Employee	X	Y	$(X-\bar{X})$	$(X-\bar{X})^2$	$(Y-\bar{Y})$	$(Y-\bar{Y})^2$	$(X-\bar{X})(Y-\bar{Y})$
A. Selber	72	92	16.4	268.96	11.4	129.96	186.96
B. Franklin	31	65	−24.6	605.16	−15.6	243.36	383.76
C. Nichols	56	91	0.4	.16	10.4	108.16	4.16
D. Vitello	63	85	7.4	54.76	4.4	19.36	32.56
E. Grado	56	70	0.4	.16	−10.6	112.36	−4.24
Total	278	403		929.2		613.2	603.2

$$\sum(X-\bar{X})(Y-\bar{Y})$$
$$\downarrow$$

$$\sum(X-\bar{X})^2 \dashrightarrow r = \frac{603.2}{\sqrt{(929.2)(613.2)}} \dashleftarrow \sum(Y-\bar{Y})^2$$

$$= -0.7991$$

primarily upon a test of statistical significance, but use the 4/5ths rule of thumb as a practical and easy-to-administer measure of whether differences in selection rates are substantial. Many decisions in day-to-day life are made without reliance upon a test of statistical significance.[33]

The preference appears to favor ease of use by EEOC investigators. Note that the use of tests of significance is not prohibited—the 4/5ths rule is merely preferred. From a practical selection standpoint, employers should have conducted a test of significance. The reason for this is a practical one. The real purpose behind validation is to ensure that the employer has an accurate prediction of future job performance. Tests of significance help reduce the likelihood that the correlations are merely a random error.

Construct Validity

Of the three validation methods, **construct validity** is probably the most complicated because it involves demonstrating that abstract characteristics (i.e., decisiveness, innovation, sound judgment, etc.) are necessary for successful job performance and that the employer has a means of accurately measuring these characteristics.[34] Unfortunately, those constructs are often hard to measure. Hence, an overriding factor in deciding to use construct validation is the availability of personnel with the high level of expertise in this type of statistical analysis.[35]

As defined, construct validity is really two validation studies: (1) the employer must prove the construct or trait is essential for the successful performance of the job in question (i.e., participative leadership style may be vital to the position of branch manager) and (2) the construct (leadership style) can be accurately measured. This means extensive job analysis must be conducted to identify critical work behaviors.[36] Ultimately, the employer is responsible for providing proof that the selection procedures measure the degree to which candidates possess the identifiable construct determined important for successful job performance.[37]

Assume an employer has demonstrated that "decisiveness" is a very important characteristic for a branch manager. However, the personality assessment test that the employer uses to evaluate "decisiveness" in candidates for the position is a poor predictor of that construct. Though the behavioral trait, "decisiveness," is critical to job performance, the personality test does not accurately identify the trait in applicants. Consequently, the selection process lacks construct validity.

On the other hand, if the personality assessment test could accurately identify the level of decisiveness possessed by a candidate, but the construct was not essential for the job's performance, the selection process would again lack construct validity. Imagine the level of "decisiveness" required by a bank teller to perform the essential functions of the job compared to a branch manager. As always, the importance of thorough job analysis cannot be overstated.

The skills requirements to conduct construct validation are such that most organizations must employ an in-house psychometrician or hire a consultant. The major organizational consideration when pursuing this validation strategy or the other two is the availability of an individual with psychometric skills and expertise needed for this level of analysis.[38]

Other Methods of Validation

Validation is not just limited to statistical validation methods. There may be situations and circumstances under which criterion-related, content, and construct validation would not be practical. As the Supreme Court noted in *Teamsters v. United States,*

> Statistics are . . . competent in proving employment discrimination. We caution only that statistics are not irrefutable; they come in infinite variety and, like any other kind of evidence, they may be rebutted. In short, their usefulness depends on all the surrounding facts and circumstances.[39]

One of these surrounding facts and circumstances results when the safety of coworkers, customers, or other parties can be shown to be an essential function of the job.[40] In one instance, applicants for positions with the New York City transit authority filed an EEOC complaint alleging the transit authority's policy of not hiring applicants who received methadone treatments created an adverse impact on African Americans and Hispanics. Methadone is a drug given to persons undergoing rehabilitation for narcotics addiction. It is a narcotic and indicates addiction to serious drugs (heroin, morphine, and other opiates).

The complaining parties offered evidence that the transit authority's policy had a disparate impact because 81 percent of the applicants it affected were African Americans or Hispanics.[41] In fact, at the time, 62 to 65 percent of all methadone-maintained persons in

New York City were African Americans or Hispanics.[42] Despite the obvious impact this policy had on the two protected classes (it resulted in more African Americans and Hispanics being excluded from eligibility than any other ethnic group), the safety concerns for the passengers using the transit authority's services easily established the job-relatedness/business necessity of this requirement.

In the case of *Spurlock v. United Airlines,*[43] the question arose as to whether work experience can be job-related in the absence of a statistical validation study. In *Spurlock,* any applicant for flight officer on a United Airlines crew had to have a minimum of 500 hours of flight time, a college degree, a commercial pilot's license, and an instrument rating.

The court accepted the argument that the college degree was considered necessary to substantiate an applicant's ability to understand and retain information during training. The 500 hours of flight experience were important for successful completion of the airline's flight training program and reducing training costs.[44] Applicants without the 500 hours took longer to train and had a lower passing rate than applicants who possessed the previous flight experience.

Under similar circumstances in *Washington v. Davis,* the Supreme Court concluded that a verbal skills test that predicted applicant success in training was job related, despite its disproportionate effect on African Americans.[45] Though the test had not been validated for job performance, it had been correlated with police academy training scores. The verbal skills test was held to be an accurate predictor of an applicant's ability to successfully complete training.

THE COMPLAINING PARTY'S REBUTTAL

Even if the employer is able to establish the job-relatedness/business necessity of the employment practice creating the statistical imbalance, the complaining party is afforded one last opportunity to challenge that practice. The complaining party can offer evidence that there are other practices that would accomplish the same objective as the challenged practice, but would have less disparate impact on the protected class. Accordingly:

> If [complaining parties], having established a *prima facie* case, come forward with alternatives to [respondents'] hiring practices that reduce the racially disparate impact of practices currently being used, and [respondents] refuse to adopt these alternatives, such a refusal would belie a claim by [respondents] that their incumbent practices are being employed for nondiscriminatory reasons.[46]

Employers could be directed to adopt another selection criterion or test that would have less disparate impact. However, this "criterion" would have to accomplish the same end as the rejected criterion. This is more easily said than done.

For HR professionals, this means that current selection processes need to be validated. Those that create disparate impact should be more closely reviewed and analyzed for possible replacement by a less exclusive process. It may be unrealistic to assume that all practices can be replaced, but some can. The effort to do so would not only reduce the likelihood of losing a case in court but also could increase the pool of qualified applicants available to the organization.

If, in our opening scenario, the complaining party was able to demonstrate that applicants with online degree certificates could perform the programmer/analysts' jobs as well as graduates from accredited universities, the employer would be required to change the requirement.

PERFORMANCE APPRAISALS AND EMPLOYMENT DISCRIMINATION

Since the discussion of disparate impact and disparate treatment is complete, perhaps it would be a good time to look at an employment practice likely to get an employer in trouble with both. Performance appraisals are at the very heart of HR management. Besides being a valuable tool (when they are properly conducted) for employee feedback, performance appraisals are used by many organizations to provide information needed to make important employment decisions. Ask a manager who should get the largest pay raise, and most will respond that it should go to the best worker. But who is the best worker? Usually it is the worker with the best performance evaluation/appraisal. Not surprisingly, individual employee performance appraisals are a major factor in determining pay raises, promotions, bonuses, transfers, retentions, layoffs, and terminations.[47]

When done properly, performance evaluations serve as an invaluable management tool. Unfortunately, when they are not done properly, they can become a potential EEO complaint or an embarrassment during any subsequent investigation or trial. From a strictly legal perspective, performance appraisals are treated as "tests."[48] Just as with any other test, a performance appraisal must be validated—it is useless to an employer if it cannot be shown to accurately measure the essential functions of the job it alleges to evaluate.

In some instances, an organization's own formal performance evaluations have been used against the employer in court as evidence of unlawful discrimination.[49] This is especially true when evaluations are highly subjective and reflect only the rater's opinion about an employee's abilities (as opposed to an objective assessment of actual work performance). Sometimes evaluations might even be tainted by the rater's conscious or unconscious prejudices.[50]

Some of the common performance appraisal methods are open to abuse. Performance appraisals known as graphic rating scales (see Figure 15.3) may be particularly susceptible to a high degree of subjectivity. Evaluation criteria such as "attitude" are especially nebulous and may have little to do with successful job accomplishment.

Regardless of the performance appraisal methods used, Bernardin and Beatty in their seminal work[51] recommend the following guidelines on the likelihood of defending an organization's performance management systems. First and foremost, all standards for performance appraisal should be based on job analysis. Next, the performance standards do the employer no good unless they are communicated to the employee. In order to ensure that appropriate feedback is being provided, employees should be evaluated on specific dimensions of job performance rather than a global (overall) measure. After

Figure 15.3 **Graphic Rating Scale**

	Poor	Below Average	Average	Above Average	Outstanding
Makes sound decisions	1	2	3	4	5
Displays a proper attitude toward work	1	2	3	4	5
Cooperates with coworkers	1	2	3	4	5
Demonstrates job knowledge	1	2	3	4	5
Demonstrates maturity in problem solving	1	2	3	4	5
Maintains a professional attitude	1	2	3	4	5

all, what guidance is being communicated if the employee is told, "your performance is substandard, unless you get at least 'average' ratings, you will be fired." What has the employee specifically done to be rated as "substandard"? More to the point, what guidance has been given to the employee to improve her performance?

Individual raters also should be assessed for reliability and validity in their ratings. This ensures consistency in their evaluations. Whenever possible, steps should be taken to ensure that more than one rater is used. This permits a second opinion regarding the individual's performance, and provides a safeguard against personal animosity corrupting the evaluation. To preclude rating inflation or overly harsh evaluations, documentation of extreme ratings (i.e., "poor" and "outstanding") should be required. In essence, the rater would have to explain and provide justification for very good evaluations as well as very poor ones. Also, a formal appeal process should be established. This ensures that an employee is afforded due process.

SUMMARY

The importance of maintaining records and documentation of the validation of each employment practice cannot be overstated. This means that HR professionals must review performance appraisals to ensure they accurately measure essential job functions and do not overemphasize non-job-related behaviors. It also means that documentation must be maintained to prove that adverse employment actions (i.e., discharge, demotion, and denial of promotions and pay raises) are based on the employee's work-related behavior and actions. It is always important to remember that once disparate impact occurs, the employer bears the burden of justifying the job-relatedness of the imbalance (whether it is a performance appraisal, test score, physical requirement, or educational requirement).

Any employment requirement or measure used to predict job performance is viewed as a "test" by the EEOC, and it is the employer's burden to demonstrate that such requirements predict legitimate work-related outcomes. Whether the employer uses cognitive ability, physical ability, education, or work experience (or any combination thereof), all variables used in the decision process must be justified.

Justification for any employment practice creating disparate impact should begin with validation. It becomes immaterial if a practice results in adverse impact so long as the employer can show that it is job-related. Validation of employment practices not only provides the employer with a legal defense against disparate impact allegations, but, more importantly, assures that selection is predicated on performance-based applicant characteristics. Validation is a sound business practice, which also provides a nondiscriminatory justification for selection decisions.

The decision as to which of the three EEOC-recognized validation strategies is appropriate (content, construct, or criterion-related) is a function of the nature of the job, its complexity, and the level of statistical expertise needed for analysis.

KEY TERMS AND CONCEPTS

Cognitive tests
Concurrent validation
Construct validity
Content validity
Credit checks
Criminal background checks

Criterion-related validity
Job specifications
Language proficiency tests
Personality tests
Physical ability tests
Predictive validation

DISCUSSION QUESTIONS

1. Why is job-relatedness/business necessity important for employers in making selection decisions from a legal perspective? Why is job-relatedness important from an HR selection perspective?
2. Identify four types of tests recognized by the EEOC and differentiate each.
3. What are the three methods of conducting a validity study recognized under the *Uniform Guidelines*? How do they differ from one another?
4. What are the seven legal standards that a performance appraisal must meet?

CASES

Case 1

Given the information in the earlier Pearson's scenario, assume that another test has been developed for assessing applicants' knowledge of EEO laws and regulations. The new scores for the current EEO specialists are listed in Table 15.5.

  a. Conduct criterion-related validation in the new test.
  b. Using this new data, what is the Pearson's r for the new test?
  c. What is its magnitude and direction (strong negative, moderate negative, weak positive, etc.)?
  d. Considering how previous "tests" were analyzed in the text, which test would you recommend the employer adopt and why?

Table 15.5

Case 1

Employee	New Exam Score	Mean Performance Appraisal Score (out of 100)
Briggs	96	92
Franklin	56	65
Nichols	84	91
Vitello	88	85
Grado	72	70

Case 2

Given the information in Table 15.6 and using Pearson's Product Moment Correlation Coefficient:

    a. Conduct criterion-related validation in the new test.
    b. Using this new data, what is the Pearson's r for the new test?
    c. What is its magnitude and direction (strong negative, moderate negative, weak positive, etc.)?
    d. Considering how previous "tests" were analyzed in the text, which test would you recommend the employer adopt and why?

Table 15.6

Case 2

Employee	Score on Personality Assessment	Mean Performance Appraisal Score (out of 200)
Briggs	28	155
Franklin	36	162
Nichols	24	176
Vitello	38	152
Grado	25	186
Cooper	38	146

Case 3

East Colorado Motor Freight, an interstate trucking company employing 20 full-time drivers, 4 mechanics, and 7 office staff has become concerned about employment litigation because a competitor was recently sued for disparate impact under Title VII.

Currently, position announcements for drivers only require an applicant to possess a commercial license and pass a driving course. The owner knows that if the company is ever challenged in court, he must be able to prove that the complaining party was not selected because of business necessity.

a. Which validation study recognized by the *Uniform Guidelines on Employee Selection Procedures* is the most appropriate for drivers?

b. Justify your answer.

NOTES

1. 29 C.F.R. § 1607.4(D) (2012).

2. 29 C.F.R. § 1607.

3. B. Lindeman, "Diversifying the Work Place: Affirmative Action in the Private Sector After 1991," *South Dakota Law Review* 42 (1997): 434–468.

4. 29 C.F.R. part 1600.

5. U.S. EEOC, Fact Sheet on Employment Tests and Selection Procedures (February 25, 2008), www.eeoc.gov/policy/docs/factemployment_procedures.html (accessed May 1, 2008).

6. 29 C.F.R. §1607.14 (D)(3).

7. C.E. Miller and G.V. Barrett, "The Coachability and Fakability of Personality-based Selection Tests Used for Police Selection," *Public Personnel Management* 37, no. 1 (2008): 339–352; C. Viswesvaran and D.S. Ones, "Meta-analysis of Fakability Estimates: Implications for Personality Measurement," *Educational and Psychological Measurement* 59, no. 2 (1999): 197–210.

8. R.J. Karren and L. Zacharias, "Integrity Tests: Critical Issues," *Human Resource Management Review* 17, no. 2 (2007): 221–234; S.G. LoBello and B.N. Sims, "Fakability of a Commercially Produced Pre-employment Integrity Test," *Journal of Business and Psychology* 8, no. 2 (1993): 265–273.

9. U.S. EEOC, "Questions and Answers About Race and Color Discrimination in Employment" (May 6, 2006), www.eeoc.gov/policy/docs/qanda_race_color.html (accessed March 19, 2013).

10. *Albemarle Paper Co. v. Moody,* 422 U.S. 405 (1975).

11. *Firefighters Institute for Racial Equality v. City of St. Louis,* 588 F.2d 235 (8th Cir.) cert. denied 443 U.S. 904 (1978).

12. 29 C.F.R. §§ 1607.1(B) and 1607.3.

13. 29 C.F.R. § 1607.5(B).

14. 29 C.F.R. § 1607.5.

15. 29 C.F.R. § 1607.14C(1).

16. *Guardians Assn. of Police Depts. v. Civil Service Commission of New York,* 633 F.2d 232, 242 (2nd Cir. 1980).

17. *Zamlen v. City of Cleveland,* 906 F.2d 209 (6th Cir. 1990).

18. Ibid. at 218.; *U.S. v. City of Wichita Falls,* 704 F.Supp. 709, 714 (N.D. Tex. 1988).

19. *Legault v. Russo,* 842 F.Supp. 1479 (D.N.H. 1994).

20. *Police Officers for Equal Rights v. City of Columbus,* 916 F.2d 1092, 1100 (6th Cir. 1990).

21. 21 C.F.R. § 1607.5(F).

22. *Guardians Assn.,* 630 F.2d 79.

23. *Gilbert v. City of Little Rock,* 799 F.2d 1210 (8th Cir. 1986).

24. R.D. Gatewood and H.S. Field, *Human Resource Selection,* 4th ed. (Fort Worth, TX: The Dryden Press, 1998), p. 166.

25. 29 C.F.R. § 1607.7.

26. G.V. Barrett, J.S. Phillips, and R.A. Alexander, "Concurrent and Predictive Validity Designs: A Critical Reanalysis," *Journal of Applied Psychology* 66 (1981): 1–6.

27. W.J. Conover, *Practical Nonparametric Statistics,* 3d ed. (New York: John Wiley & Sons, 1999), pp. 234–239.

28. Ibid.

29. Ibid.

30. T. C. Urdan, *Statistics in Plain English,* 2nd ed. (Hillsdale, NJ: Lawrence Erlbaum, 2005), p. 76.

31. C.W. Emory and D.R. Cooper, *Business Research Methods,* 4th ed. (Homewood, IL: Irwin, 1991), pp. 521–526; J. Cohen and P. Cohen, *Applied Multiple Regression/Correlation Analysis of the Behavioral Sciences,* 2d ed. (Hillsdale, NJ: Lawrence Erlbuam Associates, 1983), p. 166.

32. U.S. EEOC, *Adoption of Questions and Answers To Clarify and Provide a Common Interpretation of the Uniform Guidelines on Employee Selection Procedures* (April 24, 2008), www.eeoc.gov/policy/docs/qanda_clarify_procedures.html (accessed March 19, 2013).

33. Ibid.

34. U.S. EEOC, *Questions and Answers to Clarify and Provide a Common Interpretation of the Uniform Guidelines as Employee Selection Procedures* (April 24, 2008), www.eeoc.gov/policy/docs/qanda_clarify_procedures.html (accessed March 19, 2013).

35. 44 Fed. Reg. 11996 (1979); 45 Fed. Reg. 29530 (1980).

36. 29 C.F.R. § 1607.14D.

37. 29 C.F.R. § 1607.16E.

38. U.S. EEOC, "Questions and Answers to Clarify and Provide a Common Interpretation of the Uniform Guidelines as Employee Selection Procedures."

39. 431 U.S. 324, 339–340 (1977).

40. *New York City Transit Authority v. Beazer,* 440 U.S. 568, 587 (1979).

41. Ibid. at 578.

42. Ibid.

43. 475 F.2d 216 (10th Cir. 1972).

44. Ibid. at 218–219.

45. 426 U.S. 229, 252 (1976).

46. *Watson v. Fort Worth Bank & Trust,* 487 U.S. 977, 998 (O'Connor, J.) (1988).

47. R.D. Arvey and R.H. Faley, *Fairness in Selecting Employees,* 2d ed. (Reading, MA: Addison-Wesley, 1988).

48. 29 C.F.R. § 1607.16Q, *Albemarle Paper Co. v. Moody,* 422 U.S. 405 (1975).

49. *Burney v. Rheem Manufacturing Co., Inc.*, 196 F.R.D. 659, 672 (M.D.Ala. 2000).

50. L.S. Kleiman and R.L. Durham, "Performance Appraisal, Promotion and the Courts: A Critical Review," *Personnel Psychology* 34, no. 1 (2006): 103–121.

51. H.J. Bernardin and R.W. Beatty, *Performance Appraisal: Assessing Human Behavior at Work* (Kent Human Resource Management Series) (Boston: PWS-Kent, 1984).

GLOSSARY

Absolute bar: An exclusion from consideration for any position of all parties who are not members of the preferred group.

Absolute privilege: A situation where an employer is protected from liability, regardless of the motive, for publishing information about an employee in question and regardless of the truth or untruth of the information.

Action plan: An action-oriented program designed to eliminate problems and attain previously established goals and objectives.

Actionable discrimination: Discrimination for which redress can be sought under a specific statute.

Adverse impact: The theory responsible for the current preoccupation with proportional representation in the workplace; see disparate impact.

Affirmative action plan: A formalized program designed to remedy the present effects of past discrimination or to keep eligibility for federal contracts and grants that is comprised of utilization analysis, goals and timetables, and an action plan.

Applicant flow analysis: An assessment of disparate impact that examines the effect of the questioned selection criterion only on the actual candidates who applied for the position.

Assumption of risk defense: The philosophy that a person accepts the inherent risks involved in a job, thus absolving the employer of responsibility of injuries or illnesses incurred as a result of normal job risks.

Back pay: Wages (plus interest) that accrues from the time discrimination first occurs to the date of ordered reinstatement of the complaining party.

Black Codes: Following the passage of the Thirteenth Amendment, states passed these laws to prevent freedmen from enjoying the benefits of citizenship, such as denying the rights to bear arms, to assemble after sunset, to serve on juries, and to vote.

***Bona fide* occupational qualification (BFOQ):** A justification by an organization of its employment decision that allows only persons of a certain sex, religion, or national origin to be considered as qualified for a job.

Bottom-line statistics: The selection rates of protected class members at the conclusion of the selection process.

Business necessity: Employment practice that is validated as job related; see job-related defense.

Cognitive tests: Tests designed to measure the test-taker's reasoning, mathematical, and reading comprehension skills (i.e., cognitive ability tests).

Collective bargaining agreement (CBA): A negotiated contract between an employer and a labor union that represents some, or all, of the employees in the business. It specifies the compensation, terms, and conditions of employment for the affected employees during the term of the CBA.

Compelling government interest: The first part of a two-part test that a state or local government pass in order to engage in preferential affirmative action. First, it must clearly identify present effects that can be traced to some previously discriminatory practices. Next, it must show that it actually implemented the discriminatory policy or practice.

Compensable time: Time for which employees are owed compensation; time spent by employees performing work-related tasks is time for which they are due compensation, or compensable.

Compensatory damages: Damages imposed by a court to compensate a complaining party for monetary and nonmonetary harm suffered as a result of discrimination.

Compensatory time: Time off granted from a job in lieu of overtime compensation.

Competency-based job analysis: The antithesis of traditional job analysis methods, this focuses on those individual skills, abilities, and characteristics that can be linked to successful job performance—for example, ability to adapt to changing conditions, decisiveness, ability to work in ambiguous situations (e.g., worker-based or behaviorally based).

Complaining party: The person or persons making the complaint of unlawful discrimination.

Conciliation: A process whose aim is to bring about a negotiated settlement with a complaining party.

Concurrent validation: Determination of the correlation coefficients between test and performance by administering the test to current employees and correlating the test scores to their individual performance evaluations.

Congressional intent: What Congress was trying to accomplish at the time the statute was enacted; courts must view legal decisions in terms of this intent.

Construct validity: Method for evaluating abstract characteristics (i.e., decisiveness, innovation, sound judgment) that are important for successful job performance.

Constructive discharge: Occurs when job conditions have become so unpleasant that a reasonable person feels compelled to resign.

Content validity: Involves having an applicant perform a "fair sample" of work associated with the actual job for which he or she is applying.

Contributory negligence defense: A situation in which an employer claims that the damages for injuries were due, at least in part, to the negligence of the affected employee.

Corporate legitimacy: The extent to which an organization's objectives, actions, and activities are viewed as being consistent with society's expectations.

Countervailing statistics: Evidence in the form of alternative mathematical analysis submitted by an employer in the course of a disparate impact investigation, if the employer discerns problems or deficiencies in the data offered by the plaintiff.

Credit checks: Background checks that focus on the applicant's financial and credit history.

Criminal background checks: Background checks conducted to see if an applicant has an arrest or conviction record.

Criterion-related validity: Demonstrated by empirical data showing that a selection procedure is predictive of the important elements of the job in question.

De minimus **violation:** An OSHA violation at a place of employment that arises from a nonserious condition that has no direct or immediate relationship to safety or health.

Defamation: In the case of employment, an injury to an employee's reputation by an employer's disclosure of highly personal matters, such as details of the employee's qualifications and performance.

Defined benefit plans: Programs developed by an employer that identify how much a retiring employee will receive each month for the remainder of his or her life.

Defined contribution plans: Programs based on a prescribed amount invested periodically into an individual account for each employee.

Direct liability: A situation in which an employer is liable for the hostile environment sexual harassment of its employee, only if the employer knew, or should have known, that the harassment was occurring.

Direct threat: A significant risk of substantial harm to the health or safety of the individual employee or others that cannot be eliminated or reduced by reasonable accommodation in the workplace.

Disability: A physical or mental impairment that substantially limits one or more of the major life activities of an individual, a record of such impairment, or regarding an individual as having such an impairment.

Dismissal: When the EEOC stops an investigation without any determination being made.

Disparate impact: A statistical imbalance in a workforce that has the effect of disproportionately harming certain racial and/or ethnic groups, and that is often unintentional and is characterized by imposing the same standards on all people with different outcomes for different groups; sometimes called adverse impact.

Disparate treatment: Results from treating individuals in the workplace differently because of their membership in a protected class.

Due process: An employee's right to fair and consistent treatment in regard to terms and conditions of employment.

Emergency standard: Safety and health standard based on the need to protect employees from grave danger.

Employment-at-will: Old common law concept based on the premise that if an employee can terminate his or her employment relationship with an employer anytime he or she sees fit, and for any reason, the employer is entitled to do the same.

English-only work rules: Rules that require employees to speak English in certain work situations as a condition of employment.

Equal Protection Clause: The Fourteenth Amendment's clause that states: "No State shall make or enforce any law which shall abridge the privileges or immunities of citizens of the United States; nor shall any State deprive any person of life, liberty, or property without due process of law, or deny to any person within its jurisdiction the equal protection of the laws."

Ergonomics: The science of adapting a job to the biomechanical needs of a worker by using a human engineering process of matching the physical requirements of the job and the physical capacity of the worker.

E-verify: Also known as electronically verify, this is a way to check the employment eligibility status of all newly hired employees.

Exclusivity principle: The fundamental rationale for workers' compensation legislation stating that an employee injured in the course of employment receives fixed compensation described statutorily as the employee's "exclusive remedy" against the employer.

Exempt employees: Employees who are specifically excluded from the Fair Labor Standards Act's protection for minimum wage and overtime.

Explicit contract: A written document (in most instances) that represents an agreement between the two parties (the employer and the employee) establishing the terms of employment.

Extraterritorial application: The enforcement of a U.S. law beyond the boundaries of the United States.

Fair Employment Practice Agency (FEPA): A term that collectively refers to state agencies authorized by the EEOC to investigate employment discrimination allegations under Title VII.

Family and medical leave: Provided for by the Family and Medical Leave Act of 1993; requires that eligible employees receive up to twelve weeks of unpaid leave for any of the following reasons: (1) birth of a child; (2) adoption of a child; (3) care of an immediate family member (spouse, child, or parent) suffering from a "serious health condition"; or (4) recovery from a personal "serious health condition."

Fellow-servant-rule defense: An employer's assertion that an employee's injuries or illnesses were derived from the actions, whether accidental or intentional, of another employee.

Fiduciary: A person who is placed in a position of trust and confidence to exercise a standard of care in the administration or management of an activity.

Form I-9: An immigration document submitted with proof that establishes the applicant's identity and his or her authorization to work in the United States. Employers are required to verify that all employees are legally authorized to work in the United States by having every employee hired after November 6, 1986, complete a Form I-9.

Front pay: Money awarded for lost compensation during the period between judgment and reinstatement, or in lieu of the reinstatement.

Genetic Information Nondiscrimination Act (GINA): Signed into law on May 21,

2008, to prohibit the use of genetic information in either health insurance eligibility issues or employment.

H-1B visa: A nonimmigrant visa that only permits the holder to temporarily work in the United States. Only 65,000 such visas are issued annually, and a noncitizen can maintain his or her H-1B status for a maximum of six years.

Hostile environment sexual harassment: Unwelcome harassment that is severe or pervasive enough to alter the terms or conditions of employment and that creates an abusive work environment.

HR compliance: The area of human resource management that deals with the relationship between managers and employees in a regulated, but nonunionized, work environment.

Imminent danger violation: A violation that occurs when death or serious physical harm to an employee is imminent (i.e., an open flame in a fireworks factory); the offending organization must stop the activity immediately, and work cannot be resumed until the specified danger has been eliminated or corrected.

Implied contract: An agreement inferred by the actions or conduct of the parties rather than an openly expressed offer and acceptance.

Independent agencies: Those federal agencies that report directly to the President of the United States. They are not subject to or under the control of a cabinet officer.

Independent contractors: Independent individuals who contract with employers to perform specific duties; independent contractors are not employees of the companies with which they contract.

Injunctive relief: An order by the court for the employer to cease and desist unlawful practices.

Inpatriation: The recruiting and selection of foreign employees to work at facilities in the United States.

Interim standards: Temporary standards that the secretary of labor was given the power to establish for two years following the effective date of the Occupational Safety and Health Act of 1970; these were generally taken from preexisting national consensus standards.

Involuntary affirmative action: A remedy imposed by a court when an employer has been found in violation of Title VII or the Equal Protection Clause.

Jim Crow laws: Racially discriminatory laws named for a character in minstrel shows that were a means to get around the Civil Rights Acts of 1866, 1870, 1871, and 1875.

Job description: Reports that identify essential tasks, duties, and responsibilities of jobs in question.

Job-related defense: A defense that says even though a requirement causes adverse impact, it is absolutely essential to performing the job in question.

Job specification: The knowledge, skills, and abilities that an employee or applicant must possess in order to adequately perform the essential tasks, duties, and responsibilities contained in a job description.

Joint employers: Refers to two or more employers who employ the same individual.

Judicial activism: Occurs when judges go beyond their power of merely interpreting the law to actually making law.

Judicial restraint: The avoidance of judicial activism; essentially the court refrains from law making and restricts its activities to the settlement of legal conflicts.

Just cause statute: Laws enacted by a state that limit employers to discharging employees only for reasons of misconduct, such as poor performance, or financial exigency. The state essentially eliminates employment-at-will.

Language proficiency tests: Tests used to determine how well an individual can speak or write in a specific language.

Legitimate nondiscriminatory reason: An argument made by an employer that the decision to hire, fire, promote, or lay off any employee is based on sound business rationale and not the individual's protected class status.

Major life activities: Defined by the Americans with Disabilities Amendment Act of 2008 as (1) caring for one's self; (2) performing manual tasks; (3) seeing; (4) hearing; (5) eating; (6) sleeping; (7) walking; (8) standing; (9) sitting; (10) reaching; (11) lifting; (12) bending; (13) speaking; (14) breathing; (15) learning; (16) reading; (17) concentrating; (18) thinking; (19) communicating; (20) interacting; and (21) working.

Mandatory benefits: Benefits mandated or required by law such as social security, unemployment compensation, workers' compensation, and family and medical leave.

Mass layoff: Defined under the Worker Adjustment and Retraining Notification Act of 1988, a reduction in force that is not the result of a plant closing but involves at least one-third (33 percent) of the employees (excluding part-time employees), and at least fifty employees are laid off for at least a thirty-day period.

Mixed motive: Term describing an employment decision that is affected by at least two reasons: (1) a legitimate (job related) reason, and (2) an illegitimate reason (i.e., sex stereotyping).

Narrowly tailored: Preferential treatment of an affirmative action program designed in such a way as to minimize the harm to innocent third parties.

Negligent hiring: When an employer fails to exercise ordinary care in hiring or retaining an employee and that employee creates a foreseeable risk of harm to a third party.

Negligent misrepresentation: The conscious omission on the part of an employer of information regarding incidents of workplace violence, inability to perform critical work tasks, or sexual harassment on the part of a former employee. The former employer may be held responsible for acts of workplace violence or incompetence at the employee's new place of employment if he or she provided a positive recommendation or evaluation of the former employee's performance despite this knowledge.

Negligent retention: Retaining an employee with the knowledge that the employee presents a danger to coworkers or other third parties (through violent behavior or even incompetence); also known as negligent supervision.

Negligent supervision: See negligent retention.

No cause: Term used when no sufficient evidence is found in an investigation to establish that an unlawful employment practice has occurred.

Nonexempt employee: Any employee who is entitled to protection under the Fair Labor Standards Act's minimum wage and overtime provisions.

Nonpreferred group: Includes all employees or applicants *not* entitled to preferential treatment under an affirmative action program, including those who are members of protected classes; also known as nonfavored group.

Notice of right to sue: Notice issued by Equal Employment Opportunity Commission that is requested by a complaining party within ninety days of being formally notified of the agency's no cause determination; it allows the complaining party to still bring suit against the employer in federal court.

Other-than-serious violation: Safety and health violation involving a situation in which the most serious illness or injury would probably not result in death or serious physical harm.

Overtime: Legally defined as any hours worked in excess of 40 during a 168 consecutive-hour workweek.

Performance standards: The minimum levels of activity and output that an employee must attain if the essential tasks and duties of the job are to be accomplished.

Permanent standards: Safety and health standards that are newly created or revised from original interim standards and are issued on an as-needed basis or evolve from emergency standards.

Permanent variance: Waiver granted to an employer who can prove that conditions or particular methods provide as safe a work site as those that would exist through compliance with the Occupational Safety and Health Act standards.

Personality tests: Tests used to assess traits that predict a job candidate's predisposition to react in a given way to environmental stimuli.

Physical ability tests: Tests that measure an individual's physical strength, endurance, and stamina, as well as hand-eye coordination or ability to carry particular loads.

Plant closing: Defined under the Worker Adjustment and Retraining Notification Act of 1988. The permanent or temporary shutdown of a single site of employment or one or more facilities or operating units within a single site of employment, provided that the shutdown results in an employment loss of fifty or more employees (excluding part-time employees) at the single site during any thirty-day period.

Precedent: Based on the legal principle of *stare decisis,* the adherence to norms established in previously decided cases.

Predictive validation: A means of establishing criterion-related validity by giving a validation test to applicants rather than to current employees.

Preferred group: Includes all employees or applicants entitled to preferential treatment under an affirmative action plan.

Pretext: An apparently legitimate justification for actions by an employer in the effort to hide unlawful discrimination.

Prevailing wage: The minimum wage established for each class of workers as determined by the secretary of labor.

Procedural due process: Refers to the fairness of the procedure used by an organization in determining whether its work rules or policies have been violated.

Protected classes: The original five categories—race, color, religion, sex, or national origin—along with age and disability, against which discrimination is prohibited.

Public policy: A condition in which an employee cannot be discharged for refusing to violate a law or ordinance, fired for refusing to avoid a civic duty or obligation (i.e., jury duty or when summoned as a witness), or terminated for exercising a legal right.

Punitive damages: Compensation awarded to a complaining party, imposed to punish and to be a painful reminder to an employer of the consequences of blatantly violating Title VII.

Qualified individual with a disability: One who can perform the essential functions of the job in question with reasonable accommodation.

Qualified privilege: A conditional privilege in which an employer is protected from liability based on the fact that a statement is made in the performance of some judicial, social, or personal duty.

Qualifying events: Certain conditions that require continued coverage under the Consolidated Omnibus Budget Reconciliation Act.

Quid pro **quo sexual harassment:** Harassment that occurs by withholding or granting of tangible employment benefits in exchange for sexual favors.

Reasonable accommodation: Modifications that would permit an individual with a disability to perform the essential functions of a job, provided that these modifications do not create an undue hardship for the employer.

Reasonable cause: When the Equal Employment Opportunity Commission's investigation finds enough evidence to believe that an unlawful employment practice has occurred.

Relevant labor market: Geographic area from which an employer normally recruits individuals with the requisite qualifications for a specific job.

Religious accommodation: Employers must refrain from considering an individual's religious beliefs in making hiring decisions, and they must make accommodations for those beliefs after employment.

Religious exemption: Occurs when religious organizations are permitted to make hiring and discharge decisions based on an applicant's or employee's religious affiliation if they can show some connection between the position and the religion.

Remand: Process in which the Court of Appeals may vacate part of a decision, instruct the lower court where it erred (improperly interpreted the law), and then return the case to the district court for reexamination under the Court of Appeals' previous instructions on the point of the law.

Respondent: The party against whom a complaint is made.

Revised Order No: 4: Contains the guidance of the Office of Federal Contract Compliance Programs for constructing affirmative action programs that would meet their standards of review.

Serious violation: Occurs when there is substantial probability that death or serious physical harm could result and that the employer knows, or should have known, of the hazard.

Sex discrimination: Discrimination based on an individual's sex; the second largest source of Title VII violations after race discrimination.

Sex-plus discrimination: Occurs when members of one sex who possess a specific characteristic or condition are treated differently from members of the opposite sex who have the same characteristic.

Sex stereotyping: Generalized belief about behaviors or characteristics attributed to a certain sex.

Sick building syndrome: Term used to encompass a number of medical ailments associated with physical workplace settings.

Statutory law: Laws, referred to as statutes, created by legislative bodies and enacted by the federal government.

Stock analysis: Statistical study of the composition of an employer's workforce and how that workforce compares to its relevant labor market.

Strict scrutiny: Under the Fifth Amendment, requires the public employer to first establish that any preferences serve a "compelling government interest" and, second, that the preferences are "narrowly tailored" to achieve that interest.

Substantive due process: Assures employees that no disciplinary action will be taken against them unless there is clear and convincing evidence that they have committed a disciplinary offense.

Successor employer: An employer who replaces an earlier employer; if one company was acquired by another company, the acquiring company is the successor employer.

Systematic job analysis: The planned collection of information about a job in order to establish how the work in question is performed (the tasks, duties, and responsibilities) and what particular traits or characteristics (knowledge, skills, and abilities) a person must possess in order to perform the work properly.

Temporary variance: An extension granted when an employer cannot meet the requirement to comply with a safety and health standard by its effective date.

Testers: Individuals who apply for positions of employment for the sole purpose of determining whether a "tested" employer is engaging in discriminatory hiring practices.

Title VII: Part of the Civil Rights Act of 1964, the foundation of most of the laws and regulations that affect equal employment opportunity in the workplace.

Underrepresented: A protected class that has become underutilized in the workplace because of the employer's past discriminatory hiring or promoting practices.

Underutilized protected group: A protected group under Title VII that is underrepresented in the workforce in proportion to the relevant external market.

Undue hardship: Determination made under the Americans with Disabilities Act that requires consideration of five factors in the hiring of persons with disabilities: (1) costs; (2) resources; (3) type of operation; and (4) impact of hardship.

Unemployment compensation: An unemployment insurance program to offset workers' lost income during periods of involuntary unemployment and to help unemployed workers locate new employment.

Unfair immigration-related employment practices: Violations of the antidiscrimination provisions in the Immigration Reform and Control Act of 1986 (IRCA).

Unnecessarily trammels: An affirmative action program that unduly restricts the rights of individuals who are members of nonpreferred groups is said to unnecessarily trammel their rights.

Utilization analysis: Analysis used to determine the extent to which ethnic minorities and/or women are being "underutilized" by an organization in question.

Vacate: Term indicating the reversal of the district court's decision by the Court of Appeals.

Vesting: Occurs when an individual has a nonforfeitable right to pension benefits.

Vicarious liability: An employer can be found liable for the wrongful actions of its agent, regardless of whether or not the employer knew, or should have known, of the agent's sexual harassment.

Voluntary affirmative action: Affirmative action programs not imposed by a court, including: (1) consent agreements; (2) programs developed for eligibility in certain federal programs; and (3) programs created by an employer for the express purpose of eliminating the effects of past discriminatory policies and practices.

Voluntary benefits: Benefits that are not required by law, such as medical insurance, paid vacation time, or retirement programs.

Waivers: Private agreements between an employer and a former employee excusing the employer of certain obligations.

Whistleblower clauses: Rules that protect employees from being retaliated against for reporting violations of the specific law in question.

Willful and repeated violation: Occurs when an employer is notified of a safety and health violation by a compliance officer and refuses or fails to take corrective action.

Workers' compensation: Provision of cash benefits for work-related injuries and deaths for which workers are eligible by law.

Writ of certiorari: Applied for when requesting an appeal; if approved, it would compel the Court of Appeals to provide records of a case for review by the Supreme Court.

INDEX

Page numbers in *italics* indicate figures and tables

ABOUT THE AUTHORS

Robert Kirkland Robinson (Ph.D., SPHR) is the Michael S. Starnes Professor of Management and the Chair of the Management Department in the School of Business Administration at the University of Mississippi. Dr. Robinson's research interests involve federal regulation of the workplace, affirmative action policies, sexual harassment, business ethics, and employee recruiting and selection. He has written over 100 articles that have appeared in many different business and public administration journals. He coauthored *The Regulatory Environment of Human Resource Management* (2002).

Geralyn McClure Franklin (Ph.D.) has served as dean of business at three different academic institutions. In July of 2012, she began serving as Interim Dean of the Nelson Rusche College of Business at Stephen F. Austin State University. Dr. Franklin has published more than 100 journal articles on human resource management, employment law, and small business management and entrepreneurship issues. In addition, she has coauthored *Human Resource Management* (1995), *Management* (1997), and *The Regulatory Environment of Human Resource Management* (2002).